Elizabeth Barrett Browning

Elizabeth Barrett Browning

A LIFE

BY

DOROTHY HEWLETT

ALFRED A. KNOPF

NEW YORK

1952

L. C. CATALOG CARD NUMBER: 51–13218

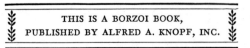

THIS IS A BORZOI BOOK,
PUBLISHED BY ALFRED A. KNOPF, INC.

FIRST EDITION

To

Gertrude Reese Hudson,

of the University of Texas,

in affection and

gratitude

PREFACE

THIS life of Mrs. Browning was undertaken partly to please myself and partly because it seemed to fill a need; Elizabeth has for far too many years been remembered as the wife of Robert Browning, the heroine of a romantic love story, rather than as a poet in her own right. Little of her except the lively, eloquent letters was read, though there are now signs that her poetry is attracting new attention; indeed, Mr. Gardner B. Taplin, of Indiana University, with whom I have had the advantage of discussing our respective plans, is at present writing a critical work.

In her own time, and for many years after, the world agreed with Browning in placing her, not far below, but higher than himself. Then, for some forty years or more, she was practically unread, jeered at as "Victorian," "sentimental." It is probable that we of this generation value her with more accuracy; admitting that a lack of sustained strength is, to an appreciable extent, atoned for by the sensitive quality of her writing. Indeed, a modern poet and critic whose judgment most of us place very high in poetic perception has gone so far as to assert—at least in private—that Mrs. Browning is a "finer" poet than her husband. Her handicap—particularly exemplified in *Aurora Leigh*—he considers to have been an experience comparatively narrow.

Interest in the Brownings is to-day far stronger in America than in their native land; therefore it is fitting that this book comes first before the American public.

The main book sources of my biography are given at the end of this volume: to all concerned—writers, editors, publishers, and those kind American friends who sent me the newest ones —I render grateful thanks. Mrs. Gertrude Reese Hudson has been particularly generous, not only in the provision of books difficult to obtain in England, but in answering queries and in supplying me with a whole sheaf of notes collected for her life of Robert Browning. Miss Jeannette Marks was kind enough to obtain for me a copy of her *The Family of the Barrett*. I should like particularly to mention two collections of letters which came over by gift and, by their admirable editorship, enabled me to clarify various points: Mr. Edward C. McAleer's *Dearest Isa* and his article "New Letters of Mrs. Browning to Isa Blagden" in *PMLA*, September 1951. On one point alone am I at issue with Mr. McAleer: he says that the pronunciation of Elizabeth's pet name should be "Bay," short for "baby." I have talked with members of the Barrett family, including her niece, the late Miss Mary Altham, and they all called her Aunt "Bah." And would Kenyon have spoken of Elizabeth's "bay"-lambishness?

In regard to unpublished material, Mr. and Mrs. John J. Hagedorn, of St. Louis, Missouri, most generously put at my disposal their valuable collection in the original. The Henry E. Huntington Library, the Pierpont Morgan Library, and the Henry W. and Albert Berg Collection, New York Public Library, have also allowed me to quote material in their possession. Wellesley College has delved for me into its wealth of material, and Miss Hannah French, their Research Librarian, has been both prompt and kind in answering questions. As always, I am indebted to my friends, Mr. Maurice Buxton Forman and Dr. Willard B. Pope. Mr. Buxton Forman has given me unpublished letters to Haydon. Dr. Willard B. Pope has given me others from Haydon, and has also pointed out the Marsh papers in the Wilbur Library of the University of Vermont, which I am permitted to quote. Other unpublished material in the form of letters or illustrations has been supplied by Miss Henrietta Altham, Mrs. Violet Altham, Mr. Stephen Ballard, Signor G. G. Giannini, of Florence, Mr. E. R. Moulton-Barrett, Mrs. K. J. Moulton-Barrett, Miss Winifred Myers, of Bond Street, London, Mrs. Rayner Wood, of Old Colwall; Balliol College, Oxford; the Bodleian, the National Library of Scotland, and the Torquay Natural History Society. The use of unpublished Barrett Browning material without fee has been generously conceded by the copyright owner, Sir John Murray.

Information personally given me by members of the family —Miss Henrietta Altham, the late Miss Mary Altham, the late Mr. J. A. S. Altham, and Mrs. Violet Altham, Lieutenant-Colonel E. F. Moulton-Barrett of Jamaica, Mr. E. R. Moulton-

Barrett, and Mrs. K. J. Moulton-Barrett—has been particularly helpful. In talking with them I found odd scraps of information falling into place when combined with others they were able, from family sources or tradition, to supply. They have all been extraordinarily kind and patient with an inquiring author.

For help and advice I have particularly to thank Mr. H. Phillipson, of the Tavistock Clinic, London, for clarifying a psychological problem, Dr. Maurice Campbell, of Guy's Hospital, for discussing with me Elizabeth's malady, and my husband, Norman Kilgour, whose patient help has sustained me in a long and exhausting task. Others to whom I am indebted are Mr. T. B. Layton, of Guy's, Mr. Edmund Blunden, Mlle Berthe Esseiva, of Paris, Mr. A. Farquharson, of Ledbury, Dr. G. H. Gibbens, of the Devonshire Association, Sir Frederic Kenyon, Mr. Percy Lubbock, Mr. J. W. Lucas, Miss P. Morgan, of the Malvern and the Hereford Public Libraries, Mr. F. Morley, of Malvern, Signora Franca Adamo Paoletti, of Siena, Miss Janet E. Payne, Mrs. J. Hughes Preston, Mr. Neville Rogers, Signorina Toscanella Roster, of Florence, Mrs. Rosamund Rubens, Mr. A. Stonebridge, of the St. Marylebone Public Library, Miss Signe Toksvig, the Misses Woods, Mrs. Anne Page, who found both books and manuscripts for me in London shops, and Mr. Herbert Weinstock, of Alfred A. Knopf, Inc., for detecting certain small errors and inconsistencies.

Never before in my literary career has a book of mine been published first in America; that this book so appears is to me a peculiar gratification, not only for the reason given above, but because, apart from kindnesses detailed above, and many others in the past, Americans have always been particularly generous and understanding toward my work. I can only hope that in return I may give some pleasure and profit to readers who are bodily so far away but near in spirit.

DOROTHY HEWLETT

Hampstead, London
November 1951

CONTENTS

ILLUSTRATIONS

Elizabeth Barrett Browning

ELIZABETH BARRETT BROWNING

CHAPTER 1

HER FAMILY AND EARLY YEARS

In or about the year 1795 two Creole boys and a girl, the grandchildren of Edward Barrett of Cinnamon Hill, Jamaica, came to England to be educated. The eldest, named after his grandfather, was heir through the death of his uncles to the greater part of a vast fortune.

Young Edward Barrett Moulton (soon to become by royal licence Edward Barrett Moulton Barrett) was sent to Harrow School. There, according to time-honoured custom, he had to "fag" for a senior boy; a bleak change of circumstance to a lad pampered and petted in early years by slave attendants. He who had almost certainly never done a hand's turn for himself was now expected to fetch and carry, to perform such duties as blacking boots and preparing breakfast before school began at half past seven in the morning. One can imagine him neither efficient nor resigned: soon, in the words of Robert Browning, he "received there so savage a punishment for a supposed offence ('burning the toast') . . . that he was withdrawn from the school by his mother, and the delinquent was expelled."

Charles Moulton, the father of the children, was still living but had early separated from his wife and children; even consenting, though his name was ancient and honourable, to allow his sons as inheritors of their grandfather to bear the name of Barrett. When the grandfather died, in 1798, James Scarlett, later the celebrated judge Lord Abinger, became their guardian.

Elizabeth Moulton (she never resumed her maiden name of Barrett) returned to Jamaica some time before her father's death in 1798, and it was during the years of her absence that Edward stayed with the family of John Graham Clarke, a rich merchant of Newcastle-on-Tyne closely tied in friendship and business relations to the Barrett family. For the rest all we know of him at this period is that he "frequently accompanied" James Scarlett "in his post-chaise while on circuit."

At the age of eighteen Edward was entered at Trinity College, Cambridge. One of his fellow-students there was John Kenyon, a West Indian cousin who had been at school with the son of another Jamaican family, Robert Browning, the father of the poet. Edward remained only one year at Trinity.

Edward Moulton Barrett is depicted for us about this time in a miniature by Hoppner [1] as a large-eyed youth with oval face, high forehead, longish nose, short upper lip, and slightly receding chin. A strong sensibility is apparent.

John Graham Clarke had five daughters. While still at Cambridge Edward declared his love for the eldest, Mary, a beautiful gentle girl of twenty-four. Probably because of his youth and the disparity in ages, Scarlett at first made strong objections to the match, but a meeting with Mary Graham Clarke overcame them. He exclaimed: "I can hold out no longer—she is far too good for him!"

Edward Moulton Barrett's determination to have his own way, to dominate his family, has become legend, a legend unfairly distorted: that he was essentially a fine character there is no doubt. He was upright, scrupulous, and kind. His children loved and respected him. As a man and as a father he must not be judged by the standards of today. Rich and apparently little controlled from an early age, the child of long generations of arbitrary slave-owners, he married while still at a formative age and soon came to the management of a large estate: power was native to him, a power confirmed by family obligations and sanctified by religious faith. In the words of his daughter, he took "it to be his duty to rule like the Kings of Christendom, by divine right."

Perhaps James Scarlett in finally consenting had, on consider-

---

[1] Reproduced in Jeannette Marks: *The Family of the Barrett* (New York: The Macmillan Company; 1938).

ation, thought the marriage of his ward with a woman older than himself might prove a salutary check on self-will. A wife of twenty-five, even in those days of legal and approved feminine subservience, could hardly be expected to submit herself completely to the whims of a youth of nineteen. But Mary's more mature age benefited neither herself nor her future family; she being, in the words of her daughter, "one of those women who never can resist . . . too womanly she was—it was her only fault." Frequent childbearing, twelve children in nineteen years, must have helped to weaken any manifestation of resistance Mrs. Barrett might have nerved herself to make: in yielding, the gentle nature did not itself escape harm, being, her daughter added, by the "thunder a little turned from its sweetness—as when it turns milk."

So far as can be gathered from incomplete evidence, Edward Barrett was a man to be pitied rather than wholly blamed. With his own high honour, his proud rigidity and self-exaltation as an instrument of God, he must have been a lonely man; a man increasingly alone as each family loss—some later of his own making—bereft him of cherished companions. The first bereavement came early with the death of his only sister, a pretty, lively child commemorated for us in paint by Sir Thomas Lawrence as "Pinkie." Miss Marks has pointed out how, like his daughter, Mr. Barrett reacted bodily to loss, anxiety, or grief, being subject to a sharp attack of the rheumatic complaint that early plagued him. We may guess him to have been in sorrow or in personal anxiety as inarticulate as she; but unlike her Mr. Barrett was no poet with a power to relieve feeling at least partially in the written word.

Such a nature must wound itself; and perhaps there was a hidden knife for Edward Barrett to twist in his essential probity. Noncomformity, to which he leaned in religion, was an acknowledged and active accuser of the system of slavery. It was by slaves, however humanely worked, that Edward Barrett lived: by slavery his ancestors had piled up great wealth. Custom and tradition may have enabled him generally to accept the system as a natural phenomenon, but those of his religion were constantly questioning and attacking it.

Edward took his wife to Coxhoe Hall, Kelloe, Northumberland, the property of his bride's father, and there on March 6, 1806, at seven o'clock in the evening, his eldest child was born.

As first born, and in the right of her own delightful gifted little self, Elizabeth early became a child cherished and especially favoured. She had the privilege of visiting her father's room in the morning, scrambling up with an effort on to the high white bed. Laughing, she would bury her head in his pillow and whisper: "*Baisez-moi.*" She seems to have spoken French, or at least some phrases, at a very early age, talking in that language, with a "*venez ici*" or "*couchez*" to Havannah, a poodle who was supposed to understand French better than English. Elizabeth, looking back at this early and tender introduction to a foreign tongue, declared that she liked this kind of French far better than French verbs, an atrocious invention, "probably Boney's own."

To her Uncle Sam, Edward Barrett's brother, always plain Sam to her, "Dear Sam," the child was a delight: he would jealously exclaim that he loved her more than did her own father. At his comparatively early death he left to her, and to her alone in the family, investments amounting to some four thousand pounds.

Elizabeth's name, a family one, was not given her officially until after the birth of her brother Edward a year later: when Edward was six months old the two children were christened together. This was an odd custom Mr. Barrett kept up to the end of his long family. Always two at a time were dispatched at the font; perhaps in a gesture of contempt for the State religion, with which he was out of sympathy. His early attitude to the Church seems to have been a mixed one: he apparently admitted the services but repudiated her large claim. On the title page of Elizabeth's Prayer Book (dated 1813 and with her name stamped in gold on the cover) "Church of England" is altered to "Church *in* England"; in "with notes by a member of the Established Church" the word "Established" is struck through.

The little Elizabeth, affectionately called Ba in her family, was small, dark, lively, and a self-willed child. At fourteen, looking backward on her life, she wrote:

*I was always of a determined and if thwarted violent disposi-
tion. My actions and temper were infinitely more inflexible at
three years than now at fourteen. At an early age I can perfectly remember reigning in the Nursery and being renowned
amongst the servants for self love and excessive passion.*
In her paroxysms of baby rage she was given to knocking over
small articles of furniture.

To a father so young this first child may have been a pretty
toy: we hear of one trick he played, lifting her on to a high
mantelshelf and exhorting her to be a hero and stand up
straight; which she did (to quote her own words):
*straighter and straighter, and then suddenly was "ware" . . .
of the walls growing alive behind me and extending two stony
hands to push me down that frightful precipice to the rug,
where the dog lay . . dear old Havannah, . . and where he
and I were likely to be dashed to pieces together and mix our
uncanonised bones.*

In 1809 Henrietta (Addles in the nursery), the first of her
sisters, was born. In 1810 the family removed to Hope End,
near Ledbury in Herefordshire, their home for twenty-two
years and the birthplace of eight more of the children.

Mary, the first born at Hope End, died four years later in
tragic circumstances: during an illness leeches were put upon
her with fatal effect. It is typical of Elizabeth Barrett Browning's reticence in grief that even in her youthful reminiscences
of the nursery Mary is never mentioned. Mary was the only one
of the children to be buried with the parents at Ledbury.

There followed over the years, and up to 1824, when Eliza-
beth was eighteen, Samuel, Arabella, Charles John (Stormie),
George Goodin, Henry, Alfred Price (Daisy), Septimus James
(Sette), and Butler Octavius, the youngest, familiarly called
Occy, or Occyta.

The father of these children, himself a young man, enjoyed
among them a benevolent autocracy, perhaps at first only to a
degree common in those days, but heightened because the
mother was weak. Among the elder boys he, who retained his
youthful appearance far beyond this period, must have looked
like a brother; and as a loved elder brother he seems to have
behaved, playing cricket with them and laughing among them

in a loud boyish way. Though the tone of the birthday odes
customary in this family are in his case reverential, his sons'
letters from school to their "Puppy" are not constrained: to
them their father was far from being an ogre. Through years of
arbitrary treatment they loved and respected him. The few
letters too I have seen from him to his children are friendly,
affectionate—even playful. When conveying his wishes he is
firm but not dictatorial, often leaving it to them to make their
own decisions. There is no doubt that his anger was sometimes
capricious and to be feared, but there is no hint of the physical
punishment usual in those days; and where temporary injustice
might be felt there were always two devoted women in the
house to run to for comfort, the weak loving mother and an
aunt, her sister Arabella Graham Clarke, oddly called Bummy.

The lot of these children was cast in pleasant places: set in
a wooded valley within sight of Malvern Hills, the estate,
though now neglected, wild, is richly beautiful. Around the old
house, now pulled down, Mr. Barrett laid out gardens, one of
which was reached by a subterranean passage. By 1822 at
least [2] there were "some fine pieces of water" and what appears to have been a primitive rock garden, "a very large projec-
tion of rock, which the taste of the owner has highly ornamented
with a fine collection of plants." At some time during Mr. Barrett's ownership a cascade was constructed.

The house, originally a farm dwelling, was not well situated,
being at the narrowest part of the valley, shaded from the sun
and with a restricted view. The immediate surroundings, however, were serenely beautiful. Elizabeth describes in *Aurora
Leigh* what was to be seen from the window of her own room:

> *First the lime,*
> *(I had enough there, of the lime, be sure,—*
> *My morning-dream was often hummed away*
> *By the bees in it;) past the lime, the lawn,*
> *Which, after sweeping broadly round the house,*
> *Went trickling through the shrubberies in a stream*
> *Of tender turf, and wore and lost itself*
> *Among the acacias, over which you saw*

---

[2] See Mary Southall: *A Description of Malvern* (London: Longman, Hurst,
Rees, Orme & Brown; 1822).

The irregular line of elms by the deep lane
Which stopped the grounds and dammed the overflow
Of arbutus and laurel.

Above the elms and deep hidden lane there rose "the folded hills, striped up and down with hedges," planted with burly oaks and fed upon at that time by many sheep.

The children lived out of doors in fair weather:

If the rain fell, there was sorrow,
Little head leant on the pane,
Little finger drawing down it
The long trailing drops upon it,
And the "Rain, rain, come tomorrow,"
Said for charm against the rain.

In spring, after lovely west-country fashion, there were drifts of fruit blossom in the glades; in the grounds a fine pear and chestnuts with their fairy cones of pink and white. About Hope End there were woods and rich deep meadows, a home farm to visit, and, more immediate joy, the children's own garden, where they dug and planted their plots in long narrow beds at the end of which was an ancient thorn.

In this Eden there was a reptile; not a snake, or the little green frogs which, to the horror of her nurses, Elizabeth loved to pick up and make leap from hand to hand, but an old toad who lived in the hollow root of the thorn. Elizabeth would stoop and peep fearfully into the blackness of the hole, convinced she could see glittering there the "jewel in his head." When he chose to come out and "sate swelling his black sides" she would skirt the garden through shrubberies, nearly waist deep in wet grass and nettles, to avoid passing him; afraid that he might spit poison that would strike her dead.

The pride of these gardens was Elizabeth's own white roses, which she grew to perfection. All over the estates were trees, young ones planted by her father—among them an avenue of oaks—and giants the children could climb; Elizabeth, scorning the limitations of her sex, being foremost in the sport. In this she was more fortunate than girls later in the century, her garments being light, almost petticoatless, with probably little more than long trouser drawers and a muslin frock to tear.

The house, a spacious Georgian edifice, must have been a

delight and pride to the children: as an expression of perhaps a smothered fantasy, a hidden luxuriance of temperament, Edward Barrett had entirely refaced it in a "Turkish style," "crowded with minarets and domes, and crowned with metal spires and crescents." But to at least one of the children when thunder rolled among the Malvern Hills, "where great storms most do congregate," the house was a source of fear; fear heightened by the comments of neighbours who declared its minarets and spires to be a provocation "to every lightning of heaven." "Once," Elizabeth later told Robert Browning, "a storm of storms happened," and they thought the house was struck.

A tree was so really, within two hundred yards of the windows while I looked out—the bark rent from top to bottom . . torn into long ribbons by the dreadful fiery hands, and dashed out into the air, over the heads of other trees, or left twisted in their branches—torn into shreds in a moment, as a flower might be, by a child! . . . The whole trunk of that tree was bared and peeled—and up that new whiteness of it ran the finger-mark of the lightning in a bright beautiful rose-colour . . . the fever-sign of the certain death—though the branches themselves were for the most part untouched, and spread from the peeled trunk in their full summer foliage; and birds singing in them three hours afterwards!

To the personal horror was added another when the girl heard that two people had been struck dead out on the Malvern Hills.

But storms were mere interruptions in the idyll of summer at Hope End: the serene rich beauty spreading about that fantastic house lived on nostalgically, haunted with bird-song, in Elizabeth's mind, so that she wrote lovingly of it in middle age. At nine years old she herself added a small distinction, a giant ("Call him Hector, son of Priam!") cut in turf under the shadow of the pear tree and picked out in flowers:

> *Eyes of gentianella azure,*
> *Staring, winking at the skies;*
> *Nose of gillyflowers and box;*
> *Scented grasses put for locks,*
> *Which a little breeze at pleasure,*
> *Set a-waving round his eyes.*

> *Brazen helm of daffodillies,*
> > *With a glitter toward the light;*
> *Purple violets for the mouth,*
> > *Breathing perfumes west and south;*
> *And a sword of flashing lilies,*
> > *Holden ready for the fight.*

> *And a breastplate made of daisies,*
> > *Closely fitting, leaf on leaf;*
> *Periwinkles interlaced*
> > *Drawn for belt about the waist;*
> *While the brown bees, humming praises,*
> > *Shot their arrows round the chief.*

This child of genius was precocious, but at the same time a normal little girl, loving games, climbing, riding her pony, and cherishing dolls. Out in her garden bower overhung with white roses, or in "Elizabeth's room" (probably the library), a lofty place lit by a stained-glass window, she would read Homer in the original holding the book in one hand and hugging a doll with the other. Having already formed her habit of sitting on the floor, she would lean against a wall bending over with her dark hair falling about her face.

But though Elizabeth was encouraged to, perhaps carefully nurtured for a literary life, she was not always approved. We catch hints of music studies neglected and a murmur from her grandmother, Elizabeth Moulton, a lady of the old school who would "far rather see Elizabeth's hemming more carefully finished than hear of all this Greek." Elizabeth detested the stock accomplishments of a gentlewoman, needlework, music, and drawing. She acquired enough skill in drawing, however, to be able, later on her travels, to make quite adequately those little commemorative sketches expected of ladies at that time.

In the great hall of the house there was an organ on which some member of the household regularly played, as we can learn from some verses written by Elizabeth at thirteen describing daily life at Hope End:

To school till five! & then again we fly
To play & joy & mirth & pleasures ply.
Some dance, some fight, some laugh, some play, some squall,

And the loud organ's thunder circles all.
And then at tea we snatch a short repast
As long as one large plate of toast doth last.
At nine fatigued upon the grateful bed
We stretch out weary limbs and rest our head.

These children acted plays in the nursery, some written by
Elizabeth, and had their own small charitable works. Over all
there hung, as we may deduce from an observation on her own
boy's freer upbringing, a certain air of evangelical strictness; a
strictness common to many families at that time, which a large
group of children, with their private jokes and activities, could
resist without too much damage to young and tender consciences. Mr. Barrett was certainly no killjoy: he dressed up as
"Grand Mufti" to amuse the children [3] and may even have taken
part in their performances (see Appendix 1). In summer the
family, in whole or part, was taken to the seaside. Elizabeth
herself, as we shall see, even made an excursion abroad.

Elizabeth was early a leader among the children. On attaining the age of six, she rejoiced that there was in the nursery
"no UPSTART" to dispute her authority, Henrietta being too
young and Bro a gentle child who "never allowed the rage for
power to injure the endearing sweetness of his temper."
Though, as they grew in size and weight, brothers less pliant
probably disputed this authority in the person of an elder sister
who was exceptionally small for her age, Elizabeth stood
out among them by a natural supremacy of mind. Bro and Sam
could write verses, and at least two of the younger boys were
precocious in development, but none had the same power of
learning, the same fluency of expression. And within this child's
veins ran the strange ichor of genius.

At the age of four she first "mounted Pegasus" and in her
sixth year, for some lines on "Virtue" carefully written out, received from her father a ten-shilling note enclosed in a letter
addressed to the *Poet Laureate of Hope End.*

[3] Juvenile family letter in the possession of Mrs. K. I. Moulton-Barrett.

CHAPTER 2

THE POET LAUREATE OF HOPE END

Ah! the poor lad in yonder boat
Forced from his wife, his Friends, his home,
Now gentle Maiden how can you
Look at the misery of his doom?

THESE LINES, the earliest recorded, and written in or before her eighth year, "on the Cruelty of Forcement to Man; Alluding to the Press Gang," are of double significance in the pattern of Elizabeth Barrett Browning's life; recalling not only those strongly humanitarian poems which moved the world, "The Cry of the Children" and "The Runaway Slave at Pilgrim's Point," but also the age in which the poet was born.

War, memory of war, rumour of war and an abortive peace, unrest among the hungry workers manifest in the notorious "Peterloo," a growing feeling for individual liberty arising out of the French Revolution, abhorrence of the slave trade, and its abolishment, at least officially, in 1807; widespread misery and want, revolt physical and spiritual, all culminating in civil disturbance and in strong Government repression with, in 1817, suspension of Habeas Corpus. Though deep in the lovely retirement of Hope End, the little girl, daughter of a Liberal, could not escape the impact of this turmoil upon a sensitive spirit. The misery of the agricultural poor was only too evident around her, the poor who were taken by her father as his special province beyond the formal duties of a landowner and Justice of the Peace. It is a local tradition that he opened a school in which each of his children had his own pupils; he certainly moved among the people, giving them active sympathy, ministering to soul as well as body.

In these ministrations, these unofficial visitings of the sick, little Elizabeth often accompanied him, seeing at close range dire poverty, a rural population starving amid plenty because of bad harvests and the oppressive Corn Laws. In the neatly

written manuscript book of which the lines on the Press Gang
form the first entry we find this appeal:

> *Open, Oh Charity, thy bounteous hand!*
> *Soften the Sufferings of the tortured poor;*
> *Blow out the flame of Vice's lifted brand;*
> *To Virtue's bower shew out the golden Door!*

The children of Hope End worked actively to relieve suffering:
the set of verses, the second of which I quote, and four others
were "written for the shop to be held in the Children's Garden,
the profits of which to be charitably used." An emphasis on
virtue in the poor, on the connection between a decent standard of living and a decency of behaviour, arose probably as
much from individual observation, from parental homily, as
from a convention in the moral verse of the time. The little
poet in "To the Muse" sets out certain definite aims:

> *Come forth my Muse, and tune the lyre so bright,*
> *The darkest soul illume with purer light*
> *And pour instruction o'er the embarrassed Mind*
> *And Godly Virtue in the Wicked find:*
> *Thus like the Sun who darts his brighter beam*
> *And shines with awe, and lights the shadowed realm;*
> *So strike my muse! and through the gloomiest way*
> *Shew Virtue's path and sing beneath her Sway.*

From this purpose, culminating in *Aurora Leigh,* she never
wholly departed.

In this mood, self-conscious enough in an evangelical household where every action was probably approved, censured, or
exalted by prayer both public and private, we have a "cau-
tionary tale," that of a naughty girl eaten by a lion in a forbidden wood. To this moral work, repeated in essence more
than once, we might perhaps give a personal application: the
woods lay thick about Hope End to draw little feet astray.

Other poems in this early manuscript book, quaint and
charming enough in their degree—homilies on virtue, lines on
cottage maidens, virtuous or otherwise—are not beyond the
capacity of any clever child in stimulating surroundings, but in
"A Song," written on July 2, 1814, we have a foreshadowing of
genius:

> *Peter Quarry he called all his vices together*
> *To meet on the green field, or bright yellow meadow*
> *Says he our acquaintance I fear will be short,*
> *For of going to virtue I've a great thought.*
> > *Singing fal lal, etc.*

> *So you must begone*
> *With your weeds and your bushes,*
> *And sweet virtue must come*
> *With her larks and her thrushes.*
> > *Singing fal lal, etc.*

Elizabeth never once, so far as I am aware, mentions Blake, but surely the *Songs of Innocence* and *Songs of Experience* were on the nursery book-shelf?

Many of the poems are celebrations of nature, often in the square-toed eighteenth-century manner of personification and moral deduction, but some a direct outcome of bright-eyed observation:

> *Wild were the windings of the stream*
> *And every plant and tree looked green—*
> *The violets raised their heads so blue*
> *And grass so green around them grew—*
> *Upon a bank of roses red*
> *Laborious bees on honey fed—*
> *A boy there wasted many an hour*
> *Watching the Bees suck honey from the flower.*

"Had this portentous little girl," asked H. Buxton Forman, "an 'anticipated cognition' of Shelley's poet watching

> *'from dawn to gloom*
> *The lake-reflected sun illume*
> *The yellow bees in the ivy bloom?'* "

In this album, apart from the domestic tributes and celebrations mentioned in the previous chapter, we have certain verses of more dramatic quality, such as "On an Eruption of Mount Etna: 8th May 1814," beginning:

> *Loud blows October's chilly blast*
> *And Etna's firebrands rudely cast,*

> *Many a cottage burns upon the ground—*
> *Many a thundering hissing's heard around—*

and (with a flavour of William Cowper) "On first seeing the
Sea at Tynemouth" in the summer of 1814:

> *The German Ocean rolls upon my sight,*
> *A wat'ry world of brilliant light;*
> *The proud rocks overhang the sea,*
> *The sands afford a walk for me*
> *When there, the mighty hand of God*
> *I saw in every step I trod!*

In the same year she wrote "Hannibal's Passage of the Alps,"
describing in such stirring lines as these the effect on the
Phœnician army of attacks by stoning from above the pass:

> *Down the steep hills fell Elephants and Men,*
> *Into vast Gulphs or solitary den—*
> *Where horrid fiends were gathering far and near,*
> *Such were their feelings amid War and fear,*
> *Where ne'er was heard the blithely singing Lark,*
> *Death takes them for his bloody arrow's mark. . . .*

Of Elizabeth's lifelong interest in novels there is indication in
small prose works of fiction written this year, 1814. The prose
is remarkably well constructed for so young a child. We know
that certain poems were composed for sale in aid of charity:
perhaps a note appended to a prose work "Sebastian" was written with an agreeably childish eye upon pocket-money. The
tale is dedicated to her mother:

Madam,—

    I request you to accept this little story for three shil-
lings, and to write copies to be sold to the public.

I am, Madam,
Your most ob't Humble Servant,
Elizabeth Barrett

N.B. You owe me 8d. for other things:—

At the end of another tale we have a further reminder that
capital, commercial or charitable, was sometimes made out of
poems and stories:

ELIZABETH BARRETT AS A BABY
from the lid of a snuff-box

HOPE END
from an early photograph

EDWARD MOULTON BARRETT
probably painted about 1820

Madam,—

> *It would give me great pleasure if you could dispose of "The Way to humble Pride" as you have done of the other stories— I am, Madam,*
>
> > *Your most ob't Humble Serv't—*
> > *Elizabeth Barrett.*

Added to these are short moral essays "Of Prophesy," "An Address to Truth," in an elevated style of copybook maxim; in the main conventional enough, though one beginning "Where can happiness be found?" having its answer in:

To rise early and to let industry have a share in your time—to open your eyes, and your ears to the voice of the beggar,— to press humanity to your breast, and at the last, to ascend to Heaven, and to receive the reward of your labors—

suggests an early conviction resolutely adhered to through years of illness and sorrow. We do not know whether Elizabeth in health willingly practised the chilly virtue of early rising, but in a life restricted by ill health she achieved much for the cause of humanity; in herself attaining at length to a degree of spirituality so fine that one who saw her a few years before her death exclaimed: "I have never seen a human frame which seemed so nearly a transparent veil for a celestial and immortal spirit."

This manuscript book extends, with few verses for the last year, to 1816, the final entries including one scene of an original tragedy upon Regulus in French excellent for her age; but Elizabeth was now turning from original work, postponing it until she was older and wiser. "I read," she tells us, "that I might write." Study became an absorption. "I felt the most ardent desire to understand the learned languages. To comprehend even the Greek alphabet was delight inexpressible." She studied Latin and Greek under Mr. McSwiney, Bro's tutor, studies rendered the more delightful because they were shared with one dearest to her in life. "Literature was the star which in prospect illuminated my future days—it was the spur which prompted me . . the aim . . the very seal of my being."

At nine years of age, though she derived much pleasure "from effusions of my imagination . . . nothing could com-

pensate for the regret I felt in laying down a book to take up
a pen." She had first felt real delight in poetry a year before;
reading *Paradise Lost,* Shakespeare's plays, Pope's translation
of Homer, and Beattie's *The Minstrel.* It is an instance of the
remarkable sagacity of this child that at fourteen she could
analyse her attitude to poetry. The greater works mainly interested her for the story. "I was then too young to feel the
loveliness of simple beauty,—I required something dazzling to
strike my mind. The brilliant imagery, the fine metaphors and
flowing numbers of 'The Minstrel' truly astonished me."

Of particular interest to a biographer is the occasional verse
of this family, mostly birthday odes and tributes, a form of
compliment in which the mother herself joined. The following,
written by Elizabeth on April 27th, 1814 exhibits her father in
a particularly pleasant light:

TO MY DEAREST PAPA!

Sweet Parent! dear to me as kind
Who sowed the very bottom of my mind
And raised the very inmost of my heart
To taste the sweets of Nature you impart!

I hope you will let us drink tea with you, and have your fiddle
to-night—
　　Your dear child Elizabeth
An answer to the Nursery.

She writes a lively and facetious "Epistle to Dearest Papa in
London," another in the same vein to her sister Henrietta suffering from a cold ("Altho' dear Addles far too much you eat"),
ending:

And I am, dearest Henrietta!
Your very dear Elizabeth Barrett
Compared to you, a chatting parrott.

More seriously, the recovery of Baby Arabella from a dangerous illness is celebrated in a birthday address to her father. A
visit to Matlock is described from the carriage stop at "the neat
and smiling Inn" through a climb up shaggy hills to a limestone
cave with underground stream:

Here heedless Ba, with magic wonder struck
Her eyes upraised, she gave her foot a duck;

> *The cavern dark, Papa's laugh resounded;*
> *Mama's, Bro's, Addles's all loud rebounded;*

and the glittering beauty of petrified spars with this comment:

> *The massive rocks upon an angle rest,*
> *Nature bears all these wonders in her breast.*

Then came the return to "the morning sun," quitting "the shadowy cave with vapours hung." After running down the hill,

> *Papa, so ever kind, our joys to swell,*
> *Led us to see the petrifying well,*
> *Where heads, wigs, baskets, eggs, lie on the ground*
> *Soon turned to stone, in dropping waters drowned.*

The last poem to be quoted reminds us of a young attachment too soon to be broken by absence, that to her Uncle Sam, written on a visit to his home at Carlton, Yorkshire:

> *Dear Sam, accept my humble lay,*
> *How dear to me I need not say,*
> *And when from Carlton I am gone,*
> *I'll never cease thy love to mourn;*
> *At childhood's age these faults forgive,*
> *When I am older, if I live,*
> *I'll offer better verse to thee,*
> *Who's been so very kind to me.*

"I'll never cease thy love to mourn . . ." This is more than mere childish riming verbiage. To this remarkable girl, later to become a woman of such deep feeling, every loss was, in greater or lesser degree, a memory lifelong. When in 1860, a year before her own death, Henrietta died far from her, out of reach of an ailing woman, Browning wrote: "She has borne it, on the whole, as well as I should have thought possible, but the wounds in that heart never heal altogether, tho' they may film over."

CHAPTER 3

A TRIP TO PARIS [1815]

"I WAS VERY MUCH delighted when I set off for France, and have never repented my resolution to go."

This beginning to "Notes on a Trip to Paris, October and November 1815," comes oddly from a child of nine: the story behind it, revealed in a letter [1] written from Paris by Mrs. Barrett to her mother, Mrs. Graham Clarke, is that "after the carriage was ordered dear Ba seemed so unhappy at our going" that the parents gave way and "she jumped into the carriage with us."

This was in London at five o'clock on the evening of the 17th of October. In the carriage were Mr. and Mrs. Barrett, the triumphant child, a friend, a Mr. Wyatt,[2] and a woman servant. Elizabeth "sat quite still and contented listening to Papa's and Mr. Wyatt's discourse which pleased me much, as Mr. W. told some very entertaining Anecdotes." Later she fell asleep.

She awoke at Rochester, where they spent the night. When next day they arrived at Dover, "only just in time for the packet," our travellers "were very struck . . . with the Castle, pile on pile, heaped on chalky rocks which tell the passing stranger it is England,—England the only asylum for the forlorn and the helpless!"

The crossing took two hours, "an excellent passage," the mother says, though all were seasick; Elizabeth and her mother not seriously and "more from hunger than anything else." At Calais French boats came out to meet them and a band of noisy, quarrelling, half-naked men walked out in the sea eager "to have the honor of carrying us ashore" and looking to the child's eyes "more like monkeys than men." Mr. Barrett at first refused to be carried; "however it was all in vain, they hoisted him off on their shoulders & away we went & were set down on

---

[1] This has been partly drawn upon in the following narrative.

[2] Probably the artist and landscape gardener who had laid out the grounds of Hope End.

the very fine sands from whence we had to climb a ladder to the magnificent pier."

After "an excellent supper and champagne" (the best champagne was seven shillings a bottle) at "Monsr. Quillac's fine hotel" and a good night's rest in clean and handsome rooms, the little student of the classics awoke "as soon as Aurora had thrown off the veil which covered the earth" to see out of the window preparations to drive a light vehicle out of the inn yard. She was "much amused with the postillion's great boots, and their thin half starved and plough tired horses with rope harness, and nearly died of laughing at the nodding Cabriolet, and the slow motion of the horses, as they dragged it out of the yard." This callous laughter at the suffering beasts in one so gentle and pitying must remind us not only of her youth but of the age in which she was born. Horses were but a means of locomotion: the Royal Society for the Prevention of Cruelty to Animals was not founded until 1824.

The party set off in a hired "German barouche" drawn by four horses. In describing the journey to Paris Elizabeth very naturally dwells upon good and unusual food. In Abbeville at the Hôtel de l'Europe "the dishes alone were enough to tempt any one from America to eat them; the wine too was without exception the most delicious I had drunk in France." At Amiens they admired the Cathedral and at Clermont found "the country full of Prussian soldiery," a reminder to us that this was a France occupied by the victorious Allies. Waterloo had been fought only the previous June. Finding but poor accommodation in a town packed with troops, they did not stay to breakfast at Clermont but drove on to Chantilly, where they took the opportunity of visiting "the remains of the magnificent stables" of the Prince de Condé, damaged when the chateau was destroyed in the Revolution.

On the evening of the 22nd they reached Paris, having their first view of "the superb Church of St. Denis where the King was buried." The martyrdom of Louis XVI on the scaffold in January 1793 was still fresh in the minds of travellers.

In Paris, the old city of ancient streets, they found "a very disagreeable smell." As they passed Napoleon's pillar in the Place Vendôme the wheel of the carriage came off "and obliged

us to alight." When the wheel was put on again, they drove in
weary search for rooms in a Paris crowded with troops and
sightseers. Much of the accommodation was *"trop cher."* They
found at last top rooms five storeys up in the Hôtel de Rivoli "at
seven napoleons a week" (£7). Mrs. Barrett tells us the apartment, self-contained, consisted of five rooms "magnificently
furnished" self-contained, consisted of five rooms and a kitchen.
Out of French windows leading on to a balcony they could see
the new Bourbon King, Louis XVIII, whenever he left the Tuil-
leries "and when he shews himself at the windows, which is
once every day after Mass." Mrs. Barrett, though the stairs put
her out of breath, was "delighted with our abode," where, even
from her bed, she could see the beautiful Tuileries gardens.
She acted as interpreter to her husband and Mr. Wyatt, neither
of whom understood a word of French.

Here was Elizabeth in Paris for the first time among the people she was to love and defend so ardently in the person of the
defeated Emperor's nephew. She visited the Louvre (where
much of Napoleon's loot of European art treasures was being
taken down to return to its owners), the Palais Bourbon, St.
Cloud, Versailles, Malmaison (seeing the room and bed in
which Josephine had died the previous year), china, carpet,
glass manufactories, and the Temple of mournful memory.
Here, having heard an anecdote of Louis XVI in prison, she
remarked in parenthesis, having apparently already a healthy
suspicion of official guides: "I ought not entirely [to] believe
what every body says." In the Pantheon she was most interested in the tomb of Voltaire, an author with whom this precocious little girl was perhaps already discreetly acquainted.
One case in her father's library containing among other books
Gibbon's *History* and *Tom Jones* was forbidden her; so, she
told Robert Browning many years after, "I was very obedient
and never touched the books on *that* side, and only read instead Tom Paine's 'Age of Reason,' and Voltaire's 'Philosophical
Dictionary,' and Hume's 'Essays' and Werther and Rousseau
and Mary Wollstonecraft . . books I was never suspected of
looking towards."

Our travellers spent a busy fortnight of sightseeing in Paris,
even relaxing their British and evangelical prejudices enough

to go twice to Mass. Mr. Barrett and his friend spent many
hours in curiosity shops, then crammed with soldiers' loot,
keeping poor Costa, their *"laquais de place,"* quite "out of
breath running about." Mrs. Barrett indulged in a feminine
pastime later to be loved by her daughter, shopping. She
bought for £2 (having been asked double at a fashionable
milliner's) "a highcrowned Spanish black velvet cap" trimmed
with plumes of high black feathers "as Edward could not bear
the great French bonnets."

But perhaps, even more than the Jardin des Plantes with its
live animals, to little Elizabeth the most stirring sight was the
Elephant, some forty feet high, erected in the south-east corner
of the Place de la Bastille, a preliminary model for a grandiose
monument Napoleon had intended to set up to the glory of his
Egyptian campaign. Its trunk, she tells us, "is to cast up water,
and there is to be a staircase up one of its legs into a room for
people to walk up and down in, in its body." This symbol of
egomania, of a power once thought invincible, was in his crum-
bling old age to be immortalized at last by Victor Hugo in *Les
Misérables* as the night refuge of that lively street arab *"le petit
Gavroche."*

Uncle Sam, intending to spend two years abroad, arrived
with friends on November 10. Elizabeth was taken twice to
the theatre, to hear Talma, in whom she was disappointed, and
to a ballet at the Opéra-Comique. Through a delay in getting
passports, two more precious days were spent with "dear Sam,"
who took rooms on the ground floor of the hotel, before they
set off for home. "I could not help being sorry that we left Paris
so soon." This sentiment had been prospectively echoed with
a qualification in Mrs. Barrett's letter to her mother: " The
amusement is varied & unceasing & nothing but seeing my dar-
lings would reconcile me to quitting France so soon as we propose to do." At home in England there were now five other children including Charles John, a baby eleven months old.

They went back through St. Germain, "where we were obliged to sleep in the same room we dined in," and on to Meulan,
where again Elizabeth had the excitement of a wheel coming
off the carriage: it was fastened on for a few francs, securely
enough to carry them on to Vernons, by those handy men the

English soldiers, some of whom were passing. At Gaillon there was the further novelty of sleeping, when the beds were found to be damp, on an extempore couch made of four chairs. Papa and Mamma, dozing uneasily upright, did not fare so well. At Formerie, the child records, they breakfasted on honey, butter, tea, pears, and eggs.

At Port St. Omer, Papa gave money to an old beggar woman who "crossed herself, then said her prayers, crossed herself again, kissed the ground, and stood by the door curtseying—as the horses came out of the yard, she pushed them away, because she said, it was holy ground." This would seem rather excessive thanks for a sou. Papa gave her another "to try if she would repeat her devotions, which she did, and as the carriage drove off she curtseyed, saying she hoped the carriage would not tumble over before we got to the end of our journey." Elizabeth's comment, "poor thing, she was, we were told, foolish," seems superfluous.

On the road to Rouen the child admired the Seine, with its wooded islets, flowing through thick trees and hills. At Rouen they found the Hôtel de France extremely dirty, and again were obliged to sleep in the room they dined in. The inside of the Cathedral Elizabeth thought "scarcely worth seeing." She was more interested in the immense tower, which had "tumbled down three times." They saw where Joan of Arc was burned, had a bad dinner, went to bed, and set off in the dark at seven o'clock next morning for Abbeville. There, on finding the former excellent cook replaced by one decidedly inferior, the small moralist observed: "On such little causes, how much of human happiness is founded!" They sailed from Boulogne on "a fine still evening, and the translucent water reflected the sides of our ship."

"Farewell to France," the little creature exclaims, "and to a people, tho' perhaps extravagant in their praise, yet fascinating in the kindness of their manners." Soon she rejoiced to find herself "by a good comfortable English fireside which, even foreigners must allow, is preferable to all the luxuries of the world."

Elizabeth at home was perhaps confirmed in complacence: a visit to Paris, and so soon after the termination of hostilities,

must have given further distinction to the child prodigy petted
and adulated. Some of this complacence, this good conceit of
herself which she deplores on looking back from the lofty pinnacle of fourteen years, was the result perhaps of a too rapid
development of mind. We find her logical where authority demanded that she should be respectful and obedient. One day
she fell over Uncle Sam's foot and did not apologize. When
asked why, she replied: "I did not mean to do it, it was an accident—why should I beg pardon?" And on meeting her father
one morning on the stairs she merely smiled at him. "Not a
word?" he inquired. She told him she had nothing to say. "Will
you not ask me if I am well?" "No—if you had been ill, you
would have told me."

Her father led her by the hand into the breakfast room.
"Here is a little girl who thinks it too much trouble to ask her
father how he is."

"In short," commented the sage of fourteen, "I was in infinite
danger of being as vain as I was inexperienced."

The sense of superiority given by studies in Latin and Greek
—the rapid power of assimilation and possibly a daily feeling
of triumph over Bro as they worked with Mr. McSwiney—was
heightened the following summer during a visit to Ramsgate,
where "the heated imagination was perhaps increased by the
intoxicating gaieties of a watering place." Here she began her
epic poem "The Battle of Marathon." Let us continue the story
in her own words: "When we came home one day after having
written a page of poetry I considered models of beauty I ran
downstairs to the library to seek Pope's Homer in order to compare them that I might enjoy my own SUPERIORITY. . . . I read
fifty lines from the glorious Father of the lyre.—It was enough
. . . I felt the whole extent of my immense and mortifying in-
feriority."

She burst into tears of humiliation. For a time she "could find
no pleasure in any book but Homer."

CHAPTER 4

THE BATTLE OF MARATHON [1820]

"AT TWELVE," Elizabeth tells us, looking back two years, "I enjoyed a literary life in all its pleasures. Metaphysics were my highest delight and having read a page of Locke my mind not only felt edified but exalted." It was the direct influence of Locke that led her to examine her own mind so minutely.

This exaltation led to a healthy recovery of ambition. Perhaps strengthened by the composing of an epic poem in four books, Elizabeth felt equal to dealing with the loftier subject of theology and "was in great danger of becoming the founder of a religion of my own." In the heat of imagination, an unbridled fantasy, the plain worship in her own home could not then satisfy her. "I worshipped God, heart and soul, but I forgot that my prayers should be pure and simple as the Father I adored. They were composed extempore and full of figurative and florid apostrophes to the Deity." There had been a time when this child worshipped false gods, kindling altar fires in the garden to Athena with matches stolen from the housemaid's cupboard, but now she was fervently Christian. "I shall always," she wrote at fourteen, "look back to this time as the happiest of my life."

It was perhaps inevitable, in a household where too much emphasis was openly laid upon religion for the comfort of the young, that this precocious mind in a body approaching adolescence should be painfully disturbed. A happy state of religious certainty could not endure. Having omitted a prayer one day, the little girl feared she "had so offended the God of my salvation that I hardly hoped for pardon." Her prayers were long and agonizing. "My God, my God," she cried, "why hast thou forsaken me?" It was a dark morning, "a dingy mist floated in the mid air . . . a veil of loneliness." Then a flood of sunlight illuminated the child's room. "My imagination took fire and I believed that my God had forgiven me."

This paroxysm of conscience over, Elizabeth was reading and studying to but one end: "to gain ideas, not to indulge my fancy and I studied the works of those critics whose attention was directed to my favorite authors." Milton was read all through, Shakespeare studied; Pope's Homer was still a cherished book. Her "religious enthusiasm" having subsided, she took upon herself to advocate the cause of the Church of England, but whether in the presence of her father or the seclusion of the nursery she does not say.

In this year we get a hint of wholesome discipline. A petition was put up to Papa and Mamma in neat couplets, with this argument:

> *But if a hungry chicken wants to eat*
> *The hen throws victuals close, before its feet.*
> *Then let me to the Music Meeting go—*
> *The pleasure it would give me none can know;*
> *If you are troubled for my night's repose*
> *Half of Bum's bed is open to my woes.*

The petition, though, one may guess, supported by an indulgent aunt, was refused.

By the summer of 1817, we learn from a letter to her mother, she was already at work upon the preface to *The Battle of Marathon*, but the poem was not printed until 1820, when she was fourteen.

This youthful epic is both vigorous and sonorous, though perhaps an observation of her own in the preface may serve as a major criticism: "The battle of Marathon is not, perhaps, a subject calculated to exercise the powers of the imagination, or of poetic fancy, the incidents being so limited." Two quotations may suffice, the first being the opening of Book 3:

> *When from the deep the hour's eternal sway*
> *Impels the coursers of the flaming day,*
> *The long-haired Greeks with brazen arms prepare*
> *Their freedom to preserve and wage the war.*
> *First Aristides from the couch arose,*
> *While his great mind with all Minerva glows;*
> *His mighty limbs his golden arms invest,*
> *The cuirass blazes on his ample breast,*
> *The glittering cuisses both his legs enfold,*

And the huge shield's on fire with burnished gold;
His hands two spears uphold of equal size,
And fame's bright glories kindle in his eyes;
Upon his helmet plumes of horse-hair nod,
And forth he moved, majestic as a God!

These are the last lines of the epic:

By vengeance fired, the Grecians from the deep
With rage and shouting scale the lofty ship,
Then in the briny bosom of the main
They hurl in heaps the living and the slain;
Thro' the wide shores resound triumphant cries,
Fill all the seas, and thunder thro' the skies.

It is conceivable (though I know of no example) that a clever imitative child without genius, deeply read in Homer and Pope, might accomplish such an epic, though few could stay the course through four books; but the preface, dated 1819, with its close reasoning, its clear expression and disclosure of a strong critical faculty, could only have been written by the Elizabeth Barrett who contributed so much to that important book of 1844, *A New Spirit of the Age.* After commenting that "Now, even the female may drive her Pegasus through the realms of Parnassus, without being saluted with the most equivocal of all appellations, a learned lady," she continues in the following paragraph:

In these reading days there need be little vulgar anxiety among poets for the fate of their works: the public taste is no longer so epicurean. As the press pours forth profusion, the literary multitude eagerly receive its lavish offerings, while the sublimity of Homer, and the majesty of Virgil, those grand and solitary specimens of ancient poetic excellence, so renowned through the lapse of ages, are by many read only as schoolbooks, and are justly estimated alone by the comparative few. . . .

There are real poets among these prolific rimers "though they be mingled with an inferior multitude of the common herd." Here we, with the romantic age behind us, might expect the names of Wordsworth, Coleridge, Keats, and Shelley, but in 1819 these poets, so clearly to us the great ones, were little

known or respected in the average cultured home: the stars in
Elizabeth's firmament were Byron, Moore, and Scott.

Of Pope, whose couplets she imitated in this work, the girl
wrote:

*No one who has read his translation of Homer, can refuse him
the immortality which he merits so well, and for which he laboured so long. He it was who planted rime for ever in the
regions of Parnassus, and uniting elegance with strength, and
sublimity with beauty, raised the English language to the highest degree of smoothness and purity.*

Some twenty years later, freed from the strait jacket of pseudo-
classical prose and poetry, she wrote of Wordsworth:

*He laid his hand on the Pegasean mane, and testified that it
was not floss silk. He testified that the ground was not all lawn
or bowling-green; that the forest trees were not clipped upon
a pattern. He scorned to be contented with a tradition of
beauty, or with an abstraction of the beautiful.*

Truly in this preface to her first printed work the child was
mother to the woman.

One light-hearted family criticism came from Elizabeth's
grandmother, Mrs. Moulton: "Your preface my dear Elizabeth was so formidable that I expected it would end in nothing less than a call on me to pay the national debt or the seven
millions which it is said will be required to build the Prince a
new palace."

The volume was announced on its title page as "printed for
W. Lindsell, 87, Wimpole Street, Cavendish Square," but probably the whole issue of fifty copies came down eventually, if
not at first, to Hope End. There are now only seven known
examples, and of these not one was of Elizabeth's own possession. Browning, indeed, doubted its existence, writing to
Thomas Wise in 1888 (with, by the way, a delicious unconscious irony): "I have a doubt whether *The Battle of Marathon*
. . . may not be a fabrication." Elizabeth herself, who called
it in later years "Pope's Homer done over again, or rather undone," probably wished this juvenile performance to be buried
and forgotten.

In 1820 when, after the publication of this ambitious piece,

she wrote down those revealing "Glimpses into my own life
and Literary Character" from which I have largely quoted,
Elizabeth was suffering from her first loss. Bro, her constant
and adored companion, was now away from her for many
months of the year in London at Charterhouse School.[1] In her
new loneliness the earnest child prayed for his preservation
from the dangers of a public school. "Heaven knows my heart
that I would unhesitatingly buy his happiness with my own
misery! But oh if there is a bitterness worse than death, if
there is any pang which surpasses human wretchedness in
agony it would be that with which I should behold him were
he ever to stray from the path of honorable rectitude!"

At this maternal anxiety in a girl of fourteen over a brother
a year younger we can smile, but it must be with tenderness,
commiseration: in a few years she was to know the full loss of
that brother.

After dwelling in imagination on the possible behaviour of
Bro "when the laugh of dissipation assails" him, she ends this
remarkable document with a final self-examination. "My dis-
position is haughty, impatient and fiery but I trust my heart is
good—I am confident it is grateful." She is "capable of patriotism, enthusiastic and sincere," and must express her anger at
"the base and servile aristocracy of my beloved country"; that
aristocracy which was, in 1820, trying for adultery "our mag-
nanimous and unfortunate Queen" at the instigation of a monarch notoriously unfaithful. Like most Liberals, large and small,
Elizabeth whole-heartedly supported Queen Caroline. "The
dearest wish of my heart would be to serve her—to serve the
glorious Queen of my native isle." Elizabeth vented indignation in dramatic form, writing a first scene in very tolerable
blank verse. A line and a half of it may embody a painful personal reminiscence of the trip to France five years before:
"Think of me sometimes Charlotte! . . . I must pass that terrible ocean." The scene ends with this couplet:

> *And I—I go to cross the dark blue sea*
> *Th'abused—the desolate—but yet the free.*

This recalls, both in phrase and content, another object of
scandal whose affairs, amorous and matrimonial, were attract-

[1] He was there at the same time as Thackeray.

ing attention that year. Lord Byron's all-pervading influence is apparent in the rhapsody which follows in the "Glimpses":

I have remembered the littleness of Man when compared to the Majesty of God and my heart has throbbed almost wildly with a strange and undefined feeling!—I have gazed on the fleeting clouds which rolled their light columns over the dark blue sky and wept while I felt that such was the futility of life.

But hers was not a nature to give way more than dramatically to that cultivated melancholy, termed Byronic, which had its roots in the eighteenth-century "graveyard school" of writers. Her feelings were acute, there is too much sentiment and "too little rational reflection" in her being, but she could control herself, and so rigidly that "I often appear to my dearest friends to lack common feeling!" This restraint went deeper than mere self-control: to the end of her life and even with the supremely beloved, Mrs. Browning remained dumb in suffering, only partially able to relieve herself in poetry. She never could speak of those lost to her.

Even in Byronic mood Elizabeth was not going to admit her outlook on life to be a gloomy one: she had far too much of native high spirits for that. Although there had been moments of acute disillusionment, "my views on every subject are naturally cheerful and light as the first young vision of aerial hope."

In some notes made in maturity on her childhood (which have already been slightly drawn upon here) Elizabeth gives a less self-consciously austere picture of her young self, telling how at ten years of age she was by no means indifferent to her personal appearance, but would tiptoe to her mother's triple pier-glass to admire herself "multiplied by three." It was perhaps at this time she demanded that her hair should grow from the fashionable short crop of childhood to the long tresses we associate with her: now as she gazed the child reflected that when her hair was down to her feet, perhaps when she was fifteen ("the age when all the princesses in the fairy tales were fallen in love"), she might be as pretty as Peggy, a local rustic beauty. She intended to be very much in love. Her lover's name should be Henry—unless, of course, he happened to be Lord Byron.

But at times another dream arising out of an early dislike and contempt for femininity, a resentment she had not been born a boy, dominated Elizabeth's thoughts. She was, of course, to be a poet, among women as Homer was among men: she would wear men's clothes and live on a Greek island girt by a sea turquoise-blue, or perhaps in a cave upon Mount Parnassus, feeding on cresses and Helicon water.

This girl, later to be such an ardent friend to women, then despised them all, with the possible exception of Madame de Staël. The fashionable mincing delicacies, the tender nerves and affectations annoyed her. She herself was not "feminine." She could run fast and jump high, and though her hands were "miserably small to be sure," her wrists were strong. She could climb and slide, and liked fishing, though she didn't often catch anything. She liked bows and arrows, squirts and pop-guns; but best of all riding, "galloping till the trees raced past her and the clouds were shot over her head like arrows from a giant's bow," on her black pony, Moses, who had a tail "longer by nine times than the patriarch's beard."

At fifteen she would arm herself in complete steel and ride along the banks of the Danube, singing her own poetry as she went and collecting many warriors. At Istanbul she would be the chief of a battalion, destroy the Turkish Empire and deliver Greece. These were fine dreams, in essence not wholly abandoned: Elizabeth was to do battle, not with an army but with marshalled words, for the enslaved at home and abroad, and in later years to exhaust her frail body in excited championship of the Italian *Risorgimento*.

But by the age of fifteen this little creature's fiery energy was to receive a sobering check: some accident or illness laid her on her back for several years, driving her spirit inward on itself and making her more completely the companion of books, of the mighty dead.

CHAPTER 5

LEARNED LADY

ELIZABETH'S FIRST PERIOD OF SERIOUS ILLNESS was attributed by
Lady Ritchie (*Dictionary of National Biography*) to a fall: impatient for her ride, the girl had tried to equip a pony herself
and, falling with the heavy saddle upon her, had injured her
spine. Pen Browning, Elizabeth's son, however, stated that the
spine injury, not suspected at first, was caused by a strain while
tightening the pony's girths. Perhaps, as Elizabeth remained so
small in person, this pony was still Moses, an animal fiery and
impatient as his mistress; loving his freedom and escaping when
he could into the Malvern Hills.

If, as Pen Browning said, the injury was not at first suspected,
a derangement of the nervous system may have been wrongly
and painfully treated. On March 8, 1821 we find a Dr. Carden
recommending shower baths and outdoor exercise. In the following June, Dr. William Coker diagnosed "the case of Miss
Barrett, that prodigy in intellectual powers and acquirements,"
as a serious affection of the nerves, manifesting itself in severe
bouts of pain:

*The suffering is agony, and the paroxysms continue from a
quarter of an hour to an hour and upwards, accompanied by
convulsive twitches of the muscles, in which the diaphragm is
particularly concerned.*

During the progress of an attack, which would cease as it
reached its terrible climax, "the mind is for the most part conscious of surrounding objects, but towards its close, there is
generally some, and occasionally, very considerable confusion
produced by it." On looking back in 1843 to this period of torture, Elizabeth told R. H. Horne: "at fifteen I nearly died."

Elizabeth, no longer able to take an active part in the children's games, was driven in upon herself: "in a retirement
happy in many ways" she read "Greek as hard under the trees as
some of your Oxonians in the Bodleian; gathered visions from

Plato and the dramatists, and eat and drank Greek and made my
head ache with it." Her life was, she told Browning years later,
lonely, "growing green like the grass around it. Books and
dreams were what I lived in—and domestic life only seemed to
buzz gently around, like the bees about the grass." She was fast
developing in interests, in intellectual power away from the
family in general. "My sympathies drooped towards the ground
like an untrained honeysuckle—and but for *one*, in my own
house—but of this I cannot speak." This "one" was, of course,
Bro, that loved brother finally to be lost in circumstances of
bitter tragedy. Bro, however, was at this time away from home
many months of the year at Charterhouse School. Sam, a lively
companion too, in his way, soon joined him there.[1]

On her recovery Elizabeth seems to have led a fairly active
life again, though riding is no longer mentioned. She drove fast
in a pony carriage about the steep leafy Herefordshire lanes;
when her father went to Ledbury on business she would accompany him. Late in the century old people remembered the
young girl with the pale spiritual face sitting waiting in the carriage for her father at the toll-gate outside Ledbury. She seldom
entered the busy market town.

In these years, before the illness and after, she continued her
studies, not only in Greek but in Latin and Italian. Of her translations there have survived examples from Moschus, Horace,
Cicero, Claudian, Anacreon, and Dante. Later she learned German, probably some Spanish, and acquired enough Hebrew to
read her Old Testament through in the original from beginning
to end. On looking back in 1859 Elizabeth considered this period of intensive study, although she covered "a wider surface
than most scholars perhaps," as a loss of time "and life." On her
Greek, which included the reading of "nearly every word extant," she commented: "never was a vainer kind of smattering!"
"I *believe*," she added, "that nothing helps the general faculties
so little as the study of languages." But, even if we can accept
her conclusion, surely a survey of so wide a field was a fruitful
substitute for the "life" available to a young woman of her period and circumstance, one largely limited to family, drawing-
room, and a remote countryside.

[1] Family letters.

Of her studies in and about 1820 I have before me evidence in the form of small exercises, Latin, Greek, French, and Italian, some in the form of letters and—more important in the development of a poet—essays in Italian verse [2] (see Appendix 1), attempts which must have gone to produce that "strange music" which haunted Robert Browning and enchanted the Rossetti brothers. These small poems, for all their necessary faults, are lively and living products of the poet. Her Italian master was quite evidently a man skilled in the practice of verse in conventional eighteenth-century metres.

The subject matter of the majority of these poems is of vital interest to a biographer: she who in her last years was to be obsessed with Italy's struggle for freedom now sang of enslaved Greece, of the bid for freedom in Spain and the death by execution of Riego, the great Spanish patriot, of tyranny in Italy and the fleeing of her patriots to Great Britain. But in 1820 the emancipation of oppressed peoples, both white and coloured, British or alien, was in the air, heralding in minds and hearts the liberal reforms of the century.

These exercises in verse and prose, the probes of a genius rather than the regular product of a student, show signs of that impatience in learning, a desire to take all knowledge too rapidly for her province, which made the Italian master call her, in an effort to convey the adjective "headlong," "*testa lunga.*" The Latin of a letter [3] containing quotations that are probably hits at her brother's lessons in that language is lively but not too correct. It is addressed on its outward fold: *Puero eruditissimo et elegantissimo Bro a menu stultissimi Sam de puella impudentissima—*

"*Scribimus docti indoctique*"   "*O tempora o mores*"
           Horace   *Cicero*

On four octavo sheets pinned together [4] there are, besides Anacreontic Greek verses and short translations from Greek fables, letters in lively French dated 1820, to Socrates, to Pindar, and "Au Seigneur Homère, Les Champs Elyseès, Pres du Palais de Pluton, L'Enfers." She expresses friendship, though telling Homer (with a suggestion that schoolroom hours under Mr.

---

[2] Hagedorn Collection.   [4] Hewlett Collection.
[3] Hewlett Collection.

McSwiney were not always idyllically peaceful): *"Je vous as-sure que vous devez etre bien poli aupres de moi car Je vous ai toujours traitée en ami et J'ai soufferte beaucoup à cause de vous et du plaisir et du douleur—par l'esprit et par les oreilles!"* Cavil-ling at Virgil, who, professing friendship for Homer, stole from him, she calls Virgil *"un lurion, un coquin, un lache, un poltron"* —adding: *"Je l'appellerais tous les noms dont Je peux me sou-venir."* She hopes *"le Seigneur Mercure"* will be sure to deliver the letter, says she has no time to write more, and assures Ho-mer of her *"amitie eternelle."*

The letter to Socrates is more flippant. She doesn't know him perfectly but writes with as sincere a friendship as she is ca-pable of. She had heard he has *"les manieres bien dures"* and a grave face, and that his beard is long and majestic. Her *"dis-cours"* may seem to him *"trop gai"* though she is trying not to laugh and make faces. She would like to compose *"une harangue philosophique sur la materialite du corps ou sur l'immortalité de l'esprit"* just to please him, but can't *"à cause de mon papier et de mon humeur que n'est pas bien adapté aux sujets philoso-phiques."* But her *"amour propre"* flatters her he will be charmed with her because he is not too accustomed to polite-ness—at any rate *"Madame notre Femme"* is not at all *"douce."* She asks him to convey her compliments to *"notre bon ami Platon,"* protests friendship, and ends in a postscript with: *"J'espere que Je vous verrai souvent quand Je viens dans l'enfer—"*

To "Electric Pindar, quick as fear," [5] she writes her last let-ter, telling him she loves him *"a la folie"* though she can't un-derstand him perfectly and has to use translations. She refers to Horace's complimentary ode to him (Book IV, ii) and at the end professes her love for him in these pretty words: *"Je vous aime au tel point que la mort seroit depouilée de toutes ses ter-reurs, croyez moi pour le seul plaisir de vous voir—Adieu—"*

It will be seen that the French is careless, especially in point of accents, but the idiom lively and characteristic. There is gen-uine appreciation and understanding of these great men; un-derstanding to be expressed tersely in poetic form some twenty years later in "A Vision of Poets." Of the depth and breadth of

---

[5] "A Vision of Poets."

her reading before and during those twenty years we can turn to the "Vision" and see enshrined there Homer, Æschylus, Euripides, Sophocles, Pindar, Theocritus, Sappho, Aristophanes, Virgil, Lucretius; Ariosto, Dante, Alfieri, Berni, Tasso, Petrarch; Racine, Corneille; Camoëns, Calderòn, Lope de Vega; Goethe, Schiller; and a host of English poets pseudo-classical and romantic.

Of the classical studies, vigorously pursued again later with the help of the blind scholar Hugh Boyd, evidences remain in the form of volumes with her name written in them; many of them in duodecimo because, Browning tells us, her hands were so small she could not with comfort hold larger books.

But this brilliant girl was primarily poet, not scholar. The poetic ambitions were not forgotten. By 1822 she had completed a long poem and sent it to Thomas Campbell, the popular poet and editor of the *New Monthly Magazine*.

On August 28 Campbell wrote a tactful and kindly letter [6] in which, though he held out no hope that this poem was "likely to be popularly admired," he contrived without direct praise to encourage the young author; ending with:

I trust you will believe you have a

> *Sincere & respectful well wisher*
> *Thos. Campbell.*

This very naturally elated the girl: unwisely she sent him more poems, one of which appears from the evidence of a title page and dedication [7] to have been "Leila, an Eastern Tale." This title page of "Leila" bears a quotation that in its modest humour, combined as it was with a truly handsome tribute to himself, might further have softened the poet's heart:

> "*Duke. And what's her history?*
> *Viola. A blank, my lord.*"
> *Twelfth Night.*

On December 1 Campbell wrote again, this time altering his previous formal address as "Madam" to "My dear Young Lady." As he had already applauded the symptoms of promising talent, "it was very natural for your youth & ingenuousness to throw yourself again on my confidence." He liked her "nothing

---

[6] MS. 1807, f. 79. Small Collections, National Library of Scotland.
[7] Hagedorn Collection.

the worse for a mistake originating in simplicity," but he was a busy editor; far too busy to "admit of renew'd applications for criticisms on the works of young authors, however promising they may be—I have neither eye-sight nor leisure for it." There, so far as we know, the correspondence ended.

To one of these manuscripts, probably that of "Leila," there is a preface in draft [8] which shows that the young author was contemplating the publication of another volume. This, however, perhaps because of Campbell's discouragement, did not materialize: it was not until 1826 that Elizabeth published *An Essay on Mind.*

Of Elizabeth's life in the years 1822 and 1823 we have little knowledge: she was writing, while perhaps working on "An Essay on Mind," pieces in the style of Byron and Campbell. Her brother Septimus was born, and William Wordsworth visited Uvedale Price at Foxley Park, only seven and a half miles from Hope End. Uvedale Price, landscape gardener, classical scholar, and musician, may already have been a friend of the Barretts, but it is almost certain that Elizabeth did not meet Wordsworth either on this occasion or in 1827, when he came to Foxley once more; however, in verses written at the end of this year on Storm's birthday (printed among the poems appended to "An Essay on Mind" as "Memory") his influence might for the first time be apparent in such lines as

> *My Fancy's steps have often strayed*
> *To some fair vale the hills have made;*
> *Where sparkling waters travel o'er,*
> *And hold a mirror to the shore.*

But as in these verses Elizabeth says her "chatting pen runs on," it would appear that she still did not regard the easier style as more than suitable to occasional verse; indeed, the later stanzas catch up the first line's personification of Fancy with Thought and Memory, Virtue and Learning in the old Popean way.

The year 1825 marked her first entry into the public press; a form of publication she was to favour even in her days of fame. William Jerdan printed in the *Literary Gazette*, November 19, "The Rose and Zephyr," a fanciful little piece of the love of a zephyr for a faithless flower. On May 6, 1826, the *Gazette* pub-

---

[8] Hewlett Collection.

lished her "Irregular Stanzas," lines of interest to us both as an
early expression of interest in Liberalism and liberty and as an
involuntary prophecy:

> *Oh! should I ever live to be*
> *On the sunlit plains of Italy,*
> *I would walk as they walk beside the dead,*
> *With voiceless lips and a soundless tread!*

Italy should be for her no land of mere art, of "Pleasure, cold
and light":

> *. . . Glory was her ancient spouse,*
> *And her heart remembers its early vows.*

The mind goes forward in reading these stanzas to *Casa Guidi
Windows*, to the *"O bella libertà, o bella!"* the singing child outside, and to the poet's declaration:

> *And I, a singer also, from my youth,*
> *Prefer to sing with these who are awake,*
> *With birds, with babes, with men who will not fear*
> *The baptism of the holy morning dew . . .*
>
> *Than join those old thin voices with my new,*
> *And sigh for Italy with some safe sigh*
> *Cooped up in music 'twixt an oh and ah,—*
> *Nay, hand in hand with that young child, will I*
> *Go singing rather, "Bella libertà,"*
> *Than, with those poets, croon the dead or cry*
> *"Se tu men bella fossi, Italia!"*

That year of 1826 was to see the publication of her second
volume of verse, *An Essay on Mind*.

CHAPTER   6

AN ESSAY ON MIND, WITH OTHER POEMS [1826]

To HER SECOND VOLUME of verse, published anonymously, Elizabeth attached a modest line from Tasso: "*Brama assai, poco spera, e nulla chiede.*" [1] Perhaps the choice of this motto denoted a determination to test public opinion: *An Essay on Mind* was, priced at five shillings, obviously not intended purely for private circulation.

Whatever may have been Elizabeth's original estimate of the title work in 1843 she wrote of it to R. H. Horne as
A didactic poem . . . long repented of as worthy of all repentance. The poem is imitative in its form, yet is not without traces of an individual thinking and feeling—the bird pecks through the shell of it. With this it has a pertness and pedantry which did not even then belong to the character of the author, and which I regret now more than I do the literary defectiveness.

The "pertness" or, more strictly, mild wit of some lines leavens a heavy lump for the reader of today, revealing more than in any other work, except *Aurora Leigh,* that innate humour which makes her letters so delightful. Its main interest perhaps lies in the passages on poetry and poets. Elizabeth and her world have, by 1826, changed in poetic taste: Wordsworth has done his work. We are invited to roam with "the musing poet" and with Nature to "steal instruction from her classic tome." There is an amusing scornful passage (though prefaced by a tribute to Pope as the poet of Reason) on the pseudo-classical drama of France:

> *—'twere mean*
> *To leave the path of Nature for Racine;*
> *When Nero's parent, 'midst her woe, defines*
> *The wrong that tortures—in two hundred lines:*
> *Or when Orestes, maddened by his crime,*
> *Forgets life, joy, and everything—but rime.*

[1] Desire much, hope for little, and demand nothing.

This girl, forestalling Victor Hugo's attack, pleaded for poetry

> *Not clogged by useless drapery, not beset*
> *By the superfluous word or epithet,*
> *Wherein Conception only dies in state,*
> *As Draco smothered by the garments' weight—*

Among the thirteen poems attached to "An Essay on Mind" we find ample evidence again of that deep interest in Continental struggles for freedom. In style a use of obsolete words and phrases points to a growing absorption in the old literature, hinting at a mediævalism that she was to be among the first to make popular in later years. We get too a touch of that nervous, almost apocalyptic mysticism which her contemporary critics stigmatized as "dreamy"; a mysticism in which there is already a vein of sad foreboding. Among these minor poems is one astonishingly mature, the beautiful "Song" beginning "Weep, as if you thought of laughter!"

When copies of *An Essay on Mind* arrived at Hope End, Elizabeth was from home: Mrs. Barrett wrote to her of the family's excitement. The copies came about dinner-time, but both parents were too excited to do justice to the dishes of a cook with the charmingly apt name of Mrs. Tuckem. When the children were in bed—having had some of the poems read to them by Arabel—Elizabeth's parents sat close to the fire turning over the leaves of this "wondrous little book."

The volume attracted little attention: William Jerdan, who had published verses of hers in the *Literary Gazette*, and to whom the secret of authorship may have been revealed, printed a short review on July 15, in which her own advice to poets was returned on her: "All that we ask of the fair author is to address herself more to nature, and undress herself from the deep *blue* in which she is now attired." H. Buxton Forman suggested that the notice was written by L. E. L., a frequent contributor to the *Literary Gazette*.

It may have been a copy of *An Essay on Mind* that drew to the learned young lady serious attention from a distinguished neighbour, Uvedale Price of Foxley Park—though Elizabeth in a birthday poem to him in 1827 suggests a longer interest.

Uvedale Price, already known as a writer upon landscape

gardening, published at the age of eighty "a most ingenious work" (to quote his friend William Wordsworth) "on ancient metres and the proper mode of reading Greek and Latin verse." "If he be right," Wordsworth added, "we have been all wrong, and I think he is." This old man, "all life and spirits," still with a heart for youth, asked the young author of *An Essay on Mind* to read and comment on the proofs of this book. Elizabeth was "greatly struck by the original chain of argument." About the chapter on hexameters, with quotations from the English poets, she made criticisms, remarking on the omission of Dante from his catalogue of poets who "have done all that was possible in less perfect languages and metres," and citing as an "instance of metrical felicity" the last line of Canto V of the *Inferno:*

E caddi come corpo morto cade

with the comment: "It is almost superfluous to observe what a different character is here given to the iambi—(no longer *celeres*)—by the monotony of consonants and vowels—how much heaviness and falling and stiffness we have instead—how much of the 'Corpo morto.'"

There ensued a long and learned correspondence [2] and the development of a stronger intellectual intimacy. "Mr. Price's friendship," Elizabeth recorded in a private memorandum, "has given me more continual happiness than any single circumstance ever did—and I pray for *him,* as the grateful pray." Uvedale Price appears to have done much to encourage the young poet, thereby poaching perhaps on a preserve the loving proud father felt to be his own: certainly from a scrutiny of the memorandum quoted above, and from other papers before him, H. Buxton Forman thought he detected distinct signs of parental jealousy. But if Price did trouble the domestic peace it was not for long. He died in 1829, one year after being created a baronet.

It is probable too that another and longer friendship arose from the publication of *An Essay on Mind.* In Malvern there lived a blind classical scholar, Hugh Stuart Boyd, with whom Elizabeth corresponded. In 1827 a meeting was discussed; but, although Boyd was a middle-aged married man with a daughter, Elizabeth's father objected. When they did meet for the

---

[2] Unpublished, in the Wellesley Collection.

first time in March 1828, it was in a somewhat violent and dramatic manner.

Boyd is known to have lived in two houses at Malvern (then but a series of villages): Ruby Cottage, Malvern Wells, and Woodland Lodge, Great Malvern. There is also a strong local tradition that he was at one time in Rose Cottage, Barnard's Green. It must, however, from the internal evidence of Elizabeth's account of their first meeting, have been Ruby Cottage, or more correctly "The Ruby," which Boyd inhabited in 1827; probably as a lodger, since many of the houses already provided apartments for the people who came to take the pure spring water of the wells.

When Boyd wrote a long reproachful letter saying that he might soon be leaving Malvern, Elizabeth went in distress to her father and begged permission to visit him. Mr. Barrett told her she might do as she liked. A few days later she set out with Bro, Arabel, and Henrietta; Bro to pay the visit with her, and the girls to await them at a house close by belonging to some friends named Trant. Elizabeth was eager but intensely nervous, expecting in the learned man's conversation "something particularly awful and abrupt."

As they came to that precipitous hill on the old road beyond the Wyche,[3] Bro noticed that there was no drag chain to the carriage; but, having been driven down without one by a friend a few days before, Elizabeth urged her brother to take the risk. The pony, with the vehicle pressing behind him, rushed down the steep. Bro cried out: "Hold tight! don't touch the reins!" but Elizabeth, losing her head, seized hold of one. Soon they were all thrown out; fortunately landing on a bank at the side of the road. Only Henrietta sustained injury, and slightly, escaping with a bumped forehead and sprained ankle.

A coach going by at that moment, Bro put Henrietta inside and set off on foot with his other two sisters. Further on they came to the carriage, but the pony seems to have been out of action, or too frightened to handle. Bro unharnessed him, tied him to a tree and took the shafts of the carriage himself. He pulled Elizabeth along until, fearing he might be tired, she was getting out when Mr. and Mrs. Boyd appeared.

[3] Cars are not now permitted to drive down it.

Poor Elizabeth, covered in dust, pelisse torn and bonnet bent, had no choice but to go up as boldly as possible to Mr. Boyd and hold out her hand. Mrs. Boyd, distressed over the accident, offered assistance at her house, but Elizabeth felt that she must deny herself the visit and go to Henrietta at the Trants' house. Mr. and Mrs. Boyd walked along with them. Boyd, a man of natural gloom, reproached himself for having been the cause of the accident. "But this is ominous, Miss Barrett—I *hope* you do not believe in omens." She assured him that "a merciful preservation could not be considered a bad omen."

Elizabeth gave an account of this adventure in a letter intended for her grandmother, Mrs. Moulton, but on second thoughts preserved by herself for future reference. Of Boyd she wrote:

My eccentric friend is a rather young looking man than otherwise, moderately tall, and slightly formed. His features are good —his face very pale, with an expression of placidity and mildness. . . . His voice is very harmonious and gentle and low— and seems to have naturally a melancholy cadence and tone!— which is affecting when you look at his quenched and deadened eyes—totally and hopelessly blind. I did not see him smile once.
Even before she had left the Trants' house a note in fervent tone came to her from Boyd.

The key of his mind, one feels, was attuned to her own. It was not the mere accident of his blindness, of a retreat from the world, that later made Hugh Boyd the only confidant in the matter of her coming marriage. This man

> *Permitted, with his wandering eyes light-proof,*
> *To catch fair visions, rendered full enough*
> *By many a ministrant accomplished ghost,—*
> *Still seeing, to sounds of softly-turned book-leaves,*
> *Sappho's crown-rose, and Meleager's spring,*
> *And Gregory's starlight on Greek-burnished eves!*
> *Till Sensuous and Unsensuous seemed one thing,*
> *Viewed from one level,—earth's reapers at the sheaves*
> *Scarce plainer than Heaven's angels on the wing!*

—this man had much of her own spirituality and mysticism: his translations of the Christian Fathers were not wholly a mere work of scholarship. Though of an older generation, bound by

classic conceptions in poetry and religious dogma of a Calvin-
istic cast, his mind could range as freely between earth and
heaven as hers.

It was on Wednesday, April 16, 1828 that Elizabeth paid her
first call in less hazardous circumstances: a month later she
came to read with her new friend "the opening of Œdipus
Tyrannus." These two facts were recorded by him in his copy of
An Essay on Mind.[4]

This man was no compromising friend: as she read Greek to
him in his learned darkness he would reprove her sharply for
speaking too low, or at too high a pitch. He was captious, hard
to please, critical of her work: perhaps a certain astringent quality in him had its value to the girl so much admired at home.
She wrote at his dictation, corrected at least one set of proofs,
exchanged books with him, and, above all, drew on the resources of his classical learning. For a while she stayed with
him at Woodland Lodge [5] working in particular upon the *Aga-
memnon*, but it would seem as if the major part of their reading
together was done at "The Ruby." Of the three houses the position of "The Ruby" fits in best with the verse in which she recalled those "golden hours" in "Wine of Cyprus":

> *When, betwixt the folio's turnings,*
> *Solemn flowed the rhythmic Greek:*
> *Past the pane the mountain spreading,*
> *Swept the sheep-bell's tinkling noise*
> *While a girlish voice was reading,*
> *Somewhat low for αι's and οι's.*

"The Ruby" is built right against a steep slope so that the sheep
—formerly so numerous as to be, in the words of the present
owner of the house, "a great nuisance"—might have come right
down outside the back windows.

The friends could not at this time have met daily, as later at
Sidmouth: there were some seven miles between them and, perhaps, certain duties and anxieties at Hope End. Mrs. Barrett
was by now an invalid. But these two, the girl of genius and
the learned man, soon became intimate. In her letters ranging
from 1828 to 1832, written in a clear hand for the easier reading

---

[4] In Wellesley College Collection.
[5] Mentioned in a family letter, undated.

aloud to one blind, but unfortunately not dated, the mode of address passed from "My dear Mr. Boyd" to " My dearest friend." In later unhappy days when her mother was dead, the home of childhood already threatened, and Mr. Boyd himself intending to leave Malvern, she referred to his companionship as "the greatest & indeed only happiness which it is possible for me now to possess."

It was about this time that the Martins of the great banking family, already friends of the Barretts, came to live at Old Colwall, a mile away: they and the Peytons at Barton Court were among the closest associates of the family at Hope End. The Martins were childless, but at Barton Court there were children, one of whom, Harry Peyton, is thought in the family to have been attached to Elizabeth. The Barretts were also on friendly terms with the owner of Eastnor Castle, Earl Somers, whose estate was adjacent: at one time Elizabeth was staying with his wife, Lady Caroline.[6] There were also those friends, the Trants, who lived somewhere on the way to Malvern.

It is the Martins we know most about, because Elizabeth's letters to Mr. and Mrs. James Martin have survived. They are published unfortunately in somewhat shortened form; as, when the Martins were abroad, it was Elizabeth's pleasant custom to retail the gossip of the neighbourhood, these letters in their entirety would give us a more complete picture of the Barretts' social surroundings.

Mrs. Martin, though some years older than Elizabeth, became a close friend and confidante: it is from letters to her that we gather much of Elizabeth's emotion and thought. As her maiden name was Julia Vignoles it seems likely she was of French descent. Her portrait, which I have been privileged to see at Old Colwall, shows a pretty, dark, vivacious woman. At Old Colwall, but a mile away, Elizabeth must have spent many happy hours; walking perhaps in the ancient yew alley or sitting in a stone summerhouse of classic design erected by Mr. Martin.

It is from a note written by Bro to Mrs. Martin [7] that we learn of an illness of Elizabeth's about the time of her mother's death

---

[6] Family letters.   [7] Rayner Wood Collection at Old Colwall.

in October 1827. Mrs. Barrett died not at home, but at Cheltenham Spa: Elizabeth was absent from her mother's side at the last. Mrs. Barrett had been ailing for some years, though in the spring of 1827 her health had seemed to improve.

How far Mrs. Barrett had in her quiet way fostered Elizabeth's genius after the years of precocious babyhood we do not know; but we do know her loss was a material one. A tender love for her children is mirrored in the exquisite little water-colour drawings that she made of them,[8] the beauty of which cannot be guessed at from the uncoloured portrait of Elizabeth, drawn in 1823 during her illness, given in the volume of her letters to Henrietta.

To Mr. Barrett his wife's loss was certainly a severe one though, we are told in one of Elizabeth's letters, he gave courage to his family in their grief "by his own surpassing fortitude." The bereaved husband must have been lonelier because of an intense native reserve: he took Septimus, now a lively child of six, to sleep in his room.

There were other anxieties to harass Elizabeth's father at this time: we do not know how early Mr. Barrett found himself in financial difficulties, but it is certain that not until after his wife's death did embarrassment become apparent. There had been heavy losses to the Jamaican estate through enforced litigation arising out of the grandfather's will, and perhaps Mr. Barrett had spent too much on Hope End, embellishing at a heavy cost the interior of the house, making a show garden, and extending the estate. A reverse in fortune was carefully kept from his ailing wife: it may have been to this end that the estate was heavily mortgaged.

In or about 1832 the mortgagees [9] decided to foreclose, and we find Elizabeth writing to Boyd of intruding men measuring in the estate. When her young brother Henry asked them what they were doing, he was told: "making a new map and putting down all the improvements."

The inventory of the sale, which took place in London, at Garraway's Coffee House, Change Alley, Cornhill, gives de-

---

[8] In family possession.

[9] One of them, curiously enough, bore another name destined to be known in literature: he was a London solicitor, Sacheverell Sitwell.

tails of the elaboration of house and grounds. The drawing-room had been decorated by Italian artists and, according to a local tradition, took seven years to complete. Many of the doors were inlaid with mother-of-pearl. The billiards room was ornamented with Moorish views, the walls of the library stuccoed. There were windows of stained glass. The cascade was described as "a chef d'œuvre unrivalled in this kingdom." Mr. Barrett's gardens indeed were celebrated in the neighbourhood: it is said in the family that Princess Victoria came to visit them when she was staying at Malvern in 1831. While she was there the young Princess opened the new Victoria Parade, now Foley Terrace. Mr. Boyd wrote some courtly verses on the royal presence to which Elizabeth replied in more democratic tones.[1]

Mr. Barrett remained in possession of Hope End for some period after the sale; refusing to allow the purchaser, Thomas Heywood, to set foot in the grounds. Heywood, as a neighbour jocularly put it, was only able to view his property with a spy glass from the top of Herefordshire Beacon.

Mr. Barrett was so severely wounded in his pride, so hurt by these losses, that he secluded himself, even giving up attendance on religious societies which in Ledbury, his daughter wrote, "he was so much pledged to support, and so interested in supporting." He no longer visited the surrounding families, even neglecting the Martins: for this Elizabeth apologized in a letter to Mrs. Martin after the family had left Herefordshire, remarking that "painful circumstances produce—as we have often had occasion to observe—different effects upon different minds." This proud withdrawal Elizabeth could not approve, though she could understand.

There were other preoccupations to exercise the mind of Elizabeth's harassed father, and these perhaps not entirely unconnected with those religious societies in Ledbury he was now avoiding. Evangelical agitation against slavery, at home in Parliament and in Jamaica by certain earnest preachers there, had steadily increased during the preceding twenty years. The slave trade had been abolished as early as 1807, only to make harder the work of those slaves remaining in Jamaica, or born

[1] In Hewlett Collection.

ELIZABETH BARRETT
from a tinted drawing by her brother Alfred

HENRIETTA MOULTON
BARRETT
from a miniature

ARABELLA MOULTON BARRETT
from a photograph

there; although good masters, such as the Barretts, treated them with humanity. Samuel Barrett provided a mission home for an ardent Presbyterian missionary, Hope Waddell, and his wife helped to educate black children. In the words of Waddell himself, Samuel tried to "improve the condition of his people both for time and eternity."

But these measures, even if known at home, could only be soothing balm to a running sore in the public conscience. The institution of slavery must go. The slaves themselves, with a hope of freedom in sight, grew restive to the point of insurrection: in February 1832 news reached London of fifty-two plantations destroyed by them. Barrett property was unharmed, but the danger signal could not be ignored. The abolition of slavery, sooner perhaps than expected, was now inevitable.

At some time after Mrs. Barrett's death, Annie Boyd entered the household in a responsible capacity; in January 1831 she left rather hurriedly. It would appear from a letter to Annie written by Henrietta that there was some sort of trouble in the house which led to a desire to part with her services. Henrietta tried to soften the matter by adding: "we did not doubt your kindness, dear Annie, we know very well however painful it would have been to yourself you would have staid with us if we had asked it." This sudden departure took place after some illness of Elizabeth's; perhaps at the time of her mother's death. On the reverse sheet she herself wrote to Mrs. Boyd:

I am afraid I must have seemed in all your opinions weak & miserable lately. Weak I know myself to be on many points—but if you knew all, you might not think the weakness on this occasion, quite inexcusable. If you knew how she has nursed me in sickness & been indulgent to me in health & loved me always— how she has been considered by us all, as a second—that which we have lost—you could not think so. I cannot recollect that she ever by one act of positive or negative unkindness—by waywardness, or neglect or any other means, ever for an instant gave me pain.

This episode is somewhat puzzling: as Annie Boyd could hardly have been more than thirty (Hugh Boyd was fifty in 1831) she would appear rather young to be regarded as a second mother by young women in their twenties. Unless, indeed, Annie was not Boyd's daughter,[2] but the child of his wife by a previous marriage.

Probably Mr. Barrett was from home when this letter was written. About January 15 his mother, Elizabeth Moulton, died at her house in Baker Street, London. Of six thousand pounds at her disposal two thousand were left to Mary Trepsack (a ward of Elizabeth's grandfather, nurse to her father in childhood and long Mrs. Moulton's companion) and four thousand to her eldest grandchild. Elizabeth, through the grandmother's benefaction and money later to come to her from her uncle, was the only member of the Barrett family financially independent of its head.

Apart from this domestic loss, Mr. Barrett must have been much away from Hope End that year: it was perhaps because of frequent absences that he put Annie Boyd in charge. Business cares were heavy and a new dwelling-place must be found. In the spring of 1832 we find him writing to his brother in Jamaica:

I expect soon to return into Herefordshire, altho' it will be for a distressing object—the packing up of all my things for removing hence; God knows where; but He knows best. I dread much the effect on my dear Children in tearing them away from their most happy associations.

Edward Barrett must bear this burden alone. His natural reticence, a self-made barrier between himself and his children, prevented confidence even to Elizabeth. But his courage was notable. When in late summer the break came, "though he had not power to say *one word,* he could play at cricket with the boys on the very last evening."

Escorted by their Aunt "Bummy," the family were to travel together to a temporary home in Sidmouth, Devon, leaving behind at Hope End only the father and Bro; but "half an hour before we set off," Elizabeth told Mrs. Martin in her first letter from Sidmouth, "papa found out that he *could not* part with Sette, who sleeps with him, and is always an amusing companion to him." Unwilling, however, to separate him "from his lit-

---

[2] In the only account (undocumented) we have of Boyd's life his daughter's name is given as Henrietta.

tle playfellows," Mr. Barrett asked the child if he very much wished to go. "Sette's heart was quite full, but he answered immediately, 'Oh, no, papa, I would *much* rather stay with *you.*'"

To Elizabeth the parting from Hope End was inexpressibly painful: she drove off in the carriage weeping bitterly. Of her grief some old servants who stayed behind spoke to a tender-hearted intelligent little girl of four, Mary Heywood, the daughter of Hope End's new proprietor. With "a sort of loyal sympathy" the child tended Elizabeth's favourite flowers in her own small garden and thought how happy she was "to live in such a lovely home while she was pining somewhere far away." [3]

The night of their departure the family slept at York House, Bath, proceeding through country that Elizabeth, with the memory of Hope End so painfully before her, could not admire. They arrived late at Sidmouth to find themselves, although it was almost dark, "besieged by a crowd of disinterested tradespeople, who *would* attend us through the town to our house, to help to unload the carriages." To their dismay they found their new home in total darkness, "not a rushlight burning," and nobody to welcome them: their arrival, which had been daily expected for three weeks, had now been despaired of.

At Sidmouth the Barretts were to live three years; years happy and unhappy to Elizabeth, but spent by a sea which could as yet bring her only joy.

[3] *Mary Sumner, her Life and Work* (1921). Mary Heywood, as Mrs. Sumner, was the founder of "The Mothers' Union."

C H A P T E R   7

AT SIDMOUTH; *PROMETHEUS BOUND* [1832–5]

THE HOUSE TO WHICH the Barretts came in the dusk of a summer evening was 8, Fortfield Terrace, facing the sea; standing then on open land "with pleasant green hills and trees behind." It is singled out by a plaque on the pediment above bearing a double-headed eagle commemorating a short stay there in 1831 of the Grand Duchess Helena, a member of the Russian royal family.

All, with the exception of Aunt Arabella, took an immediate liking to Sidmouth. Elizabeth especially enjoyed the view from the drawing-room windows. "I always thought," she told Mrs. Martin, "that the sea was the sublimest object in nature. . . . *There*, the Almighty's form glasses itself in tempests—and not only in tempests, but in calm—in space, in eternal motion, in eternal regularity. How can we look at it, and consider our puny sorrows, and not say, 'We are dumb—because *Thou* didst it'?" In a few years, however, when a loss more dire than that of mother and home afflicted her, Elizabeth could derive no comfort, experience no resignation from an aspect of that sea.

She rode on a donkey sometimes at the sea's edge, slept soundly in the mild air, and admired the myrtle, the verbena, and hydrangeas tall and luxuriant in that southern climate. By the end of the month the rest of the family had joined them, "dear papa in good spirits, and not only satisfied but pleased with this place." Every day Elizabeth, on donkey-back, accompanied the children in their walks, and often the father came too. Even more than donkey rides she enjoyed a family excursion in their boat. But the memory of Hope End, or home as she was to call it yearningly in her thoughts, overshadowed these pleasures for Elizabeth; and soon there was added anxiety when sporadic but fatal cases of cholera were reported in the town.

Happily untouched by this foul result of bad drainage, the younger children tasted true seaside delights. Alfred, Sette, and Occy, in studying "the art of catching shrimps," soaked themselves up to their waists "like professors." For the older Barretts there was trout fishing in the Otter and the "noble river Sid." Although yearning for her native Herefordshire, Elizabeth had to admit the country round to be beautiful, its green shady lanes unrivalled: her own "love of water" concentrated "itself in the boat" when the sea was calm. It was here at Sidmouth that her poem "The Sea-mew," so justly admired by Miss Mitford, was written.

The more social members of the family, Sam and Henrietta among them, could enjoy intercourse with people of their own class inhabiting pretty thatched houses termed "cottages" in echo of an earlier fashionable rusticity. Elizabeth, however, tended to move, perhaps in company with her father, in a more serious circle, the centre of which was the Reverend George Barrett Hunter,[1] a Nonconformist minister.

One loss Elizabeth must have felt keenly on leaving Hope End was the learned companionship of Hugh Stuart Boyd: an intercourse with him entirely on paper was particularly unsatisfactory because her correspondent was a blind man. Boyd was able to write his own letters, but naturally he could not read them through. Her irascible friend was apt to fling his thoughts or feelings on to paper without regard to the susceptibilities of the recipient. "It has always been my habit," he had written her directly after their first meeting, "to express what I feel at the moment whether it be judicious or not." Once Boyd expressed impatience at the length of her letters from Sidmouth, making Elizabeth fear that his affection for her had cooled. She wrote humbly:

I consider the fault to be, in all probability, not yours but mine. I have observed that people in general who have liked me best, have liked me better at first than afterwards: and I used once to imagine (in my infinite modesty) that this was caused by my not being very apt to like them in return. I do not understand why people should like me better at first: for I am very certain of not pretending to be what I am not, & of there being in my

---

[1] Was he related to the Barretts?

dull shy manner, no purpureus pannus, *to catch the eye in an exordium.*

But Boyd, who appears to have left Malvern about the same time as the Barretts removed from Hope End, soon came to live at Sidmouth, and not five minutes distant from Elizabeth. Now the old communion of minds was re-established, strengthened by frequent meeting. Elizabeth would see him most days, sometimes running the short distance between their houses that she might not lose a moment of her friend's company. They resumed their Greek studies; and she had the privilege of writing down those translations of the Christian Fathers made in a learned darkness. In 1834 extracts from these translations were presented in a work published by a Sidmouth bookseller, *The Fathers not Papists, or Six Discourses by the most eloquent Fathers of the Church.* This title gives a clue to another aspect of Boyd, his passionate Protestantism.

Between the two there was friendly rivalry as to who had the best memory for classic verse: in 1832, on the anniversary of her mother's birthday, Elizabeth set down on paper the "Number of Lines which I can repeat," 3,280 in Greek prose, ranging from the Septuagint and Greek Testament through the Christian Fathers to "a few passages of Heathen writers," and in Greek verse 4,420, among which Æschylus stands first with 1,800 and the Hymns of Synesius second with 1,310.

That lines from Æschylus should be the most numerous was natural since Elizabeth was now translating, or contemplating the translation of, *Prometheus Vinctus.* This was published in 1833 by J. A. Valpy, of Red Lion Court, Fleet Street, priced five shillings, as "by the author of *An Essay on Mind.*"

In some fine verses accompanying a copy to a friend, almost certainly Hugh Boyd, she wrote:

> *To thee, acquaint with each*
> *Divinest song the Attic muses bring*
> *In golden urns from out that ancient spring*
> *Of their own charmèd speech,*
> *How dark and dank this water will beseem*
> *Among whose trembling reeds*
> *A pale thin echo feeds*
> *Upon the distant tune of fairer stream.*

This modesty was to grow into positive shame: of the merits of her translation other than its accuracy, Elizabeth wrote in 1845 to another student of Greek, Robert Browning, that it was "the whole together as cold as Caucasus, and as flat as the nearest plain." The first had been hurriedly made in less than a fortnight: in 1844, or early 1845, Elizabeth was employing the long slow hours of an invalid life in a new rendering to "wash away the transgression." This fine and accurate translation admirably catches the spirit of the original: the progress she had made in handling language can be realized by comparing the two presentations of Prometheus' first great speech beginning in both versions as "O holy æther, and swift-wingèd winds."

While some ten years later Elizabeth was making this atonement the unsold copies of the 1833 edition lay "safely locked in the wardrobe of papa's bedroom, entombed as safely as Œdipus among the olives." Ultimately, one supposes they were, as Elizabeth herself wished, destroyed: the edition is very scarce today. Of original work included in this volume she wrote to Horne in 1843: "A few of the fugitive poems connected with that translation may be worth a little perhaps; but they have not so much goodness as to overcome the badness of the blasphemy of Æschylus."

The volume, like its predecessor, attracted little notice: the *Athenæum,* later to do her high honour and publish much of her work, merely advised "those who adventure into the hazardous lists of poetic translation to touch anyone rather than Æschylus; and they may take warning by the author before us." This critic ignored the 'fugitive poems'; poems that included "The Picture Gallery at Penshurst."

There is in these poems a sorrowfulness of tone, a sense of personal loss which it would be tempting, if such easy speculations were not dangerous, to attribute to frustrated love: certainly in "Idols" there is one direct expression of the unsatisfying quality of all earthly things; her "oldest worshipping" of natural beauty, that—almost as early—of "Moloch Fame," and

> *Last, human Love, thy Lares greeting,*
> *To rest and warmth I vowed my years,*
> *To rest? how wild my pulse is beating!*
> *To warmth? ah me! my burning tears.*

This surely would appear an overstatement of any purely domestic trouble or loss; unless, of course, the piece is merely dramatic, Byronic in tone. But we find the same melancholy note
in a sad poem "The Autumn" where this woman nearing the
age of thirty laments:

> *Youth fades; and then, the joys of youth,*
> *Which once refreshed our mind,*
> *Shall come—as, on these sighing winds,*
> *The chilling autumn wind.*

She is turning more and more to God, saying boldly that all
true values are spiritual; crying out "How beautiful is earth!"
but seeing it as in an apocalyptic vision. The last lines of that
strong fragment "The Tempest," in which the end of the world
is depicted in horrible detail, claim through the salvation of
Christ a protection against natural human fear:

> *High-seeming Death, I dare thee! and have hope,*
> *In God's good time, of showing to thy face*
> *An unsuccumbing spirit, which sublime*
> *May cast away the low anxieties*
> *That wait upon the flesh; the reptile moods;*
> *And enter that eternity to come,*
> *Where live the dead, and only Death can die.*

That there was within Elizabeth at this time a deep psychological conflict is clear from a powerful and curious poem not
published in her lifetime, "A True Dream." This account of a
horrible nightmare she experienced in 1833 is told, significantly
enough, in the verse form of "The Ancient Mariner": indeed,
both the poetic narrative and the symbolism would appear to
formulate a similar guilt complex to that of the killer of the Al-
batross. In Elizabeth's dream, after the calling up by a magic
spell of sinister menacing figures, a swart man and a delusively
beautiful child, three serpents "besprent with noisome poison
slime" writhe before her. Here a brother comes into the dream,
Bro personifying herself perhaps, and he endeavours in vain to
kill the serpents by pouring on them oil of vitriol; but the serpents, as they shriek in pain, grow larger, bringing to her a personal agony. Like the Ancient Mariner, she finds herself unable
to pray.

> *And in my anguish I prayed and named*
>   *Aloud the holy name,*
> *The impious mocking serpent voice*
>   *Did echo back the same.*

Other conflicts are apparent here, but in the main her deep trouble would appear to be an unfulfilment, symbolized by the serpents. Elizabeth was a woman of strong feeling whose dominant father would not permit his children to marry. Normal desire, thwarted, smothered in maiden ignorance, can take strange channels, and in Elizabeth's case feelings of guilt and intense conflict were surely inevitable. The strong Evangelical concept of a personal God, represented on earth in this case by a possessive father to whom she was devoted, would change natural desire into a sense of sin and a craving for death.

One factor in this disturbance—tending perhaps in Elizabeth's present state of mind to lay too strong an emphasis upon religion—was her friendship with the Reverend George Barrett Hunter; a friendship probably heightened after Boyd left Sidmouth to live in Bath. Boyd, it is true, was a religious man himself, but the main feature of her association with that older friend was a concentration on something outside herself, upon classical lore.

If we are to judge by a poem written to him eleven years later, the Nonconformist clergyman was a dominant figure in Elizabeth's life at this time. Indeed, that the thought, the memory of him even lingered on long after their lives had fallen apart is clear from verses addressed to Hunter and written on the fly leaf of a presentation copy of *Poems*, 1844, sent together with *The Seraphim* (1838). In these volumes, her only published work since Sidmouth days, Hunter's name, she pointed out, was not mentioned, but

> *There is a silence which includes*
>   *Much speaking and completest,—*
> *As oft, in sylvan solitudes,*
>   *Society grows sweetest.*

In poems of the country, in reference to books, to poetry itself, and to religion, his spirit, she told him, was still with her. These presentation verses end thus:

By feelings tried, by memories kept
As fervid friendship vows them, .
Accept the volumes . . and ACCEPT
The silence which endows them!

As there had been a gap of seven years since the publication
of *An Essay on Mind,* it is possible that the verses attached to
Prometheus Bound may be the outcome of earlier experience:
for work known to have been done at Sidmouth we must go
forward to 1838 and *The Seraphim.* Among poems composed
there are "An Island," "The Sleep," "The Sea-mew," "A Sabbath Morning at Sea," and "The Little Friend," the last being
written to Hunter's small daughter, Mary.

We have little knowledge of the Reverend George Hunter
beyond Elizabeth's own indirect testimony to him as a man of
strong, sensitive personality, of stern yet kindly religion. He
conserved some of her verse in manuscript. Before the Barretts
left Sidmouth he went to live in Axminster. Of correspondence
between these friends there remains, so far as I am informed,
nothing beyond that charming fanciful rimed epistle of February 22, 1837 purporting to come from Elizabeth's doves in London to Mary Hunter's canary at "Cage House, Axminster."

There is however, a letter that might by inference be ascribed
to Hunter, the signature of which is said to be indecipherable.
It was written from Axminster in September 1838 after reading
The Seraphim. The tone of this letter is rather morbidly warm,
perhaps too warm for mere friendship. The writer claims a personal association with certain poems, and especially with "A
Sabbath Morning at Sea," declaring it to be "most beautiful and
dear, and it too *is* mine. I cannot, may not tell you how & what
I feel of your kindness, while I call that and others—*Mine*—and
the feeling is so intense as it is because you taught me to call it
so." The writer speaks of her regard for "him" as "dearer to me
than of all the world besides."

"A Sabbath Morning at Sea," undoubtedly written at Sidmouth, suggests a voyage that involved a parting from one
dear to her:

For parting tears and present sleep
Have weighed mine eyelids downward.

This poem commemorates the new experience of dawn over

the water; an experience sharpened by personal emotion. In pre-railway days it was common enough for people to travel between the southern coastal parts of England by sea. Later Elizabeth herself was to make most of her journey to Torquay by water. That this particular voyage meant the loss, temporary or otherwise, of a cherished companion is clear, but who he was we can only conjecture. We can, however, be fairly certain that Hunter (if it was he who wrote the letter from Axminster) was present on board to share in a feeling of awed wonder when, as light broke,

> *Heaven, ocean, did alone partake*
> *The sacrament of morning.*

There may have been preoccupation at home further to cast a general shadow over Elizabeth's mind: financial anxiety was begining to weigh upon the family. A Bill for the abolition of slavery hung above their heads. West Indians, Mr. Barrett declared, would be irreparably ruined: "nobody in his senses would think of even attempting the culture of sugar . . . they had better hang weights to the sides of the island of Jamaica and sink it at once." At the end of August 1833 the Bill was passed. "The consternation here," Elizabeth wrote, "is very great. Nevertheless I am glad, and always shall be, that the negroes are—virtually—free!"

Edward Barrett, knowing that his brother would need help and support in the emergency, decided to send out his eldest son to Jamaica. This meant a separation of those two, twins not in the flesh but in soul, for more than a year. "Our beloved Ba," he wrote to Samuel, "upon the colour I put upon the project, namely as being profitable to Bro's interest, has consented in a spirit that has, if possible, raised her still higher in my estimation." Surely, at least in 1833, Edward Moulton Barrett was no arbitrary tyrant.

Another and more immediate danger threatened this family at Sidmouth: the house in which they were then living—not, it is thought, 8, Fortfield Terrace—was in a ruinous condition. One chimney had already been pulled down for safety. Before the winds of winter raged they must go. But where would they go? Would they leave Sidmouth? Elizabeth lived from day to day, but with faith in her father. "Of one thing," she wrote to Mrs.

Martin, "I have a comforting certainty—that wherever we may go or stay, the decree which moves or fixes us will and must be the 'wisest virtuousest discreetest best!' "

Whether they actually spent a perilous winter in this house is not known, but certainly in the autumn of next year they were established at "Belle Vue," a thatched house with a veranda, bowered in trees and "with a green lawn bounded by a Devonshire lane." [2] Here Mr. Barrett left them for some months, living in a London hotel to transact his business; perhaps that opening of an estate office or agency to which he, born a country gentleman, was soon heroically to bind himself during long hours for six days of the week. In London's damp fogs Mr. Barrett fell ill of his old rheumatic complaint. The children took a daring decision: so that he should not be suffering alone in a hotel, a brother must go to him. Bro was probably still in Jamaica: Sam, the next in age, either was not available or perhaps was not considered to be the right person. Storm and George were studying at Glasgow University. It was therefore the seventeen-year-old Henry who was sent up by coach to tend his father.

Elizabeth awaited a scolding. "We were not scolded: but my prayer to be permitted to follow Henry was condemned to silence." The unsatisfactory reports received from Henry made her "anxious and fearful." Apart from the personal loss, which would be severe, a fatal end of Mr. Barrett's illness would deprive his family, three of whom were still young, of its mainstay. "You know he is *all* left to us—" Elizabeth wrote to Mrs. Martin, "and without him we should indeed be orphans and desolate." Elizabeth's thoughts would naturally turn to the beloved uncle in Jamaica; but he was far away and necessarily occupied at such a dangerous moment in the Barrett affairs.

But happily the father recovered: by Christmas he was with his family at "Belle Vue," the pleasant house that they must soon leave. "Belle Vue" had been sold and might be handed over to a new owner in March. At least one of the family, Henrietta, was heartily tired of Sidmouth: the two months' stay first projected there had extended to three years. Elizabeth herself

2 Now Cedar Shade Hotel, and in the middle of the town.

felt that she would "very much grieve to leave it." But decisions in this family rested with only one person.

It was ostensibly for George's sake that Mr. Barrett determined at least to try the experiment of settling his family in London. George, who at nineteen had become a Bachelor of Arts with distinction, was to be entered at the Bar. Charles John (Stormie) was leaving Glasgow University without a degree; not because he was less prepared than George, but because a hesitancy of speech had made him too nervous to face an oral examination.

In the late summer or autumn of 1835 the family moved to a furnished house in the London parish of St. Marylebone, an area that had already been inhabited by Barretts in several generations, including Elizabeth's grandmother, Mrs. Moulton.

CHAPTER 8

LONDON AND *THE SERAPHIM* [1835–8]

'Twas hard to sing by Babel's steam—
More hard, in Babel's street!
But if the soulless creatures deem
Their music not unmeet
For sunless walls—let us begin,
Who wear immortal wings within!

My Doves

THE HOUSE Mr. Barrett rented was 74 (now 99) Gloucester Place, at the end of a long row of the terrace houses. Boyd, who had preceded Elizabeth to London, was now living, a widower, in Hampstead; Mrs. Boyd had died at Bath.

The heights of Hampstead were considerably more inaccessible from Gloucester Place at that time, yet they were well within driving-distance. It is true that in London Mr. Barrett kept no carriage, but surely some vehicle might have been hired to convey Elizabeth to her old and bereaved friend; yet she did not visit him for some time. We find her writing to him that autumn: "Don't be angry because I have not visited you immediately. You know—or you *will* know, if you consider—I cannot open the window and fly."

Perhaps on first coming to London she was unwell: certainly Gloucester Place, though but on the fringe of London proper at that time, and near to Regent's Park, was a sad change to a woman country-bred. A New Year's letter to Mrs. Martin would imply, if not illness, at least in its nostalgia a physical oppression. "Half my soul . . . seems to have stayed behind on the sea-shore, which I love more than ever now that I cannot walk on it in the body. London is wrapped up like a mummy, in a yellow mist, so closely that I have had scarcely a glimpse of its countenance since we came. Well, I am trying to like it all very much." London was then for a good part of the year under a miasma of reeking chimneys, its streets covered with liquid mud, and with an odour of defective drainage too often apparent; no place for a woman weak upon the chest. When, however, Miss Mitford, introduced by John Kenyon, met Elizabeth on May 27, 1836, there was in her appearance no suggestion of invalidism.

A closer acquaintance with John Kenyon, a Jamaican cousin of Edward Barrett, was one of the immediate advantages to Elizabeth in London. Kenyon, a middle-aged wealthy man, was highly intelligent, a friend and patron of literature and himself a respectable practitioner in verse.

Kenyon, taking his old friend Mary Mitford, up from the country, to see the new giraffes at the Zoological Gardens, called first upon Elizabeth. That evening Miss Mitford wrote to her father:

A sweet young woman, whom we called for in Gloucester Place, went with us—a Miss Barrett—who reads Greek as I do French, has published some translations from Æschylus, and some striking poems. She is a delightful young creature; shy and timid and modest. Nothing but her desire to see me got her out at all.

"She is so sweet and gentle," Miss Mitford wrote the next day, "and so pretty, that one looks at her as if she were some bright flower."

Allowing for dear Miss Mitford's rose-coloured spectacles, the delightful picture of Elizabeth at this time which she later drew for a young friend seems to suggest an appearance of perfect health:

a slight, girlish figure, very delicate, with exquisite hands and feet, a round face, with a most noble forehead, a large mouth beautifully formed, and full of expression, lips like parted coral, teeth large, regular and glittering with healthy whiteness, large dark eyes, with such eyelashes, resting on the cheek when cast down; when turned upward, touching the flexible and expressive eyebrow; a dark complexion, with cheeks literally as bright as the dark China rose, a profusion of silky, dark curls, and a look of youth and of modesty hardly to be expressed. This, added to the very simple but graceful and costly dress by which all the family are distinguished, is an exact portrait of her some years ago.

Miss Mitford found her "one of the most interesting persons I had ever seen," with "a smile like a sunbeam."

Because of Miss Mitford's country residence, and also the circumstance of Elizabeth's coming illness, most of the intercourse between these two, the famous elderly writer and the younger poet on the verge of fame, must be on paper; but Miss Mitford's warm heart and intimate pen soon overcame formality. Elizabeth was to her "my dear love," "my dearest love," a being to whom she felt as a mother might to a son of genius. The friendship sprang up rapidly: during Miss Mitford's week in town that spring Elizabeth was with her a part of every day.

Having faced one pleasant literary lion, Elizabeth was emboldened to dine with Mr. Kenyon next evening and meet, among other celebrities, Landor and Wordsworth; of whom she wrote to Mrs. Martin: (Wordsworth's) "manners are very simple, and his conversation not at all *prominent*—if you quite understand what I mean by *that*. I do myself, for I saw at the same time Landor—the brilliant Landor!—and *felt* the difference between great genius and eminent talent."

Wordsworth "was very kind to me, and let me hear his conversation." The wide-eyed admiration of this girl must indeed have been balm to the aged Wordsworth, who, we know, sometimes missed the incense of the home shrine in his visits to London. As a woman friend drove him one day with Miss Mitford and Elizabeth to Chiswick, Miss Mitford took her apart to inquire whether Miss Barrett was "out," so much a child did she still look at the age of thirty.

At Kenyon's reception, Landor, "in whose hands the ashes of antiquity burn again," had talked for some ten minutes with Elizabeth and had given her two Greek epigrams lately made by himself, one being upon Napoleon. Bro, now again in England, and with whom Elizabeth had the happiness of attending this gathering, afterwards "abused Landor for '*ambitious* singularity and affectation.'"

On reading Miss Mitford's letters to her father it is strange to note that on May 26, a day before Kenyon's party, she had been dining at Serjeant Talfourd's table with Wordsworth, Landor, and other writers, among whom was the young author of "Paracelsus," a poet already hailed in that limited circle though the

public would have none of him. Browning's father had been at
school with John Kenyon: Kenyon's interest in his old companion's brilliant son was almost as strong as that felt for his cousin.
There is indirect evidence that Elizabeth herself at once recognized the quality of "Paracelsus" "as the expression of a new
mind"; but it does not appear as if she ever expressed a desire
to meet Mr. Kenyon's young friend.

But this excursion into literary society at Mr. Kenyon's table
appears to have been Elizabeth's first and last before marriage:
her time was spent in Gloucester Place quietly at work to the
background of the cooing doves in her room. She saw Boyd
from time to time, letting him hear her verses. That captious
old-fashioned man became, as Elizabeth developed on lines
modern in her day, more and more inclined to carp and criticize: his criticisms usually provoked a lively and spirited
defence.

In 1836 writings of hers appeared both in the *Athenæum* (an
article in prose, "A Thought on Thoughts"), under the editorship of Charles Dilke, and in the *New Monthly Magazine,* edited by Bulwer, afterwards Lord Lytton. Dilke, as yet unaware
of the identity of "E. B. B.," in his review of current magazines
noted that ambitious long poem "A Poet's Vow" as "a fine almost too dreamy ballad" and exhorted "him," the author, to
"greater clearness of expression and less quaintness in his choice
of phraseology." To us, accustomed to the intricacies and wide
word range of modern poets, it is difficult to realize that her own
generation linked Elizabeth with Robert Browning as obscure.
So conscious was Elizabeth of this accusation that, she told
Miss Mitford, "my fear of it makes me sometimes feel quite
nervous and thought-tied in composition."

In the October of 1836 Elizabeth embarked upon her most
daring adventure of the mind, an exercise in sublimity itself:
"The Seraphim," which was to be the title poem of her next volume. In that beautifully balanced piece of prose, her preface,
she tells how even in translating *Prometheus Bound* the thought
of the greatest Christian Martyrdom was with her: how from
the victim of Zeus, punished for bringing benefit to man, her
mind went forward "to the multitudes, whose victim was their
Saviour; to the Victim, whose sustaining thought beneath an

unexampled agony, was not the Titanic 'I can revenge,' but the celestial 'I can forgive!' "

If the level of the white spiritual beauty of the opening of this poem could have been sustained, surely Elizabeth Barrett Browning must have been hailed as a poet of very high rank; but always in those longer poems her hand seems to falter. Perhaps the texture of her verse is too thin, or perhaps the inhibitions of her age and sex made her self-conscious. Perhaps in this particular case the poem suffered from a broken treatment: the manuscript submitted to the *New Monthly* was lost by Colburn, its publisher. "Partly from a very rough copy, and partly from memory," Elizabeth reconstructed it, adding a second part of about twice the length.[1]

The exalted plane, the spirituality, of this work, an apex in her religious expression, can touch us perhaps more in this professedly unreligious age, when men have suffered a crucifixion of mind and body, than in her own time, when life for all but the inarticulate toiling masses was comfortable and safe. Our minds too may, because of the extent of modern outer-world discovery, be empowered to soar more easily up into space, to the lingering Seraphim momentarily disobeying a Command to follow down to the Cross those angels

> *The roar of whose descent has died*
> *To a still sound, as thunder into rain.*
> *Immeasurable space spreads magnified*
> *With that thick life, along the plane*
> *The worlds slid out on. What a fall*
> *And eddy of wings innumerous, crossed*
> *By trailing curls that have not lost*
> *The glitter of the God-smile shed*
> *On every prostrate angel's head!*
> *What gleaming up of hands that fling*
> *Their homage in retorted rays,*
> *From high instinct of worshipping,*
> *And habitude of praise.*[2]

.   .   .

[1] Letter to Kenyon, in Hagedorn Collection.
[2] Quoted in the later revised version.

For nearly two years more the Barrett family lived uneasily in a furnished house with dirty carpets, Elizabeth without her books and armchair, Henrietta without a pianoforte. Confidence in the house could not have been increased when, during the great storm of December 1836, a chimney-stack crashed through a skylight and, descending to ground level, broke the stone stairs; stairs on which the beloved Bro had five minutes before been standing. Sarah, the housemaid, who "looked up accidentally and saw the nodding chimneys," had run shrieking into the drawing-room where Mr. Barrett was sitting. She escaped "with one graze on the hand from one brick."

During these two years there was for Elizabeth no escape from town; but, though yearning for the lost Hope End, she now admitted to many advantages in London: "if we can't see even a leaf or a sparrow without soot on it, there are the parrots at the Zoological Gardens and the pictures at the Royal Academy; and real live poets above all, with their heads full of the trees and birds and sunshine of paradise." These poets were no new constellations in her sky, but those two she had met in 1836. Her only contact with a poet at this time, and he a very minor one, was in the increasing and fruitful friendship with her cousin, John Kenyon.

The year 1837 had, except for composition and fugitive publication, little to offer us and nothing in the way of event beyond the marriage, at which she was present, of Annie Boyd early that year or at the end of 1836. In the summer Elizabeth, to help Henry, who was going to Germany, joined with Bro in studying German. German, the last to be learned, was perhaps to be enjoyed latest in point of time: during illness towards the end of her life Elizabeth read many German books and translated a few lyrics.

1838 was, on the other hand, an outstanding year: it was to see the beginning of her long invalidism, the first publication (beyond the privately printed *Battle of Marathon*) with her name attached, and to connect her with that famous address, 50, Wimpole Street.

The family had for months been looking forward with dislike to this removal which took them to a similar house in a street parallel with Gloucester Place. But at least they had no longer to live with other people's furniture: their own came up from store in Ledbury. Elizabeth had her books back, and Henrietta a pianoforte.

Elizabeth's illness early that year began with the breaking of a blood vessel in the chest. Dr. William Frederick Chambers, physician-in-ordinary to the Queen, was called in, but though the rupture apparently healed he was unable to cure her of a persistent cough.

1838 was a year of bereavement: Samuel Moulton Barrett died at Kingston, Jamaica, on December 23, 1837. News of his death must have reached London in the February of 1838. As Elizabeth's uncle had been ill for some time, and her brother Sam was with him, the family could not have been wholly unprepared, but her grief for the loss of him who had been "more than an uncle" was profound. His love and thought for her were expressed in a legacy that helped to make her independent. Among tokens of their mutual affection was a locket he had given her, which she habitually wore; a locket intended for perfume, but later to contain some of Robert Browning's hair.

Although sales of *The Seraphim* were not large enough to warrant a second edition, its publication in May of this year secured for Elizabeth a definite place among the English poets. The *Athenæum,* though to some extent disappointed, declared it

an extraordinary volume—especially welcome as an evidence of female genius and accomplishment. . . . Miss Barrett's genius is of a high order; active, vigorous, and versatile, but unaccompanied by discriminating taste. A thousand strange and beautiful views flit across her mind, but she cannot look at them with a steady gaze. . . .

Perhaps this criticism is just and may be partially explained by inhibitions of sex, time, and position in society. Elizabeth born and reared in the remoteness of a Haworth Parsonage might have been a stronger poet, though she could hardly have been a more sensitive one.

The *Athenæum* also spoke of a certain want "of unaffected earnestness." This accusation Elizabeth vigorously repudiated in a letter to Boyd: "I have always written too naturally (that is, too much from the impulse of thought and feeling) to have studied *attitudes.*" Later she was to write to R. H. Horne: " 'The Seraphim' has faults enough—and weaknesses, besides—but my voice is in it, in its individual tones, and not inarticulately."

The *Atlas,* a powerful newspaper whose criticisms were read with attention, laid more stress upon the faults of the volume, though admitting "occasional passages of great beauty, and full of deep poetical feeling." In considering "The Romaunt of Margret" it brought for the first time a charge which, great as was her admiration for the poet, always irritated Elizabeth: that she was strongly influenced by Tennyson. When "The Romaunt of Margret" was composed she had not yet read a line of Tennyson. "I came from the country," she told Robert Browning in 1846, "with my eyes only half open, and he had not penetrated where I had been living and sleeping."

"The Romaunt of Margret" is perhaps to a biographer the most interesting poem in the volume, embodying as it does, linked with the *Alcestis* theme, that German mystical notion of a *Doppelgänger,* a man's soul or self facing himself. It is an idea that persisted in Elizabeth's mind, growing stronger and becoming a thread in the allegory of her life.

The story, given in mediæval vein, may in its eerie atmosphere be not unfavourably compared with "Christabel":

> *The ladye doth not move—*
> *The ladye doth not dream—*
> *Yet she seeth her shade no longer laid*
> *In rest upon the stream!*
> *It shaketh without wind—*
> *It parteth from the tide—*
> *It standeth upright in the cleft moonlight—*
> *It sitteth at her side.*
>
> *Margret, Margret!*

To Margret, sitting in happy thoughtful mood by the stream at night, her shadow announces the doom of certain death unless she can lay claim to some human being whom she loves and who loves her "more truly than the sun." The only one she can so claim is no longer living:

> *"Behold! the death-worm to his heart*
> *Is a nearer thing than* thou."
>
> *Margret, Margret.*

Hearing that her lover is dead, the ladye casts herself into the water.

Of the other poems in this volume all are instinct with personality, all pervaded with a yearning towards God less fully expressed in previous published work. Some poems are heavily coloured with that rather self-conscious mediævalism which was to fascinate and conquer the Pre-Raphaelites: nearly all have fine opening stanzas. Her themes are striking and varied; the self-sacrifice of a poet; the beauty of motherhood in "Isobel's Child" and "To the Child Jesus"; of contemporary life in the poems of young Queen Victoria; in "The Soul's Travelling" and other poems a nostalgia for green country. Her own life is revealed to us in at least three, "The Deserted Garden," "My Doves," and "The Name." Her verse now reads more smoothly and easily to the ear. The two pieces longest to endure in popularity are "The Sea-mew" and "Cowper's Grave."

The summer of 1838 brought little improvement in Elizabeth's condition: Dr. Chambers had hoped that its warmth might prove a healing agent. In June we hear of him "shaking his head as awfully as if it bore all Jupiter's ambrosial curls." Some plan must be made for a winter abroad, a plan Mr. Barrett did not approve but which Elizabeth was for a time determined to carry out. To her brother George, now a barrister and away on circuit, she wrote:

Still it is hard to think of going out of this room to the South of Europe . . . leaving gravity in Papa's eyes, and perhaps displeasure deeper within him! If he should be displeased! But his manner is most affectionate to me—affectionate in a marked manner & measure! which indeed was needed to stroke down & smooth a little my poor ruffled feathers, after that hard cold letter of his. Perhaps he had relented in his thoughts of me! or perhaps, George, (which I conjecture sometimes) perhaps he takes for granted that I have given up the scheme, & his good nature is meant for my compensation.

These children might love their father, but between the typical arbitrary parent of a hundred years ago and even so affectionate and well-loved a daughter as Elizabeth there could be little real confidence. One characteristic trait of both stood, too, in the way of easy intercourse; their reticence and a difficulty in the expression of feeling in speech.

But some sort of compromise must be reached. It was decided that Elizabeth should go to Torquay, where apparently an aunt (perhaps Mrs. Hedley) was then living. In September 1838 she was taken most of the way there by sea, Bro, George, and Henrietta accompanying her. One sister was to remain at Torquay, Arabel later taking the place of Henrietta. Elizabeth wrote to Boyd on the eve of sailing:

And all this companionship is more than I hoped for, & I ought to be contented with it—& thankful for every brightness which has fallen, beyond my hope, upon my present circumstances. But still I cannot help being very sorrowful even while I write about the brightness! May God bless you. It may please Him for me to return & visit you again.

She was to return after three long, weary years, years fraught with pain, distress, and infinite sorrow.

CHAPTER 9

TORQUAY [1838–41]

BRO HAD ORDERS from his father to put Elizabeth in the care of her aunt and then return home; but Elizabeth, weakened by illness, perhaps thinking in despair that she might never see this beloved brother again, clung to him in tears. Her aunt, kissing those tears away, sat down immediately and wrote a protest to Mr. Barrett: if he should call Bro back he would break his sister's heart ("as if," Elizabeth commented bitterly seven years later to Robert Browning in a revelation of the tragedy of her life, "hearts were broken *so!*"). The father's reply, which she could never forget, was that "under such circumstances he did not refuse to suspend his purpose, but that he considered it to be *very wrong in me to exact such a thing.*"

The well-beloved brother is, oddly enough, seldom mentioned in Elizabeth's letters: we know so little about him we can only conjecture that he was, beyond the known year in Jamaica, much away from home in the 'thirties. Of what he did in town, and whether as eldest son he helped his father in business, we are quite ignorant. Perhaps Mr. Barrett's "purpose" at this time was the serious one of sending Bro out once more to Jamaica: since the death of Elizabeth's uncle, Sam, not so reliable a son, had been the only family representative there.

Of Elizabeth's first year at Torquay I can gather little except that there was a plan, of which she feared her father would disapprove, to winter abroad; that her poem "A Romance of the Ganges" was printed in *Finden's Tableaux*, edited by Miss Mitford; and that she was reading with intense enjoyment Beaumont and Fletcher.

One of her solaces in exile was frequent letters from Mary Mitford, those delightful letters full of literary gossip and containing from time to time delectable descriptions of an English countryside. In November 1839 [1] we hear of a gift of seeds from

---

[1] Wrongly dated 1838 in L'Estrange's *Friendships of Mary Mitford.*

Miss Mitford to the Barrett family, some of which came from Wordsworth's garden. Seeds from this precious packet, Elizabeth wrote her, were to be reserved by Arabel for Elizabeth's own use in a flower-pot for her window "if it should please God to permit my return to London."

In this letter Elizabeth mentions Theodosia Garrow,[2] a precocious child who, through Landor, had contributed a poem to *The Book of Beauty* edited by Lady Blessington. The Garrows, living at a house called "The Braddons" in Torquay, were friends of Mr. Kenyon. Elizabeth and Theodosia, a delicate girl, were attended by the same doctor.

Theodosia sent fruit and vegetables to the admired Miss Barrett, whom she longed to visit, but, at least in 1839, Elizabeth was too ill to admit strangers. In 1840 Theodosia contributed to a second *Book of Beauty* some verses "Presenting a Young Invalid with a Bunch of Early Violets," sending the two Annuals for Elizabeth to read. Elizabeth wrote a gracious note of thanks regretting that she could not receive Miss Garrow; anyhow "a visit to an invalid condemned to the *peine forte et dure* of being very silent, notwithstanding her womanhood" would be "a gloomy thing." Elizabeth's sense of humour, evidently not submerged by illness, may have been tickled, in the second set of verses intended for her, by a certain youthful tactlessness in such lines as "Thine innocent life, ebbing fast away . . . Innocent beings like thee fade with a gentle decay."

A record of this episode, of Theodosia, the flowers, vegetables, and verse, might not have survived the years if, in time, Theodosia had not become Mrs. Thomas Trollope, destined to meet again with Elizabeth and under happier auspices.

By November 24, 1839 Elizabeth was moved to 1, Beacon Terrace, "a still warmer nest." "Her brother," Miss Mitford wrote to Henry Chorley, "means to fold her in a cloak and carry her to the new house in his arms."

Beacon Terrace overlooks the sweep of Torbay and, in the harbour below, a bustle of business and pleasure craft. Elizabeth had long loved the sea, bitterly regretting its loss on leaving Sidmouth:

[2] Mistranscribed as "Farren" by L'Estrange.

> *. . . the glorious sea! from side to side*
> *Swinging the grandeur of his foamy strength,*
> *And undersweeping the horizon,—on—*
> *On—with his life and voice inscrutable*

was to her a living entity. Soon, however, the sea was to bring
her tragedy and a lasting grief.

That year Mr. Barrett was at Torquay in January. How long
he stayed then we do not know, but we do know that nine
months later, on November 11, there was between his daughter
and himself a parting more emotional than circumstance would
seem to warrant: he was to be absent only a fortnight. As Elizabeth let fall those tears always near her eyelids in sorrow and
in happiness, Mr. Barrett wept openly. In at least one mind,
Elizabeth's, there was a sense of ill omen, the memory of a
dream she had frequently during illness. "I used," she told Miss
Mitford,

> *to start out of fragments of dreams, broken from all parts of the*
> *universe, with the cry from my own lips, "Oh, papa, papa!" I*
> *could not trace it back to the dream behind, yet there it always*
> *was very curiously, and touchingly too, to my own heart, seem-*
> *ing scared of me, though it came from me, at once waking me*
> *with, and welcoming me to, the old straight humanities.*

In other words, and in the light of future events, sorrow was to
come through her to the beloved father. At the time Elizabeth's
interpretation of both dream and grief at parting was a fear that
she might be ill again during the fortnight's absence.

It may well be that Mr. Barrett had, in addition to the worry
of a cherished daughter's health, a more distant preoccupation:
word had come that his son's behaviour in Jamaica was not,
from his own strict standard, all that it should be. The little we
know of Sam suggests a gay, volatile spirit of some sensibility,
one who wrote verses and was fond of company. Perhaps he
found the father's control too rigid. There is a family letter [3] to
Sam with the signature torn away, obviously written from
Hope End, which suggests this artistic bias to Sam's character.
After saying that, on a question of Bro's return, "Papa's thoughts
on the subject are to us as inscrutable as if we had been all tru-
ants and adhered to the fourth form," the writer adds: "There

[3] Hewlett Collection.

is a great difference between yourself, and him, at least in *one* respect—for if your reveries are *upon* a rose, *his* are *under* it." Others, even the devoted Elizabeth herself, were, we know, exasperated by the Olympian attitude of their father towards his children.

Whatever Sam's temperament, the temptations of Jamaica and its climate to the white man appear to have been too much for him: this much we know from the account of his missionary life in the West Indies [4] written by the Reverend Hope Masterman Waddell. By February 17, 1840 the Jamaican climate had exacted a final toll. Sam was dead of the fever.

All this had been entirely forgotten, even in the family, until Miss Marks discovered it, thereby explaining the reference in a letter to R. H. Horne, on May 17, to an expression of sympathy that had touched Elizabeth "so nearly and deeply." The shock of the news, which must have come to England in the previous month, had thrown her into a fever so that she had "been too weak to hold a pen." "It was a heavy blow, for all of us—and I, being weak, you see, was struck down by a *bodily* blow, in a moment, without having time for tears." But she could find comfort in "God's will . . . manifested in Jesus Christ. Only *that* holds our hearts together when He shatters the world." But Elizabeth's world, as she was to discover in a few months' time, was not yet shattered.

The pen friendship with Horne had progressed, with her father's approval: he brought her a copy of Horne's poetic play *Gregory VII*, exclaiming at her look of pleasure: "Ah! I thought that would move you." We find her rather shyly sending Horne some Devonshire cream and, more boldly, criticizing or praising his work; praise that sounds oddly to us who have almost forgotten R. H. Horne, "the farthing poet." To Elizabeth he was at this time "one of the very first poets of the day."

At the end of May we hear in a letter to Mr. Boyd that Elizabeth was still confined to her bed and even when lifted out on to the sofa inclined to faint: she was blistered every few days. It was considered she would never again "be fit for anything like exertion."

But in spite of physical weakness mental activity continued:

[4] *Twenty-nine Years in the West Indies and Central Africa* (London, 1863).

her correspondence with Miss Mitford, Harriet Martineau, Horne, and others was not abandoned and she was able to compose. Poems known to have been written at this period are "The Lay of the Early Rose" (containing some beauties, especially of rhythm, but reading too much like a metrical exercise) and "Crowned and Buried," the subject of which was suggested by her Torquay physician.

In this year, 1840, Napoleon's remains were brought back from St. Helena to be given to France for more ceremonial burial: in July 1815 Napoleon had lain four days on board the *Bellerophon* in the waters of Torbay. Elizabeth, though she could not condone his crimes against humanity, felt, together with many Liberals, that Great Britain was to be censured in her treatment of him:

> *Because it was not well, it was not well,*
> *Nor tuneful with thy lofty-chanted part*
> *Among the Oceanides,—that Heart*
> *To bind and bare and vex with vulture fell.*
> *I would, my noble England! men might seek*
> *All crimson stains upon thy breast—not cheek!*
>
> *I would that hostile fleets had scarred Torbay,*
> *Instead of the lone ship which waited moored*
> *Until thy princely purpose was assured. . . .*

One day Elizabeth was to see the evils of arbitrary power at close quarters; though always she was to honour the name of Napoleon in a lesser man, his nephew.

But soon a far greater test of endurance than the second brother's death in Jamaica was demanded of that weak body. In the first bereavement Bro had been beside her, remaining there though his father must have sorely needed him; declaring, as he held his sister's hand, that he loved her better than them all and would not leave her until she was well again. It was not Mr. Barrett's eldest son but the third, Charles John (Stormie), who was sent out to Jamaica after Sam's death.

On July 11 Bro went out with two friends in a sailing-boat, *La Belle Sauvage*. Elizabeth, perhaps fretful at being left, let him go "with a pettish word." The day was fine, the sea smooth, but at the appointed hour the boat did not return. In Elizabeth's own words to Robert Browning:

For three days we waited—and I hoped while I could—oh—that
awful agony of three days! And the sun shone as it shines to-day,
and there was no more wind than now; and the sea under the
windows was like this paper for smoothness—and my sisters
drew the curtains back that I might see for myself how smooth
the sea was, and how it could hurt nobody—and other boats
came back one by one.

"Remember," Elizabeth continued in that account of the tragedy which unburdened her soul five years after, "how you wrote in your 'Gismond'

> *What says the body when they spring*
> *Some monstrous torture-engine's whole*
> *Strength on it? No more says the soul,*

and you never wrote anything which *lived* with me more than *that*. It is such a dreadful truth."

What remained of young Edward Barrett was thrown up by the sea and buried in Tor churchyard: the final agony remained. Face to face with her father, Elizabeth was bowed down with a load of guilt. She had robbed him of his son, his eldest son, by a selfish weakness in keeping Bro by her. Perhaps too, in the painful encounter, the father had a load on his conscience, needing all the consolation a favourite daughter might otherwise have given him: Bro had been in love, had wanted to marry, but, lacking money, could not do so against Mr. Barrett's prohibition. Elizabeth had wanted to make over to him her own income, but this was not permitted.

A great love for her father, hitherto second only in her affection, filled the wounded heart. "The crown of his house had fallen" but Edward Barrett, great in forbearance, uttered no word of reproach. "I felt," she told Robert, "that he stood nearest to me on the closed grave . . or by the unclosing sea." From the moment of loss this woman, so loving, so sensitive, ceased for many years properly to live, though the suffering lasted on.

In that fanciful poem "An Island," published with "The Seraphim," Elizabeth had pictured a solitude withdrawn from the world, alone but for a chosen few "whom dreams fantastic please as well," and beside the sea "within the sounding coral caves."

> *Choose me the loftiest cave of all,*
>   *To make a place for prayer;*
> *And I will choose a praying voice*
>   *To pour our spirits there.*
> *How silverly the echoes run—*
> *Thy will be done—thy will be done!*

But now, slowly emerging from the stupor into which the shock of Bro's death had first plunged her, she must drag out an existence spiritually alone by that sea, a cruel sea bringing no thought of resignation. The power of prayer might return, but even one so devout, so near to God, could no longer cry with a full heart "Thy will be done."

Only to Robert Browning could Elizabeth ever write directly of that loss so closely intertwined by a tender conscience with guilt, and even to him she never spoke of it. Her heart was too stricken for tears or lamentation. When composition was again possible she wrote in a moving sonnet:

> *I tell you, hopeless grief is passionless;*
> *That only men incredulous of despair,*
> *Half-taught in anguish, through the midnight air*
> *Beat upward to God's throne in loud access*
> *Of shrieking and reproach.*

This, "De Profundis," and other sonnets of her sorrow, are moving, but in a more dramatic presentment of misery, "The Mask," one can feel more fully the heart-break. This poem is so important in the presentment of her life that, at a risk of being over-lengthy, I feel it must be quoted in full. That she herself put on this poem high value as an expression of feeling we may guess by the care lavished on it. There are three separate, widely differing, drafts extant:

> *I have a smiling face, she said,*
>   *I have a jest for all I meet,*
> *I have a garland for my head*
>   *And all its flowers are sweet,—*
> *And so you call me gay, she said.*

Grief taught to me this smile, she said,
  And Wrong did teach this jesting bold;
These flowers were plucked from garden-bed
  While a death-chime was tolled.
And what now will you say?—she said.

Behind no prison-grate, she said,
  Which slurs the sunshine half a mile,
Live captives so uncomforted
  As souls behind a smile.
God's pity let us pray, she said.

I know my face is bright, she said,—
  Such brightness, dying suns diffuse;
I bear upon my forehead shed
  The sign of what I lose,—
The ending of my day, she said.

If I dared leave this smile, she said,
  And take a moan upon my mouth,
And tie a cypress round my head,
  And let my tears run smooth,—
It were the happier way, she said.

And since that must not be, she said,
  I fain your bitter world would leave.
How calmly, calmly, smile the Dead,
  Who do not, therefore, grieve!
The yea of Heaven is yea, she said.

But in your bitter world, she said,
  Face-joy's a costly mask to wear.
'Tis bought with pangs long nourishèd,
  And rounded to despair.
Grief's earnest makes life's play, she said.

Ye weep for those who weep? she said—
  Ah fools! I bid you pass them by.
Go, weep for those whose hearts have bled
  What time their eyes were dry.
Whom sadder can I say? she said.

There were other ties to bind her, a loved father to whom she poured out gratitude, affectionate sisters and brothers: weak, arid of soul, she must forge for herself some sort of armour, a mask in which to front the world. Her natural cheerfulness, a sense of humour, enveloped the husk that remained. Feverishly she lived a life of the intellect, seeking for consolation, as the first bitterness left her, in the love of God.

But the expression of grief, a living on in profound abnegation, was for the future. Now for many months Elizabeth lay in the shadow of death. There is a gap in her correspondence: the next letter available to me, dated December 11, is to her old friend Mrs. Martin, to whom she wrote:

do believe that although grief has so changed me from myself and warped me from my old instincts, as to prevent my looking forwards with pleasure to seeing you again, yet that full amends are made in the looking back with a pleasure more true because more tender than any old retrospections.

She was thankful to be able to report that Stormie was back in England. "It is a mercy which makes me very thankful, and would make me joyful if anything could. But the meanings of some words change as we live on." After the drowning of one brother Elizabeth was to dread for those left all journeyings by sea. Indeed, she may have had to face the cruel anxiety in regard to her father at this time: from another passage in the letter we might conjecture that he found it necessary to go over to Jamaica.

The correspondence with Horne was now resumed over a bold project: to follow in the footsteps of Dryden and present Chaucer in modern language. Among others Wordsworth, Leigh Hunt, Monckton Milnes (afterwards Lord Houghton) were asked to contribute with Horne as editor. Of distinguished writers approached only Landor refused, declaring "I will have no hand in breaking his dun but richly-painted glass, to put in (if clearer) much thinner panes." All but Leigh Hunt agreed that Chaucer's language should be adhered to as closely as possible. Elizabeth modernized "Queen Annelida and False Arcite."

From a letter dated December 17, 1840 it is clear that Horne submitted preface and translations for her opinion. She considered that some of the contributors were too wide of the mark,

that "You, yourself, and Wordsworth are most devoutly near."
Though all such modernizations must lose the original in essence, Elizabeth's own rendering is perhaps as near as may be.

We also learn from this letter that Mr. Barrett, proud of the
connection, or perhaps out of gratitude to one who had helped
to rouse his ailing daughter from a lethargy of grief, had left his
card on Horne in London. Elizabeth asked Horne to pay a visit
in Wimpole Street "some day when you are in the neighbourhood—before I am there . . . it would give them such real
pleasure to know you, I am very sure." Later we hear of the gift
of a jar of West Indian tamarinds.

Another work in which she was more closely associated with
Horne at this time was a lyrical drama after the Greek manner
to be called "Psyche Apocalyptè," which they were to compose
together; he to devise the characters, interlocutors, choruses,
semi-choruses, and she to present the part of Psyche and provide the lyrical portion. As may be guessed, the theme was Elizabeth's, "the terror attending spiritual consciousness—the man's
soul to the man," exalting the *Doppelgänger* conception on to
a spiritual plane. "There are moments when we are startled at
the footsteps of our own being, more than at the thunders of
God." Perhaps the working-out of this theme on her own might
to some extent have eased Elizabeth's burdened, guilt-shad-
owed soul; but as it was, she wrote only a few isolated lyrics
after the general plan had been mapped out. The project was
never openly abandoned, though perhaps tacitly dropped. Such
a collaboration at arm's length, and on paper, seemed doomed
to failure from the start.

At the end of March 1841, Elizabeth wrote to Mrs. Martin:
*my faculties seem to hang heavily now, like flappers when the
spring is broken. My spring is broken, and a separate exertion is
necessary for the lifting up of each—and then it falls down
again. . . . Nevertheless, I don't give up much to the perni-
cious languor—the tendency to lie down to sleep among the
snows of a weary journey—I don't give up much to it.*
That she could think and write at all seems a miracle, weakened as she was by being kept in bed in a room with the windows papered up in winter to exclude every breath of fresh air
and, in addition, dosed with brandy and opium. We gather that

she was left to brood, perhaps at her own desire, many hours by
herself. That spring, however, a solace was provided in her invalid life by Miss Mitford: a cocker spaniel, a faithful creature
never to be forgotten. "Flush amuses me sometimes when I am
inclined to be amused by nothing else," Elizabeth told her
brother George.

With some slight return of bodily power, Elizabeth was now
yearning to go home, to leave Beacon Terrace, where the sound
of the sea was always with her. Anyhow, she wrote to her
brother, Dr. Scully said she must remain in her room all the
winter, so what did it matter where she lived? No decision on
her future fate, however, could be obtained from Mr. Barrett.
One would have thought the cruelty of keeping his daughter so
long by that engulfing sea would have been evident to a father
at heart so devoted, but Mr. Barrett himself made no move in
the matter. Perhaps he kept Elizabeth at Torquay all that summer because his plans in life were unsettled. He was contemplating the removal of his family from London: there was even
one wild scheme of a migration to the Schwarzwald in Germany. "These Black Mountains," Elizabeth commented, "are
black indeed."

In June a new anxiety possessed her. Mr. Barrett talked of
making Clifton, the spa near Bristol, a halting-place for a month
or two before she should come home. Elizabeth was afraid a
short stay there might prolong itself into the winter. "My
mind," she wrote to George, "turns round & round in wondering
about Papa's fancy for Clifton, that hot, white, dusty vapory
place." It is possible that Mr. Barrett's fancy for Clifton origi-
nated in youthful memories: his grandmother, the wife of Edward Barrett of Jamaica, may have lived there. She certainly
died at Bristol in 1804, being buried in the Cathedral.

In the meantime Elizabeth was composing: probably "The
Romaunt of the Page," one of her most popular poems when it
appeared, and certainly "The House of Clouds," a particular favourite with her father, were written about this time.

In early summer Elizabeth was so far improved in health as to
be able to sit up out of bed for an hour without fainting: though
there must necessarily be a risk, Dr. Scully pronounced her fit
for travel. Patiently, "tied hand and foot and gagged" at Tor-

quay, she awaited her release. During August her father disappeared into Herefordshire without giving a date for her departure, but at length, in September, by stages of twenty-five miles a day, she made the journey in a patent invalid carriage with "a thousand springs."

But though Torquay was left behind, although Elizabeth need no longer listen through long sleepless nights to a sound of waves on the shore, there could be no escape. An echo lingered on. "I seem now," she told Robert Browning years later, "always to hear the sea *in* the wind, voice within voice."

CHAPTER 10

A CONFIRMED INVALID [1841–3]

BACK IN WIMPOLE STREET, Elizabeth told Boyd in a letter of October 2, 1841, she was "more happy—that is, nearing to the feeling of happiness now—than a month since I could believe possible to a heart so bruised and crushed as mine. . . . To be at home is a blessing and a relief beyond what these words can say." Not only had Elizabeth escaped from that place of doom overlooking a terrible sea, but she had not now to reproach herself with tearing her family asunder, with depriving Mr. Barrett of the company and ministrations of his two younger daughters, both of whom he had lately insisted should remain with her.

An intellectual life grew daily stronger in home surroundings. "Part of me," she wrote, "is worn out; but the poetical part— that is, the *love* of poetry—is growing in me as freshly and strongly as if it were watered every day."

The exact nature of Elizabeth's illness has never been thoroughly diagnosed. I have wondered whether the first hæmorrhage came from some accidental injury to the lungs. There is, however, an interesting letter [1] written later from Italy to an old friend, Fanny Dowglass, which sheds some light. Mrs. Dowglass had been ordered to Italy because of a threat of tuberculosis. Elizabeth warned her friend not to take the prediction too seriously:

The stethoscope is not an infallible searcher—that I have "heard sain" by several medical men who trusted much to it: and I know in my own case besides several others, that differences of opinion have been elicited from the very same instrument. Congestion & tuberculation will equally produce unsatisfactory responses to an ear resting on the stethoscope—& congestion is the much less serious evil. In my own case "extensive tuberculation" was declared by one physician while by two or three oth-

[1] *c.* 1850; Huntington Library Collection.

ers the existence of anything beside congestion has been sted-
fastly denied, positively denied—& circumstances at present
seem quite to confirm the softer judgment.

By 1840 the "softer judgment" had been given by four able
physicians in the west country who pronounced the affection of
her lungs to be not tubercular consumption, but the result of a
"decline," that word which in earlier medical days so elegantly
concealed a lack of precise knowledge.

On her return to London Mr. Boyd urged that her case should
be put before a Mr. Jago, but this Elizabeth refused at first.
Later Mr. Jago was to be a trusted adviser, relied upon even in
far-away Italy.

In refusing Boyd's request Elizabeth told him that, though
unequal to meeting people in general, she would gladly see her
old friend. We have, however, no record of a visit from Boyd.
It seems likely that Boyd, now living alone, was already fast
sinking into that mood of valetudinarian apathy which was to
make his last years so tragic to beholders. He spent long hours
brooding in his chair, his ear refreshed only by the striking and
chiming of the many clocks of which he was a collector. Perhaps the marriage of his daughter in 1836, or '37, had been,
apart from the loss of her company, a serious blow to the
staunch Protestant. If "Henrietta" was in truth Annie, her husband, Henry Hayes, or Heyes, was a Roman Catholic and later
his wife became a convert.

A link with Boyd at this time was Elizabeth's work on the
Greek Christian Fathers. In January 1842 she had sent to the
Athenæum, without much hope of acceptance, translations with
a prefatory note, from Gregory Nazianzen. "You will comprehend my surprise," she wrote to Boyd, "on receiving last night
a courteous note from the editor, which I would send to you if
it were legible to anybody except people used to learn reading
from the pyramids." Those familiar with Keats's letters will remember his comment on Dilke's handwriting: "like the speaking
of a child, three years old, very understandable to its father but
to no one else."

Not only did Dilke print these translations but he welcomed
a suggestion from her that she should write an article upon the
Greek Christian Fathers (begging her to keep away from theol-

ogy). This, although it meant further hard reading, she accomplished in time for part publication in the next issue. The first
instalment begins with a fine passage on the Greek language
and its great exponents. I give the opening sentences:

*The Greek language was a strong intellectual life, stronger than
any similar one which has lived in the breath of "articulately
speaking men," and survived it. No other language has lived so
long and died so hard,—pang by pang, each with a dolphin colour—yielding reluctantly to that doom of death and silence
which must come at last to the speaker and the speech.*

Though "the instrument of the Greek tongue was, at the
Christian era, an antique instrument, somewhat worn," the
Christian Fathers had, as compared with the better-known
Latin ecclesiastical poets, "that higher distinction inherent in
brain and breast, of vivid thought and quick sensibility."

They must be estimated, however stiff and stammering, as
religious poets. To Elizabeth all true poets must be in essence
religious, and at this time the state of the human soul before its
God was preoccupying her. She was to sing, or perhaps had already sung, in "The Soul's Travelling" of man's spirit adventur-
ing in the world of men, but

. . . very vain

> *The greatest speed of all these souls of men,*
> *Unless they travel upward to the throne,*
> *Where sittest* THOU, *the satisfying* ONE,
> *With help for sins and holy perfectings*
> *For all requirements—while the archangel, raising*
> *Unto Thy face his full ecstatic gazing,*
> *Forgets the rush and rapture of his wings.*

It is clear from a reference in "The Greek Christian Fathers"
that in her preoccupation with man's soul, Goethe, in the person
of his Wilhelm Meister, was impressing her mind. The wounded
spirit was climbing from its abyss though its earthly shell remained weak and crushed. Boyd, perhaps fearing that her love
of Greek poetry was weakening, put a direct question and received a lively answer: she had in Devonshire kept up her
knowledge of Euripides, Æschylus, and Sophocles. "You know
I have gone through every line of the three tragedians long
ago, in the way of regular, consecutive reading." The reading of

Plato, although already extensive, she had to complete "as soon as I can take breath from Mr. Dilke." She would also round off her knowledge of Aristotle.

Mr. Kenyon, who was fast becoming a close friend, disapproved of the work on the Christian Fathers as "labour thrown away, from the unpopularity of the subject." Mrs. Jameson, however, in the first reference we have of Elizabeth's to her, although no Grecian, "read them with 'great pleasure' unconsciously of the author": "Mr. Horne the poet and Mr. Browning the poet were not behind in approbation."

Dilke had suggested that Elizabeth should also give him a series of papers on the English poets, linking it loosely as a review with a recent anthology entitled *The Book of the Poets* and rounded off with a review of Wordsworth's latest volume, *Poems, chiefly of early and late years.* This she did well enough to please even that stern critic Mr. Boyd, who, she confided delightedly to George, commented that "of the whole passage about Shakespeare, nobody can find the least sign of its being written '*by a female.*'"

Chaucer is understandingly analysed and his "true music" defended against those who still maintained that he wrote by accent only. Most interesting perhaps to modern ears is her passage on Skelton and "his influence for good upon our language. He was a writer singularly fitted for beating out the knots of the cordage, and strain the lengths to extension; a rough worker at rough work." Our modern admiration of Donne she could hardly share in 1842; Donne, "having a dumb *angel,* and knowing more noble poetry than he articulates." In a rapid survey of Elizabethan drama she asserts that, in the history of its development, "Kyd's blank verse is probably the first breaking of the true soil; and certainly far better and more dramatic than Marlowe's is—crowned poet as the latter stands before us— . . . Marlowe was more essentially a poet than a dramatist . . . Kyd . . . more essentially, with all his dramatic faults, a dramatist than a poet."

In dealing with Shakespeare and linking him with Homer, she roundly declared:

We, who have no leaning to the popular cant of Romanticism and Classicism, and believe the old Greek BEAUTY *to be both*

new and old, and as alive and not more grey in Webster's
Duchess of Malfy *than in Æschylus's* Eumenides, *do reverence
this Homer and this Shakespeare as the colossal borderers of
the two intellectual departments of the world's age—do behold
from their feet the antique and modern literatures sweep outwardly away.*

In speaking of the Augustan age, and the "idol-worship of
rime," Elizabeth gave a fine analysis of the earlier employment
of rime as "a felicitous adjunct, a musical accompaniment, the
tinkling of a cymbal through the choral harmonies." Dryden,
"eloquent above the sons of men," though it was then the fashion to speak of him not as a poet but an influence, "was a poet—
an excellent poet—in marble. . . . He was a poet without passion. . . . He had a large soul for a man, containing sundry
Queen Anne's men, one within the other, like quartetto tables;
but it was not a large soul for a poet. . . ." Our language and
our literature, however, remain, in certain respects, the greater
for his greatness. She could not fully join in the new fashionable
decrying of "Pope, the perfecter," the idol of her childhood, but,
with the true historic sense of a born critic, gave him his just
due, placing him as a practitioner even higher than Dryden for
*a delicate fineness of tact, of which the precise contrary is un-
pleasantly obvious in his great master . . . there is nothing of
[Dryden's] coarseness of the senses about Pope; the little pale
Queen Anne's valetudinarian had a nature fine enough to stand
erect upon the point of a needle like a schoolman's angel; and
whatever he wrote coarsely he did not write from inward impulse, but from external conventionality, from a bad social
Swift-sympathy.*

Of chief interest to a biographer in these first articles are not
only a wide understanding knowledge of the earlier poets, but
her general remarks upon poetry and nature. The true poet of
nature is not he who uses merely the language, the scenery of
nature—Nature is but "chief secretary to the creative Word."
"Nature is where God is," and so, in a larger sense, is poetry:
*In the loudest hum of your machinery, in the dunnest volume of
your steam, in the foulest street of your city—there as surely as
in the Brocken pine-woods and the watery thunders of Niagara*

*—there, as surely as He is above all, lie Nature and Poetry in full
life.*

Though she herself was to contribute largely to the fashionable
escape of a materialistic age to mediævalism, to island, to cloudy
refuge, she was also to strike the note of modernity; to culmi-
nate in *Aurora Leigh,* a story of contemporary life.

Her article on Wordsworth continued the history of poetry
into the romantic age, beginning with, in a reference to him in
a previous article, Cowper, the forerunner. Though clearly familiar with *Poems,* 1817, she did not, oddly enough to us, in
dealing with the early nineteenth-century revolt against pseudo-
classic conventions, refer to Keats's direct attack upon the
Popean school and the rules of Boileau; but Keats, awaiting the
publication of Lord Houghton's *Life and Letters* in 1848, had
not yet come into his own.

She did honour to Wordsworth for his greatness as a pioneer,
a true Christian poet and interpreter of Nature, though pointing out that in part the challenge of the *Lyrical Ballads* was
founded on a false premise: "Betty Foys of the Lake school (so
called) may be as subject to convention as Pope's Lady Bettys."
These poems of the master presented in the new volume were
not the finest of his productions. She quoted from "The Borderers," the early verse play now for the first time published,
calling it "strong black writing," though not true Wordsworth,
gave four of his sonnets, including the beautiful "Airey-Force
Valley," and in her last tribute to his greatness protested against
certain critics who

*utter melancholy frenzies, that poetry is worn out for ever. . . .
In the meantime the hopeful and believing will hope—trust on;
and better still, the Tennysons and the Brownings, and other
high-gifted spirits, will work, wait on, until as Mr. Horne has
said—*

> *Strong deeds awake,
> And clamouring, throng the portals of the hour.*

This, her first public mention of Browning, did singular honour
to a poet as yet unknown outside literary circles; perhaps hardly
beyond the discriminate few among which her cousin Kenyon
moved.

The footsteps are now coming nearer, only to recede. In the March of this year Mr. Kenyon wanted to bring to her sofa-side "Mr. Browning the poet . . . who was so honor-giving as to wish something of the sort: I was pleased at the thought of his wishing it—for the rest, no!" Kenyon had told her that Browning was discouraged by his reception with the public. "Poor Browning!" said Mr. Kenyon.

"And why poor Browning?"

"Because nobody reads him."

"Rather then," Elizabeth retorted, "poor readers. Mr. Carlyle is his friend—a good substitute for a crowd's shouting!"

When reporting this to George, Elizabeth commented: "you are aware how I estimate . . . admire (what is the sufficient word?) that true poet—however he may prophesy darkly." We know from Browning himself that he was physically near, at this time or another, probably for a moment or two under the same roof: Kenyon had announced him but reported her too unwell to receive him.

In the modernity of her spirit Elizabeth, in spite of enforced seclusion, kept close touch with contemporary writers. Carlyle was reverenced, and she was now reading Emerson. Novels were eagerly devoured, many of them French, her passion for French fiction being shared by Miss Mitford, with whom there was a constant exchange of recommendations. For Balzac she had, and was later to share with her husband, an immense admiration, Victor Hugo was for her far above the popular Dickens, and George Sand one of the greatest women of the age.

An interest in contemporary life had been manifest in December of the last year in verses (published in the *Athenæum*) upon the marriage of Queen Victoria with the deliberate echo-title in "Crowned and Wedded" of the previous year's "Crowned and Buried," the verses upon Napoleon Bonaparte. "Crowned and Wedded," called by the partial Miss Mitford "the most magnificent poem ever written by woman," written in a measure that does not fall too happily on modern ears, is for us redeemed from utter commonplace only by her references to the Dead "who lie in rows beneath the minster floor," the scene of the royal wedding:

The statesman whose clean palm will kiss no bribe,
                                    whate'er it be,
The courtier who for no fair queen, will rise up on his
                                    knee;
The court-dame who, for no court-tire, will leave her
                                    shroud behind;
The laureate who no courtlier rime than "dust to dust"
                                    can find;
The kings and queens who having made that vow and worn
                                    that crown,
Descended into lower thrones and darker, deep adown!
Sentiments more worthily expressed in the fine "Epitaph" beginning "Beauty who softly walkest all thy days," published with the translation of "Prometheus Bound."

To Miss Mitford Elizabeth was now writing some two or three times a week, letters of which that enthusiastic friend wrote: "Put Mdme de Sevigné and Cowper together, and you can fancy them." Though Elizabeth's letters cannot, perhaps, be placed in that high class, they are lively, penetrating, humorous, philosophic; and speak, according to the testimony of those who knew her, in her own authentic voice.

By an ever widening correspondence she kept contact with the outer world in letters to distinguished men of the day, most of whom were writers: an exception, and one of the most interesting, was the painter and priest of "high art" Benjamin Robert Haydon, with whom she had a lively exchange between 1842 and 1845. Haydon was probably put into communication with her by their common friend Miss Mitford.

A part of Elizabeth's side of this correspondence has been printed, a few letters in Haydon's *Correspondence* and some twenty by Miss Shackford, but a good number of Haydon's letters to her remain unpublished; [2] and from these I am privileged to quote.

Haydon, as natural a writer as herself, fell quickly into a tone of intimacy, commenting in his large way: "there is something so original in a couple of Geniuses corresponding, becoming acquainted, knowing each other thoroughly and yet never seeing each other, that I revelled in the Idea beyond expression."

[2] Pope Collection.

Once he had called in Wimpole Street, only to receive the usual reply that her health did not permit her to receive visitors.

He, as man of the world, an artist and a man of wide reading and interests, had much to give this recluse; perhaps more than we know in the way of drawing her back to life. He wrote lively reminiscences of illustrious people he had met twenty years before, including Keats, sent her drawings to look at, two portraits, successively, of Wordsworth upon Helvellyn to hang in her room, and his autobiography in manuscript. She on her part lent him books, including a black-letter Chaucer, helped him in the planning of his Chaucer picture, and, not the least, gave the unfortunate man sympathy, delicate feminine praise, at a time when he craved for it. When in 1843 his cartoons for the Houses of Parliament were rejected, Elizabeth tried to soften the blow, pointing out that all great men have been attacked in their generation. But it was in vain that she, the most modest of artists, combated against his overweening vanity, his enormous sense of grievance at failure.

In refusing Haydon's request that they should "change portraits royally," declaring she has no likeness to send him, Elizabeth gave, as "scanty data" to his fancy, a verbal portrait of herself that is worth quoting if only because it settles one point on which descriptions of her are at variance, the colour of her eyes:

I am "little and black" like Sappho, en attendant the immortality—five feet one high; as the latitude, straight to correspond—eyes of various colours as the sun shines,—called blue and black, without being accidentally black and blue—affidavit-ed for grey —sworn at for hazel—and set down by myself (according to my "private view" in the glass) as dark-green-brown—grounded with brown, and green otherwise; what is called "invisible green" in invisible garden-fences. . . . Not much nose of any kind; certes no superfluity of nose; but to make up for it, a mouth suitable to a larger personality—oh, and a very very little voice, to which Cordelia's was a happy medium. Dark hair and complexion— Small face and sundries.

In discussing his autobiography Elizabeth begs him to "*spare the provocative,*" to cultivate reserve, especially in regard to himself. "When the lion roars, he need not say 'I am a lion' . . .

if he SHOULD say 'I am a lion,' all the monkeys on the palm trees are sworn to cry out . . . 'No lion! but a jackall.'" To this, in his inflated estimate of his own genius, Haydon retorted, did she want him to act the hypocrite?

A subject of mutual interest was Napoleon. On Elizabeth's expression of her country's dishonour in the banishment to St. Helena, after the Emperor had surrendered to the Prince Regent, Haydon commented: "The Rock was melancholy! but it was poetical! It surrounded his latter days with a halo of Romance." Much as he admired Napoleon's genius, it must be admitted that security of his person was, after twenty-five years of war, the first object. "His word of honour was nothing": at large he must always have remained a danger. Looking at the first Dictator with a detachment surprising in one so partial, so emotional, Haydon added: "Napoleon threw the cause of Genius, 100 years back, the good he did was accidental, the Evil certain." As Elizabeth held to her point he teased her, calling her his "little Napoleonette," "You Ingenious little darling invisible."

In this connection he gave her reminiscences of his visit to Paris, in 1814 soon after Napoleon's abdication, where he examined "his haunts," "doating on his Genius," even seeing "the extinguisher on the last candle he read by, at Fontainebleau." Elizabeth, always reticent about her age, did not, so far as we know, reveal the fact that she had to some extent followed his footsteps in 1815.

From Napoleon they passed naturally to the Empress Marie Louise and from her, as one of two women who had left their husbands, to Lady Byron. Elizabeth always hated Byron's wife even after she came to know Anna Jameson, a close friend of that unhappy lady. Haydon told her how twice he had come in contact with Lady Byron, "that double X icicle": "and we quarrelled without hope, the second time—the first day, I thought Byron a brute—the second day I was convinced *she* was—a *Mathematician*. The morning dress was dimity, the Evening silk." [3]

On December 30, 1842 Haydon made a precious gift to his "little darling invisible": the last sixty lines in holograph of "I

[3] See *Don Juan*, Canto I, st. xii.

stood tip-toe upon a little hill." Keats, loved and read then by
comparatively few, Elizabeth had in 1838 already honoured
in "A Vision of Poets"; later, in *Aurora Leigh*, she was to give
the world an "epitaph" of him which set a seal on the new estimate of a poet who, by 1857, had entered into his kingdom.

At the end of June 1843 Haydon, rendered desperate by the
rejection of his cartoons and expecting daily executions for
debt, sent for safety to Elizabeth "two jars of oil (1816) twenty-
seven years old," and several boxes containing papers, books,
and letters. These boxes were to be, at Haydon's tragic death,
a source of embarrassment and annoyance to her.

In the spring of that year Haydon, who, to do him justice, arrogant being though he was, felt to the full his high privilege in
consorting with the great of his generation, sent her an urn
upon which he had inscribed the names of those "immortals"
who had taken tea drawn from it: though she might not drink
at his own table, Elizabeth must join this illustrious band. On
the 29th Elizabeth wrote, expressing both inward amusement
and natural modesty: "This is my certificate, my dear Mr. Haydon that I have taken and quaffed a cup of amreeta [4] from your
urn of the Immortals!" And as Flush had taken "a quaff from
the lees of my cup" she made "a humble suggestion" that he
"inscribe the worthy name of Flush first and my name afterwards . . we two completing together a very perfect antithesis
to your *Dii Majores*."

Flush is now among the immortals and perhaps it is unnecessary to write much of him: the spaniel was her constant companion and consolation, her "loving friend." His beauty and devotion have been fitly celebrated in those well-known lines "To
Flush, my Dog." A less familiar tribute is the sonnet "Flush or
Faunus," which is perhaps worth quoting in full:

> *You see this dog. It was but yesterday*
> *I mused forgetful of his presence here*
> *Till thought on thought drew downward tear on tear,*
> *When from the pillow, where wet-cheeked I lay,*
> *A head as hairy as Faunus, thrust its way*
> *Right sudden against my face,—two golden-clear*

[4] "The Amreeta-cup of immortality." See Canto XXIV, st. 9, l. 11, Southey's
The Curse of Kehama.

Great eyes astonished mine,—a drooping ear
Did flap me on either cheek to dry the spray!
I started first, as some Arcadian,
Amazed by goatly god in twilight grove;
But, as the bearded vision closelier ran
My tears off, I knew Flush, and rose above
Surprise and sadness,—thanking the true PAN,
Who, by low creatures, leads to heights of love.

In a letter of September 1842 we find another reference to the god Pan, who was to form the subject of two of her best-known poems: Elizabeth asked Kenyon for permission to keep a little longer his translation of Schiller's "Gods of Greece." She thanked him for two volumes of Tennyson's *Poems* recently published and, in comparing old poems with new, observed with her usual critical acumen:

nothing appears to me quite equal to "Œnone," and perhaps a few besides of my ancient favorites. . . . There is, in fact, more thought—more bare brave working of the intellect—in the latter poems, even if we miss something of the high ideality, and the music that goes with it, of the older ones.

But, though she might criticize him, Tennyson remained for Elizabeth almost an object of adoration: six months later we find her treasuring "a very kind note" from him. "I am," she wrote to George, "sensible of the honour of being written to by Mr. Tennyson, & I am ready to kiss his shoe-tyes any day. This is not in joke—it is grave, solemn, earnest." She looked eagerly for any news of Tennyson her brother might obtain. When George, on meeting the great man, reported that he wore a dirty shirt, Elizabeth countered mischievously: "I waive the dirty shirt—it is by way of lyrical transition into the society of lawyers with dirty consciences." The smoking of a pipe in society, a solecism of which Tennyson was often guilty, she was also prepared to overlook. "I envied you notwithstanding the tobacco smoke."

The summer of 1842 was a warm one, with a consequent improvement in Elizabeth's health. By the end of September she was free from the blood spittings that had been such a disturbing symptom of her illness, was able to go downstairs several times and even out in her chair. "At the end of such a double summer," she wrote to Boyd, "I might be able to go to see you at Hampstead. Nevertheless, winters and adversities are more fit for us than a constant sun."

One "adversity," if a minor one, at this time was "dearest Miss Mitford's letters from the deathbed of her father," which *make my heart ache as surely almost as the post comes. . . . If I were in her circumstances, I should sit paralysed—it would be impossible for me to write or to cry. And she, who loves and feels with the intensity of a nature warm in everything, seems to turn to sympathy by the very instinct of grief, and sits at the deathbed of her last relative, writing there, in letter after letter, every symptom, physical or moral—even to the very words of the raving of a delirium, and those, heart-breaking words!*

Practical sympathy was expressed during Dr. Mitford's illness by gifts, some West Indian in origin, of delicacies probably beyond the purse and certainly beyond the reach of his devoted daughter.

To Boyd in the December of this year Elizabeth gave, in reply to a charge of Calvinism, a clear avowal of her religious faith:

I believe simply that the saved are saved by grace, and that they shall hereafter know it fully; that the lost are lost by their choice and free will—by choosing to sin and die; and I believe absolutely that the deepest damned of all the lost will not dare to whisper to the nearest devil that reproach of Martha: "If the Lord had been near me, I had not died."

For the rest she was agnostic. "But of the means of the workings of God's grace, and the time of the formation of the Divine counsels, I know nothing, guess nothing, and struggle to guess nothing." She refuses to examine the "brickbats of controversy—there is more than enough to think of in truths clearly revealed."

It was probably at this time that she composed a group of religious sonnets. In one of the finest we get a painful glimpse into miseries silently endured in that upper room, the pains of the rack:

> *All tortured states*
> *Suppose a straitened place.*

With Mr. Boyd Elizabeth was carrying on a lively literary correspondence. Boyd in his old-fashioned way was refusing to acknowledge the merits of Wordsworth; and, curiously enough, appeared only now, in 1843, to be "discovering" Ossian, whom —more astonishingly still in a classical scholar—he claimed as superior to Homer. "The fact," Elizabeth commented succinctly, "appears to me that anomalous thing among believers —a miracle without an occasion."

About this time R. H. Horne delighted her with the loan of an original portrait of Keats, one which seems to be unrecorded. Of it she wrote: "It is a Vandyke—all but the form and color—to be sure! So, being just, I can't remonstrate against your resolution of keeping it to yourself, though I sh.ᵈ like very much to see your lines of correction." She noted a singular resemblance to a portrait of Horne himself.

In this letter [5] she discussed the question of euthanasia, remarking:

Intense pain & light & serenity of soul do often go together— & spectators & physicians cannot always judge of the actual condition of the patient. And pain does good to us often—& God's grace often is flowing in an undercurrent under the seemingly most rocky ground.

Elizabeth herself had, of course, known searing pain at an early age and was not now exempt from it: a bitter east wind, penetrating even to that closed room, could affect her heart.

Elizabeth had now material enough for a new volume of poems. Thinking that her literary reputation now warranted it, she offered her copyright to Saunders & Otley, the publishers of *The Seraphim,* if they would undertake publication without expense to herself. On their refusal she asked Horne to advise her as to "the most poetical bookseller" of his acquaintance. Again she was willing to surrender the copyright. It was, however, two years before "the most poetical bookseller," Edward Moxon, put out those two volumes which were to bring her both fame and happiness.

As with many English writers, and the majority of our poets in the first half of the last century, Elizabeth's reputation in

[5] Forman Collection, January 7, 1843.

America was higher than here. At the end of 1842 *Graham's Magazine* gave an enthusiastic review of her work: in the spring we find her writing to Cornelius Mathews, its editor and himself a writer of distinction, sending him poems for publication, recommending English writers, and giving the literary gossip of the day. Once in return Mathews sent her a notice of "A Blot in the 'Scutcheon," apparently not favourable, under the impression that she was personally acquainted with Browning. Elizabeth replied:

I do assure you I never saw him in my life—do not know him even by correspondence—and yet, whether through fellow-feeling for Eleusinian mysteries, or whether through the more generous motive of appreciation of his powers, I am very sensitive to the thousand and one stripes with which the assembly of critics doth expound its vocation over him, and the "Athenæum," for instance, made me quite cross and misanthropical last week.⁶ The truth is—and the world should know the truth— it is easier to find a more faultless writer than a poet of equal genius.

"Don't," she added quaintly, "let us fall into the category of the sons of Noah. Noah was once drunk, indeed, but once he built the ark."

⁶ In a review of *Dramatic Lyrics*.

CHAPTER 11

THE RECLUSE OF WIMPOLE STREET [1843–4]

FROM LETTERS at this time we can build up a picture of Elizabeth's surroundings in the Wimpole Street house, one of an attached row, running parallel with Gloucester Place, "whose walls look so much like Newgate's turned inside out." The house itself has been pulled down, but it can be mentally reconstructed from those remaining; with their dignified reception rooms below, the great drawing-room on the first floor and bedrooms piled above. Elizabeth's room was at the back on the second floor with Henrietta's directly above her.

That room which she hardly left for five years had a wide bay window, a window that in its noble proportions would seem to demand a fine view. It looked, however, over dark houses and chimney-pots. In a deep window box that summer of 1843 there were scarlet runners, convolvuluses, nasturtiums: a large ivy root given her by John Kenyon, and destined to veil the urban view, had recently been planted. Very soon it covered all the panes, its trailing branches even reaching up to Henrietta's window.

This greenery, these flowers brought wistful memory of gardens lost, of the countryside over which she had so freely run, ridden, or driven in and about Hope End. "I have never," she wrote Mrs. Martin, "cared so much in my life for flowers as since being shut out from gardens." But in winter this joy must be but transitory: in that close atmosphere plants and flowers quickly died.

An effort was made to disguise the fact that in this room Elizabeth slept as well as lived: the bed was "like a sofa," the wash-stand turned into a cabinet on which stood shelves home-carpentered by "Sette and Co." Similar shelves covered with crimson merino topped a chest of drawers. The wardrobe, an uncompromising piece of furniture in Victorian days, could not be disguised. In the middle of the room stood a large table to hold books and papers. Her sofa opposed an armchair, the gift of her uncle so many years before.

In the window hung an Æolian harp, given her by Mr. Barrett, of which she wrote to Boyd in friendly rivalry with his chiming clocks: "nothing below the spherical harmonies is so sweet and soft and mournfully wild." Flush was jealous of this harp, thinking it alive; always taking it "as very hard that I should say 'beautiful' to anything else except his ears!" Boyd was now living at 3, Circus Road, St. John's Wood. In attempting to induce him to walk across Regent's Park to visit her, Elizabeth told Boyd that in this retreat, her "prison," no sound should affront the over-sensitive ears of a blind man:

We live on the verge of the town rather than in it, and our noises are cousins to silence; and you should pass into a room where the silence is most absolute. Flush's breathing is my loudest sound, and then the watch's tickings, and then my heart when it beats too turbulently.

But around this quiet room, sometimes irrupting into it, was life enough in that large household. The sisters were Elizabeth's most constant companions, the lively auburn-haired Henrietta and gentler, soberer Arabel. Of these two women, neither of them girls now, Elizabeth has drawn pen portraits for us in the sonnets "Two Sketches." Henrietta, she tells us, had a Grecian profile, but a face too full at front view and rather high-coloured, her main beauty being

> *A smile that turns the sunny side o' the heart*
> *On all the world, as if herself did win*
> *By what she lavished on an open mart!*
> *Let no man call that liberal sweetness, sin,—*

Henrietta was perhaps a flirt and certainly a woman attractive to men. There was more than one eager to marry her though she was now well past the age of thirty.

Arabel, her eyes blue, dark-lashed, her head covered with fair drooping curls,

> *As many to each cheek as you might see*
> *Green leaves to a wild rose!*

was a woman born to serve, of a natural saintliness:

> *To smell this flower, come near it! such can grow*
> *In that sole garden where Christ's brow dropped blood.*

Henrietta loved balls and parties, but Arabel's deep joy was in religion, in the Paddington Chapel to which she went early each morning. She, Elizabeth's favourite sister, slept in her room.

The brothers, so far as we know, were all living at home. It is not easy to gather, except in the case of George, how they occupied themselves: Septimus later became a barrister, Occy was at one time studying architecture, and Alfred, ultimately a King's Messenger, seems in the middle forties to have had some connection with the Great Western Railway.

We are best informed about Elizabeth's relations with George because the letters written to him while he was on circuit are available. George took a lively interest in the literary society of his day and, as has been said, brought her news of Mr. Tennyson. The eldest surviving son, Charles John, or Stormie, may have helped his father at the London office, but we hear nothing of it: certainly he seems to have had enough freedom to travel in Mr. Barrett's ships when he wished. Though now the eldest, being of a softer, gentler nature than George, he tacitly ceded a place as leading spirit in the family to that more vigorous personality.

There was also in the house a pretty fair-haired girl of ten years, Elizabeth Georgina, daughter of Captain George Goodin Barrett, who, being out in Jamaica, had left her in charge of his cousin, Mr. Barrett. Elizabeth Georgina, or Lizzie, was a favourite, just the quiet kind of child to be welcome in an invalid's room:

> *Choosing pleasures, for the rest,*
> *Which come softly—just as she,*
> *When she nestles at your knee.*

Her voice murmured "lowly, as a silver stream may run." This charming child, the pet of the family, was later to become Elizabeth's sister-in-law.

At the head of this household ranging from childhood to early middle age (as age was reckoned then) was an enigmatic man who, from certain misrepresentations and a radical change in family customs, has come to be popularly regarded as one larger than life, a sinister figure: actually Mr. Barrett, though spoiled as were so many men before the emancipation of women, though arbitrary in relation to his children, seems to have been, but for one odd and distressing kink in his nature, a typical conscientious early nineteenth-century father who held firmly that a parent should command and a child obey.

In the evening, on his return after long hours in the City, Mr. Barrett liked to enjoy the society of his family, to have none else at table but his own invited guests. His nature was robust, his face and figure youthful. He took pleasure in his house, his pictures (more believed in as Old Masters by himself, it would appear, than by his children), and was not ashamed to take a feminine interest in flowers. We hear of a branch of some Australian bush (possibly wattle), sent by Mrs. Martin at Christmas, being carried by him all over the house. His laugh was frequent and hearty. When he was away from home the eldest daughter, nearest to him in spirit, felt as if some strong supporting power was withdrawn from her. As with Elizabeth, religion was in him fervent and deep-seated. Of the general influence of his strong personality, of the deep affection between Elizabeth and himself, more must be written later.

It was in 1842 that Miss Mitford gave to an enthusiastic young friend a description of Elizabeth in 1836 (see p. 63): to balance this description Miss Mitford also gave one of her as she appeared that year:

Now she has totally lost the rich, bright colouring, which certainly made the greater part of her beauty. She is dark and pallid; the hair is almost entirely hidden; the look of youth gone (I think she now looks as much beyond her actual age as, formerly, she looked behind it); nothing remaining but the noble forehead, the matchless eyes, and the fine form of the mouth and teeth; even now their whiteness is healthy . . . a symptom favourable to our beloved friend's restoration. The expression, too, is completely changed; the sweetness remains, but it is accompanied with more shrewdness, more gaiety, the look not merely of a woman of genius—that she always had—but of a superlatively clever woman.

Miss Mitford spoke of Elizabeth's ripened talent for conversation, her loss of the early shyness, "an odd effect of absence from general society":

When I first saw her, her talk, delightful as it was, had some-
thing too much of the lamp—she spoke too well—and her let-
ters were rather too much like the very best books. Now all that
is gone; the fine thoughts come gushing and sparkling as water
down a hillside, clear, bright, and sparkling in the sunshine.

However slowly Elizabeth might be progressing towards that
recovery her optimistic friend looked forward to (with a prescience not given to either Elizabeth herself or those about
her), there was in the invalid a growing force of mind that revealed itself in her work: in the spring of 1843 she composed
one of her strongest and finest poems, "The Dead Pan"; one that
Kenyon, having helped to inspire, felt to be almost his own
property. To him she strenuously defended a strong religious
note that he thought likely to injure her popularity. "What pa-
gan poet ever thought of casting his gods out of his poetry? And
what, she asked, was popularity beside "truth and earnestness
in all things?" If in "The Dead Pan" "Christ's name is improperly
spoken . . . then indeed is Schiller right, and the true gods of
poetry are to be sighed for mournfully." But feeling the poem to
belong peculiarly to her cousin, she was willing to withhold it
from publication, if he so desired. In the question of loose rimes
Elizabeth was not so firm: some she altered at Kenyon's request.

Incidentally Kenyon was wrong in his estimate of injured
popularity: it was in part the earnest Christian note in Elizabeth's poetry that made her so popular with a large section of
the Victorian community.

Kenyon's enthusiasm for "The Dead Pan" increased Elizabeth's reputation in the literary world; he taking care to bring
it to the notice of his circle, of Landor, Browning, and "several
other of the demi gods." Kenyon even ventured to send several
stanzas of it to Wordsworth in the hope that his appetite might
be whetted for more. From what we know of the old egoist,
however, it is unlikely that Wordsworth did ask for more,
though he had in the previous month expressed his personal
value for Elizabeth by sending her the somewhat embarrassing
gift of his uninspired verses upon a heroine of the hour, Grace
Darling.

Kenyon had also rendered Elizabeth a more immediately

practical service by finding in the flesh that "most poetical bookseller" she had shadowed forth to Horne a year before: Edward Moxon, lover and publisher of poets, maker of verses himself. When Moxon reported Tennyson as saying: "There is only one female poet whom I wish to see, and that is Miss Barrett," Kenyon seized the opportunity, asking: "Why, did you not once refuse a volume of Miss Barrett's poems?" In Elizabeth's light-hearted words to George, "Moxon answered pathetically in the affirmative, & went on to affirm that he had never had a night's sound sleep since for the aching of his bibliopolic heart . . . that he was suffering agonies of remorse . . . wore sackcloth under his linen and ashes in the crown of his hat." Moxon at once offered "to ruin himself for me, & me alone, by accepting any MS. I might please to send him."

Perhaps from the stimulus of a growing reputation, Elizabeth's health was improving: in the July of 1843 we hear of her again going downstairs some seven or eight times, of "meditating *the chair*" (a bath chair), when "something between cramp and rheumatism" temporarily set her back. The mind, however, was active. She told her brother:

I am in a poetical fit just now. . . . I am writing such poems—allegorical-philosophical-poetical-ethical—synthetically arranged! I am in a fit of writing—could write all day & night, & long to live by myself for three months in a forest of chestnuts and cedars, in an hourly succession of poetical paragraphs & morphine draughts.

Then perhaps with a consciousness that a resort to drugs for sleep and calm nerves was becoming with her a habit, she quickly added:

Not that I do such a thing. . . . Nota bene! You are not to say a word of morphine when you write next.

One result of this poetic activity was "The Cry of the Children," published in the August number of *Blackwood's Magazine,* the outcome of a harrowing report issued by R. H. Horne as assistant commissioner on the employment of children in mines and factories. "The Cry of the Children" both stirred and embodied public conscience.

The mental energy, even the physical labour, of this invalid was amazing. In addition to the many poems composed that year—which included the long, finely-wrought "A Vision of Poets"—and the letters she wrote to George, to Miss Mitford, to Miss Martineau (most of them unhappily lost to us), to Boyd, to Kenyon and others, Elizabeth was at work in collaboration with Horne on a daring book to be published the following year, *A New Spirit of the Age.*

CHAPTER 12

A NEW SPIRIT OF THE AGE [1844]

In 1825, Henry Colburn published *The Spirit of the Age: or Contemporary Portraits*. The work was anonymous though it must have been fairly generally known that the author was William Hazlitt.

This was an age of giants. Of the twenty-four people appraised or criticized in the second edition—writers, social theorists, reformers, or fighters for freedom of thought and expression—thirteen at least are among the great who formed the thought, modes of living, and taste of coming generations, and the rest are familiar to anyone only tolerably acquainted with the period.

Nearly twenty years later R. H. Horne, admittedly as writer and critic far below Hazlitt, set himself to prepare *A New Spirit of the Age*. Thirty-seven personalities were celebrated and others glanced at by the way: of these thirty-seven, Wordsworth, Leigh Hunt, Carlyle, Landor, Browning and Tennyson, Lord Shaftesbury and Dr. Pusey, Hood and "Thomas Ingoldsby," Macready, Dickens, Harrison Ainsworth, and Mary Shelley are the only names that ring familiarly to the plain man of this generation, and of these Wordsworth, Leigh Hunt, and Landor must more truly be said to represent the Georgian era.

The most marked difference in these analyses of two generations is the gentler, less politically biased tone of the second: when allowance has been made for Hazlitt's combative spirit and injured feelings, it must be conceded that his provocative tone towards Tory writers, Tory editors and journals was common among the Liberals. They gave as good as they got. To us, looking at the battle from afar, Hazlitt's brilliant attacks add interest to his contemporary portraits but, fine true critic though he was, they are not without an element of harsh caricature. The spirit of Rowlandson, of Gillray, informed his age; whereas

Horne's critical comments have in them the keen but more kindly humour of that new and typical voice in the land, *Punch, or the London Charivari*. In this connection it is curious to note that it was Horne, not Hazlitt, who presented the wits of twenty-five years before, Theodore Hook and Sydney Smith.

Another change in outlook, in mental atmosphere, is the more humanitarian feeling displayed, the indignation at certain social abuses, especially that of which Horne in his official capacity had first-hand knowledge: the employment of children. Emphasis, too, is laid upon the advance, the popularisation of science, the new mechanical aids to living, with a warning, in the person of Carlyle, of the dangers to the soul of material comfort, of an easiness of life. In this connection stress might have been laid on the mental and spiritual discipline called for by the High Church movement, but in dealing with Dr. Pusey the opportunity to show one clear facet of early Victorian life is missed; if indeed it was not yet too soon to realize its meaning. Dr. Pusey is represented not as a spiritual force, a man of saintly life, but as a doctrinaire, a militant theologian. It was perhaps also a natural inability always to see one's own age completely in focus that made Horne print what appears to us an entirely wrong-headed, a quite humourless criticism of another member of the Church, the Reverend R. H. Barham, "Thomas Ingoldsby." Even a stern moral outlook must, for healthiness, have its jester, and to the Victorian age at its strictest surely Thomas Ingoldsby was that jester.

There are two more differences, one being the number of women writers celebrated by Horne, and the inclusion of many novelists of both sexes: Hazlitt does not include one woman and the only two novelists he admits are Scott and Godwin, both men with a prior fame in other forms of writing.

Horne's work suffers less than one would think from a difference in method. Hazlitt's book was entirely written by himself, and anonymously, whereas Horne, though he took responsibility as editor for the whole, and wrote much himself, had collaborators, the chief being Robert Bell, once editor of the *Atlas*, a powerful London journal, and Elizabeth Barrett. The whole, however, is cleverly co-ordinated, seldom patchy in effect. The collaborators wisely remained anonymous: it was

Horne who bore the brunt of subsequent attacks from parties who felt themselves injured, by either criticism or omission.

Elizabeth's co-operation, earnest and thorough, was given selflessly, without material gain. "The most valuable friend and counsellor in a book affecting contemporaries," Horne wrote some thirty years after, is

one who, possessing a finely suitable intellect for the matter in question, and having gathered together the requisite knowledge, is dwelling comparatively out of the world and its conflicting people and opinions, yet taking a deep interest in the best things that are going on, coupled with a due indignation at the worst, and who has magnanimity to admire, as well as moral courage to demur or denounce, ever holding within, as at a shrine, an unmixed love and spirit of truth. Such a friend and counsellor . . . I had in Miss Barrett.

Another advantage to Horne, perhaps only fully realizable by one looking back on the age, is that suggested by his use of the word "shrine." Elizabeth brought to the work a spirit of religion which was also that of many of the best of her time, a spirit reverencing art as an expression of the beauty and truth of God.

Their method of collaboration, one that could only have been pursued by two persons entirely with their eye on the object and not out to ride their own particular hobby-horses, was that of separate manuscripts submitted one to the other for interpolation. The mottoes heading each article, which are beautifully apt in every case and drawn from a long range of English literature, were for the most part supplied by Elizabeth and another friend of Horne's, Robert Browning; presenting a biographer with yet another false start towards the great climax of her story. What, if only Elizabeth had not insisted on absolute anonymity, would have been more natural than that these two should have consulted one another in the delicate and important operation of choosing quotations appropriate to each author?

The article upon Landor, considered by Horne to be one of the finest, was mainly written by Elizabeth, the following extract being among the most striking:

He writes criticism for critics, and poetry for poets: his drama, when he is dramatic, will suppose neither pit nor gallery, nor critics, nor dramatic laws. He is not a publican among poets— he does not sell his Amreeta cups upon the highway. He delivers them rather with the dignity of a giver, to ticketted persons; analysing their flavour and fragrance with a learned delicacy, and an appeal to the esoteric. His very spelling of English is uncommon and theoretic. He has a vein of humour which by its own nature is peculiarly subtle and evasive; he therefore refines upon it, by his art, in order to prevent anybody discovering it without a grave, solicitous, and courtly approach, which is unspeakably ridiculous to all the parties concerned, and which no doubt the author secretly enjoys. And as if poetry were not, in English, a sufficiently unpopular dead language, he has had recourse to writing poetry in Latin; with dissertations on the Latin tongue, to fence it out doubly from the populace. "Odi profanum vulgus, et arceo."

On Landor's style she commented: "In marble indeed, he seems to work; for there is an angularity in the workmanship, whether of prose or verse, which the very exquisiteness of the polish renders more conspicuous. You may complain too of hearing the chisel; but after all you applaud the work . . . his smaller poems . . . for quiet classical grace and tenderness, and exquisite care in their polish, may best be compared with beautiful cameos and vases of the antique."

When one considers the influence of Landor upon the great romantics, and his established reputation among the finer spirits of the Georgian era, it seems strange that Hazlitt did not even mention him in *The Spirit of the Age;* perhaps because he had in 1825 been so long out of England, or perhaps because of his disdainful attitude towards criticism. "His feeling towards this department of literature," wrote Elizabeth of him in a lively account of his career, "may be estimated by his offer of a hot penny roll and a pint of stout, for breakfast (!) to any critic who could write one of his Imaginary Conversations—an indigestible pleasantry which horribly enraged more than one critic of the time."

The article upon Wordsworth and Leigh Hunt, largely Elizabeth's work, compares admirably with those by Hazlitt: it is typical of a change in attitude that the two veterans were linked together by Horne, whereas Hunt, known personally to Hazlitt in his younger, more volatile days, is linked in a critique with Tom Moore. Hazlitt's article on Wordsworth, though brilliant, is marred by a veiled personal attack on the man who had abandoned early revolutionary principles and accepted a Government appointment: in *A New Spirit of the Age* Wordsworth is presented reverently as accepted poet (though as sometimes dull and prolix), as father of the romantic school and an earnest Christian moralist. In her analysis of Wordsworth as poet Elizabeth surely puts a finger on the very heart of romanticism: "Chaucer and Burns made the most of a daisy, but left it still a daisy; Wordsworth leaves it transformed into *his* thoughts. This is the sublime of egotism, disinterested as extreme."

In dealing with Leigh Hunt as the founder of the so-called "Cockney School" she gives an eloquent catalogue of its illustrious members: "Lamb, who stammered out in child-like simplicity, his wit beautiful with wisdom"; "Coleridge, so full of genius and all rare acquirements"; "Hazlitt, who dwelt gloriously with philosophy in a chamber of imagery"; "Shelley with his wings of golden fire"; "Keats who saw divine visions, and the pure Greek ideal, because he had the essence in his soul"; "Leigh Hunt (now the sole survivor of all these) true poet and exquisite essayist."

In the correspondence over Leigh Hunt between Elizabeth and Horne it is interesting to note the difference in moral attitude: Horne, certainly with the advantage of a long acquaintanceship with Hunt, could, drawing from his roots in the Liberalism of the Georgian era, firmly assert that the criticism Hunt had provoked of an inability, of disinclination to draw a line between good and evil, was not a fair one: in his own lovable nature and infinite charity it was persons, not principles, Hunt was utterly unable to condemn. This, though admitting that "the cordiality and benignity of his genius are essentially Christian," Elizabeth could not admit, though she conceded that he had cancelled offending passages in later editions of his works. The general attitude of many readers in this Evangelical age is given by her in a reference to "our dear friend, Miss Mitford—no prude—no fanatic—yet one who said, or implied to me once, that a woman should not be eager to praise Leigh Hunt."

In the critique on Hunt—not, perhaps because of this outlook, so well co-ordinated as some on which they worked together—the following analysis is surely Elizabeth's:

His blank verse is the most successfully original in its freedom, of any that has appeared since the time of Beaumont and Fletcher. His images are commonly beautiful, if often fantastic—clustering like bees, or like grapes—sometimes too many for the vines—a good fault in these bare modern days. . . . His gatherings from nature are true to nature. . . . His nature, however, is seldom moor-land and mountain-land; nor is it, for the most part, English nature—we have hints of fauns and the nymphs lying in the shadow of the old Italian woods; and the sky overhead is several tints too blue for home experiences . . . it is nature by memory and phantasy; true, but touched with an exotic purple.

In the critique on Alfred Tennyson, a joint production, a lively retort is given to a reference in *The Times* of December 26, 1842 to poems of Keats as "the half-finished works of this young, miseducated, and unripe genius" which "have had the greatest influence on that which is now the popular poetry." That influence could not be denied but Keats, "divine," unique, could have no "single mechanical imitator": in regard to mere popular poetry, rather "the pure Greek wine of Keats has been set aside for the thin gruel of Kirke White."

Of the three full pages upon Keats much must have been written by Horne himself, who had walked and talked with him, but surely it was Elizabeth who wrote of his effect upon the better part of contemporary literature as:

spiritual in its ideality; it has been classical in its revivification of the forms and images of the antique, which he inspired with a new soul; it has been romantic in its spells, and dreams, and legendary associations; and it has been pastoral in its fresh gatherings from the wild forests and fields, and as little as possible from the garden, and never from the hot-house and the flower-shows.

The influence of Keats upon Tennyson might be apparent, but he was "undoubtedly one of the most original poets that ever lived." As an instance of Tennyson's "enchanted reverie," his skill in subjective scene-painting, the opening to Elizabeth's favourite poem "Œnone" is given. To most of us in the present day this critique on Tennyson will seem over-enthusiastic, over-long but, as in the case of Elizabeth herself—so soon to be accepted as a major poet—it must be remembered that this "silver-tongued romantic," as a modern poet has so happily called him, was then to be contrasted only with far lesser men and women, and in a generation that still read poetry where now only novels would be tolerated.

Elizabeth herself remained to the end of her life under the spell of Tennyson; at first as a verbal enchantment and, when she had met that large demanding personality, of a personal charm. But her intellect in regard to him was not entirely drowsed by the spell. From the first she recognized, or suspected, his lack of essential content, writing to Horne: "He is a divine poet; but I have found it difficult to analyse his divinity, and to determine (even to myself) his particular aspect as a writer. What is the reason of it?" And to another correspondent, Thomas Westwood, a literary son of Charles and Mary Lamb's landlord at Enfield: "the poet is a preacher and must look to his doctrine. Perhaps Mr. Tennyson will grow more solemn, like the sun, as his day goes on. . . . He is one of God's singers, whether he knows it or does not know it."

To us this long eulogy of Tennyson must seem out of proportion to the space given to Robert Browning, who shares attention with J. W. Marston, a poet now entirely forgotten; but it must be remembered that at this time Browning's only major works before the public were "Paracelsus," a few plays, and "Sordello" with its "broken, mazy, dancing sort of narrative no-outline, which has occasioned so much trouble, if not despair, to his most patient and pains-taking admirers." In a generation unaccustomed to trouble the intellect with its poetry it is amazing that, even among his few but fervid admirers, any were found poring over this difficult work: it is a tribute to the unique fascination of Browning, both as poet and as man.

Horne gives us no hint of how much Elizabeth contributed to this critique, nor is there in those published of the letters they exchanged any mention of this poet so soon to mingle his life

with hers. One would like to think that the climax of an affectionate and whimsical judgment of "Sordello" (unfortunately
too long to quote in its entirety) was written by Elizabeth:

*It abounds in things addressed to a second sight, and we are of-
ten required to see double in order to apprehend its meaning.
The poet may be considered the Columbus of an impossible
discovery. It is a promised land, spotted all over with disap-
pointments, and yet most truly a land of promise, if ever so rich
and rare a chaos can be developed into form and order by revision, and its southern fulness of tumultuous heart and scattered
vineyards be ever reduced to given proportion, and wrought
into a shape that will fit the average mental vision and harmonize with the more equable pulsations of mankind.*

This revision, as we know, Browning did attempt but failed to
achieve.

Browning, his work published as yet in cheap little paper-
covered booklets paid for by his father, was a poet for the elect,
barely known to the general public, and only then as one to be
reviled and ridiculed: Elizabeth, on the other hand, though
handled in *A New Spirit of the Age* with a note of suitable con-
descension as "a poetess," had, apart from her growing popularity, a legendary existence of which the writer of the critique
upon herself and Mrs. Norton made the most. Elizabeth had
sent Horne ample details of her life on which a biographer
gratefully draws today, but this had to be embroidered upon.
In an exaltation of her learning, the composition of Latin verses
is attributed to her, and the period of seclusion of this "fair
shade" magnified into "six or seven years" of imprisonment
"during many weeks at a time, in darkness almost equal to that
of night." A human touch is added to the legend by a mention of
her love of novel-reading. With an extract from "The Seraphim," Elizabeth's poetry is characterized as "the struggles of
a soul towards heaven." "Miss Barrett often wanders amidst
the supernatural darkness of Calvary sometimes with anguish
and tears of blood, sometimes like one who echoes the songs of
triumphal quires." In comparison with Mrs. Norton "one is all
womanhood; the other all wings." As poet "Miss Barrett has
great inventiveness, but not an equal power of construction."
This incomplete picture of Elizabeth, ignoring a strong inter-

est in the world about her, was surely not written by her assiduous correspondent R. H. Horne.

The critique on Carlyle, now in full strength as a writer, was probably, though Horne does not directly state it, largely contributed by Elizabeth: certainly she wrote many letters on the subject to Horne, though only two, one of which was too late to be incorporated, are published. It is a fine analysis of this rugged rock of a writer, this Northern crag looming over the softer Southerner.

After an acknowledgment of Carlyle's own doctrine of Heroes, the article continues, I think in the words of Elizabeth:

That Mr. Carlyle is one of the men of genius thus referred to, and that he has knocked out his window from the blind wall of his century, we may add without fear of contradiction. We may say, too, that it is a window to the east; and that some men complain of a certain bleakness in the wind which enters at it, when they should rather congratulate themselves and him on the aspect of the new sun beheld through it, the orient hope of which he has so discovered to their eyes.

An integral part of this new message to mankind was the strange language in which it was couched. If not "style" and classicism, "it was something better; it was soul-language. There was a divinity at the shaping of these rough-hewn periods. . . . He uses no moulds in his modelling, as you may see by the impression of his thumb-nail upon the clay. He throws his truth with so much vehemence, that the print of the palm of his hand is left on it."

Against the charge that Carlyle brought no specific plan of action before mankind, that his was largely a philosophy of dissatisfaction, and inclined to be little material progress, the writer asserted that his teaching, however vague in import, was essentially Christian. "Life suggests to him the cradle, the grave, and eternity, with scarce a step between." Man is exhorted sometimes to work, sometimes to sit still and think. "He [Carlyle] is dazzled by the continual contemplation of a soul beating its tiny wings amidst the pale vapours of Infinity." In such a contemplation our corporeal condition, our physical wants, seem transitory, of small significance.

Carlyle, veering, to the bewilderment of the plain man, from

Tory to Radical, from Radical to Tory, was at heart a poet and therefore "*too* poetical to be philosophical . . . *so* poetical as to be philosophical in essence when treating of things." His dramatic sense too brought about a close and often misleading identification of himself with the man portrayed. His use of images was poetical. "His illustrations not only illustrate, but bear a part in the reasoning;—the images standing out, like grand and beautiful caryatides, to sustain the heights of the argument."

The most notable omission in this brave assessment of the spirit of the age is that of Miss Mitford, whose "prose-pastorals" have only passing mention; that a full-dress portrait was intended is clear from one of Elizabeth's letters. Perhaps Horne feared to embroil himself with an old and valued friend by a true estimate of those acted tragedies which the author put high above such works as *Our Village* and *Belford Regis;* perhaps he merely intended to reserve her for a future volume.

A New Spirit of the Age is illustrated by fine etched portraits, a set of which Horne gave to Elizabeth, including one from a drawing, made by his friend the Comte Amédée de Ripert-Monclar, of Robert Browning; a presentation perhaps too conventionally poetical for the Browning of 1844, but having in the eyes a direct vision, about the mouth and chin a set determination, and in the large curving nose a hint of quest, of keen scent. Browning, when Elizabeth's reply to his first letter reached him on January 11, 1845, was less informed than she: no portrait of her had appeared in *A New Spirit of the Age* or elsewhere. "There is no portrait of me at all which is considered like—except one," she told Horne, "painted in my infancy, where I appear in the character of a fugitive angel, which papa swears by all the gods is very like me to this day, and which perhaps may be like—about the wings." This charming presentation of the baby Elizabeth, on the lid of a snuff-box, we have already seen.

C H A P T E R   1 3

BOOKS AND THOUGHTS [1843–4]

IN THE LATTER HALF of 1843 Elizabeth was actively engaged, not only on the work for Horne, but in the preparation of her new volume: at least one long poem remained to be completed.

At the end of summer an even flow of writing was interrupted by certain anxieties, the first being one which touched into life that aching memory of Torquay. George and Storm wanted to spend a holiday abroad together on the Rhine. Elizabeth took an elder-sisterly share in the diplomacy needed to gain Mr. Barrett's consent, but against her own feeling. It was, she told Mrs. Martin, "a hard, terrible struggle with me to be calm and see them go. But *that* was childish, and when I had heard from them at Ostend I grew more satisfied again, and attained to think less of the fatal influences of *my star.*"

A spell of hot August weather with some dangerous drops in temperature further tried the invalid, but we hear of her being "very well for *me*" and making use of the chair for outdoor exercise. But in an enjoyment of comparative health, the happiness of knowing that her brothers were safely across the sea in enjoyment of their holiday, fresh and more immediate trouble came to her in the person of Flush. First the spaniel had been worried and wounded by another dog inmate of the house, a savage Cuban bloodhound, and then in mid-September, while out taking his exercise, he gave a sudden cry and vanished, a prey to those pests of early Victorian London, the dog-stealers.

Elizabeth spent three days without eating or sleeping, "nor could do anything much more rational than cry" amid accusations of "silliness" and "childishness" from robuster folk around her. Grief was less over the loss of Flush's companionship than from "the consideration of how he was breaking his heart, cast upon a cruel world." Even when prevented from sleeping on his mistress's bed Flush would spend the night in moaning, and often he would refuse to eat from a strange hand.

With difficulty the "dog-banditti" were hunted down and bribed into giving up the spaniel. "The audacity of the wretched men was marvellous," Elizabeth commented in anger. "They said they had been 'about stealing Flush these two years,' and warned us plainly to take care of him for the future." These scoundrels were in a strong position, and knew it. As a dog was not at that time legal property, its owner had no redress.

On his return Elizabeth wrote to Boyd:

The joy of the meeting between Flush and me would be a good subject for a Greek ode—I recommend it to you. It might take rank next to the epical parting of Hector and Andromache. He dashed up the stairs into my room and into my arms, where I hugged him and kissed him, black as he was—black as if imbued in a distillation of St. Giles's.

"You had better give your dog something to eat," said the thief who yielded up his prey to a brother, "for he has tasted nothing since he has been with us." "And yet," Flush's mistress wrote to Horne, "his heart was so full when he came home he could not eat, but shrank away from the plate and laid down his head on my shoulder. The spirit of love conquered the animal appetite even in that dog. He is worth loving. Is he not?"

All these anxieties broke in upon a period of steady work: in the letter to Boyd of September 19 quoted above, Elizabeth spoke of having just finished "A Vision of Poets," "philosophical, allegorical—anything but popular." She intended to print "as much as I can find and make room for," feeling, except in moments of bleak doubt, that she had made "some general progress in strength and expression."

But later in the autumn doubt spread about her like a seasonable London fog. "A Drama of Exile," that ambitious poem about the Expulsion from Eden, was composed rapidly from a fragment written some time before: when it was completed her mind misgave her. Was the poem worth printing, worth even preserving? She was on the point of thrusting it into the fire when her cousin Kenyon, now a privileged visitor, came in. "In the kindest way he took it into his hands, and proposed to carry it home and read it," saying: "You know I have a prejudice against these sacred subjects for poetry, but then I have another prejudice for *you*, and one may neutralise the other."

Elizabeth awaited the return of her manuscript in trepidation but, except for a few minor criticisms, Kenyon approved, considering "A Drama of Exile" "very superior as a whole to anything I ever did before—more sustained, and fuller in power."

In the spring of 1844, a short time before publication, all this was rather unwisely reported to Mr. Boyd, that older and jealous mentor. Boyd wrote immediately warning Elizabeth against taking "the man's" opinion. She told him, surely with a gleam of amusement:

The "man" is highly refined in his tastes, and leaning to the classical (I was going to say to your classical, only suddenly I thought of Ossian) a good deal more than I do. . . . If I had hesitated about the conclusiveness of his judgments, it would have been because of his confessed indisposition towards subjects religious and ways mystical, and his occasional insufficient indulgence for rhymes and rhythms which he calls "Barrettian."

Elizabeth declared to her old friend that she feared his own judgment both of this poem and of others in the new work; but clearly she no longer offered manuscripts for his old-fashioned, sweeping, and condemnatory criticism.

What Elizabeth did not tell Boyd was the depth of her despair. The supposed failure of this poem was, it is clear from a letter to Kenyon, but a passing cause, a symptom of a deeper ailment of the spirit. His encouragement saved her from a break in that high valour with which she faced life. "The book may fail signally after all—*that* is another question; but *I* shall not fail, to begin with, and *that* I owe to *you*, for I was falling to pieces in nerves and spirits when you came to help me. . . . It was a long compressed feeling breaking suddenly into words."

Elizabeth regretted a "note of weak because unavailing complaint" which she had sent him, the more so as it was accompanied by a letter from Miss Martineau "of heroic cheerfulness." That strong-hearted woman facing severe illness, the terrible threat of cancer, with great courage, had brought the power of her mind to bear upon an analysis of her condition in *Life in a Sick Room*.

It is in the November of 1843 that we first become aware of an interest in the supernatural, or extra-natural, later to become so strong a preoccupation with spiritualism. This began as a rather horrified fascination by hypnotism or "animal magnetism," soon to become a fashionable theme of the hour. The subject was, so far as I know, first discussed on paper with B. R. Haydon.[1] Haydon, "being always inclined to believe in the wonderful . . . went to ascertain the fact of Mesmerism" at the house of one John Elliotson, a physician who had been forced to resign a professorship at London University because of his avowed interest in the subject. Although the letter is unfortunately incomplete, it is obvious that Haydon considered the performance he witnessed to be fraudulent. Elizabeth's own interest in mesmerism is clearly implied.

In December a friend, accepting the current notion that "animal magnetism" could cure a variety of diseases, pressed Elizabeth to send a lock of hair to "a chief Rabbi of the magnetisers" in Paris so that he might diagnose her condition. Apart from a conviction that magnetism was of no avail in cases of the chest—that it might even be harmful—Elizabeth feared her own imagination; writing to Boyd, who urged a trial of the treatment:

If I had parted with that lock of hair, Queen Mab would have been with me day and night. I should have seen visions and dreamt dreams. And, through the thick of them, a great French disembodied spirit would have floated, peering about the room, and causing my flesh to creep with cold magnetic testimonies of a "Presence."

And then, do you remember the harm which all the old witches (whom I am beginning to believe in) did with a lock of hair?

A day's visit from Miss Mitford, that "very precious friend" and a sensible, understanding woman, must have strengthened Elizabeth's determination. Miss Mitford agreed with Kenyon that Elizabeth was wise to refuse. Mary Mitford, "sprinkled as to the soul with meadow dews," brought, with her cheerful rosy face, a taste of country joys lost, the sharp pleasure of her pointed conversation and gossip from the literary world; a salutary interlude in the long feverish preoccupation with words and books.

[1] Pope Collection, November 9, 1843.

With Miss Mitford, however, the subject uppermost in Elizabeth's mind, her work for *A New Spirit of the Age,* must be avoided. Already there had been one alarm: a Mr. Reade had informed Horne that he knew Miss Barrett was collaborating with him. To a reproachful Horne Elizabeth had protested her entire innocence in the matter: to neither Miss Mitford, Kenyon, nor even her own father had she even mentioned the name of the book. Perhaps Miss Mitford, herself a wide correspondent, had gathered from some source that Elizabeth was to be the subject of a critique, and perhaps this information, misunderstood, had been passed on to Reade. If Mr. Reade really meant what he was reported as saying, "he must have had it from especial revelation of the angels."

On the early spring of 1844 there is little correspondence available to me except that with Horne. In one letter Elizabeth made the interesting claim that Dickens was strongly influenced by the French school of imaginative literature. She asked Horne to compare the "powerful, the wonderfully powerful" "Trois Jours d'un Condamné" with the trial of Fagin in Dickens's latest novel, *Oliver Twist.* She expressed an ever-growing admiration for French novelists:

we have no such romance-writer as Victor Hugo,—let us be as anti-Gallic as we please. . . . The indelicacy and want of elemental morality make another side of the question: but the genius is just as undeniable to me, as the sun would be in Italy. George Sand, for instance, is the greatest female genius the world ever saw—at least, since Sappho, who broke off a fragment of her soul to be guessed by—as creation did by its fossils. . . . And then Balzac—Eugene Sue—even the Soulies, and the grade lower—we cannot wish *them to be popular in England, for obvious reasons, but it is melancholy to look round and see no such bloom of intellectual glory on our own literature, in shutting our doors against theirs.*

In March 1844 a "painful vexation" agitated the invalid: the probable loss of a personal maid who had been with her throughout illness. Apart from a natural attachment to this woman, the idea of a stranger about her was "scarcely tolerable" to the recluse. Who this maid was and whether she now left Elizabeth's service we do not know: if she remained, and the service was unbroken, we must later acclaim her as that faithful friend Elizabeth Wilson, a young north-country woman who so cheerfully embarked with her mistress on the great adventure of 1846.

But all this was for the future: at present Robert Browning, "meditating a new poem, and an excursion on the Continent," was only a young poet of whom Elizabeth heard much that was interesting from her cousin Kenyon; a man of "many noble capabilities" at criticism of whom Elizabeth felt an oddly personal resentment; whose portrait, pronounced by Kenyon to be "rather like," hung framed on the wall of her room together with those of Carlyle, Wordsworth, Harriet Martineau, and Tennyson. But probably the most cherished of these was the portrait of Alfred Tennyson, before whom, though her intellect could not fully tell her why, she burned a delicate incense. Although Elizabeth treasured a note of Browning's written to Kenyon in praise of "The Dead Pan," she probably set higher value on one from Tennyson to herself; Tennyson of whom she demanded from George, her courier of news in the world, every fragment of "Tennysoniana" he could gather. And if any dim presage of a passionate lover, in the person of Robert Browning or any other, could have entered the mind of this invalid of thirty-eight years, she would have instantly thrust it from her.

"Books and thoughts," she wrote of herself in the autumn of 1843, "and dreams (almost too consciously *dreamed,* however, for me—the illusion of them has almost passed) and domestic tenderness can and ought to leave nobody lamenting. Also God's wisdom, deeply steeped in His love, *is* as far as we can stretch out our hands."

CHAPTER 14

POEMS [1844]

MOXON DECIDED TO PRINT an edition of fifteen hundred copies with half profits to the author; the work to begin with that poem Elizabeth had at first intended as a title piece, "A Drama of Exile," and to end with "The Dead Pan" as, she said, "a flourish of trumpets and to please Mr. Kenyon."

Her manuscript went to press at the end of March but publication was delayed: Miss Mitford is reported as saying that she "never heard of so slow-footed a book." Elizabeth, though admitting to certain alterations in proof, declared: "in my opinion, it is a good deal more the fault of Mr. Moxon's not being in a hurry, than in the excessive virtue of my patience, or vice of my indolence."

Only at the end of July were the volumes discovered to be of unequal length. "Mr. Moxon," Elizabeth told Boyd, "uttered a cry of reprehension, and wished to tear me to pieces by his printers, as the Bacchantes did Orpheus. . . . He wanted to tear away several poems from the end of the second volume, and tie them on to the end of the first!" This would mean shifting the position of "The Dead Pan," which, with the backing of her father's opinion, Elizabeth was determined not to allow. "So there was nothing for it but to finish a ballad poem called 'Lady Geraldine's Courtship,' which was lying by me, and I did so by writing, i.e. composing, *one hundred and forty lines last Saturday!*" Mr. Moxon was now as precipitous as he had once been dawdling: the *Poems* came out in the second week of August.

If, as Landor said, variety and invention are essential in any poet beyond the second-rate, *Poems*, 1844, certainly meets that qualification. There are personal utterances, ranging from sonnets to biographical poems such as "A Flower in a Letter," "The Lost Bower," to the more fanciful one of "The House of Clouds," a favourite with her father; mystical allegories such as "A Drama of Exile," "A Vision of Poets"; personal tributes to Miss

Mitford, George Sand, and to Boyd in "Wine of Cyprus"; poems
of life around her, as "The Cry of the Children," "Crowned and
Buried," "Crowned and Wedded"; poems quasi-philosophical,
quasi-religious such as "The Cry of the Human," "A Rhapsody
of Life's Progress"; the stories, all told picturesquely in styles so
different as that of "The Rime of the Duchess May" and "Lady
Geraldine's Courtship"; love poems, as that favourite with
Browning, "Caterina to Camoens" and "The Lady's Yes"; all in
forms varying from blank verse to the triple disyllabic rimed
stanzas of "A Vision of Poets."

Elizabeth was at once acclaimed, not only as an established
poet, but as first in rank among "poetesses," a compliment she
regarded as left-handed; there being in her opinion no single
poetess worthy of the name before Joanna Baillie. Chorley in
the *Athenæum* defined her position as a woman poet in declaring that between Miss Barrett's "poems and the slighter lyrics
of most of her sisterhood, there is all the difference which exists
between the putting-on of 'singing robes' for altar service, and
the taking of lute or harp to enchant an indulgent circle of
friends and kindred." In this perhaps Chorley might have excepted one woman poet who had died comparatively young
only a few years before, Felicia Hemans, who is now perhaps
undeservedly neglected: at least her "The Forest Sanctuary" is
beyond simple feminine enchantment and needs no indulgence.

Blackwood's, giving the *Poems* a whole article, found Elizabeth's poetical merits far to outweigh her defects. "Her genius
is profound, unsullied, and without a flaw." John Forster in the
Examiner boldly claimed her for posterity: the *Atlas* acknowledged extraordinary power and genius "abating the failings of
which the followers of Tennyson are guilty." This, repeated in
other reviews, annoyed Elizabeth, who, though yielding to none
in admiration of Tennyson, claimed at least her faults to be her
own. The chief peculiarity attributed to Tennyson and his
"school" was the use of compound words; a "fault," as Elizabeth pointed out, common, not only to Greek and German
poets, but to our own both in earlier times and—nearer to herself—Keats, Shelley, and Leigh Hunt.

Most of the reviews also accused her of a fault entirely her
own, that of defective or careless riming. In this Elizabeth paid

a pioneer's penalty as advocate of a freedom in verse not generally recognized until some eighty years after. She employed loose rimes and assonance with deliberate intent, asserting that in a language deficient in light end-vowels a variety in rime was needed. Her innovations were most apparent in disyllabic rimes, a fondness for which was, no doubt, a legacy from an early acquaintance with Italian literature.

"A Drama of Exile" was the poem on which Elizabeth had built a hope of enhanced reputation. She had written it at white heat, modelling her form on that of Greek tragedy. "A Drama of Exile" tells the story of Adam and Eve after they were driven into the wilderness, "with a peculiar reference to Eve's allotted grief, which, considering that self-sacrifice belonging to her womanhood, and the consciousness of originating the Fall to her offence, appeared to me imperfectly apprehended hitherto; and more expressible by a woman than a man." This is how Elizabeth phrased her intention in a preface to *Poems,* 1844, but in a letter she put it more intimately: "the subject being . . . especially the grief of Eve, under that reproach of her soul which must have afflicted her with so peculiar an agony." The personal application is implicit. No Eve could have been more tortured by remorse, could have known "so peculiar an agony" as this sensitive woman convinced that she had sent a beloved brother and treasured eldest son to his death.

"A Drama of Exile" was not, however, well received. As Browning later remarked, her individual gift in poetry was for speaking out, for that direct expression of emotion denied to himself. With the exception of the harrowing "The Mask," but slightly dramatized, it was in the most personal form, the sonnet, that Elizabeth most poignantly set down emotional statements about grief, religious feeling; sonnets which in these volumes anticipate with a sure touch the matured power of those "from the Portuguese."

Elizabeth was surprised and not a little chagrined to discover that the poem acclaimed by reviewers and public alike was not "A Drama of Exile" but that which Sir Frederic Kenyon has happily called a masterpiece of rhetorical sentimentality, "Lady Geraldine's Courtship." Amusement was added to the mixed emotion when she knew it to be an avowed favourite with

Carlyle and Miss Martineau. This unexpected popularity of "a romance of the age," "treating of railroads, routes, and all manner of 'temporalities,' and in so radical a temper," was to confirm in Elizabeth's mind that assertion of 1842 that a poet could find matter to his hand in the world around him, however drab, mundane, and industrialized that world might appear to be. A ballad poem cast in as a make-weight led clearly on to that verse novel in the thick of contemporary life, *Aurora Leigh*.

"Lady Geraldine's Courtship" has for us another significance: it was the reading of some lines in it that led directly to Robert Browning's first approach to his future wife early in 1845. Opening the first volume of *Poems* on his return from Italy he saw how Geraldine's lover would read to her:

. . . *at times a modern volume,—Wordsworth's solemn-
    thoughted idyl,*
Howitt's ballad-verse, or Tennyson's enchanted reverie,—
*Or from Browning some "Pomegranate," which, if cut deep
    down the middle,*
Shows a heart within blood-tinctured, of a veined humanity.

"The Rime of the Duchess May," a pseudo-mediæval ballad, which Elizabeth herself disliked and had considered omitting, was another favourite. This ballad is an example of how well she could tell a story, in this case a grim drama of love, revenge, and violent death; even overcoming by sheer skill in narration tiresome and sometimes strained internal rimes in two lines of each of the one hundred and twelve four-line stanzas. Of it Elizabeth wrote to Boyd:

*I did not think that you would much like the "Duchess May";
but among the* profanum vulgus *you cannot think how successful it has been. There was an account in one of the fugitive reviews of a lady falling into hysterics on the perusal of it, although that was nothing to the gush of tears of which there is
a tradition, down the Plutonian cheeks of a lawyer unknown,
over "Bertha in the Lane." But these things should not make
anybody vain. It is the story that has power over people, just
what you do not care for!*

"Bertha in the Lane," a vivid rather morbid delineation of two sisters, the elder dying, in love with the same man, has a Pre-Raphaelitish air of gloom.

Other favourites with the *profanum vulgus* were "The Romance of the Swan's Nest," a fanciful glimpse into the mind of a bookish romantic child, perhaps Elizabeth herself, and the highly personal "To Flush, my Dog," which the fastidious Mr. Boyd had besought Elizabeth to omit. She, though surely realizing the verses to be far from her best, protested that she could not in loyalty do this. "The Flushes have their laurels as well as the Cæsars."

Another poem of biographical interest is "The Lay of the Brown Rosary," which plays again upon the theme of "The Romaunt of Margret," though in more sinister vein. A girl is preserved from death by the powers of darkness so that she may marry her lover: the ceremony over, her husband falls dead on the altar steps. In both this poem and "The Romaunt of Margret" it is love that may preserve the woman's life, though in "The Lay of the Brown Rosary" it brings disaster to the loved one. Here, even if there may have been nothing of the shadowy prescience one is tempted to claim, is at least a clear thread in the story, the allegory of Elizabeth Barrett Browning's life. Love did pluck her back from death and, though not met by death itself, with a measure of disaster in the loss of her father's affection and the temporary alienation of her brothers:

> . . . *a mystic Shape did move*
> *Behind me, and drew me backward by the hair,*
> *And a voice said in mastery while I strove, . .*
> *"Guess now who holds thee?"—"Death," I said. But, there,*
> *The silver answer rang, . . "Not Death, but Love."*

In this ending to the first sonnet written after she knew that Robert Browning loved her is no shadowy prescience, but knowledge.

In 1844, however, this invalid, bruised by the tragedy of Bro's death, already considered at that time a middle-aged woman and solacing her "sweet sad years, the melancholy years" with poetry, with domestic affections and the comfort of God, could not foresee a miracle. Her conscious utterance of life's bitterness and loss are in the sonnets placed, perhaps with deliberate intent, after that opening "A Drama of Exile" which seems to embody her own deep-rooted sense of guilt. Of these the key-sonnet to her life is the beautiful "Past and Future":

My future will not copy fair my past
On any leaf but Heaven's. Be fully done,
Supernal Will! I would not fain be one
Who, satisfying thirst and breaking fast
Upon the fullness of the heart, at last
Says no grace after meat. My wine has run
Indeed out of my cup, and there is none
To gather up the bread of my repast
Scattered and trampled,—yet I find some good
In earth's green herbs, and streams that bubble up
Clear from the darkling ground,—content until
I sit with angels before better food.
Dear Christ! when Thy new vintage fills my cup,
This hand shall shake no more, nor that wine spill.

CHAPTER 15

MR. BARRETT OF WIMPOLE STREET

DEDICATION

TO MY FATHER

When your eyes fall upon this page of dedication, and you start to see to whom it is inscribed, your first thought will be of the time far off when I was a child and wrote verses, and when I dedicated them to you who were my public and my critic. Of all that such a recollection implies of saddest and sweetest to both of us, it would become neither of us to speak before the world; nor would it be possible for us to speak of it to one another, with voices that did not falter. Enough, that what is in my heart when I write thus, will be fully known to yours.

And my desire is that you, who are a witness how if this art of poetry had been a less earnest object to me, it must have fallen from exhausted hands before this day,—that you, who have shared with me in things bitter and sweet, softening or enhancing them, every day,—that you, who hold with me over all sense of loss and transiency, one hope by one Name,—may accept from me the inscription of these volumes, the exponents of a few years of an existence which has been sustained and comforted by you as well as given. Somewhat more faint-hearted than I used to be, it is my fancy thus to seem to return to a visible personal dependence on you, as if indeed I were a child again; to conjure your beloved image between myself and the public, so as to be sure of one smile,—and to satisfy my heart while I sanctify my ambition, by associating with the great pursuit of my life its tenderest and holiest affection.

Your
E. B. B.

On the 10th of August Elizabeth sent her *Poems* down to Mr. Barrett cut at the page of the above dedication. "When he came upstairs at one o'clock" (to continue in her own words to George), "he seemed pleased & touched by it—only the satisfaction to myself of expressing my natural feeling, is deeper (must be) certainly than any his tenderness could receive."

From the entirely personal tone of her dedication it is clear that Elizabeth's father was no longer in the old position of public and critic. As a poet she had grown from him, perhaps in imaginative power, perhaps in a fashion of poetry too new for one born in the previous century: nor did he (in her own words) "over-value poetry even in his daughter." Pride in the phenomenon he had begotten had its basis in possession, in family feeling. His measure of life was apt to be a worldly one, though deeply tinged with religion.

Mr. Barrett's strong belief in a personal God was shared by Elizabeth: it was a bond between them. It was his habit to come up to her at about eleven o'clock at night, before retiring, to pray with her. But in their religious outlook was an essential difference: Mr. Barrett's communings with his Creator produced no humility of mind. Consciously, or unconsciously, he regarded himself as His vice-regent in family affairs.

Love for his children, a native kindliness, and a certain inattention to detail made, however, that self-imposed duty "to rule like the Kings of Christendom, by divine right," less irksome than it might appear: indeed, though she might privately complain in family letters of an Olympian detachment, a reserve as to plans of life vitally affecting herself, on Elizabeth the yoke sat lightly. She had never, beyond childhood, felt a strong "will for the common things of life . . . though every now and then there must be of course a crossing and vexation—but in one's mere pleasures and fantasies, one would rather be crossed and vexed a little than vex a person one loves." In her own case, too, the word "literature" covered a certain permitted licence; and where the accepted obedience of child to father might be strained there was solemn joy in negation of self before this man whom she, by an act of weakness, had robbed of his eldest son. Not the least of her debt to him had been Mr. Barrett's tender, unreproaching kindness in her grief and during prolonged illness.

The other children of Edward Barrett, the youngest now

twenty, were, in the uncompromising words of that loving daughter, "constrained *bodily* into submission . . apparent submission at least . . by that worst and most dishonoring of necessities, the necessity of *living*"; every one of them except herself "being dependent in money-matters on the inflexible will." In the Moulton-Barrett family it is thought that Mr. Barrett was generous enough to his sons and not exigent in terms of work, but this subservience inevitably brought with it a "concealment from the heart naturally nearest to us . . . disengenuousness—the cowardice—the 'vices of slaves.' "

Yet this arbitrary rule gave the Barrett family a curious liberty: not being able to confide in the father, they took their own paths, doing in his daily absence in the City of London more or less as they wished, asking to the house whom they pleased. No friend might be invited to dinner, but before the hour of six Mr. Barrett's children were tolerably secure for six days of the week: questions were seldom asked and breaches of discipline in general not noticed unless they came directly under the paternal eye. Probably, taking the short view, this circumscribed liberty had for some of them its own fearful joy in that element of danger, of being found out, dear to a young adventurous heart. Papa might not know, or inquire, but he might from time to time guess. Mr. Barrett was not, Elizabeth told Robert, "a nice observer, but, at intervals very wide, he is subject to lightnings—call them fancies, sometimes right, sometimes wrong."

There seems to have been among the brothers and sisters little deep-seated resentment of restraint: as Elizabeth observed, "it is possible to get used to the harness and run easily in it at last." Such domestic harness was common enough in many households up to the end of the last century and beyond: children did not then expect to rule their parents. It is certain that two of the sons who lived well into living memory,[1] Octavius and Charles John, adored their father and would hear nothing against him.

But, extreme type of kindly, arbitrary old-fashioned parent though he was, Mr. Barrett differed in one strange particular. He would not have his children marry, or even discuss marriage.

---

[1] Charles John (Stormie) died in 1905, Octavius in 1910.

He who had taken a wife at nineteen, who came of a family so anxious to preserve the principle of primogeniture that his own surname had been changed to uphold it, would not have his children marry. In this he departed radically from the typical early Victorian parent who so valued family life that he would often himself arrange early marriages for his daughters, and sometimes even for his sons. The Barrett sons, except Alfred, remained bachelors until his death in 1857: of those children who married during his lifetime, Elizabeth, Alfred, and Henrietta, all were cast off.

Once when the daughters were discussing this strange idiosyncrasy of Mr. Barrett Elizabeth said in jest: "If a prince of Eldorado should come, with a pedigree of lineal descent from some signory in the moon on one hand, and a ticket of good-behaviour from the nearest Independent chapel in the other—?"

"Why even *then*," said her sister Arabel, "it would not *do*."

To Elizabeth, with as yet no temptation to defy him on this or any other count, her father was a comfort, a support: she felt and enjoyed his strength as father, as man. Resentments, anxieties she might feel, but these were largely vicarious; as when Arabel deprived herself of a holiday with a friend because her father had frowned when the visit was proposed; or when Henry packed his carpet bag and announced he was going to spend a day and night with friends at Dover, a journey Papa had already discountenanced. When Henry did not appear at breakfast next morning Mr. Barrett was put off with the fiction that his son was lying late abed. The rest of the story, possibly a turbulent one, is tantalizingly not given us. Henrietta's enterprises brought Elizabeth's heart into her mouth more than once; a "polka" given at the house during Mr. Barrett's absence in Cornwall, an unauthorized carriage excursion for a picnic of strawberries and cream to Three Mile Cross, the home of Miss Mitford.

All we know definitely of Mr. Barrett's activity in the City of London is that he attended at the Jamaica Coffee-house, St. Michael's Alley, Cornhill,[2] which was a subscription house for merchants and captains trading with Madeira and the West Indies, and where they could obtain accurate West Indian intelli-

[2] Family information.

gence. He had also certain enterprising side lines; having shares
in a Cornish mine and, even so far back as Hope End days, a
certain practical interest in shipping. Recently he had bought a
craft and, under his own control, was employing her in what
Elizabeth called "his favourite 'Via Lactea' of speculations." In
1844 she sailed to Alexandria with a cargo of coal. When Storm
and Henry wrung from their father a reluctant permission to
travel on board, nothing was said to Elizabeth of the journey
until a few days before departure.

It was perhaps a sign of renewing health that Elizabeth did
not, during their absence on a sea voyage, feel that gnawing
anxiety of the year before when George and Storm were merely
crossing the Channel. Though naturally looking forward to the
travellers' return, she was not, to her own surprise, unduly
worried.

One concomitant of the possessive spirit, jealousy, we can
only tentatively guess at in Edward Barrett. Perhaps, knowing
that her heart was his, he was content to share an influence over
his daughter's mind and work; perhaps after her release from
poetic leading-strings he resigned himself to a growth of mind
and method beyond his scope—be it as it may, his attitude to
John Kenyon, now a strong influence and an admired friend,
was curious.

This kindly man, who had done so much to introduce Elizabeth to a chosen public, a cousin living near by and probably
acquainted with Mr. Barrett at least from Cambridge days,
never came to dine; nor was Elizabeth allowed to invite him
to Mr. Barrett's table. As to Boyd, that older friend and mentor,
we hear nothing of any message to him from Elizabeth's father.
Apart from certain slight courtesies to R. H. Horne, Edward
Barrett appears to have taken little direct interest in his daughter's growing list of literary acquaintances: her world of friends
remained curiously apart from this man she so greatly loved
and depended on. We never hear of him making a third in a
colloquy with Miss Mitford or any other woman friend privileged to visit Elizabeth. Although Robert Browning's calls upon
her, or a known proportion of them, were later allowed and
even approved with some measure of pride, Mr. Barrett made
no effort to meet Browning himself.

In Elizabeth, a poet of fast growing reputation, Mr. Barrett might take a healthy pride, but it was soon to appear as if he took a pride unhealthy, but typical of many of his generation, in his daughter as an incurable invalid. In a condition of helplessness there might be both an unconscious gratification and a sense of security. She, the treasure of his house, was physically dependent on him for moral support and comfort; always at home, fixed in her room, a refuge for himself, and a pivot around which family affairs could circle in the absence of that wife he had lost. With this first child, the eldest daughter, a woman with an unusual grasp of mind and a wide sympathy, perhaps this reserved man came as near to confidence as he was able. She was always there, dependable, never giving him anxiety, her heart being wholly his.

Of the second daughter Mr. Barrett might well be distrustful; that daughter whose besetting sin was, according to her sister, "an over-pleasure in pleasing; a sin made venial by a native softness of heart." Henrietta was too fond of dancing, too fond of male admiration, even going so far as to desire a husband. Mr. Barrett had had trouble with Henrietta in her youth, though certainly she had then obeyed him as a daughter should, very properly giving up her lover instantly at command. In the words of Elizabeth, "a child never submitted more meekly to a revoked holiday."

But Henrietta's submission had only seemed further to incense this man inexorable to mania on one subject. "Oh, the dreadful scenes!" Elizabeth confided to Browning in considering her own more flagrant breach of family discipline,
and only because she had seemed to feel so little. . . . I hear how her knees were made to ring upon the floor, now! She was carried out of the room in strong hysterics and I, who rose up to follow her, though I was quite well at the time and suffering only by sympathy, fell flat down upon my face in a fainting-fit. Arabel thought I was dead.

But such insubordination was not to be expected from the treasured Ba, the eldest and dearest child. Her thoughts were not of the world, not of the flesh but of the spirit. Secure in the fortress of his home, in her own weak condition and native purity, Mr. Barrett would not in the wildest flight of imagination suspect that a man unknown to him, or only slightly by reputation, could wrest his daughter from him; could within the space of a year disturb her spirit and tamper with that obedience she owed him, her father.

But any attempted portrait of Edward Barrett must be tentative, full of hesitations. Of one thing we may be certain; the depicting of this man in a certain play as a monster, a mass of cruel selfishness, was a deliberate falsification for dramatic purposes. That Mr. Barrett was arbitrary, indulged from his youth up, in possession of wealth and power too early in life, all will admit; but, however peculiar his attitude in regard to marriage within his family may appear to us of a freer generation, he could only have applauded himself in the performance of a moral duty, a duty towards his Maker. On what ground he objected to the marriage of his children none can know. No one but the ghost of himself could satisfactorily interpret that enigma; and, self-deluding as most of us are, perhaps even he in the spirit would not be equal to the task.

CHAPTER 16

ON THE THRESHOLD [1844]

IN THESE LAST MONTHS of 1844 we, who know her history, listen for coming footsteps, the steps of one privileged to release Elizabeth from bondage; a bondage of both enforced and encouraged invalidism during which limbs and heart had weakened. A bondage made more sinister by sleep and periods of false calm "red with the hood of poppies."

But, vitiated though Elizabeth inevitably was, partially drugged, sequestered in an airless room, there were signs of a lustier life: a headier draught was already taking the place of that plain water she took as her own in the sonnet quoted. The wine of success, of acclamation as a major poet of her age, was there now for her to sip, if only "like a fly." She might feel, in that cleavage of self which had distressed her so long, Elizabeth Barrett, the poet, to be but a "factitious personality" associated with her work only, but there is no doubt that there was natural gratification.

She had sung of that "Wine of Cyprus" sent her by Mr. Boyd, a wine so aromatic, so dulcet to the palate that

> . . . *the brown bees of Hymettus*
> *Make their honey not so sweet.*

Elizabeth could sip her wine, the wine of success, with pleasure, not mistaking it for a cup more sacramental; nor could she guess that God, already so near in affliction, would soon come closer to her in a gift of human love.

In this period of unconscious waiting Elizabeth's heart was warmed by the world's praise, a praise swelling to a pæan when the *Poems* were issued in America that October. One voice there was to mix criticism, some justifiable criticism, with adulation, that of Edgar Allan Poe; but he was to soften a certain harshness by a handsome dedication of his next volume to Elizabeth.

Amid the public acclamation of this already accepted but

newly popular poet several voices spoke privately, among them
Miss Martineau, a public figure, and especially revered by Elizabeth as a gifted, logical, strong-minded, and courageous
woman. Henry Chorley, the *Athenæum* critic, added to official
praise a private letter, in his enthusiasm breaking through an
unwritten law of the press.

But, though Elizabeth might in a sense be roused by success,
any emotion, pleasurable or otherwise, must bring strain to a
worn spirit weakened by drugs and seclusion. It was perhaps
fortunate that at this time a woman came into her life who,
though to prove a devoted friend, had in her something of the
strength—and the resilience—of high-tempered steel. When
Mrs. Jameson, who had already expressed an admiration of the
Poems, asked for an interview, Elizabeth at first refused, but
when Mrs. Jameson came to stay nearly on her own doorstep,
at 51, Wimpole Street, Elizabeth wavered. A tactfully kind note
left at the door finally softened her. Mrs. Jameson was admitted.

As Mrs. Jameson came upstairs Elizabeth, unused to strangers, always dreading a fresh human contact, felt her "heart
beat itself almost to pieces for fear of seeing her." Perhaps Mrs.
Jameson's reputation as a woman outwardly somewhat hardened by circumstance, trenchantly critical to the point of pedantry, had reached her through Kenyon, a friend of this once
distinguished woman now almost forgotten but for her association with the Brownings.

Mrs. Jameson's fox-like appearance could not have soothed
the nervous invalid: in Elizabeth's own words, "she is very light
—has the lightest of eyes, the lightest of complexions; no eyebrows, and what looked to me like very pale red hair, and thin
lips of no colour at all . . . a nose and chin projective without
breadth." Elizabeth found, as she had expected, "the tone of her
conversation rather analytical and critical than spontaneous
and impulsive." Mrs. Jameson's acute mind would permit no
vagueness of thought either in herself or in others.

But an infinite kindness towards her soon set Elizabeth at
ease. Although in a letter to Horne she could not but compare
Mrs. Jameson unfavourably with "our friend of Three Mile
Cross who 'wears her heart upon her sleeve,' and shakes out its
perfume at every moment," it is possible that Anna Jameson's

sharper quality, tempered with an Irish vivacity, was just the astringent Elizabeth needed in her emotional state. Though she could not readily weep, tears always came easily to her eyes: one feels in studying the life of Mrs. Jameson that, for all her strong kindness of heart, tears were not a commodity in which she dealt.

Perhaps in comparing the two women Elizabeth had in mind that struggle common to both to maintain themselves by the pen; Miss Mitford in support of a selfish extravagant father and Mrs. Jameson of mother and sisters. Mrs. Jameson's lot was made the more bitter by the memory of a husband once loved, as selfish and unreliable as Dr. Mitford, who, after two unsatisfactory spells of life together, only unwillingly supported her.

Not without a painful travail of spirit, Anna Brownell Jameson had built up for herself a place in the world of art criticism, or rather art appreciation, and had written, among others, successful travel books, beginning eighteen years earlier with the popular *Diary of an Ennuyée,* the fruit of an excursion on the Continent as a governess. One practical aspect of her life-work was the first compilation of handbooks to Art Collections, private and public. A more idealistic aspect was an emphasis upon women in literature and society: the encouragement given by her to Bessie Rayner Parkes, Barbara Bodichon, and other pioneers of woman's emancipation was in itself a valuable contribution to the cause of human freedom. Her closest friend at this time was one whom the contemporary outlook on marriage had done much to injure, Lady Byron. She would often talk of her friend to Elizabeth, telling her that the true story of the separation reflected nothing but credit on Byron's wife, but Elizabeth, obstinate in prejudice, would not be influenced.

Whatever may have been in Elizabeth's mind at this first interview lasting nearly an hour, she at once "ran into what my sisters call 'one of my sudden intimacies' and there was an embrace for a farewell." There are indications that this early liking was later modified for a time, but soon a potent influence was brought to bear. Browning liked and admired Mrs. Jameson.

Among agitations less pleasurable this autumn was the third loss of Flush. This time he was filched away on his own doorstep while waiting with Arabel to be let into the house. So that a Jovean anger might not descend upon a favourite sister, who had taken the dog without a chain, Elizabeth was forced to conceal from her father not only Flush's absence but sleepless nights, tears, and neglect of food; by "a very convenient bad headache" avoiding contact with him when her eyes were reddest.

The thieves, yielding up Flush for six and a half guineas, announced that next time the price would be ten pounds. Part of the anxiety to keep Flush's loss from Mr. Barrett was his natural and outspoken annoyance at a member of his family being the subject of blackmail; but to one who loved the devoted animal this objection could be but a "kicking against the pricks."

Another agitation more remote, though disturbing to a sensitive secluded spirit, was the revival of interest in animal magnetism through an article in the *Athenæum* by Harriet Martineau, a firm believer in its medical efficacy and one who claimed its cure in herself of a cancerous malady. To Elizabeth, who had herself been urged to take the treatment, this apparent cure, though she could not but rejoice in it, brought a tremor of the soul. In a happier future she was, under the wing of Swedenborg, to take wondering pleasure, even delight, in supernatural questionings, but now she agreed whole-heartedly with the sturdier Mrs. Jameson who had said during their first interview "that if there was *anything* in it, there was *so much*, it became scarcely possible to limit consequences, and the subject grew awful to contemplate." "The agency," Elizabeth added for herself to Mr. Martin, who was inclined to laugh, "seems to me like the shaking of the flood-gates placed by the Divine Creator between the unprepared soul and the unseen world."

Bitter attacks were made upon Miss Martineau, who had so courageously, but not cautiously, revealed her own experiences in print. "I would rather fall into the hands of God than of man," Elizabeth told that old friend James Martin, "and suffer as she did in the body, instead of being the mark of these cruel observations." But Miss Martineau, a born fighter, took the attacks in her stride: this was not the first time she had challenged public opinion.

One lighter reference among the letters to the Martins of this autumn is perhaps worth noticing by the way; it being one to which we in this age must give hearty endorsement. "Do you take in 'Punch'? If not, you *ought*." Mr. Punch was, of course, at this time only three years old and so perhaps needing encouragement in his march forward through time. A part of Elizabeth's interest in this journal was its radical tone. In those earlier days *Punch* was a champion of the suffering poor.

That summer there had been exterior decorating at 50, Wimpole Street: Elizabeth's ivy, temporarily torn down, had been damaged. It was perhaps to replace in some measure the ivy screen that in the autumn Elizabeth added to her room a fanciful touch: a transparent green blind scene-painted, with "a castle gate-way and two walks, and several peasants, and groves of trees," all harmonizing well with new green damask curtains. "The effect is beautiful," Elizabeth told Mrs. Martin, "and the whole room catches a light from it." Mr. Kenyon joined nearly every inmate of the house in admiration of this blind: even the one dissentient, Mr. Barrett, had to give it grudging praise when the sun lit up the castle, though insulting his daughter's taste "with the analogy of a back window in a confectioner's shop." Another and more practical change in her room was a large table, the gift of Mr. Kenyon, "with a rail round it to consecrate it from Flush's paws, and large enough to hold all my variety of vanities."

In December intense cold robbed Elizabeth of her voice, forcing her to refuse, in a charming note, an interview with Mrs. Jameson: "You are not to think that I should not have been delighted to have you in a monodram, as I heard Mr. Kenyon one morning when he came and talked for an hour, as he can talk, while the audience could only clap her hands or shake her head for the yea and nay . . . but with you I was too much a stranger to propose such a thing."

In a December letter which told Mrs. Martin of a gradual recovery from this loss of voice we have our first mention of Elizabeth Wilson, that minor but important actress in the drama to come. Wilson was pleased with a pair of woollen boots sent as a present to her mistress by Mrs. Martin because "they can't be kicked off." Elizabeth adds a note of gratification: she need now not be at the trouble of pulling on her stockings in the morning.

This month two rather odd and incongruous tributes came to

Elizabeth which pleased and amused her: a "sonnet from Gutter Lane, Cheapside," and information that the fashionable
"Count D'Orsay had written one of the stanzas of 'Crowned
and Buried' at the bottom of an engraving of Napoleon which
hangs in his room." The sonnet from Gutter Lane was followed
by a highly laudatory review of her *Poems* in the *League* (the
anti-Corn Law paper) praising her for "courage in opposing
war and monopoly" and rumoured to have been written by
Richard Cobden, "an enthusiast for poetry." "If I thought so to
the point of conviction, *do you know*," Elizabeth wrote to John
Kenyon, himself of advanced Liberal opinion, "*I should be much
pleased?* You remember that I am a sort of (magna) chartist—
only going a little farther!"

Good news had come throughout the autumn from Gibraltar,
from Malta and Alexandria, to relieve an underlying anxiety:
on January 12 in the new year Elizabeth told Mrs. Martin that
Henry and Stormie were on the way home, "bringing with
them as a companion for Flushie, a little gazelle." Elizabeth in
reporting this seems to disregard the incongruity of a gazelle in
Wimpole Street: perhaps she was anyhow only keeping up a
humorous pretence in what was but a brotherly joke.

All that remains to us of this letter ends thus: "And I had a
letter from Browning the poet last night, which threw me into
ecstasies—Browning, the author of 'Paracelsus,' and king of the
mystics."

C H A P T E R   1 7

ROBERT BROWNING [1845]

*I love your verses with all my heart, dear Miss Barrett,—and
this is no off-hand complimentary letter that I shall write,—
whatever else, no prompt matter-of-course recognition of your
genius, and there a grateful and natural end of the thing.
Since the day last week when I first read your poems, I quite
laugh to remember how I have been turning and turning again
in my mind what I should be able to tell you of their effect upon
me, for in the first flush of delight I thought I would this once
get out of my habit of purely passive enjoyment, when I do really enjoy, and thoroughly justify my admiration—perhaps even,
as a loyal fellow-craftsman should, try and find fault and do you
some little good to be proud of hereafter!—but nothing comes
of it all—so into me has it gone, and part of me has it become,
this great living poetry of yours, not a flower of which but took
root and grew— Oh, how different this is from lying to be dried
and pressed flat, and prized highly, and put in a book with a
proper account at top and bottom, and shut up and put away
. . . and the book called a "Flora," besides! After all, I need not
give up a thought of doing that, too, in time; because even now,
talking with whoever is worthy, I can give a reason for my
faith in one and another excellence, the fresh strange music, the
affluent language, the exquisite pathos and true brave new
thought; but in this addressing myself to you—your own self,
and for the first time, my feeling rises altogether. I do, as I say,
love these books with all my heart—and I love you too.*

THIS LETTER of January 10, 1845, written with the encouragement of her cousin, John Kenyon, continued with an account of
this missed meeting three years before:
*I feel as at some untoward passage in my travels, as if I had
been close, so close to some world's-wonder in chapel or crypt,
only a screen to push and I might have entered, but there was*

some slight, so it now seems, slight and just sufficient bar to ad-
mission, and the half-opened door shut, and I went home my
thousands of miles, and the sight was never to be?

Elizabeth wrote back immediately expressing her delight, her
gratitude; asking that if he ever did emerge without inconvenient effort from his "passive state," would he please point out
any obvious and important faults in her work. She did not "pretend to any extraordinary meekness under criticism" but felt
that a "general observation" from such a poet on her "master-
faults" must be of value.

If he had entered that "crypt," she told him, he "might have
caught cold, or been tired to death, and *wished*" himself "a
thousand miles off": "what I have lost by one chance I may recover by some future one. Winters shut me up as they do dor-
mouse's eyes; in the spring, *we shall see:* and I am so much
better that I seem to be turning round to the outward world
again." This nervous invalid who had trembled at the advent of
Mrs. Jameson, who had so resolutely kept away from her presence older acquaintances, was eager, bold in a desire to meet
Robert Browning.

The admired and revered Tennyson had expressed a desire
through a friend to meet her, but we hear of no invitation from
Elizabeth. With Browning, however, perhaps as much admired
though with some qualification, she had long been linked; as
poets alike labelled mystical, obscure, and as the common friend
of John Kenyon. Hostile criticism of Browning as poet Elizabeth
had long resented in a curiously personal way, and of Browning
the man she had heard much, and much to his credit, from her
cousin. So linked, so familiar already to her in the mind, a step
forward to meeting was easier than in the case of others who
would seem to have had a prior claim.

She ended her letter with: "I will say that while I live to
follow this divine art of poetry, in proportion to my love for it
and my devotion to it, I must be a devout admirer and student
of your works. This is in my heart to say to you—and I say it."

Browning, himself of West Indian planter stock on his father's side, came of a family of more intellect and character
than gentle birth; such birth as Elizabeth could proudly claim
if, as a Radical, she had not discounted it as "honourable ver-

digris." The elder Robert Browning, apart from creative genius as remarkable a personality as his son, had, after a brief period in Jamaica, relinquished his inheritance there for conscience's sake. He would be no party to the institution of slavery. This man, profoundly intellectual, something of an artist, gave up the prospect of a large measure of freedom for a clerk's position in the Bank of England.

In the elder Browning, a quiet man living happily among his family and books, ambition was centred in the brilliant son who, he determined, should have that freedom necessary for the development of poetic power. Indeed, from earliest years there had been little interference with a child's natural growth: Mr. Browning himself had suffered too acutely from the tyranny of a selfish grasping father to impose even disciplinary restraint on his children.

Browning's mother, of Scottish-German stock, delicate, gentle, with a great love of flowers and music, was adored by her son: however late his engagements in Town might be, he would walk five miles to the outlying village of New Cross that he might sleep in a room beside her, with a door open between them. Browning indeed cherished a superstition that, so close was the bond between mother and son, whenever she was ill he himself was indisposed. Both mother and father were his loving, admiring friends. Unlike Mr. Barrett, they demanded no obedience: on the other hand, so great was his affection for them that in the small things of life he was content to be a child still, to fall in with their way of life.

In this idyllic home there was another intimate friend, Sarianna Browning, a clever lively girl, who, after the fashion of those days, lived in self-abnegation as daughter and sister.

Like the Barrett family the Brownings were, here through the influence of the mother, Dissenters: as with Elizabeth, Browning admitted, however, nothing of a Dissenter's narrowness of outlook: indeed, an innate catholicism of mind took him further towards agnosticism. In spiritual quality Elizabeth transcended his more worldly nature.

Browning, a monarch in the small kingdom of home, took his freedom with a proud pleasure; a freedom, with the small income allowed him by his father, to write and study untram-

melled, to travel in a modest way, to lead his own life within
the limits of few personal wants. Freedom, a power of self-
determination, was to him infinitely dear. The Brownings, he
would declare, always got what they wanted.

He was now in his thirty-second year. His worldly fame as a
poet was qualified, limited, his reputation as a poetic dramatist somewhat wider, though all ambition in the theatre had
been angrily abandoned after a split with Macready. His popularity as an urbane, amusing, clever, well-dressed, and handsome young man overflowed purely literary circles. Dancing,
dining out, parties were becoming wearisome to him. As once
he had felt impatience with the immediate narrow, suburban
circle about his early Camberwell home, now he was discon-
tented in a wider London world. Popularity with women had
never touched his heart more than superficially: he thought
that he could never fall in love, never lose a proud freedom of
mind and action.

Elizabeth had on her wall a portrait which, though misleading, at least gave some impression of her new correspondent:
of Elizabeth Browning had but a vague notion, founded, it
would seem, more upon general gossip than on any information Kenyon might have given him. His first advances were
made believing her to be suffering from an incurable injury to
the spine.

He followed up her reply the day after receiving it with a
typical tumultuous, allusive letter, expressing joy at the thought
of obtaining in spring his "Chapel-sight after all" and confessing himself, on consideration, unable, unwilling to find fault:
*your poetry must be, cannot but be, infinitely more to me than
mine to you—for you do what I always wanted, hoped to do,
and only seem now likely to do for the first time. You speak out,
you,—I only make men and women speak—give you truth
broken into prismatic hues, and fear the pure white light, even
if it is in me, but I am going to try . . . it seems bleak, melancholy work, this talking to the wind (for I have begun)—yet I
don't think I shall let you hear, after all, the savage things about
Popes and imaginative religions that I must say.*

"What 'struck me as faults,'" he told her, "were not matters
on the removal of which, one was to have—poetry, or high po-

Yours very truly,
Robert Browning.

ROBERT BROWNING
from an engraving in A New Spirit of the Age *(1844); a copy of this*
hung in Elizabeth's room in Wimpole Street

ELIZABETH BARRETT BROWNING
from a daguerreotype taken at Le Havre in 1858

etry,—but the very highest poetry, so I thought, and that, to universal recognition." He seems to imply that her main fault—in
itself dear to a fellow-artist because it revealed herself—was a
laboured detail or method of expression; but, as so often with
Browning, to whom prose was an awkward instrument, the exact meaning, only half-expressed, is hard to define.

Elizabeth, poring over this letter in her quiet room, came to
a different solution; considering, wrongly as he later pointed
out, that he was but renewing that charge, so often in Kenyon's
mouth, of careless writing. She protested in her next letter that,
though by nature headlong, impatient, there was in the pursuit
of art "love strong enough, even in me, to overcome nature.
. . . What no mere critic sees, but what you, an artist, know, is
the difference between the idea in the writer's mind and the
eidōlon cast off in his work." She praised his art, its "immense
grasp," its power of dealing "both with abstract thought and
with human passion . . . you are 'masculine' to the height—
and I, as a woman, have studied some of your gestures of language and intonation wistfully, as a thing beyond me far: and
more admirable for being beyond." She was delighted to be told
of new work and hoped he would develop his dramatic sense
in plays for the closet rather than the stage. With reference to
his anticipation of a delight in her friendship she offered it
"*now*, if you please, at this moment, for fear of worldly
mutabilities."

It was nearly a fortnight before Browning replied. He had
been trying to "find fault," but could only say that, when his
head was aching from work, he would open one of her green-
covered volumes at his elbow and there find "so much fresh
trefoil to feel in one's hands this winter-time." He would, however, go so far as to mark in pencil passages most and least admired. Browning then went off into one of those absurd stories
which pepper so pleasantly this long correspondence between
them; of a man who, volunteering to criticize "a sonnet-writing
somebody," had recourse in despair to "badder, badderer, bad-
derest" and "worster, worsterer, worsterest." Of that immediate
friendship she offered, he wrote "(and here Juliet's word rises to
my lips)—I feel sure once and for ever."

In the last paragraph he begged Elizabeth not to write if she

hated writing letters "as I hate writing to nearly everybody."
In a few days she answered, protesting: "Why how could I hate
to write to you, dear Mr. Browning? Could you believe in such
a thing? . . . As for me, I have done most of my talking by post
of late years—as people shut up in dungeons take up with
scrawling mottoes on the walls." She would gladly make him
one of those few regular correspondents, in company with Miss
Mitford, who had "filled a large drawer in this room with delightful letters, heart-warm and soul-warm," if he would promise to do away with all ceremony as between the sexes and
treat her *"en bon camarade."* "You will find me an honest man
on the whole, if rather hasty and prejudging, which is a different thing from prejudice at the worst." At the end of a long letter she gives us the first example of a feature of these letters, a
playful misunderstanding of his own words: "you might indeed
repent your quotation from Juliet—which I guessed at once—
and of course—

I have no joy in this contract to-day!
It is too unadvised, too rash and sudden."

At the end of January Elizabeth told Mrs. Martin: "I am getting deeper and deeper into correspondence with Robert
Browning, poet and mystic, and we are growing to be the truest
of friends. If I live a little longer shut up in this room, I shall
certainly know everybody in the world."

Their correspondence over the next three months, so full of
self-revelation, especially on her part—on his, giving many interesting stories of his friend Carlyle, and other writers of the
day—can be little more than indicated in outline: indeed these
amazing letters, two volumes of them, demand a separate work,
so full are they of literary and classical allusions, anecdotes,
thoughts on life, on poetry, and on good writing. Her letters are
the finer, more lucid, more finished, but his contain, beside rich
passages, a mine of unsifted wisdom, thought often incom-
pletely, awkwardly expressed.

There was discussion of their work; his upon "Luria" and "A
Soul's Tragedy," hers a new translation of *Prometheus Vinctus*
to take the place of that earlier one which Elizabeth considered
"the most miserable of all miserable versions of the class." She
consulted him on difficult and obscure passages.

By the end of February Robert was exclaiming with impatience: "Real warm Spring, dear Miss Barrett, and the birds know it; and in Spring I shall see you, surely see you—for when did I once fail to get whatever I had set my heart upon? As I ask myself sometimes, with a strange fear." Elizabeth protested:

Yes, but, dear Mr. Browning, I want the spring according to the new "style" (mine), and not the old one of you and the rest of the poets. To me unhappily, the snowdrop is much the same as the snow—it feels as cold underfoot—and I have grown sceptical about "the voice of the turtle," the east winds blow so loud. April is a Parthian with a dart, and May (at least the early part of it) a spy in the camp. . . . A little later comes my spring; and indeed after such severe weather, from which I have just escaped with my life, I may thank it for coming at all.

On May 3 he wrote wistfully: "Surely the wind that sets my chestnut-tree dancing, all its baby-cone-blossoms, green now, rocking like fairy castles on a hill in an earthquake,—that is South West, surely!" In her reply Elizabeth made no reference to this veiled request, wishing nervously to postpone their meeting. He had asked to be allowed to collaborate with her: she told him that such an idea, though welcome to her, was impossible because the "Psyche" drama begun with his friend Horne "in my dreary Devonshire days, when I was his debtor for various little kindnesses," had never been completed.

In referring to this abortive collaboration, and the subject chosen by her, Elizabeth uncovered for this new friend a hidden place: that cleft in her nature furrowed deep by sorrow in the dark days at Torquay. "Did you ever feel afraid of your own soul, as I have done?"

In Browning, so complete a man, untouched by grief, there was already a disturbance, a weakening of self-sufficiency—a premonition. This woman with whom he was now so intimate on paper had power to move him strangely. Elizabeth's careless exaggerated invalid's statement that from the rigours of winter she had "just escaped with her life" touched a tragic chord on his "life's harp" to which, he said, she had added "octaves on octaves of new golden strings." The thought of Elizabeth Barrett was already an agitation, if a sweet one, in his planned poetic life, his life of a chartered freedom. We hear of an ache, a singing in the head, denoting nervous strain. Why will she not see him, he demanded. Did she mistrust him?

Elizabeth did not mistrust him, but she was shy: however, on a strict understanding that he kept silent about the visit, she would receive him. "I *cannot* admit visitors in a general way— and putting the question of health quite aside, it would be unbecoming to lie here on the sofa and make a company-show of an infirmity, and hold a beggar's hat for sympathy."

The only other man friend Elizabeth had consented to receive had been Horne, who, in 1844, before he went to Germany, would not take a first denial but begged for an interview in a letter "expressive of mortification and vexation." When Horne had not kept the engagement Elizabeth "clapped her hands with joy when I felt my danger to be passed"; and yet she liked, admired Horne, and had worked on familiar terms with him. Browning was but comparatively a new acquaintance and yet already he had singularly affected her. "For instance," she wrote him nine months later, "by two or three half words you made me see you, and other people had delivered orations on the same subject quite without effect. I surprised everybody in this house by consenting to see you." Most of the letters this romantic celebrity received from men anxious to get a sight of her went directly on to the fire.

He fixed a call three days ahead so that, if unequal to their meeting, Elizabeth might have time to write. A great part of this letter is taken up with a jaunty and rather tactless tale of a mythical "Simpson" who came to pay homage to a literary idol and departed ejaculating "mentally—'Well, I *did* expect to see something different from that little yellow commonplace man.' "

Browning's intention, his own apprehension, is clear to us: would she feel disappointed in one so long admired as a poet? But Elizabeth's humility, her consciousness of a lost hold on the words, led her to give a twist to the story. "I think you should have made out the case in some such way as it was in nature— viz. that you had lashed yourself up to an exorbitant wishing to see me . . . because I was unfortunate enough to be shut up in a room and silly enough to make a fuss about opening the door."

From his growing warmth, from an impatience to meet her, Elizabeth feared that Browning might expect more than he would find; that he might have to substitute for some enchanted princess poet a mere sickly invalid. And from these earlier letters, throbbing with the beat of a strong heart, we cannot doubt, I think, that Robert Browning came to Wimpole Street on May 20, 1845 ready to fall in love.

In a spasm of shyness Elizabeth had removed his portrait from where it hung under Wordsworth, pulling down Tennyson as well "in a fit of justice." The over-poetical portrait, which later she was to condemn as "a vulgarized caricature," could have given her little hint of the man who did appear; a handsome man, but with none of the traditional bearing of a poet. Even less could Elizabeth link this urbane courteous man with the writer of impulsive, affectionate letters.

Elizabeth did not, however, feel that profound disappointment Browning was to bring to many in the years of celebrity: she did not think he looked like a gentleman farmer, or a mere intelligent man of affairs. What struck her particularly was his eyes; the most serene, the most spiritual she had ever seen.

He stayed an hour and a half, and when he went a memory of him lingered in that quiet room. "I had a sense of your presence constantly," Elizabeth told him nine months later. There was, however, in her no presentiment of what was to come. Next morning she said to her father: "It is most extraordinary how the idea of Mr. Browning does beset me—I suppose it is not being used to see strangers, in some degree—but it haunts me . . it is a persecution."

Mr. Barrett, happily for all three of them also without presentiment, smiled and told her "it is not grateful to your friend to use such a word."

On his return home Browning noted on her last letter the date and length of his visit. He then sent a note asking whether he had behaved as he should, talked softly enough, and not stayed too long. His "great happiness, such as it will be if I see you, as this morning, from time to time," must "be obtained at a cost of as little inconvenience to you as we can contrive." On his part there was one objection: "do not humiliate me—*do not* again,—by calling me 'kind' in that way."

She wrote back at once protesting. There must be no restriction on "our vocabulary." A kindness felt must be expressed. "It is hard for you to understand what my mental position is after the peculiar experience I have suffered and what τί ἐμοὶ καὶ σοί,[1] a sort of feeling irrepressible from me to you, when, from the height of your brilliant happy sphere, you ask, as you did ask, for personal intercourse with me." He was to come again in a week's time—"and again, when you like and can together—and it will not be more 'inconvenient' to me to be pleased, I suppose, than it is to people in general."

Elizabeth has written impulsively before and regretted it; yet even if in this case time had been given for consideration, she could not have thought that a sight of her, a wan invalid no longer young, could inflame any man. The next day he wrote to her "intemperate things"; an open declaration of love.

After a lapse of two days there came an agitated reply:
You do not know what pain you give me in speaking so wildly. . . . You remember—surely you do—that I am in the most exceptional of positions; and that, just because of it, I am able to receive you as I did on Tuesday. . . . Now, if there should be one word of answer attempted to this; or of reference; I must not . . . I will not see you again—and you will justify me later in your heart . . . spare me the sadness of having to break through an intercourse just as it was promising pleasure to me; to me who have so many sadnesses and so few pleasures. . . . Your mistakes in me . . which I cannot mistake (—and which have so humbled me by too much honoring—) I put away gently, and with grateful tears in my eyes. . . .
She begged him to "forget *at once*, and *for ever*" what he had written: "and which (so) will die out between *you and me alone*, like a misprint between you and the printer."

A new paragraph began on a note of calm friendship. With an excuse, perhaps to give herself time to regain composure, she put off his visit for a week because of relations now in London. On their next meeting he should criticize her "Prometheus." The end of this pitiful letter is tremulous with emotion:
You are not displeased with me? . . . I do not write as I might, of some words of yours—but you know I am not a stone, even if

---

[1] "What have I to do with thee?"

silent like one. And if in the unsilence, *I have said one word to
vex you, pity me for having had to say it—and for the rest, may
God bless you far beyond the reach of vexation from my words
or my deeds!*

This brilliant man, Elizabeth told herself, had fallen in love, not
with a worn-out woman, but with a poet romantically secluded.

Robert Browning, for a proved psychologist, acted so stu-
pidly on receiving this that one can only suppose he lost his
head; fearing to lose what had just been gained. Into her delay
of a week he read an intention to deny him admittance unless
"the past avowal" was "blotted out." Instead of allowing her
letter to pass, as she had requested, in silence, he wrote the
next day falsely, almost jauntily:

*Don't you remember I told you, once on a time, that you "knew
nothing of me"? whereat you demurred—but I meant what I
said, and knew it was so. To be grand in a simile, for every poor
speck of a Vesuvius or a Stromboli in my microcosm there are
huge layers of ice and pits of black cold water—and I make the
most of my two or three fire-eyes, because I know by experience, alas, how these tend to extinction—and the ice grows and
grows—still this last is true part of me, most characteristic part,
best part perhaps, and I disown nothing—only,—when you
talked of "knowing me"! Still, I am utterly unused, of these late
years particularly, to dream of communicating anything about
that to another person (all my writings are purely dramatic as
I am always anxious to say) that when I make never so little an
attempt, no wonder if I bungle notably—"language," too, is an
organ that never studded this heavy heavy head of mine. Will
you not think me very brutal if I tell you I could almost smile at
your misapprehension of what I meant to write?*

What he had hurriedly written must "have looked absurd
enough as seen apart from the horrible counterbalancing never-
to-be-written *rest of me*—by the side of which, could it be written and put before you, my note would sink to its proper and
relative place, and become a mere 'thank you' for your good
opinion."

On this theme he embroidered rather incoherently for what
fills another page of print; reproaching himself for having given
her pain, assuring her that next Tuesday she will find him "pre-

cisely the same mild man-about-town you were gracious to the other morning." A postscript, written rather in the tone of a man who wants to suppress the evidence of an indiscretion, asked her to return his note that he might destroy it.

This blundering male effort to set matters right, to put Elizabeth's mind at rest, hampered his future courtship. Even when her love for him was avowed; a possibility with renewed health of marriage admitted, Elizabeth could not entirely rid herself of the feeling that it was an idea Browning worshipped, a sublimation of combined poet and woman. In her own phrase nine months later, "the lava of that letter has kept running down into my thought of you too much." This doubt was intensified by a long continued inability wholly to identify Browning, the writer of ardent letters, with the quiet, self-controlled man, declared lover though he was, who visited her.

Even in her morbid state of self-abasement Elizabeth might well have been offended by this extraordinary declaration: but, quite angelically, she wrote tendering humble apologies
for having spent so much solemnity on so simple a matter. . . . I am quite as much ashamed of myself as I ought to be, which is not a little. You will find it difficult to believe me perhaps when I assure you that I never made such a mistake (I mean of over-seriousness to indefinite compliments), no, never in my life before—indeed my sisters have often jested with me (in matters of which they were cognizant) on my supernatural indifference to a superlative degree in general, as if it meant nothing in grammar. . . . I wrote what I wrote so unfortunately, through reverence for you, *and not at all from vanity on my own account . .*
though, she added with a touch of humour, no man "who ever lived in the world (not even *you*) could be expected to believe" this "though said, sung and sworn."

She then again protested his superiority to her. This protestation, now from her, and now from him to her, becomes in these letters an almost wearisome ding-dong of self-depreciation.

After some general literary chat Elizabeth appointed a further meeting when "I, for one, shall have forgotten everything by that time; being quick at forgetting my own faults usually."

Still Browning could not leave well alone:

Nay—I must have the last word—as all people in the wrong de-
sire to have—and then no more of the subject. You said I had
given you great pain—so long as I stop that, think anything of
me you choose or can! But before your former letter came, I
saw the preordained uselessness of mine . . . since the offering
to cut off one's right-hand to save anybody a head-ache, is in
vile taste, even for our melodramas, seeing that it was never yet
believed in on the stage or off it,—how much worse to make the
ugly chop, and afterwards come sheepishly in, one's arm in a
black sling, and find the delectable gift had changed aching to
nausea! There! And now "exit prompt-side, nearest door, Luria"
—and enter Robert Browning—next Wednesday—as boldly as he
suspects most people do just after they have been soundly
frightened!

Unless in her heart Elizabeth did suspect that "ugly chop,"
the denial of his true feelings, to be a mere dramatization in a
sense other than that in which he had first presented it to her,
this letter could only have bewildered. Be it as it may, his letter and the whole painful subject were now ignored by her,
though at the next meeting embarrassment could hardly have
been confined to him. It was long before those beautiful eyes,
so admired by Miss Mitford, were again raised in Browning's
presence.

His own constraint, an effort to conceal the love that had
proved so perilous, is implied in a short note of mid-June: a request that she will not allow him to run on in conversation
about matters on which he is ignorant. "I tell you plainly I
only trench on them, and intrench in them, from gaucherie, pure
and respectable . . . I should certainly grow instructive upon
the prospects of hay-crops and pasture-land if deprived of this
resource." A safe and congenial subject, both in the mouth and
on paper, was the poems Robert was gathering together for his
next volume.

The essential nervousness of Robert Browning's temperament, bodily robust though he was, manifested itself at this
time of trial in frequent headaches. For him, a man who boasted
somewhat arrogantly that he always got what he wanted, the
first setback must have been a serious blow apart from natural
disappointment in love. Whether from accident or design—since

nothing appeals so much to an unselfish invalid as other people's symptoms—he spoke freely of these headaches. She took them, and other signs of temporary indisposition in a healthy man, very seriously indeed: surely he must have smiled when she attributed a slight cold to having carried flowers to her unwrapped, the wet stalks in his bare hand.

Soon a fresh embarrassment was to beset Elizabeth. With the coming of summer, friends and relations began to descend upon Wimpole Street: there was further need for caution. So many, friends of Browning among them, had been denied entrance that she did not want his visits to be known. This necessity of concealment meant an anxious watch upon dates and, from time to time, some alterations. Only to Miss Mitford, for sheer love of truth with an intimate friend, had Elizabeth admitted to one single visit from Robert Browning. Kenyon soon knew of their interviews, though from whom it is not clear: no attempt was made to conceal the weekly calls from Elizabeth's father, who, curiously enough, though he did not "overvalue poetry," appears to have taken pride in them.

In regard to a secrecy so alien to his nature Browning himself declared:

Indeed, though on other grounds I should be all so proud of being known for your friend by everybody, yet there's no denying the deep delight of playing the Eastern Jew's part here in this London—they go about . . . with the tokens of extreme destitution and misery, and steal by blind ways and by-paths to some blank dreary house, one obscure door in it—which being well shut behind them, they grope on through a dark corridor or so, and then, a blaze follows the lifting a curtain or the like, for they are in a palace-hall with fountains and light, and marble and gold, of which the envious are never to dream!

He was clearly plucking up courage in love. "Pomegranates you may cut down the middle and see into," he had written on June 25, "but not hearts,—so why should I try and speak?" He ended this short note with "and so your own R. B."

On July 8 Elizabeth took a first faltering step towards recovery; leaving not only her room but the house, going out for a short carriage drive. Only her sister's prudence in this first venture prevented her from entering Regent's Park and also from leaving a card "vaingloriously" at Kenyon's house in Harley Place. The experiment was not altogether pleasant to one so weakened with long seclusion, but Elizabeth was determined to repeat it. "I walk," she told her brother George, "as well as most children of two years old."

In the course of a long letter of July 18 Elizabeth made one of her many protests against the false position in which Robert nailed her up with his "gold-headed nails of chivalry." Perhaps with a certain dreary purpose of discouraging him, she claimed the doubtful advantage of *"being older by years."* But Elizabeth did not disclose how many years: indeed, it is thought in the family that while she lived Browning never knew her real age.

It is clear from a postscript to Browning's letter of July 22 that a plan to recover health abroad was being discussed. He was proud of her praise of his work—"when will the blame come?—at Malta?" Not "from Malta," be it noted, but "at Malta." Clearly if Elizabeth goes to Malta Robert will follow.

To Mrs. Martin on July 29 Elizabeth revealed a growing strength. "I have been *getting well,*" she wrote exultantly, "—going out into the carriage two or three times a week, abdicating my sofa for my armchair, moving from one room to another now and then, and walking about mine quite as well as, and with considerably more complacency than, a child of two years old. . . . I look in the looking-glass with a better conscience." But if this summer good was not to be undone she must go abroad for the winter.

In spite of a determination not to admit Robert's love, not to be the means of ruffling his smooth path "by so much as one of my flint-stones," Elizabeth was, there is no doubt, drawing strength, deep joy, from their communion. Sure of his interest, she wrote much of her own nature, feelings, and childhood, and of her development as a poet. On both sides the friendship, the pure friendship she was determined to maintain, was quite frankly tinged with emotion. His letters fast gathered in warmth.

By August she could have been in no doubt that, even if his love might be three parts ideal worship of a dream woman, the love was there, and she returned it with all her heart. When he

urged her to tell him what she was writing she mentioned casually "lyrics for the most part, which lie illegibly in pure Egyptian," but "nothing worth speaking of." "Oh, there is time
enough," she exclaimed, "and too much, perhaps! and so let me
be idle a little now, and enjoy your poems while I can. It is pure
enjoyment and must be—" Elizabeth, one may guess, far removed as she was from girlhood, was enjoying that curious drift
of emotion, that awareness of another, which is a part of un-
declared love: to her was added the peculiar joy, the soul-
shaking experience of a return to throbbing human life:

> . . . *a mystic Shape did move*
> *Behind me, and drew me backward by the hair,*
> *And a voice said in mastery while I strove, . .*
> *"Guess now who holds thee?"—"Death," I said, But, there,*
> *The silver answer rang, . . "Not Death, but Love."*

Robert is exhorting her to exercise, to grow stronger: "Never,
pray, *pray,* never lose one sunny day or propitious hour to 'go
out and walk about.'" "But do not surprise *me,*" he added
boldly, "one of these mornings, by 'walking' up to me when I
am introduced . . or I shall infallibly, in spite of all the after
repentance and begging pardon—I shall . . ." There follow
some words effaced, the purport of which it does not take an
expert in love to guess.

Towards the end of August, when after a long fine summer
they must look forward to the fogs and winds of autumn, Malta
is again mentioned, and this time by Elizabeth: Mr. Kenyon had
"talked homilies of it last Sunday and wanted to speak to
Papa." On the question Mr. Barrett himself, the head of the
house, the acknowledged arbiter of her fate, remained curiously, ominously silent. He had been the first to suggest that a
winter spent in Malta might help to restore his daughter's
health, and at a time when illness and a lack of interest in living had made her indifferent in the matter, but now he was silent. From something Elizabeth had written earlier in the summer of an angry word from her father, it looks as if at this time
he was persuading himself that her continued illness was perversely due to a determination not to take nourishing food, to
"obstinacy and dry toast." An excuse, albeit an unconscious one,

must be made for keeping the dearest child, his comfort, near
to him.

In a momentous letter of August 25 Elizabeth rather disin-
genuously asked Browning why, with freedom and the world
before him, he had at their last meeting declared himself weary
of the world. Perhaps it was because he was unwell.

Then, in a long passage covering some four printed pages,
there followed a confession which eased her burdened soul.
Starting off from some remark she had made to him about her
father, Elizabeth spoke of Mr. Barrett's domination, but of a
deep tender affection behind it, and of the reason why she herself should submit gladly to that imperial will. Then the whole
tragic story of Bro's death was told to this man who now possessed her heart. "I have never said so much to a living being—
I never *could* speak or write of it." This grief of her life was
never again mentioned, even to him, until the tactless words of
a friend reopened the wound years later.

To Browning this revelation, tragic though it was, brought
hope of winning her. In a short note he said: "There is a better
thing than being happy in your happiness; I feel, now that you
teach me, it is so."

Elizabeth had said at the beginning of her letter, and in solemn earnest, that she was "always expecting to hear or to see
how tired you are at last of me!" Picking up this phrase, he
wrote: "I *could* blot that out of your mind for ever by a very
few words *now*,—for you *would believe* me at this moment,
close on the other subject:—but I will take no such advantage—
I will wait." "May God bless you," he ended, "—in what is past
and to come! I pray that from my heart, being yours R. B."

To a letter crossing his, written that same day, Robert made
no reply. Three days later Elizabeth asked in an agitated note,
had she vexed him? Would he please write? In the meantime
she heard from him. Sitting alone on an autumn evening, the
sun coming golden into his room, Browning was thinking of her,
but the words would not come. "It must be for another time
. . after Monday, when I am to see you."

But a lover's impatience overcame him that night: he wrote
a second letter:

I believe in you absolutely, utterly—I believe that when you bade me, that time, be silent—that such was your bidding, and I was silent—dare I say I think you did not know at that time the power I have over myself, that I could sit and speak and listen as I have done since? Let me say now—this only once—that I loved you from my soul, and gave you my life, so much of it as you would take,—and all that is done, not to be altered now: it was, in the nature of the proceeding, wholly independent of any return on your part. . . . If I thought you were like other women I have known, I should say so much!—but—(my first and last word—I believe in you!)—what you could and would give me, of your affection, you would give nobly and simply and as a giver—you would not need that I tell you—(tell you!)—what would be supreme happiness to me in the event—however distant . . . I will never recur to this, nor shall you see the least difference in my manner next Monday.

A postscript makes it clear that now there was a project for a winter in Italy. "I trust," he wrote, "you see your . . dare I say your *duty* in the Pisa affair, as all else *must* see it—"

In reply Elizabeth asked, with some simplicity, how she could have provoked this letter?

Can I forgive myself for having even seemed to provoke it? and will you believe me that if for the past's sake you sent it, it was unnecessary, and if for the future's, irrelevant? . . . if a thousand more such words were said by you to me, how could they operate upon the future or present, supposing me to choose to keep the possible modification of your feelings, as a probability, in my sight and yours?

Clearly that first denial of love was still having an effect: it might be now a mere noble pity this chivalrous poet felt for her.

She did not deny her own feeling:

I cannot help adding that, of us two, yours has not been quite the hardest part . . I mean, to a generous nature like your own, to which every sort of nobleness comes easily. Mine has been more difficult—and I have sunk under it again and again: and the sinking and the effort to recover the duty of a lost position, may have given me an appearance of vacillation and lightness, unworthy at least of you, and perhaps of both of us.

She never could allow him to take

the step of wasting, in a sense, your best feelings . . of empty-
ing your water gourds into the sand . . . you may well trust
me *to remember to my life's end, as the grateful remember; and*
to feel, as those do who have felt sorrow (for where these pits
are dug, the water will stand), the full price of your regard.

The journey to Pisa was now arranged: if Elizabeth could
bring herself, in defiance of her father, to involve the brother
and sister needed to accompany her, she would soon be on her
way. Browning had his plans too. "You were in jest," she wrote,
"about being at Pisa *before or as soon as we were?*—oh no—that
must not be indeed—we must wait a little!—even if you determine to go at all, which is a question of doubtful expediency."
Elizabeth might have been unselfish, humble in self-abnegation,
but she was also in love. There was now no question of taking
the obvious way, by forbidding him to follow, of putting an end
to the danger of being as a flint stone in the smoothness of his
path.

This letter was not sent until well after their meeting the next
day, September 1: Elizabeth seems to have waited to be examined by Dr. Chambers before posting it. On the 3rd an anxious
Browning sent her a note: "Will you not tell me something
about you—the head; and that too, *too* warm hand . . or
was it my fancy? Surely the report of Dr. Chambers is most
satisfactory,—all seems to rest with yourself." Later that day
he received the letter and wrote again. "Before you leave
London, I will answer your letter—all my attempts end in nothing now."

Six letters passed between them, friendly, informative, before Browning wrote that one in his heart. If he could win her
affection—he did not dare to aspire to her love—Elizabeth might
be sure that he would be content:

I am not what your generous self-forgetting appreciation would
sometimes make me out—but it is not since yesterday, nor ten
nor twenty years before, that I began to look into my own life,
and study its end, and requirements, what would turn to its
good or its loss—and I know, *if one may know anything, that to*
make that life yours and increase it by union with yours, would
render me supremely happy, *as I said, and say, and feel. My*
whole suit to you is, in that sense, selfish—*not that I am ignorant*

that your *nature would most surely attain happiness in being
conscious that it made another happy—but* that best, best end
of all, *would, like the rest, come from yourself, be a reflection of
your own gift.*

Browning's chosen way of life had included no wife in its
scheme:

*for my own future way in the world I have always refused to
care—anyone who can live a couple of years and more on bread
and potatoes as I did once on a time, and who prefers a blouse
and a blue shirt (such as I now write in) to all manner of
dress and gentlemanly appointment, and who can, if necessary,
groom a horse not so badly . . . such an one need not very
much concern himself beyond considering the lilies how they
grow. But now I see you near this life, all changes—and at a
word, I will do all that ought to be done . . . and let "all my
powers find sweet employ" as Dr. Watts sings, in getting whatever is to be got—not very much, surely. I would print these
things, get them away, and do this now, and go to you at Pisa
with the news—at Pisa where one may live for some £100 a
year.*

Charles Kean has offered him £500 for a play, and Mr. Colburn, the publisher, wants "more than his dinner" a novel on
the subject of Napoleon. "So may one make money, if one does
not live in a house in a row."

On the 16th Elizabeth wrote sadly affirming the impossibility
of marriage. God had put a barrier between them. "As dear Mr.
Kenyon said to me to-day in his smiling kindness . . 'In ten
years you may be strong perhaps.'" Browning must give up all
thought of her but as a friend.

There was another obstacle, her father's implacability in the
matter of marriage: "if he knew that you had written to me *so,*
and that I had answered you—*so,* even, [he] would not forgive
me at the end of ten years—" Poverty could be in itself no bar,
since if she "*wished* to be very poor, in the world's sense of poverty," she could not be so "with three or four hundred a year of
which no living will can dispossess me."

"The obstacles then are of another character, and the stronger
for being so. . . . The subject will not bear consideration—it
breaks in our hands."

But Browning, in his great tenderness, his innate wisdom, could handle the subject gently enough to preserve it fresh: "Those obstacles are solely for *you* to see and to declare . . . and perhaps they strike me the more from my true, honest unfeigned inability to imagine what they are. . . . Your regard for me is *all* success—let the rest come, or not come." He can hardly promise to change his affections,

put them elsewhere &c. &c. That would be pure foolish talking, and quite foreign to the practical results which you will attain in a better way from a higher motive . . . in sober earnest, it is not because I renounced once for all oxen and the owning and having to do with them, that I will obstinately turn away from any unicorn when such an apparition blesses me . . but meantime I shall walk at peace on our hills here nor go looking in all corners for the bright curved horn! . . .

One final word on the other matters—the "worldly matters"— I shall own I alluded to them rather ostentatiously because—because—that would be the one poor sacrifice I could make you— one I would cheerfully make, but a sacrifice, and the only one: this careless "sweet habitude of living" . . . I feel sure that whenever I make up my mind to that, I can be rich enough and to spare—because along with what you have thought genius in me, is certainly talent, that the world recognizes as such.

He gave her an instance of ability: at the time his "Paracelsus" was laughed to scorn in the press ten years before, an Elementary French book, on a new plan, was praised; "which I 'did' for my old French master, and he published—'that was really an useful work'!"

At the end Robert broke into the first directly tender words he had permitted himself, calling her: dearest, my dearest, dearest. "I will wait. God bless you and reward you—I kiss your hands *now*." The postscript, practical again, mentioned his inquiries into shipping to Leghorn.

A letter crossed his: "it is all over with Pisa. . . . I spoke face to face and quite firmly—so as to pass with my sisters for the 'bravest person in the house' without contestation." The next day Elizabeth wrote telling Robert that, precarious as her health must always be, she would not accept sacrifices from him, and in no case could she permit "an exchange of higher work for lower work." In the last paragraph there is a touch of bitterness. "I had done *living*, I thought, when you came and sought me out! and why? and to what end? *That*, I cannot help thinking now." The hope of Pisa was not, however, entirely extinct, though but feebly flickering. On the same day, September 18, she wrote again:

Papa has been walking to and fro in this room, looking thoughtfully and talking leisurely—and every moment I have expected I confess, some word (that did not come) about Pisa. Mr. Kenyon thinks it cannot end so—and I do sometimes—and in the meantime I do confess to a little "savageness" also—at heart! All I asked him to say the other day, was that he was not displeased with me—and he wouldn't; and for me to walk across his displeasure spread on the threshold of the door, and moreover take a sister and brother with me, and do such a thing for the sake of going to Italy and securing a personal advantage, were altogether impossible, obviously impossible! So poor Papa is quite in disgrace with me just now—if he would but care for that!

Browning, before he received this, wisely keeping that tone of sweet reason most salutary to her agitated state of mind, remarked in his letter that all he desired of life was

to live and just write out certain things which are in me, and so save my soul. . . . That you cannot dance like Cerito does not materially disarrange this plan—nor . . . the incidental, particular and unexpected happiness of being allowed when not working to rather occupy myself with watching you . . . this, also, does not constitute an obstacle, as I see obstacles.

But Elizabeth, though she may have been softened, would not relent: "we cannot see the same thing in the same light." She advised him to go, for the sake of his health, to Pisa, with some Italian friends.

Her own plan for Pisa was not yet entirely given up. George had come home: he and she would speak. Arabel had offered to go with her "at whatever hazard," but this Elizabeth could not allow. On the heels of this letter Elizabeth spoke again to her father without result, "only with bitterer feelings on one side. If I go or stay they *must* be bitter: words have been said that I cannot easily forget, nor remember without pain." Mr. Barrett had complained about the "undutifulness and rebellion" of everyone in the house. When told that she felt her prospects of health depended on going abroad that winter

but that through my affection for him, I was ready to sacrifice those to his pleasure if he exacted it—only it was necessary to my self-satisfaction in future years, to understand definitely that the sacrifice was exacted by him and was made to him, . . and not thrown away blindly and by a misapprehension. And he would not answer that. I might do my own way, he said —he would not speak—he would not say that he was not displeased with me, nor the contrary:—I had better do what I liked:—for his part, he washed his hands of me altogether.

Elizabeth might have extracted some sort of comfort from an admission that it was his love that held her there, to the detriment of health, but even this Mr. Barrett would not concede, though she gave him an opening.

We know that Elizabeth, so lucid on paper, found it always difficult to express feeling in words: her father had not even this consolation, the relief of a born writer. It seems unlikely that the case was put so clearly or so well as it was in her lettter. As with many inarticulate people, they both probably said foolish, hurtful, and misleading things. The tragedy between father and daughter had begun. Mr. Barrett could not have been the more placated if he knew that the brother who proposed to go with her was the gentle, affectionate Stormie, now his eldest son.

George advised her to continue preparations for the voyage: he at the last minute would again state the case to the "highest authority" and judge whether it would be possible for her to go with brother and sister. She asked Browning's advice. George considered that the father's displeasure would fall upon her in either case, whether she went or stayed.

Browning had hitherto restrained himself from comment on Elizabeth's father but now he wrote: "I truly wish *you* may never feel what I have to bear in looking on, quite powerless, and silent, while you are subjected to this treatment, which I refuse to characterize—so blind is it *for* blindness." She must nerve herself to action:

all passive obedience and implicit submission of will and intellect is by far too easy, if well considered, to be the course prescribed by God to Man in this life of probation—for they evade

probation altogether, though foolish people think otherwise.
Chop off your legs, you will never go astray. . . .

Circumstances had now shifted, placing her in what he could
only consider the veriest slavery:

and I who could *free you from it, I am here scarcely daring to*
write . . though I know you must feel for me and forgive
what forces itself from me . . what retires so mutely into my
heart at your least word. . . . *Now, while I* dream, *let me once*
dream! I would marry you now and thus—I would come when
you let me, and go when you bade me—I would be no more than
one of your brothers—"no more"— . . . *when your head ached*
I should be here.

When Elizabeth again made her answer of self-abnegation,
of a determination not to take "a base advantage of certain noble extravagances," she could not, as an unmarried woman, have
realized to the full the greatness of this lover's gesture; though
perhaps, even if knowing what such a statement meant to a natural man, she might still have felt that it was made out of love
for an idea, or from pity. However Browning might protest,
that foolish letter about ice-pits and fire-eyes was still having
its effect. But this last letter, his generous offer, did move her to
promise that if God

should free me within a moderate time from the trailing chain
of this weakness, I will then be to you whatever at that hour
you shall choose . . whether friend or more than friend . .
a friend to the last in any case . . . only in the meanwhile you
are most absolutely free . . "unentangled" (as they call it)
by the breadth of a thread . . . you cannot force me to think
contrary to my first thought . . that it were better for you to
forget me at once in one relation.

A note came to her on that same day: "oh, do not fear I am
'*entangled*'—my crown is loose on my head, not nailed there—
my pearl lies in my hand—I may return it to the sea, if I will!"
One can hear a joyful laugh in the very words.

Elizabeth was now making plans to sail in almost a month's
time: but the decision to break away from her father was not
yet final. Her "foot is in the air," she told Horne, "balanced on
the probability of a departure from England." To Browning she
sent a plea not to think too hardly of "poor Papa. You have his

wrong side . . his side of peculiar wrongness . . to you just now. When you have walked round him you will have other thoughts of him."

To an expressed wish that she should take this momentous journey wrapped in a cloak of his, Elizabeth must say no: "do you remember . . do you consider . . how many talkers there are in this house, and what would be talked—or that it is not worth while to provoke it all? And Papa, knowing it, would not like it." It is clear that Mr. Barrett was aware of Browning's continued visits though probably not that they were weekly: to the end there seems to have been no suspicion that Robert was anything more than a literary acquaintance.

The plan of destination veered from Pisa to Malta, from Malta and Pisa, as steamers seemed at the moment most convenient and possible, but by October 6 Pisa was fixed upon. "Oh, to be in Pisa. Now that E. B. B. is there!" Browning wrote happily. "And I *shall* be there . ."

On October 11 Elizabeth is wavering: "no: I shall not go." It remained for George to speak to her father. Mr. Barrett was still relentless in his disapproval of insubordination. His evening visits to her room had been wholly withdrawn; those precious moments of confidence always ending with prayer offered up both together, and separately by him on his daughter's account, humbly upon his knees before God:

the thing is quite expressively significant. Not that I pretend to complain, nor to have reason to complain. One should not be grateful for kindness, only while it lasts: that would be a short-breathed gratitude. I just tell you the fact, proving that it cannot be accidental.

A new anxiety was upon her: Occy had been seized with "a fever of the typhoid character" which the doctor thought might be infectious. Browning, who robustly disbelieved in contagion from fevers, refused to forgo his next visit, scouting Elizabeth's fear for him. This scepticism showed more fortitude than it would in our own day: to the London of the 'forties, with its filthy, pullulating slums, its contaminated water and lack of sanitation, typhoid was an ugly, a terrifying word indeed.

On October 13, with an arrangement made to sail on the 17th, George spoke to his father, pressing the matter with some an-

ger. Mr. Barrett's pronouncement settled the question; that she
might go if she pleased, "but that going it would be under his
heaviest displeasure." Mr. Kenyon had said one day that under
her "Ba-lambishness" there was a tigress-nature "distinctly cog-
nizable": in defence of health and happiness Elizabeth might
have stood out against her father, but she could not involve
Arabel and Stormie in that heaviest of displeasures. The "Ba-
lambishness," family affection, must prevail. Perhaps in this decision was some measure of relief: before George had spoken
Elizabeth had felt "as if the house stood upon gunpowder, and
as if I had held Guy Fawkes's lantern in my right hand." The
habit of years, a long obedience, was not for this frail woman,
however nerved by love, easy to break through. Her brother's
entreaty had not even softened Mr. Barrett into permission for
at least a removal to a warmer part of England. In a man who
had sacrificed domestic comfort in 1840, and allowed Bro to
stay on with Elizabeth at Torquay, this decision against a compromise that would have kept her within reach seems inexplica-
ble except by the thesis that, with advancing years, an absolute
power had twisted the man's nature.

The kindness of Elizabeth's sisters, who begged her not to
consider them, made Elizabeth the more determined not to embroil her family. She would take up her chain once more, a
chain made heavier by Mr. Barrett's continued displeasure. His
visits to her room were now confined to a hasty five minutes before dressing for dinner. "The bitterest 'fact' of all is, that I believed Papa to have loved me more than he obviously does: but
I never regret knowledge . . I mean I never would *un*know
anything . . even were it the taste of the apples by the Dead
sea—and this must be accepted like the rest." George went further in an estimate of his father's attitude to Elizabeth, asserting roundly more than once: "He does not love you—you need
not think it."

Browning declared bravely that their disappointment would
"be seen for the best in the end." With a dream of perfect happiness cruelly postponed now that Elizabeth's health was again
imperilled by a London winter, he must be content with
snatches of joy, the letters and many more months of those visits; visits which must secretly humiliate a proud man since they

were, and in those days of formal etiquette, made to the house
of one who would not take the trouble to receive him. Moreover, he went under a false pretence of mere friendship: if it
should come to Mr. Barrett's knowledge that Browning was his
daughter's lover he would be summarily ejected.

Elizabeth composed herself to resignation. "My cage is not
worse but better since you brought the green groundsel to it—
and to dash oneself against the wires of it will not open the
door."

Better still, the caged bird was not now an ailing one. A state
of chronic invalidism had turned to hope, and the sick soul from
the grave. With Elizabeth all was changed.

> "My future will not copy fair my past"—
> *I wrote that once; and thinking at my side*
> *My ministering life-angel justified*
> *The word by his appealing look upcast*
> *To the white throne of God, I turned at last,*
> *And there, instead, saw thee, not unallied*
> *To angels in thy soul! Then I, long tried*
> *By natural ills, received the comfort fast.*
> *While budding, at thy sight, my pilgrim's staff*
> *Gave out green leaves with morning dews impearled.*
> *I seek no copy now of life's first half:*
> *Leave here the pages with long musing curled,*
> *And write me new my future's epigraph*
> *New angel mine, unhoped for in the world!*

CHAPTER 18

LOVE AND EXPECTATION [1845–6]

LOVE, NOW ACKNOWLEDGED, made Browning's visits dearer but
more fearful. The one weekly visit of which Mr. Barrett knew
was "a thing established," and perhaps a more frequent call
might be risked now and then. But, Elizabeth wrote, "I am Cas-
sandra, you know, and smell the slaughter in the bath-room."

Elizabeth did not stop to consider how this impulsive and sinister dramatization might agitate a lover. What sort of danger
could she be in from an angry man, one of whom he, Browning,
had no personal knowledge? How far would Elizabeth in her
unselfishness conceal persecution, indignities from him? Not
wishing perhaps further to disturb her, Robert made no direct
reference to the situation but when they met, and the question
of visits arose, he evidently tried cautiously to draw her. From
his attitude Elizabeth thought that he had not fully grasped
the implications.

On October 22 she wrote him a difficult letter; a letter tremulous with apprehension, emotion, to which she begged him not
to reply. There might be an occasional second call in the week
"if there is no habit . . do you understand? I may be prudent
in an extreme perhaps—and certainly everybody in the house is
not equally prudent!" Her father's anger at discovery of the
true position "the tongue of men and of angels would not mod-
ify so as to render less full of vexations to you." Only now had
she fully considered the extent to which, in the case of open
conflict, Robert might suffer. Perhaps it would be better if he
went abroad at once; indeed, retreat from the engagement altogether. They had been too carried away by recent events and
had forgotten "the other obvious evils, which the late decision
about Pisa has aggravated beyond calculation . . for as the
smoke rolls off we see the harm done by the fire." For her part,
she would have his letters and could hope to see him on his return. The decision must be taken for both their sakes:

*If it should be your choice not to make an end now, . . why
I shall understand* that *by your not going . . or you may say
"no" in a word . . for I require no "protestations" indeed—
and* you *may trust to* me . . *it shall be as you choose.* You
will consider my happiness most by considering your own . .
and that is my last word.

But Browning would never allow his woman her last word;
knowing perhaps intuitively that inarticulate people should not
be allowed to brood. Gently he wrote telling her that his concern was for her only. "In this case, knowing you, I was sure that
if any imaginable form of displeasure could touch you without
reaching me, I should not hear of it too soon—so I spoke."

With a large gesture he swept aside her scruples, "the grace
of your imaginary self-denial, and fidelity to a given word, and
noble constancy; but it all happens to be none of mine, none in
the least."

*I love you because I love you; I see you "once a week" because
I cannot see you all day long; I think of you all day long, because I most certainly could not think of you once an hour less,
if I tried, or went to Pisa, or "abroad" (in every sense) in order
to "be happy" . . a kind of adventure which you seem to suppose you have in some way interfered with. . . . Do, for this
once, think, and never after, on the impossibility of your ever
(you know I must talk your own language, so I shall say—) hin-
dering any scheme of mine, stopping any supposable advance-
ment of mine. Do you really think that before I found you, I
was going about the world seeking whom I might devour, that
is, be devoured by, in the shape of a wife . . do you suppose
I ever dreamed of marrying?*

This virile assertion of Browning's went a long way towards
expunging the traces of doubt left by that "ice-pit" "fire-eyes"
letter of six months before: "really and truly," Elizabeth told
him, "I have sometimes felt jealous of myself . . of my own
infirmities, . . and thought that you cared for me only because your chivalry touched them with a silver sound—"

Her caution, she must repeat, referred not to her brothers
and sisters, who would "be glad if I was glad," but "to one person alone. In relation to *whom*, however, there will be no 'getting over'—you might as well think to sweep off a third of the

stars of Heaven with the motion of your eyelashes—" But, though she had been a submissive and was still a loving daughter, Elizabeth had always reserved a right over her own affections "even though I *never* thought (except perhaps when the door of life was just about to open . . before it opened) never thought it probable or possible that I should have occasion for the exercise; from without and from within at once."

One reason for hesitation over the retreat to Pisa must, though it is never mentioned in the letters, have been the serious character of her brother's illness: by the end of October, however, Occy's worst symptom was "too great an appetite . . a monster-appetite indeed." During this month of anxiety, of disappointed hope, a distraction and consolation was the preparation of Robert's proofs. The new *Bells and Pomegranates* was to present to the world many of Browning's most popular poems: "The Lost Leader," "How They Brought the Good News," "The Lost Mistress," the lovely song "Nay, but you who do not love her," "The Last Ride Together," "Saul," and "Home Thoughts from Abroad." Alterations suggested by Elizabeth for the sake of harmony and of clarity were gratefully adopted by the poet.

Browning, working with a distracted mind on the closet-drama "Luria," begged Elizabeth to make every effort to improve her health. "Why, we shall see Italy together! I could, would, *will* shut myself in four walls of a room with you and never leave you and be most of all *then* 'a lord of infinite space' —but, to travel with you to Italy, or Greece."

As always with lovers, Elizabeth's world of feeling and interest dwindled to smaller proportions: the old pleasure in a visit from Miss Mitford was marred by a new fatigue, a fear "of questions with a pair of woman's eyes behind them; and these are worse than Mr. Kenyon's, when he puts on his spectacles." To Kenyon she thought it wise to confess to "visits 'generally once a week' . . . he has looked at me with scanning spectacles already and talked of its being a mystery to him how you made your way here." Those spectacles were to become more searching, more alarming as the months went by.

In this letter of November 6 Elizabeth conquered her shyness and spoke out on a subject at which she had been hinting ever since they were betrothed: the return to her of the first rash declaration of love. But "that untoward letter" was irretrievably lost. "I burned it," Robert told her, "and cried 'serve it right!' Poor letter,—yet I should have been vexed and offended *then* to be told that I *could* love you better than I did already."

In the middle of November comes the first mention of her "amreeta draught," her "elixir," the morphine that Elizabeth took under medical orders

to keep the pulse from fluttering and fainting . . to give the right composure and point of balance to the nervous system. I don't take it for my "spirits" in the usual sense; you must not think such a thing. . . . I do not suffer from it in any way, as people usually do who take opium. I am not even subject to an opium-headache.

And even, when in despair, when a lowness of spirit might seem justified, she could always be cheerful, so cheerful that it was frequently remarked upon:

Nobody has known that it was an effort (a habit of effort) to throw the light on the outside,—I do abhor so that ignoble groaning aloud of "the groans of Testy and Sensitive" [1]—*yet I may say that for three years I never was conscious of one movement of pleasure in anything.*

This effort of will, this fortitude, is hardly the attribute of a drugged woman: if Elizabeth's words are literally true, that she took forty drops of laudanum a day, it would seem as if she had a quite exceptional constitution, an immunity found in general only among Eastern peoples. It is, however, possible that Elizabeth only thought that she habitually took so strong a dose: invalids have been deceived before in such matters by those around them. But that she had contracted a habit, and one not approved by her father, is suggested by the earlier admonition to George not to mention opium in his letters. Doctors might prescribe, might in a lesser or greater degree encourage the drug-taking, but Browning, wiser than his own generation, exhorted her to abandon it. She consulted her medical advisers and, three months later, we hear of a determination gradually to lessen the doses to that end: "after all the lotus-eaters are

---

[1] Mistranscribed as "Sensitude" in the *Letters*. See Rev. James Beresford: *The Miseries of Human Life, or The Groans of Timothy Testy and Samuel Sensitive* (1806).

blessed beyond the opium-eaters; and the best of lotuses are
such thoughts as I know."

The conception of Browning as in love with an idea was not
entirely done away with. Robert found it necessary to declare
categorically: "if you COULD tell me when I next sit by you—'I
will undeceive you, I am not *the* Miss B.—she is up-stairs and
you shall see her—I only wrote those letters, and am what you
see, that is all now left you,' " and if by some chance this misunderstanding could have been none of Elizabeth's doing, it
would make no difference to his love. Indeed, he might love her
the more, "having a right to expect more strength with the
strange emergency." If he had approached her only from admiration of her work, he might have done so years before: it was
the mention of himself in "Lady Geraldine's Courtship" that
had led him to write that first letter:

on the whole, UNWILLINGLY *. . with consciousness of having*
to speak on a subject which I felt thoroughly concerning, and
could not be satisfied with an imperfect expression of. As for ex-
pecting THEN *what has followed . . I shall only say I was*
scheming how to get done with England and go to my heart in
Italy.

And now, my love—I am round you . . my whole life is
wound up and down and over you . . I feel you stir every-
where. I am not conscious of thinking or feeling but about you,
with some reference to you—so will I live, so may I die!

He had been reading her sonnet "Past and Future," which
affected him more than any other poem of hers. The companion sonnet, with its deep joy in a renewal of life, Robert was not
to see until three years after marriage; but that it was written
now, in mute answer to the sadder lyric, is clear. In her reply
Elizabeth told him: "I sate by while the angel stirred the water,
and I called it *Miracle.* Do not blame me now . . *my* angel!"

At the end of November Browning complained whimsically
that, although by some process she seemed to know whether he
was looking well or ill, he had not had a glimpse of her eyes
since the day on which they first met. "I only know yours are
there, and have to use that memory as if one carried dried flowers about when fairly inside the garden-enclosure." The beauty
of Elizabeth's eyes, veiled by long eyelashes, was praised by

others than Miss Mitford: the brilliant look of them, redeeming
a sickly face, would linger long in the memory of the beholder.
So shy was Elizabeth still of Robert that on sending him a ring
containing her hair she begged him not to refer to it when they
met. At Browning's request she gave him too a curl of that dark
hair: at his death a gold locket containing it was taken from
about his neck. For this lock she demanded one of his:

> *The soul's Rialto hath its merchandise;*
> *I barter curl for curl upon that mart.*

Their letters now—soon, with few omissions, to be written every
day of the week—are full of that recapitulation, so dear to lovers, of the growth of love, of a knitting together of personal
relations.

Mr. Kenyon, perhaps suspecting the case, began to ask Elizabeth awkward questions about Browning's visits: Browning's
name was naturally much in his mouth because of an ecstatic
delight in the new *Bells and Pomegranates*, "Dramatic Romances and Lyrics," published in November 1845 and dedicated
to Kenyon. "Saul," his favourite, Kenyon read every night before going to sleep "to put his dreams in order."

This little paper-covered volume, as modest as its predeces-
sors and published again at the expense of Browning's father,
strongly stimulated that lively but limited literary interest
aroused by the poet; and especially among the youthful Pre-
Raphaelites to whom Browning became an idol to be worshipped, conned over, illustrated in paint and pencil. The greatest honour to "Dramatic Romances," bringing particular pride
and pleasure to all those in Browning's immediate circle, was a
poetical tribute from the revered Landor, "There is delight in
singing," printed in the *Morning Chronicle* after it had been
privately circulated among friends by the elder Browning.

With Elizabeth there was, beyond the love sonnets, no composition during this period of waiting: she was content to be—
perhaps for the first time in life—deliciously idle, "leaning out of
some turret-window of the castle of Indolence and watching
the new sunrise." Her only published work was for an annual
volume that summer and some small translations from the
Greek for a book of Mrs. Jameson's in the spring of 1846. When
in October a request came from America that the *Athenæum*

prose papers might be issued in book form, there and in England, Elizabeth could not apparently bring herself to make the revision she considered necessary: the papers were not collected together until 1862, after her death.

One of the minor miracles of love in that turret room of the Castle of Indolence was the continued life of flowers that Robert brought her; so long as the season lasted, from his mother's garden. In that close room where plants and flowers withered and died, his offerings remained fresh; perhaps because Elizabeth cared for them tenderly. There were some little blue blossoms that she particularly cherished: "while I was putting them in water," she wrote him once, "I thought your visit went on all the time."

These visits, so dear to them both, Robert had from the beginning recorded. At the end of November, putting the precious minutes together, he had spent the equivalent of two whole days with her. "I enter the room determining to get up and go sooner . . and I go away into the light street repenting that I went so soon by I don't know how many minutes."

One of Browning's minor pleasures was an acquaintance in the world outside with George, whom he met at Kenyon's and elsewhere. He liked the grave legal brother: "It comforts me that he is yours." Though there can be little space for the many good stories told in these letters by Browning, perhaps one may be mentioned here. Browning and George met at the house of Serjeant Talfourd, famous in his day for the poetic drama "Ion." On a side table they found a "portentous book lettered and thick as a law-book" of congratulatory letters upon "Ion." Browning discovered his own and two of Elizabeth's [2] bound and indexed. This piece of bad taste, though it was annoying, amused them all. George in particular enjoyed his sister's discomfiture when at first she had thought that her rather effusive girlish letters had been read by Browning. But Browning, who was very short-sighted in one eye, could not see the open page as George held the book, and a closer scrutiny of "what was so unfairly exposed to view" he had neither sought nor desired.

Browning's anxiety for Elizabeth, mutely defying her father within the castle of home, was not allayed: there seems to have

[2] One is in the Hagedorn Collection.

been within him an underlying fear that he might lose her, that she might not have strength to resist Mr. Barrett's anger. This, she assured him, could never be "since I am yours, while I am of any worth to you at all." He had suggested a certain sealed letter, perhaps to be put directly into her father's hand in case of discovery; but, Elizabeth wrote, such a note would be no defence to her. "Only one person holds the thunder—and I shall be thundered at; I shall not be reasoned with—it is impossible." And really they stood in little danger. "Let there be ever so many suspectors, there will be no informers." "Why not," she asked, "leave that future to itself? For me, I sit in the track of the avalanche quite calmly . . so calmly so as to surprise myself at intervals—and yet I know the reason of the calmness well." Browning, with a lover's apprehension, a poet's imagination, and his own vivid sense of drama could not view the position so calmly: the very contrast of the Barrett household to his own home, so free from parental tyranny, must have aggravated the sore in his mind. It is no wonder that headaches, the nervous tension, continued.

In the middle of January Robert again expressed that gnawing anxiety: "as I sate by you, so full of the truest life, for this world as for the next,—and was struck by the possibility, all that might happen were I away, in the case of you continuing to acquiesce—dearest it *is* horrible—I could not but speak." When she felt strong enough and ready to come to him he must, in their approach to her father, have "the man's right of first speech. *I* stipulate, too, and require to say my own speech in my own words, or by letter—remember! But this living without you is too tormenting now. So begin thinking,—as for Spring, as for a New Year, as for a new life."

In her reply Elizabeth disabused his mind as to any idea of a normal approach to Mr. Barrett:

from the moment of a suspicion entering one *mind, we should be able to meet never again in this room, nor to have intercourse by letter through the ordinary channel. I mean, that letters of yours, addressed to me here, would infallibly be stopped and destroyed—if not opened. Therefore it is advisable to hurry on nothing—on these grounds it is advisable. What should I do if I did not see you nor hear from you, without being able to feel that it was for your happiness? What should I do for a month even? And then, I might be thrown out of the window or its equivalent—I look back shuddering to the dreadful scenes in which poor Henrietta was involved who never offended as I have offended.*

Elizabeth then told him the story of Henrietta and the lover whom she had been forced to reject; how, suffering from sympathy, she herself, though perfectly well at the time, had fallen into a dead faint in trying to follow Henrietta from the room. Both sisters now knew of the engagement and fully approved; indeed, Henrietta was in a like position to herself.

The situation was made harder to Browning by his own inherent love of freedom, his hatred of tyranny. He told her of a familiar nightmare dream: "I stand by (powerless to interpose by a word even) and see the infliction of tyranny on the unresisting man or beast (generally the last)—and I wake just in time not to die: let no one try this kind of experiment on me or mine!" He then told her the story of a man, his host, who had insulted a meek wife before guests. Browning had bided his time, but at the first opportunity had expressed his contempt for the husband "and at the end marched out of the room." His host followed him to the front door completely bewildered. "What *can* have possessed you, my *dear* B?"

In the middle of January, on an exceptionally warm day, Elizabeth took one more step towards freedom by walking downstairs into the drawing-room, surprising her family "as much as if I had walked out of the window instead."

The naturally sanguine Robert was, by February 6, eagerly looking forward:

Then see the bright weather while I write—lilacs, hawthorn, plum-trees all in bud; elders in leaf, rose-bushes with great red shoots; thrushes, whitethroats, hedge sparrows in full song— there can, let us hope, be nothing worse in store than a sharp wind, a week of it perhaps—and then comes what shall come—

In five days winter had descended once more: the pond before Browning's window was frozen over.

It has been said that Elizabeth, feeling reserve with them and fearing questions, now found irksome the visits of friends, of Kenyon and Miss Mitford in particular. There must be restraint

ELIZABETH BARRETT BROWNING
*a bust executed after her death by William Wetmore Story; an
example of it is in the Keats-Shelley Memorial House, Rome*

ROBERT WIEDEMAN ("PEN") BROWNING
from a photograph taken in Rome in 1861

too in letters: to Mrs. Martin however this spring she hinted at
a change of circumstance. Mrs. Martin, recovering from an illness at Hastings, wished Elizabeth could be there too. "I can
lose nothing here," Elizabeth wrote to this old friend, "shut up
in my prison, and the nightingales come to my windows and
sing through the sooty panes." A direct reference to Browning
could not be kept out: "A friend of mine too—one of the greatest poets in England—brought me primroses and polyanthuses
the other day, as they are grown in Surrey!"

The cold spell did not last long: the rest of the winter and the
spring were mercifully mild that year. On February 27 Elizabeth went down alone to the drawing-room and surprised Henrietta singing at the pianoforte. Henrietta tried to persuade her
to remain in order to "see the great sight of Capt. Surtees Cook
—*plus* his regimentals—fresh from the royal presence at St.
James's." It would also be Elizabeth's first introduction to Henrietta's accepted lover, William Surtees Cook, who had, by
sheer perseverance and a strong emotional appeal, ousted two
other suitors. Captain Surtees Cook had one decided advantage
over his rivals in being a cousin of Mr. Barrett: he had therefore
a licence to come and go in the house, though hardly to pay his
addresses. His courtship was necessarily as clandestine as
Browning's.

A knock came at the front door. It was not the decorative
Captain who was announced, but Mrs. Jameson. Elizabeth,
who could not face Mrs. Jameson in the drawing-room "with
the prospect of the military descent in combination," begged
Henrietta to take Mrs. Jameson directly upstairs that she might
follow in a minute or two: "and the corollary of all this interesting history is," she wrote to Browning, "that being able to
talk at all after all that 'fuss,' and after walking 'upstairs and
downstairs' . . . proves my gigantic strength—now doesn't it?"

Mrs. Jameson, "kind beyond speaking of," brought a new
light to the lovers, a prospect of escape from open conflict.
Might she herself take Elizabeth to Italy? Others had offered to
do the same, but Elizabeth had so far hesitated that she had not
revealed this to Robert. Now she wanted his opinion. To this he
made no reply on paper, so we cannot tell what he thought.

At the beginning of March Mr. Barrett encountered Browning in the house one morning. Coming to Elizabeth's room for a moment before dressing for dinner, he showed a certain displeasure. "I was not *scolded*, do you understand. It was more manner, but my sisters thought as I did of the significance:— and it was enough to prove to me (if I had not known) what a desperate game we should be playing if we depended on a yielding nerve *there*."

Robert's anger against the domineering father, held in check till now, burst out a few days later in writing:

That a father choosing to give out of his whole day some five minutes to a daughter, supposed to be prevented from participating in what he, probably, in common with a whole world of sensible men, as distinguished from poets and dreamers, consider every pleasure of life, by a complete foregoing of society— that he, after the Pisa business and the enforced continuance, and as he must believe, permanence of this state in which any other human being would go mad—I do dare say, for the justification of God, who gave the mind to be used in this world, . . . that, under these circumstances, finding . . . what, you say, unless he thinks he does find, he would close the door of his house instantly; a mere sympathizing man, of the same literary tastes, who comes good-naturedly, on a proper and unexceptionable introduction, to chat with and amuse a little that invalid daughter, once a month, so far as is known, for an hour perhaps,—that such a father should show himself "not pleased plainly," at such a circumstance . . My Ba, it is SHOCKING!

He exhorted her to take advantage of the mild weather, to get strong in expectation of going to Italy before next winter.

Elizabeth in her reply wisely ignored the anger in Robert's outburst, explaining gently that it was not his visit as such which offended.

It was a sort of instinctive indisposition towards seeing you here, unexplained to himself, I have no doubt—of course unexplained, or he would have desired me to receive you never again, that would have been done at once and unscrupulously. But without defining his own feeling, he rather disliked seeing you here—it just touched one of his vibratory wires, brushed by and touched it—oh, we understand in this house.

She did her best to explain Mr. Barrett's attitude: "after using one's children as one's chattels for a time, the children drop lower and lower towards the level of the chattels, and the duty of human sympathy to them becomes difficult in proportion."

Robert wrote back more temperately:

I dare say I am unjust—hasty certainly . . . but if I ever see it right, exercising my intellect, to treat any human beings like my "chattels"—I shall pay for that mistake one day or another, I am convinced—and I very much fear that you would soon discover what one fault of mine is, if you were to hear anyone assert such a right in my presence.

Enjoying freedom, an apostle of freedom, Robert could not know or pity the inhibited man as proud in his own way and as secure of right; a man soon to receive a harsh blow from one dearest to him. Elizabeth, near to her father, loving him in spite of tyranny, could pity his loneliness, an alienation from his own children. When he was once laying down the law "about passive obedience, and particularly in respect to marriage," one by one his sons left the room. Captain Surtees Cook alone remained: to a meek question from the young man ambitious to be Mr. Barrett's son-in-law, "if children were to be considered slaves," Mr. Barrett's reply is unfortunately not recorded.

Browning, having finished "Luria," was now at work upon "A Soul's Tragedy." The first act Elizabeth found, was bound to find, gripping: it is one of Browning's finest pieces of dramatic writing. But of the whole she evidently thought it safer to generalize:

It is a new work with your mark on it. That is . . it would make some six or sixteen works for other people, if "cut up into little stars"—rolled out . . diluted with rain-water. But it is your work as it is—and if you do not care for that, I care, and shall remember to care on. It is a work full of power and significance.

If she had known him only by "Luria" and "A Soul's Tragedy," although "Luria" was "the completer work," it would have been "A Soul's Tragedy" that would have led her to attribute to its author "more power and a higher faculty."

All this is true, known to posterity to be true, but Browning himself could not but be dissatisfied with that heavy-footed

"Luria" and with the ill-made "A Soul's Tragedy." Both had been written with the surface of his mind. Obsessed as he was, tormented by the thought of Elizabeth, his heart, his soul, was not free enough for composition.

Elizabeth herself, not driven by the money urge, wisely abstained from any serious work beyond those sonnets which were a direct expression, a relief to an overcharged heart. Browning, who could not express himself so, had no such relief: love poetry was not for him until he was safely married. Rather reluctantly he sent those two valuable but imperfect works, the dramas of the first year of their engagement, to Moxon. "Luria" and "A Soul's Tragedy" were published in April as the last of the series *Bells and Pomegranates*.

A cold spell at the end of March, with winds and snow, prevented Elizabeth from those strengthening walks down to the drawing-room, but her health continued good. One night a howling melancholy wind brought her the sound of the sea and old sorrow, but with a difference: in happiness and a hope for the future the old surging misery echoed more remotely now. She could even feel glad of the estrangement from her father, because if he were kind and affectionate she would be the less willing to give him pain. "Ah well!" she added, "in any case I should have ended probably, in giving up all for you."

On April 4 Elizabeth went downstairs and, finding the drawing-room empty, came up again, meeting Flush half way. Flush, who had been sleeping when she left the room, leaped up against her "in such an ecstasy of astonished joy, that I nearly fell backward down the stairs." Flush was probably at this time disturbed in his faithful dog soul: he did not like this new affectionate visitor of hers, especially as he was of the wrong sex. "He hates," his mistress told Robert, "all unpetticoated people." When, later in the year, Browning arrived with an umbrella in his hand Flush openly flew at him. His contrition afterwards, when alone with his mistress, was profound: a certain bribery with cakes helped to smooth over a difficult situation.

That same day of Flush's agitation Robert started a subject which led to their first difference of opinion, that of duelling. Curiously enough he spoke in defence of it. Elizabeth, astonished, alarmed, spoke her mind. If Robert were ever to commit such an act in a fancied defence of honour she would "just *call in the police*, though you were to throw me out of the window afterwards." "Ever dearest," she begged, "do *you* promise me that you will never be provoked into such an act—never?" The next day she wrote nervously: "So I spoke my mind—and you are vexed with me, which I feel in the air. May God bless you dearest, dearest! Forgive as you can, best, Your Ba."

Browning wrote a long reasoned defence, with exemplars, of the custom of duelling on serious counts. Though giving no specific promise to abstain from duelling, he got very neatly out of the dilemma. He did not care enough, and had often reproached himself, for the ways of the world to go to an extreme in defence of righteous opinion: "*I*, angry! oh, how you misinterpret, misunderstand the motions of my mind! In all that I said, or write here, I speak of others—others, if you please, of limited natures: I say why *they* may be excused . . that is all. . . . Now, love, let this be a moot point to settle among the flowers one day."

Elizabeth, with her clear mind, detecting certain fallacies in his argument, maintained her position, that duelling was morally wrong. "Why should we see things so differently, ever dearest? If anyone had asked me, I could have answered for you that you saw it quite otherwise." But, with sweet femininity, she yielded a point. "You may be right and I wrong, of course—I only speak as I *see*. And will not speak any more last words . . taking pardon for these."

Elizabeth took his rather perverse arguments so much to heart that, brooding on what might arise from their dangerous situation, she worried herself into the old fears. Perhaps it would be better that they should part, that he should never be placed in a position where insult would be inevitable: perhaps in her feverous cloistered mind she even envisaged a clash, demanding a trial of honour, between Browning and a brother. He could not know what insult he might have to endure: "no, you *do not understand* . . you *cannot*, perhaps!" Such was her distress that Robert begged her to marry him at once and end those despairing fears, the need on his part so constantly to reaffirm his love: in an apology she told him that "through my want of familiarity with any happiness" "these weights of flowers" would drop "again and again out of weak hands."

Elizabeth escaped from the subject into news of Mr. Kenyon, who, "with those detestable spectacles—like the Greek burning glasses" turned full on her face, had said: "I suppose now that Mr. Browning's book is done and there are no more excuses for coming, he will come without excuses."

Some comment of Kenyon's on Browning's way of living, a worldly view of his lack of prospects, led Elizabeth to request that no reference should ever be made to their mutual circumstances; as "it is not of the least importance to either of us, as long as we live, whether the sixpence, we live by, came most from you or from me . . and as it will be as much mine as yours, and yours as mine, when we are together . . why let us join in throwing a little dust in all the winking eyes around," even those of her own family. This Robert agreed for the moment to do, though reserving to himself a right to speak on the subject later: almost certainly he had already determined on that marriage settlement which was his first care once they were well settled in Italy.

On April 16 Elizabeth wrote momentous news: she had been buying a bonnet. "And having chosen one a little like a Quaker's, as I thought to myself, I am immediately assured by the learned that 'nothing can be more fashionable.' " This preparation for "going out, walking out, driving out" delighted Robert, who, as a year before when he craved for a sight of Miss Barrett, wrote happily of spring, lambs bleating in a field behind the house, "beautiful sunshine . . . and a chestnut tree leafy all over, in a faint trembling chilly way, to be sure . . . and blossomed trees over the garden wall."

Two days later Kenyon came again, "spectacles and all. He sleeps in those spectacles now, I think." His first question was: "Have you seen Mr. Browning? And what did he come for again, pray?" Robert, fearing a more personal question to himself, wondered whether they should let Kenyon into their secret, but Elizabeth was firm. It was far better that nobody should be informed on what was strictly their own concern.

A cold wind came again, an east wind that confined Elizabeth to her room. On the 26th, in spite of a late spring, Robert was able to bring her a branch of sweetbriar to unfold its leaves in her room; by the first week of May its promise was fulfilled by a sudden warmth. On the 12th Elizabeth enclosed in her letter a laburnum blossom actually plucked by herself in Regent's Park:

we stopped the carriage and got out and walked, and I put both my feet on the grass, . . which was the strangest feeling! . . and gathered this laburnum for you. . . . . I never enjoyed any of my excursions as I did to-day's—the standing under the trees and on the grass, was so delightful. It was like a bit of that Dreamland which is your especial dominion. . . . It seemed illogical, *not to see you close by.*

"My Ba," Robert replied, "your flower is the one flower I have seen, or see, or shall see."

Mr. Barrett, who seems to have been kinder of late, brought his daughter some flowers; flowers which quickly died while Robert's remained triumphantly blooming. The contrast, the unexpected gift, brought sadness to Elizabeth. "I cannot draw a glad omen—I wish he had not given me these." It would appear strange that the constant presence of flowers in Ba's room aroused no suspicion in the dominating father's mind.

Mrs. Jameson's visits were almost as embarrassing as Kenyon's: Elizabeth wanted to talk to her of Robert, to praise him, and yet she must dread every reference. The two were linked one day in an alarming manner. Mr. Kenyon turned "those horrible spectacles" full upon Elizabeth and asked: "Does Mrs. Jameson know that Mr. Browning comes here?" "No," said Elizabeth, "suddenly abashed." "Well, then, I advise you to give directions to the servants that when she or anyone else asks for you, they should not say *Mr. Browning is with you,*—as they did the other day to Miss Bayley, who told me of it."

It was clear that behind those spectacles there was some measure of calculation. Elizabeth did not fear that he, or any other of her friends who knew the peculiarity of the household, would disapprove her marriage, or the proposed means of attaining it, but she did not want unduly to worry Mr. Kenyon, or jeopardize his friendship with the Barrett family. Her father would, on the slightest suspicion, be only too apt to say that

Kenyon had engineered the whole affair. Later this consideration for her cousin grew into a nervous anxiety: his cautious nature might lead him to attempt to divide them.

A Miss Heaton called and talked Elizabeth into complete exhaustion. In a knowing manner she gave some information
about Browning: how he had been engaged, with a strong attachment on both sides, to a lady who had broken off the engagement on the score of religious differences. This, given with
a request for secrecy, had "helped to tire" Elizabeth. Breaking
that implied promise she at once wrote of it to Browning. He,
no doubt amused and pleased by the small twinge of jealousy
clear in her words, wrote back light-heartedly: "they used to
get up better stories of Lord Byron."

Elizabeth, already accustomed as poet and romantic recluse
to letters adulatory, half amorous, eccentric, from strangers,
was now, with the amelioration of her health, to suffer a more
determined attack from those people who had tried in vain to
penetrate the house. One lady, encamped at 16, Wimpole
Street, frightened her by writing on the card attached to a
votive rose tree: "When are you going to Italy?" However close
the lovers might wrap themselves round with their secret some
fringe of it was bound to brush the public. Perhaps even some
dim consciousness of their love, or at least a close friendship,
had escaped the enchanted circle: Elizabeth again heard that
Browning was engaged to be married, this time to a Miss Campbell.

That her brothers well knew the situation was clear. On the
occasion of her next "Sunday-levée," when she was in the habit
of receiving all her brothers and sisters at once, a remark that
Ba and Mr. Browning were such *very* intimate friends met with
a wave of laughter: "on which, without any transition and with
an exceeding impertinence, Alfred threw himself down on the
sofa and declared that he felt inclined to be very ill, . . for
that then perhaps (such things being heard of) some young
lady might come to visit *him,* to talk sympathetically on the
broad and narrow gauge!"

In this letter Elizabeth told of a walk downstairs, out of doors,
and then up again with only a few rests on the stairs—"see how
vain-glorious I am. And what a summer-sense in the air—and

how lovely the strips of sky between the houses!" In a few days
the length of her walk had so far extended that Elizabeth was
obliged to allow Stormie to carry her upstairs. These walks
were, however, never more than a very short stroll: it is a measure of Elizabeth's weakness of body only a few months before
setting out on the great adventure that it was a matter of self-
congratulation when, on May 28, she posted a letter to Browning with her own hands at the office in Great Marylebone
Street,[3] just round the corner, a matter of some seventy yards
from the house. In Great Marylebone Street, at no. 6, was
Hodgson's, the bookseller, where she often rested on her way.
A chair awaited her: Flush soon began to consider the shop
sufficiently his own to snap at the shopboy. The dog's delight at
these outings, especially in the carriage, was almost, his mistress thought, beyond a natural thing. One day, while waiting
in the back drawing-room, she said: "Flush! go and see if the
carriage is come!" He ran at once to the front window, stood on
his hind legs, and looked up and down the street.

On the 30th Elizabeth walked in the Botanical Gardens, Regent's Park, again picking a flower to send to Robert; one this
time of especial significance:

Transie de peur, I was, . . listening to Arabel's declaration
that all gathering of flowers in these gardens is highly improper,
—and I made her finish her discourse, standing between me and
the gardeners—to prove that I was the better for it. . . .

The flower she picked, a pansy, was one peculiarly connected
with Dr. Paracelsus, "Cintrinula (flammula) herba Paracelso
multum familiaris"; confirming Robert when he received it in a
particularly happy and hopeful mood: "all bright things seem
possible."

Elizabeth continued in her letter:

What I enjoy most to see, is the green under the green . .
where the grass stretches under trees. . . . And to stand under
a tree and feel the green shadow of a tree! I never knew before
the difference of the sensation of a green shadow and a brown
one. I seemed to feel that green shadow through and through
me, till it went out at the soles of my feet and mixed with the
other green below. Is it nonsense, or not?

[3] Now a continuation of New Cavendish Street.

On coming home, so tired that she had to be carried upstairs, Elizabeth found Miss Bayley, a literary friend of Kenyon's, waiting to see her. "Then she sate with me an hour—and oh, such kind, insisting, persisting plans about Italy!" Very soon it was to appear as if half the world was going to Italy and wanted to escort her there.

With summer more visitors arrived to disrupt plans of quiet meeting. Among them were relations, the Hedleys, come over from their Paris home to prepare for the wedding in London of their daughter, Arabella. It was Mrs. Hedley whom Elizabeth particularly dreaded as a potential danger to her secret. Aunt Hedley was a tactless woman ever; in her niece's words, "doing a wrong with a right intention."

Mr. Kenyon now suggested that he should bring Sarianna Browning to call upon Elizabeth. Elizabeth felt obliged to refuse: in Mr. Kenyon's presence her future sister-in-law must be treated as a mere acquaintance. She shrank from the meeting too from a fear that Sarianna might not like her enough, a nervous feeling perhaps increased by a comment Browning had passed on. Looking at a portrait of Elizabeth, considered by its subject to be both flattering and unlike, Sarianna, veiling her comment because of a third person in the room, had murmured: *"molto bella."*

On June 3 Elizabeth paid her first visit to a friend, that old friend Miss Trepsack, or Treppy. Ba's coming was celebrated with ice cream, cakes, and cherry brandy. Ba herself was "kissed to pieces as the darlingest of children." The food, which Elizabeth and Arabel found difficult to face an hour after dinner, was welcomed by Flush, who highly approved of "that class of hospitable attentions." The visit, as a new thing, tired Elizabeth excessively.

On June 6 she set down on paper her "first word written out of my room, these five years, I think"; writing in the back drawing-room on a hot stormy evening "half out of the window for air," and curled up on the sofa. The rest of the family were at church or chapel. On June 9 she drove to Hampstead, then in open country, and pulled a dog-rose for Robert.

On June 14 Elizabeth, who had been dreading an invitation

to drive with Mr. Kenyon in his carriage, found even that frightening innovation improved upon: her cousin took her to see the Great Western train come in: "we left the carriage and had chairs—and the rush of the people and the earth-thunder of the engine almost overcame me . . not being used to such sights and sounds in this room, remember!!"

The weather remained hot and close. On the 17th, as a carriage was waiting to take Henrietta out to an evening engagement, Elizabeth took advantage of it to get into the air, driving at half past seven in the evening, with her small cousin Lizzie and Flush, into Hyde Park. On the Serpentine lake "shadows were gathering in quite fast, shade upon shade; and at last the silvery water seemed to hold all the light left, as on the flat of a hand. . . . And, as we came home, the gas was in the shops . . another strange sight for me."

On the 18th of this month, so eventful for a quiet invalid, Mrs. Jameson took her for a drive in Regent's Park. Softening as she was at every meeting to this valiant woman, Elizabeth now melted into a half confidence, telling Mrs. Jameson "what might be told," admitting at least a friendship with Robert Browning. Mrs. Jameson spoke warmly in admiration of him, delighting her companion more than she could know. It seems curious that this new friend and not the old intimate, Miss Mitford, was first confided in; but, as Elizabeth said, Miss Mitford had no sympathy with love, no knowledge of it. Her opinion too of Browning as a poet was not high. Elizabeth expected Miss Mitford to speak angrily about her marriage.

There are signs at this time in the letters that Browning was more hard pressed in spirit than his Ba, girt about though she might be with difficulty and danger: his continued headaches are a symptom. He had hesitated whether to write another poem before they should leave England, or whether he should accept a diplomatic post "Young England," in the person of Richard Monckton Milnes (afterward Lord Houghton), was offering. It is evident that the money question was weighing upon a prudent, upright mind. Ways and means were always more of a preoccupation with him than with her, and after all, it would be his wife's money on which, in present circumstances, he must live. Concealment too of the situation from his parents, requested by Elizabeth so that they should not be implicated in Mr. Barrett's wrath, was painful to the loving son. This must have weighed more heavily as his delicate mother was unwell. Later it was to be through her that he paid the only personal price for his marriage.

On the evening of the 19th, while the family were at dinner and Wilson out, Elizabeth put on her bonnet "as a knight of old took his sword," went downstairs and into the street "And, with just Flush, I walked there, up and down in glorious independence." Flush, however, who had "a very good, stout vain-glory of his own, and although adoring" his mistress, had no idea of "being ruled over" by her, chose to walk on the other side of the way. Every moment Elizabeth expected him to "disappear into some bag of the dogstealers."

On June 22 Arabel went to visit Mr. Boyd, and Elizabeth accompanied her. Hugh Boyd, always a nervous man, and now living alone, had worried himself into a state of valetudinarianism: he never went out, or left his chair. It was thought wiser, as both these old friends dreaded a first meeting after years of separation, that Arabel alone should enter the house, telling Boyd that Ba was outside in the carriage.

The next day Elizabeth had an emotional experience of a different nature; driving with Mrs. Jameson to the house of Rogers, the old poet and rich banker, to see his art treasures. Pictures and statuary, under an expert guidance, she admired in a bewildered amazement, and among them the portrait of Rembrandt by himself: "such a rugged dark, deep subterraneous face . . yet inspired—! seeming to realize that God took clay and breathed into the nostrils of it." She also saw the bookseller's agreement for the purchase of *Paradise Lost,* with Milton's signature and seal. "How was it possible not to feel giddy with such sights!" As they were leaving, Mrs. Jameson led her up to a picture of Napoleon on St. Helena by B. R. Haydon.

Next day came the news of the terrible death by his own hand. Haydon must have been in that last bloody phrenzy of despair when Elizabeth was looking at his picture. The shock was great: remorse flooded the tender heart. "Could anyone— *could my own hand even . . have averted what has hap-*

pened?" She had been told again and again that "to give money *there,* was to drop it into a hole in the ground," but "if to have dropped it so, dust to dust, would have saved a living man— when then?" Though he had written to her three times in the previous week, no suspicion of the man's state of mind had come to her: he had been bitter, but light-heartedly bitter about the grotesquerie of the Tom Thumb show that had killed his own exhibition of pictures: but in the last letter now mournfully re-read, Haydon had repeated "an old phrase of his, which I had heard from him often before, and which now rings hollowly to the ears of my memory . . that he *couldn't and wouldn't die."* Her private epitaph on this extraordinary man is acute in its analysis:

He was a man, you see, who carried his whole being and sensibility on the outside of him; nay, worse than so, since in the thoughts and opinions of the world. All the audacity and bravery and self-exultation which drew on him so much ridicule were an agony in disguise—he could not live without reputation, and he wrestled for it, struggled for it, kicked for it, forgetting grace of attitude in the pang. When all was vain, he went mad and died.

Annoyance was added to remorse and pity: Elizabeth was given to understand—although there is no evidence available today that he did so appoint her—that Haydon had named her as literary executor, asking that she should arrange for the publication of those journals left in her care. Browning soon relieved her mind of any fancied necessity to pay serious attention to this, only "part and parcel of his insanity." Anyhow Haydon's papers were the property of his creditors. Browning thought, and others supported him in the view, that Haydon, "being quite of the average astuteness in worldly matters when his own vanity and selfishness were not concerned," had hoped that Elizabeth, in her ignorance of life, would publish the journals in their libellous entirety: Talfourd had been approached to act as literary executor, and refused.

Elizabeth herself, having felt the charm and power of the man, could not so easily dismiss Haydon as insane and selfish: *His conscience was not a sufficient witness, . . nor was God. He must also have the Royal Academy and the appreciators of*

*Tom Thumb. A "weak man," of course he was,—for all vain men
are weak men. . . . But that he had in him the elements of
greatness—that he looked to noble aims in art and life, however
distractedly, . . that his thoughts and feelings were not those
of a common man, . . it is true, it is undeniable.*

On July 1 Elizabeth drove to Boyd's house, this time to visit
him. Arabel rallied her on her nervousness. "Oh, Ba, such a
coward as *you* are, never will be . . . married while the world
lasts." The rest shall be told in her own words:

*I stood at last, at the door of poor Mr. Boyd's dark little room,
and saw him sitting . . as if he had not moved these seven
years—these seven heavy, changeful years. Seeing him, my
heart was too full to speak at first, but I stooped and kissed his
poor bent-down forehead, which he never lifts up, his chin being quite buried in his breast.*

As the two women sipped his Cyprus wine Mr. Boyd began
to talk of Ossian, proving that the Adamic fall and corruption
of human nature were "never so disgustingly exemplified" as in
the literary controversy over this work. To Elizabeth, on the
threshold of a new life, it must have been as the stirring of
dead bones.

On that same day the man who now in place of this old failing scholar, and to a greater degree, ruled her life, wrote a
laughing protest: only once had he heard her call him by his
Christian name. This Elizabeth strenuously denied. "If you
heard me say 'Robert,' it was on a stair-landing in the House of
Dreams . . . and now I have got the name, shall I have courage to say it?" To her, having known no Robert except the favourite uncle whom she called "Uncle Hedley," it was entirely
new. "So it is a white name to take into life."

All those, Uncle Hedley and other relations in Town who
might disturb hours with or thoughts of this dear Robert,
moved her now but little. A visit from Miss Mitford was not
welcomed in the old way. "Why have you turned my heart into
such hard porphyry? Once, when it was plain clay, every finger (of these womanly fingers) left a mark on it."

On July 3 Elizabeth drove out as far as Harrow, seeing London as a cloud "quite far over the tops of the trees." The lanes
and hedgerows, "so silent, so full of repose," gave her serene

pleasure. She was able to read Robert's last letter alone under the trees while Arabel took Flush for a run in a field.

Her letter of the next morning gives a contemporary view of marriage which is worth quoting, if only because it can partially explain Mr. Barrett's conduct:

I think, at least, that if I were inclined to fear for my own hap-piness apart from yours (which, as God knows, is a fear that never comes into my head), I should have sense to reason my-self clear of it all by seeing in you none of the common ramp-ant man-vices which tread down a woman's peace—and which begin the work often long before marriage. Oh, I understand perfectly, how as soon as ever a common man is sure of a wom-an's affections, he takes up the tone of right and might . . and he will have it so . . and he won't have it so! I have heard of the bitterest tears being shed by the victim as soon as ever, by one word of hers, she had placed herself in his power. Of such are "Lovers' quarrels" for the most part. The growth of power on one side . . and the struggle against it, by means legal and illegal, on the other.

Add to this that the girls of the family were expected, for the most part, to give way to, to wait on their brothers, and we have the perfect basis for a tyrannical father.

With preparations going forward for Arabella Hedley's wed-ding, the institution of marriage was necessarily much in Eliz-abeth's mind of late. The paraphernalia of a fashionable cere-mony tired and disgusted her: no marriage service, she felt, should be conducted in public.

With relations constantly in the house their next meeting was postponed. Elizabeth, tried by sudden changes in the weather, from hot to sudden cold, from cold to hot, felt her old weakness upon her: on the day of writing this last letter she fainted. This indisposition made a few days of entire separa-tion from Robert hard to bear. In spite of a determination to be prudent, to take no risk of discovery until the house should be free of these people, Elizabeth wrote on the 8th: "*I must and will see you to-morrow—I cannot do otherwise. It is just as if Flush had been shut up in a box for so many days. My spirits flag. .*"

One evening Aunt Hedley said to Mr. Barrett over the dinner

table: "I have not seen Ba all day—and when I went to her room a gentleman was sitting there."

Arabel, in answer to her father's look of inquiry, said: "Mr. Browning called here to-day." "And Ba bowed her head," continued the well-meaning aunt, "as if she meant to signify to me that I was not to come in." Henrietta interposed quickly. "Oh, *that* must have been a mistake of yours. Perhaps she meant just the contrary." Mr. Barrett, happily unconscious of the powder-mine under his feet, merely remarked: "You should have gone in and seen the *poet*."

This was in itself alarming; but later the affectionate Stormie added his own corollary: "Oh, Mr. Browning is a *great* friend of Ba's! He comes here twice a week—is it twice a week or once, Arabel?"

This was enough to form the basis of an innocent raillery on the part of Aunt Hedley. Introducing her future son-in-law to Elizabeth, she told him knowingly that he must consider it a great honour, "for she never lets anybody come here except Mr. Kenyon, . . and a few other gentlemen."

Mr. Barrett corrected her. "Only *one* other gentleman indeed. Only Mr. Browning, the poet—the man of the pomegranates."

These incidents, though embarrassing enough, brought a measure of relief in the knowledge of Mr. Barrett's complaisance. Robert, to whom they were reported, felt positively grateful. "I dare say he is infinitely kind at bottom—I think so, that is, on my own account,—because, come what will or may, I shall never see otherwise than with your sight."

Mr. Barrett, in high good humour, was again calling her "my love" or "my puss." Before these renewed endearments Elizabeth must quail as from "so many knife-strokes. . . . Anything but his *kindness*, I can bear now." But she was glad for Browning to have at least a glimpse of her father's other side, that not "of peculiar wrongness."

"The difficulty, (almost the despair!) has been with me, to make you understand the two ends of truth . . both that he is *not* stone . . and that he *is* immovable *as* stone. . . . We must be humble and beseeching *afterwards* at least, and try to get forgiven." An application to him before marriage might lessen her father's pain, but it would not gain consent; and she herself might not be strong enough to abide the immediate consequences. They would be "hindered from writing . . hindered from meeting."

The next day Uncle Hedley, of whom Elizabeth was particularly fond, came to sit with her. She must, he told her, make up her mind to act. "If you don't go to Italy this year, you will never go." He looked forward to receiving her in his Paris home as she went through. Elizabeth told him sadly that when the time came he might cast her off. The kind man protested, asking in vain for an explanation of her words. "Do you mean," he insisted, "because you will be a rebel and a runaway?" He laughed, promising never to cast her off.

Kenyon, though he too now accepted Browning's visits as a custom established, was pleased to joke about them. No use visiting Ba—Browning had taken his place. Elizabeth was appalled to hear he intended to stay in London the whole summer. Those spectacles, though perhaps not now as inquisitorial, were too noticing for comfort; and the visits of one now so much dearer might be interrupted.

On July 21 Robert stayed with her three whole hours, hours of fearful pleasure since Aunt Hedley was about the house. Flush, perhaps misinterpreting an embrace, again behaved badly and had to be put out of the room. On his return Elizabeth would not forgive him until late evening, and even then he did not get the placating bag of cakes Browning had left lying on the table. Poor Flush! The lot of a displaced lover is hard and beyond a dog's understanding. Even Wilson, as tender to him as his mistress, had shown no sympathy, though the "whipping" she gave him, with tears of compunction in her eyes, amounted to little more than a few soft slaps of the hand. The next morning, after sniffing the chair on which his enemy had sat, Flush was given the cakes with a scolding, and expressed his contrition in doglike manner. Elizabeth threatened him with the indignity of a muzzle, but this Browning would not permit. A muzzle in his presence would only fix a dislike in Flush.

There was another lover, or jealous old friend, who resented

Browning's visits: an old unnamed admirer whom Elizabeth called "Chiappino"[4] when writing of him. He was now so plaguing her with importunities and "insolent letters" that the angry Browning talked of interfering personally, as one who had a right to protect her. Elizabeth gave an analysis of the man: "a sort of dumb Rousseau. . . . A miserable man, first by constitution and next by fortune. . . . I have told him sometimes that he had a talent for anger!" This mysterious person, a friend of some twelve or fourteen years' standing, evidently had the right of entry to Mr. Barrett's house and even to his daughter's room. Of late, however, she had refused to receive him unless Arabel were present.

One day this unhappy man "white with passion" followed Browning upstairs. Afterwards in Elizabeth's room "there was an explosion that day among the many—and I had to tell him as a consequence, that if he chose to make himself the fable and jest of the whole house, he was the master, but that I should insist upon his not involving my name in the discussion of his violences." Though the miserable "Chiappino" was jealous of Browning, sneering at him as her "New Cross Knight," it is evident that Elizabeth feared no betrayal from that quarter.

The lovers were now discussing their future life, a life necessarily to be one of the simplicity they both preferred. One extravagance, urged by her sisters, Elizabeth did propose: the taking of Wilson with her, at least for the first year. After that she might be "rather less sublimely helpless and impotent." With Wilson's connivance, too, it might be easier to slip luggage out of the house without the knowledge of her sisters, whom she was anxious to keep ignorant of the affair. Wilson had already declared she would go anywhere with her mistress, both from devotion to her and from a desire to travel. Last year when the plan for Pisa had gone awry Wilson had seemed disappointed. One drawback was the extra expense in cost of travel and in wages, Wilson being an expensive servant—at sixteen pounds a year. Browning replied that without Wilson, or some other personal maid, he would be "simply, exactly, INSANE to move a step."

One solemn preliminary on which Robert insisted was com-

4 See "A Soul's Tragedy."

plied with, not without protest, by Elizabeth: the writing of a
formal paper expressing a wish that her future husband should,
in the event of her death before him, leave her property in
equal parts to her sisters; or, failing them, to her surviving
brothers leaving out Stormie, on whom the Jamaica estates
were entailed. Elizabeth's income, of course, before the Married Woman's Property Act, became Browning's by law on
their marriage. In acknowledging this paper Robert hinted at
a pleasing contingency that might render this paper unnecessary. "There may be even a *claimant*, instead of a recipient, of
whatever either of us can bequeath—who knows?"

Towards the end of July Kenyon was pressing Elizabeth's sisters to urge an acceptance of Mrs. Jameson's offer to escort
Elizabeth to Italy: he had himself informed Mrs. Jameson of
the position, that Elizabeth might be " 'cast off' as for a crime."
The sisters, somewhat embarrassed, declared that they could
not interfere in the matter. "Ba must do everything for herself."
"But how?" Mr. Kenyon very naturally asked. "She has determination of character. She will surprise everybody some day."
Kenyon looked uneasy. This renewed offer of Mrs. Jameson's
placed Elizabeth in an awkward situation. Mrs. Jameson must
both be thanked and offered some sort of excuse for the refusal
of such a generous offer.

Kenyon's visit was doubly unwelcome that day. Robert had
been with her. Hearing of Kenyon's arrival in the house he felt
obliged to go three-quarters of an hour before his time. On the
way down he met Kenyon, who further embarrassed him by an
invitation to join himself and Landor for travel in Italy that
year. Browning, confused, resentful because his visit was cut
short, acutely aware of a half-open door near them, managed
to maintain an easy manner, joking with the intruder and telling him a good story, the purport of which he was quite unable
to recollect when Elizabeth told him how Mr. Kenyon had enjoyed the anecdote.

Browning, Mr. Kenyon told Elizabeth, when invited to Italy
with him, "did not seem to encourage the idea." Perhaps behind those spectacles, as he watched Elizabeth's conscious expression, there was a twinkle: perhaps this offer was generously
made with the idea that these two might the more easily come

together away from a home where love was forbidden. It seems unlikely that suspicion was not already aroused in that acute kindly mind.

September, and a journey to Pisa partly by water, was now fixed upon. An easy motion by river and canal boat across France would be less fatiguing for the invalid. Elizabeth made the suggestion that they should jointly accept Mrs. Jameson's offer, travelling with her; but Robert, though agreeing if Ba felt it for her own good, implied a wish that they should be alone.

In regard to Kenyon, Browning was inclined to think that he would only, if he guessed at their love, shake his head good-naturedly: Elizabeth, however, reflecting on her cousin's native caution, feared that "just in proportion to the affection he bears each of us, would he labour to drive us apart . . . *he fears like a mere man of the world.*"

On the last day of July Elizabeth had an experience that painfully exposed a continued weakness of the nerves: going for a quiet visit to Westminster Abbey she found a service was just beginning. As the great organ boomed out, after enduring the sound for a minute or so she fled in panic "being so disused to music, it affects me quite absurdly." Even a song heard in the drawing-room had lately made her weep. Music always recalled to her those lost happy days with Bro and the chasm of grief which lay between: the organ perhaps had an especial potency as a reminder of childhood when, after lessons, they had played before supper "while the loud organ's thunder circles all."

On August 2 danger seemed to threaten the lovers. A thunderstorm, exceptionally heavy, had kept Robert by Elizabeth's side for many hours. When he came to her room about seven o'clock Mr. Barrett found Elizabeth in a white dressing-gown. He "looked a little as if the thunder had passed into him, and asked, 'Has this been your costume since the morning, pray?'

" 'Oh, no,' Elizabeth answered, 'only just now, because of the heat.' 'Well,' he resumed with a still graver aspect, 'it appears, Ba, that *that man* has spent the whole day with you.'

"To which I replied as quietly as I could, that you had several times meant to go away, but that the rain would not let you,—and there the colloquy ended. Brief enough—but it took my breath away."

Part of Mr. Barrett's concern had been for the storm, which he knew always frightened Elizabeth. Arabel was reproved for having left Ba, who might have been ill from fear, "with only Mr. Browning in the room."

The storm, threefold that day, had, in spite of a comforting presence during some hours of it, upset the nervous woman. She was racked by apprehension of her father, of Mr. Kenyon linking up the loose threads put into his hand by one and another, and of fate in general. Foreboding had already been with her: "I had a presentiment which oppressed me during two days . . a presentiment that it would end *ill*, through some sudden accident or misery of some kind." To Robert, impotent in his distance from her, the receipt of this letter must have brought—though her candid confessions to him were sweet—a new torture of spirit which, on second thought, she might have spared him. But his Ba was to remain headlong to the end.

When Mr. Kenyon came that day to see her "through a special interposition of guardian-angels" he had broken his spectacles and carried them in his hand. "On which I caught at the opportunity and told him they were the most unbecoming things in the world, and that fervently (and sincerely) I hoped never to see them mended." But she was not to be let off the inquisition. "Did you see Browning yesterday?" Mr. Kenyon had stayed away just because he thought Browning would be with her. Elizabeth was, however, reassured by his manner especially as, without spectacles, he could not see her confusion.

Her embarrassment was not lessened, however, by the next question: was there an attachment between her sister and Surtees Cook? She said: "Why, Mr. Kenyon? What extraordinary questions, opening into unspeakable secrets, you ask."

Mr. Kenyon did not think the question extraordinary: the Captain was so often at Wimpole Street that he thought "the affair might be an arranged one by anybody's consent."

"But you ought to know," Elizabeth answered, "that such

things are never permitted in this house." She begged him to ask no questions. Was Mr. Kenyon fumbling after another secret? All Elizabeth's nervousness returned.

Mr. Kenyon, even in his awkward questions, might well have been anxious only to give these other lovers a friendly warning to tread delicately. This Browning himself thought, declaring it "the beginning of his considerate, cautious kindness . . . his own spectacled *acumen*."

Robert was, for his part, now tormented with a new fear: that Mr. Barrett, if he made the discovery, would suddenly take Elizabeth out of London—say into Sussex, or even Devonshire. Alarmed by Elizabeth's report of her father's displeasure on the day of the storm he now took a precaution, preparing himself with a letter or parcel to leave at the door if approach were indicated as dangerous: "any man's anger to me is Flushie's barking, without the respectability of motive,—but, once the door is shut on me, if he took to biting you!" Mr. Barrett's anger towards himself might be mere clamour on the air, but the thought of a sudden suspicious return to the house on the father's part, an open scene in front of Elizabeth was unendurable: "my own tied tongue, and a system of patience I can well *resolve* upon, but not be *sure* of, as experience makes sure."

His presentiment that Elizabeth might be removed from London, and perhaps into Sussex, proved literally true: next day Elizabeth told him that, as the house was to be thoroughly cleaned, papered, and painted, a retreat to either Sussex or Kent was discussed. However, the same plans had been made for several summers back, and there they had remained in Wimpole Street; so nothing might come of it.

Aunt Hedley was the immediate threat to their comfort with her arch jokes about lovers and gentlemen visitors; jokes naturally in the air with a marriage in making. On the wedding day, August 5, the lovers fancied themselves secure as the reception was to be held at an hotel, but the bridal party came back unexpectedly "to change their costume into something wearable for comfort . . into gowns which had not a devil, torturing the wearer with a morbid sense of flounces." Browning fled, not, however, in time to prevent Aunt Hedley from knowing he had been there. He left a disappointed woman behind him, but a contented dog: Flush, heavily bribed with cakes, had graciously consented to take Robert into favour.

It being necessary to know how much money they could count upon, Stormie, the eldest brother, was asked to supply the information. Elizabeth had £8,000 in the Funds, an investment in the Eastern Railroad, a share in the ship *David Lyon* bringing a little under £200 a year, and "ten shares in Drury Lane Theatre—out of which come nothing." She drew £40 a quarter, which, Storm told her, did not represent her whole income.

Robert would wonder, Elizabeth wrote, how she could spend £40 a quarter. She did spend it, but not all on herself: her dress never exceeded £20 a year. "My greatest personal expense lately has been the *morphine*. Still the money flows out of window and door—you will understand how it flows like a stream." Browning, who kept within a limited allowance, and that a small one, must have smiled over this: his Ba had never known what it was to lack money. A natural prudence in himself was to counterbalance her heedlessness in financial matters.

The practical difficulty now, however, could not escape her attention: Mr. Barrett held a power of attorney over her income, and the allowance for that quarter was spent, or accounted for. "We might either wait on the road till the required sum be called for and sent—or get a hundred pounds advanced by someone for a few weeks until everything is settled . . what would be pleasanter, if possible. Poor Papa's first act will be to abandon his management." Elizabeth added with generous pity: "Ah, may God grant him to do it rather angrily than painfully."

"When you write so of caring to be with me," she added, "my heart seems to *rock* with pleasure."

In the midst of one of those storms which always frayed Elizabeth's nerves Mrs. Jameson came to renew her offer as escort. Had the idea been given up because Mr. Kenyon had discouraged it? When Elizabeth, faintly thanking her, begged Mrs. Jameson not to reopen the subject with her cousin, that acute woman looked at her curiously: before she went Elizabeth had to face questions more pertinent. "But you will go?" "And with efficient companionship?" "And happily and quietly?" To the

last Elizabeth was unable to give a full "yes." It died away in
her throat.

In spite of anxieties, Elizabeth's improvement in health was
so marked that those about her noticed it. Henrietta cried out
in loud astonishment to Treppy: "Did you ever see anyone
looking so much better? It really is wonderful, the difference
within these last few weeks." Miss Trepsack, in her ancient wisdom, had seen more than Elizabeth's improvement in health.
Walking with Arabel a few days later she revealed a very
shrewd guess at the real state of affairs: that Ba would marry
and go to Italy. Elizabeth knew the old adoring friend would
do nothing to bring one of her "children" into trouble, but officially she must know nothing. "To occasion a schism between
her and this house, would be to embitter the remainder of her
days."

The day Elizabeth wrote of this, Robert was employing himself in putting all her letters "into rings—twenty together—and
they look now as they should—'infinite treasure in a little
room.' " Not only did Browning carefully preserve these letters,
a "treasure" to both himself and us, but he even kept the paper
and string about parcels which her fingers had touched. No
man is too great for the charming imbecilities of love.

On August 15 Kenyon, inconsiderately lingering in Town that
summer, drove Elizabeth to a bridge outside London so that
she might watch the Birmingham train as it came down the line.
As they waited, Elizabeth cut short an observation of her cousin's upon Browning's phenomenal memory with a remark about
the weather. This unadroit move brought the spectacles upon
her. Arabel, moved to mischief, asked Mr. Kenyon if he did not
think Elizabeth should try travelling on the railroad before she
undertook a journey to Italy? Kenyon asserted that Ba would
not go.

"Yes, she will, perhaps—Ba is inclined to be a great deal too
wild, and now that she is getting well . . ."

"To sit on thorns," Elizabeth commented, "would express
rather a 'velvet cushion' than where I was sitting, while she
talked this foolishness." On their return home Arabel was well
scolded.

"But we saw the great, roaring, grinding Thing . . a great,

blind mole, it looked for blackness. We got out of the carriage
to see closer—and Flush was so frightened at the roar of it, that
he leapt upon the coach-box." This novelty of the railroad, now
cutting its way all over England, was perhaps a startling portent of the changed life to come. As they watched there was a
sudden shower of rain: the experience of rain spattering upon
her gown and face was not new, but so remote that it pleased
Elizabeth "nearly as much as the railroad sight."

Her report of this adventure heartened Browning: "once you
crossed the room to look out Shelley's age in a book, and were
not tired—now you cross London to see the trains arrive and (I
trust) are not tired. . *So*—you are stronger."

Kenyon may have had a mild suspicion, but an older friend,
his curiosity roused by something Elizabeth had written, was
fumbling after the truth. That something, a mere passing remark, nobody else "would have paused to think over; but he,
like a prisoner in a dungeon, sounds every stone of the walls
round him, and discerns a hollowness, detects a wooden beam,
. . patiently pricks out the mortar with a pin—all this, in his
rayless, companionless Dark—poor Mr. Boyd!"

There was to be some change in the life of this cherished dis-
ciple of his. Did she intend, Boyd asked, to become a nun? On
the following visit he put a direct question. Elizabeth, secure
in his love, his honour and isolation from the world, gave him
the truth. Boyd, rather surprisingly in so conservative a man,
expressed full approval exhorting her, with quotations from
the moral philosophers, to keep to her purpose. A certain element in this approval may have been a natural gratification at
having deduced so much from a trifling clue: a larger part was
undoubtedly an old jealousy and dislike of Mr. Barrett. The
tyranny of his refusal to allow her to go to Italy the previous
year had further hardened Boyd against Elizabeth's dominating
father. As to Browning, he had but barely heard his name as a
poet. Elizabeth, knowing how even the now well-established
Wordsworth offended his eighteenth-century ear, was content
to leave it at that.

On August 19 Elizabeth drove to Finchley and there, lured
by a pretty rose-covered cottage and five young children, she
left the carriage to join Arabel in a visit to a married friend.

Some time spent with the eager, clamouring children, ending
with the treat of a carriage ride, left Elizabeth comparatively
fresh. The woman whose heart beat wildly on hearing Mrs.
Jameson's foot on the stairs had travelled far towards recovery.

On the 22nd Elizabeth went to St. John's Wood, where she
could enjoy the relief of talking openly. Mr. Boyd was flushed
with the old enthusiasm. "The very triumph of reason and
righteousness, he considers the whole affair," Elizabeth told
Browning, "taking us up exactly as if we were Ossian and Macpherson, or a criticism of Porson's, or a new chapter of Bentley
on Phalaris."

The following Sunday she tested her strength by attendance
at a Scotch church[5] in which, as a visiting parson was preaching
in French, Arabel thought they might expect a small congregation. Elizabeth should sit near the door so as to leave quietly
before the singing, which would excite her too much. The
church, however, filled rapidly and, with tears in her eyes, Elizabeth retreated. "One gets nervous among all these people if a
straw stirs." Arabel put her in a cab and she drove back alone
to Wimpole Street.

That Sunday, perhaps because George was come home from
circuit, the brothers had been talking about their eldest sister:
Stormie asked Arabel outright whether there was an engagement between "Mr. Browning and Ba." Arabel, taken unawares,
managed to reply: "You had better ask them, if you want to
know. What nonsense, Storm."

Storm said he would ask Ba when they came up to her room
that evening. "George was by, looking as grave, as if antedat-
ing his judgeship." Elizabeth, informed of the conversation,
awaited them nervously, but no question was put to her.
Browning, alarmed on hearing this, wondered whether it would
not be wiser to forgo their meetings in future. "To hazard a
whole life of such delight for the want of self-denial during a
little month,—that would be horrible." Elizabeth compromised
by limiting his visits to "nearly a week apart, perhaps."

This self-denial did not bring a reward: the postponed meeting was interrupted by the advent of Kenyon. Browning, losing his nerve, beat so rapid a retreat as to draw the attention of

---

[5] Was this the Scotch Chapel in Wells Street, Tottenham Court Road?

the household upon himself. Never had he stayed for so short a time.

It was the brothers whom Browning now feared: exact knowledge on their part might bring either harm to Ba and himself or, if they were content to acquiesce, a vengeance upon themselves. Elizabeth thought none of those around her would disapprove of their marriage, though some might "be vexed at the occasion given to conversation and so on." Also, if the proposed flight were known, there were those among them who might press her to make formal application to marry, "and I might perhaps, in the storm excited among so many opinions and feelings, fail to myself and you, through weakness of body. Not of the *Will!*"

Wondering whether a sea voyage would be less dangerous to his Ba than "railroad noises and the like," Robert gave prices which are interesting to compare; £21 first-class by sea to Leghorn and £10 only as far as Pisa through France, partly along the waterways, one presumes, since it was their intention to travel on them. He reckoned out that on the total expenses a sea voyage would add quite £20. This, of course, was in the early days of distance steamers. Robert thought that, after all, the journey by sea, at least as far as Gibraltar, would be more tiring than over land.

Browning now revealed to his father, through the mediation of that more intimate friend, his mother, what must in part have been for some time an open secret. Like the perfect parents they were, Mr. and Mrs. Browning received the news of their son's coming marriage with at least outward equanimity. "They have never been used to interfere with," Browning told Elizabeth, "or act for me—and they trust me. If you care for any love, purely love,—you will have theirs—they give it to you, whether you take it or no." His father was more than willing to advance money to cover the cost of their journey.

Browning was now considering whether it might not be as well to travel at least as far as Orléans with Mrs. Jameson, who was still embarrassing Elizabeth, though in the kindest manner, with questions about the Italian journey. Elizabeth, nervous of any further disclosure, offered objections. Mr. Kenyon would think he should have been confided in—Mrs. Jameson herself

might disapprove of their marriage. She postponed a decision
to travel with Mrs. Jameson with an obvious sense of relief.
Mrs. Jameson was to make her departure in the second week of
September: perhaps they might join her at Orléans.

The kindness of relations was now more teasing to Elizabeth than their raillery. The Hedleys, both realizing that some
sort of plan for a winter in Italy was made, asked no inconvenient questions but, appearing to assume that Elizabeth might
be planning to join Henrietta and Surtees Cook in a flight
abroad, her aunt said firmly that Henrietta should not, out of
respect, marry without at least a formal request to Mr. Barrett.
What, Elizabeth thought, would her aunt and uncle think of
her own omission?

While they talked her father came in. Aunt Hedley commented on Elizabeth's healthy appearance. Mr. Barrett seemed
surprised.

"Why," the aunt insisted, "do not *you* think so? Do you pretend to say you see no surprising difference in her?"

"Oh, I don't know," Mr. Barrett replied. "She is mumpish, I
think—she does not talk." Aunt Hedley suggested, not too happily, that perhaps Ba was nervous.

"Mumpish!" Elizabeth commented. "The expression proved
a displeasure. Yet I am sure I have shown as little sullenness as
was possible. To be very talkative and vivacious under such circumstances as those of mine, would argue insensibility, and
was certainly beyond my power."

On Sunday August 31, Elizabeth again entered a place of
worship, this time sitting in the vestry of Paddington Chapel
with the door ajar so that she might hear the service in private.
This was but a half-hearted attempt at courage. A certain fray-
ing of the nerves was betrayed in another and more important
instance. Elizabeth now seemed inclined to postpone her marriage and flight until October.

Plainly showing that he could not endure his own hateful
position much longer, Browning asked her what was to be
gained by a month's delay? Indeed, with cold mornings and
dark evenings, much might be lost. As delicately as possible he
hinted that, if by a journey at a bad season of the year her

health was "irretrievably shaken" (in plainer language, if it should prove fatal to her), "the happiest fate" he could "pray for would be to live and die in some corner where I might never hear a word of the English language, much less a comment in it on my own wretched imbecility,—to disappear and be forgotten." Elizabeth agreed to go in a few weeks' time.

On the second day of September Elizabeth's general anxiety was increased by a woeful concern for her more humble lover, Flush. This time the thieves snatched him from under the wheels of the carriage just as Elizabeth herself, having done some shopping in Vere Street, was stepping in.

Arabel, alarmed by her sudden pallor at the shock, comforted Elizabeth with a reminder that the bandits had themselves promised to secure the spaniel's return on payment of £10. But, Elizabeth commented, "*Flush* doesn't know that we can recover him, and he is in the extremest despair all this while, poor darling Flush, with his fretful fears, and pretty whims, and his fancy of being near me. All this night he will howl and lament, I know perfectly,—for I fear we shall not ransom him to-night." Elizabeth tried to console herself with the thought that Flush, who was going with them, would in Pisa be safe from the London dog-stealers.

Henry, having to deal with these vile men, was naturally angry. Elizabeth begged her brother not to haggle with the thieves: there had been a dreadful story current that a lady who demurred at the price demanded had received a parcel containing her dog's head.

Browning, rashly anticipating that Elizabeth would have Flush back when she received his letter, wrote somewhat hardly: "I would not have given five shillings on that fellow's application." He would threaten the thief with punishment, the band of thieves with extermination by all the powers he possessed. "How will the poor owners fare," he argued, "who have not enough money for their dogs' redemption?" His peevishness, his open expression of anger, might be put down to a "sick vile headache." "Dearest, I am not inclined to be even as tolerant as usual." Later in the day, being now so bilious that he had to throw himself on the bed, he wrote confirming his views, but softened them by adding: "I ought to have told you (un-less you divined it, as you might) that I would give all I am ever to be worth to get your Flush back for you."

Elizabeth indeed had not taken her lover too seriously; com-menting, not without mischief:

Do you mean to say that if the banditti came down on us in It-aly and carried me off to the mountains, and, sending to you one of my ears, to show you my probable fate if you did not let them have . . how much may I venture to say I am worth? . . five or six scudi . . . would your answer be "Not so many crazie . . . ?" Would you, dearest? Because it is as well to know beforehand, perhaps.

Elizabeth's distress was not mitigated by the two days' yell-ing and moaning of some dog shut up in the mews behind Wimpole Street. "Think of Flush he seemed to say."

On September 5 she determined to interview Taylor, the cap-tain of the banditti, in person. She found her "hero not at home." Remaining in the cab at the request of Wilson, who was terrified in that rough quarter, Elizabeth parleyed with "an immense feminine bandit." Mrs. Taylor reassured her with the most gracious of smiles. "She was sure that Taylor would give his very best attention."

Mr. Taylor came to Wimpole Street, but without Flush. He demanded six guineas and confidence in his honour. Unfortu-nately as the money was about to be paid over on Elizabeth's behalf Alfred met "the archfiend" in the hall and called him swindler, liar, and thief. "Which no gentleman could bear, of course." Therefore with reiterated oaths Taylor swore " 'as he hoped to be saved, we should never see our dog again'—and rushed out of the house."

Mr. Kenyon's gentle Ba-lamb became a tigress. Alfred was not spared. With the thought of that dog's head in her mind, she went downstairs determined to go in person and "save the victim at any price." It was already getting dark. The whole family cried out against her. "At last, Sette said that *he* would do it, promising to be as civil as I could wish, and got me to be 'in a good humour and go up to my room again.' "

Sette prevailed. Flush came back at eight o'clock, dashing up to her door and drinking from his cup of water, filled three times over. His joy at reunion was not so great as formerly. He seemed frightened, bewildered, and, when his mistress commiserated with him, "put up his head and moaned and yelled." Mr. Taylor had magnanimously allowed the return of the dog for no more than the six guineas: perhaps Alfred's anger had had its effect in frightening the scoundrel.

Browning was this time really unwell. On September 10 he was not able to come to her. That day she sent him serious news: the project of house painting was decided upon. George was going the next day to look for a temporary dwelling, to be hired for a month, at Dover, Reigate, or Tunbridge. The thorough cleaning of 50, Wimpole Street would probably take more than the month allotted. A matter so long delayed was now to be settled in a rush. This was Wednesday: Elizabeth might well be taken out of London on the Monday following.

Browning, having gone up to Town, did not receive her note until midday. "If you *do* go on Monday, our marriage will be impossible for another year—the misery! . . . We must be *married directly* and go to Italy."

C H A P T E R   1 9

MARRIAGE [1846]

ON ELIZABETH'S LETTER of September 11 Browning wrote: "Saturday, Septr. 12, 1846, ¼11–11¼ A.M. (91)." At their ninety-first meeting, the only meeting away from her father's house, they had been married in St. Marylebone Parish Church with Wilson and Browning's cousin, James Silverthorne, as witnesses.

On the evening of the 11th Elizabeth had tried to make the way smooth for their secret marriage by telling Arabel of an arrangement for the next morning; probably saying that she would walk to the cabstand with Wilson, driving with her to Mr. Boyd's house, and then send Wilson home. After her visit to Boyd her sisters should pick her up in a carriage and take her for a drive. This is the story so far as one can piece it together.

Before going to bed Elizabeth took Wilson more completely into her confidence. The maid was "very kind, very affectionate."

Elizabeth could not sleep that night. Next morning, as they walked to Marylebone Street, so great was her emotion and fatigue that she fainted and had to be revived with sal volatile in a chemist's shop. She left the cab at Marylebone Church looking, in the words of her lover, "more dead than alive."

At this wedding there could be no pews filled with friends and relations, no watching eyes beyond those of maid and cousin. Elizabeth would not have had a crowd at her marriage, but there must have been some, and some perhaps not then living, with whom she might wistfully in imagination have peopled the church. This, however, could be only a passing regret as she stood there at the altar beside Browning: there came into her mind a thought of those many women "who have stood where I stood . . . not one of them all perhaps, not one perhaps, since that building was a church, has had reasons strong as mine, for an absolute trust and devotion towards the man she married,—not one!" With this strong faith in her future husband it seemed to her only simple justice that she should stand there alone, unsupported by family and friends.

At half past eleven husband and wife parted. Hardly had the wedding ring been put on Elizabeth's finger but it must be taken off. Elizabeth returned to the cab and drove to St. John's Wood.

Fortunately Mr. Boyd was engaged with his doctor; so Elizabeth, having sent Wilson back in the cab, was able to settle quietly on a sofa alone to rest and try to regain composure. When she was called up to her old friend, who was in the secret, he, perhaps not as self-centred as she thought him, had the tact to demand the effort of conversation from her as she sipped his Cyprus wine. She talked and waited, but her sisters did not come. Boyd, guessing at the pallor of those thin cheeks, insisted on a luncheon of bread and butter to put some colour into her. She must not arouse suspicion.

At Wimpole Street there was considerable alarm when mistress and maid were found to be absent: perhaps a hysterical dog betrayed them, since it does not appear that Flush attended the wedding—Flush, who was used to accompanying his mistress everywhere.

Arabel, either from genuine inattention, or from a desire to help her sister by a delay, seems to have ignored the arrangement of the night before. It is known that, if not now, certainly later that day she guessed at the marriage. Presumably it was on Wilson's return that Henrietta first knew Ba was awaiting them in St. John's Wood.

The sisters came at last to Circus Road bearing marks of agitation. The gravity of their eyes, and especially Arabel's, made Elizabeth tremble, but she maintained as bold a front as she could. These two dear beings must not be implicated in her "crime." "What nonsense," she protested as they spoke of their alarm, "what fancies you have, to be sure."

She drove with them to Hampstead, as far as the Heath, chattering of this and that with a calm that surprised herself. "How necessity makes heroes—or heroines at least!" she commented to her husband by letter that afternoon. "It seems all like a dream! When we drove past that church again, I and my sisters, there was a cloud before my eyes." Knowing by in-

tuition whom this hasty marriage might most hurt, though un-
complainingly, Elizabeth added: "Ask your mother to forgive
me, Robert. If *I* had not been there, *she* would have been there,
perhaps." A certain remorse was still touching her happiness: "if
either of us two is to suffer injury and sorrow for what happened there to-day—I pray that it may all fall upon *me*! Nor
should I suffer the most pain *that* way, as I know, and God
knows."

Browning had been right in thinking, and her condition when
he met her outside the church must have confirmed this opinion,
that Elizabeth could not have endured the fatigue and excitement of both marriage and flight on one day. When the date of
the wedding had been hastily fixed, with a threat of removal
to Little Bookham on Monday, it seemed as if the double event
might have to take place, but departure from Wimpole Street
was postponed.

The delay thus gained did not, however, prove a happy one
for Elizabeth at least, forced as she was to endure day after
day of embarrassment, living under a false guise among her
family and with no confidant beyond Wilson: it had been a
fixed condition of the marriage that Browning should not again
visit her in her father's house. We are not told how she contrived to explain the absence of so constant a visitor. Surely
questions must have been asked, if not by the sisters, by the
teasing brothers.

To Browning himself this enforced absence from his wife,
painful though it must have been, brought a sense of relief:
never could he, a man of fundamental honesty, ask for Elizabeth in her maiden name at Mr. Barrett's door. Such a false-
hood would have stuck in his throat.

It was unfortunate that the next day was a Sunday when the
family all came to Elizabeth's room. That morning her head
"seemed splitting in two (one half on each shoulder)" from
fear of arousing suspicion. The noise made by her brothers, all
excited at the prospect of the removal from Town, was torture,
but she dared not protest. Several women friends up from Herefordshire called: it seemed as if they would never go. Treppy
came too. "It was like having a sort of fever."

In the midst of all this disturbance and din some church bells rang out. One of the provincial ladies asked: "What bells are those?" Henrietta, standing behind Elizabeth's chair, answered her: "Marylebone Church bells."

Later in the day, when Elizabeth was sitting quietly alone writing to her husband, Mr. Kenyon came in "with his spectacles, looking as if his eyes reached to their rim all the way round." Almost his first question was: "When did you see Browning?" and his last: "When do you see Browning again?"

In the midst of this agony of embarrassment Elizabeth was looking with longing "over the palms to Troy—I feel happy and exulting to belong to you, past every opposition, out of sight of every will of man—none can put us asunder, now, at least." She was still conscious of that enforced lack of courtesy towards Robert's people. "I feel so as if I had slipped down over the wall into somebody's garden—I feel ashamed."

Browning, returning to a home where there need be no concealment, wrote to Elizabeth: "my father and mother and sister love you thoroughly." His mother wished so much she had felt well enough to write to her new daughter-in-law. She must be content to send a message. As for himself, Browning told her: "Dearest, I woke this morning *quite well*—quite free from the sensation in the head. I have not woke *so*, for two years perhaps—what have you been doing to me?" The long period of nervous tension was over. There was only pure happiness to look forward to now. "Come what will my life has borne flower and fruit—it is a glorious, successful, felicitous life. I thank God and you."

The few days ahead were busy ones for Wilson and Elizabeth: there must be a careful packing of luggage so as to minimize cost since at that time every ounce was charged for, arrangements made for its private dispatch to Nine Elms Station (then the terminus of the London & South Western Railway) and, above all, there were letters to write.

While composing that difficult letter to her father Elizabeth aroused something of the suspicion she dreaded: many tears shed over the paper before her, as she sat with hesitant pen, made her look so pale that the family wondered what was amiss. In the only one of these farewell letters to survive, Elizabeth's agitation is manifest in the broken style and wavering blurred script:

My dearest George I throw myself on your affection for me &
beseech of God that it may hold under the weight—Dearest
George, go to your room & read this letter—and I entreat you
by all that we both hold dearest, to hold me still dear after this
communication which it remains to me to make to yourself and
to leave to you in order to be communicated to others in the
way that shall seem best to your judgement. And oh, love me
George, while you are reading it—Love me—that I may find par-
don in your heart for me after it is read.

She told of Browning's early attachment and her determination to refuse him; an attachment that she had thought "a little more light on my ghastly face" would soon bring to a natural end. But Browning's love was too strong. Upon herself
she took the entire responsibility of an "omission of the usual
application to my father and friends." Browning himself had
been only too anxious to make a formal approach. She insisted
that everyone in the house was ignorant of the whole affair
"and innocent of all participation in this act of my own."

It was not to the eldest brother, the gentle, affectionate
Storm, that Elizabeth entrusted a letter to her father, but to this
stronger-natured George; and it was with tolerable confidence
in his understanding and sympathy that she did so. George had
always encouraged her to break away in search of health, had
himself spoken with anger on the subject to his father and knew
well that her sacrifice in forgoing the Pisa trip the previous
year had brought upon her only severe and prolonged displeasure.

George, after reading through the letter enclosed "for my
dearest Papa," should break the news gently before giving it.
Elizabeth also begged that her father would "deign to read"
this letter to her brother. The forgiving replies for which she
hoped were to be directed to her at Orléans.

Elizabeth was nursing a hope of her father's forgiveness:
after all, he had been kind to her of late, so kind as to fill her
with remorse. But the hope was a faint one. Once he had been
heard to say: "Ba is the purest woman I ever knew." At the
time this had amused her: what Mr. Barrett meant to convey,

she thought, was that his eldest daughter had never troubled him with love affairs "or any impropriety of seeming to think about being married," but now the words seemed of graver import: "the whole sex will go down with me to the perdition of faith in any of us. See the effect of my wickedness!—'These women!' "

She urged upon Browning a complete submission. "I will put myself under his feet, to be forgiven a little, . . enough to be taken up again into his arms. I love him—he is my father—he has good and high qualities after all: he is my father *above* all." Over that difficult, tear-blotted letter Elizabeth argued to herself: "surely I may say to him, too . . 'with the exception of this act, I have submitted to the least of your wishes all my life long. Set the life against the act, and forgive me, for the sake of the daughter you once loved.' " She would remind him of her long years of suffering.

From now until the 19th their letters are short, containing little more than the discussion of necessary details, the marriage announcements, routes, and what luggage to take. There was soon real need for haste: the family were to travel to Little Bookham, Surrey, on Monday, September 21.

One of Elizabeth's last acts in her old home, characteristically impulsive, was to bring vivid regret: remembering that *Blackwood's Magazine* had said it would welcome lyrics from her, and no doubt with the possibility of an early shortage of ready money in mind, she swept her desk clear of old unpublished pieces with hardly a glance over them. These poems *Blackwood's*, perhaps with a journalistic eye on what we should now call the "news value" of the celebrated Miss Barrett who had become Mrs. Browning in circumstances that were the talk of literary circles, published hard on the flight from home, in October. They were not poems Elizabeth would have chosen to come so soon under the eye of a father she hoped to soften.

On the afternoon of Saturday, September 19, between half past three and four, two days before the departure for Little Bookham, Elizabeth and Wilson began their journey carrying with them only small bags of necessaries. It was, fortunately for the delicate woman—as Browning lovingly recalled in after years—"a delicious day."

Their greatest embarrassment in stealing out of the house un-
observed was that living piece of luggage Flush, who could not
be left behind to pine his heart out, and perhaps be slightingly
treated as a relic of his defecting mistress. Flush, however, who
seemed to understand the situation when it was put to him, behaved admirably; entirely restraining a natural noisy excitement at the prospect of an outing.

Outside Hodgson's, that friendly bookshop in which Elizabeth had so often rested, they met Browning and entered a cab
bound for Nine Elms Station. Elizabeth was soon to be on the
railroad she had only viewed with interest and alarm. One
wonders which of them, she or Flush, was most frightened by
the bustle, din, and confusion of a railway terminus, of the flying monster that carried them to Southampton on the first stage
of a journey to freedom.

At Wimpole Street Elizabeth's absence was discovered long
before its reason was explained. Her letters to the family,
posted that morning, either did not arrive before late evening
or, if they were enclosed in one envelope to George, were de-
liberately held back.

Elizabeth had appealed to George in vain: his heart was hard
against her. He seems to have refused the cruel task of inform-
ing Mr. Barrett. It was Henrietta who told her father of Ba's
flight. Mr. Barrett was standing on the stairs with a heavy book
in his hand: in angry amazement he dropped the book. Henrietta slipped and fell, so giving rise to a preposterous legend
that, on hearing the news of the flight of his eldest, Mr. Barrett threw his second daughter down the stairs.

It was not long before Kenyon came to him, no doubt pressing the claim of Robert Browning to be honourably received as
a son-in-law. Mr. Barrett is said to have remarked: "I have no
objection to the young man, but my daughter should have been
thinking of another world."

It is not clear whether Mr. Barrett accompanied his family to
Little Bookham on the Monday, or whether he stayed behind,
nourishing his grief and anger alone. Some sort of inquisition
must have been held before their departure. George in his reply to Elizabeth's letter accused both Arabel and Minnie, the
housekeeper and former nurse, of connivance. This Mrs. Brown-

ing denied, but it is hard to believe there was no one partially in their secret, or how could Wilson have smuggled their boxes out of the house?

Mr. Barrett wrote an obdurate letter, casting Elizabeth from him. On the return of his family to Wimpole Street the wounded man, embattled in strong pride, kept a bold face towards a world not yet entirely done with gossip about the marriage. In high spirits, spirits perhaps unnaturally high, he entertained friends to dinner every night. He never again referred to his daughter. She was to him as one long dead and forgotten.

A notice of the marriage, giving no date so as not unduly to embarrass the Barrett family, was inserted in leading papers. When a proof of the *Daily News* reached John Forster, its editor and Browning's friend, he took it for a hoax, some poor sort of joke. Falling into "a great passion" he called for the head compositor, telling him to bring up the manuscript. As this was in a familiar hand, that of Sarianna, Forster had to believe the evidence of his eyes. The two poets, not even known to the world as acquaintances, were, in sober fact, man and wife.

To Elizabeth's friends the news of the marriage and flight brought both astonishment and apprehension. Miss Mitford wrote to a correspondent that it was "as if I had heard that Dr. Chambers had given her over when I got the letter announcing her marriage, and found she was about to cross to France. I never had an idea of her reaching Pisa alive."

CHAPTER   20

PISA [1846–7]

THE BROWNINGS ARRIVED at Southampton an hour before the boat sailed; at nine o'clock they embarked at the Royal Pier for Dieppe. It was to be five years before they returned to England.

The journey from Southampton to Paris took nineteen hours and a half. In France travel was partly by rail, partly by *diligence*. We do not know whether they rested by the way, or the exact date on which they arrived in Paris.

Mrs. Jameson was travelling too, on her way to Italy with a young niece, Gerardine Bate. She was staying in the Rue de la Ville-l'Evêque, at the Hôtel de la Ville de Paris, when an astounding piece of information reached her: Robert Browning wrote to inform her that he and his bride had just arrived from London, and that the lady was Elizabeth Barrett. Elizabeth had been wrong in thinking that her friend had divined at least part of the truth; that when, unable to bid Mrs. Jameson good-bye, she had written of herself as "forced to be satisfied with the sofa and silence," Mrs. Jameson could read a certain message in that discreet phrase. The news came like a thunderbolt.

Her aunt's astonishment, Gerardine tells us, was "something almost comical." Surprise was soon lost in delight. Mrs. Jameson hurried to the Brownings' hotel. Opening her arms to them both, calling them "children of light," she gave that instant approval for which Elizabeth, disturbed in conscience, was craving from her friends. What misgiving she had Mrs. Jameson kept to herself, reserving for a friend comment on these "two celebrities who have run away and married under circumstances peculiarly interesting, and such as to render imprudence the height of prudence." "God help them!" she added, "for I know not how the two poet heads and poet hearts will get on through this prosaic world."

Finding Elizabeth exhausted and ill, Mrs. Jameson persuaded

them to take a week's rest in Paris at her own quiet hotel. She would accompany them to Pisa and help to take care of the invalid. Robert, thoroughly frightened over his wife's condition, agreed gratefully. Elizabeth herself felt private regret that they could not hurry forward; anxious as she was to reach Orléans, where the fateful letters from father and family would be awaiting her.

It was but natural, since the party had met together in Paris, that the world should credit Mrs. Jameson with having taken a large part in the arrangement of the marriage. Her absolute denial friends took to be merely discreet, shaking their heads, as Elizabeth put it in her vivid way, "incredulously over writing paper of various sizes."

"The week at Paris!" Elizabeth wrote to Miss Mitford. "Such a strange week it was, altogether like a vision. Whether in the body or out of the body I cannot tell scarcely." In her exhaustion she had to be "satisfied with the *idea* of Paris" except for one visit to the Louvre. To Miss Mitford she talked of Balzac, that exponent of Parisian society ardently and half guiltily admired by herself and her friend. One thing she did not mention to Miss Mitford, or to any other correspondent (at least in any letter I have seen), and that was her own earlier visit so far back as 1815.

This feminine reticence may serve to remind us that, together with so many of her family, the father included, Elizabeth did not look her age in spite of frail health. Browning, too, kept an appearance of youth. We find him called a young man by people who met him years later in Italy. The little Gerardine, really young at seventeen, an age when even thirty seems mature, did not regard these two as elderly and beyond romance. True, romance was heightened by the memory of a visit to Elizabeth's secluded invalid room, and newly consummated love must have put the flushed and happy lovers in a good light; but, even so, they must have appeared nearer to Gerardine than actual years would warrant. So charming, so full of delight was the coming journey, the vicarious honeymoon through beautiful France, to a young untravelled girl, that every detail remained with her in the sterner years ahead. Of this journey she wrote in or about 1877:

. . . the temptation is great to linger upon the memory of a journey so enchanting, made in the fairest days of youth, and with such companionship. The loves of the poets could not have been put into more delightful reality before the eyes of a dazzled and enthusiastic beholder; but the recollections have been rendered sacred by death as well as by love.

They travelled partly by train and *diligence*, but also in a more leisurely way by steamer on the Loire, the Saône, and the Rhone. While Gerardine was intoxicating herself in an aura of love with the beauty of landscape, Mrs. Jameson was watching the man to whom this delicate friend had given herself; a man admired, liked, but possibly not as well known as the former Miss Barrett. Her approval was whole-hearted. She "never knew anyone of so affluent a mind and imagination combined with a nature and manner so sunshiney and captivating."

Though at times the strain of that journey must have been almost unbearable to a man functionally nervous, even though an experienced and older woman was present to watch over Elizabeth, Browning was ever thoughtful for their comfort, "witty and wise, (and foolish too in the right place)." He charmed cross old women in the *diligence*, talked "latin to the priests who enquire at three in the morning whether Newman and Pusey are likely '*lapsare in erroribus*' . . . and forgets nothing and nobody . . except himself, it is the only omission."

One criticism, and one only, Mrs. Jameson had to make as she watched this couple so perfectly fitted for one another, and that was Browning's adoption of the pet family name; but Browning, who liked "Ba" as well as Elizabeth herself, could not be talked out of it. Ba might well consider herself the Baby of early days, so carefully was she cherished, pillowed by arms and knees at night against the shaking of the *diligence*; carried, laughing, protesting, upstairs and put instantly to bed when they halted on the way. Already Elizabeth was feeling a little stronger. Travel, change of air, always did her good, and now they were journeying south in perfect sunshine.

Our two minor actors in the drama, Wilson and Flush, were both delighted with their new experience, though in one case with an important reservation. Flush, now getting almost as much attention as his mistress, was perfectly reconciled to his new master, enjoying a strange freedom, but behaving admirably so far, absorbed as he was by strange sights, sounds, and scents; but when on the railroad inexorable authority clapped him into a box, his protests were loud in wailing and moaning.

As they rushed on to Orléans by train it might have been hard to say who was the more unhappy, Flush or his mistress. Elizabeth was suffering in anticipation the first sight of those letters awaiting her, an ordeal she called her "death-warrant." The rest can be told in her own words to her sisters:

Robert brought in a great packet of letters . . and I held them in my hands, not able to open one, and growing paler and colder every moment.

He wanted to sit by me while I read them, but I would not let him. I had resolved never to let him do that, before the moment came—so, after some beseeching, I got him to go away for ten minutes, to meet the agony alone, and with more courage so, according to my old habit you know. And besides, it was right not to let him read. . They were very hard letters, those from dearest Papa and dearest George— To the first I had to bow my head—I do not seem to myself to have deserved that full cup, in the intentions of this act—but he is my father and he takes his own view, of course, of what is before him to judge of. But for George, I thought it hard, I confess, that he should have written to me so with a sword.

But her brother wrote "in excitement and ignorance."

The sisters' letters were pure balm to the wound George had inflicted. When Robert returned, Elizabeth put them in his hands. Browning, with tears in his eyes, kissing the kind words as he read them through a second time, declared his affection for Henrietta and Arabel: "I am inexpressibly grateful to them, — It shall be the object of my life to justify this trust, as they express it here."

There was the "kindest letter" from Miss Mitford and one from Mr. Kenyon. It was Kenyon's verdict on the marriage, and perhaps Kenyon's alone among his friends, that Browning personally dreaded, but to his relief it was one of complete approval. Kenyon wrote: "Nothing but what is generous in thought and action could come from you and Browning. And the very peculiar circumstances of your case have transmuted what might have been otherwise called 'Imprudence' into 'Prudence,' and apparent wilfulness into real necessity." Kenyon begged his "Ba and very dear cousin" to regard him as her banker if money should prove to be temporarily short.

Of Mr. Barrett's flint-hearted letter we know nothing, except that he accused his daughter of having sold her soul for genius. "Which I might have done," Elizabeth commented, "when I was younger, if I had had the opportunity; but am in no danger of doing now."

When Elizabeth had spoken to him of Mr. Barrett's obdurate letter, Robert, with no sign of resentment at the position into which circumstances had forced him, swept her up in a wave of tenderness, laying her down on the bed, sitting by her for hours, and promising to win back for her, with God's help, the affection of those of her family who were incensed against her.

When some months before it had appeared as if her father cared little, Elizabeth had said that she was always glad to know the worst, however bitter the pill might be: now, one may guess, once the draught was taken, she was better able to enjoy the south, sun and blue sky, the certainty of love. Life was expanding for her, who had once put it so resolutely behind her, in a warmth, a fullness, an inevitability.

Gerardine Bate, looking back on that enchanted journey, a journey almost too sacred to be spoken of, permitted herself one revelation. The party rested for a couple of days at Avignon that they might make a poetical pilgrimage to Vaucluse, the home of Laura.

There, at the very source of the "chiare, fresche e dolci acque," Mr. Browning took his wife in his arms, and, carrying her across the shallow curling waters, seated her on a rock that rose throne-like in the middle of the stream. Thus love and poetry took a new possession of the spot immortalised by Petrarch's loving fancy.

The fountain, Mrs. Browning herself wrote to Westwood, was swollen by rains, flashing and roaring in its dark prison of rocks "louder and fuller than usual . . . and Flush, though by no means born to be a hero, considered my position so outrageous that he dashed through the water to me, splashing me all over, so he is baptised in Petrarch's name."

At Avignon Elizabeth was delighted by another poetically symbolic episode, this time with the charm of complete surprise. A friendly stranger approached the party to offer a pomegranate, and of the three ladies Elizabeth was the one chosen for this significant gift. She, who had never seen the fruit before, immediately took a knife and cut it "deep down the middle." But at this point the pomegranate of happy omen dwindled to an unfamiliar fruit: Mrs. Browning found it unpalatable.

By easy stages they reached Marseilles and there took ship for Genoa. Elizabeth sat on deck enjoying a new vision of "mountains, six or seven deep" as they coasted along the Riviera. From Genoa they sailed southward to Leghorn, passing Shelley country at Viareggio and the Gulf of Spezia. On reaching the port of Leghorn Browning had an odd encounter.

There was at this time a certain eccentric exuberant personality in the world of letters, Francis Mahoney, once a Jesuit Father, and then a priest. Abandoning his clerical vocation, though still retaining "an uneradicable air of the priest and seminarist" in amusing contrast to his Bohemian way of life, Mahoney contributed to *Frazer's Magazine* learned, entertaining, and poetically charged articles as "Father Prout," a name by which he soon became generally known. Of late years he had been much in London, though with frequent excursions to the Continent. Browning had already told Elizabeth how he was always "meeting that Lion in strange out of the way places roaring wildly," and had many times encountered him abroad "whenever the sight was least expected." Let us continue the story in Elizabeth's own words:

Well—while we travelled across France, my fellow-traveller laughed a little as he told me that in crossing Poland Street with our passport, just at that crisis, he met—Father Prout—"oh, of course, he met him just then"— It was a moment worthy to be signalized! . . . On our landing at Leghorn, at nine o'clock in the morning, our boat which was rowed from the steamer to the shore, passed close to a bare jutting piece of rock on which stood a man wrapt in a cloak, he also having just landed from an English vessel bound from Southampton—Father Prout!! Robert cried: "Good Heavens, there he is again!— There's Father Prout!" At the inn after breakfast "the reverend Lion" entered and was just as amazed as Browning at the meeting; more so, surely, as the poet had a wife with him, and she one far more celebrated than himself. Feeling shy and tired, Elizabeth kept to the other side of the room sheltering behind a black veil, though a slight formal introduction had to be gone through. As Father Prout was going, or returning to Rome, where he was now acting as correspondent for Dickens's paper the *Daily News*, the Brownings were to meet him again. Once at least he was to burst in dramatically upon them, and at that time more opportunely.

At Pisa, which they reached by train, Browning, after a few days of hotel life with Mrs. Jameson, took rooms for his wife and himself in the Collegio Ferdinando, a great building erected by Vasari near the Cathedral. From their windows they could see that abiding marvel, the Leaning Tower and the Cathedral behind it, with the Baptistery and peaceful Campo Santo close at hand.

The first ten days were wet but at length the sun came out, the sky was a cloudless blue and the temperature that is a warm English June. Pisa, that ancient place from which history, almost life itself, had at this time receded, Elizabeth at first found enchanting, "full of repose, yet not desolate: it is rather the repose of sleep than of death." The Cathedral, the Baptistery, the Leaning Tower are beautiful enough against a grey sky, but now they shone out in all their candour of beauty. Never was there such a complete contrast in homes than Pisa and Wimpole Street, the southern city in its pure clean air and the sooty, foggy London of 1846. Every day Elizabeth was out walking "while the golden oranges look at me over the walls, and when I am tired Robert and I sit on a stone to watch the lizards."

Flush, too, highly approved of Pisa, "going out every day and speaking Italian to the little dogs." Flush was no longer so discreet, so well behaved as when the changing vicissitudes of a journey occupied his attention. He was vociferous, arrogant, "overbearing," tyrannizing over his new master; appearing, Robert declared, to consider him "to be created for the special purpose of doing him service."

There were expeditions to the Mediterranean shore, where,

in far mist, the island of Gorgona might be seen "beautiful and blue"; to the foot of Monti Pisani, where mountain heights could be seen reflected in the pure waters of Lake Ascuno and great pines climbed upward in the silence of the woods. Elizabeth had too the unexpected delight of meeting with camels, camels loaded with faggots. These exotic beasts were bred at the Cascine di San Rossore, a farm founded by the Medici.

Once during their stay at Pisa the Brownings visited the Lanfranchi Palace, the home of Byron, a poet admired by both. There in the garden they picked a bay leaf: this leaf Browning later had mounted with a lock of Elizabeth's hair, adding a note that it was gathered in the first year of their marriage.[1]

Over the fire found necessary morning and evening in their rather too cool rooms, husband and wife would sit day-dreaming, planning future travels over roasted chestnuts and grapes. Excellent and plentiful meals came in from the *trattoria,* of which Elizabeth ate well, drinking and enjoying too the light Chianti with which Robert would dose her until she dropped asleep. At night, in spite of an uncomfortable bed stuffed with orange-tree shavings, she slept soundly. By the end of the year she had so far progressed from the old state of nervous invalidism as to be present on Christmas Eve at midnight Mass in the Cathedral.

All the strength of a great heart and mind was concentrated on assuring Elizabeth's welfare. Browning not only surrounded her with care, but put forth his best powers of entertainment, talking wisdom or foolery as the mood of his beloved seemed to demand. Elizabeth was not now, or ever in their married life, burdened with the slightest household care; all was kept in Robert's hands. Scrupulous, fidgety as he always was over money matters, bills were cast up and settled weekly, much to the amusement of Mrs. Jameson, who declared that the married poets reminded her "of the children in a poem of Heine's who set up housekeeping in a tub, and inquired gravely the price of coffee."

Browning was prudent but not calculating. Although he had lived a good deal in Italy, a present comparative cost of living

---

[1] In the possession of Miss Henrietta Altham.

impressed him so that he fell an easy victim to a system of systematic extortion; foreigners, at that time, and especially the English, being considered lawful prey.

Later, at Florence, the Brownings were to discover by contrast how rough was the accommodation provided here at a high price, but now, such was their state of innocence, their *padrone* was the envy of other Pisan landlords. One living opposite, to sustain his dignity, let it be known that Mrs. Browning ("mark," Elizabeth interpolated in telling of this, "Mrs. Browning") had offered him a fabulous price for his rooms if he would break a prior engagement with a certain Major's wife. This lady, "being a woman of masculine understanding, (and superstructure besides)," walked about Pisa abusing Mrs. Browning "in good set terms." Browning felt obliged to send her a peremptory note refuting the rival landlord.

Towards the end of their stay in Pisa, a kindly English neighbour took Wilson to the shops and showed her how to avoid the most barefaced cheatings, but even so, apart from the rent, Browning was soon aware that they were living at a far higher rate than was necessary. "For two hundred and fifty pounds a year," Elizabeth commented, "we might and ought to live in excellent apartments, and keep our own carriage and two horses; and a man servant to boot."

Mrs. Jameson and Gerardine remained in Pisa three weeks, spending what leisure they had with the Brownings; but much of Mrs. Jameson's time was occupied in a close study of art treasures, drawing, arranging, and classifying sometimes far into the evening.

In this labour, Gerardine, or "Geddie" as she was familiarly called, helped her aunt, though not with the assiduity that hard-working and enthusiastic art-lover demanded. Geddie, she was constantly complaining to her friends, was indolent, preferring to lounge in bed in the morning and play with Flush at night. Mrs. Jameson adored her niece, and was sacrificing much in bringing her abroad for an art training. Elizabeth, with whom the "pretty, accomplished, gentle little girl" was a favourite, was privately of the opinion that Gerardine "was no more fitted to be what Mrs. Jameson desired, a *laborious artist*, than to fly to Heaven like a lark." As with many adoring per-

sons, Mrs. Jameson was by turns too easy and too hard with
her young niece. Browning was almost tactlessly outspoken on
the subject of Geddie's defects, especially when her aunt was
over-enthusiastic, but Elizabeth privately sided with the pretty
mismanaged child, often making excuses for her.

Mrs. Jameson's approval of the marriage was now complete:
Elizabeth, she reported to the anxious Miss Mitford, was "not
merely improved but transformed." For her Elizabeth's admiration grew daily stronger. Both she and Robert were now affectionately calling her "Aunt Nina." When at the end of three
weeks Mrs. Jameson decided to move on to Rome, she made
Browning promise that if Elizabeth were taken ill he would at
once write to her: if anywhere in Italy she could come to them
immediately. This from a woman who was abroad on business,
studying art with a view to making money in a new work, was
no light promise. It says much for her warmth of heart, her
tact, that these two, naturally absorbed in each other, found
parting from Mrs. Jameson genuinely painful.

The weather turned prematurely cold, unusually cold: Pisans
went about "muffled in vast cloaks, with little earthenware pots
full of live embers to warm their fingers." In December snow
fell, the first for five years, and the cold intensified in spite of a
hot sun. Their English eyes were treated to the incongruous
sight of women wrapped in furs and carrying parasols. Untouched by the sun in their shaded rooms Elizabeth was languid, feeling a touch of the old discomfort in her throat.
Browning, nervous about her, heaped wood on the fire, richly-
burning pine from the Grand Duke's woods. Elizabeth was almost as nervous herself: "If I were to be ill after all," she wrote
home, "I feel I should deserve to be stoned for having married."
Robert would hardly leave her chair, having to be driven out
each day for an hour's solitary exercise.

Life, now that Mrs. Jameson had gone, was completely intimate, isolated; nor did they wish it otherwise, though they
would have been glad to practice the Italian language a little.
The only Italian of their acquaintance, a Professor Ferucci,
who lent them books, spoke French "as by a point of honour."
The English were numerous in Pisa, but Robert was determined to keep them out, even at the cost of an almost open in-

civility. Those many admirers in Wimpole Street days excluded from "the shrine," as Elizabeth herself light-heartedly called it, could now feel that they had an easier approach and perhaps a legitimate one, since congratulations on her marriage could be offered to the romantic celebrity. Robert dreaded too "the horrors of a mixed society," foreigners not of the best who sought the company of the English, and certain of the English themselves, lion-hunters, or refugees from conventional British morality.

Apparently neither of the Brownings was yet at work: some time of the day they spent over novels from a lending library, dull novels over which Robert yawned uncontrollably, but many hours were spent happily in talk, talk "with ever so many reflections and varieties." They laughed a good deal and chattered lovers' nonsense. They wrote long letters to family and friends.

C H A P T E R   2 1

LETTERS, AND DEPARTURE FOR FLORENCE [1846–7]

IT IS FROM LETTERS written to her sisters from Pisa, in a correspondence kept inviolate, that we get the most intimate details
of the new life. Since Browning was only to see what Elizabeth
might think fit to show him, these three could still talk freely
and intimately on paper. Robert's own letters to his family
were kept as private, but of these we have not the benefit since
they were later destroyed; but from a few of his to Arabel and
Henrietta we get the tones of his voice.

Perhaps feeling on arrival "at our great journey's end" her situation to be more real, more actual, Elizabeth sat back and
contemplated her marriage. "I can only wonder increasingly,"
she wrote, "at the fact of his selecting *me* out of the world of
women." Like all sensible folk, she nerved herself to expect that
a honeymoon must soon be over, that they must settle down
to the more humdrum friendship of marriage, but with the
Brownings this was never to happen. As she put it herself, the
stars kept them in light.

Elizabeth poured out love and admiration for Robert to sisters and friends, writing in a long explanatory letter to Mrs.
Martin:

*Now may I not tell you that his genius, and all but miraculous
attainments, are the least things in him, the moral nature being
of the very noblest, as all who ever knew him admit? Then he
has had that wide experience of men which ends by throwing
the mind back on itself and God; there is nothing incomplete
in him, except as all humanity is incompleteness.*

To her sisters Elizabeth was more explicit, more rapturous,
speaking of a love far deeper than "in the Wimpole Street days
of adoration." With a smile she begins "to wonder naturally
whether I may not be some sort of a real angel after all." Then,
serious again: "It is not so bad a thing, be sure, for a woman to
be loved by a man of imagination. He loves her through a lus-

trous atmosphere which not only keeps back the faults, but produces continual novelty, through its own changes."

Browning, in letters to his sisters-in-law, wrote of Elizabeth with an expansion rare in this reserved man:

I, however, thought I knew her, while every day and hour reveals more and more to me the divine goodness and infinite tenderness of her heart,—while that wonderful mind of hers, with its inexhaustible affluence and power, continues unceasingly to impress me. I shall not attempt to tell you what she is to me. Her entire sweetness of temper makes it a delight to breathe the same air with her—and I cannot imagine any condition of life, however full of hardship, which her presence would not render not merely supportable but delicious— It is nothing to me that my whole life shall be devoted to such a woman,—its only happiness will consist in such a devotion.

At this time he was celebrating the anniversary day of their marriage every week.

But Browning's common sense, so evident in his work and letters, saved him from fatuity. Elizabeth told a little story of a mistake made in a letter home, impetuously and rather peevishly fathered on him. When she found herself to be the culprit and made a gracious acknowledgment, instead of the pretty speech she expected, her husband answered quietly: "It is a satisfaction, at any rate that you should admit it."

This same common sense, a logicality of mind, made Browning attempt to use reason with Elizabeth's angry brothers. Taking advantage of news that England was in the grip of an abnormal cold, which had even touched Pisa with an icy finger, he tried to convince them that their marriage, and the manner of it, had been inevitable: the invalid was now out of reach of a London winter, which would seriously have harmed her. To the sisters he wrote:

if, on a consideration of all the facts, your brothers can honestly come to the opinion that, by any of the ordinary methods applicable to any other case, I could have effected the same result,—that any amount of exertion on my part, any extent of sacrifice, would have availed to render extreme measures unnecessary,—then, I will express all the sorrow they can desire—

tho' at the same time I shall expect some forgiveness for a very involuntary error—assuring them, as I do, that I believed—and believe—that their sister's life depended upon my acting as I acted.

When at the end of January Sette wrote a letter full of affection for Elizabeth, but unrelenting towards Robert, she wrote back sharply, through the medium of Henrietta, that her brothers *ought to be able to see, what every other person of sense sees in an instant, that to have* given them my confidence *and have destroyed their prospects in the same breath, would have been an act of the most atrocious selfishness on my part, and impossible to one who loved them as I did and do.*

Elizabeth's strong and affectionate interest in her brothers was not lessened by their intransigeance. Soon she was worrying over news that Stormie might go to Jamaica; a natural destination, one would think, for a son on whom the family estates were entailed. But Storm was the eldest son because of two losses, the first of which had been, directly or indirectly, due to the Jamaican climate. "Dearest Storm," she wrote Henrietta with characteristic impetuosity, should "turn his eyes another way . . any other way in the world." Why could he not come, if the *Statira* passed through the Mediterranean that year, to visit her? Or could not he, George, Sette, and Occy travel up the Rhine that summer and meet them in the Luganean mountains? She and Robert were not rooted in Italy—indeed, they were even talking of going to Jerusalem—and an early visit must be made home, to England.

In this new life permeated by love, in a new liberty of action, the rigour of her father's control of the family, his anger with herself, seem partly to have been forgotten; perhaps appearing almost as a bad dream. In company with her husband under an Italian sky Elizabeth could even look hopefully towards a moment when "my dearest papa will be melted . . . into a clearer understanding of motives and intentions; I cannot believe that he will forget me, as he says he will, and go on thinking me to be dead rather than alive and happy."

Her thirst for news from Wimpole Street was insatiable, even to such detail as the colour of a fresh carpet. At first her letters were tinged with anxiety over the welfare of her family after the marriage and sudden departure; as early as November, however, she had heard that "everybody is well and happy, and dear Papa *in high spirits* and *having people to dine with him every day,* so that I have not really done anyone harm in doing myself all this good." Some natural bitterness of soul Elizabeth must conceal from her correspondent, Mrs. Jameson, but later, writing to Henrietta of her good fortune in being out of England in a severe winter, she commented: "only this is no argument to those who wish me dead!" It is presumed, since letters to Henrietta and Arabel were addressed care of Miss Trepsack at 5, Upper Montague Street, that there was even a fear of Mr. Barrett intercepting them if they were sent direct to Wimpole Street.

It had been a pleasure to hear through the Martins in Paris that Uncle Hedley unreservedly took the lovers' part against his brother-in-law. Of other relatives "Bummy," the aunt so closely connected with childhood, still took the father's side.

One genuine twinge of conscience Elizabeth had in regard to Mr. Barrett: he might read, and regard as an impudent flouting of himself, those lyrics, the hasty sweepings of her desk before flight, which *Blackwood's* printed in October. Five of these lyrics, though all clearly written before she knew Browning, dealt with the love of man and woman and, of the other two, "Hector in the Garden" vividly recalled a happy childhood at Hope End.

By the middle of October the Brownings were wishing they had not taken their apartment for six months: there was little to see in Pisa, the country round was monotonously flat for Robert's walking, and their position near the Cathedral rather noisy. The bells, Elizabeth told Boyd, who was a connoisseur in them, beginning at four o'clock in the morning, "rang my dreams apart." The fourth bell, with a profound note, called *Pasquareccia,* which was tolled on the occasion of an execution, had a ghastly effect "dropped into the deep of night like a thought of death." Sometimes all the bells of all the churches would be shaken together in a peculiar discordance. Nor was the position of the Collegio Ferdinando of the most cheerful:

*The funerals throng past our windows. The monks, sometimes
all in black, and sometimes all in white (according to the order), chant in a train, carrying torches . . and on the bier
comes the corpse . . openfaced . . except just a veil. At first,
we both used to wish to see the sight . . but the horror (my
old horror, tell Arabel) grew too strong for me soon . . and he
[Robert] feels it too, and attends to me often when I say, "Oh,
don't go to the window." But sometimes he cries out . . "I
can't help it, Ba—it draws me." Such horrible, hoarse chanting,
it is.— Like the croaking of death itself.*

Pisa was too, we are told by others, full of coughing invalids
come there for a supposed benefit to the chest. An Italian impression of the city was summed up in a jingling tag, *Pisa pesa
a chi posa*.[1]

We may guess that to a man of Browning's essentially nervous temperament this life was, for all its perfect happiness, a
considerable strain. Apart from his tendency to worry over
ways and means, seclusion for most of the day in a warm room
was not good for one who was a social man and a great walker.
Elizabeth pressed him to a couple of small extravagances, a
subscription to a good library where newspapers and French
books could be obtained, and a pianoforte. To the first he conceded, but was obdurate on the second point, Elizabeth having
imprudently admitted that she did not perform. "The idea of
even *seeming to have anything for himself* . . (though I have
talked myself hoarse about my love of music and so on) is quite
enough to make Robert turn back determinedly. He calls it a
foolish expense."

Some little relief from the strain of this close, concentrated
life, the more exhausting because of his ardent love for the
fragile woman, Browning now found in work upon a collected
edition. Elizabeth, for her part, was composing an anti-slavery
poem "too ferocious, perhaps, for the Americans to publish:
but they asked for a poem, and shall have it." This was "The
Runaway Slave at Hurst Point" ("Pilgrim's Point" in English
collected editions). It was printed in the *Liberty Bell*, on sale
at the Boston Anti-Slavery Bazaar of 1848.

[1] "Pisa weighs down upon him who stays there."

At the end of January the Brownings had their first touch of domestic trouble: Wilson was taken ill while she was attending on her mistress at bedtime. Dr. Cook, being sought by Robert, pronounced her to be suffering from delayed seasickness on a stomach already disordered. Wilson was put to bed with five leeches on her side. One guesses from the doctor's remarks, conveyed by Elizabeth to her sisters in a dramatic account of Wilson's illness, that the maid had aggravated her case by indulgence in good things from the *trattoria*.

Elizabeth, who had been sitting with her feet in hot water when Wilson collapsed, had run to Robert's room with feet bare: for this she was well scolded ("I wanted to kill him. . . . I played with his life, etc., etc!"). Now she, who perhaps had never attempted such tasks before, had to dress herself, to do her own hair and perform Wilson's household duties. The nursing and preparation of breakfast was undertaken by "The Signorina," perhaps the daughter of their landlord, who had already shown them attention in the way of gifts of fine oranges and of Italian dishes not always agreeable to the English palate; a general benevolence not uncalled for since he was so heavily overcharging them for the apartment.

Frightened by her illness, Elizabeth suggested that Wilson should return home to be nearer her own people, but Wilson wanted to remain. Apart from a devotion to her mistress, and a growing interest in this new country, the maid had an easy place with plenty of opportunity for outdoor exercise. In a few months it was to prove particularly fortunate that Wilson had decided to stay.

It was in March that the Brownings' happiness was broken into by a minor tragedy, a natural event made unnatural by the heedlessness of a woman who perhaps thought herself unlikely at her age to bear children: a miscarriage at five months' date. Wilson had suspected her condition, but she had apparently been only too zealous in predicting it since the marriage: Elizabeth had taken no notice of her. The maid too had hinted that in case of pregnancy the morphia Elizabeth continued to take, though in diminished quantity, might affect herself and the child.

Elizabeth, attacked now with pains in the night, submitted

to a doubt and, at last genuinely frightened, wrote over to Mr.
Jago to ask his opinion in regard to the drug-taking. But, still
convinced in her own mind that she was not pregnant, she refused to see Dr. Cook, putting off Robert in his urgency "with
ever so many impertinent speeches, and obstinate ones." She
had but contracted an internal chill.

The pains, however, getting more severe, Dr. Cook was summoned. He spoke sternly of a lack of precaution, of unsuitable
conditions, "the room at seventy, a scandalous fire, a wrong
posture"; sitting for hours at a time on a low stool before the
blazing pine logs. Elizabeth still refused to believe in a patent
fact. Then came the crisis, painful, but doing her no injury.
Browning's agony was intense: when readmitted to her room he
"threw himself down on the bed in a passion of tears, sobbing
like a child . . he who has not the eyes of a ready-weeper."

Six days later Elizabeth, pronounced rather benefited than
harmed by the miscarriage, was carried to her sofa in the sitting-room; by March 30 she was allowed to walk a little. They
need not abandon their plan, said Dr. Cook, of joining Mrs.
Jameson at Florence in a fortnight's time, but there must be no
travelling northward first as had been intended.

Already Elizabeth was making projects for the autumn, projects hardly to be dreamed of a year ago, of riding up mountains, of travel north, "a week at Bologna to visit Rossini," and
eventually a winter in Venice, where they might meet Mr. Kenyon. Lying in bed while she recovered, Elizabeth had been
thinking with ever-increasing gratitude of Mr. Kenyon. Her
cousin had not only pressed them to regard him as banker in
case of need, but had praised Browning to an angry father and
undertaken the task, so uncongenial to a man by temperament
inclined to avoid unpleasant encounters, of arranging the trans-
fer of investments to Elizabeth's husband.

In appearance, when again "all dressed up and ringleted,"
Elizabeth considered herself, though a little pale, rather improved than otherwise. Again at the open window, she could
enjoy exquisite weather. "The air seems to float its balmy softness *into* you."

Browning, perhaps as a result of the strain put upon him by
his wife's illness, was working himself up into a state of agita-

tion. They were going to Florence where, even more than in
Pisa, there was danger of being plagued by members of "a
mixed society"; the English living abroad, often of doubtful
reputation, and foreigners, not of the best, who courted their
company. Walking up and down the room he would point out
the experience of Mrs. Jameson, whose entrance into that mixed
society had gained her "nothing . . except the acquaintance
of two interesting foreigners" neither of whom she considered
fit for Gerardine to associate with.

"Those people will spoil all our happiness, if we once let
them in,—you will see— If you speak of your health and save
yourself on that plea, they will seize upon *me*—oh, don't I know
them!"

Elizabeth, lying placidly back in her chair, would try to turn
the subject, but Browning had worked himself up into a state
beyond jest or reason. "There is that coarse, vulgar Mrs. Trollope—I do hope, Ba, if you don't wish to give me the greatest
pain, that you won't receive that vulgar, pushing, woman who
is not fit to speak to you."

Elizabeth became more urgent. "Well . . now we are at
Mrs. Trollope! you will have your headache in a minute—now
do sit down, and let us talk of something else, and be quite sure
that if we get into such scrapes, it won't be my fault."

Their landlord at the Collegio Ferdinando, having made such
an excellent profit, was reluctant to part with the Brownings,
hoping fondly to the last, Elizabeth averred, that she might
have a relapse, so as not to be able to leave his rooms. Browning
declared that, if they stayed much longer in this apartment,
they would have "fallen fixed into barbaric habits"; would have
been inviting visitors to "take a mug of coffee" or request them,
in the absence of any bells, to "be so good as to thump with
your fist on that door," a knock being their only means of sum-
moning Wilson.

They set off on April 17, travelling uncomfortably in the
coupé of a *diligence*. For most of the journey Elizabeth lay
across her husband's knees to avoid the worst of the swaying.
The Tuscan scene, soon to grow familiar, passed them by; the
intensely cultivated hedgerows festooned with ropes of vine,
hills topped with little ancient towns, "the abrupt black line of

cypresses," the tall umbrella pines, the river Arno curling, winding on its way to Florence; all, in both colour and form, in sharp contrast to the scene of childhood, the soft English green of meadow and sheep-dotted down, the gentle undulating curve of Malvern Hills.

CHAPTER 22

FLORENCE [1847–9]

THE BROWNINGS ARRIVED in Florence on April 20, settling down in an excellent apartment in the Via delle Belle Donne at £4 a month, about thirty shillings less than in Pisa for far greater comfort; a sofa, a spring chair, real cups instead of the "famous mugs of Pisa." Luxury extended to decanters and champagne glasses. Wilson's comment on the new order of things was succinct but eloquent: "It's something like!" All that remained to be hired was a pianoforte at a price surely well within even Robert's range of economy, ten shillings a month including the hire of music.

Elizabeth, still weak from the miscarriage and affected by the jolting coach, had to spend a week lying down; having caught but one tantalizing glimpse of the beautiful ancient city as they entered. It pleased her to think of "our dear old yellow Arno" flowing through Florence, a living link with Pisa.

Mrs. Jameson and Gerardine were to join them as guests on the 24th. On the evening of the 23rd, however, they arrived unexpectedly, Mrs. Jameson with a bottle of wine in her hand; having thought it appropriate that she should be with the two poets on that date to drink to the immortal memory. She found Elizabeth on a sofa listening to Robert at the pianoforte. The tune he played was "The Light of Love," an air reputed to be a favourite with Shakespeare.

"Everybody was delighted to meet everybody," Elizabeth told Mrs. Martin, "and Roman news and Pisan dullness were properly discussed on every side."

In this letter to Mrs. Martin Elizabeth gives us our first intimation of interest in the Italian struggle for freedom with which she was so closely to identify herself.

Italy was at this time a series of small states dominated by the Hapsburg and Bourbon dynasties, with one notable exception, that of the Kingdom of Sardinia, which included the ducal crowns of Piedmont and Savoy (including Nice) and the former Republic of Genoa with its capital at Turin. The King of Sardinia was Italy's only native ruler, and one who, with the possession of Savoy and Piedmont, straddled the Alpine barrier to the north, thus holding a strategic position in Europe. His determination one day to oppose Austria in Italy was by 1846 made clear in the preparation of armies.

All these states were reactionary, priest-ridden, and seething with discontent. "Young Italy," led by the republican patriot Giuseppe Mazzini, had already attempted to raise a banner of revolution in Savoy. The worst oppression was in the Neapolitan states, which included the Sicilies, and in the Papal States.

But, curiously enough, it was in the most reactionary, the most backward, the Papal State, that some measure of Liberal reform began. At Rome Pope Pius IX, in his first year of office, was now astonishing the world by a line of conduct wholly new in Papal policy; granting an amnesty to political adversaries, giving permission for the installation of railroads and gas in the Papal States, and showing concern for the education of his people. He went about daily on foot and, without a guard, would make evening visits to the houses of the poor, "a sort of Christian Haroun el Raschid of the nineteenth century." He lived, Mrs. Jameson told the Brownings, "in an atmosphere of love and admiration," and "doing *what he can*"; in other words, combating by example the injustice, the backward social conditions in other Italian states by Austrian tyranny, but necessarily wielding a power in its essence opposed to freedom of thought. Browning's comment on this remark of Mrs. Jameson's is characteristic: "A dreadful situation, after all, for a man of understanding and honesty! I pity him from my soul, for he can, at best, only temporise with truth." That supple mind was later to present in *The Ring and the Book* a moral dilemma of the Vicar of Christ at once so powerful and hedged in by the rigour of tradition. These were subtleties not at once appreciated by his wife with her more direct vision. Elizabeth's comment here was: "but human nature is doomed to pay a high price for its opportunities." Where Browning could see the legitimacy of moral doubt, she would be aware with heart and soul of a clear duty to be performed.

Browning's interest in Pope Pius IX prepared him to go further than sympathy: already in Pisa he had written to Richard Monckton Milnes (one of the first to congratulate him on his marriage) of "this tiptoe expectation of poor Italy" and a desire to give practical help. Thinking, only too hopefully, that the British Government might send a mission to this enlightened Pope, he offered himself as secretary.

The Brownings, with Mrs. Jameson and Gerardine as their guests, were enjoying the new pleasure of hospitality, and certainly not at a cost beyond their purse: the local *trattoria* could provide an excellent dinner of five courses for the four of them, with enough left over for Wilson, at a total cost of 4s. 6d. Wine was proportionately cheap. Their only handicap as hosts was Robert's inability, neat-handed man though he was, to carve a joint. Mrs. Jameson, able to watch him in his own home, was more than ever struck with Browning's devotion and his wise care of a delicate wife. His inexhaustible spirits amazed her.

It was a disappointment that Elizabeth was unable to visit the art galleries under Mrs. Jameson's expert guidance, but her fine and stimulating talk helped to restore the invalid. Some element of vexation there was, however: Gerardine, who was in her aunt's opinions so half-hearted a student, had while in Rome "completed her offences by falling in love with a bad artist! an unrefined gentleman!! a Roman catholic! (converted from protestantism!) a poor man!! with a red beard!!! what ever Geddie could mean by it was what Mrs. Jameson in her agony couldn't divine." Indeed, Mrs. Jameson was inclined to put the blame for this mishap upon the Brownings. It was their love and happiness, the disappointed aunt decided, that had infected "the dear child who never thought in her whole life before of love and marriage."

Elizabeth, privately sympathizing, had to listen to Geddie's own version of the affair. Mr. Macpherson was so good, generous, and handsome; "likely to be a good artist *when he tries*," likely to revert to Protestantism. Mr. Macpherson had "left off smoking just to please aunt Nina, and was very firm."

Geddie and her aunt left Florence early on the 30th, kissing Elizabeth good-bye as she lay between sleeping and waking. It

was the last time she was to see Mrs. Jameson before her return
to England.

In Elizabeth's affection for Mrs. Jameson there was, one may
guess, a certain intermingled admiration and pity; the generous
pity of a happy sheltered woman and admiration for one who
was a partisan of the oppressed, pioneer for the freedom of her
sex. "To be a *road-maker,*" Elizabeth wrote to her, "is weary
work, even across the Apennines of life. We have not science
enough for it if we have strength, which we haven't either." A
hidden feeling for young love breaks out in this letter to Geddie's aunt: "My sympathies to go with you entirely, while I wish
your dear Gerardine to be happy; I wish it from my heart." Elizabeth pressed Mrs. Jameson to come back to Italy soon and
stay with Robert and herself, or near them if she preferred so.
With this warm-hearted impulsive woman the Brownings were
even willing to share their solitude.

Elizabeth was still not strong enough for the full enjoyment
of Florence, but there had been "an inglorious glorious drive
round the Piazza Gran Duca, past the Duomo, outside the walls,
and in again at the Cascine. It was like the trail of a vision in
the evening sun. I saw the Perseus in a sort of flash." "Oh this
cathedral!" she wrote to Henrietta, "so grand it is, with its pile
of tesselated domes. . . . Think of a mountainous marble
Dome, veined with inlaid marbles—marble running through
marble: like a mountain for size, like a mosaic for curious art—
rivers of colour inter-flowing, but all dimly." They had taken
two walks in the cool evening, the second "as far as the Bap-
tistry where we sat down in the half dark and talked of Dante."
And at Florence, Dante's Florence, "the river rushes through
the midst of its palaces like a crystal arrow" beneath the four
bridges,

> *Bent bridges, seeming to strain off like bows*
> *And tremble while the arrowy undertide*
> *Shoots on and cleaves the marble as it goes.*

She marked how at sunset the river reflects in faithful sem-
blance churches, houses, windows, bridges, and people walking, the only difference being that "down below, there is double
movement; the movement of the stream beside the movement
of life."

Soon the heat increased. Elizabeth sat with doors open, French windows thrown back wide, and green blinds drawn. It was true that she had felt the heat of a London summer more oppressive, but this was as yet only May.

Every afternoon, after their three o'clock dinner, Robert would wheel a great chair into his dressing-room—the coolest in the afternoon—sit her comfortably back and apply eau-de-cologne to hands and forehead. At six in the evening, when the "muslin curtains seemed to sigh themselves out—blowing to and fro," they would walk out to enjoy sweet air blowing along the ground. In spite of the heat Elizabeth was gaining strength.

But Flush could not so soon become acclimatized: there were two days of misery while he was seriously ill. Robert declared that Elizabeth "gave up loving him and only thought of Flush." The dog had fits of screaming. If they pulled him out from some dark hiding-place he would stare wildly as if he knew none of them. He refused to drink. His human friends thought miserably of hydrophobia, but after two doses of castor oil in one day, administered by Browning while his mistress hid herself in the furthest room, their patient recovered. Flush took the nauseous draught quietly, as if he knew it would cure him; though, doglike, making capital out of sweet sympathy, moaning piteously to Elizabeth. A lump of sugar made him forget grief, and he was soon as "insolent as ever," though on the whole behaving better than at Pisa.

On May 21 Elizabeth ventured into the Tribuna, with some friends of the Barretts who were visiting Florence, and saw for the first time those "divine" Raphaels, dulcet, smooth, placed so high in the realm of art by the earlier Victorians. She drove to other shrines of historic beauty, entering the Cathedral, doing reverence at the tomb of Michelangelo in Santa Croce. These friends, the Hanfords, acted as witnesses to the Brownings' marriage settlement. Neither husband nor wife, hating such mundane detail, would read it through, though Elizabeth at a glance discovered that the document provided for "a countless progeny! and all 'future husbands'!!"

They were now admitting a few strangers within their enchanted circle, the first being, fittingly enough in view of their many friendships in the coming years, an American "on the

point of leaving Florence and very tame and inoffensive" who
desired to "pay his respects." Their first acquaintance was
American too, Hiram Powers, the sculptor once so popular
whose "tinted Venus" was so much admired, and whose "Greek
Slave," later to be a major exhibit at the Great Exhibition of
1851, was (in the words of Henry James) "so undressed, yet so
refined, even so pensive, in sugar-white alabaster, exposed under little domed glass covers in such American homes as could
bring themselves to think such things right." Elizabeth thought
Powers "of the most charming simplicity, with those great
burning eyes of his . . . like a wild Indian's, so black and full
of light."

The eternal charm of Florence having taken hold of them,
the poets decided only to leave in full summer's heat, and to return in the autumn. Elizabeth set her heart on a retirement for
the hot season to Vallombrosa, then fully occupied by the Monastery of San Guilberto, high up on a slope of the Protomagno
mountains; a retreat cool in shade, rich in beauty and in association, but seemingly impossible for a woman, and a delicate
one at that.

But to Vallombrosa she would go, and to no other place.
When there appeared to be no chance of obtaining permission
Elizabeth went on "crying for my moon like a spoilt child in a
pet." After some delay however they secured a letter recom-
mending them "for various rare and valuable qualities" to the
Abbot, and requesting him to allow them to make a stay there.

In early July the heat became almost unbearable. They were
"being burnt up, suffocated, exterminated." Flush, creeping under sofas, "turned his head away from warm milk, and his tail
from soft cushions." The Brownings longed to leave Florence
but Elizabeth, waywardly infected on a sudden by Robert's
economic frame of mind, put off the decision from day to day.
The Italian almanac, in which they had strong faith, prophesied
rain which *mitiferà l'eccessivo caldo*—why therefore should
they sacrifice three weeks' rent by leaving before their period
was up, on the 22nd of the month? But a week before the 22nd
Elizabeth gave in. They set off for Vallombrosa.

It would seem as if a measure of common prudence should
have made Browning deny her "moon" to his wife, so frail, so

impetuous, so childlike in feverish desire: the journey to Vallombrosa entailed at that time some forty miles of rough travelling, and on arrival they could not be sure of their reception.
Elizabeth herself was half anticipating a rebuff. "They will take
Robert into the monastery," she predicted, "and leave Wilson
and me on the outside with other unclean beasts. We shall not
be let dine together, even, I dare say! Perhaps we may have
coffee sometimes, or walk out—but otherwise there will be a
divorce." But so far as his wife's health was concerned, Robert's
faith, or temerity, was justified: she survived without mishap
the journey up and a return down the mountains a few days
later.

They started out at three o'clock in the morning, and, happily
anticipating a two months' stay, armed with a dozen of port for
Elizabeth's daily fortification. At Pelago they left the road and
proceeded for the last five miles up winding paths between the
trees, Robert on horseback, Flush and the women in wine-
basket sledges drawn by two white bullocks. This last lap of the
journey lasted four hours. On arrival at the monastery, Elizabeth was so tired she had scarcely appetite for the beef and
oil they were offered at the House of Strangers. Food was a first
disappointment: they had hoped to live on eggs, milk, bread
and butter, but found they might as well have expected manna
from heaven. Bread could be got, but, with its fetid smell, it
"stuck in the throat like Macbeth's amen!" This bread Elizabeth
disposed of by the schoolgirl trick of slipping it under the table.

The Monastery of San Guilberto was an austere retreat: its
monks, all of high birth, even mortified themselves by cleaning
out the pigsties with bare hands. Its little red-faced Abbot provided the second and most severe disappointment, declaring
that no permit from Authority in Florence should override his
strict rule that a sojourn in the House of Strangers should be but
a brief one. One concession he did make, that these visitors
might remain two days beyond the allotted three, but then they
must go. Up here on the holy mountain, Elizabeth commented
sadly, the filth of a pigsty was less uncleanly to monkish hands
than the little finger of a woman.

As a second Eve she was driven out of her Eden, that same

Vallombrosa which it is said moved Milton to his description of Paradise; from the hanging forests of chestnut and beech, the "great, silent, ink-black pine-wood" where they had walked so happily. Even she had seen eagles in flight. They went down again to Florence in the glory of an unforgettable daybreak and found their apartment stifling.

One member of the party rejoiced, however, in spite of a breathless contrast with mountain air: Flush had hated Vallombrosa, was frightened in the pine forest and, in short, preferred "civilised life, and the society of little dogs with turned-up tails." The one flaw in doggy content was the fleas that at times afflicted Flush to the verge of despair. His master and mistress would kneel patiently by him with comb and a basin of water, but with little relief to him. Elizabeth could hardly bear to watch him tearing at his pretty curls. In the end Robert was to take the drastic remedy of shaving off those curls in the hottest weather.

They spent the rest of the summer in a new apartment on the Pitti side of the Arno, close to the Grand Duke's palace, in the Via Maggio, a fashionable situation only within their means because this was the dead season in Florence. They occupied a spacious suite of well-furnished first-floor rooms in the Palazzo Guidi, later more familiar to us as Casa Guidi and their permanent home. The rent, no higher than in the Via delle Belle Donne, included admission to the large and beautiful Boboli Gardens close by.

One side of Casa Guidi faces the old grey wall of San Felice Church, so that on a balcony outside their drawing-room they could walk in the moonlit cool of the evening in absolute privacy. They were to find the nights rather noisy on the Via Maggio, but by day the position was an ideal one for the woman who was so to identify herself with the Italian people: all the processions in time of *festa* or national rejoicing passed down Via Maggio into the Pitti Square, where stood the palace of the Grand Duke of Tuscany.

Here in this lovely city, alone with her husband, Elizabeth lay back and enjoyed to the full her new existence. "I take it for pure magic, this life of mine," she told Miss Mitford. "Surely

nobody was ever so happy before. I shall wake some morning
with my hair all dripping out of the enchanted bucket, or if not
we shall both claim the 'Flitch' next September."

Life outside the Casa Guidi seemed as yet to Elizabeth untouched by care:

*For what helps to charm here is the innocent gaiety of the peo-
ple, who, for ever at feast day and holiday celebrations, come
and go along the streets, the women in elegant dresses and with
glittering fans, shining away every thought of Northern cares
and taxes, such as make people grave in England. No little or-
phan on a house step but seems to inherit naturally his slice of
water-melon and bunch of purple grapes, and the rich frater-
nise with the poor as we are unaccustomed to see them, listening to the same music and walking in the same gardens, and
looking at the same Raphaels even! Also we were glad to be
here just now, when there is new animation and energy given to
Italy by this new wonderful Pope, who is a great man and doing greatly.*

"And the spark spreads!" she added happily. The Grand Duke,
inspired by the Pope's example, had allowed the formation of a
Civic Guard in open defiance of Austrian prohibition. Her Liberal heart rejoiced. "The world learns, it is pleasant to observe."

The celebration of their wedding day on September 12 was
doubly happy: that day the world outside rejoiced too: Florence, packed with people, was celebrating in a great festa the
establishment of a Civic Guard. A long procession passed down
Via Maggio to the Pitti, where the Grand Duke and his family
stood at a palace window to receive them. Past windows bright
with silks and carpets hung out, Florence in ever dignified aspect, the Magistrates, the Priests, the Lawyers, the Artists, the
Trade Guilds, marched rich with flowing banners, followed by
representatives with their ensigns of each Tuscan state, and
sympathizers, Greek, English, French. All this colour, this elation of spirit, went into Elizabeth's poem *Casa Guidi Windows*,
treasured up now in her heart as she hung over a window
draped with crimson silk waving a handkerchief until her wrist
ached. For three and a half hours they marched by:

> *At which the stones seemed breaking into thanks*
> *And rattling up the sky, such sounds in proof*

> *Arose; the very house-walls seemed to bend;*
> *The very windows, up from door to roof,*
> *Flashed out a rapture of bright heads.*

But "on the famous evening of that famous day," an anniversary so worthily celebrated, Flush put an end to private rejoicing. He had been watching beside her, his paws hanging over the window-sill, but, thinking "they were rather long about it, particularly as it had nothing to do with dinner and chicken bones and subjects of consequence," he slipped out of doors and did not return that night. At nine o'clock next morning he was found waiting at the door of their apartment. "I imagine," Elizabeth wrote, "he was bewildered with the crowd and the illumination, only as he *did* look so very guilty and conscious of evil on his return, there's room for suspecting him of having been very much amused, 'motu proprio,' as our Grand Duke says in the edict."

They were meeting a few more people now, though Powers remained their chief friend. One of them, a "vivacious little person, with sparkling talk enough," Mary Boyle, niece to the Earl of Cork, was present with them as they watched the procession. Mary Boyle would descend on the Brownings most evenings before going on to late parties, and, though her society was welcome, sometimes she tired Elizabeth by staying on too long. Miss Boyle, in her reminiscences, gives us a pleasant picture of Mrs. Browning as she appeared during those "hours of enchantment" spent at the Casa Guidi; Elizabeth would be lying on a sofa with Flush in her lap. "The pale thin hand of his mistress rested on the glossy head of that 'gentle fellow-creature' like a benediction."

I have never, in the course of my life seen a more spiritual face, or one in which the soul looked more clearly from the windows; clusters of long curls, in a fashion now obsolete, framed her small delicate face, and ever shrouded its outline, and her form was so fragile as to appear but an etherial covering.

Among the most interesting new acquaintances were the Hoppners, Byron's friends in Venice, and the Storys. William Wetmore Story, son of the famous Judge Story of Boston, was himself a lawyer of note, but now hesitating on the brink of a new career as sculptor. Story and his charming wife, strongly attracted towards the Brownings on this first encounter, were, on their return to Italy in 1851, to become fast friends.

A two months' tenancy at Casa Guidi came to an end: as the Brownings had decided to winter in Rome it was perhaps at first only for a short period that they took a new apartment in the Via Maggio, an apartment they found both quieter and cooler. But Elizabeth was again pregnant.[1] In October, when they had decided to go, her doctor, making a mistake in the date on which the child should be born,[2] prohibited the journey. Elizabeth was very disappointed. Apart from an ardent desire to see Rome, she wished to join an old friend there, a Mrs. Fanny Dowglass; she was the more annoyed because of a conviction that the doctor was wrong. But, as she told her friend, "I made a mistake at Pisa & therefore had no right to be persistent."

The Via Maggio apartment, from being cool, proved to be cold when autumn came. At a sacrifice of six months' rent, which he could ill afford, Browning removed his wife at the end of October to "funny rabbit-hutch rooms" drenched in sunlight on the Piazza Pitti, exactly opposite the Duke's palace. There Elizabeth could enjoy a grand-stand view of Italian life and politics: it was probably there that she wrote the first part of *Casa Guidi Windows*, called at first "A Meditation in Tuscany," which *Blackwood's*, reflecting a general lack of interest in Italian politics at home, refused to publish.

Here on the Piazza Pitti their new Civic Guard, in helmets and epaulets, daily delighted crowds of admiring Florentines. Robert, looking at the Guard with more realistic eye, said musingly: "Surely after all this, they would *use* those muskets." It was rumoured that the Guard, very naturally liking its uniform to be admired, had proposed it should only do day service, leaving the unspectacular and tedious night work to the "ancient military." This "triviality and innocent vanity of children" at first only amused Elizabeth, but later she was to be exasperated by what appeared the supine attitude of her Florentines to Austrian tyranny; but Austrian though he was, tyranny in the

---

[1] Unpublished letter to Mrs. Fanny Dowglass, October 26, 1847, Huntington Library Collection.

[2] Unpublished letter to Fanny Dowglass, April 6, 1848, Huntington Library Collection.

person of the stupid but kindly Gran Duca, called affectionately the *"gran ciuca"* (great ass), was not unacceptable to many Tuscans. Because the Duke was a wealthy man taxes were light and the fine *mezzeria* system of agriculture in his realm made the peasants happier, more prosperous than anywhere else in Italy. Never had these people known real freedom. Besides, any gesture for freedom might entail summary punishment from Vienna, which kept close control; perhaps imprisonment in the infamous fortress of Spielberg.

Sitting together in their rooms "under the very eyelids of the sun" Robert and Elizabeth read, wrote, talked, and enjoyed music. News of the outside world, of Miss Martineau in her new Ambleside home, of Tennyson's last poems, and, above all, of family affairs, came to them mostly through letters; though they did hear of Mrs. Jameson and Geddie in Rome from Father Prout, who, being but two hours in Florence, "of course, according to contract of spirits of the air," met Robert, kissing him in the open street before he disappeared inside a *diligence.*

Florence was quiet enough that winter, but the early months of 1848 brought hope and joy to those who longed for Italian liberty: January saw risings in Falerno and Naples. In February there was revolution in Paris, overthrowing the Bourbon dynasty, a declaration of independence in Sicily, revolutions in the German states, and agitation even in Vienna itself. The Emperor of Austria abdicated, the powerful, sinister Metternich was driven into exile.

The Grand Duke of Tuscany, taking heart to oppose his masters in Vienna, granted a constitution. His popularity with the warm-hearted Florentines grew to fever pitch.

One night as Elizabeth was preparing for bed, Robert called her to the window. Through darkness below, "a great flock of stars seemed sweeping up the Piazza." The people of Florence, having recognized their Duke on a private visit to the Opera, were bringing him home in triumph amid a cluster of waxen torches. The *Evvivas* were deafening. "So glad I was," this enthusiastic childlike woman wrote to her friend Miss Mitford, "I, too, stood at the window and clapped my hands. If ever Grand Duke deserved benediction this Duke does."

During this sunny Italian winter Elizabeth was well, putting on flesh, visiting the galleries; but in early March there came an abrupt check, a second miscarriage,[3] this time partly brought about, Browning declared, by "the long, long, far too long letters that she *would* write the day before."

Elizabeth was kept in bed for a week. Again she suffered no harm, her doctor declaring that "the constitution has shown an astonishing energy." Though naturally disappointed by this further mishap, she wrote bravely to Fanny Dowglass: "the right thought suggests itself naturally, that God has blessed me so abundantly in some things, there is scarcely room for a greater weight of blessing. Children may be kept for those, who have not such a husband as I, perhaps!"

Delicious spring weather helped her to gain strength. At the first moment possible she drove out with Robert in a hired carriage "to our old Paradise—the Cascine, and saw the elms as green as ever they mean to be, and the grass like emeralds, and the pheasants all alive and flying." In order to reach the Cascine Gardens they passed by ancient buildings rich with association: "such a door where Lapo stood, and past the famous stone where Dante drew his chair out to sit. Strange, to have all this old-world life about us, and the blue sky so bright besides, and ever so much talk on our lips about the new French revolution, and the King of Prussia's cunning, and the fuss in Germany and elsewhere."

There were stirring events nearer home to discuss as they rode: the Austrians had been driven from Milan, from Venice, and the republics declared. The puppet princes of Modena and Parma had fled.

Inspired by a wave of popular enthusiasm in the north, Carlo Alberto, King of Sardinia, Duke of Savoy and Piedmont, the only active ruler in Italy, put himself at the head of an army. The Grand Duke, after a stirring proclamation, sent a contingent of his troops. There was war in Lombardy.

At the end of March Florence was illuminated, lit up in the peculiarly lovely Italian manner, "the Grand Duke throwing his Pitti palace in fire upon the sky." The Austrians had suffered an initial defeat. On the night before there had been turbulence

[3] Unpublished letter, April 6, 1848 to Fanny Dowglass, Huntington Library Collection.

before the Brownings' windows; a turbulence that in no wise
daunted Elizabeth. Amid a "shriek of curses" the crowd had
rushed to the Austrian Embassy, torn down the arms of Austria,
and burnt them before the Duke's palace; afterwards giving a
"*Viva Leopoldo secondo*" and dispersing peacefully.

During this time of stress foreigners, and especially the many
English living in Florence, had taken flight. The Brownings
were by no means disposed to follow this prudent example, but
rather to identify themselves more closely with the Florentines
by making a home there; a home from which they might take
wing when they chose. Indeed, without acquiring a still cheaper
apartment, with the additional advantage of being able to let it
in their absence, a plan to spend future summers in England
could not be carried out. Elizabeth's income from the ship
money was already reduced by £100 a year and likely to be
further lessened. Neither felt they could wait until more prosperous time to see their families again. Robert in particular
yearned for his mother: not a day passed without him speaking of her. In Italy unfurnished apartments were so inexpensive
that the fine suite in Casa Guidi, to which they were soon to return, only cost twenty-five guineas a year. Furniture, bought
out of their two years' earnings by writing, they could acquire
very cheaply now that so many people were rushing away from
Florence. They decided furthermore to add to their personal
comfort, probably without more expense, by engaging a man
servant who would be responsible for meals in future; one Alessandro, who proved to be highly efficient, if somewhat con-
sequential.

The suite they occupied on the first floor was that which the
last Count Guidi had occupied: his arms were in scagliola on
Elizabeth's bedroom floor. They had six large high-ceilinged
rooms, "three of them quite palace rooms and opening on a
terrace." Furniture must be antique, worthy of the place. The
terrace Elizabeth determined to throng with orange trees and
camellias.

Casa Guidi is now so cut up into modern flats that it is difficult to visualize these fine rooms, this spacious apartment, but
the building still stands outwardly as it did, rather grim and forbidding in wedge shape against the Pitti Square.

A bust of Browning stands in the entrance way and on the outer wall a tablet placed there after Elizabeth's death by "a grateful Florence" and celebrating, in the words of the poet Tommaseo, the woman *"che in cuore di donna conciliava scienza di dotto e spirito di poeta e fece del suo verso aureo anello fra Italia e Inghilterra.*[4] Another tablet on the wall overlooking San Felice Church gives the beautiful first lines of her poem *Casa Guidi Windows,* commencing "I heard last night a little child go singing."

Elizabeth's first days in the Casa Guidi were saddened by news of the death of Hugh Boyd on May 10. Although it could not but be felt as a merciful end to many years of patient suffering, Elizabeth must grieve over the passing of this

> Steadfast friend
> *Who never didst my heart or life misknow,*
> *Nor either's faults too keenly apprehend,—*

Her heart was further touched when later she heard he had left to her the copies of Æschylus and Gregory Nazianzen from which she used to read to him, and a clock

> *Chiming the gradual hours out like a flock*
> *Of stars whose motion is melodious.*

On June 20 she told Mrs. Martin: "I am very well and quite strong again, or rather, stronger than ever, and able to walk as far as Cellini's Perseus in the moonlight evenings, on the other side of the Arno. Oh, that Arno in the sunset, with the moon and evening star standing by, how divine it is! . ." The statue of Perseus in the Loggia, springing forward with the Gorgon's severed head in his upraised hand, was to her a symbol of that Italy now upsurging to combat tyranny.

The furnishing of their apartment, proceeding slowly since nothing was to be admitted unworthy of the fine rooms, was Robert's concern: not only could he circulate more freely than Elizabeth, but he had the more sensitive eye for surroundings and, for all his earlier protestation of devotion to a simple life, a greater love of luxury. So particular was Browning about appearances that Elizabeth would be admonished for wearing

---

[4] "who in her woman's heart combined learning and poetry and made of her verse a golden ring linking Italy and England."

soiled gloves. The furniture, in the taste of the period and suiting their palatial rooms, was ornate, richly carved.

There was peace in Florence that summer, a sober peace during which the inhabitants indulged in no huzzas, illuminations, or fireworks, but concentrated on collecting all the money they could for the Army in Lombardy. The Brownings contributed according to their income.

A question was exercising Italian minds, one politically dangerous because the great patriot and prophet of Italian revolution, Mazzini, was a republican: whether the new Italy should be a kingdom under Charles Albert, or a series of federated republican states. France, their prototype in revolution, was now a Republic, but a troubled one. Some remarks on the news of a massacre there, coming to Mrs. Browning on July 4, made her reflect this indecision. Robert had belief in a French Republic though "with melancholy intermediate prospects," but Elizabeth thought the French would soon be impatient for a kingship. "How did you feel," she wrote to that other enthusiast for France, Miss Mitford, "when the cry was raised 'Vive l'Empereur'? Only Prince Napoleon is a Napoleon cut out in paper after all."

The hot season was now advancing. In July the Brownings sought change and coolness by going (deluded by Murray's Guide Book) to Fano "for the benefit of the sea air and the oysters." They found Fano unbearably hot, scorched up, "the very air swooning in the sun." Their only gains there were making the acquaintance of Mrs. Wiseman, mother of Dr. (later Cardinal) Wiseman, and seeing "a divine picture of Guercino's" which moved Browning to write "The Guardian-Angel":

> *We were at Fano, and three times we went*
> *To sit and see him in his chapel there,*
> *And drink his beauty to our soul's content*
> *—My angel with me too.*

After three days they left Fano for Ancona, "a striking sea city holding up against the brown rocks and elbowing out the purple tides, beautiful to look upon." There they stayed a week "living upon fish and cold water." The place was no cooler than Fano. All the long sun-hot hours Elizabeth lay on a sofa "with dishevelled hair at full length and 'sans gown, sans stays, sans shoes, sans everything' except a petticoat and a white dressing wrapper."

They wound up their holiday with "un bel giro," visiting Loreto, Sinigaglia, Pesaro, Rimini, Ravenna, Forli. The varied scenery drew constant admiration from every traveller except Flush, that urban dog, who had "a supreme contempt" for the beauty of landscape, only putting his head out of the window as they passed through a town or village.

Ravenna they found beautiful, "holding an atmosphere of purple glory," but oppressive: "the marshes on all sides send up stenches new and old, till the hot air is sick with them." Unarmed with a special permission, they were denied entrance to Dante's tomb: too angry to apply for one, they contented themselves with peering through the grated window. This was at an early hour, between three and four in the morning; that same night they passed on to Florence from the tomb of her exiled poet, arriving in the coolness of dawn.

After a three weeks' absence, Elizabeth was delighted to get back to Casa Guidi, now justly to be called home. "Florence seemed as cool as an oven after the fire; indeed, we called it quite cool, and I took possession of my own chair and put up my feet on the cushions and was charmed, both with having been so far and coming back so soon."

By now the forces of Charles Albert had been defeated at Custozza by Marshal Radetzky: the King had been obliged to retire beyond the Ticino and beg for an armistice. Though Garibaldi continued to harass the occupation army with his irregulars, Tuscany came again under the domination of Austria: the Pope, who had at first taken up the Liberal cause, now declared against the war.

The Florentines appeared to take their defeat tamely, "eating ices and keeping the feast of the Madonna," but putting up at a review in the Cascine Gardens a show of some 10,000 men. Mrs. Browning was bitter about an apparent lack of spirit. "Dante's soul has died out of the land."

One factor in Florentine acquiescence, apart from a natural fear of Austria's hard hand and a personal affection for the Duke, was an element in revolt of Mazzinian republicanism with its hostility to the Pope and established religion; constituting a pitiful and dangerous schism in Liberal ranks. These complications were perhaps not clear to Elizabeth, who as yet had no intimate acquaintance with Italians.

Autumn brought serious news from Rome. The Pope's support of Austrian tyranny had aroused anger in the republican party led by Mazzini. In November Count Pelligrino Rossi, a minister of Liberal tendencies appointed in Rome under the new Constitution, was foully assassinated, and there were threats of further violence if the Pope did not give in to republican terms. "The poor Pope I deeply pity," Elizabeth wrote; "he is a weak man with the noblest and the most disinterested intentions. . . . He should have gone out to them and so died, but having missed that opportunity, nothing remained but flight." Pio Nono, disguising himself, had escaped to Gaeta into the arms of the reactionary King Ferdinand of Naples, whom not long before he had denounced as a rogue.

Some Roman news was brought to them by word of mouth: William Wetmore Story had been in Rome with his wife and family. These vivacious, cultivated people had made their acquaintance during a brief visit to Florence in the spring of that year, but now an autumn there was to warm that acquaintance into the beginnings of a close friendship. It is worth perhaps regarding Robert and Elizabeth at this period with Story's keen eye.

In Elizabeth, sitting quietly deep in a large easy chair, he found "nothing of that peculiarity which one would expect from reading her poems. . . . Very unaffected and pleasant and simple-hearted is she." Robert he thought a man of "great vivacity, but not the least humour, some sarcasm, considerable critical faculty, and very great frankness and friendliness of manner and mind." It seems to us strange that anyone, especially a man so congenial, could find no humour in Browning, but perhaps at this time he was not his normal self. Story also speaks of twitching of the eyes and a general nervousness of manner. In September Robert was seriously ill.

He had been laid up for nearly a month with fever and an ulcerated sore throat; and, greatly to Elizabeth's anxiety, refused to see a doctor.

When Elizabeth was feeling particularly unhappy Father Prout made his next appearance and, ignoring the old adage about starving a fever, mixed a potion of eggs and port wine while Alessandro, the Brownings' man servant, lifted his eyes in horror, crying: "O, Inglesi, Inglesi!"

Not only this "eccentric prescription," which sent Robert off into a healing sleep, but Father Prout's own quaint and hearty manner did them both good. He called Elizabeth a "bambina" for being frightened. They were now to see him every day; "he came to doctor and remained to talk." "Not refined," Elizabeth commented on him, "in a social sense by any manner of means, yet a most accomplished scholar and vibrating all over with learned associations and vivid combinations of fancy and experience." He must also have brought them vital and intimate news from Rome, where he was closely in touch with workers for liberation; writing on their behalf for his journal, the *Daily News*, a forceful series of articles.

But the society of the unrefined Father Prout had its disadvantages: he was apt to stay too late over wine, to smoke heavily in Elizabeth's presence, and to demand a spittoon. He flourished a dubious handkerchief. His native cynicism too, and his malicious talk jarred on them both. He further offended by calling his hostess "Ba," that name the prerogative of those dearest to her.

But at length Father Prout left for Rome, though not without a threat, happily coming to nothing, of returning soon. Husband and wife settled down again to their quiet evenings of uninterrupted happiness.

Robert's devotion to his wife increased, if that were possible: Elizabeth was again with child. In order to run no risk this time she resolutely broke her long habit of taking a laudanum sedative. Apart from this effort, which must have required considerable courage and strength of mind, she had nothing to do but rest and wait, attended by her husband and Wilson.

Wilson, getting rapidly Italianized, had now an engaged lover in the rather lordly and handsome person of Mr. Righi, son of a medical man and a member of the Ducal Guard. The only flaw in Wilson's content was her fellow-servant, Alessandro, whose own efficiency made him touchy and overbearing.

On the grounds of being a travelled man, he claimed to know everything. Alessandro was graciously pleased, however, to approve his employers, whose domestic happiness appeared to him quite exceptional. The Signor was an angel "and the Signora was rather an angel too—she never spent two thousand scudi on her dress at once, as *he* had seen women do—so the Signor might well be fond of the Signora—but still for a Signor to be always sitting with his wife in that way, was most extraordinary."

The December of 1848 found Elizabeth despondent over chances of Liberal success. The Florentines around her appeared supine, effeminate; a downpour of rain seeming enough to damp revolutionary enthusiasm. France, the mother of Revolution, had now elected Prince Louis Napoleon as President on no better grounds, she considered, than that he was "*le neveu de son oncle.*" Italy was again in the grip of reaction and, although allowance must be made for the ferment of new wine, it was impossible, hearing news of anarchy in Rome, "to sympathise, to go along with the *people* to whom and to whose cause all my natural sympathies yearn"; these people who were too apt to assassinate, to destroy. "The holiness of liberty is desecrated by the sign of the ass's hoof."

One may guess that she was physically weighed down. Even that which had been earlier a pleasing interest, was now termed "the slow agonies of furnishing our apartment." Elizabeth was by nature too impatient to admire the caution with which Robert acquired belongings, keeping sternly within the limits of money earned, and the more constitutional slowness of the Italian race made her rail against delays in curtaining the windows. There was pure pleasure, however, to be got out of the news that Robert's new edition would soon be out, and that a performance by Phelps at Sadler's Wells Theatre of *A Blot in the 'Scutcheon* was a decided success. There were flowers too, about the house this December, "white roses as in June."

In January the Grand Duke, seeing that might was no longer on his side, himself fled to Gaeta, going there, ironically enough, by the aid of a free nation in the British war vessel *Bulldog*. A republican party, headed by men from Leghorn, strangers to Florence, took charge against the wishes of many Florentines who wanted their Duke back. The spirit of revolution was now abroad in Florence. The English who were still in residence packed their bags ready for instant flight.

The Brownings, however, remained both from choice and necessity: Elizabeth was not now in a condition to travel. Of those at Casa Guidi Wilson was the most disturbed since the future of her *fidanzato* depended on that of the Grand Duke. She wanted her lover to leave the Duke's service and settle down as a shopkeeper in Prato on money offered as a loan by a rich tradesman brother, but Mr. Righi seemed to be fonder of himself and his own dignity than of Wilson. Later, when the Duke's bodyguard was disbanded, Mr. Righi went to Prato.

Flush, that town dog, probably welcomed street disturbances: Elizabeth, who knew he would ultimately return, no longer worried over the dog's disappearances. With his hair grown again into glossy curls after the summer's shaving, Flush was full of insolence and liveliness, seeming with advancing age to grow "preternaturally wise." In the house he would sit apart and growl singularly, appearing to commune with himself. Robert had long been accepted, not as a rival, but a friend over whom to tyrannize: Flush could not foresee that a few months would bring another claimant on his mistress's affection.

CHAPTER 2 3

BIRTH AND DEATH; *CASA GUIDI WINDOWS* [1849–51]

AT A QUARTER PAST TWO in the morning of March 9, 1849, Elizabeth's son was born after some twenty-one hours of labour, a strong well-nourished child. During the long day and night of bitter pain Browning was with her whenever possible, holding her hand, and for the rest he waited in the drawing-room. To the end of his life he would point out the chair on which he sat.

To the sisters, and also presumably to his parents, though the letter has not survived, Browning wrote in the early hours of the morning. To Miss Mitford he sent the news minutely written on a scrap of paper, the whole folded up to the size of a postage stamp.

Elizabeth herself, exhausted but happy, would not see her child until Robert could bring him to her in his arms. As the doctor did not think she could feed him herself, a wet nurse had to be found. Four persons were tried, the one chosen being "a mighty woman, that would cut up into twenty Bas . . . good natured and intelligent spite of her fat cheeks which overflow her neck as she bends down." Three little tufts of hair were cut off the baby's head, one for the sisters, one for Treppy, to whom Elizabeth was "favourite child," and a third for Robert's mother.

While Elizabeth lay recovering from the birth much was happening outside Casa Guidi windows. The town was in a ferment, some calling (to the same tune, Elizabeth said) *"Viva la repubblica!"* and others *"Viva Leopoldo!"* Agitation for the return of the Duke was in part, Elizabeth declared, literally a *counter* revolution, since great indignation was aroused by the unwillingness of the Livornese, who dominated the republican party, to pay their café bills. This fact may have influenced certain waverers, but undoubtedly the peasants were wholehearted in their invitation to Duke Leopold to return: all they demanded of him was a promise to respect the new Constitution. The Duke, perhaps pardonably nervous at the general turn of events, hesitated.

In that disastrous month King Charles Albert took the offensive again, only to be overwhelmingly defeated at Novara on March 23. Out of this defeat, however, though it meant eleven more years of Austrian rule in northern Italy, a strength was to come. Convinced republicans might hold resolutely to their idea of federated states, but general opinion moved towards the more human conception of a united Italy under the House of Savoy, a conception unexpectedly strengthened by the provision of a royal martyr to the cause of freedom. Charles Albert, abdicating on the field of battle in favour of his son, the wise and intrepid Victor Emmanuel, died broken-hearted after a few months of illness. Thousands made pilgrimage to his tomb, as to that of a saint, and under a new, more severe oppression a fervour for liberty was kept up.

In Rome all at first seemed to augur well for the type of freedom favoured by the republican followers of Mazzini until, on April 25, General Oudinot landed with 8,000 men at Civitavecchia sent by Louis Napoleon to extinguish, in the name of the French Republic, all hope of Republican freedom in Rome. Garibaldi, after an heroic march into Rome at the head of a small band of irregulars, only escaped by a hairsbreadth.

This action of the First Consul, on the face of it cynical, ironic, was a severe blow to the cause of Italian freedom and a stunning shock to Liberal minds; the more so because the rise to power of a second Napoleon had heartened men to revolt, remembering as they did how in 1796 Napoleon himself had come as deliverer, though an arbitrary rapacious deliverer, from the thrall of Austria and her puppet princes. And had not this Napoleon, the nephew, himself in 1831 fought with the Carbonari against Papal troops in an abortive revolt at Cività Castellana? Now French forces were arriving in his name to restore Papal dominion. But Louis Napoleon, tortuous, astute, had his reasons: ambitious for an imperial crown and the old Napoleonic power in Europe, he must conciliate French Catholic opinion and strengthen his hand against Austria.

Of the man who had used power ruthlessly to drive Liberals from Rome, Elizabeth was not yet an unqualified admirer but, though she must condemn an action that "cast Rome helpless and bound into the hands of priests," she was willing to admit his position to be a difficult one. Up to a point, in her opinion, he had shown himself "an upright man with noble impulses." Her deep-rooted affection for France had perhaps first been aroused in a heart already warm with Napoleon-worship during that childish expedition of 1815. Later, in her close room, the novels of Balzac and other French writers brought a pulsing vicarious life to the invalid; so that now, from gratitude and habit, she identified herself almost as closely with France as with her beloved Italy.

At home in England, though they must often have been disturbed at the thought of Ba being so many miles away among those excitable subversive foreigners, the sisters were rejoicing over the birth of their first nephew, though with some amusement. "Tell Arabel," Elizabeth wrote them after receiving letters from Wimpole Street, "that her insult about my carrying him by the head is quite gratuitous." But she had to acknowledge that Robert seemed the more natural baby-minder.

At Hatcham there was little rejoicing, or rather a rejoicing amid sorrow: the elder Mrs. Browning, taken suddenly ill with an unsuspected ossification of the heart, lay in an unconsciousness preceding death. She could not know of the existence of her grandson. A few days later she died.

Sarianna broke the news gently to Robert, writing twice, telling of illness, and of its increasing seriousness, when in actual fact Robert's mother was dead. Even with this preparation he fell into a state of deep anguish, the excitement of his son's birth having laid him open the more to reaction. His was at first a stony grief, unable to find relief in tears. His only consolation could be, Elizabeth wrote, if his father and Sarianna could come to him at once. This, of course, was out of the question while the elder Browning was tied to an office chair. Elizabeth decided that as soon as possible she must get a change of scene for her husband, "but where to go? England looks terrible now. He says it would break his heart to see his mother's roses over the wall, and the place where she used to lay her scissors and gloves."

Outside Casa Guidi there was now open conflict between

the two parties. Shooting began: one day Robert had barely time to escape the fray. "The tree of Liberty," Elizabeth wrote, so proudly erected by republicans, had "come down with a crash." The baby in his cradle at Casa Guidi would be startled from sleep by noisy festas, rejoicings, first about this Liberty tree and then over its fall, each accompanied by the continual firing of guns and cannon.

"For my part," Elizabeth commented in May, "I am altogether *blasée* about revolutions and invasions. . . . Oh heavens! how ignoble it all has been and is! A revolution made by boys and *vivas,* and unmade by boys and *vivas*—no, there was blood shed in the unmaking—some horror and terror, but not as much patriotism and truth as could lift up the blood from the kennel." On the behaviour of her "beloved French" in Rome, Elizabeth was resolved to withhold judgment until the facts were clearer.

At the beginning of May the Grand Duke, having decided to accept an invitation from his loving subjects, came back, but accompanied by Austrian troops. Elizabeth, who had defended him against Robert's harsher opinion, now had to admit his treachery. "I give him up, having fought for him gallantly." With Austrian soldiers in the streets of Florence she was the more inclined to take a favourable view of Louis Napoleon's action, writing to Henrietta: "The French intervention has been awkwardly managed, but the *intention* . . . is, in my opinion, noble and upright—nothing else could have saved Rome, with Austria at the doors, and Russia behind Austria." Mazzini should have welcomed the French: in that case Napoleon could not have been reproached, as representative of one republic, for having put down another.

In this letter Elizabeth described the coming of the Austrians. The nurse called: "*Signora, signora, ecco i Tedeschi!*"
We ran out on the terrace together—and up from the end of the street and close under our windows came the artillery and baggage waggons—the soldiers sitting upon the cannons motionless, like dusty statues. Slowly the hateful procession filed under our windows. The people shrank back to let them pass, in the deepest silence—not a word spoken, scarcely a breath drawn. . . . For my part I felt my throat swelling with grief

and indignation. Oh, to think of our ever seeing such a sight from these windows. I wish we were a thousand miles away.
Robert came in, telling her that the Austrian General's proclamation, posted up, began with the words "Invited by your Grand Duke."

In this atmosphere of reaction and oppression Robert's grief over the loss of his mother remained sharp. Elizabeth, while sharing it in part—with some feeling of guilt since it was she who had parted those two close friends—had her own quieter sorrow: the birth of a grandson had not softened her father.

Mr. Barrett gave no sign. The brothers too remained inexorable except one who had written kindly and sent a note on the birth of her child. As her letters to him were not returned, Elizabeth tried to nourish a hope that her father at least took enough interest in her to read them: on this point she was later to be roughly disillusioned.

The baby, now two months old, was fat and rosy, reminding his mother of the Infant Christ in a reproduction of Raphael's "Virgin and Child" which used to hang in her room at Wimpole Street. He was full of life. *"O, questo bambino,"* said his proud nurse, *"è proprio rabbioso!"* In public he drew much admiration and attention. The nurse considered him to be not at all like an English child: in English children there was always *qualche cosa di strana*—something a bit queer.

On July 25 he was christened at the French Evangelical Protestant Church, a chapel at the Prussian Legation. His names, chosen by Elizabeth, were Robert Wiedeman, the second being the maiden name of Browning's mother. As Wiedeman the little creature was to be known, thus keeping alive in a manner she herself would have liked the memory of that grandmother who never knew him.

The heats of summer were beginning: with some difficulty Elizabeth persuaded Browning to leave Florence. They retired to the Bagni di Lucca high up in the mountains, taking with them the three servants. Little Wiedeman, now short-coated, was already babbling in baby language, a smiling friendly child. Robert, away from the place where grief first overwhelmed him, began to rally.

Flush, who had been sulking over the baby's advent, now

recovered his spirits too, running about in the fresher air and bathing—perhaps getting rid thus of the tiresome fleas of summer—in the hot springs, one of which gushed up close to the house. He became gracious towards Wiedeman, though always the child's love for him, rather too demonstrative, was stronger than his for the boy. This elderly animal, though he endured it with affection, could not be expected to welcome a heavy child scrambling on his back.

The Baths of Lucca were a favourite resort for coolness in summer; sheltered as they were by even higher mountains, so that a day of normal sunshine there was curtailed by four hours. The Grand Duke did all he could to attract visitors with balls, receptions, and other attractions. The Brownings stayed in the highest of the three villages called, because the Duke's estate was there, La Villa. Their house was "a sort of eagle's nest" that only donkeys and carrying-chairs could reach, lying *at the heart of a hundred mountains sung to continually by a rushing mountain stream. The sound of the river and of the cicala is all the noise we hear. Austrian drums and carriage wheels cannot vex us; God be thanked for it; the silence is full of joy and consolation.*

The Baths, which Browning had dreaded as "a sort of wasp's nest of scandal and gaming, with everything trodden flat by the Continental English," they found pleasantly deserted in this time of political trouble. Living was even cheaper than in Florence. Chestnut forests clustered thickly on the mountain; at night, so thick were the fireflies, they seemed to be "living among the stars." We hear nothing of mosquitoes on this healthy height; those mosquitoes Elizabeth feared far more than the Austrians.

But the Brownings were not entirely free to enjoy their Eden: anxiety haunted them. Cholera was raging in and about London. Near Hatcham it was virulent. Sarianna, who had promised to visit them in the autumn, would not now leave her father. Elizabeth herself was miserably aware that no danger would deter Mr. Barrett from remaining in Town, from going daily into the crowded City then so unsanitary with its stinking alley ways and horrible piled-up graveyards. "Love," she wrote sadly to Miss Mitford, "runs dreadful risks in the world."

There was a great event over which to rejoice within their owned charmed circle: "Baby has cut a tooth." The bright, healthy laughing boy was forward for his age in every particular.

About the child's upbringing there was one dispute between husband and wife: Robert very naturally wanting his son to grow up an Englishman, reproached Ba for talking to him in Italian. But, she protested, the child heard Italian all day from his voluble nurse, and from Wilson when she talked with the other servants. To hear English spoken would only confuse his small mind. When they visited England next year he could learn his native tongue in the natural way.

Elizabeth's recovered health enabled her to walk up and down steep hillside paths and even to ride, as they did one day, five miles on donkey-back to the Prato Fiorito, a velvety dome of flower-strewn grass deep in rugged mountains. They set off at half past eight in the morning and stayed out until six, riding where at some points a single slip of a donkey's foot would have meant precipitation into a deep ravine. The baby went with them, riding in turns with Wilson and the nurse.

While the Brownings were at Lucca, Elizabeth, coming quietly behind Robert as he stood looking out of the window, slipped into his hand a small book of manuscript: her love sonnets, the last written two days before marriage. She had delayed so long in giving them because of something he had said "against putting one's loves into verse." "A strange, heavy crown, that wreath of sonnets," her poet husband called them in writing of the event three years after her death to Julia Wedgwood.

On their return to Florence in October Robert was working on "Christmas Eve and Easter Day" and Elizabeth upon a collected edition. In this edition, published in 1850, the love poems were first published, lightly veiled under the title of "Sonnets from the Portuguese," chosen because "Caterina to Camoens" was a favourite with Browning. An attempt was made further to deflect attention from the personal character of the series by banishing to the last page of Volume I the sonnet beginning:

"My future will not copy fair my past"—
I wrote that once . . .

which linked up with that quoted here on page 127. Later, in
the 1856 edition, it was put back in its rightful place as Sonnet
XLIV.

In this new edition, and in that of 1856, Elizabeth, assisted
by Browning, made many revisions: a number of the unorthodox loose rimes, or assonances, were altered to suit conventional
ears, archaisms removed and certain lines rewritten; not always, I think, improving on the original. That her second
thoughts were not always best—at least to modern readers—is
perhaps most evident in the love sonnets if one compares with
those published a set in early manuscript form [1] where the language is more direct, less "literary," and therefore more moving. I give as an example Sonnet XVI (Appendix 3).

In late autumn there is a pause in the correspondence. Elizabeth was again ill. By December 1 she had recovered but not,
to Robert's disappointment, enough to resume the "grand walking expeditions." If, said Elizabeth, her husband was vain about
anything, it had been of those new walking-powers, boasting
of them as if, she told him teasingly, "a wife with a pair of feet
was a miracle of nature."

During this illness Elizabeth had the continued comfort of
Wilson's care: the maid's engagement to Mr. Righi had been
broken off. Mr. Righi had not written as often as he should, and
on her return to Florence did not hasten over from Prato to see
her. Wilson, convinced of his unworthiness, grieved at first, but
soon recovered.

More friends were now being admitted to Casa Guidi, still in
the main American. The Brownings seem to have been closer in
spirit to these members of a newer nation: their early appreciation of Browning's true worth warmed Elizabeth's heart to
them. Americans too paid a practical homage not generally accorded by their own countrymen. Of them Elizabeth wrote in
1860:

*English people will come and stare at me sometimes, but physi-
cians, dentists, who serve me and refuse their fees, artists who*

---

[1] In the Pierpont Morgan Library.

give me pictures, friends who give up their carriages and make
other practical sacrifices, are not English—*no—*
Also, many of the English abroad kept up a style of living beyond the Brownings' means.

Among American friends was Margaret Fuller, a rather wild
woman of socialistic ideas, an advocate of women's rights, and
a convinced republican. During the siege of Rome she had
served Italy nobly in the hospitals and now, French troops being
in occupation and the forces of reaction at work, she retired to
Florence bringing with her the Marquis Ossoli, an Italian husband, and a child a year old. Until the siege of Rome was at
its height none of her friends had known of the existence of a
husband, and certainly not of a child. With the Marquis Ossoli
Mrs. Browning was not impressed, though admitting his one
important qualification as Margaret Fuller's husband, that of a
good listener.

There was another home in Florence where Americans were
welcomed, that of Miss Jane Isabella Blagden, a writer of forgotten novels and verse whose fame now rests upon her hospitality. Isa Blagden's origins were obscure: she was certainly of
mixed blood, perhaps a Eurasian. Browning called her "a
bright, delicate, electric woman." Although forced to eke out a
small income by sharing her home with a woman friend and
writing "bread-and-butter" novels, she created by her generous
and lively personality a salon rivalling that of the Trollopes. Isa
Blagden was to be closely identified with the Brownings, both
in happy and in darker hours. It was—fittingly enough as their
most intimate friend—she who gave to each of them a ring of
fine chased gold in the Etruscan style; a ring commemorated for
us in *The Ring and the Book.*

For economy's sake Isa lived outside the walls, but it was not
until 1856 that she inhabited Villa Bricchieri, that "house at
Florence on the hill of Bellosguardo." Villa Bricchieri became
almost a second home to Browning: several evenings a week,
when his wife had retired for the night, he would walk up there
to enjoy a few hours of lively conversation with Isa and her
guests.

April brought news from England. Henrietta, at the age of

forty-one, had at length summoned courage to defy her father. When asked for a formal consent Mr. Barrett had intimated that she must either give up the engagement of five years' standing or leave his house. Elizabeth, who had already written a private letter of encouragement, was delighted to hear of Henrietta's marriage. As Surtees Cook's [2] income was restricted she combined strong personal desire with prudence by advising them to come and live in Florence. But for the Barrett family, so invincibly British, the Continent was for an occasional holiday and no more.

Mr. Barrett, strongly entrenched in his own bitterness, cut this second daughter out of his heart. He would "never let her name be mentioned again in his hearing."

On April 23, 1850 Wordsworth died: a new Poet Laureate must be appointed. The *Athenæum,* anonymously but in the voice of Henry Chorley, strongly pressed Elizabeth's claim as one peculiarly appropriate because a woman sat on the Throne. Elizabeth herself wished that the aged Leigh Hunt might be appointed as some compensation for early neglect and opprobrium. It is a measure of the slightness of Browning's fame at this period that his name was not seriously put forward. When Alfred Tennyson, that poet typical of the Victorian age at its height, was appointed, approbation was general.

Elizabeth's heart and mind were turning towards England. She longed to go back on a visit, to see her sisters and to "authenticate" Wiedeman, "for, as Robert says, all our fine stories about him will go for nothing, and he will be set down as a sham child."

Elizabeth's reading in her own language was constant: with Miss Mitford she discussed such new English books as could be obtained in Florence, though with some delay. She expressed disappointment in Tennyson's *The Princess,* pronounced the author of *Jane Eyre* to be certainly a woman, found *Vanity Fair* very clever, very effective, but cruel to human nature"; praised two poems in Matthew Arnold's new volume—one of them "The Forsaken Merman"—and took a personal interest, as one who had herself long planned a verse novel, in Clough's *Bothie of Tober-na-Vuolich*. Perhaps there were moments when she

[2] Later he changed his name to Altham.

longed to encounter those literary personalities whose books she read, and who were out of reach in far Florence.

Two years before, John Kenyon had made an earnest request to his cousin to draw upon him in case of need, and now he pressed the offer again; hoping perhaps to have the comfort of their presence in England once more. After his son's birth in 1849 Browning had accepted an allowance of £100 a year from Kenyon, but beyond this his pride, a horror of contracting debt, would not allow him to go. Even to bring his wife pleasure, he wrote, it would be "a vile habit, to say no worse, that of looking wistfully up at the clouds, on all occasions, to see what facilities may drop down." If he and Elizabeth could not raise the money between them they must remain in Italy.

When Browning decided to postpone a long and expensive journey to England he had another and a very good reason for doing so: it might be that next year they would be living in Paris, within easy access of London. But before she left Italy, perhaps for good, Ba must see Rome. This, he told Kenyon, was well within his resources.

But plans for Paris, for Rome, must be much in the air. Soon it was clear that another child might be born in January; perhaps the girl for whom Elizabeth longed. This was, however, not to be: on Sunday, July 28, Elizabeth had a serious miscarriage with great loss of blood. "Four of these mishaps, besides the advent of our babe, amount to a serious drain on such a constitution as hers." In telling Kenyon this, and not sparing the painful detail, Robert added:

how otherwise can I put you in my place, and make you fancy that, after sitting all night by the little patient white face, that could smile so much more easily than speak, your letter and its proposal for her good reached me? You surely feel that whatever I say presently, the real business is over and indeed, in the truest sense I have, as you express it, "already accepted" this last of your kindnesses, and laid it away with its fellows in my heart forever.

Elizabeth was slow in recovery: her condition was not improved by the shock of terrible news in August about a woman who, though a recent friend, was an admired one. Margaret Fuller was dead, and she had died in a manner peculiarly agonizing to Elizabeth. In late April she and the Marquis Ossoli had sailed with their child to America. They spent their last evening in Florence at Casa Guidi. Over the friends so soon to part a sad premonition brooded. The Marquis had been warned by a fortune-teller that the sea would be fatal to him. His wife turned smiling to Mrs. Browning and said: "Our ship is called the 'Elizabeth,' and I accept the omen." Before leaving that night she inscribed a Bible, as from her child to Wiedeman, "In memory of Angelo Eugene Ossoli."

The *Elizabeth* had sunk beneath the Atlantic. Robert would have preferred to keep the news from his ailing wife, but so close was their intimacy that any reserve between them was difficult: he thought it wiser to tell her at once. In writing to Miss Mitford Elizabeth told how the loss had affected her more deeply "through association with the past, when the arrowhead of anguish was broken too deeply into my life ever to be quite drawn out." Unhappiness was deepened by a personal anxiety. For twenty-four hours her child lay ill with sunstroke. "Terrible the silence that fell suddenly upon the house, without the small pattering feet and the singing voice."

Her doctor having ordered a change of air, on August 31 the Brownings left for Siena, travelling by railroad; Elizabeth, having to be lifted on the journey, "looking ghostly rather than ghastly."

They stayed a week in a hotel, probably the Villa di Londra, and then settled in a house standing in its own grounds two miles out of Siena on the *Poggio dei Venti,* Hill of the Winds. For the seven-roomed furnished villa, a vineyard, an olive ground, an orchard, a flower garden, taken for a month, the rent worked out at 11s. 1½d. a week.

The views from that hill, at their finest from a *specola,* or belvedere at the top of the house, are magnificent and today little changed. From one window the Brownings could see the ancient city, so close in that clear air, like some bright medi-æval illumination; from another over a vast sweep of marshy land to the mountains of Rome, and from a third—to quote Elizabeth's own words, as true today as a hundred years ago—"the whole country leaps under the sun, alive with verdure and vineyards." There may be more villas now on the hill of the winds, but there are still "English lanes with bowery tops of trees, and brambles and blackberries, and not a wall anywhere" except house walls. The air, too, has an English quality without its dampness.

At first Elizabeth could enjoy little more than "the enchanting silence" (perhaps even more enchanting today after the noise of modern Florence) and the magnificent views as she moved with difficulty from room to room. Wiedeman, able to get out of doors, soon got back the colour in his fat cheeks, revelling in such new delights as pigeons, a pig, a donkey, and a big yellow dog; though, his mother commented, being a town baby he really preferred a military band, even if it were Austrian.

There were certain drawbacks: the doors would not shut and the house was so small that "Robert and I had to whisper all our talk whenever Wiedeman was asleep." One unexpected pleasure, however, was a good and cheap library in Siena of which the Brownings took full advantage, though lamenting that now they could never read a new Balzac: the great novelist died on August 19, 1850.

On leaving Siena in October they grew "rather pathetical" and "shrank from parting with the pig." The road home probably included a week in Siena to enjoy the art treasures and some divergence from the straight path back to Florence. Dr. Harding had prescribed a frequent change of air for his patient. This prescription both would have willingly followed over many months of their year if their income had allowed. "Every now and then we take out the road-books, calculate the expenses, and groan in the spirit when it's proved for the hundredth time that we cannot do it." Both had a fever for roaming.

We hear this autumn little about work. Elizabeth declared that she spent half the day doing nothing but admire her boy. But visitors to Casa Guidi have recorded that, although the Brownings were busy workers, they never appeared to be so, always having leisure for friends at any hour. Elizabeth at this time must have been writing or revising the second part of *Casa Guidi Windows.*

Her attitude to the Florentines about her is clearly set out in

this second part. Perhaps not realizing the effect of long oppression, of terrible odds, the rank and file of Italians,

> *those oil-eaters, with large, live mobile mouths*
> *Agape for macaroni,*

now appeared to her as cheerfully submitting to tyranny so long
as they might be entertained with festas, illuminations, military
reviews and bands. A rigorous domination was imposed, not
only by the Austrian-controlled State, but the Church: when in
profound disillusionment with the Pope many flocked to Protestant churches these churches were threatened with expulsion
from Italy if they allowed Catholics within their walls.

It was all very well for Elizabeth, born in free England, to
admonish that

> *Austrian Metternich*
> *Can fix no yoke unless the neck agree:*

she herself was not an Italian held in subjection for many generations by Church usurping State. Nor did she take fully into
account the widespread hatred of republicanism, and the personal popularity of the Grand Duke.

But Elizabeth herself would perhaps have been the first to
acknowledge a certain lack of full comprehension: as she says
in her preface to the published poem, it was but "a simple story
of personal impressions" of political events.

The second half of the poem seems to lack the fire of the
first. Perhaps, as the outcome of disappointment, the shattering
of high hopes in a woman of frail physique, it was bound to be
flatter in effect: though in the part that was written in 1850
there are strong passages, such as that upon the futility of military oppression, its perverse power to arouse in the end a sense
of freedom, of nationality:

> *Behold, the people waits,*
> *Like God. As He, in His serene of might,*
> *So they, in their endurance of long straits.*
> *Ye stamp no nation out, though day and night*
> *Ye tread them with that absolute heel which grates*
> *And grinds them flat from all attempted height.*
> *You kill worms sooner with a garden-spade*
> *Than you kill peoples: peoples will not die;*
> *The tail curls stronger when you lop the head;*

> *They writhe at every wound and multiply,*
> *   And shudder into a heap of life that's made*
> *Thus vital from God's own vitality.*

This poem was sent in early spring for Sarianna to copy and see through the press.

In the December of 1850 Elizabeth read *In Memoriam,* a poem eagerly looked forward to, for which her appetite had been whetted by review extracts. It was inevitable, from the very theme of the work, that it should go "to her heart and soul." When Miss Mitford complained of its monotony, Elizabeth replied:

The sea is monotonous, and so is lasting grief. Your complaint is against fate and humanity rather than against the poet Tennyson. Who that has suffered has not felt wave after wave break dully against one rock, till brain and heart, with all their radiances, seemed lost in a single shadow? So the effect of the book is artistic, I think, and indeed I do not wonder at the opinion . . . that Tennyson stands higher through having written it. You see, what he appeared to want . . . was an earnest personality and direct purpose.

Elizabeth had one criticism: "All I wish away is the marriage hymn at the end, and *that* for every reason I wish away—it's a discord in the music."

There was one old friend of Miss Mitford's whom till now Elizabeth had not met in Florence; and, indeed, at Robert's wish had sedulously avoided, "that coarse, vulgar Mrs. Trollope" over whom he had so worked himself up at Pisa. His objection, still maintained, seemed to arise from "a sort of vow never to sit in the same room with the author of certain books directed against liberal institutions and Victor Hugo's poetry."

This obstinacy Elizabeth had been forced to combat, and in other directions. She who was apt to be (except in certain enthusiasms) less prejudiced, found people—as in the case of Margaret Fuller—"better than their books, than their principles, and even their everyday actions, sometimes. I am always crying out: 'Blessed be the inconsistency of men.'" She hated, besides, to seem "ungracious and unkind."

Mrs. Trollope and her daughter, at length invited to Casa Guidi, proved "very agreeable, and kind, and good-natured," with an additional charm of talking much about Miss Mitford. The Brownings were to return their visit privately, avoiding Mrs. Trollope's public days "in the full flood and flow of Florentine society."

To Miss Mitford, curiously enough, Elizabeth made no mention of Mrs. Trollope's daughter-in-law, the former Theodosia Garrow, now the wife of Thomas Trollope, whom, either in 1840, or perhaps in London in 1838, Elizabeth had met. Part of Browning's reluctance to know the Trollopes may have arisen from the effect of certain malicious gossip that at one time was circulating in Florence about the lively, impulsive Theodosia. It was inevitable, of course, that the two women should encounter one another again but, although Elizabeth appreciated Theodosia's work for Italian freedom in her news-letters to the *Athenæum,* there seems, from a few letters which have survived, little personal link beyond a childish acquaintance between her young son and Beatrice, or Bice, the Trollopes' daughter. Later the children rode together. In the reminiscences of his old age Thomas Trollope appears to lay too much emphasis on friendship between the two; perhaps because he was uneasily aware of this cloud once upon his dead wife which any sort of suggested intimacy with such a woman as Elizabeth might lift in the memory.

By April 1851 the Brownings' great plan of living in Paris, closer to their people in England, was coming at least to experiment; the Florentine apartment was, however, to be retained and only temporarily let in case the Paris winter should prove dangerous to Elizabeth. That spring, fortified with the proceeds of their books and rent from the apartment, they were to take a long, lingering farewell of Italy beginning with Rome and visiting Naples, Venice, and Milan. Across the Alps they were to reach as far north as Brussels, then to Paris and, ultimately, London.

At the end of April their luggage was actually packed and a carriage to Rome bargained for, when doubt assailed them. It was late in the season, late for the festas. Rome in May might be too hot for the boy. Two journeys, south then north again, might put too much strain on their purse. They decided instead to go, on their way north, to Venice.

CHAPTER 24

VENICE; PARIS; ENGLAND [1851–2]

TRAVEL, always a pleasure, was enhanced in 1851 by discomfort left behind, the discomfort of decorators in Casa Guidi. "My head and Robert's," Elizabeth wrote, "ring again with the confusion of it all."

Elizabeth had expected to find in Venice "a dreary sort of desolation": instead she was charmed by its "soothing, lulling, rocking atmosphere."

Never had I touched the skirts of so celestial a place. The beauty of the architecture, the silver trails of water up between all that gorgeous colour and carving, the enchanting silence, the moonlight, the music, the gondolas—I mix it all up together, and maintain that nothing is like it, nothing equal to it.

They had planned at least a fortnight there, but "alas for these mortal Venices—so exquisite and so bilious!" Robert was soon in a nervous condition, unable to eat or sleep. Wilson was plagued with headaches and continual bouts of sickness. From Venice they must go.

In the meantime they "swam in gondolas," enjoyed the opera from a box on the ground floor (at two shillings and eightpence), sat taking excellent coffee by moonlight in the great Piazza San Marco, and went out to Chioggia for a festa.

On leaving Venice they made a short stay at Padua, visiting Arqua, where Petrarch spent his declining years. "And didn't it move you," Elizabeth wrote to Kenyon, "the sight of that little room where the great soul exhaled itself? Even Robert's man's eyes had tears in them as we stood there, and looked through the window at the green-peaked hills."

They passed through Brescia at night, under a full moon, entering Milan in the morning. During their two days there Elizabeth excelled herself in those performances on her two feet of which Robert boasted, climbing three hundred and fifty stairs to the topmost pinnacle of the Cathedral. At Milan and

other places passed through they visited the galleries. At Parma
they saw the "sublime" Correggios, a memory of which lingered
in Browning's mind, to be immortalized in that fine poem "A
Face," written in 1852 after he had met Coventry Patmore's
strangely beautiful wife.

> *I know, Correggio loves to mass, in rifts*
> *Of heaven, his angel faces, orb on orb*
> *Breaking its outline. . . .*

This poem Browning did not publish until 1864, after the death
of both his wife and Emily Patmore. For herself, Elizabeth
found Correggio's angel faces in very likeness of her own child.

Pausing at Como to enjoy the beauties of the Italian lakes,
the Brownings crossed into Switzerland through the great St.
Gotthard pass. Snow was unusually thick that year: a "passage
through it, cut for the carriage, left the snow-walls nodding
over us at a great height on each side." Although the cold was
intense Elizabeth sat out for a while in the coupé so that she
might have an unimpeded view. It was overwhelming, "like
standing in the presence of God when He is terrible. . . . I
think I never *saw* the sublime before."

Although they found Lucerne even more beautiful than the
Italian lakes, there was no time to linger. They went on, traveling from Strasbourg to Paris in twenty-four hours. Their child,
already an intrepid traveller, was in no way put out by the rapid
motion. Little Wiedeman, a painter in the future, had indeed
appeared to take delight in the beauties of their journey, both
of nature and architectural. Paris, however, was to the town
baby a supreme joy. His mother wrote to Kenyon:

Well, now we are in Paris and have to forget the "belle chiese":
we have beautiful shops instead, false teeth grinning at the cor-
ners of the streets, and disreputable prints, and fascinating hats
and caps, and brilliant restaurants, and M. le Président in a
cocked hat and with a train of cavalry, passing like a rocket
along the boulevards to an occasional yell from the Red. Oh yes,
and don't mistake me! for I like it all extremely, it's a splendid
city—a city in the country, as Venice is a city in the sea. And
I'm as much amused as Wiedeman, who stands in the streets
before the printshops (to Wilson's great discomfort) and roars
at the lions.

This was the Paris of Daumier and Gavarni, a Paris in which luxury, the pursuit of pleasure, was daily increasing, to reach its zenith under the Second Empire: a Paris, for all its subcurrents of revolution, more self-confident than the defeated city Elizabeth had visited in 1815. Many of the mediæval streets had gone, with their fetid smells, to make way for the boulevards. To Elizabeth's eye, accustomed to the ancient close towns of Italy, the trees and gardens of this "city in the country" were a constant delight.

The great event of their month's stay was a meeting with Tennyson and his wife. So anxious was Elizabeth to make the acquaintance of this poetic hero of long standing that, although tired "half to death" by a visit to the Louvre, she rose from her sofa "in a decided state of resurrection" to take tea with him at a near-by hotel. She found Mrs. Tennyson "a very sweet person": her reaction to the poet is not specifically given, but one gathers that she was not disenchanted. Although Tennyson had only met Browning casually in London society, he went so far in friendliness now as to offer them—if it was not already let—his Twickenham home as a refuge while in England. This, according to Miss Mitford (though Elizabeth herself does not mention it) was countered by putting at his disposal their apartment in Casa Guidi, at present unoccupied.

To this momentous tea-drinking Robert induced his wife to go without a cap, claiming a promise extracted from her in Florence "after a revolutionary scene (besides various *emeutes*)." This cap was perhaps ampler than the black net she usually wore: Elizabeth's hair had apparently been cut, or greatly thinned, in illness. It was now as thick as ever.

They crossed the Channel at the end of July. Robert was eager to join his family, looking forward after a "five years' hunger" to talk with Carlyle; but much as Elizabeth longed to see her own people again, her thoughts of England must be full of bitterness, past and present. Even the physical circumstances of a return to her native land were unpropitious. She stepped ashore "into a puddle and a fog" and began to cough before reaching London. The weather was cold and windy.

They lodged at 26, Devonshire Street, Marylebone, living in three rooms which cost them £2 a week—precisely what they had paid for a luxuriously furnished seven-roomed apartment *au premier* in the most fashionable quarter. The advantage gained, however, was nearness to both Arabella and Mr. Kenyon.

Elizabeth had proposed to live the life of a hermit, only seeing her family, Kenyon, and a few old friends, but this proved impossible. The Brownings were "overwhelmed with kindnesses, crushed with gifts, like the Roman lady." The door bell was constantly ringing.

One of their first visits was to Carlyle. Elizabeth liked Carlyle "infinitely more in his personality" than she had expected; finding him "one of the most interesting men I could imagine even, deeply interesting to me. . . . All the bitterness is love with the point reversed." Mrs. Carlyle she could meet without any preconception: that fascinating woman soon became "a great favorite of mine: full of thought, and feeling, and character, it seems to me."

Miss Mitford came up to London for a week. "A strange thing," she wrote to a friend, "it was to see Miss Barrett walking about like other people." Miss Mitford was shocked in her English soul to hear people of her own race—Robert, Elizabeth, Wilson—talking in Italian to the Brownings' "pretty little boy." "I suppose next year they will all talk to him in French, and when English will take its turn, God knows."

However uneasy Elizabeth, for reasons both personal and political, might feel in this country of hers, reunion with her sisters was undiluted joy. Arabel she saw daily; Henrietta, with her first baby, stayed near her for a week or so. The brothers, though they do not appear to have been over-attentive, made their peace. A rather emotional reconciliation with George, the strongest character among them and bitterest against her marriage, brought Elizabeth great happiness.

Another attempt was made to reconcile her father, or at least to induce him to see his first grandson. Browning wrote him "a manly, true, straightforward letter," touching to Elizabeth, "generous and conciliating."

In reply he had a very violent and unsparing letter, with all the letters I had written to papa through these five years sent back unopened, the seals unbroken. *What went most to my heart was*

*that some of the seals were black with black-edged envelopes;
so that he might have thought my child or husband dead, yet
never cared to solve the doubt by breaking the seal.*

It must have deepened tragedy for this warped, innately affectionate man that he, who had lived in such intimacy with his
own children when young, was too stiff in fanatic pride to receive his own grandchild.

By the other grandfather, "the dear nonno," little Wiedeman
was instantly "taken into adoration." Personal contact with the
family at Hatcham, though strengthening a new and affectionate tie, must have brought pain to Elizabeth. The simple-
hearted devotion of his father was in poignant contrast to Mr.
Barrett's possessive passion for his children.

Elizabeth was far from well, so unwell that Robert contemplated a rapid return to Paris, but soon the weather improved.
Elizabeth was forced to take a much needed rest by an event
which, paradoxically, gave her little repose. Wilson left to
spend a fortnight's holiday with her mother in the north. At
first it had been arranged that the child should go with her, but
Elizabeth decided to keep him: the maid should have leisure
to enjoy a well-earned holiday. Wiedeman, suddenly bereft of
"Lilli," fearing desperately that his mother might also be
snatched away, clung to Elizabeth "like a little old man of the
mountain." As he craved constantly to be carried, to be in her
arms for comfort, it was perhaps fortunate that the heavy baby
had fined down into a small light-boned boy. To a woman unaccustomed even to care for her own person this was, though
it must bring to a mother compensatory joy, "a dreadful state
of slavery." Elizabeth learned to value more highly the ministrations of Wilson.

Elizabeth had been constantly urging Henrietta to live in
Paris, for both cheapness and pleasure: now, seeing at close
range her sister's happiness, making acquaintance with little
Altham, the baby son who might later be a companion for her
own boy, she exercised all her power of persuasion to extract
a promise that the Surtees Cooks would come to live near her
that winter. But there were ready arguments against the
scheme, such as expense and the danger of revolution in these
disturbed times.

On Wilson's return an accumulation of engagements "broke on" Elizabeth. "I had to go here and there in all directions, and see and write and talk till I was out of breath."

One engagement, though perhaps in the period before Wilson went north, was to dine with Mr. Kenyon. Elizabeth went to Devonshire Place alone. It was a fairly general rule with Kenyon not to invite husband and wife together (the Sydney Smiths were a notable exception) because he considered that they spoilt each other's conversation.

Mrs. Andrew Crosse, wife of the electrician who had been at school with Kenyon and the elder Browning, has given us an account of the dinner party at which Elizabeth was a guest of honour. Mrs. Crosse, who looked forward perhaps too eagerly to meeting a favourite poet, found herself disappointed. To her Mrs. Browning was "hard featured," "non-sympathetic," though her brow was "a noble soul-case" and her eyes "dark and penetrating." "The mouth was hard and immobile for any play of expression, while the lower jaw showed something of the strength of obstinacy."

She wore her hair in long ringlets, which, falling very much over her face, and when seen in profile, suggested the unpleasing idea of blinkers, that harshly cut across the graceful curves of brow and cheek. It was this style of arranging the hair that made Mrs. Browning look, not old fashioned—for that would have been a touch of sentiment—but strangely out of fashion. Her slight pretty figure was rather disguised than set off by garments that fell lopping round her; but thank Heaven! she was entirely and utterly free from the bad taste of the self-styled clever women, who acknowledge themselves to be failures, as women, by aping a masculine style of dress and address.

Mrs. Crosse thought Elizabeth showed "a proud aloofness of manner." This impression, in direct contradiction to that of others who met her, was perhaps on that particular occasion inevitable. Physically oppressed by the London air, modest, shy, unused to much society even in the healthy days of youth, Elizabeth found herself the lion of the party alone, torn apart from the man who for five years had been her constant companion, her other self; a man, too, accustomed to take the lead in conversation.

She seems to have cast something of a damp on the company: "there was a listening reticence in her attitude that did not help the playful tossing to and fro of talk." What remarks Elizabeth did throw into the conversation, however, were "weighed, measured, and full of sense and purpose."

Crabb Robinson, also present, though partly in agreement with Mrs. Crosse, found Elizabeth "very interesting and pleasing." Being a persistent talker himself, he appreciated a good listener.

But though these excursions into London society were a strain upon Elizabeth, she found a distinct fascination in the new environment, in "a great dazzling heap of things new and strange." Among Browning's older friends introduced to her was Forster, who gave a dinner party in Browning's honour at Thames Ditton "in sight of the swans," B. W. Procter, and Fanny Haworth, a gifted woman Browning had fervently admired in youth. Fanny Haworth became a friend in her own right, a correspondent: it was she who introduced Elizabeth to the works of Swedenborg, that visionary thinker who so influenced her latter years. Swedenborgian doctrines, mesmerism, spiritualism, those subjects which caught Elizabeth on her "weak side" of the "love of wonder," were all equally potent with this new acquaintance.

Of old friends, Mrs. Jameson, at work upon her *Legends of the Madonna*, was met with again; and Elizabeth had the pleasure of at last meeting in the flesh R. H. Horne, that former intimate correspondent.

One lion of London in this year, and the most popular, was not a man but a building, a portent: the Great Exhibition of 1851 housed under glass in Hyde Park, promoted by Prince Albert to foster commerce, the arts, and world peace. From far-off Florence Elizabeth had guessed at its materialism, its lack of real meaning in a troubled Europe.

> *O Magi of the east and of the west,*
> *Your incense, gold and myrrh are excellent!—*
> *What gifts for Christ, then, bring ye with the rest?*

she had written in *Casa Guidi Windows,* asking pertinently, did
this palace of peace and plenty shed

> *No light*
> *Of teaching, liberal nations, for the poor*
> *Who sit in darkness when it is not night?*
> *No cure for wicked children? Christ,—no cure!*
> *No help for women sobbing out of sight*
> *Because men made the laws?*

But these questionings, a realization of the hollowness of this
temple of peace in a world of strife and oppression, surely did
not prevent Elizabeth from a childlike enjoyment of its compli-
cated splendours. That the highly original building, then in its
first glitter of beauty, fascinated her is clear from a letter to
Mrs. Jameson in which she asked:

But if the Crystal Palace vanishes from the face of the earth,
who shall trust any more in castles? Will they really pull it
down, do you think? If it's a bubble, it's a glass bubble, and not
meant, therefore, for bursting in the air, it seems to me. And
you do want a place in England for sculpture, and also to show
people how olives grow. What a beautiful winter garden it
would be!

Mrs. Jameson had a personal contact with the Exhibition,
having drawn up a Guide to the Court of Modern Sculpture;
she also had other and more vital contacts in London which
had led her, herself an ill-used struggling woman, to speak
openly, to work for the emancipation of women. In the lines
quoted above: "No help for women sobbing out of sight because men made the laws," we have Elizabeth's own first protest, soon to be in *Aurora Leigh* a clarion call, against the oppression of women in law and society. At this time, and for
many years after, a married woman was merged in her husband,
having no legal right even to her own child and certainly not to
her income, earned or unearned. It was generally thought a
moral duty of woman to conceal from the world any suffering
her husband might inflict on her; if she must weep, "sobbing
out of sight." Elizabeth's innate feminism, an early critical attitude to marriage, a pity for those cringing women who put up
a silent prayer at meal time that the chops might be well done,
was given full play by Browning, a husband who so abhorred

the exercise of power by one individual over another that, as has been said, it was the basis of a vivid and distressing nightmare. Any suggestion of submission to his will on Elizabeth's part hurt and excited him.

With this mutual concern for human freedom it is more than likely that the Brownings desired to meet, through Mrs. Jameson, Barbara Leigh Smith, that intrepid young pioneer of woman's rights and cousin to Florence Nightingale. Better known now as Madame Bodichon, she was soon to make, with John Stuart Mill as willing instrument and mouthpiece, a first protest in the House of Commons against the power of a husband to confiscate his wife's earnings. Later we hear of Elizabeth collecting signatures for this petition in Paris.

One of their last evenings in London was spent with the poet Rogers, now nearly ninety and confined to his armchair as the result of an accident a year before. Elizabeth would infinitely have preferred to be with Arabel, since time was so short, but could not refuse a particular request to meet her from a man of Rogers's age. On "the last melancholy packing-up evening" she did have Arabel with her, and Treppy too.

The Brownings left London on September 25, driving from their lodgings, for a few moments poignant to Elizabeth, through Wimpole Street. There was now no hope of softening her father. The house itself she had found on her return to be, except for Arabel's own room, dismal in effect, the old familiar drawing-rooms appearing smaller, darker, with a general lack of comfort; "bachelor-looking" in appearance. The whole house needed a thorough cleansing.

At the station they met Carlyle, who, having been invited to join the Ashburtons in Paris, had not, helpless being as he was, known how to arrive there unaided. He put himself entirely into Browning's hands, sitting back to admire that energetic poet's capacity for dealing with porters, passports, and custom-houses. To both fellow-travellers, however, Carlyle made the journey wholly delightful "except the sea-part which was horrible"; rough, stormy, and lasting eight hours. All were sick including Elizabeth, who was considered a good sailor. "As to baby, he rather liked it, and rose in conscious dignity when he had used the basin." Flush, a victim too, was ordered off the deck. This is Elizabeth's first mention of Flush—at least in the letters available to me—during the whole three months of their travel; Flush, who, before the advent of a child, was constantly referred to on their journeyings.

Elizabeth set foot in France with a lighter heart in spite of seasickness:

Leaving love behind is always terrible, but it was not all love that I left, and there was relief in the state of mind with which I threw myself on the sofa at Dieppe—yes, indeed. Robert felt differently from me for once, as was natural, for it had been pure joy to him with his family and friends. . . . Oh England! I love and hate it at once. Or rather, where love of country ought to be in the heart, there is the mark of the burning iron in mine, and the depth of the scar shows the depth of the root of it.

"After all," she added, "I wasn't made to live in England, or I should not cough there perpetually." In the light, cleaner air of Paris the cough at once left her.

It would seem as if Kenyon either was in Paris, or expected there: "to please Mr. Kenyon and to be near his hotel" Browning looked for apartments near the Madeleine but, Paris being very full, sunny rooms in that quarter were both scarce and dear. He found at the suburban end of the Champs-Elysées an apartment on the second floor, "bathed in the sun and comfortably furnished, with a large Terrace and beautiful view upon the great avenue, and all for two hundred francs a month, about the same as they paid in London for "miserable accommodation" out of season.

True, the situation of 138, Champs-Elysées, now one of a row of busy shops, was then a retired one outside Paris itself, but opposite them was a stand for fiacres, any of which would carry them to the other end of Paris for half-a-crown including a generous tip. In addition there was a continual stream of omnibuses on which you could travel the same distance for six sous. In trying to persuade her sister to come over and settle in the same house Elizabeth mentioned these humble vehicles rather apologetically: Henrietta was always more fashionably inclined than herself. The cost of a journey from London to Paris, first class, was then twenty-two shillings.

Elizabeth had the delight of finding her Aunt Jane, the favourite Uncle Hedley, and a cousin settled in the Faubourg St. Honoré. It was perhaps through Aunt Jane that an invitation came from Lady Elgin, which the Brownings gladly accepted, knowing that at her house they would meet many French celebrities: Elizabeth was determined to make the best of the remaining fine weather before winter shut her up again.

They found society in Paris delightfully informal and frugal, a cup of weak tea being the usual evening refreshment. "Lady Elgin was prodigal and gave us bread and butter." Soon they were visiting Madame Mohl, an Englishwoman reared in France whose *salon* was famous.

It was but natural that Henrietta should soon be asking her sister about Paris fashions. Elizabeth had bought a bonnet of drawn maroon satin trimmed with velvet and with purple flowers inside the brim; a bonnet approved even by the critical Robert. As she was imprudent enough to go to a fashionable milliner it cost her sixteen shillings. "Polkas" were the latest mode and basqued dresses a good deal worn. Wiedeman—whom now we may call by his more familiar name of Penini, his own attempt to pronounce this rather outlandish name—was wearing "trowsers" now, trousers to the knee and long white knitted gaiters. His costume was completed by a white felt hat, white satin ribbons, and feathers with a trimming of blue satin inside at each cheek. "It's a beautiful costume," Elizabeth assured her sister, "and he is much admired." Penini was soon chattering French to Désirée, the *femme de service*.

With an appetite whetted by a long study of Balzac's novels, Elizabeth perhaps expected more from French society than she found: men of letters, the writers and journalists "of all colours, from white to red," she thought much more interesting and amusing. Mazzini having, through the Carlyles, promised them a letter of introduction to George Sand, Elizabeth was now looking forward with excitement to a meeting with that remarkable and notorious woman of genius.

Paris, seething below the surface with political excitement, was bright with emotional colour. Troops passed down the Champs-Elysées every few days to be reviewed: it was expected they would soon be bringing the President back with them as Emperor. Napoleon's popularity had enormously increased after the Assembly had defied him in May when he demanded the restoration of universal suffrage: so had a potential despot confused the real issue in the eyes of people only too ready, remembering old glory, to cry *"Vive l'Empereur!"* Elizabeth, for all her liberal leanings, was ready to echo that cry.

A personal gratification had been a laudatory article on Browning in the *Revue des Deux Mondes* for August, second in a series on English poetry since Byron, by Joseph Milsand, soon to become a close friend. After the mixed reception of Browning's work in his own country this understanding appreciation by a Frenchman was particularly gratifying to both husband and wife; and especially, one may guess, to Elizabeth, who from the first had, in spite of the popular suffrage, been under no illusion as to which was the greater poet.

In October they had the pleasure of a three weeks' visit from Browning's father and sister. Perhaps the elder Browning had already decided to make a future home in Paris. "They are an affectionate family," Elizabeth told Miss Mitford, "and not easy when removed one from another." Sarianna she admired for her cleverness, sense, and even temper: "devoted to her father as she was to her mother: indeed, the relations of life seem reversed in their case, and the father appears the child of the child."

By December 1 an intense and abnormal cold had shut Elizabeth up in their rooms. The cough returned and she lost flesh, but the lighter air of Paris secured her from actual illness. The warmth of a French apartment, with its lack of draughty passages and staircases, was a comfort. Paris was still a delight to her, but one can detect a certain yearning for Florence. "I love Italy, and like Paris—there's the difference."

She would not permit Robert to immure himself with her: he must visit Lady Elgin, Madame Mohl, and others, in a lively social intercourse "which really is good for him, with his temperament." Browning, the widower in London, the inveterate diner-out, was no new Browning but an intensification in loneliness of the old.

Elizabeth herself received but little. One evening when Lady Elgin and Madame Mohl were both present, she enjoyed "a great long talk about Shelley and the poets generally." Shelley was now a familiar topic in this household. Moxon was bringing out an edition of "Shelley" letters which proved to be forgeries by George Byron and were withdrawn; but not before the completion by Browning of a fine preface, both a contribution to literature and a pronouncement of his own poetic faith.

On December 2 Louis Napoleon executed his *coup d'état*, promulgating a sham constitution that enormously pleased the majority of Parisians, so they were willing to overlook the illegality of his action and the breaking of that solemn oath to the French Republic he had taken on being elected President. Elizabeth, though not yet so whole-heartedly for the future Emperor of the French as she was later to be, exonerated him on the score of expediency:

The situation was in a deadlock, and all the conflicting parties were full of dangerous hope of taking advantage of it; and I don't see, for my part, what better could be done for the French nation than to sweep the board clear and bid them begin again. . . . He [Napoleon] has broken, certainly, the husk of an oath, but fidelity to the intention of it seems to me reconcilable with the breach; and if he had not felt that he had the great mass of the people to back him, he is at least too able a man, be certain, if not too honest a man, to have dared what he has dared.

But in France there can be no political change without bloodshed. The army, that more tangible backing to a new power, had to kill citizens and disfigure buildings with cannon shot. Elizabeth, too excited to go to bed, sat up until one o'clock listening to the sound of firing.

To his elders the thought of "Frenchman against Frenchman" must bring pain, but to little Penini all was pure joy. On the fatal second day of December he had watched the entrance of troops into Paris, screaming and shouting with delight. Elizabeth wrote to her sister:

the military music and the shouting of the people, as the president rode under our windows, the manœuvring of the splendid cavalry, the white horses, glittering helmets, all the "pomp and circumstance," might well move older children than our babe. Though the author of the *coup d'état* rode in their midst, Elizabeth would not admit this parade of soldiers to be a symbol of military despotism. Was not the French army, she wrote to Mrs. Martin, "eminently *civic*, flesh of the people's flesh? . . . Every man is a citizen, and every citizen is or has been a soldier."

Repressive measures there must be in a state of emergency but, she urged, "grant the righteousness of the movement, and you must accept its conditions." Elizabeth in 1851 could not know the full danger of this plea, this unrighteous cloak of a rebel strong enough to impose his will on a nation.

Robert, though he did not reveal until long after Elizabeth's death his full hatred of Louis Napoleon and all he stood for, held his own in domestic argument, but he too was a little dazzled; confessing to his wife that "the excessive and contradictory nonsense he had heard among Legitimists, Orleanists and *English*" against the movement inclined him almost to a revulsion of feeling. As the President rode under their windows that 2nd of December "through a shout extending from the Carrousel to the Arc de l'Etoile," even his keen mind might well have been deluded into thinking this was a popular movement.

The disturbances in Paris, magnified as they so often are in foreign presses as bloody revolutions, effectively frightened the Surtees Cooks into a definite and final decision not to come to Paris. This disappointment to Elizabeth was followed by the minor one of missing her literary heroine, George Sand, during a short, private visit to the capital.

There followed on the *coup d'état* a period of material prosperity. Trade increased. In January the sun shone and festivities of the first of the year filled the city with fairs and fine things to buy. Penini was all the more charmed with Paris, "its magnificent Punches, and roundabouts, and balloons." Unconsciously expressing his mother's attitude of mind, one day he shouted "Viva Peone" (Napoleone) in at the President's carriage window.

In the middle of January the clumsy but well-meant action of one of Elizabeth's dearest friends brought her infinite pain: Miss Mitford's *Recollections of a Literary Life*, out at last, contained a long detailed passage revealing the loss of Bro. Miss Mitford, with her sturdy common sense and a certain lack of perception, had considered that grief must now be softened after a lapse of eleven years; that a woman so domestically happy could not be unduly distressed by this revelation, private though it might be. "Now," wrote Elizabeth in great distress to Mrs. Martin, "I shall be liable to see recollections dreadful to me, thrust into every vulgar notice of my books." Indeed, the *Athenæum* had already repeated the story in a long extract.

Elizabeth's letter on the subject to Miss Mitford was tender, generous, and forgiving, but did not disguise her pain. The *Athenæum* extract she could not herself read, but Robert had assured her that the facts "could not possibly be given with greater delicacy. . . . And I will add for myself, that for them to be related by anyone during my life, I would rather have *you* to relate them than another." But even so she was badly hurt. "See what a deep wound I must have in me, to be pained by the touch of such a hand."

George Sand was now making one of her infrequent returns to Paris: the letter of introduction from Mazzini having arrived, means had to be found of conveying it. They were told that Madame Sand never received strangers, that she was only in Paris for a few days "and under a new name to escape the plague of notoriety." Browning himself did not show much energy in trying to deliver the letter; seeming inclined rather to "sit in his chair and be proud a little." Nor did he approve of his wife, a woman of utter purity, coming in contact with George Sand, the freedom of whose life was common knowledge.

Mazzini's introduction was at length sent under cover of a personal note signed by both, passed mysteriously by a friend to a friend who knew where Madame Sand was concealing herself. There was an immediate reply with an invitation for the following Sunday night. Elizabeth, though this was February, determined to muffle herself up, head and all, proceeding to 3, Rue Racine in a closed carriage and armed with a respirator.

She approached her literary lioness with a beating heart, stooped, and kissed her hand. George Sand raised her quickly with a *"Mais non, je ne veux pas,"* and kissed Elizabeth on the lips. Every detail of the famous writer's appearance was noted and reported to that lover of celebrities John Kenyon. Her rather disdainful manner, "a scorn of pleasing," at first repelled Elizabeth. "But I liked her. I did not love her, but I felt the burning soul through all that quietness, and was not disappointed in George Sand."

They found her sitting in a circle of eight or nine young men, giving them directions and quiet advice; obviously *"the man* in that company." During the three-quarters of an hour the Brownings spent with her, there was little conversation. Madame Sand sat "at a corner of the fire, and warming her feet quietly, in a general silence of the most profound deference." Browning was impressed in spite of himself, saying afterwards: "If any other mistress of a house had behaved so, I would have walked out of the room." But this was George Sand. At parting she gave them, after a little indirect prompting from Elizabeth, an invitation to come again next Sunday.

To Mrs. Martin, Elizabeth commented freely on French characteristics, the love of pure ideas, and of the socialists, so strong in Paris:

I quite agree with you that various of them, yes, and some of their chief men, are full of pure and noble aspiration, the most virtuous of men and the most benevolent. Still, they hold in their hands, in their clean hands, ideas that kill, ideas which defile, ideas which, if carried out, would be the worst and most crushing kind of despotism. I would rather live under the feet of the Czar than in those states of perfectibility imagined by Fourier and Cabet, if I might choose my "pis aller."

A hundred years have not yet fully brought home to mankind this dreadful truth.

At this time the Brownings were worried about Penini, now nearly three years old: the child was too excitable, too intense. Lately he had "been attacked at night with a sort of slight hysterical seizure . . involuntary laughter & spasmodic thrills through the frame." [1] Though his parents professed to do all they could to keep him back, Penini was for ever "drawing, writing, singing, dancing." It was perhaps this early drain on vitality, living with such gifted, vivacious parents, travelling, speaking three languages, that helped to make Pen Browning the indolent man he undoubtedly was in middle life; a man who wasted a decided talent as a painter.

---

[1] Unpublished letter to Fanny Dowglass, March 5, 1852, Huntington Library Collection.

A second visit to George Sand brought to Browning an increased disgust, but to Elizabeth a lively sense of pity:

She seems to live in the abomination of desolation, as far as regards society—crowds of ill-bred men who adore her à genoux bas, *betwixt a puff of smoke and an ejection of saliva. Society of the ragged Red diluted with the lower theatrical. She herself so different, so apart, as alone in her melancholy disdain! I was deeply interested in that poor woman, I felt a profound compassion for her.*

They were both well aware that, for all her protestations, Madame Sand had no real interest in them. "Perhaps she doesn't care for anybody by this time—who knows? . . . we always felt that we couldn't penetrate—couldn't really *touch* her—it was all in vain."

By the second week in April Elizabeth was able to walk about with her husband enjoying the sunshine, the beauty of Paris, "the sentiment of southern life" as she watched men, women, and children, all classes mixing as in Italy, sitting out of doors enjoying their coffee or wine. She went to the Vaudeville to see *La Dame aux Camélias* and found it not immoral, but moral and human; moving her to the point of distress. Even Robert, "who gives himself out for *blasé* on dramatic matters," shed some tears.

In May Elizabeth caught cold, a cold that led unhappily to "*an attack* after the ancient fashion," considerably weakening her, but by mid-June all that remained, in beautiful summer weather, was a slight cough. That month Mrs. Jameson came to stay with them, perhaps to enjoy a well-earned rest: not only did her *Legends of the Madonna* come out that year but also an early travel book in second edition and heavily revised. Mrs. Jameson never really liked Paris, and took none of Elizabeth's eager interest in what she termed "vile French politics." Her social interests were more general: within the circle about Lady Byron Mrs. Jameson was becoming more and more active in the advocacy of legal and social reform to benefit women and children.

By July 23 the Brownings were in England again, this time in more comfortable rooms at a moderate price, in Welbeck Street. Henrietta was in London too, staying some twenty doors off.

The one drawback at 58, Welbeck Street was a screaming baby
in the house.

There was a notable encounter this year with Giuseppe Mazzini, whom his friend Mrs. Carlyle brought to visit them. Mazzini, now working on behalf of his country's freedom as president of the National Italian Committee in London, made a
profound impression "with that pale spiritual face of his, and
those intense eyes full of melancholy illusions." Telling Miss
Mitford of the meeting Elizabeth added:

*I was thinking, while he sate there, on what Italian turf he
would lie at last with a bullet in his heart, or perhaps with a
knife in his back, for to one of those ends it will surely come.*

At this time Mazzini had not only Austrian antagonists: he was
under sentence of death pronounced in 1833 by Italy's only
Italian ruler, the King of Sardinia, for having stirred up active
revolution within the Sardinian army.

Mrs. Carlyle, who, though she had a strong affection for Mazzini, knew as a close friend his whims and oddities, commented
tartly on the occasion: "Oh, such a fuss the Brownings made
over Mazzini the other day! My private opinion of Browning is,
in spite of Mr. C.'s favour for him, that he is 'nothing,' or very
little more 'but a fluff of feathers!' *She* is *true* and *good*, and the
most *womanly* creature." Elizabeth wrote to Miss Mitford of
Jane Carlyle: "She is a great favorite of mine: full of thought,
and feeling, and character, it seems to me." How valuable, how
entertaining a correspondence we might have had between
these two fine letter-writers; but Mrs. Carlyle's antipathy for
Browning, which increased when they met again that summer,
touched his wife also. In September Mrs. Carlyle declared to
her husband "even she does not grow on me."

Again the Brownings had a multiplicity of engagements, engagements that kept them tied to London; though they did
manage a visit to Farnham and an encounter with Charles
Kingsley. On Elizabeth, though she might disapprove his the-
ories, Kingsley made a strong impression as a man of pure
ideals and good heart. Later she met another friend of Miss
Mitford's, young Mr. Ruskin, whom the Brownings soon
counted as "among the valuable acquaintances made this year

in England." The inevitable Father Prout was in London and found them out in Welbeck Street.

By the middle of September chilly days were already warning Elizabeth that she must take care: "the horrible climate is beginning to put out its gripes." She was again cherishing a plan to winter in Rome.

Business, however, unpleasant business, detained Browning in London. A "strange and calamitous visitation," evidently some form of blackmail, was cruelly disturbing his father's quiet scholarly life. By the middle of January 1853 the elder Browning was driven into retiring from the bank, accepting a two-thirds pension, and exiling himself in Paris. There he settled down to reading at the Library, book-hunting, drawing at the Louvre, and, said his son, " 'shaping his old course in a country new,' like Lear's Kent."

Browning, having done what he could for the moment to help his father, determined to take Elizabeth away from London cold and fog on October 5, but the journey was again delayed and this time by a pleasanter cause: Tennyson wanted the Brownings to be present at the christening of his son Hallam. Elizabeth accepted the invitations for both with pleasure, but perhaps it was fortunate that she was unable to go. Tennyson was reported by Robert as "talking vehemently against the French President and the French."

On September 28 another child, the niece Elizabeth had predicted, was born to Henrietta. "Since she is yours," Elizabeth wrote, "I won't covet her—and you must accept that abnegation as a proof of love." The child, christened Mary, survived until June 7, 1951, to the end taking an interest in her famous aunt, though she barely remembered her.

In mid-October the Brownings left London at six in the morning for Paris, where they stayed for a while in the Rue de la Ville-l'Evêque. Elizabeth's cough persisted: it was soon evident that she could not pass a winter there this year. By November they had decided to return to Florence.

While in Paris Elizabeth was able to indulge Napoleonic fervour by being present on a boulevard balcony as, under a bright sun, Louis Napoleon, now the future Emperor, swept by with "all military and civil pomp" amid a crowd of admirers. On the balcony with them was the American actress Charlotte Cushman, who, although disapproving of Louis Napoleon, was startled into exclaiming: "That's fine, I must say!" when "Napoleon showed his usual tact and courage by riding on horseback quite alone, at least ten paces between himself and his nearest escort, which of course had a striking effect, taking the French on their weak side." Penini "in a state of ecstasy" called out: *"Vive Napoleon!"* and boasted that the hero took off his hat to him.

CHAPTER 25

BACK IN FLORENCE: BAGNI DI LUCCA; ROME [1852–4]

ELIZABETH did not reach home without mishap: wanting to take the shortest route, the Brownings crossed by the Mont Cenis pass, where the cold was extreme. At Genoa she was unwell "to the extent of almost losing heart and hope," but exquisite weather, warm as June, restored her. At the end of a week she was able to spend two days in sightseeing, she told Kenyon:

my "unconquerable mind" even carried me halfway up the lighthouse for the sake of the "view," only there I had to stop ingloriously, and let Robert finish the course alone while I rested on a bench: aspiration is not everything, either in literature or lighthouses, you know. . . .

In Florence they found the people crushed, demoralized: "trodden flat in the dust of the vineyards by these mules of Austria,[1] and these asses of the Papacy."

Although she regretted having to leave Paris, and at a time of political excitement, Elizabeth was pleased to find herself at home, "everything looking exactly as if we had left it yesterday." Robert, however, found Florence "all as dull as possible" after the palpitating life of the Parisian boulevards. Admitting herself that the beloved city was dead by comparison, Elizabeth added: "but it's a beautiful death, and what with the lovely climate, and the lovely associations, and the sense of repose, I could turn myself on my pillow and sleep on here to the end of my life; only be sure that I *shall do no such thing.*"

Browning's early restlessness soon left him: they subsided happily into their "former soundless, stirless hermit life" with a few visitors dropping in for tea and talk. One resident in Florence, Frederick Tennyson, a poet obscured by his younger brother, was a particular favourite with both and became a close friend of Robert. In November Elizabeth had the pleasure of meeting a cousin, Robin Hedley, and his bride: it was

[1] For a small human sidelight on the Austrian occupation see Appendix 2.

probably he who introduced into Casa Guidi a Miss Jane Wills Sandford, a woman of means who placed no undue value on money. With Miss Sandford Elizabeth fell "into a sudden intimacy."

One interesting new acquaintance was Robert Lytton, son of Edward Bulwer Lytton and himself a poet known as "Owen Meredith." Young Lytton shared to the full Elizabeth's interest in the supernatural. Powers, the sculptor, an older friend, had also by this time "made up his mind . . . upon the truth of the American rapping spirits." Elizabeth's own attitude to spiritualism is defined in a letter to Isa Blagden of March 1853:

Profane or not, I am resolved on getting as near to a solution of the spirit question as I can, and I don't believe in the least risk of profanity, seeing that whatever is, must be permitted; and that the contemplation of whatever is, must be permitted also, where the intentions are pure and reverent. I can discern no more danger in psychology than in mineralogy, only intensely a greater interest. As to the spirits, I care less about what they are capable of communicating, than of the fact of their being communications. . . . They seem abundantly foolish, one must admit. There is probably, however, a mixture of good spirits and bad, foolish and wise, of the lower orders, perhaps in both kinds. . . .

A winter was spent indoors revising for the third edition of her collected poems, and at work upon a new one; "meditating Socialism and mysticism of very various kinds," reading French novels, and eagerly listening to accounts of "my rapping spirits, of whom our American guests bring us relays of witnesses."

Among American guests was George Perkins Marsh, American Minister at Constantinople, in Florence because of a change in Presidency. Hearing that Mrs. Marsh, although an invalid and almost blind, had travelled to Jerusalem—even being carried to the top of Mount Horeb—there was a revival of that old dream of visiting the Holy Land. But it could be but a dream: even an invitation from their new friends to visit Constantinople as their guests had to be refused that year. No money was to be expected from their books for a while: until the new edition was ready Elizabeth's collected poems were out of print. *Casa Guidi Windows* had proved less popular than former works.

The winter was warm: Elizabeth was so well, busy, and happy that spring surprised her almost with regret at having to emerge from retirement. Two subjects of great interest at this moment were the French situation and a new attack on the American institution of slavery.

Elizabeth's admiration for Louis Napoleon—though still with some qualification—was rapidly growing. That astute man, elected Emperor by plebiscite in the previous November, had sealed his popularity by marriage with a beautiful girl, Eugénie de Montijo, Countess of Téba. Elizabeth "as a democrat to the bone" could still see the danger of despotism in a continued censorship of the press, but felt convinced that it was but a temporary measure. This optimism proved false: later, because of Louis Napoleon's need for Church support, severe censorship was extended to books, involving, as we know, a public prosecution of the author of *Madame Bovary*.

The new attack on slavery came in fictional form with *Uncle Tom's Cabin*, the instant and immense popularity of which soon spead from America across Europe. Rather surprisingly Mrs. Jameson appears to have shown some disapproval of its author, Harriet Beecher Stowe, and her choice of subject. Elizabeth protested:

Oh, and is it possible that you think a woman has no business with questions like the question of slavery? Then she had better use a pen no more. She had better subside into slavery and concubinage herself, I think, as in the times of old, shut herself up with the Penelopes in the "women's apartment," and take no rank among thinkers and speakers. Certainly you are not in earnest in these things. A difficult question—yes! All virtue is difficult. England found it difficult. France found it difficult. But we did not make ourselves an arm-chair of our sins. As for America, I honor America in much; but I would not be an American for the world while she wears that shameful scar upon her brow.

Penini, now four years old, was beginning to have his social successes; and Elizabeth wrote to his Aunt Henrietta: "Penini is extremely fond of society, you must understand." Robert, having more good sense in the matter than the adoring mother, would not allow Elizabeth to take the child with them on morning visits, but Elizabeth was not inclined to acquiesce in this decision, writing to her sisters:

See if I won't have my own way and work my vanity into light just as I please. Penini, too, who is just made to be carried about and shown off, with his long purple feather shaking over his trailing golden ringlets, and the small black silk jacket I have just finished embroidering for him! He does look like a fairy king of a child—and is intended to be looked at accordingly.

This feminine garb for a small boy was by no means unpermissible in the middle of the last century, though Elizabeth in her fondness (and perhaps subconsciously from a frustrated desire for a girl child) kept up this custom rather beyond the usual age, decking Penini in feathers, velvet, and embroidery up to the time of her death in 1861. It seems unlikely that the virile Browning approved: indeed, in less than a month after her death Browning reported to his sister that "the golden curls and fantastic dress, is gone just as Ba is gone: he has short hair, worn boy-wise, long trousers, is a common boy all at once"; alleging the difficulty of keeping Pen in his old garb without the assistance of a maid.

Penini would insist on being dressed up in the evening in a hope that he could keep awake long enough to help receive his mother's visitors; visitors who increased in number as the spring advanced. There was a greater influx of Americans, "a sort of fluent society," Elizabeth told her sister, "which comes and passes."

These Americans stimulated an interest in "table-tapping," which, in the spring of 1853, became a veritable rage in Florence. "When people gather round a table it isn't to play whist." Robert remained obstinately a sceptic as Elizabeth's faith in spiritualism grew, though even he was forced to admit that some evidence appeared valid; as when several clairvoyants, unknown to one another, predicted an accident to Robert Lytton's father.

In July the Brownings retired again to La Villa, Bagni di Lucca, taking Casa Tolomei, a pleasant house with a *specola* facing the village green and embowered in trees. For the next three months they worked hard to earn their holiday and perhaps a winter in Rome.

Elizabeth carried with her to Lucca a particularly happy memory, which is best told in her own words:

The evening before our last at Florence, we had tea and straw-berries on the terrace of Mr. Lytton's villa, on the heights of Bellosguardo; meeting there our friends, Mr. Powers and Mr. Tennyson. It was a bachelor's party, and I made tea like a bach-elor, in an awkward way I believe, but nobody minded it be-tween the fireflies and the stars, and Florence dissolving in the valley beneath us in that seething, purple light which had run down from the hills. Seldom have I enjoyed anything so much.[2]

This passage we may perhaps link up with one in that book on which Elizabeth was at work, *Aurora Leigh*. She described the seething purple light filling up the valley below, flooding the city; and, as the darkness deepens:

> *The duomo-bell*
> *Strikes ten, as if it struck ten fathoms down,*
> *So deep; and twenty churches answer it*
> *The same, with twenty various instances.*
> *Some gaslights tremble along squares and streets;*
> *The Pitti's palace front is drawn in fire.*

But here, deep in the mountains, were few lights beyond the village except those of

> *fireflies, that suspire*
> *In short soft lapses of transported flame*
> *Across the tingling Dark, while overhead*
> *The constant and inviolable stars*
> *Outburn those light-of-love:*

The large solitude these two claimed for work at Lucca was soon interrupted, pleasantly interrupted by the advent of Mr. and Mrs. Story, with whom a friendship had been prosperously begun in 1848. The Storys, staying at the Bagni Caldi, took them by surprise one day. Up to their house higher in the mountain Elizabeth would go on donkey-back, Robert holding the reins, "to tea-drinking and gossiping." The Storys had two children, Edith, nine years of age, and Joe, six. With Edith little Pen soon fell in childish love. Later he was to take lessons with her from an Italian tutor.

---

[2] Unpublished letter, July 19, 1853, from the Marsh papers in the Library of the University of Vermont.

Through the Storys the Brownings came to visit others, to join in "omnivorous teas—of hams and tarts and fruits and cakes, and coffee etc." With their American friends they rode, drove, walked, and took meals in the open.

For a fortnight Robert Lytton stayed with them at Casa Tolomei. While he was there Elizabeth wrote a poetical tribute to him so adulatory in tone that it is difficult to accept it as from a famous woman to a young man, however promising he might be as poet and seer. She called him "our leader and king of us all," declaring "There is none we can honor above you," and "We'd die for you gladly, if need be":

All that strength! all that power! yet so pliant!
    You're so great we could never come near you,
Were it not that the child with the giant
    Is mixed—and we honor –not fear you.

One can only suppose—if, indeed, this piece was meant to be taken seriously—that Lytton's youthful charm, his curly hair, intensely blue eyes, combined with an active interest in spiritualism to blur true vision. In later years Browning himself showed a strong dislike for Lytton and it was not long before Elizabeth was to disagree with the young diplomat on a question of Austrian power politics. Also it seems likely that there was some sort of love affair between Lytton and Isa Blagden in which the Brownings considered that he had not behaved well: certainly while in Florence Lytton was suffering from an attachment he felt to be hopeless. For a young diplomat, one destined eventually to become Viceroy of India, union with a Eurasian (if so Isa Blagden was) would have been impossible. Isa too was some ten years older than he.

But, however it might be in the future, Lytton was now a highly valued companion, with his "wit that walks forth silvershod," his smile like "a rainbow that arches the deeps."

One day he accompanied them, with the Storys, on a long expedition to the Prato Fiorito. They went, led by guides, on horse- or donkey-back. "It was like going up and down a wall, without the smoothness." On their return all were tired out, though Robert refused to admit his fatigue. No wonder Elizabeth "could not stir for days after." But, she added with spirit to Mrs. Martin, "who wouldn't see heaven and die? Such a vision of divine scenery . . ." The Italian countryside that July was, we learn from a letter of Browning's to Allingham, peculiarly beautiful, vivid in colour, after a mild winter and heavy rains in spring.

There was one alarming incident which is best told in Elizabeth's own words:

The other day we were walking, and I, attracted by a picturesque sort of ladder-bridge of loose planks thrown across the river, ventured on it, without thinking of venturing. Robert held my hand. When we were in the middle the bridge swayed, rocked backwards and forwards, and it was difficult for either of us to keep footing. A gallant colonel who was following us went down upon his hands and knees and crept. In the meantime a peasant was assuring our admiring friends that the river was deep at that spot, and that four persons had been lost from the bridge. I was so sick with fright that I could scarcely stand when all was over, never having contemplated an heroic act. "Why, what a courageous creature you are!" said our friends. So reputations are made. . . .

When October came, with broken weather, the Brownings were glad at last to leave their mountain paradise. "This poor place," Robert wrote to Story, who had preceded them to Florence, "has given up the ghost now."

From Casa Guidi we have in a letter to Thomas Westwood one of Elizabeth's acute criticisms, this time of Coventry Patmore's early work. She found him defective "in the intellectual part of poetry."

His images are flowers thrown to him by the gods, beautiful and fragrant, but having no root either in Enna or Olympus. There's no unity and holding together, no reality properly so called, no thinking of any kind.

In this letter we find her recommending *Villette* as a "strong book."

That autumn the visit to Rome, so long desired, so often delayed, seemed at last possible: after a few weeks in Florence they set out on November 12, being eight days on the road, pausing at Assisi and having a vision of the Torni fall, "that passion of the waters which makes the heart seem so still." Excited, exalted, they entered Rome in the highest spirits, "Robert and Penini singing actually; for the child was radiant and flushed with the continual change of air and scene."

It was in the dusk they entered: at their apartment, 43, Bocca di Leone, they found "lighted fires and lamps as if coming home" and the smiling faces of friends, the Storys, who had prepared this welcome.

Happiness, however, was delusory, short-lived: in Elizabeth's own words, their "first step into Rome was a fall, not into a catacomb but a fresh grave."

The next morning, their first in Rome, had begun badly with a distinct shock for Elizabeth. Browning, who had woken in a state of bilious irritability, probably from over-exposure to the sun on their journey,

in a fit of suicidal impatience shaved away his whole beard, whiskers and all! I cried when I saw him, I was so horror-struck. I might have gone into hysterics and still been reasonable; for no human being was ever so disfigured by so simple an act. Of course I said when I recovered breath and voice, that everything was at an end between him and me if he didn't let it grow again directly.

As a "just punishment of the gods" Robert's beard grew, not the old full rich black, but grey; though Elizabeth thought "the argentine touch" becoming enough.

That morning, begun so inauspiciously, ended in anxiety and grief: a servant came from the Storys' apartment bringing little Edith to them. Her brother had been taken with convulsions. The Brownings hurried to their friends. Their first day in Rome was spent by a deathbed: that evening the boy died of gastric fever.

While they were away Edith Story had been taken ill: because space was wanting in the apartment she was taken down to another below, where Page, the American artist, another friend of Story's, lived. To add to horror and confusion, the Storys' nurse was taken seriously ill of the same fever, and soon Page's youngest daughter sickened.

Elizabeth, distraught with sympathy and shock, was in deadly fear for her own loved ones, although the physicians, among them the great Roman doctor Panteleoni, assured her that there was no danger through contagion. Though the other patients soon recovered, it was January before Edith was well again, a feverish ague following on the original gastric trouble.

Elizabeth's first drive out in the city she had so longed to visit was with Mrs. Story to the Protestant Cemetery,
where poor little Joe is laid close to Shelley's heart (Cor cordium, *says the epitaph), and where the mother insisted on going. . . . I am horribly weak about such things. I can't look on the earth-side of death; I flinch from corpses and graves, and never meet a common funeral without a sort of horror. When I look deathwards I look over death, and upwards, or I can't look that way at all. So that it was a struggle with me to sit upright in that carriage in which the poor stricken mother sat so calmly —not to drop from the seat, which would have been worse than absurd of me.*

Well, all this has blackened Rome to me. I can't think about the Cæsars in the old strain of thought; the antique words get muddled and blurred with warm dashes of modern every-day tears and fresh grave-clay.

It is possible that, whether she realized it or no, Rome was blackened for her by another aspect of that ancient city: travellers tell us that even when Tuscany was most oppressed under Austrian grand-ducal rule, a crossing over the frontier into the Papal States revealed oppression, social conditions far worse. As one put it in a *Cornhill* article (December 1860): "With quiet, almost stealthy pace, downcast look, and submissive bearing, the native Roman creeps noiselessly along the thoroughfares of his city; his gait and appearance harmonize in sad sort with the death-stricken aspect of the morally and physically dilapidated world around him." French soldiers in occupation were the only cheerful bustling people.

By the end of December Elizabeth's naturally good spirits were beginning to rise again. The invalids were convalescent and there were many visitors in the Bocca di Leone. Rome suited her: their rooms, high up in the building, were flooded with sun even in that narrow street. On Christmas morning she attended mass at St. Peter's, with an excellent view of "pope and cardinals and all"; giving herself without reserve to the beauty of service, music, and the "sight of the crowding multitudes."

Among new friends in Rome were the fascinating Mrs. Sartoris, formerly the singer Adelaide Kemble, and her more famous sister Fanny, a woman of fine intellect and majestic mien; one of those who had suffered in a miserable marriage by the law as it then stood. Staying with Mrs. Sartoris was that ancient enemy of romantic poets John Lockhart, now old and ill, near to death. Lockhart liked Browning; declaring that he wasn't in the least like "a damned literary man." And, Elizabeth told Miss Mitford, "if anybody wants small-talk by handfuls of glittering dust swept out of salons, here's Mr. Thackeray besides."

Although there was never complete ease between Elizabeth and Thackeray, they had one interest in common. Lady Ritchie has given us a picture of the two talking of spiritualism, Mrs. Browning very small, very brown, quiet, smiling, with a manner full of charm and kindness, and dressed in soft-falling flounces of black silk, a thin gold chain about her neck. Thackeray's huge bulk loomed over the dark head with its heavy curls dropping about an eager face. As they talked Browning would interrupt in his loud resonant voice, sweeping away arguments. His wife would protest, "her own weak voice in a faint minor chord, slightly lisping, 'Robert!'"

Lady Ritchie, then Annie Thackeray, would often be invited with her sister to spend an evening with Mrs. Browning while Browning and her father were out visiting: Annie conceived a profound admiration for Elizabeth, recording in her diary: "I think Mrs. Browning the greatest woman I ever knew in my life."

At a children's party given by Thackeray he drew for his fortunate little guests pictures to illustrate *The Rose and the Ring*. By the bedside of Edith Story, now slowly recovering, he would sit, soft-hearted man as he was under a crust of worldliness, reading to her from the manuscript of that book which was soon to delight in print children of many generations.

Isa Blagden was in Rome that spring, staying at 28, Corso: in the apartment above was what Story flippantly termed a "harem (scarem)" of young American women, "emancipated," artists and writers. Through them and Isa, Elizabeth came to know Hatty Hosmer, a young sculptress of great promise who lived alone, dined and breakfasted "at the *cafés* precisely as a young man would," worked at her art from morning till night "and this with an absence of pretension and simplicity of manners which accord rather with the childish dimples in her rosy cheeks than with her broad forehead and high aims." The diminutive, merry, gallant little creature became "a great pet" of the Brownings. Hatty Hosmer was the more welcome to Elizabeth because she was a visionary and a writing medium.

In March Elizabeth wrote to Sarianna: "I don't like Rome, I never shall; and as they have put it in the English newspapers that I don't, I might as well acknowledge the barbarism." One aspect, however, of Roman society which pleased her was Penini's undoubted social success. Her son was "generally acknowledged as the king of the children here." Mrs. Page, of the apartment below, gave a party, perhaps on his birthday, in Penini's honour. The self-possessed, precocious child would even talk on equal terms with that queen of tragedy Mrs. Kemble, who, his mother said, " 'dashes' most people."

Elizabeth's dislike for Rome was soon deepened by a loss of colour and vitality in her child, who was affected, in the increasing warmth of spring, by the climate of a city pervaded by miasma from the Campagna marshes, which had perhaps brought Joe Story to untimely death. It was with relief that she left for home on May 22, intending to stay there a few weeks and then set off for England.

England, and particularly London, had lately been present to Elizabeth under its grimmest aspect: she had written, for sale at a bazaar in aid of Arabel's particular work, "A Plea for the Ragged Schools of London." The "Plea" is not imbued with the direct passion of "The Cry of the Children," but its best verses are affecting enough to those who know from harrowing research the plight of many homeless waifs in Victorian England:

> *Ragged children, hungry-eyed,*
> *Huddled up out of the coldness*
> *On our doorsteps, side by side,*
> *Till your footman damns their boldness.*

To this Browning added his singular and attractive piece "The Twins" (Date and Dabitur): the two were sold on a leaflet for sixpence.

One of their first evenings in Florence was spent like the last, at Lytton's villa on Bellosguardo:

We walked home to the song of nightingales by starlight and firefly light. Florence looks to us more beautiful than ever after Rome. I love the very stones of it, to say nothing of the cypresses and river.

Hampered by lack of money, they lingered on in Florence: it soon became evident that there could be no visit to England, or even to Paris, this summer. The ship shares were yielding no income, but loss. By June the Brownings had only £100 to cover the next six months.

About June 17 Elizabeth lost her oldest companion, the comfort of unhappy years. In one sense Flush's death, however, was a relief. He had scarcely a hair on his back and the odour of him was far from pleasant. To her sister Elizabeth wrote:

dear Flush. He is gone, Arabel— He died quite quietly— I am sorry to say Penini found him, & screamed in anguish. There was no pain, nothing to regret in that way—and our grief for him is the less that his infirmities had become so great that he lost no joy in losing life. He was old you know—though dogs of his kind have lived much longer—and the climate acted unfavourably upon him . . . it has been quite a shock to me & a sadness—a dear dog he was.[3]

Flush lies buried in a cellar beneath Casa Guidi. So far as we know, his place was never taken by another animal.

In August the Brownings were really anxious about money: Mr. Kenyon had forgotten to pay the half-yearly instalment on his allowance. Chapman & Hall's accounts that summer showed little balance in their favour. *Casa Guidi Windows* was selling but slowly. They must perforce remain in Florence that summer.

In late August or early September news reached Elizabeth of an accident to her father. Mr. Barrett was knocked down by a cab [4] with a resultant lameness that, the doctors said, might be permanent; a serious blow to a man of active habits. Elizabeth wrote a letter expressing her sorrow and solicitude, taking the precaution of having it posted in London. The envelope was

[3] Unpublished letter, June 17–18, 1854, New York Public Library.
[4] Family information.

addressed by Pen. Thus his daughter's message of love must have been received and opened by Mr. Barrett, who, however, made no sign.

It would seem as if by the wedding anniversary, on September 12, the Brownings' temporary embarrassment was at an end: Robert celebrated their eight years of happiness by the gift of "a beautiful malachite brooch . . . mystically marked and of as deep a green as the Elysian ghosts walk in when the poets guide them." Wilson too, who was in a sense part of their marriage, received a present.

In the autumn of 1854 a general gloom began to overshadow the British, whether at home or abroad; a shadow familiar in our time, but strangely heavy upon a generation of which only the older members could have lively memories of war. War and revolution were to the younger subjects of Queen Victoria only for backward foreigners. There was war in the Crimea, war against Russia. News was bad, culminating in November with tidings of the bloody battle of Inkerman. Elizabeth had two cousins at the front.

There were, however, aspects of the war which Elizabeth must rejoice in; first, the alliance between France and England, which she hoped might cure her country of the growing fear of French aggression, and, secondly (though curiously enough she does not mention it), Vittorio Emmanuele's decision to send a large army of troops to the Crimea. This bold move brought Sardinia in on the side of two major powers at the later Congress of Paris, and gave the astute Cavour an opportunity to make public protest against conditions in Italy under Austrian rule. Participation in the Crimean War, where the Sardinians acquitted themselves well, also brought compensatory renown to an army that had been so thoroughly routed at Novara.

Indeed, perhaps the only benefits of this cruel conflict came to the minor participant: Louis Napoleon, for some reason never fully explained, threw away the full fruit of victory by bringing the war to an abrupt end.

Penini, of course, took a small boy's delight in war, pretending to read from the newspaper about *"bellissimi regimenti"* and how his friend Napoleon had sent 80,000 men to Turkey. Pen was progressing well with pianoforte-playing under his father's strict tuition, and developing a love for opera. Finding himself unable to accompany his own rendering of "La Donna è mobile" he found compensation in making an opera of his own about Napoleon and the milkman, "an intimate enemy" who always when he called pretended to take away the child's favourite gun. From his mother's description it would seem that Penini had the right idea:

In the opera the milkman brings bad cream and milk for the "soldati francesi" in arms against the Russians, and so Napoleon comes out against him in vengeance! "è fusillato—è morto!" . . . and then comes the burial—"misericordia," "campo santo" —and all—and an immense noise of "pieti" and bells.

The year wore on to a close, darkly enough for English minds. 1855 opened with frost, snow, and a bitter wind even in Florence. Elizabeth was taken ill, seriously ill for the first time since her marriage, of the old chest complaint. Recovery was slow, leaving a depression of spirit.

Early in the year, news came of Miss Mitford's death after a long martyrdom of illness heroically borne. Never again would Elizabeth receive another of those letters full of pleasant gossip, redolent of the English countryside and full of affection; letters which came so regularly—one, indeed, arriving just before Miss Mitford's death—that any omission on a certain date of the month caused some alarm for the writer's well-being. A minor consolation for this loss, a link snapped with the old life, was a letter from a man who had been Miss Mitford's good friend in her last years, John Ruskin. Between Elizabeth and Ruskin a correspondence was to be agreeably though fitfully carried on to the end of her life.

News from the Crimea, of the sufferings of men neglected by their own rulers in an exceptionally severe winter, continued to reach shocked English ears: the sending out of Florence Nightingale with the first contingent of women nurses was of personal interest to Elizabeth, who had met her in London and remembered clearly "her face and her graceful manner, and the flowers she sent me afterwards."

With Mrs. Jameson's happy assertion that Florence Nightingale's appointment meant a distinct advance in the position of their sex, Elizabeth did not agree:

*Every man is on his knees before ladies carrying lint, calling
them "angelic she's," whereas, if they stir an inch as thinkers or
artists from the beaten line (involving more good to general humanity than is involved in lint), the very same men would curse
the impudence of the very same women and stop there. . . .
Apart from the exceptional miseries of the war . . . I do not
consider the best use to which we can put a gifted and accomplished woman is to* make her a hospital nurse.

Elizabeth could not then know of Florence Nightingale's ad-
ministrative powers, forcefully though tactfully used to penetrate an obstinate male stronghold for the benefit of humanity
as a whole.

The miseries, the cruelties and blunders of the Crimean War
do not appear in themselves to have shocked Elizabeth greatly:
she took them to be but a small and symptomatic part of general misery, stupidity, and corruption. "This and that poisonous
berry is pulled off leisurely," but the root of it all, the system,
remained. "I begin to think that nothing will do for England but
a good revolution and a 'besom of destruction' used daunt-
lessly." She denounced the evils of nepotism:

*we have soldiers, and soldiers should have military education as
well as red coats, and be led by properly qualified officers, instead of Lord Nincompoop's youngest sons. As it is in the army,
so it is in the State. Places given away, here and there, to incom-
petent heads; nobody being responsible, no unity of idea and
purpose anywhere—the individual interest always in the way of
the general good.*

This year travel was no longer impossible: at the beginning of
May both the Brownings were working hard in preparation for
a journey to London, and later Paris. Each determined to take
at least eight thousand lines for the printer, entering into a playful rivalry as to who should complete them first. Robert won,
but Elizabeth pleaded the feminine cares of the wardrobe; especially in regard to Penini, whose "little trowsers" must be
"creditably frilled and tucked." There were visits to pay after
the seclusion of winter, many letters to write, and Penini's lessons to be attended to. Altogether, Elizabeth wrote, "my head
swims and my heart ticks before the day's done, with positive
weariness."

The serious illness of that winter had left its mark: Elizabeth had, with the warmth of spring, appeared to gain strength, but already in her letters we begin to detect a certain failing of powers so valiantly recovered nine years before. This year Elizabeth left Casa Guidi with reluctance and a certain pain. "I do love Florence so! When Penini says 'Sono Italiano, voglio essere Italiano,'⁵ I agree with him perfectly." And this time Italy was to be left for a long absence, for another experiment of wintering in Paris: perhaps indeed Casa Guidi might no longer be called home.

⁵ "I'm Italian—I want to be Italian."

CHAPTER 26

PARIS; LONDON [1855–6]

THE BROWNINGS TRAVELLED by sea to Marseilles and thence to Paris, arriving in June. At Marseilles a box was lost containing "all Penini's pretty dresses, trowsers, collars," everything Elizabeth had been so diligently collecting in Florence so that she might present her son worthily to his uncles and aunts; that this box also contained the manuscript of *Aurora Leigh* Elizabeth did not mention in writing of the disaster to Arabel.

In Paris Elizabeth had the pleasure of meeting her brother Alfred, there perhaps as a lover: in two months' time he was to marry his cousin, Elizabeth Georgina (Lizzie) Barrett, at the British Embassy in Paris. It was Alfred who later found the precious box at Marseilles lying in the custom-house.

In Paris there was another marriage nearer in view: Ferdinando, Robert's servant, and Peni's particular friend, had been courting Wilson for two years. In May they had become engaged. The Brownings approved though they saw legal difficulties. Ferdinando was a foreigner and a Catholic: the marriage must be perfectly in order for Wilson's sake. In Paris Ferdinando tried to press on the ceremony, but it was difficult to find a priest sufficiently unorthodox to perform it. But somehow the problem was solved to the satisfaction of master and mistress. In July 1855 Wilson became Elizabeth Romagnoli.

In July the Brownings left France, arriving in London very early on the 12th after a rough crossing that upset them all. Seasickness, however, was but a passing physical disability: to Henrietta Elizabeth wrote: "there's always a weight on my heart when I arrive. The land-sickness is worse than the sea's."

Arabel, always her chief darling among the family, she found "wonderfully well—quite brilliant" and wearing a Parisian bonnet. This bonnet, worn "dropping off behind," was not comfortable or of the most becoming: when Robert insisted on his wife "wearing hats like other people" and Elizabeth reluctantly wore one, she felt "an immense grudge" towards the Empress Eugénie, arbitress of women's fashions, "for tormenting me so, just because she likes to show her own beautiful face!"

Penini, to his mother's joy, took "a great passion of love" for her favourite sister. Nine years later his Aunt Arabel was to act in part as mother to a bereaved child.

The Brownings took comfortable lodgings at 13, Dorset Street, Baker Street, where they were at once overwhelmed with visitors, people who "want to see," Elizabeth wrote, "if Italy has cut off our noses, or what!" Two days after arrival they breakfasted with Mr. Kenyon—"to meet half America and a quarter of London."

There was one man in London, a man causing considerable sensation, whom Elizabeth particularly wanted to meet. Daniel Dunglas Home (pronounced "Hume" and always spelt so by Mrs. Browning) was a Scot brought up in America. His great mediumistic powers are, I believe, no longer disputed, but in 1855 a battle of opinion raged about his head.

An opportunity came: stimulated by tales of manifestations witnessed by Lytton and his father, the Brownings went out to Ealing, where, through Home's able guidance, the spirits were singularly courteous to Elizabeth. After such general manifestations as table-rappings and the touch of ghostly fingers,

at the request of the medium, the spiritual hands took from the table a garland which lay there, and placed it upon my head. The particular hand which did this was of the largest human size, as white as snow, and very beautiful. It was as near to me as this hand I write with, and I saw it as distinctly. I was perfectly calm! not troubled in any way, and felt convinced in my own mind that no spirit belonging to me was present on the occasion. The hands which appeared at a distance from me I put up my glass to look at—proving that it was not a mere mental impression. . . . These hands seemed to Robert and me to come from under the table, but Mr. Lytton saw them rise out of the wood of the table—

In telling Henrietta of this phenomenon Elizabeth asked her not to mention it in her reply; spiritualism being "a *tabooed* subject in this house—Robert and I taking completely different views." Browning openly alleged trickery: it was probably this year that Home had the temerity to call upon him and was threatened with forcible ejection. In revenge Home sedulously fostered a ridiculous rumour that Browning was jealous of the wreath that had crowned his wife's head; had even moved behind her chair in the hope that it might descend on his own brow. Later Browning was to pillory Home as "Mr. Sludge, 'The Medium.'"

Elizabeth had to admit that at the conclusion of the séance Home, in a trance, "talked a great deal of much such twaddle as may be heard in any fifth rate conventicle."

Henrietta, out of health this year because of the coming of a child, Elizabeth was destined not to see: lack of means prevented the Brownings from going to her in Somerset. Mr. Barrett, still resolute in a determination not to receive his daughter, sent the family off to Eastbourne: again shortage of money prevented the Brownings from following them. Bereft of her family, and especially of Arabel, Elizabeth felt London to be "an empty nutshell—just to be thrown away." Even Mr. Kenyon, occupied at his Isle of Wight home with a brother recently come from Austria, they did not see again until October, just on the point of their departure for France.

An invitation came from Mrs. Martin but, apart from the cost of a journey west, Elizabeth, her mind haunted by ancient memory, felt unequal even to set foot in Herefordshire; much less to stay at Old Colwall, so near to Hope End:
I could as soon open a coffin as do it: there's the truth. The place is nothing to me, of course, only the string round a faggot burnt or scattered. But if I went there, the thought of one face which never ceases to be present with me (and which I parted from for ever in my poor blind unconsciousness with a pettish word) would rise up, put down all the rest, and prevent my having one moment of ordinary calm intercourse with you, so don't ask me; set it down to mania or obstinacy, but I never could go into that neighbourhood, except to die, which I think sometimes I should like.
There was an added note of apology to her old friend:
Foolish to write all this! As if any human being could know thoroughly what he was to me. It must seem so extravagant, and

perhaps affected, even to you, *who are large-hearted and make allowance. After these years!*

The weather that summer was dull and wet. Elizabeth felt breathing difficult. But there were compensations in meeting people unattainable in far Florence: Ruskin, the Carlyles, Thackeray, Monckton Milnes, Leigh Hunt, Kinglake, the Procters, and above all, Tennyson. One memorable evening she had an experience unforgettable to more than herself.

Tennyson was now enjoying success: "Maud," published earlier that year, though unfavourably received by the critics, was ardently welcomed in the Victorian home. In a few months five thousand copies were sold. Morbidly sensitive as he was to criticism, Tennyson's enjoyment was to some extent marred: a need for personal reassurance was felt. Elizabeth admired the poem with some qualification, bewailing the earlier Tennyson, but her devotion to the poet himself was unwavering.

Tennyson, up a few days from the Isle of Wight, spent two of them with the Brownings, dining, smoking, drinking port; and, on September 27, ended their communing with a magnificent and emotional declamation of "Maud." Elizabeth, enduring tobacco smoke for love of the man, was charmed with "his frankness, confidingness, and unexampled *naïveté!*" Tennyson would now and then pause in his reading to remark: "There's a wonderful touch!" "That's very tender," or "How beautiful that is!" The Rossetti brothers were present: as Tennyson was reading Dante Gabriel made two sketches of him, one of which he gave to Elizabeth.

When Tennyson had finished, Browning took his place, giving, in strong contrast to the heavy romanticism of "Maud," his own "Fra Lippo Lippi" with (said William Rossetti) "as much of sprightly variation as there was in Tennyson of sustained continuity. Truly a night of the gods, not to be remembered without pride or pang." The friends parted at half past two in the morning.

At the beginning of October, Robert's *Men and Women* being now in print, the Brownings decided to leave England, but were delayed by the return of Mr. Kenyon, who pressed them to stay a few days longer so that he might enjoy their company. Arabel risked the parental displeasure by coming up to Town.

She begged that her nephew might return with her for a few
days at Eastbourne: with some heart-searching Elizabeth consented to part with her child for the first time. Penini himself at
first refused but, changing his mind at the last minute on account of "a little dog which was going to Eastbourne, and
which he was wanted to take care of—some temptation about
shells and the sea," he set out with Arabel "in the greatest state
of excitement and dignity of a carpet bag."

While still in London Elizabeth embarked upon a small adventure of her own; going out to shop unaccompanied. In this
congenial occupation time slipped by until she had been out a
full hour. Robert worked himself up into a frenzy of fright: as
she came back Wilson was just putting on her hat to go out in
search of "the stray Ba-lamb."

On October 18 the Brownings left for Paris, where they
lodged at first in unsuitable apartments at 102, Rue de Grenelle,
near the elder Browning's home. After six weeks of discomfort,
during which Elizabeth was far from well, they moved to 3,
Rue du Colysée, a turning off the Champs-Elysées. To Mrs.
Jameson Elizabeth gave a lively account of her transference on
a cold December day:

That darling Robert carried me into the carriage, swathed past
possible breathing, over face and respirator in woollen shawls.
No, he wouldn't set me down even to walk up the fiacre steps,
but shoved me in upside down, in a struggling bundle—I strug-
gling for breath—he accounting to the concierge for "his mur-
dered man" (rather woman) in a way which threw me into fits
of laughter afterwards to remember. "Elle se porte très bien!
elle se porte extrêmement bien. Ce n'est rien que les poumons."
Nothing but lungs! No air in them, which was the worst! Think
how the concierge must have wondered ever since about "cet
original d'Anglais," and the peculiar way of treating wives when
they are in excellent health. "Sacre."

In London there had been little time for writing: now, in retirement for the winter, Elizabeth was working hard to complete *Aurora Leigh*. Although the winter was mild her health
was affected, partly through lack of air. In Florence she remained cloistered for months, but in apartments large and lofty.
These rooms in the Rue du Colysée were small, low-ceilinged. It

was April before she was fit enough to go driving in the Bois de Boulogne.

In that letter always written on March 4, Henrietta's birthday, Elizabeth spoke with envy of the coming of her sister's third child, hoping again for a niece. On April 11 she wrote to Arabel of another baby, the Emperor's son, born on March 16, 1856. Tales of Napoleon's tears and refusal to eat during the birth Arabel, probably representing the majority of her countrymen, refused to believe. To the British Louis Napoleon was a hard-hearted, treacherous intriguer.

At the beginning of May news came from England both good and bad. Henrietta's second son, Edward Altham, was born, and John Kenyon was seriously ill.

On the choice of a name for Henrietta's son Elizabeth would not comment, merely saying that for her part she didn't much care to use beloved names over again, having even a sort of regret at having called her own child Robert. Henrietta's decision to name her son Edward touched an old wound: it was not his grandfather who was commemorated, but the lost Bro.

When news came of Kenyon's illness Browning's impulse was to go over at once to the childless man; but his scrupulous nature held him back from one who was already a benefactor. He had already asked twice for permission to go, receiving the first time "a kind negative" and to the second request no answer. "It is easier for a rich man to enter, after all, into the kingdom of heaven than into the full advantages of real human tenderness," Elizabeth commented sadly.

A certain weakening of the nerves now begins to be evident in Elizabeth's letters: if Arabel neglected to write she worried unduly. Arabel, she told herself, was overworked, slaving at the Refuge and at organizing bazaars. Mr. Barrett too had never fully recovered from his accident. Liable now to asthma, he was a good deal confined to the house. Anxiety over the beloved cousin was constant. "I get so frightened by silences," Elizabeth wrote to Henrietta. Concentrated work on *Aurora Leigh* was tiring her too.

Although, apart from French celebrities she liked and admired, there were interesting people in Paris that spring—

among them Cavour, Monckton Milnes, Dickens, Macready, and, on the stage, Madame Ristori—Elizabeth appears to have gone out in public little, or not at all.

The Brownings returned to London at the end of June, to cold weather and a house full of sad association because of its owner's illness: at Mr. Kenyon's invitation they stayed at his new home, 39, Devonshire Place. As Elizabeth was working against time on her poem few invitations were accepted, but "bells ring and knockers knock." Browning was now something of a lion in his own right, at least with one advanced set of young men, the Pre-Raphaelites.

In London, Wimpole Street must be Elizabeth's chief centre of interest, but that was now an anxiety. Her father was far from well, Arabel so obviously overworked and getting rapidly set in the ways of charity and self-denial. Much as Elizabeth admired her saintlike devotion to a chosen duty, she felt that "a new set of mental associations" would greatly benefit Arabel; something less dreary than constant good works to compensate for a lack of society at home.

During a hot spell in August, "heavy stifling English heat," Elizabeth was detained in Town by the necessity of proof-reading the 11,000 lines of *Aurora Leigh*. Another trial not long to be avoided was the "heavy, damp, stifling English dinners"—at that time portentously lengthy functions. One of their pleasantest evening visits was to the Hallés' house in Bryanston Square, where they heard the musician himself "play Beethoven divinely" and the singing of their friend Adelaide Sartoris.

It was some while this summer before Mr. Barrett discovered the presence of that first offending daughter; once aware of it he sent Arabel, in early September, with some of her brothers to Ventnor, Isle of Wight. But Mr. Barrett's object was defeated: the Brownings at once followed, joining in a happy family party. Penini especially enjoyed himself by the sea in the unaccustomed company of indulgent uncles. A move to Mr. Kenyon's quiet house at West Cowes was a sad change for the child; and sadder still for his parents, who saw their cousin and friend lying dangerously ill.

When an invitation came from the Surtees Cooks at Taunton,

Somerset, Elizabeth was overjoyed and determined to go as soon as it was at all safe to leave Mr. Kenyon. The only blot on her happiness was the dismal fact that Arabel could not join them "for fear of an arrival from London." Arabel, angry at having been sent to Ventnor, disliked the place and longed to get away. Elizabeth, though Robert told her she was very wrong even to wish it, was inclined to press her to take the risk.

Elizabeth bore with her more than one burden as she crossed the Solent towards her sister's home. Apart from the heavy task of proof-reading, which must accompany her, and anxiety about Mr. Kenyon, there was that sorrow, always deeper when in England, over her father's attitude; humiliation too in her child's wonder at the estrangement. Pen, now seven years old, had come to a conclusion that his mother must "have done something very wicked to make my father what he is." Once he came to her and said earnestly: "Mama, if you've been very, very naughty—if you've *broken china*, I advise you to go into the room and say, 'Papa, I'll be dood.'" Pen's idea of a heinous crime, his mother told Mrs. Martin, was breaking china. Elizabeth felt almost inclined to take the child's advice, but on consideration decided there was much against it.

Elizabeth, after enjoying to the full a week or so of serene family life, left Taunton at the end of September. There was between the sisters a final parting, though neither of them could then suspect that they were never to meet again in life.

It was now October: fog was touching London with a damp and chilly finger. An east wind blew. Elizabeth was coughing half the night.

The remaining three weeks in England were busy and not too cheerful. There was anxiety, over not only Mr. Kenyon but her father, now with his family in the Isle of Wight. Ventnor was too damp for him. Laborious days were spent in proof-reading and, having put off the painful task as long as possible, looking through her dear Miss Mitford's letters to see what might be given to the world in a collected edition. It was probably at this time that Elizabeth recovered a box of papers left behind at Wimpole Street in 1846.

Aurora Leigh being now made ready for her launching in England and America, the Brownings set out for Florence on

October 23. A perilous ship indeed Elizabeth felt her new poem
to be, containing as it did so many challenges to public opinion,
decorum, and accepted religion; or, as she put it in that dedication to John Kenyon he was not to see, her "highest convictions
upon Life and Art."

CHAPTER 27

AURORA LEIGH [1857]

THE POETICAL NOVEL planned by Elizabeth as far back as 1844 was to be more than a mere story; it was to comprehend "the aspect and manners of modern life, and flinching at nothing of the conventional." This representation of life around him was, she considered, the true vocation of a modern poet, who must "never flinch" but

> . . . *catch*
>
> *Upon the burning lava of a song*
> *The full-veined, heaving, double-breasted Age:*
> *That, when the next shall come, the men of that*
> *May touch the impress with reverend hand, and say*
> *"Behold,—behold the paps we all have sucked!*
> *This bosom seems to beat still, or at least*
> *It sets ours beating. This is living art,*
> *Which thus presents, and thus records true life."*

How far does this ambitious poem fulfil that aim? To the next generation it was indeed living art, but a later tendency was to regard *Aurora Leigh* as a mere museum specimen. In our time, however, high praise from that delicate, perceptive critic Mr. Clifford Bax has led to a new evaluation. "Period piece" the poem undoubtedly is, but one which has much in it to interest and delight us in a changed world.

Readers may, it is true, be at first repelled by a story in some respects banal, faded enough to a generation nurtured on Trollope and Jane Austen; though at the time this was no stumbling-block: it was the daring thought and expression, much to us now long accepted, that brought down a hail of criticism.

It has been stated that as a result of this criticism Elizabeth altered, softened much in the fourth [1] edition (1859), but this is not so. Apart from obvious corrections, a few verbal changes were made—not always for the better—and the system of punc-

---

[1] Given wrongly as 5th edition, 1860, by Wise.

tuation revised; but that was all. No concession was made to mealy-mouthed readers that I can discover except perhaps the altering of "chaste wife" to "perfect wife," "right damnable" to "unmerciful," and "appetite" (a man's physical appetite in marriage) to "fantasy." "Coarse" references to "the stews," street-walkers, the coupling of beasts, sweat, such verbs as "stink," all remain to shock contemporary "over-delicate ears." No bold statement or thesis is abandoned either. Elizabeth, already thoughtful in social matters, was, after her marriage with Browning, in touch with many advanced and outspoken people in her life on the Continent: it is herself she echoes in putting into the mouth of Aurora Leigh: "I've known the pregnant thinkers of my time."

The intertwined themes of Elizabeth's greatest poem are important, both for themselves and as illustration for her life and character; a strong firm claim for woman's freedom, a passionate avowal of the true artist's integrity of mind and purpose, dedicated to God's service, and the supreme importance of married love.

Aurora Leigh is perhaps no longer a living influence, but once it was a direct inspiration to women sighing out their lives in close parental drawing-rooms, longing to escape; proving to them that there were other duties beyond submission. To illustrate this point I quote from an unpublished lecture by that distinguished educationalist the late Miss Alice Woods, who died at the age of ninety-one in 1941. Miss Woods, after telling how what she and her sisters longed for, above all, was work, so that they envied girls who had to gain a living, continued:

Few writers did more to strengthen the desire than Elizabeth Barrett Browning. Aurora Leigh *had been published as early as 1856 but did not fall into my hands until about 1873, when I found the poem had living expression to my longing.*

> *. . . get leave to work*
> *In this world—'t is the best you get at all*
> *For God in cursing gives us better gifts*
> *Than men in benediction. . . .*
>
> *. . . get work, get work.*
> *Be sure 'tis better than what you work to get.*

And again:

> *The honest earnest man must stand and work.*
> *The woman also,—otherwise she drops*
> *At once below the dignity of man*
> *Accepting serfdom. Free men freely work.*

Only those partly enfranchised can speak on behalf of slaves: Elizabeth was more fortunate than most girls of the early nineteenth century. She was highly educated, had freedom to work on her own lines, and, in spite of a strict upbringing, was apparently subject to few of the restrictions that hampered and intimidated little girls well into living memory. She worked and played on equal terms with her brothers, climbed trees, rushed about on her pony. When comparatively late in life marriage came to her it was not as bondage, but release.

Aurora Leigh is written in blank verse, flowing verse the technical skill of which can be appreciated by a comparison with that of "A Drama of Exile," written in 1843. Dialogue, that pitfall of the novelist in verse, is on the whole well managed, particularly in the masterly church scene where fashionable folk are occupying the pews on one side and denizens of the slum of St. Giles on the other; all assembled to witness the deliberate marriage of socialistic Romney Leigh to Marian Erle, a woman of the people. The men and women of fashion twitter gossip:

> —"*Yes, really, if we need to wait in church*
> *We need to talk there." "She? 't is Lady Ayr,*
> *In blue—not purple! that's the dowager."*
> —"*She looks as young"—"She flirts as young, you mean!"*

When after a lengthy wait the bride does not appear, Romney tells the slum folk to go off and enjoy the marriage-feast prepared for them on Hampstead Heath. After an ominous moment of sullen silence a man speaks gratingly:

> "*Now, look to it, coves, that all the beef and drink*
> *Be not filched from us like the other fun.*
> *For beer's spilt easier than a woman's lost!*
> *This gentry is not honest with the poor;*
> *They bring us up, to trick us."*

Suspecting that some trick has been played on Marian, determined to "see her righted," the angry mob rise up and rush at

Romney. As an example of vivid presentment I give the ensu-
ing panic:

> From end to end, the church
> Rocked round us like the sea in storm, and then
> Broke up like the earth in earthquake. Men cried out
> "Police"—and women stood and shrieked for God,
> Or dropt and swooned; or, like a herd of deer,
> (For whom the black woods suddenly grow alive,
> Unleashing their wild shadows down the wind
> To hunt the creatures into corners, back
> And forward) madly fled, or blindly fell,
> Trod screeching underneath the feet of those
> Who fled and screeched.

Beauty of description, the evocation of an atmosphere, was
already familiar in Elizabeth's work, but these swift, direct, con-
crete living pictures, heightened by metaphor, were something
new. In Elizabeth's later work the influence of her husband is,
of course, apparent, but may I also suggest that of one greater
than he, the Florentine Dante?

The degraded condition of common people, people such as
we can only imagine now in England, is vividly presented and,
from what we can read elsewhere, there is no exaggeration in
the following:

> Those, faces? 't was as if you had stirred up hell
> To heave its lowest dreg-fiends uppermost
> In fiery swirls of slime,—such strangled fronts,
> Such obdurate jaws were thrown up constantly,
> To twit you with your race, corrupt your blood,
> And grind to devilish colours all your dreams
> Henceforth. .

Elizabeth would not have to go as far as St. Giles in the London of her day to see such faces peering out of waterless, un-
drained courts, faces gaunt with hunger, swollen with cheap
drink, or covered in sores.

One offspring of this legion of the damned, the secondary
heroine of this book, is, however, unacceptable enough to a
modern reader. Marian Erle, the tramp's child, in her native
purity, her innocence and beauty of mind, her literary speech,
is to us too false a figure to stir our pity even when she is be-

trayed and hounded by respectable society; but a generation accustomed in novels to the sentimentalizing of a type of noble poor accepted Marian. Robert Lytton considered the history of Marian Erle "a sublime episode." To those not determined to bury their heads in the sand, refusing to see or hear the evil in their midst, the story of this girl, prey to a heartless woman, a procuress and a foul man, was the most moving, the most beautiful thing in the poem; the more so as they could enjoy pity with an easy conscience. Elizabeth makes it quite clear in the person of Aurora Leigh that she would in no circumstances sanction unmarried love.

The heartless woman, Lady Waldemar, who betrays Marian out of jealousy and possessive love for Romney, is also to us theatrical, unbelievable, but here again her type appears in many Victorian novels, to descend within the memory of older people to penny novelettes and Lyceum melodrama; though few authors, even at the franker end of the nineteenth century, would have had the courage to make her, knowingly or unknowingly, abet a procuress.

Romney Leigh, whose heart is governed by his head, who tries to prove his faith by marrying a girl of the people, and later by setting up in his ancestral home a "phylanstery" or communal settlement, was a type familiar in early Christian socialism, a follower, as was the father of Louisa Alcott, of François Fourier. We, who have suffered so much in this age from impractical idealists and the men in wait to exploit them, can feel the full force of this man's tragedy better perhaps than the sheltered Victorians. Elizabeth, declaring she "would rather live under the feet of the Czar than in those states of perfectibility imagined by Fourier and Cabet," was wiser in future events than she knew.

Romney's ancient home, his reputation, his sight, all perish in the vindictive flames that consume this ill-advised colony at Leigh Hall: out of a man's bloodless idealism an historic house and treasures of art are destroyed, a girl's life degraded, an illegitimate boy born, begot by a scoundrel. It is with marriage to Marian Erle that Romney proposes to atone, by a warm act of human compensation, for the failure of cold philanthropy. Perhaps if the main purpose of the theme had not been the triumph of love, it would have been more fitting, more dramatic if Aurora's cousin had made that sacrifice.

But Marian Erle, "the very lamb left mangled by the wolves" through Romney's "bad shepherding," shows more pride, more self-respect than to take the conventional course of being made an "honest woman." "Here's a hand shall keep," she declared boldly, and to the scandal of many a Victorian home, "for ever clean without a wedding-ring."

Aurora Leigh, taking to her heart that Romney she had once scornfully refused, partly in order to live her own life, to fulfil a poetic destiny, now confessed that:

> Passioned to exalt
> The artist's instinct in me at the cost
> Of putting down the woman's, I forgot
> No perfect artist is developed here
> From any imperfect woman. Flower from root,
> And spiritual from natural, grade by grade
> In all our life. . . .
>   Art is much, but love is more.
> O Art, my Art, thou'rt much, but Love is more!
> Art symbolises heaven, but Love is God
> And makes heaven.

Aurora is perhaps a little hard on herself: it was not love, the burning, selfless love of a Robert Browning, that the dismal Romney had offered her, and which she had scornfully refused. Romney had offered the poet-woman, much as St. John Rivers offered Jane Eyre, a service to humanity not her own, telling her not to "play at art." His wife was to be a little beyond the child-bearing toy of a dominant type of wealthy Victorian, but still an appanage, a chattel.

The bold and ardent feminism of *Aurora Leigh* led to much direct denunciation; the Roman Catholic *Tablet* going so far as to call the heroine "a brazen-faced woman," further implying that the story was grossly indecent. Other critics thought the language coarse. Thinkers, those more enlightened, claimed the poem as a masterpiece. Rossetti, Swinburne, and Ruskin were loud in its praise. It was soon bought up by those who admired, those who blamed or enjoyed being shocked: a second edition was called for within the fortnight and there was a steady de-

mand throughout the century. I have before me the nineteenth
edition, dated 1885; the last was, I think, that of 1898 with a
preface by Swinburne.

The first book is particularly good reading in its description
of Aurora's Italian home, the shock of coming on her father's
death to an austerer England and a rigid, virtuous aunt. It is
full of a quiet humour, the description of Miss Leigh being particularly happy:

> *The poor-club exercised her Christian gifts*
> *Of knitting stockings, stitching petticoats,*
> *Because we are of one flesh after all,*
> *And need one flannel (with a proper sense*
> *Of difference in the quality)—and still*
> *The book-club, guarded from your modern trick*
> *Of shaking dangerous questions from the crease,*
> *Preserved her intellectual. She had lived*
> *A sort of cage-bird life, born in a cage,*
> *Accounting that to leap from perch to perch*
> *Was act and joy enough for any bird.*
> *Dear heaven, how silly are the things that live*
> *In thickets, and eat berries!*

Her training of this uncongenial niece, the romantic girl half-
Italian, gives a lifelike picture of the lot of many girls at this
time with "instructed piety" its inculcation of "useful facts," its
minimum of mathematics, science, and languages, its showy
music

> *. . . shuffling off*
> *The hearer's soul through hurricanes of notes*
> *To a noisy Tophet;*

its drawing in pencil and washy water-colours, its ballroom
dancing, the spinning of glass, stuffing birds, modelling flowers
in wax, and hours of unlovely, feeble needlework. How many
frustrated intellectual girls (if allowed to read this dangerous
book) must have felt the bitterness of this passage so deeply
that the humour was lost on them:

> *I read a score of books on womanhood*
> *To prove, if women do not think at all,*
> *They may teach thinking, (to a maiden-aunt*
> *Or else the author)—books demonstrating*

Their right of comprehending husband's talk
When not too deep, and even of answering
With pretty "may it please you," or "so it is,"—
Their rapid insight and fine aptitude,
Particular worth and general missionariness,
As long as they keep quiet by the fire
And never say "no" when the world says "ay,"
For that is fatal,—their angelic reach
Of virtue, chiefly used to sit and darn,
And fatten household sinners,—their, in brief,
Potential faculty in everything
Of abdicating power in it: she owned
She liked a woman to be womanly,
And English women, she thanked God and sighed,
(Some people always sigh in thanking God)
Were models to the universe.

It is on record that the girl Elizabeth hated those womanly accomplishments, needlework, music, and drawing; but for her there were compensatory hours with Mr. McSwiney, and alone with books. To the dominant father she must often have said "may it please you," but one feels that "so it is" came less frequently from the lips of Mr. Barrett's headstrong opinionated young daughter.

Aurora's young nature is Elizabeth's, in both poetic aspiration, ambition, and an absorption in books. Her own development is shadowed out, its imitations and its high-strained tones. One aspect of her own early work is given in a passage partly known to many of those who, dismissing her—unread—as Victorian, pious, sentimental, have no use for Mrs. Browning:

By Keats's soul, the man who never stepped
In gradual progress like another man,
But, turning grandly on his central self,
Ensphered himself in twenty perfect years
And died, not young—(the life of a long life
Distilled to a mere drop, falling like a tear
Upon the world's cold cheek to make it burn
For ever;) by that strong excepted soul,
I count it strange and hard to understand
That nearly all young poets should write old,

> *That Pope was sexagenary at sixteen,*
> *And beardless Byron academical,*
> *And so with others.*

Aurora, her aunt dead, living in London poor and alone, working by day and night at her art, is not in physical circumstance the sheltered Miss Barrett, but she is the poet in essence. Faced with Lady Waldemar and her selfish love for Romney, her plotting to sever him from Marian, Aurora cries:

> *"I love love: truth's no cleaner thing than love.*
> *I comprehend a love so fiery hot*
> *It burns its natural veil of august shame,*
> *And stands sublimely in the nude, as chaste*
> *As Medicean Venus. But I know,*
> *A love that burns through veils will burn through masks,*
> *And shrivel up treachery. What, love and lie!*
> *Nay—go to the opera! your love's curable."*

To many a Victorian reader this was shameless: love in its bodily manifestation was to be hidden behind drawn bed-curtains, an affair of man imposed on quiescent woman, a woman who must never speak of, or indeed was hardly expected to enjoy, the physical side of love.

Was there in the subsequent visit to Marian's lodging a memory of that shuddering adventure into Seven Dials after the lost Flush?

> *Two hours afterward,*
> *Within St. Margaret's Court I stood alone,*
> *Close-veiled. A sick child, from an ague-fit,*
> *Whose wasted right hand gambled 'gainst his left*
> *With an old brass button in a blot of sun,*
> *Jeered weakly at me as I passed across*
> *The uneven pavement; while a woman, rouged*
> *Upon the angular cheek-bones, kerchief torn,*
> *Thin dangling locks and flat lascivious mouth,*
> *Cursed at a window both ways, in and out,*
> *By turns some bed-rid creature and myself,—*
> *"Lie still there, mother! liker the dead dog*
> *You'll be to-morrow. What we pick our way,*
> *Fine madam, with those damnable small feet!*

We cover up our face from doing good,
As if it were our purse! What brings you here,
My lady? is't to find my gentleman
Who visits his tame pigeon in the eaves? . . ."

Aurora, after Marian's disappearance before the marriage, finds the betrayed girl with her child in Paris, takes the two in her care, and carries them off to Italy. They go down through France by train. The train in a tunnel was as new an experience to many at this time as going up in an aeroplane is now:

Athrob with effort, trembling with resolve,
The fierce denouncing whistle wailing on
And dying off smothered in the shuddering dark,
While we, self-awed, drew troubled breath, oppressed
As other Titans underneath the pile
And nightmare of the mountains.

On to Marseilles

With all her ships behind her, and beyond,
The scimitar of ever-shining sea
For right-hand use, bared blue against the sky!

Then, on board ship, recalling Elizabeth's journey to Pisa those many years back, "The old miraculous mountains heaved in sight."

The house Aurora takes on Bellosguardo is thought to have Isa Blagden's home as its prototype; that villa overlooking Florence, the valley of the Arno, and facing the mountains of Vallombrosa.

No sun could die nor yet be born unseen
By dwellers at my villa: morn and eve
Were magnified before us in the pure
Illimitable space and pause of sky,
Intense as angels' garments blanched with God,
Less blue than radiant.

Here, as was fitting, Romney came, a new Romney in humility and despair, to regenerate himself in love. Here was a new dawn to an Aurora so happily named; an Aurora called so, not by happy chance, but trial and error. The heroine was at first to be Laura Leigh, then (as it appears on the manuscript) Aurora Vane; but at length Elizabeth attained to perfection in Aurora

Leigh, with its bright glow of morning, its high aspiring last vowel.

There is much more of interest in this long poem than the working-out of main themes, the enunciation of ideas, a beauty of scenic description, and a boldness in presentment: of interest too are the minor portraits of people in society; the theoretical Christian socialist, Lord Howe, Grimwald, the bilious literary critic, and Sir Blaise Delorme with so high and narrow a forehead that

> *a strong wind,*
> *You fancy, might unroof him suddenly,*
> *And blow that great top attic off his head*
> *So piled with feudal relics.*

The poem ends, as I have said, in the happiness of lovers, but a happiness which Elizabeth knew could not exist in unequal relations, that of the owner and the owned; nor in selfish absorption. These two, one an acknowledged poet and the other a man vowed to work directly for human happiness, are to experience to the full "a love of wedded souls" sanctified by God:

> *Which still presents that mystery's counterpart.*
> *Sweet shadow-rose, upon the water of life,*
> *Of such a mystic substance, Sharon gave*
> *A name to! human, vital, fructuous rose,*
> *Whose calyx holds the multitude of leaves,*
> *Loves filial, loves fraternal, neighbour-loves*
> *And civic—all fair petals, all good scents,*
> *All reddened, sweetened from one central Heart!*

The climax of this huge and intricate work, though it may make us smile rather bitterly in these days of war, frustration, and lack of faith, still has its message:

> *The world's old,*
> *But the old world waits the time to be renewed:*
> *Toward which, new hearts in individual growth*
> *Must quicken, and increase to multitude*
> *In new dynasties of the race of men,—*
> *Developed whence, shall grow spontaneously*
> *New churches, new œconomies, new laws*
> *Admitting freedom, new societies*
> *Excluding falsehood: HE shall make all new.*

My Romney!—Lifting up my hand in his,
As wheeled by Seeing spirits toward the east,
He turned instinctively, where, faint and far,
Along the tingling desert of the sky,
Beyond the circle of the conscious hills,
Were laid in jasper-stone as clear as glass
The first foundations of that new, near Day
Which should be builded out of heaven, to God.

CHAPTER 28

FLORENCE; FRANCE; WAR IN ITALY [1856–9]

THEY RETURNED TO FLORENCE in the late autumn of 1856 to find exceptionally cold weather, a bitter wind and snow already on the mountains; but, her cough having "dropped off somewhere on the road," Elizabeth felt little more than "discomfort and languor." She busied herself with the furnishing of a second drawing-room and anxiously awaited the reception of *Aurora Leigh*.

News from the Isle of Wight was "strange and sad": not only was Kenyon suffering from a relapse, but his brother had died suddenly. On December 3 Kenyon himself died. Elizabeth wrote to Mrs. Martin:

This Christmas has come to me like a cloud. I can scarcely fancy England without that bright face and sympathetic hand, that princely nature, in which you might put your trust more reasonably than in princes. These ten years back he has stood to me almost in my father's place; and now the place is empty —doubly. Since the birth of my child (seven years since) he has allowed us—rather, insisted on our accepting (for my husband was loth)—a hundred a year, and without it we should have often been in hard straits. His last act was to leave us eleven thousand pounds.

£6,500 was left to Robert and £4,500 to Elizabeth: these bequests (apart from the cousinship) were part of a general benevolence to literary people. Henrietta was left £100. Mr. Barrett, much to his annoyance, was not mentioned in the will. "If the principle of relationship had been recognised *at all*," Elizabeth wrote to her sister, "(*which it was not*) he had his undoubted claim." Because of the wealthy brother's death so near to his own some £80,000 was left unaccounted for in Kenyon's will, all of which went, as the law ordained in those days, to the residuary legatees. The trustees were dilatory: it was a full

year before the Brownings benefited by their legacies. In the
meantime Elizabeth's feelings were harrowed by many letters
of congratulation. Although she herself might materially gain
by it, the death of so loved a relative and friend could hardly
be a matter for rejoicing. In the few years remaining to her she
could never trust herself to speak of Kenyon, or even write his
name without tears. When *Aurora Leigh* came out just before
the New Year, pleasure at its immediate success was marred by
a thought that he to whom the book was dedicated could no
longer read it, or enjoy the fame it brought.

After her experience at the séance in Ealing Elizabeth's letters contain more frequent reference to Home and to spiritualism. During her absence in 1855, Home had given demonstra-
tions in Florence which had stirred society. Although he had
enemies, especially among Roman Catholics—and a certain
weakness of moral character gave them a convenient handle—
among the many who were convinced by him was Mrs. Kinney,
wife of the American chargé d'affaires at Turin, whom Elizabeth regarded as particularly "veracious and just." In 1856
Home was in Paris, not, however, holding séances: his power
had departed from him during that year. Elizabeth heard of his
presence near her husband with a certain horror: Browning had
quite worked himself up into a state of hatred of the man. He
had to promise her to be as "meek as a maid" and, if he encountered Home in the street, to pass him without recognition.

Story too was encouraging Elizabeth in her belief, writing
from America that even in "a cold conventional place like
Boston" there was enthusiasm for the spirits. Back in Florence,
Elizabeth, who had there only maintained a mild interest in
table-turning and automatic writing (of which Wilson was a
weak exponent), now heard with ever-increasing awe and interest of more thorough manifestations. To her, as to many people
in the early days of spiritualism, these manifestations were held
to be the sign of a new Revelation, of the gradual passing of human kind into a higher state of being.

In Florence there was an old and simple Englishman, Seymour Kirkup, an artist and archæologist, whose chief fame now
rests upon his discovery of Giotto's portrait of Dante in the
Bargello. Kirkup, credulous to a degree, brought marvellous

tales to Casa Guidi. Elizabeth did not always believe in his visions and spirit voices, but she did not go so far as Robert in declaring Kirkup an old humbug.

One striking case of psychometry (though it may well have been thought-transference) did, however, come to Browning's notice that year through the agency of a Count Ginnasi. Holding in his hand a gold wrist-stud of Browning's the Count declared that a voice was crying in his ear "Murder! Murder!" No one but Browning knew that the stud had been taken from the dead body of a great-uncle who had been violently killed on his estate at St. Kitts.

Life presented itself in a more frivolous aspect that spring: the February carnival of 1857 was a particularly gay one, the wearing of masks being allowed after a prohibition of some years. Peni was wholly absorbed by it, thought of nothing but carnival, and demanded a blue domino trimmed with pink. Robert prepared a domino of black silk (later made into a dress for Elizabeth) and invited friends to supper in a box at the Opera House ball. It had not been thought possible that Elizabeth should act as hostess but, the evening being exceptionally mild, she determined to be present, going out at the last minute to hire domino and mask. Let us hear the rest of the story from herself:

Do you think I was satisfied with staying in the box? No, indeed. Down I went, and Robert and I elbowed our way through the crowd to the remotest corner of the ball below. Somebody smote me on the shoulder and cried "Bella mascherina!" and I answered as imprudently as one feels under a mask.

She was much struck by the "refinement and gentleness" of these people so essentially civilized, "where no excess, no quarrelling, no rudeness nor coarseness can be observed in the course of such wild masked liberty." The Grand Duke went down among the crowd, a crowd consisting of all classes; though, uneasy in conscience as the man must have been, he did not stay long.

In Lent that year Elizabeth wrote in her usual letter to Henrietta on March 4: "everybody now is fasting and sighing,—and enlarging their petticoats." The crinoline was advancing to its final huge encirclement while Elizabeth herself was still hesitating about the mere insertion of whalebone hoops in her skirt. This curious fashion, seeming to us now an encumbrance, brought a certain freedom to women in its very lightness, discarding as they could a dragging weight of many petticoats. Elizabeth stood "lingering by that species of crinoline-petticoat called 'the tower of Malakoff.'"

In giving Henrietta this frivolous detail Elizabeth commented:

What nonsense one talks! when one has talked it, it's impossible to expect that one should be thought of except in the gayest spirits,—and yet really, Henrietta, I have had many sad and heavy thoughts this winter, many.

In March news came of the death of Miss Trepsack, the beloved "Treppy" with whom Elizabeth had been as a favourite daughter. Since this old friend was ninety years of age, tidings of her death could not come as a grievous shock, but Elizabeth was again occupied with thoughts of the past and of death. Though the trappings, the graveyard element, were abhorrent to her, of death itself Elizabeth had no fear. "Death," she wrote to Arabel, "is a bridge to cross and no more."

In the middle of March, looking forward to release from winter bondage in a burst of fine weather, Elizabeth's spirits lightened a little: by the first of April she was driving out in the Cascine Gardens and to Bellosguardo. "Beautiful, beautiful Florence. How beautiful at this time of year! The trees stand in their 'green mist' as if in a trance of joy."

The latest acquisition to Florentine society was Harriet Beecher Stowe of *Uncle Tom's Cabin* fame. Elizabeth had not thought she should like Mrs. Stowe, but found her "very simple and gentle, with a sweet voice. . . . Never did lioness roar more softly." Although Elizabeth could not admire her books "the fact is, that she above all women (yes, and men of the age) has moved the world—and *for good*." To Elizabeth's surprise she preferred her to Mrs. Gaskell, who was also in Florence.

In 1857 Victor Hugo, from his exile in Jersey, published his *Contemplations*. Elizabeth was profoundly moved by them. Grieving for Hugo, she wrote a letter to Napoleon III pleading that he, "a great poet of France," might obtain pardon.

Ah, Sire, what was written on "Napoleon le Petit" does not touch your Majesty; but what touches you is, that no historian of the age should have to write hereafter, "While Napoleon the Third reigned, Victor Hugo lived in exile."

This plea, covering four pages, began humbly with "I am only a woman," and designated the writer modestly as "the wife of an English poet." Her emotional appeal was not, however, actually sent to Napoleon; perhaps as the result of an intervention on Browning's part.

Elizabeth's passionate interest in the Emperor had grown considerably since the day when she had written that he was "a Napoleon cut out of paper after all." Her stout defence, to Mrs. Jameson and others, of him and his actions fills many letter pages in the future: one can only wonder that a being so clear-sighted in her invalid days, shut away from personal contact with the world in Wimpole Street, was now, with a greater knowledge of it, so prejudiced.

On April 17, 1857, Edward Moulton Barrett died of erysipelas, held to be a result of his accident in the autumn of 1854. He was buried in the vault of Ledbury Church, which held the remains of his wife and infant daughter. All Ledbury, with closed shops and drawn curtains, honoured him who had been a distinguished member of the congregation, a local philanthropist, and High Sheriff of the County.[1]

A few months before his death Mrs. Martin had attempted to bring about a reconciliation between Mr. Barrett and his daughters, only to meet with a firm refusal. The proud man went to his death still in a spirit, at least outwardly, of conscious rectitude.

Elizabeth was deeply affected by the news, unable to write of it to anyone outside her own family. An alleged spirit message sent her in July by Fanny Haworth reopened the wound. Elizabeth, for all her faith in spiritual communications, resolutely refused to believe in this one which touched her nearly. That it purported to be from or related to her father is not directly stated, but may well be assumed.

She was very weak now, lying much on the sofa, finding it hard to force herself into daily occupation, even though it might

---

[1] Family information.

be the teaching of her child: "I take up books—but my heart
goes walking up and down constantly through that house in
Wimpole Street, till it is tired, tired." The shock of her father's
death brought with it a return of old grief over his relentless-
ness. Robert had written to Mrs. Martin soon after the news
reached them:

*So it is all over now, all hope of better things, or a kind answer
to entreaties such as I have seen Ba write in the bitterness of
her heart. There must have been something in the organisation,
or education, at least, that would account for and extenuate all
this; but it has caused grief enough, I know; and now here is a
new grief not likely to subside very soon. Not that Ba is other
than reasonable and just to herself in the matter: she does not
reproach herself at all; it is all mere grief, as I say, that this
should have been so.*

There could be, apart from Elizabeth's weakened condition,
no visit to England this year. England would arouse too many
memories. Arabel's own wish that the Brownings should come
to stay with her, Elizabeth herself swept aside as impossible in
any case; writing to Henrietta:

There would be gêne *on both sides. The irregularities of our
house are scandalous—not immoral, observe, but scandalous.
From morning till night people are running out and in—all sorts
of people; and when we are in London we can't help it. There
are men who come and talk—talk, some of them did last summer, till one in the morning—and the freest sort of philosophy is
talked. Robert would be in agonies of annoyance even if Arabel
could bear it.*

The sisters, both children of an Evangelical home but different
in outlook, had now drifted widely apart with circumstance;
Arabel to become perhaps narrower, more devoted to bleak
duty, and Elizabeth confirmed in Liberal tendencies, less consciously religious in tone of mind.

As summer advanced, the heat became seething, "a composition of Gehenna and Paradise." The only relief was evening visits to the Bellosguardo heights and the cool villa of Isa Blagden,
now an intimate and loved friend who had a particular affection
for Penini. One delightful evening was spent on her terrace listening, with Mrs. Jameson, to new poems of Robert Lytton's

(Owen Meredith's) read by himself, "which seemed to receive modulation from the divine stars and ringing mountains." Lytton had but newly returned to Florence after nearly four years out of Italy, plunging into an atmosphere like "a perpetual vapour bath."

Another pleasure at this time was the presence of Mrs. Jameson, who had come over to the Continent in search of health after years of worry and hard work. In 1854 her dearly loved mother had died, and later that year her husband out in Canada; a husband unlamented, but whose death meant the cessation of his annual allowance of £300 a year. Nothing had been left to her. As soon as he realized her plight Thackeray had exerted himself to obtain for her in 1851 a Civil Pension of £100, a regular yearly income that was doubled by the generosity of certain friends. Mrs. Jameson came now to Florence from Rome, where Geddie lived, married to her artist and in no very flourishing circumstance although he had become a photographer—one of the first in that city.

At the end of July the Brownings again fled from the heat to La Villa, Bagni di Lucca, staying in Casa Betti, a small house in a large garden rather too closed in by trees. Soon they were followed by friends, Isa Blagden and Lytton among them, who stayed at the Pelicano opposite. In the coolness and quiet of La Villa Elizabeth found the repose she needed. "You don't know this place" she wrote, "nor how sublimely the mountains look their serenity into you." [2]

But serenity was soon darkened: Lytton, never strong, affected by the July heat in Florence, developed a serious gastric fever. Isa Blagden cared for him, refusing to hire a nurse: Browning, although he privately thought her decision a foolish one, took his share, sitting up night after night with the invalid. For six weeks there was constant anxiety until he was convalescent and able to return to Florence.

In the meantime little Pen was taking his enjoyment, riding donkeys and mountain ponies with his father and bathing in the river Lima. His mother, too weak now for much walking, went about in a *portatina*, a kind of Sedan chair. One day, run-

---

[2] Unpublished letter to Jane Wells Sandford, October 4, 1857, Hewlett Collection.

ning too fast and too far by her side, the boy too was struck down with fever, gastric fever. While he was ill his precious "Lili," the devoted Wilson, who was about to bear a child, had, after a week spent in bed, to return to Florence for her confinement. "She went all in tears, poor thing."

Oh, to see that angel face on the pillow, in the midst of its golden curls, with its scarlet cheeks and poor patient eyes! and to hear his cry of pain in the night, as I did once! It was almost more than I could bear.[3]

To add to the frail mother's difficulties the new Italian maid, Annunziata, whom Pen liked, soon went down with the fever, though not seriously. There had also been an accident to Browning, which, in his fortunate escape, helped to bring Elizabeth back to reality and present blessings. His horse had fallen over a precipice sixty feet deep, head over heels. He saved his life by catching at a crag of rock. "I might be writing to you," she told Arabel in September, "(or rather not writing to you) without a husband and without a child! . . . I feel a good deal stricken altogether."

It is possible that Elizabeth was further disturbed at this time of anxiety by a certain cooling in her friendship with Isa Blagden. We know, since Eckley had been riding with Robert at the time of his accident, that new friends were also with them at Lucca, rich Bostonians who lived in Europe for many years. The wife, Sophia Eckley,[4] was a sweet woman with a delusive air of innocence, a "white rose" of such apparent purity that, Elizabeth wrote in a poem on her, one "dared not name a sin In her presence." It was perhaps a certain gift for flattery that made Browning suspicious of her from the first. Elizabeth, however, accepted Mrs. Eckley at face value, becoming perhaps more swiftly intimate because of a mutual interest in the occult. Isa Blagden was very naturally hurt and jealous.

By October Peni was able to go out in the carriage; his mother was already making plans to travel in winter, even thinking of Egypt and the Holy Land. On their return to Florence before the 12th, the child was fully recovered and in high spirits.

[3] Hewlett Collection.
[4] She was second cousin to Louisa Alcott.

Elizabeth, to her husband's satisfaction, but Mrs. Jameson's disapproval, had now forsaken her "tower of Malakoff" to "sweep out in an excess of majestic circumference" in a hoop-petticoat: "but after all it is not an ungraceful fashion." The crinoline was, indeed, very becoming to a short woman. Elizabeth found it delightfully cool too in an Italian summer. "A hoop and a dress equips you."

There is little record of the autumn of 1857. Christmas Day found them dining at home with friends, and Penini on the verge of his own particular "festa," a festa that was to combine the typical Italian illumination, with many wax torches, and a boy's military dream in a display of toy soldiers, drums, guns, and swords.

In February came news of Felice Orsini's attempt to assassinate Napoleon III by bombs placed in his carriage. Orsini, an Italian patriot, was an agent of Mazzini. In Florence there seems to have been an almost general condemnation of Orsini's act. This episode proved to be important: it would seem as if a letter written to Napoleon by Orsini in prison finally persuaded that wayward man to intervene in Italian affairs.

The winter of 1857–8 was miserably cold even in Italy: Elizabeth was far from well but, as usual in Florence, she had no cough. A cloud hung over her spirits. "Brooding, brooding, brooding, and reading German, are not the ends of life after all—" she wrote in a fit of self-reproach to Arabel. "I must do some work this year at least, and get out of the cloud, if God lets me."

But, as usual, the sunshine of spring livened her thoughts again: plans were formed for meeting members of her family that summer on the Normandy coast, and again she dreamed of a winter in Egypt. A small but vivid interest was aroused when Home returned to Italy, though he was only a day in Florence. She reported that the manners and morals of her "*protegé prophet*" were much improved: debts previously contracted in Florence were now settled from an annuity left to him by an Englishwoman whose infidel opinions had been changed by his manifestation. Soon Elizabeth was to be amused by tidings of Home's marriage. "Think," she wrote, "of the conjugal furniture floating about the room at night."

In April we hear of a passing malady new to her, an eye in-flammation "making the *white*, one red." She was shut up in the dark for a while "with lotions instead of literature." But by April 28 she had been out driving three times.

In June we hear of Elizabeth surviving without undue fa-tigue the combined visits of the American poet William Cullen Bryant (with "a magnificent head and a long beard like snow") and his fellow-countryman Nathaniel Hawthorne. The impression Elizabeth and her child made on such a sensitive re-corder as Hawthorne is perhaps worth quoting:

. . . a pale, small person, scarcely embodied at all; at any rate, only substantial enough to put forth her slender fingers to be grasped, and to speak with a shrill, yet sweet tenuity of voice. . . . It is wonderful to see how small she is, how pale her cheek, how bright and dark her eyes. There is not such another figure in the world; and her black ringlets cluster down into her neck, and make her face the whiter by their sable profusion.

Both mother and son seemed "of the elfin race," with a strangely strong resemblance between them. Penini, he thought, was at once less childlike and less manly than a boy of nine years old should be. Hawthorne's son, Julian, nearer to Pen in age, set down his impression more bluntly: "I had the contempt for him which a philistine boy feels for a creature whom he knows he can lick with one hand tied behind his back, and I had noth-ing whatsoever to say to him."

"There is not such another figure in the world. . . ." This re-mark of Hawthorne's agrees with the general, the unique im-pression made by Elizabeth on those who met her. Though so little impressive physically, her radiant intellect, a faculty for coming at once to the point, and, above all, her spirituality, gave her a quiet power. Thomas Trollope, looking back in old age, said of her "in mind and heart she was *white*—stainless." Always he was conscious of coming away from Casa Guidi a better man, with higher views and aims. Lytton, a closer friend, a more imaginative man, wrote at her death to Forster: "a love-lier life never went back to God."

At the beginning of July the Brownings went by water to Marseilles and then on to Paris, able now to take express trains up through France. As usual travelling benefited Elizabeth in spite of seasickness. Avidly gathering together French novels and periodicals, she rejoiced in the swift isolated life of trains with "no possibility of unpleasant visitors. No fears of horrible letters. . . . Quite out of reach of the telegraph even, which you mock at as you run alongside the wires."

In Paris they stayed for a fortnight at the Hôtel Hyacinthe, Rue St. Honoré. Sarianna and "the dear nonno" were to accompany them to the sea: Elizabeth was ardently hoping that Arabel might join them and return for a short stay in Paris. Opera, theatres would be out of the question for one so strict, but there was much the sisters might enjoy together without moral questioning.

Elizabeth could no longer freely enjoy the delights of Paris. "I break suddenly like a stick," she told Henrietta, "at a certain point and it comes early." In general she contented herself with dining out with Robert and driving in the Bois de Boulogne. But change of scene and travel had so far restored her looks that Robert playfully set her down as a humbug.

Gloom was never far from Elizabeth in these late years: Lady Elgin, with whom Robert was such a favourite, was struck down by a third stroke of paralysis. She recovered enough to be sitting out in her garden before he left Paris, but entirely bereft of speech.

Two people encountered in Paris were the inevitable Father Prout "in great force and kindness," and the American Abolitionist and ex-Congressman Charles Sumner, come over in the hope of recovery from a physical assault made on him because of his opinions.

For the Brownings' seaside visit they first tried Etretat, but found accommodation there both bad and dear; soon they were "ignominiously settled at Havre, yes, at Havre, the name of which we should have scorned a week ago as a mere roaring commercial city." There they stayed in the Maison Versigny, 2, Rue de Perry, facing the sea and set in a pleasant garden.

At Le Havre Elizabeth had the experience, perhaps new to her, of being photographed (see Plate 6) so that a portrait might be engraved for the fourth, revised edition of *Aurora Leigh*. The engraving was supervised, with many letters of detailed criticism and advice from Browning, by D. G. Rossetti; to the partial satisfaction only of both. Of her face, not good in feature, William Rossetti observed: "it was a countenance of April shine and shower to which full justice could only be done by its own varying and exceptional play of expression." To us, however, who never saw Elizabeth, the engraving seems a remarkably accurate reproduction except, perhaps, about the mouth, where it is a little flattering.

Elizabeth could do little at Le Havre but drive and walk down to the shore, "sit on a bench and get strength, if it so pleased God." Soon she was delighted by the coming of Arabel, George, Henry and Henry's wife, whom he had married in the previous April. Joseph Milsand, a friend of both Browning households, joined the party for ten days in September.

They left Le Havre for Paris on September 20th with little regret, especially on Browning's part. He had found the place dull; moreover, a working-fit was upon him, and naturally there was among the family group but scant opportunity for composition. The weather too had been unkind. In Paris they stayed at 6, Rue de Castiglione, Place Vendôme. George and Arabel were with them. We hear nothing of the impact of Paris on Elizabeth's gentle Puritan sister, nor how long she remained there. The parting between them was to prove final.

William Allingham visited the Brownings in Rue de Castiglione; that their lodging was not of the best is indicated by a subsequent letter to him in which Elizabeth made whimsical apology for the fare set before him:

I often think how you consented to be starved, for the sake of our make-believe dinners, by our wicked French cook, who had been used to cook for Barmecide and to put the money in her pocket—and then I sigh and consider in myself how, in spite of your good-nature, you must have softly moralised on a certain friend's unfortunate destiny in having married a mere rhyming woman instead of an "angel in the house" capable of looking after the chops.

As Elizabeth's health was already affected by the chills of autumn, even in Paris, the Brownings left for Florence in the middle of October, taking nine days on the journey, one of which was spent

*at Chambéry, for the sake of Les Charmettes and Rousseau.
Robert played the "Dream" on the old harpsichord, the keys of
which rattled in a ghastly way, as if it were the bones of him
who once so "dreamed." Then there was the old watch hung up,
without a tick in it.*

From Chambéry the journey was difficult. Elizabeth suffered
much in crossing the Alps. On their journey from Genoa to Leghorn by sea in a wretched craft they ran into a *burrasca*, a painful combined disturbance of wind and undersea currents. So exhausted was she that they were obliged to stay the night at
Leghorn.

A consultant was evidently called in by her Florentine doctor: both advised a winter farther south. Unexpectedly severe
weather, however, delayed them in Florence. While still there,
Elizabeth was delighted with a gift from her husband of a bust
of Penini. There had been some debate over the cost: "I would
rather have given up Rome and had the bust," she told Sarianna. The sculptor, Alexander Munro, however, would only accept what the bust had cost him to make, twenty-five guineas.
And, after all, their journey to Rome cost them nothing, since
they were conveyed in the Eckleys' second carriage, and with
every comfort and personal attention. They had the carriage to
themselves and carried plenty of books.

There were, however, some frightening incidents: narrow es-
capes from spills, one over a mountain precipice, and a threatened knife-duel between two oxen-drivers whom Browning separated with only an injury to his trousers.

Weather on the week's journey was variable but they entered
Rome on a beautiful day. In their old sunny rooms high up in
the Bocca di Leone they met many friends, among them Charlotte Cushman, Hatty Hosmer, the painter Leighton, William
Page, "the American Titian," the sculptor Gibson, who had befriended Severn when he came with Keats to Italy, and, dearer
than them all, the Storys returned from America.

This time the omen of a sunny entrance was fulfilled. Elizabeth was well and happy in Rome. On Christmas morning, in
spite of intense cold, a heavy frost that hung the fountains with
icicles, she was able to hear the silver trumpets sound in St. Peter's. "I never once thought," she told Ruskin, "of the Scarlet

Lady." Her enjoyment of High Mass was complete "both æs-
thetically and devotionally, putting my own words to the music.
Was it wise, or wrong?"

In February 1859 Elizabeth wrote to Henrietta of a new hope
in Italy: "we Italians (such as Pen and I) are all trembling with
expectation. The great marriage in Piedmont . . ." This marriage between the Emperor's cousin, Prince Napoleon, and Vittorio Emmanuele's daughter was the outward symbol of a private meeting between Napoleon and the statesman Cavour, at
Plombières in the autumn of 1858. The alliance formed between
them against Austria was not divulged, but enough news of it
seeped through for the Tuscans to take fresh heart. In Florentine theatres (taking advantage of the composer's popularity)
there were shouts of *"Viva Verdi!"* That enthusiast Pen was
heard, much to the horror of his parents, instructing Romans
in the open street as to the meaning of *"Viva Verdi"* : *"Vittorio
Emmanuele Re d'Italia."*

While in Rome the Brownings were gratified by a visit from
Massimo D'Azeglio, Prime Minister of Piedmont before Cavour,
and an ardent patriot. D'Azeglio was, to Mrs. Browning's gratification, entirely on the side of Louis Napoleon, completely ex-
onerating that individual of any desire for territorial aggran-
dizement. As for Italy, he said, "it is '48 over again, with
matured actors." He spoke bitterly of British policy, and of the
European balance of power "as belonging to a past age, the rags
of old traditions."

This British policy, looking backward and forward to the
menace of Russia, of maintaining the balance of power, had perhaps more sense in it than Elizabeth and many of her *Italianissimi* friends could know. The official view was perhaps given
to Motley, the historian, by Robert Lytton in 1860:

*Austria is a slow power, moved by mediocre minds and always
behind the time, but she acts on the movements of the European machine, as the lead in the timepiece, regulating and bal-
ancing the motion of the whole; take away the weight and how
will the clock go?*

To Mrs. Browning he wrote in that year: "I think a wide distinction should be drawn between the moral support volunteered
by the public opinion of a free people and the material support

afforded by a responsible Government to conflicting parties abroad." No one could deny Lytton's own enthusiasm for Italian liberation, nor the help and support given to patriots by private British citizens and, unofficially, at times by Her Majesty's Navy. But to ardent, impatient Elizabeth, to the patriot D'Azeglio, such a distinction as Lytton's could carry little weight.

But, however anti-British Elizabeth might feel, she could not but express a feeling of delight at an honour done by the Crown to her husband. In February Edward, Prince of Wales, was in Rome with his tutor, Colonel Bruce. Colonel Bruce himself called to say that as "the society of the most eminent men in Rome" was desired for the Prince, it would "gratify the Queen that the Prince should make the acquaintance of Mr. Browning." Browning dined, apparently in public, with the Prince, "a fair, gentle youth, with a frank open countenance." Exhorted by his wife to take this golden opportunity (not knowing, perhaps, how little Her Majesty heeded the opinions of the heir to the Throne,) Robert talked, on the encouragement of a few questions, "quite naturally of the wrongs of Italy to an evidently sympathetic audience": though the well-primed Prince did not commit "his royal youthfulness in the least degree."

Another eminent man commanded to meet the Prince was Mr. Lear. Urged on by Mrs. Tennyson, who had written to him of "those wonderful spirit eyes" of Elizabeth's, Lear called in the Bocca di Leone. Elizabeth was receiving only for an hour each day, between four and five o'clock. He "thought her very nice" but too surrounded by people to make any real contact with. And, whether on any real basis, or whether because at this time he was not in a mood for society, Lear considered those people who had come to pay court to this celebrity a collection of flatterers, snobs, and bores. He occasionally met the Brownings in society, but never became more than a casual acquaintance. This we must regret; lacking as we do a lively description from Elizabeth of this odd being whom it was "pleasant to know."

Elizabeth now visited very little. Browning, however, though at first he tried to avoid it, was soon heavily involved, "some-

times two or three times deep in one night's engagements." Elizabeth having "no vocation for receiving alone" and finding
books hard to procure, perhaps found her evenings a little long,
but she went to bed early and consoled herself with Swedenborg. There was regret that Robert was not writing: "no Men
and Women. Men and women from without instead!"

Peni was enjoying society in Rome; being petted and admired. Robert encouraged his growing love of music by allowing him to go to day-concerts. An Italian version of *Monte
Cristo* was enthralling him in leisure hours.

For a woman whose physical powers were rapidly declining
it was probably not good that Elizabeth should be left to brood
in the quiet of solitary evenings on those Italian affairs taken so
much to heart. To Mrs. Jameson she wrote: "What I have endured in the last three or four months you might think I exaggerated if I told you—really physical palpitations in reading the
newspapers, or reading any thing." [5] The honour of her favourite Napoleon was, too, so much involved. When in April Austria demanded immediate disarmament of the growing forces of
Sardinia and Piedmont, and Napoleon appeared to be in agreement, she was "in anguish—I felt the sobs of rage in my throat—
Robert kept saying, 'I fear he has receded a step,' and I could
not say a word."

But when on April 29 Austria declared war on Victor Emman-
uel and crossed the river Ticino—a crossing that Napoleon had
declared would be considered as an act of aggression towards
France herself—the Emperor, to Elizabeth's supreme joy, acted.
In May he himself went to the front of battle, side by side with
King Victor Emmanuel. Italian feeling rose to a delirium. Even
in Rome, where the hand of oppression was strong, there was
a demonstration, which the Brownings witnessed, about the
French Ambassador's carriage. At cries of *"Viva la Francia,
Viva l'Italia, Viva l'Imperatore del Francesi!"* the Ambassador
"stood up in his carriage, took off his hat, and answered diplo-
matically, *'Pace ed allegria.'* " [6] The leaders of this minor demonstration of patriotism were arrested and imprisoned at the
demand of the Austrian Ambassador.

[5] Unpublished letter, postmarked May 4, 1859, Hagedorn Collection.
[6] See unpublished letter, May 14, 1859, Hagedorn Collection, as above.

In Florence that veiled "*Viva Verdi*" now rose into an open shout for a King of Italy. After a "rose-water revolution," with "an enormous amount of talking and shouting," Leopoldo, Grand Duke of Tuscany, was deposed. The *gran ciuca* went in peace, through a large crowd, this time never to return. It was, fortunately for him, not until after his departure that Florentines learned of an order he had issued: in the event of a popular movement, both fortresses should fire down on the city, and troops advance along the main thoroughfares in triple file, with fixed bayonets, those nearest the pavements firing at the windows of the houses. This order the officers in the fortresses had refused to carry out.

Naturally the Brownings' relations were worried about them: to Henrietta the intrepid Elizabeth wrote that, although steamers were crowded with English and Americans in flight from Italy, they intended to remain. "You know we are apt to flourish rather in a revolutionary atmosphere." They determined to stay in Rome until the end of May and then return to Florence by rail and *vetturino* through Siena.

Although invasion of the Sienese area was threatened, the travellers crossed it without incident "if only by a scratch." Their journey, a very pleasant one, was through "an almost absolute solitude."

CHAPTER 29

FLORENCE, SIENA, AND ROME [1859–60]

By THE TIME Elizabeth reached Florence at the beginning of June French troops had arrived there. National fervour was at its height. Florentines were admiring their allies, encamped in the Cascine Gardens, to heartfelt cries of *"La Guerra!"* Men poured in from unliberated states to join the forces. Funds for the prosecution of the war were rapidly collected. The Brownings contributed their quota, and little Penini, ardently wishing himself old enough to fight, earned his contribution of half a paul [1] a day by a good showing at lessons. He hung out two tricolour flags over the balcony, one French, one of the new Italy.

Although there was real danger of an Austrian attack the Brownings decided to remain in Florence "as long as the sun lets us." Elizabeth was naturally triumphant: Louis Napoleon was proving himself the great man she held him to be. Feeling against her own country grew more bitter as a British cry grew louder for stronger defences against possible French aggression. Even her beloved Tennyson urged on in popular verses the growth of a Volunteer movement.

On June 4 the French and Italian armies were victorious at Magenta: on the 8th they entered Milan. After the 20th patriots were sickened, disheartened by news of a terrible sack of Perugia by Papal troops; but on June 25 the fortress guns of Florence boomed out to announce victory for the combined arms at Solferino and San Martino. Excitement rose high: what was there now to stand in the way of total deliverance from foreign domination? Had not the Emperor of the French declared he would not rest until all Italy was liberated?

But Louis Napoleon was not made of the stuff of heroes: on July 8 he suddenly concluded an armistice with Austria. Various reasons have been given for this resolve not to press home the victory: a failure of nerve after witnessing the terrible car-

---

[1] About 2¾d.

nage of Solferino, a reluctance to endanger certain advantages for France by prosecuting the war in the difficult Venetian territory that lay ahead, and (the reason Mrs. Browning put forward) a fear of Prussia, which, disliking a possible access of power to the French, was already massing armies on her frontier.

The Italians very naturally took the move as pure betrayal. In Florence the many busts of this new Napoleonic "liberator" disappeared overnight: Penini was told sorrowfully by his mother that it would be wiser to take the French tricolour down from their balcony.

In the principal cities of the north there was widespread and angry agitation. Cavour, furious, thunderstruck, resigned his ministry. Victor Emmanuel himself submitted with as good a grace as possible, counting his certain gains. As yet there was no hint of a price to be paid.

In the preliminaries of peace, signed at Villafranca on July 11, Lombardy was assigned to Sardinia but the fate of Tuscany, Parma, Modena, and the Roman Legations was to be decided by plebiscite. On July 12 Pio Nono, heartened by the cessation of hostilities, appealed to Europe against Vittorio Emmanuele.

To Elizabeth, who "had been walking among the stars so many months," the news came like a physical blow, reaching her in a weakened condition: going out one very hot afternoon to the Trollopes' to see "the famous Ducal orders about bombarding Florence," she came home ill. "Violent palpitations and cough; in fact the worst attack on the chest I ever had in Italy." She would cough all the night long.

Now the little sleep she could snatch was disturbed by "political dreams . . . in inscrutable articles of peace and eternal provisional governments." To Isa Blagden she wrote of one dream of exaltation, and perhaps of prophecy:

I dreamed lately that I followed a mystic woman down a long suite of palatial rooms. She was in white, with a white mask, on her head the likeness of a crown. I knew she was Italy, but I couldn't see through the mask. . . . Walking upon the mountains of the moon, hand in hand with a Dream more beautiful

*than them all, then falling suddenly on the hard earth-ground
on one's head, no wonder that one should suffer.*

There was further torment to a fevered mind in a determination to justify Napoleon. Others must be blamed, those "selfish,
inhuman, wicked" nations which had forced his hand and
"truncated his great intentions." England, she declared, had
been in league with Prussia to "prevent the perfecting of the
greatest Deed given to men to do in these latter days."

Browning, tending his wife at night, having little sleep for
three weeks and taking over Penini's lessons by day, now shoul-
dered another and unexpected burden, the charge of an aged
and irascible genius. Walter Savage Landor, eighty-three years
of age, had of late been living with his family at the Fiesole
villa he had made over to them, together with what remained
of his income. One intensely hot day, after many violent quarrels, his wife and children turned him out of the house with
only some small change in his pocket. Either Browning found
him in a state of collapse on the road into Florence (there are
two differing accounts) or he appeared at Casa Guidi appealing
to one who had long been his ardent admirer.

Robert took Landor under his protection. Soon, however, the
wayward old man expressing a determination to go to Siena,
Browning was able temporarily to hand over charge of him to
Story, who was spending the summer in a villa outside the city.
With the help of Seymour Kirkup, Browning secured Landor's
clothes from a vindictive family and took him there in person.

Though he arrived half-crazed, his white hair streaming, in
Story's words "a case of old Lear over again," Landor soon recovered his old intellectual fire and gallantry. Back in Florence,
Browning had the unpleasant task of interviewing Mrs. Landor,
who proposed to do nothing for her aged husband. His brothers, however, stepped into the breach. Remittances amounting
to £200 a year were to be made from England to Browning for
Landor's support.

Elizabeth was now attended by Dr. Grisanowski, a German
who seems to have been on friendly terms with the Brownings
and others of their circle. He pronounced change of air as the
only hope for recovery. In early August, too weak to set foot on

the ground, she was taken like a baby in arms to Siena, where, Browning being determined not to pay the heightened price demanded for the villa he had fixed upon, they stayed a few days at the hotel. Dr. Grisanowski, refusing to accept any additional fee, had followed them by the next train. He remained with his patient for two days, "most kind and zealous."

Browning decided to rent the Villa Alberti, a house on the same hill, Poggio dei Venti, on which they had stayed in 1850, and less than a mile from Story's villa. Story was present when Browning carried his wife in from the carriage looking "like a dark shadow."

From the high *specola* of Villa Alberti, now Villa Marciano, there are the same fine wide views over hill, valley, and bright mediæval city which had delighted the Brownings nine years before. They occupied the first floor, where today, nearly one hundred years on, the furniture remains the same and frescoed walls, untouched, look as fresh in that clean dry air as they did when Elizabeth's own eye was upon them. Behind the house a garden and a small plantation of trees and bushes (*boschetta inglese*) are full of bird life. The quiet, the utter peace of the place could well bring balm to a wounded mind and spirit.

Although the heat was intense that year, even on the "windy hill," by the second week in August Elizabeth was sufficiently recovered to walk about the rooms on Robert's arm, though she remained in strict seclusion. News of Florence elections heartened her, the first election for a Tuscan parliament. Though Austria had appointed "Ferdinand IV" ruler of Tuscany, and even put ambassadors for her in Rome, Naples, and Vienna, he had little hope of entering his "Dukedom." The Liberal triumph was overwhelming. On August 16 the Assembly voted unanimously for annexation to Piedmont and adherence to King Victor.

In Italy there was still war. Garibaldi, who had fought in Tuscany, was by no means willing to accept foreign domination over other states. By July 19 he had been exhorting Italy to arm. North, in the free port of Venice, a stout resistance under siege ended in a defeat, which nevertheless demonstrated the bravery of a people long designated as soft, effeminate.

Elizabeth, remaining quiet in her lofty shaded rooms, or later out under her favourite fig tree, occupied herself with books and newspapers, English and Italian. Robert and Peni were much with the Storys. Peni rushed about those little leafy lanes, which so reminded his mother of England, on a pony "the colour of his curls," a yellow Sardinian pony soon to be his own. Landor in a cottage near by was sufficiently himself now to write Latin alcaics upon Italy's hero of the hour, Garibaldi. The harvest came. Penini rode "in the oxen carts, between heaps of *pomi d'oro*" chattering happily with the peasants. In her villa Elizabeth enjoyed "sunsets red as blood, seen every evening over deep purple hills, with intermediate tracts of green vineyards."

In the silence and repose of that leafy countryside Elizabeth recovered spirits and a measure of health, though she was never again to be active. Driving out in a hired carriage, one day Browning took her into Siena, that treasure-house of art, where in the picture gallery she looked once more on "the divine Eve of Sodoma." A visit to the Cathedral, however, proved beyond her. She could not climb the steps before it and had to be content with "the vision of it safe within me since nine years ago."

But during these months of anxiety, illness, and slow recovery, Elizabeth had not been wholly idle. On September 24 there came out in the *Athenæum* the first published of those poems written on the Italian struggle for freedom, "A Tale of Villafranca." In it she defended the action of Napoleon, postulating for him an attitude of grieved resignation:

> But HE stood sad before the sun
> (*The peoples felt their fate*).
> "*The world is many,—I am one;*
> My great Deed was too great.
> God's fruit of justice ripens slow:
> Men's souls are narrow; let them grow.
> My brothers, we must wait.*"

Towards the end of their stay at Villa Alberti Elizabeth had the pleasure of receiving guests. Isa Blagden came with her young American friend Kate Field, who lived with her and was studying art; a girl of strong feminist views who became a favourite with both the Brownings. Odo Russell, the diplomat, was a particularly interesting visitor who had much to tell Elizabeth about Napoleon and the Italian situation. Russell confirmed a rumour that the Emperor was intriguing to secure Tuscany for his cousin, Prince Napoleon. This astute move which, if successful, would have strengthened France both against the Teutonic powers and against a possible fresh rival in the new Italy, Elizabeth was unwilling to credit, though the authority for the truth of it made her waver.

Before she left Siena Elizabeth was delighted by a presentation copy of *Idylls of the King* but, on reading the work, had to admit disappointment in spite of some "exquisite things." She wrote to Allingham:

Perhaps we had been expecting too long—had made too large an idea to fit a reality. Perhaps the breathing, throbbing life around us in Italy, where a nation is being new-born, may throw King Arthur too far off and flat. But, whatever the cause, the effect was so. The colour, the temperature, the very music, left me cold. . . . I would rather have written Maud, *for instance, than half a dozen of such* Idylls.

Surely most modern critics would agree in preferring *Maud* to Tennyson's romanticized but watered-down version of old Malory.

When their time came to an end Elizabeth clung to Siena and the Villa Alberti, not wanting to leave; perhaps divining that here she had enjoyed her last untouched period of personal tranquillity. Since all desire for travel had now left her, she might have gone more happily if there had been a prospect of remaining at Casa Guidi: the condition of her lungs, however, did not permit another winter in Florence. She must flee before the tramontana, that sharp wind from mountains, southward to Rome.

But in Florence, to which they returned in November, the Brownings were detained so long that there seemed a chance that cold weather might prevent the journey: Browning's "adopted son" must be arranged for, and this took longer than they expected. When Wilson was forced by the birth of her first child to leave the Brownings' service, although Ferdinando remained with them, she took a lodging-house in the Via Nunziatina. There the Brownings settled Landor under her care. Although the arrangement would materially benefit Wilson and her husband, Elizabeth could not help feeling for her former maid: the charge was no light one. Of Landor Elizabeth wrote to her sister-in-law from Siena:

A most courteous and refined gentleman he is, of course, and very affectionate to Robert (as he ought to be) but of self-restraint he has not a grain, and of suspiciousness many grains. . . . What do you say to dashing down a plate on the floor when you don't like what's on it? And the contadini at whose house he is lodging now have been already accused of opening desks.

The "old Lion" had sharpened his teeth again. At Siena, before they left, he had been "roaring softly, to beguile the time, in Latin alcaics against his wife and Napoleon." When Elizabeth told him that one day he must write an ode to Napoleon to please her, he "laughed carnivorously." In irritable explosions of temper, in bouts of acute suspicion of those around him, Robert, whose long admiration of Landor gave him admirable patience, could calm the old man. Wilson too seems to have managed him tolerably well though once, in attempting to prevent him throwing his dinner out of the window, she was violently accused of flinging a dish in his face. As Wilson soon proved to be a victim of religious mania, partly arising from a jealousy of Elizabeth's Italian maid, Annunziata, the tiresome old man could hardly have improved her condition; unless, indeed, he proved a salutary counter-irritant.

In October Garibaldi had appealed to the Neapolitans to revolt against their Bourbon King. By November 10, when by the Treaty of Zurich Central Italy was formally established as a confederacy of states with the Pope as President, a clash of patriots and Papal troops seemed inevitable: yet the intrepid Brownings travelled south to Rome, Elizabeth declaring that "the great guns of the revolution (and even the small daggers) will be safer to encounter than any sort of tramontana."

On November 27 they started for Rome, taking six days on the road; Pen often riding triumphantly beside them on his pony, which was fastened to the carriage horses. Elizabeth, always a good traveller, was benefiting, Robert declared, by "long doses of fresh open air which she would have made no attempt to swallow in Florence." They established themselves in a sunny apartment at 28, Via del Tritone (now demolished), an apartment which, if most of the foreign population had not left Rome for fear, would have been quite beyond their means. Elizabeth was amused to find that the Pope, though fully aware of his "alarming position" (the possibility of French troops being withdrawn), yet found it in his heart to publish an edict against "crinolines, the same being forbidden to sweep the sacred pavement of St. Peter's."

At first Elizabeth rejoiced in Roman sunshine and a new wellbeing, at work in her sunny rooms preparing for the press that "thin slice of a wicked book," as she called it, *Poems Before Congress.* Robert too was at work that winter, both on lyric verse, which Elizabeth did see, and a long poem he did not show her; and for a very good reason, since it was the first draft of *Prince Hohenstiel-Schwangau* under the more direct title of "Napoleon Fallen."

Elizabeth's interest in Italian politics, the struggle for freedom, continued, and in a form more active. From Isa Blagden, through Odo Russell, the diplomat, she was apparently receiving news-letters, which she seems to have returned in kind. Once she felt real alarm at the non-arrival of one of Isa's letters, telling her that even Russell's correspondence, if it went through the post, was opened and scrutinized. But this in no way daunted her: at the same time a banned newspaper, the *Monitore,* was being sent to the Brownings from Florence, through Odo Russell, and was read by Tuscan exiles with whom Ferdinando, a patriot and former Garibaldian soldier, was in touch. These men, afraid to borrow the paper because of the many spies in Rome, came to read it at 28, Via del Tritone. "We keep a sort of café in Rome," Elizabeth told Miss Blagden, "and your 'Monitore' is necessary to us." When the authorities, noting that Russell received a *Monitore* beyond the one allowed him as a diplomat, stopped the Brownings' copy, Robert arranged that it should be sent to them direct in a plain wrapping.

In January 1860 Elizabeth's enthusiasm for her adopted land led again to illness. Swords for presentation to Napoleon and Victor Emmanuel, subscribed for by twenty thousand patriotic Romans, were ready for dispatch; a dispatch sudden and secret, as the Pope had recently denounced "all such givers as traitors to the See." One wet evening at five o'clock someone came to the Via del Tritone in a closed carriage. Late though it was, Elizabeth went with Robert to view the swords at the shop of their designer, Castellani, the famous Roman jeweller:

we were received at Castellani's most flatteringly as poets and lovers of Italy; were asked for autographs; and returned in a blaze of glory and satisfaction, to collapse (as far as I'm concerned) in a near approach to mortality. You see I can't catch a simple cold. All my bad symptoms came back. Suffocations, singular heart-action, cough tearing one to atoms.

But a "gigantic blister" and the Roman climate brought about recovery at the end of a week, though the attack left her seriously debilitated. Soon, however, she was well enough to receive two interesting visitors, both American, one a spiritualist named Thomas Hazard and the other the Unitarian minister and Abolitionist Theodore Parker. Parker, already in bad health, was soon to die. The Unitarian's lack of belief in the Godhead of Christ was to Elizabeth in bleak contrast with the fervent faith, amounting to credulity, of Hazard, but at Parker's death in May she felt a measure of sorrow. "There was something high and noble about the man—though he was not deep in proportion."

In the spring of 1860 that "thin slice of a wicked book" was published, arousing in the press much expected criticism, but with an additional sting, presenting to Elizabeth and her husband a cup of bitterness undeserved.

C H A P T E R   3 0

POEMS BEFORE CONGRESS [1860]

MISS MITFORD had dismissed *Casa Guidi Windows*, unjustly one must own, as mere pamphleteering: this accusation can be, I think, more accurately brought against *Poems Before Congress*. The emotion is there, the intense feeling for Italy, but Elizabeth was perhaps too near the events, too implicated in feeling and yet not closely enough involved, to bring a clear mind to bear.

And, although she was still to write a few fine pieces, mind and body were considerably weakened a year before death. There are flashes of poetry, some of the old bold metaphor, but on the whole, even with a strong interest in the historic and emotional background, the verses are hard to read. Contemporary critics in England less familiar with the story of Italy's struggle from day to day could feel little sympathy, accepted though Mrs. Browning was then as a major poet. And the addition, at her husband's particular request, conspicuously at the end of the volume, of one poem extraneous to the general matter completely alienated most of them, confirming the impression that Elizabeth was now openly anti-British.

In a rather natural misconception Chorley, of the *Athenæum*, leapt to a conclusion that "A Curse for a Nation," wholehearted, deep-throated, was directed against Elizabeth's native land on account of Great Britain's official attitude towards Napoleon III and the Italian struggle for freedom. No clear indication was given that in

> *Because ye have broken your own chain*
> *With the strain*
> *Of brave men climbing a Nation's height,*
> *Yet thence bear down with brand and thong*
> *On souls of others,—for this wrong*
> *This is the curse . . .*

Elizabeth was admonishing not England but America on the count of slavery. The accusation of unpatriotism was taken up by other journals.

Elizabeth, expecting "a storm of execration," was not unduly disturbed by this injustice, but Browning was enraged; declaring (not without basis in fact) that Chorley, now a bitter, disappointed man, was having his revenge for Elizabeth's criticism in a letter to himself of his novel *Roccabella*, which he had dedicated to her. Elizabeth herself was angry when the *Athenæum*, on its mistake being pointed out, did not print her letter but put in, as journals are apt to do, a correction in an inconspicuous corner; one that might well be overlooked. On finding that Chorley was not responsible for this act of discourtesy she wrote him a generous letter, adding: "I never wrote to please any of you, not even to please my own husband." She must present truth as it appeared to her. "It is one of the beatitudes of art, and attainable without putting off the flesh."

In America, where this strong piece had already appeared in the *Liberty Bell* for 1856, there was no such misconception. There *Poems Before Congress* received the respectful homage always accorded to this favourite poet. "I have," Elizabeth told a disapproving Mrs. Jameson, "extravagant praises and *prices* offered to me from 'over the western sun,' in consequence of these very 'Poems Before Congress.'" Theodore Tilton of the New York *Independent* was now offering a hundred dollars for any poem she might choose to send him; a poem that by the lack of copyright law he could have printed for nothing.

The attacks upon *Poems Before Congress* in the London press were, Elizabeth bravely considered, a justification of the poems themselves. Certainly this view was supported by Odo Russell, who held that the general censure was due solely to her support of Napoleon: for the rest, her work had succeeded in heightening sympathy for struggling Italy. *Poems Before Congress* had been published on March 17: by June Chapman & Hall were preparing to bring out a second edition.

In a letter to Chorley on May 2 Elizabeth wrote of her hero: "Observe, I may be wrong about Napoleon. He may be snake, scoundrel, devil, in his motives." "But the thing he did," she added loyally, "was done before the eyes of all." What had occurred after the French invasion might well have shaken her allegiance: Louis Napoleon had presented his bill for the partial liberation of Italy, demanding the surrender to France of Nice and Savoy, the very cradle of Italian freedom under Victor Emmanuel and his father.

This demand, held by many at the time as geographical and political common sense, was naturally to those *Italianissimi* a pure betrayal. Browning's comment was trenchant: the Emperor's intervention in Italy "was a great action; but he has taken eighteenpence for it, which is a pity." On paper, in that long poem his wife did not see, he relieved his feelings in the first draft of *Prince Hohenstiel-Schwangau.*

In Italy the political situation in early 1860 was both nebulous and critical. In only two cases were the northern Italian states definitely held; Lombardy becoming part of the Kingdom of Sardinia and Piedmont, and Venetia, including Peschiera and Mantua, to remain directly in the grip of Austria. The central states, nominally to be a separate kingdom under the presidency of the Pope, with the old Austrian rulers to return, were determined to annex themselves to Piedmont; indeed, they had direct orders from Cavour to prepare Liberal governments and acts of union. The parliament held at Turin in January included deputies from Lombardy, Tuscany, and Emilia. To the great European powers Cavour made it clear by a circular letter to agents and diplomats that, as the Italian question had not been settled satisfactorily at Zurich, Italy was now entitled to deal with internal problems herself. To Louis Napoleon he privately intimated that Nice and Savoy would be surrendered after a plebiscite judiciously arranged, and with consent of parliament, if Napoleon would support him in regard to the central states. Napoleon's reply was to march French troops into Savoy.

Elizabeth, in her Roman apartment, followed these moves, probably hearing more from diplomatic friends than the general public, with a heart "beating uncomfortably." The rushing of French troops into Savoy she was forced to stigmatize as "a haste somewhat indelicate."

March brought a personal sorrow: Mrs. Jameson died on the 17th after a short illness. The news came to Elizabeth, not gently through her husband, but thoughtlessly, abruptly in a note from Gerardine enclosed in a parcel of photographs. She could manage no more than a few agitated words in reply: Gerardine could not know to the full what she felt in "losing (as far as the loving can lose those whom they love, as far as death brings loss) that great heart, that noble human creature." In Elizabeth's frail organism the veil between life and death was becoming ever thinner. The loss of Mrs. Jameson deepened a growing depression of spirit. To Sarianna she wrote: "It's a blot more on the world to me."

A blot on Elizabeth's world at this time, and one that seriously damaged her in spirit, was the break between herself and Sophia Eckley. We do not know the actual cause of Elizabeth's disillusionment with her "white rose," but whatever it was she felt it bitterly; so bitterly that she put her emotion into that strangely harsh poem "Where's Agnes?" As for Browning, he nursed an animosity towards Mrs. Eckley for the rest of his life, writing strongly about her to Isa Blagden especially when, after his wife's death, the unworthy friend paraded affectionate letters from Elizabeth.

In March the northern states (except Venice) were annexed to Sardinia after universal plebiscite: in May, Nice and Savoy were formally ceded and French troops, except for the Roman garrison, retired from Italy. The Pope, who had lost the greater parts of his domains, was naturally enraged, excommunicating both Napoleon and Victor Emmanuel. Pen, that ardent politician, found it difficult to control his tongue; having to be "restrained into politeness and tolerance towards ecclesiastical dignitaries." To his tutor, the Italian Abbé, Pen rather neatly explained a day's bad weather "in choice Tuscan": "Of course it's the excommunication. The prophet says that a curse begins with the curser's own house; and so it is with the Holy Father's curse." The Abbé, fond of the child and secretly in sympathy, as were many priests, with the Italian struggle for freedom, found it hard to keep a straight face.

The eyes of Napoleon and Cavour were now uneasily upon Naples, that most misgoverned of kingdoms in Italy. Cavour's offer of an alliance in 1859 had already been refused: in March he heard of a plot to recover the Romagna for the Pope with Neapolitan arms. Napoleon on his side feared the annexation of Naples by Sardinia. In this event any chance of French influence in Italy might vanish. The Plenipotentiaries in Zurich were still desultorily considering the Italian situation in the light of events. Cavour felt it difficult to make an open move.

In early May, however, the question was taken out of his hands by a powerful, eccentric, and uncontrollable force. Encouraged by insurrections in Sicily, Garibaldi sailed south with his irregulars, having appealed to Cavour for open support in vain, but supplied secretly by King Victor Emmanuel with money. Napoleon, though persuaded by England not to intervene, patrolled the Sicilian straits in an effort to prevent Garibaldi from landing. It was under the unofficial cover of a British warship that the irregulars landed on the beach from their crazy old craft at Marsala on May 11.

Elizabeth watched the movements of the Sicilian expedition with a beating heart. "Garibaldi's hardy enterprise may be followed by difficult complications." Cavour too viewed the situation with alarm as Garibaldi proclaimed himself Dictator and went from triumph to triumph. That simple-hearted old warrior was under the influence of republican Mazzini: his anger over the cession of Nice, his native province, his fury against the "vulpine knave" Napoleon III might well endanger all Cavour's carefully laid plans for the uniting of Italy under his King.

Elizabeth, following the fate of her beloved Italy from day to day, had to husband a failing strength. Letter-writing, once so pleasurable to her, so active an occupation, became a weariness. For the rest, she composed a few lyrics on Italy and spent much time helping Pen with the heavy tasks set him by the Abbé. "When the sun goes down," she told her friend Isa, "I am down. At eight I generally am in bed, or little after." Visitors she found very tiring, though some were welcome. One in whom she took a strong interest was Lady Annabella Noel, granddaughter of that early hero Byron; "very quiet, and very intense, I should say." The little sculptress Hatty Hosmer remained a favourite and was often with Elizabeth.

Another visitor on intimate terms with Elizabeth this winter was Harriet Beecher Stowe. Elizabeth was amazed to find in one "coming out of a clerical and puritan *cul-de-sac* . . . a largeness and fearlessness of thought" and a strong interest in spiritualism. Perhaps when these two women, both of whom

had written on the side of human freedom, came to say good-
bye, there was a premonition that they would never meet again
on earth, Mrs. Stowe's parting words being: "Those who love
the Lord Jesus Christ never see one another for the last
time."

As she came nearer to her own end Elizabeth's interest in
spiritualism grew deeper. We find her asking news of London
activities, telling Fanny Haworth that even Robert's heart had
softened "to the point of letting me have 'The Spiritual Magazine' from England." She spoke sharply of Charles Dickens's refusal to investigate the truth of spiritualism. "This is a moral
lachêté, hard for my feminine mind to conceive of. Dickens, too,
who is so fond of ghost-stories, as long as they are impossible. ."

On June 4 the Brownings left Rome; Elizabeth with a sense
of real relief since Pen was suffering from a mild attack of fever, and there were two other cases close to their lodging. They
were four days on the road, travelling through Orvieto and
Chiusi. In spite of beautiful scenery, "interesting pictures and
tombs," the journey wearied Elizabeth. Her days of pleasure in
travel were over.

The Brownings found Landor well, living in "a chronic state
of ingratitude to the whole world except Robert, who waits for
his turn." The old man was enjoying life in the present while he
could: "he had 'quite given up thinking of a future state—he had
had thoughts of it once, but that was very early in life.'"
Though Landor was "a man of great genius, and we owe him
every attention on that ground," Elizabeth could not help confessing to her sister-in-law that "to me he is eminently unsympathetic," though she could admire his handsome person, his
"most beautiful sea-foam of a beard you ever saw, all in a curl
and white bubblement of beauty."

From Browning's letter to the Storys of June 19 [1] we learn
that not before this date did Elizabeth venture to leave the
house, having only now recovered from the journey. Her visits
were few, even to Villa Bricchieri in a carriage.

In Florence they were "all talking and dreaming Garibaldi
just now in great anxiety."

[1] Unpublished letter in Keats-Shelley Memorial House, Rome.

*Scarcely since the world was a world has there been such a feat
of arms. All modern heroes grow pale before him. It was necessary, however, for us all even here, and at Turin just as in Paris,
to be ready to disavow him. The whole good of Central Italy
was hazarded by it. If it had not been success it would have
been an evil beyond failure. The enterprise was forlorner than
a forlorn hope. The hero, if he had perished, would scarcely
have been sure of his epitaph even.*

Garibaldi, by dint of hard fighting against great odds, was
now practically in possession of Sicily. Cavour tried to claim it
for Victor Emmanuel, but Garibaldi was too incensed against
him for the loss of Nice to consent. But there was nothing to fear
of Garibaldi as a Republican. That intrepid, obstinate man had
now but one aim in view; that of prosecuting a long war until
he should reach Rome, eject the French garrison, and crown
Victor Emmanuel on the Campidoglio. As to the political complications, he cared little or nothing.

At this time George Eliot and her Mr. Lewes were in Florence; those lovers who flouted the Victorian view of marriage.
They came and went, but would return. Elizabeth declared to
her sister-in-law that, out of admiration for her books, she would
certainly receive "Miss Evans," but there is no record, so far as
I am aware, of the two writers ever meeting.

It was during this interval of a month in Florence that Browning met with the literary adventure of his life, the discovery on
a stall in Piazza San Lorenzo of the "square yellow book" for
which he gave a lira, "eightpence English just"; that bound record of the Franceschini case which was to provide a story for
his greatest work. Vividly he tells us how he started reading
leaning against the fountain, and then took his way home

> *Through fire-irons, tribes of tongs, shovels in sheaves,*
> *Skeleton bedsteads, wardrobe-drawers agape,*
> *Rows of tall slim brass lamps with dangling gear,—*
> *And worse, cast clothes a-sweetening in the sun:*

out of the market, still reading "At the Strozzi, at the Pillar, at
the Bridge," until by the time he was

> *In Casa Guidi by Felice Church,*
> *Under the doorway where the black begins*
> *With the first stone-slab on the staircase cold,*

he had mastered the contents, "knew the whole truth gathered there." Startled, obsessed as he was by the story, it must have been a disappointment to find that Elizabeth took not the slightest interest in what appeared to her merely a sordid account of crime. It was eight years before the first instalment of *The Ring and the Book* appeared: Browning did not embark upon the writing of it until three years after Elizabeth's death.

On July 7 the Brownings left Florence for Siena, probably taking with them Landor and his dog, Can 'Giallo. They stayed again in the Villa Alberti with Landor in a cottage close by, Story a mile off, and Isa Blagden but half a mile. There, in the quiet familiar house with its splendid views, Elizabeth might have attained to some measure of peace if the news had not come that Henrietta was seriously ill of a painful and fatal disease.

She fell into a melancholy state; going about her work as usual, writing, teaching Pen,

but with a sense of a black veil between me and whatever I did, sometimes feeling incapable of crawling down to sit on the cushion under my own fig-tree for an hour's vision of this beautiful country—sometimes in "des transes mortelles" of fear.

Henrietta had always seemed so strong, the most robust of the three: the more delicate Arabel was to outlive her by eight years.

Elizabeth's first impulse had been to rush over to England, but a little persuasion soon convinced her of the folly of this proceeding. All she could do was to "keep quiet and try not to give cause for trouble on my own account, to be patient and live on God's daily bread from day to day." The summer was the coolest they had known in Italy. Elizabeth added sadly: "I *could* have been very happy."

Even the news of triumphs from the south must be tempered with "a certain melancholy," since now Italian was fighting Italian. By July 20 Garibaldi's victory at Melazzo put the whole of Sicily in his hands. Another anxiety now harassed Elizabeth's tired mind: the decision of Central Italy to unite under Victor Emmanuel would lead, everyone felt sure, to a fresh war with Austria. She, who had braved war and revolutions in the past,

scorning the English who had fled away, now advised against
visiting Italy until the situation should clear.

One thing pleased her, that Thackeray, in that new magazine
the *Cornhill*, was putting the Italian situation clearly in informed articles. Among the brilliant array of writers, Anthony
Trollope, Ruskin, and Thackeray himself among them, only the
poets were not anonymous, and among those poets was Elizabeth with a war poem, "The Forced Recruit, Solferino, 1859,"
and that fine piece "A Musical Instrument."

A later contribution sent to Thackeray in the spring of 1861
put that astute editor in a difficult position. It is a curious corollary to the success of *Aurora Leigh* that when the author of
that outspoken work sent him "Lord Walter's Wife," a highly
moral piece dealing with a man who tried in vain to lure away
a friend's wife, Thackeray felt obliged to reject it. To write and
say so to the celebrated Mrs. Browning was not easy: he put it
off as long as possible. "You see," he wrote, "that our Magazine
is written not only for men and women but for boys, girls, in-
fants, sucklings almost . . . there are things *my* squeamish
public will not hear on Monday, though on Sundays they listen to them without scruple."

Elizabeth's reply was gracious, generous in tone: she agreed
that Thackeray as editor was probably right, but put her own
point of view:

*I don't like coarse subjects, or the coarse treatment of any sub-
ject. But I am deeply convinced that the corruption of our society requires not shut doors and windows, but light and air: and
that it is exactly because pure and prosperous women choose to
ignore vice, that miserable women suffer wrong by it everywhere.*

As a token of forgiveness she sent him another contribution, the
highly innocuous "Little Mattie Dead."

CHAPTER 31

THE LAST YEAR

THAT AUTUMN ELIZABETH, waiting with a sick heart for news of her sister, watched events in the south with feverish interest.

Progress was rapid. On September 7 Garibaldi entered Naples as a deliverer, without opposition. The Bourbon King fled before him. Cavour decided it was now time for him to move: having gained Napoleon's consent, he marched an army through the Papal States, lying between Tuscany and the Kingdom of Naples.

Encouraged by the near presence of Sardinian forces, Liberals within the Papal States rose in revolt. On September 11 the Sardinians crossed, facing and defeating at Castelfidardo Papal troops under that French General, Lamorcière, whom Napoleon had placed at their head. After laying siege to the city, Sardinian forces entered Ancona on the 29th.

On October 4 Victor Emmanuel took personal command of his army, and defeated the Neapolitans at Isernia on the 17th. Garibaldi was fighting on the Volturno front, but his victory on the 1st had proved too costly in men for the direct advance upon Rome he had planned. Resistance was stiff: Catholics from all over the world had naturally rushed to defend their Pope. On the 26th Garibaldi joined Victor Emmanuel at Teano, hailing him "King of Italy." After the conquerors had entered Naples in state Garibaldi sailed to his island home on Caprera, refusing all reward beyond Victor Emanuel's simple but heartfelt "I thank you." The Roman provinces, now freed, voted for annexation.

The one Neapolitan stronghold which held out was Gaeta, that ancient refuge of the Pope and Austrian puppet rulers. A siege was prolonged by the action of Napoleon, who prevented the Italian fleet from investing by sea; an action even such an ardent supporter as Elizabeth found difficult to explain, except that it must be for the good of France. The opposition to King Victor's forces put up at Castelfidardo had also been hard to account for, but this she did by repeating a rumour that General Lamorcière had, at a dinner given to his staff in Rome, drunk to the health of "Henri Cinq": Lamorcière, therefore, did not truly represent the Emperor. What Elizabeth might have admired in her hero was his agility in sitting on both sides of the fence.

During this rush of events, on October 8, the Brownings left Siena. On the 7th Elizabeth, sitting under her favourite fig tree in the garden of Villa Alberti, decided to commemorate it in pen-and-ink; perhaps with some inward premonition that tomorrow there must be a last good-bye to this place of quietude on the "windy hill."

One may suppose that the Brownings returned to Casa Guidi before they went south again to Rome; and that (if we place in 1860, as I think we should, a note to a Mrs. Matthews[1]) "a disastrous letter," perhaps containing grave news of Henrietta, made Browning hurry on the journey before November 23. "I hope," he wrote, "that the change of scene and respite from bad news for a day or two will enable her to recover strength in some degree." But the journey proved, in his own words, "a wretched business." Elizabeth was chafing to arrive that she might have fresh news from England. When in Rome they heard nothing, Browning telegraphed to George Barrett. George's reply was so serious that Browning prepared his wife for the worst: on November 23 a letter told of Henrietta's death. Elizabeth was prostrated with silent bitter grief. A little later she wrote to Fanny Haworth:

It is a great privilege to be able to talk and cry; but I cannot you know. I have suffered very much, and feel tired and beaten. Now, it's all being lived down; thrown behind or pushed before, as such things must be if we are to live: not forgetting, not feeling any tie slackened, loving unchangeably, and believing how mere a line *this is to overstep between the living and the dead.*

Perhaps some of the bitterness, a sense of personal loss extending back over the death of father and friends to a terrible summer in 1840, went into that poem called "My Heart and I"; masked though the feeling is by the fiction of a lost lover:

[1] Myers Collection.

> *Enough! we're tired, my heart and I.*
> *We sit beside the headstone thus,*
> *And wish that name were carved for us.*
> *The moss reprints more tenderly*
> *The hard types of the mason's knife,*
> *As heaven's sweet life renews earth's life*
> *With which we're tired, my heart and I.*

This time the Brownings lodged at 126, Via Felice (now Via Sestina) high up by the Pincian Gardens.[2] There Elizabeth, though in failing health and with a load of grief on her, made verses, political or in the popular vein of sentiment; and in one case turning a poem into literal Italian as a trial piece for Dall'Ongaro, that terse and witty patriotic poet, to translate. This poem, "A View across the Roman Campagna," composed in early 1861, recaptures the apocalyptic vision of earlier days. It is a direct attack upon the Papacy; an attack so outspoken that if Elizabeth had lived and Dall'Ongaro had put it into a language the Italian cardinals could read, surely no further sojourn in Rome would have been possible for this bold heretic, famous though she was.

Perhaps, at a risk of spoiling the effect of the whole strong work, some quotation may be given. The Church is imagined as a ship "heaving silently like a mighty ship in pain" while "over the dumb Campagna-sea"

> *Alone and silent as God must be,*
> *The Christ walks. Aye, but Peter's neck*
> *Is stiff to turn on the foundering deck.*

Peter, his nets "heavy with silver fish," "reckons his gains": not for him the perilous leap of faith upon heaving waters:

> *Peter, Peter! He does not speak;*
> *He is not rash as in old Galilee:*
> *Safer a ship, though it toss and leak,*
> *Than a reeling foot on a rolling sea!*
> *And he's got to be round in the girth, thinks he.*

Elizabeth was left much alone at this time. Browning, restless since last winter, unable to compose, had to seek a channel for his enormous energy beyond hard riding. Elizabeth could fill in a fallow time with books, but Browning was never able to

---

[2] A plaque commemorates the stay here, 1835–42, of Nikolai Gogol.

concentrate for long on the printed page. At one time he had amused himself with drawing, but now, inspired by his friend Story in the Palazzo Barberini close by, he threw himself to a degree beyond mere pastime into a study of sculpture, modelling in clay from the antique.

It was natural that Elizabeth should deplore this devotion to an art not his own; however much he might be discouraged by neglect, beyond the small circle of Pre-Raphaelites, of himself by the British public. Even if Robert had not already been hailed, honoured in America with public reading and study, Elizabeth would have known her husband to be a major poet. Neglect among the English extended to those in Rome, many of whom knew Browning only as the handsome amusing husband of a famous woman poet. His success in society was undoubted, but it was on his own obvious personal qualifications. "The women," Elizabeth wrote to his sister with an indulgent smile, "adore him everywhere far too much for decency."

A possible embarrassment was now occupying Elizabeth's mind as she sat so much alone. That autumn, stirred by an account in the New York *Independent* of a funeral oration by Henry Ward Beecher over the body of Annie Howard,[3] she had sent to that journal "De Profundis," written after Bro's death, the manuscript of which had probably been found again in that box of papers restored to her in London. This being published in December 1860, she feared might be taken for a lament over the loss of her sister. Explaining the situation to Isa Blagden she added:

it's not my way to grind up my green griefs to make bread of. But that poem exaggerates nothing—represents a condition from which the writer had already partly emerged, after the greatest suffering; the only time in which I have known what absolute despair *is.*

She made it clear that the cause of her misery dated back to before she met Browning, but could not mention Bro even to this intimate friend. It may be that, in the midst of new grief, Elizabeth's mind was painfully directed back to the tragic loss of her brother by a resemblance in her own child: Browning

[3] Daughter of Mrs. John T. Howard, who, with Mrs. Stowe, had visited Elizabeth in 1860.

tells us that at one period of boyhood Pen was strikingly like a drawing of Bro at the same age.

However deep sorrow might be, Elizabeth was still able to surmount it with courage: even in December she could write that life "has rolled into the ruts again and goes." She was seeing a few people, among them Val Prinsep "in the roses and lilies of youth." Prinsep, a man of magnificent physique and great strength, is now chiefly memorable, not as an artist, but as the original of Taffy in *Trilby*; he was also the grandson of that eccentric India merchant James Pattle, whose last return to England, in the spirit and partially out of spirits, has been so deliciously commemorated by Virginia Woolf.

Another Englishman met at this time brought Elizabeth news of Naples, where matters were not going too smoothly under the Italian Government. Elsewhere in Italy too there were obvious difficulties in this time of change; such as the position, especially from a financial point of view, of the Pope in Rome and the question of Venetia. "There is much talk of war in the spring," Elizabeth wrote Mrs. Martin, "and if Austria will not cede Venetia war must be." But there was no war again in Elizabeth's lifetime: Venice lay in fetters for another six years. On February 18 the first Italian parliament decreed Victor Emmanuel King of Italy. On March 31 Great Britain, the first power to do so, gave the new country official recognition.

In Rome feeling for the King was strong, but Napoleon's troops were there to protect the Holy See, and to remain for another five years. These troops were, however, on friendly terms with the people and not unsympathetic to patriots. When there was a great demonstration of twenty thousand Romans after Victor Emmanuel was decreed King of Italy, French soldiers, making sure that the Papal troops kept out of sight, marched about with them on two days. Then, Elizabeth tells us, a French officer turned to the crowds with a friendly smile and said: "*Gioventù Romana, basta così. Adesso bisogna andare a casa, poichè mi farebbe grandissimo dispiacere d'aprire ad alcuno la strada delle carceri.*" [4] "*Grazie, grazie, grazie,*" came from the people, always quick in intelligence, before they dispersed.

---

[4] "Young Romans, that's enough. You must go home now. I should hate to put any one of you on the road to prison."

Of this friendly attitude Penini, to his great satisfaction, obtained direct evidence. Falling in with French troops on the Pincio, he made friends with "ever so many captains" and marched back with them to barracks. "They hope," the boy excitedly told his mother, "that I *would not think* they were like the Papalini. No indeed. They hoped I knew the French were different quite; and that, though they protected the Holy Father, they certainly didn't mean to fight for him. What *they* wanted was V. E. King of Italy. *Napoleon veut l'Italie Libre.* I was to *understand that, and remember it.*" But Napoleon did not recognize the new state until June.

If Elizabeth was wrong in predicting war in Italy that year, she was right in regard to another land dear to her. America was on the brink of civil war. She herself held steadily to the view that the North must at all costs prevent secession, though her friend Story, an American, argued that it would be wiser to let the South go.

As a mild winter wore into spring, a spring unusually cold, Elizabeth was thinking with dread of a visit that summer to Robert's father and sister, whom he had not seen for three years now. Sadly she reflected that, because of her, that devoted family had not been together for longer than a total of three weeks in all during the last fourteen years. If Robert could have only been got to agree she would gladly have sent him and Penini without her. A bright ray, however, on the gloomy prospect of a difficult journey, one to her now even hazardous, was that in Paris, or near it, Arabel might come to her.

In April Joseph Severn, newly appointed British Consul in Rome, came to visit Elizabeth. She found him "among the persons the most interesting" to her. It was in his arms that John Keats had died:

I make him tell me the most minute details—some very painful. Keats revolted against death, on that deeply tragic ground (always so affecting to me as an artist) of his gift being undeveloped in him—of having a work to do with his right hand, which he must let fall. "In ten years," said he, "I should be a great 'poet'—and now, I have not even philosophy enough to die by. ."

In April too there came to Rome that inveterate and charming traveller Hans Christian Andersen; delighting all who met him and especially the children. At a children's party given by the Storys he read "The Ugly Duckling"; then Robert, dressed for the part, gave "The Pied Piper" and all present, men, women, children, lined up behind him. Through the great rooms of the Barberini Palace they marched and countermarched, with Story deputizing on his flute for the magic music that drew the children from Hamelin Town.

Andersen came to visit Elizabeth in emotional mood, kissing her hand, seeming indeed "in a general *verve* for embracing." She found him "very earnest, very simple, very childlike." Pen thought him "not really pretty," observing shrewdly: "He is rather like his own ugly duck, but his mind has *developed* into a swan." It is good to think that this bright being, half angel, half child, was one of the last to delight a suffering woman very near her end now. The poem she wrote upon him, "The North and the South," was to be her final poetic utterance.

But so far was the sanguine Robert, or perhaps Elizabeth herself, from realizing her condition that the Brownings were negotiating through Story for a six years' lease on an apartment in the Palazzo Barberini. One of her last preoccupations was how they should furnish this apartment.

In June they returned to Florence and there it soon became apparent that there was to be no more travelling for Elizabeth. "I am only fit," she wrote sadly to Sarianna on the 7th, "for a drag chain." That day she had heard of the sudden and untimely death of Cavour:

I can scarcely command voice or hand to name Cavour. *That great soul, which meditated and made Italy, has gone to the Diviner country. If tears or blood could have saved him to us, he should have had mine. I feel yet as if I could scarcely comprehend the greatness of the vacancy. A hundred Garibaldis for such a man.*

As Robert watched her shaking hand fly fast over the paper he knew she had written more than enough. The letter came to an abrupt end.

Even so, weak as she was, Browning had still no clue to her condition. Plans were made for a visit to Siena and for a return

to Florence next spring; not to Casa Guidi, but to a villa outside
the city gates. Perhaps this determination to abandon Casa
Guidi was in itself a sign of some impending radical change:
for years Elizabeth had clung to a home long felt to be inconvenient, too small, but where she had known much happiness.
At Casa Guidi she had borne her child, and watched from its
windows Italy in growth.

When she caught cold through sitting in a draught the usual
remedies for congestion of the lungs failed to act: at one o'clock
in the morning Robert went for Dr. Wilson.[5] Dr. Wilson reported that one lung was condensed and he suspected an ab-
scess, but even he was not unduly alarmed: his patient had
managed for so long to live on with damaged lungs. Elizabeth
herself scoffed at his verdict, saying: "It is the old story—they
don't know my case—I have been tapped and sounded so, and
condemned so, repeatedly: this time it is said the right is the affected lung while the left is free—Dr. Chambers said just the
contrary." It was not, she declared, as bad an attack as two
years before.

At first Browning carried her during the day into their cool
large drawing-room, where she sat in her chair and read the
newspapers. Later a bed was put up for her in this room.

She began to doze heavily and seemed unaware that Robert
was sitting up by her at night. Nourishment was pronounced
essential, but she would take nothing but clear soup. Still Elizabeth refused to believe in the seriousness of her case. On the
evening of Thursday, June 27, although her voice was almost
completely gone, she was discussing their future plans. When
Browning pointed out that, as she could not live in Florence either in full summer or in winter, it hardly seemed worth setting
up another home there, Elizabeth said: "But I can't leave Florence. I like Florence." As they talked her mind wandered a little, but Browning thought this merely a result of the increased
quantity of morphine the doctor had ordered.

When Isa Blagden came in on Friday evening full of an item
of political news, Robert stopped the conversation for fear of
exciting his wife, but Elizabeth waited until his back was turned
and whispered a question. Her lively interest convinced Miss

---

[5] Dr. Grisanowsky was not in Florence at this time.

Blagden that she was really better. Wilson, when she came in to visit her former mistress, was of the same opinion. Even the doctor admitted some improvement.

That night, though Elizabeth's breathing was easier, she dozed constantly, only rousing a little and smiling if her husband spoke to her. At half past three on the 29th her condition made Browning uneasy. He sent for Dr. Wilson.

As he and the maid, Annunziata, attended her, sponging with hot water, feeding her with strong fowl-jelly from a spoon, Robert wondered if she was fully aware of their presence. He asked: "Do you know me?" She kissed him, speaking words of love, and said: "Our lives are held by God." As he gave her more jelly she put her arms round him, whispering: "God bless you" and kissing him repeatedly, Browning told his sister, with such vehemence

that when I laid her down she continued to kiss the air with her lips and several times raised her own hands and kissed them; I said "Are you comfortable?" "Beautiful." . . . Then she motioned to have her hands sponged—some of the jelly annoying her—this was done, and she began to sleep again—the last.

Browning raised her up. She died peacefully in his arms, her head against his shoulder.

The memory of those last tender words and her "God bless you" Browning was to cherish in profound gratitude. Never had she spoken to him in quite those tones before, laughing "with pleasure and *youth,* and I believe in some perfectly gracious way allowed by God suffered no pain whatever."

Elizabeth looked so tranquil, "perfectly beautiful" with a smile on her lips, that it was many hours before they could believe she was dead. Her aspect was that of a young girl.

On July 1 her body was laid in the Protestant Cemetery amid an extraordinary demonstration of grief. A crowd followed the funeral procession crying aloud in lament. "The Italians," her husband commented, "seem to have understood her by an instinct." As if to mark the passing of one so loved, who had ardently loved and served her adopted land, a great comet appeared unheralded that night, soon to be blazing over half the sky.

· · ·

Robert Browning, that poet of married love, celebrated his devotion to Elizabeth Barrett in superb and characteristic verse, both directly and by implication; but there are no lines more pregnant with yearning love than those by the Florentine Dante which he transcribed in translation on a page of his lost wife's New Testament: "Thus I believe, thus I affirm, thus I am certain it is, that from this life I shall pass to another better, where that lady lives of whom my soul is enamoured."

Appendixes

APPENDIX 1. A BARRETT PLAY–BILL

THIS WRITTEN play-bill, in my possession, must be dated either 1824 or 1829. I am inclined to accept the latter date, as on the back of it are scribbled three words in Elizabeth's own writing, and these are in her more mature hand.

It will be noted that Rolla was played by Mr. E. Barrett. This would be either the father or Bro.

On Tuesday evening January twenty
at

Theatre Royal

Hope End

will be performed –

The Tragedy

of

Pizzarro

Ataliba .. Master C J Barrett. Pizzarro .. Mr Trant

Rolla .. Mr E Barrett. Davilla Master G Barrett

Alonzo ..

Valverde. Master S Barrett

Las Casas. Mr H Trant

APPENDIX 2. AN EARLY POEM IN ITALIAN
BY ELIZABETH BARRETT

THIS APPEARS to be the best of Elizabeth's girlish exercises in Italian verse, and is perhaps worth putting on record if only for her affectionate but acute estimation of James Thomson in the last two lines of stanza 1: "Phœbus in giving thee his smile [literally 'laugh'] denied thee its full splendour."

A THOMSONI

O vate dolce e semplice
Poeta grato al core
Febo suo riso dandoti
Ti nega' il suo fulgore.

Tatto tua verga magica
    orbe   *vede* [1]
L'ochi più bel si vide
E il sol con fronte amabile
Più dolcemente ride

L'Inverno pur tua musica
Sente dal trono scuro
La State [L'estate] e lumi lucidi
Scopre con vel più puro.

L'alma natura guardati
Con ammiravol' amore
E il riso bel salutati
Suo figlio e il suo pittore.

                            E. B. Barrett

---

[1] The corrections in this line are in another hand, probably that of her Italian master.

APPENDIX 3. *SONNETS FROM THE PORTUGUESE*, XVI, IN EARLY DRAFT, IN THE MORGAN LIBRARY, NEW YORK

SONNET XVI

And yet because thou art above me so,
Because thou art more strong, & like a king,
Thou canst prevail against my fears & fling
Thy purple round me till my heart shall grow
Too close against thy heart to henceforth know
Its separate trembling pulse—Oh, conquering
May prove as noble & complete a thing
In lifting upward as in beating low!
And as a soldier struck down by a sword,
Cries 'Here my strife ends' & sinks dead to earth;
Even so, beloved, I, at last, record. .
'My Doubt ends here—' If *thou* invite me forth,
I rise above abasement at the word!
Make thy love larger to enlarge my worth.

APPENDIX 4. AN ANECDOTE TOLD BY
G. G. GIANNINI

I HAVE TO THANK Signor G. G. Giannini, long an inhabitant of Florence, for the following anecdote translated from his own words:

She was a dwarfish figure with a body the size of a person of medium stature, but with legs hardly more than 30 centimetres in length.

One day she told me that she had happy recollections of a kind English lady, a poet. All she could remember of her identity was a Christian name, "Elisabetta."

As I was at that time taking a course in English and was interested in the principal English poets, I soon realized that she was talking of Mrs. Barrett Browning.

I asked her to describe the lady, but she could do nothing but repeat that she was so beautiful, with soft eyes and hair in long ringlets after the fashion of the time; and that she liked her very much.

One day I took her a portrait of Mrs. Browning, a print which I had taken out of a volume of poetry.

When I handed it to her the old woman gave a start and gazed at it in astonishment for a long time: she smiled, wept, and finished up by kissing it repeatedly.

"It is she, the kind lady: I fancy I see her now just as when I was sitting on a little stool at her feet and she was caressing me."

It was then that she was moved to give me her confidence, speaking of a youthful peccadillo.

Even she, so unkindly treated by Nature, had loved . . . and been loved in return.

"I was quite a good-looking girl," she told me, "when people saw me at the window. And it was at the window that I attracted the attention of a fair-haired Austrian officer. There was an Austrian garrison in Florence at that time, and we lived on the first floor of a house near the Pitti Palace. My father was groom to the Grand Duke. The fair officer began to court me, passing and repassing under my windows until I should appear.

I was foolish enough to encourage his attentions. At eighteen, even if Nature *had* been unkind to me, my heart beat just as with any girl of my age. It was very stupid of me—but I did want to enjoy just that one moment offered me. I flattered myself that I might be capable of winning the affection of young men."

But it couldn't last. One day she was coming out of the house with her mother when her admirer met her. His disillusionment was openly expressed in disdainful and insulting terms. It was like a blow from a bludgeon. She fainted and was carried into the house, to remain there many days in a high fever.

Her mother, being good at sewing and embroidery, numbered among her clients Elizabeth Browning. In talking with the poet the mother mentioned her daughter's plight and the pain this incident had caused her. Mrs. Browning asked the mother to bring her daughter; she would like to talk to her, to console her.

The memory of this first meeting was still vivid in the old woman's recollection. She remembered the young lady with fair [*sic*] curls deep in a big armchair, her shoulders enveloped in a wide silk shawl. She made the girl sit on a little stool at her feet and, stroking her hair, spoke many kind words, which touched her heart like a balm. After this first meeting Mrs. Browning often asked for her and many hours were passed in her company sewing. It was the girl's only joy, the only sunshine in her life, a great recompense for the cruel disillusionment of which she had been the victim.

It was a pity the old woman could not remember, so as to repeat them, the soothing phrases murmured by the English poet, phrases that succeeded in bringing back peace to her heart.

When several months later the Brownings' son had occasion to visit Florence, where he was born, I took him to old Girolama. He remembered her well, having often played with her as a child. He took an interest in her and often asked me to help her with money on his behalf.

Florence   G. G. Giannini

The old woman was named Girolama François, a name French in origin, but her father and mother were Florentines.—G.G.G.

APPENDIX 5. CHAPMAN & HALL

Why did Elizabeth in 1850 leave Moxon, "the most poetical publisher," who had been the first to publish her work at his own expense? We do not know.

We do know, however, that Browning after his marriage, recognizing perhaps that he could hardly now ask his father to continue to subsidize him, looked round for some firm who would take the risk of publication; in his case, unpopular as he still was, a real hazard. It was Chapman & Hall who, after an introduction by Browning's friend and admirer, John Forster, took that risk, publishing in 1848 an edition in two volumes containing "Paracelsus" and the contents of the eight numbers of *Bells and Pomegranates.* Whether Chapman & Hall stipulated that Browning's wife, the more popular of the two, should also become one of their authors, or whether Elizabeth merely followed her husband's lead out of loyalty or for convenience in having a common publisher, we cannot tell. There appears to have been no personal break with Moxon: the Brownings remained on good terms with him.

APPENDIX 6. A NOTE ON
ROBERT WIEDEMAN BARRETT BROWNING [1849–1912]

(For an excellent, concise account of Pen Browning's life see "Robert Browning and His Son," by Gertrude Reese, *PMLA*, Vol. LXI, September 1946.)

AFTER ELIZABETH'S DEATH Browning resolved to devote his life to her child; but his ideas as to the bringing up of a boy differed from hers. Her emphasis had been—rightly in Pen's case as it turned out—on languages and the arts, but Browning's aim was to make his boy, if not a scholar as enthusiastic as himself and his father, at least a man of the conventional acquirements of that day. Pen should go to Oxford and receive that hall-mark of an English gentleman denied to himself.

It had been said that Browning, on his wife's death, immediately shore off Pen's curls and took away his girlish attire: altered in appearance, Pen was taken from sunny Italy, from the Italians he loved, to live in a rather dreary part of London, at Paddington, by the Regent's Park Canal. There he was put to his books but, though an affectionate good-natured boy, he did not work as hard as his brilliant, ambitious father desired: it was perhaps unfortunate that Browning did defer to his wife's wishes in one respect by not sending Pen to school. He therefore lacked the stimulus of competition. When the boy was old enough for Oxford Browning tried to enter him at Balliol, a college of high attainment, but Jowett, the Master, though Browning's friend, could not bring himself to admit the lad. Pen went to Christ Church, where he ran up the usual undergraduate debts and spent a good deal of time in active sport and playing billiards.

Pen, however, had been allowed to keep up his drawing and, after leaving Oxford in 1871 with no academic distinction, expressed a wish to become an artist. Browning sent him to Antwerp to study and there, in the right atmosphere, he began to work, making rapid progress in both painting and sculpture. Browning exerted himself to obtain worldly success for his son, quite simply in his great affection using all his now not inconsiderable influence. That Pen was an artist of some ability is certain, judging both from works reproduced in the Browning Catalogue of 1913 (including portraits in paint and stone of his father) and by awards and distinctions gained in both France and Belgium.

In 1887 he married a rich American, Fanny Coddington, but the marriage was an unhappy one. It is noticeable that, once free from economic dependence on his father, he went to live in Italy: how far the sharp severance from what was practically his native land had harmed the boy we cannot know. There, in Venice, he bought the Palazzo Rezzonico and took into his household Wilson and Ferdinando. After Ferdinando's death in 1893 Wilson remained with Pen, dying in 1902. For many years her mind was enfeebled.

In 1889 Browning went to live in Italy; but on December 12 he died. Sarianna joined her nephew, whose wife left him soon after. Sarianna died in 1903, remembered by those who saw her as an intelligent, vivacious old lady.

With his powerful father no longer alive, a father he loved and was anxious to please, Pen became the lazy man he was in later life. Painting was given up and a large part of his time was spent gossiping in the street with Italians. To lovers of Browning he was a profound disappointment, a "commonplace," a "very ordinary" man, but he honoured his parents and kept up their memory; though not unfortunately to the extent of having letters, documents, and mementoes secured in any one central place after his death. At the great Browning Sale in 1913 holographs, documents, pictures, furniture, all except a few pieces kept by the Moulton-Barrett family were scattered.

In money matters Pen inherited rather the heedlessness of his mother than his father's caution: when he wanted to buy Casa Guidi in their memory he could not afford it. In Florence, where he lived towards the end of his life, Pen befriended and spent much of his time with that love of his babyhood Edith Story, who, though she had made a brilliant marriage with the Marchese Peruzzi, fell upon evil times. It was she who attended him on his deathbed at Asolo in 1912.

MAIN BOOKS OF REFERENCE

Letters of Elizabeth Barrett Browning Addressed to Richard Hengist Horne, edited by S. R. Townshend Mayer. 2 vols. Richard Bentley, 1888.

The Letters of Elizabeth Barrett Browning, edited by Frederic G. Kenyon. 2 vols. 3rd edition, Smith, Elder, 1898.

"Twenty Unpublished Letters of Elizabeth Barrett to Hugh Stuart Boyd," by Bennet Weaver. *PMLA,* Vol. LXV, No. 4, June 1950.

Letters from Elizabeth Barrett to B. R. Haydon, edited by Martha Hale Shackford (Oxford University Press, 1939).

The Letters of Robert Browning and Elizabeth Barrett Barrett, 1845–1846. 2 vols. Smith, Elder, 1899.

Elizabeth Barrett Browning: Letters to her Sister, 1846–1859, edited by Leonard Huxley. John Murray, 1929.

From Robert & Elizabeth Browning, edited by William Rose Benét. John Murray, 1936.

Robert Browning and Alfred Domett, edited by Frederic G. Kenyon. Smith, Elder, 1906.

Letters of Robert Browning collected by Thomas J. Wise, edited by Thurman L. Hood. John Murray, 1933.

Robert Browning and Julia Wedgwood, edited by Richard Curle. John Murray, 1937.

Letters to Robert Browning and Other Correspondents, edited by Thomas J. Wise. 1916.

Dearest Isa, Robert Browning's Letters to Isabella Blagden, edited by Edward C. McAleer. University of Texas Press, 1951.

"New Letters from Mrs. Browning to Isa Blagden," by Edward C. McAleer. *PMLA,* Vol. LXVI, No. 5, September 1951.

· · ·

The Family of the Barrett, by Jeannette Marks. New York: The Macmillan Company; 1938.

Life and Letters of Robert Browning, by Mrs. Sutherland Orr. 2nd edition, Smith, Elder, 1891.

The Life of Robert Browning, by W. Hall Griffin and H. C. Minchin. Revised edition, Methuen, 1938.

The Brownings, Their Life and Art, by Lilian Whiting. Hodder & Stoughton, 1911.

"Robert Browning and His Son," by Gertrude Reese. *PMLA,* Vol. LXI, No. 3, September 1946.

Hitherto Unpublished Poems and Stories, edited by H. Buxton Forman. 2 vols. The Boston Bibliophile Society, 1914.

The Poet's Enchiridion, edited by H. Buxton Forman. The Boston Bibliophile Society, 1914.

The Battle of Marathon, a Poem, by E. B. Barrett. W. Lindsell, 1820.

An Essay on Mind, with Other Poems. James Duncan, 1824.

Prometheus Bound, translated from the Greek of Æschylus, by the Author of "An Essay on Mind," with Other Poems. A. J. Valpy, 1833.

The Seraphim, and Other Poems, by Elizabeth B. Barrett. Saunders & Otley, 1838.

A New Spirit of the Age, edited by R. H. Horne. 2 vols. Smith, Elder, 1844 (contributions by Elizabeth Barrett Barrett).

Poems, by Elizabeth Barrett Barrett. 2 vols. Edward Moxon, 1844.

Poems, by Elizabeth Barrett Browning. 2 vols. 2nd edition, Chapman & Hall, 1850 (includes retranslated *Prometheus Bound* and "Sonnets from the Portuguese").

Casa Guidi Windows, A Poem, by Elizabeth Barrett Browning. Chapman & Hall, 1851.

Two Poems, by Elizabeth Barrett Browning and Robert Browning. Chapman & Hall, 1854.

Aurora Leigh, by Elizabeth Barrett Browning. Chapman & Hall, 1857.

Poems Before Congress, by Elizabeth Barrett Browning. Chapman & Hall, 1860.

Last Poems, by Elizabeth Barrett Browning. Chapman & Hall, 1863.

The Greek Christian Poets and the English Poets, by Elizabeth Barrett Browning. Chapman & Hall, 1863.

Psyche Apocalyptè: A Lyrical Drama, Projected by Elizabeth Barrett Browning and R. H. Horne. Hazell, Watson & Viney, for private circulation, 1876.

Letters to William Allingham, edited by H. Allingham and E. Baumer Williams. Longmans, Green, 1911.

Red Letter Days, by Mrs. Andrew Crosse. Richard Bentley, 1892.

Anna Jameson, Letters and Friendships, edited by Mrs. Steuart Erskine. T. Fisher Unwin, 1915.

Memoirs of the Life of Anna Jameson, by Gerardine Macpherson. Longmans, Green, 1878.

The Life and Letters of Mary Russell Mitford, edited by A. G. L'Estrange, Vols. II, III. Richard Bentley, 1870.

The Friendships of Mary Russell Mitford, edited by A. G. L'Estrange, Vol. II. Hurst & Blackett, 1882.

Mary Russell Mitford, Correspondence, edited by Elizabeth Lee. Unwin, 1914.

Letters of Anne Thackeray Ritchie, edited by Hester Ritchie. John Murray, 1924.

D. G. Rossetti, His Family Letters. Ellis & Elvey, 1895

Pre-Raphaelitism Papers, 1854–1872, edited by William Rossetti. George Allen, 1899.

William Wetmore Story and His Friends, by Henry James. 2 vols. Edinburgh: Blackwood. Boston: Houghton, Mifflin; 1903.

"Correspondence of Harriet Beecher Stowe and Elizabeth Barrett Browning," by Hazel Harrod. *Studies in English,* University of Texas, Vol. XXVII, No. 1, June 1948.

Alfred, Lord Tennyson, a Memoir by his son. Macmillan, 1906.

What I Remember, by Thomas Adolphus Trollope, Vol. II. Richard Bentley, 1888.

Catalogues, the Browning Sales, Sotheby, 1913 and 1937, and various.

INDEX

A NOTE ON THE TYPE

THE TEXT of this book is set in Caledonia, *a Linotype face designed by W. A. Dwiggins. It belongs to the family of printing types called "modern face" by printers—a term used to mark the change in style of type-letters that occurred about 1800. Caledonia borders on the general design of Scotch Modern, but is more freely drawn than that letter.*

The book was composed, printed, and bound by The Plimpton Press, Norwood, Massachusetts. The typography and binding design are by W. A. Dwiggins.

Shuttered Windows

Shuttered Windows

By

Florence Crannell Means

Illustrations by
ARMSTRONG SPERRY

HOUGHTON MIFFLIN COMPANY · BOSTON
The Riverside Press Cambridge

The Riverside Press
CAMBRIDGE · MASSACHUSETTS
PRINTED IN THE U.S.A.

TO

MATHER SCHOOL

THIS SMALL SHADOW OF ITSELF IS
GRATEFULLY DEDICATED

CONTENTS

ILLUSTRATIONS

I

Grandfather Moses

HARRIET curled up in the back seat of the car with her foot asleep and did not say a word for miles and miles.

She was usually talkative enough. Today there were good reasons for her silence. Mr. Trindle, behind the steering wheel, gave no one else a chance to slip in a word edgewise; the fifteen hundred miles between Minneapolis, Minnesota, and Charleston, South Carolina, had exhausted her vocabulary; she was soon to meet an unknown great-grandmother who was her only kin, and on the way to that great-grandmother's home visit the boarding-school where she might enroll for her senior year. In addition to all this novelty, there was Moses to hold her speechless.

Moses emerged from dim woods paths. Down the dark aisles of cypress swamps, between the swaying pennons of Spanish moss, he rowed with a rhythm of mighty shoulders. Through the sweet gum and the feathery mimosa that skirted the highway he strode with a rhythm of mighty legs.

If he disappeared like a puff of smoke in the misty mosses or on the winding paths, that was not strange:

Moses was Harriet's great-great-great-grandfather. She had always dreamed of him with fierce pride, an ancestor to boast of; but never had she seen him so clearly as now, when for the first time she came into his own place.

So she sat in the back seat, well packed about with blankets and cushions, and looked from side to side. Mr. Trindle discoursed steadily upon the rich history of the Charleston district, and Mrs. Trindle broke his flow of conversation with an occasional 'Tk! Tk!' at sight of a cart drawn by a lumbering ox, or a woman with a reed basket balanced on her head, or a vast live-oak bearded with moss. Sometimes Mr. Trindle's discourse faltered while he mopped his brow and neck and shining, beaded dome. Sometimes, but not often, Mr. Trindle paused for breath.

Unconsciously Harriet filled in those rare pauses with a phrase of song, hummed in a lilting, birdlike voice, or with a wriggle and chuckle of delight. If she could have had Helen and Iva and Jimmie with her, the experience would have been perfect. But letters were so stupid: they could never capture the sight and smell and feel of the South for the 'gang' in Minneapolis.

The distance from Minneapolis to Charleston was so much more than the fifteen hundred miles the dizzy, diagonal figures on their touring map indicated: it stretched from the world of Harriet, today, back to the world of Moses, 1836.

Here was the Ford, to be sure, and her own modern fitted traveling case at her feet. Here were other cars meeting theirs, passing it, in endless current along the smooth pavement. But — here were tall cypress trees, their silver knees rising from ink-black waters. Here were villages whose weathered, gray cabins had sat down to sleep in the forest wherever they happened to. Here were batten doors, and rude shutters swinging at glassless

2

window places, and enormous black kettles steaming over fires that smouldered on the ground.

Now and then the car flashed past a Big House straight out of a Civil War romance, its tall pillars cutting lovely white lines from ground to roof; and Charleston, behind them now, had been rich in gracious dwellings roofed with mossy tiles and flowering into ancient iron grill-work.

Somewhere in this region Taliaferro Plantation had stood in just such gracious beauty: Taliaferro, where Moses had had his being. So it was natural that Harriet should see him here.

Legend had sprung up about Moses, but the fact that it was legend made her no less proud. Even when she was small, her father had said: 'Honey-child reverts to type, Mother. Mark my word, she gets her height from Grandpa Moses; those broad little old shoulders, too, and the uppity way she flings back her head.'

Harriet liked to recall the words, with the rich laugh chuckling through them. She liked to remember all she could of the home that for a while had been so happy and complete.

After Father's death came four years when Harriet's mother served as Y.W.C.A. secretary, as she had done before her marriage: Four years in a small, bright apartment, where Harriet practised and played and grew into lanky girlhood. A year ago the small, bright apartment had been dismantled, and Harriet had gone to live with Mr. and Mrs. Trindle, a motherless as well as a fatherless girl.

Mr. Trindle had long been the pastor of their church and their friend. His house was a home, rich in books and magazines and dog-eared music and a piano shabby from the practising of Trindle children now grown and away. It was as pleasant as an adoptive home could be. The

3

insurance her mother had left took care of Harriet's small needs, though the warm fathering and mothering hearts of the Trindles would not have left her unprovided for in any case. Yet Harriet was not happy. After months of wild grieving, she had tried to settle down in her new nest, but she did not succeed very well. She felt like a visitor who must soon go on to her own home and her own people.

So far as she knew, her 'own people' numbered exactly one; her father's grandmother, living on what Harriet thought of as the old homestead, far in the mysterious deeps of the South.

Great-Grandmother was mysterious, too. Father could barely remember her, for he had been brought North in his early childhood. Every Christmas a festive box of gifts had gone to Gentlemen's Island. Other than that, there had been no communication with her. Great-Grandmother must be very old, Harriet thought; and very old people, with shaky hands and failing sight, did not often write.

Even Harriet's letter, written a few weeks after her mother's death, had not been answered by Great-Grandmother herself. She had replied by the hand of one 'R. Corwin.'

R. Corwin wrote on stationery that had evidently aged in a village store: it held definite flavors of tobacco and drugs and dried fish and perfume and kerosene. On the stale paper, in somewhat stiff phrases, R. Corwin had expressed Great-Grandmother's sympathy, and her affectionate desire to see her only living descendant.

'Your Granny,' R. Corwin had written, 'begs you will come and pay her a visit; but her deepest wish is that you live here. She says tell you there is always room in her house for you. Also there is a fine girls' school on a near island. You must have heard of it. Landers is its name, and girls in these parts have been educated there since the War Between the States. An old school and very honorable.

'Perhaps it is not right that I should tell you, but your Granny prays even in the meeting-house that her child shall come home to her before she dies. She is a respected woman: good, also very smart.'

Harriet handed that letter to Mr. and Mrs. Trindle and watched them read it. Mr. Trindle's scraggly eyebrows arched above the gold rims of his spectacles, and Mrs. Trindle clucked softly. With simultaneous question they looked at Harriet. Harriet, knitting her brows as she did when she felt strongly, answered with decision: 'I'd like to go. Maybe for a year.'

Mr. Trindle pushed out his lips and tapped them with the folded letter. 'Slowly, slowly, my child. What would be the effect of such a venture on the progress of your musical education?'

Harriet touched the piano with an unconscious hand. She was accompanist for the glee club in the big high school and was achieving a modest fame in her world. Besides, the past year had taught her to love music for its own sake. But her head went back in the 'uppity way' Father had noticed long ago. 'If my music's any good, a little interruption won't hurt it. And a great-grandmother all alone ——'

Mrs. Trindle looked past Harriet out of the window and her eyes narrowed and widened, narrowed and widened. 'What about your chums, Harrie? I don't reckon it would be so easy to pick up congenial friends ——'

Helen and Iva. Yes, and Jimmie, too. 'But a great-grandmother ought to count more than the kids you go round with.'

'Papa,' said Mrs. Trindle, with the double blink that meant that her words were a sort of code, 'don't you want to come out and open a jar for me? Seems like I haven't the strength ——'

Harriet heard them in the kitchen, Mrs. Trindle's coo answered by Mr. Trindle's astonished rumble; the coo again; the rumble, grown calmer; silences broken by coo and rumble. At the dinner table Mr. Trindle portentously cleared his throat and informed Harriet that he and Mrs. Trindle had always had the most intense desire to motor to the Deep South for their vacation.

So, when summer was waning toward autumn, the three went whirring through the country in the swift comfort of a new, gray Ford. They stopped in New York, in Washington, in Charleston. Now they were drawing near Bosquet and Landers School; drawing near Gentlemen's Island and Great-Grandmother.

Now, too, the ancestor Moses assumed more and more reality: a mighty man with the nobly held head of lofty birth. Some had said he was the son of a Mohammedan priest; some, the son of a petty king. Certain it was that he had survived the terrible Middle Passage to become a slave with other slaves on a South Carolina rice plantation.

With what satisfaction he would have regarded this descendant of his, whose head was unbowed in the land of his captivity! Harriet was as handsome as he could have been: a bronze maiden, eyes straight-gazing under brows that frowned with thought; hair cloudy black; full lips well cut; smooth, brown skin stained with dusky red.

A child of Moses — of Black Moses.

It was not until the car passed over the causeways that led across reedy waters to the old city of Bosquet that Harriet's thoughts for a little while ceased to swing between Great-Grandmother and Moses, and settled down to Landers School. The school must be their first stop, for its opening day was close upon them.

They had visited a school in Charleston, one whose pupils were called the 'colored aristocracy.' White people might laugh at the term, but it was not ludicrous: these girls and boys were the flower of generations of educated people.

But it was on Landers that Harriet had set her heart, not only because it was nearer Great-Grandmother, but because she liked the sound of it. 'An old school and very honorable,' R. Corwin had said; and 'girls in these parts have been educated there since the War Between the States.'

Seventy years! That was venerable to the girl from the Middle West. Her own high school was beautiful: endless, shining corridors; mellow woods; statues white in dim corners; a library with Gothic windows and easy study chairs and book-tapestried walls. Beautiful; but so new!

'Bosquet,' Mr. Trindle was going on with relish, 'is historically remarkable. The region hereabout is marked by some of the earliest landings on the continent. The Spanish landed in 1520 and the French Huguenot, Jean Ribaut, in 1560 or thereabouts. And within the confines of Bosquet itself, if I mistake not, exists a church edifice that dates from 1720.'

Mrs. Trindle, a plump and cozy brown pigeon of a woman, was tk-tking constantly now, for they were bowling along through the dusty, narrow streets of the town. Here more of the stately Big Houses paraded the waterfront; blossoming shrubs and garden flowers splashed the scene with color; and in the midst of the residences stood ruined, gray masonry with wrought-iron banisters leading upward to nothing, and flowers and thick leafage thrusting through the breaches everywhere. The city looked as if it had slept, charmingly, since 1864.

Harriet screwed sidewise to look out the back window

at some long buildings on the end of shadowy old grounds.

'Mr. Trindle,' she asked, 'what would those be for? With funny little high windows barred like a jail?'

Mrs. Trindle made a mournful noise, and Mr. Trindle cleared his throat. 'Slave quarters, Harrie,' he answered, handling the word gingerly, as one touches a tender scar. 'Just observe the brick wall surrounding this ancient church. Green with moss and mould. Doubtless the edifice to which I referred: 1720.'

Harriet winced, and turned her eyes from those barred windows to the old church and the old street.

More Negroes than white people walked the street: laughing, playing, quarreling children; grown people; old men, bent and shuffling; old women, peering from below white headcloths. Harriet studied the old women with her heart in her mouth. Her great-grandmother would not be like these. Harriet wanted to hurry to that meeting, and at the same time she flinched from it. She was both eager and afraid. She had not realized how different might be Harriet-of-South Carolina from Harriet-of-Minnesota.

First, however, it was necessary to visit Landers School.

Mr. Trindle inquired the way, and drove along the ribbon of black pavement that was pointed out to him.

The highway became the dark floor of a tunnel, walled and roofed with green and draped with gray. When Mr. Trindle had whizzed through the tunnel a while, he brought the car to a squealing stop, backed a little, and parked behind a trim, tan cousin Ford, with a South Carolina license. Over an aisle opening into the deep green an arched sign announced LANDERS SCHOOL.

Harriet felt herself gathered up into a tight ball of excitement as she jumped from the car and walked along the aisle with Mr. and Mrs. Trindle. This was one of Life's Moments! Who knew to what experiences this brief walk would carry her? Nothing else holds out such promises as a new school: new surroundings, new friends, new teachers, and one's self somehow a new person. Harriet surreptitiously twitched her sheer cotton dress straight and pulled her hat properly over one eye.

She had a momentary glimpse of a campus shaded by great trees; of a flame of flowers. Then her attention went to a group of people who stood facing back, apparently, toward buildings they had just left.

The people were of the type she had seen on the dusty roads, fishing in little creeks or trudging along with burdens on their heads or slung over their shoulders. The women wore the characteristic headcloths and gold hoop earrings. The man's hat was almost crownless. They were laughing and talking to each other, their voices deep and throaty.

'—— jis' gran', enty?' murmured one. 'Ever I yeddy how gran' e was.'

'But never did I reckon my chillen gwine live like white folks,' said another, her voice splitting on a note of pure awe. 'E *too* pretty, enty?'

They became aware of the Trindle group, and edged aside to let them pass, grinning and bowing and blinking curious eyes at them. Mrs. Trindle nudged Harriet along, for the girl unconsciously slowed her steps to listen. Here was a strange language, not only softly slurred, but pieced together with extra syllables — 'Nevah did Ah reckon ma chillen duh-gwan lib lak duh whi' folks' — and with strange words: 'enty,' 'yeddy.' It was as lovely as French patois. Harriet wanted to hear more.

But, urged past the trio, she looked eagerly for the grandeur that had awed them. White temples of learning, maybe, with pillared façades gleaming out of green glooms.

Another couple passed, bowing. Harriet thought idly that they were headed for the tan Ford on the highway.

The woman wore crisp white, and the man a Panama at one end and white buckskin shoes at the other: an ordinary, uninterestingly well-dressed colored man and woman.

Harriet's eyes passed them while she returned their bows; and quite suddenly she was looking at the words OFFICE above the door of a square wooden house.

They entered. Harriet felt herself falling through her bright imaginings and landing with a jolt on reality. No shining corridors here; no mellow woods and Gothic windows; instead, a splintery, scrubbed floor and plain board walls that could have made good use of a fresh coat of paint; and a shabby desk across which a serene-faced woman smiled at them.

'May I help you in some way?' asked the serene-faced woman. 'I am Miss Francis, the Principal of Landers.'

Dizzy from her bump on reality, Harriet stared at Miss Francis's pale face and honey-colored hair. The principal's lips did not smile, but her blue eyes did.

'Permit me to present Mrs. Trindle,' Mr. Trindle was enunciating deeply, 'and our young friend Miss Harriet Freeman. Of Minneapolis, Minnesota.' He drew out a card-case and laid his card on the desk.

Harriet was looking about her, still with a floating feeling as if she were dreaming the whole scene. On a bulletin board was pinned a notice headed: THE SENIORS AIM TO PLEASE. And lettered below was the information:

All are Workers in the Senior Hive.
We polish Shoes while you wait: 5¢ a Pair.
We make Dresses: 50¢ if not too fancy.
Also collars and nightgowns.

Patronize our Beauty Shop.
Hair straightened and curled.
We improve you 100%.

10

The Senior Class. That would be her class. That would *have been* her class, she corrected herself vigorously. For the dullest person could see that it would not be good sense for her to give up Centennial High and Minneapolis for Landers and South Carolina.

Noticing her intent gaze, the principal turned to her from her conversation with the Trindles. 'Every class earns money for a party and a present,' she explained. 'That is last year's bulletin. Those seniors were an energetic group. They'd do anything to earn a dollar.'

Harriet moistened her lips. 'Does it really mean — could they make a dress for fifty cents?'

'"If not too fancy." Fifty cents isn't so small a coin here as it is up North,' Miss Francis answered, her eyes warming with their unexpected smile. 'When you consider how low our fees are, at Landers, and board ——

'But wouldn't you like to see our buildings? I'll show you our newest first. Sarah B. Lawrence. We're proud of it.'

She led the way to a long brick edifice with a pillared entrance. At sight of it Harriet felt more at ease: it was not utterly different from her expectations. Downstairs were dining-rooms and living-rooms; upstairs, rows and rows of small bedrooms. The principal glowed over them, her look broodingly content, and Harriet scrutinized the plain little rooms, wondering what there was about them to make anyone so happy.

Miss Francis swayed down the corridors, tall, slender, her head bent a little to one side on her long throat. Mr. Trindle strode after her with the swing of the small man, and Mrs. Trindle pattered by his side; you almost expected her shoes to be pink, like pigeons' feet. Both Trindles made polite remarks at appropriate moments, while their faces remained blank.

'Miss Harriet would naturally be assigned to this

pleasantest dormitory,' Miss Francis explained. 'It is the upper-class hall. But it is already completely filled by the advance applications. There is, of course, always the possibility of a cancellation.'

She ushered them out and across the campus toward the other buildings, telling about fees as she went. Registration was eight dollars, board eighty-one dollars for the year, high-school books about eight dollars, music lessons two dollars a month. Harriet kept trying to figure the total, but she could never get past two times eight is sixteen, plus eighty-one is — There her mind would falter and leap to the music lessons at two dollars a month. In Minneapolis she paid two dollars for a half-hour.

Miss Francis was explaining that the students all did some housework, caring for their own rooms and corridors and taking turns waiting on tables. She broke off to usher them into a barnlike three-story house.

'This is the middle dormitory, Washington Hall. It was built shortly after the Civil War, out of lumber from Union barracks.' At the opening of the door a musty, salt-sweet odor had encompassed them, as if seventy years had made a strange potpourri. The steep stairs creaked warningly as they climbed; the hall floor creaked as they paced its length, looking into the tiny rooms.

Now Harriet understood Miss Francis's pride in Sarah B. Lawrence. Each of these Washington cubicles had space for two cot beds, a curious iron washstand that grasped in iron loops a wash basin and pitcher, and a stove like an enlarged shoe-box on legs. Across two corners curtains formed triangular clothes closets.

'You've probably noticed that none of our walls are papered,' Miss Francis observed cheerfully. 'It's too damp here: paper peels off at once.'

Harriet looked mutely at the painted wood. She was finding Mr. Trindle's steady stream of talk more agreeable than usual. He filled all conversational space, and wherever there was a hole Mrs. Trindle dropped in a word. Harriet did not have to hunt things to say. Her direct mind balked at polite untruths. She was glad she need only walk beside the others and see the buildings as they were displayed.

She saw the shabby schoolrooms and the library with its plain wooden tables for study and its miscellaneous books. She saw the cooking laboratory, with its hollow square of zinc-covered tables and its small gasoline stoves. 'The individual stoves aren't usable at present,' Miss Francis regretted, 'but it's really better for the girls to use the wood stove anyway; few of them have ever used any kind of gas; many of them probably never will.'

Harriet saw the industrial building — Jaynes Hall — one of the few new brick buildings on the campus. It held ranks of laundry tubs and files of ironing boards and stoves like old-fashioned heaters, with shelves around their sides on which clean black flatirons stood with their heating surfaces pressed against the clean, black stove walls and their handles out like ornamental curlicues.

Still dazed, she walked back to the office.

'Mrs. Trindle and Miss Harriet and myself are about to embark for Gentlemen's Island,' Mr. Trindle was rolling along in his pleasant, pompous voice. 'We shall take the matter under advisement and bring our young friend in by the opening date' — he brought his glasses to bear on the catalogue in his hand — 'the ninth, if we decide that it is advisable. I observe that the meteorologists are warning us of a West Indian hurricane heading toward the Florida Keys. Let us hope that this coast will escape such a visitation.' He was tapering off the interview with polite talk.

'I hope — I really hope Miss Harriet will decide to come to us,' Miss Francis said, for a moment holding

13

Harriet's baffled brown gaze with her intent blue one. Miss Francis was as direct as Harriet. She hadn't even noticed Mr. Trindle's tactful remarks.

'Will decide! Hmph! As if I hadn't already decided!' Harriet was thinking, while she murmured and Mrs. Trindle cooed and Mr. Trindle uttered sounding phrases, and all three bowed themselves away and walked through the shadowy aisle to the black highway.

Mr. Trindle started the car. 'Conditions differ greatly in different sections of the country,' he observed pleasantly.

'Good gracious!' agreed Harriet. She looked at Mrs. Trindle under drawn brows. 'What on earth did those people mean, calling it grand, Mrs. Trindle?'

Mrs. Trindle clucked and lifted her plump little shoulders. 'I'm beginning to think we have no idea of the sectional differences, Harrie — no idea!'

Harriet was riffling the catalogue pages. 'Listen to this,' she gurgled, and read aloud with slow weight: '"Correspondence with young men is allowed to high-school girls if parents send to the office names of those whom they approve of. Each high-school girl may write three letters each Monday." Can you imagine what Helen and Iva would say to that?'

'Southern customs — Maybe conditions make closer supervision necessary, Harrie — We may meet other surprises, too.'

Great-Grandmother: that was what Mrs. Trindle was warning her about. Harriet felt a sick churning in the middle of herself. What on earth would Great-Grandmother be like?

II

GREAT-GRANDMOTHER

A MILE away at the Bosquet wharf the boat was already tootling. Mr. Trindle drove quickly back to town and left the car in a garage, and the three hurried down where the business buildings backed onto the creaky old dock. With expectancy tightening every nerve, Harriet followed Mrs. Trindle across the gangplank and up a stairway to the next deck. Here shabbily dressed Negroes were shouting and laughing to each other, or beginning to eat lunches out of shoe-boxes and paper bags.

'There's more room on top. Let's go up there,' said Harriet, pushing toward another staircase.

Mrs. Trindle laid a hand on her arm. 'No, Harrie. That's not for us. That's the white people's deck. This — Look, honey!'

Harriet's frowning gaze followed Mrs. Trindle's pointing finger. Over the door of the enclosed deck was a large sign: COLORED. Over the staircase she had wished to climb stood a similar sign: WHITE.

Harriet sat down, feeling sick. She had of course read of the 'Jim Crow' trains and waiting-rooms, but it was the first time she had ever encountered them herself.

'Let us go out into the fresh air and sunshine,' Mr. Trindle suggested, his eyes gleaming with comprehension behind his bright glasses. Harriet followed limply.

It was impossible to remain limp, perched on a bench in the bow. Harriet took off her hat. The breeze blowing in her face cool from the water flattened her lashes and twitched at her hair and blew every curling tendril straight back. The sun struck sparks from the water and gulls called and wheeled around the boat and the foam curled up before them and swished away behind them. Even the sea smell of salt and fish and iodine was intoxicating. Harriet's spirits flew up, light as a gull. She tossed back her head and laughed aloud.

Mr. and Mrs. Trindle laughed, too. 'It certainly does make an individual thankful for the gift of life,' said Mr. Trindle, the gold fillings in his teeth and the gold rims on his glasses vying with each other in the sunshine.

They passed small, slumbrous islands where old houses dreamed among palmettos and live-oaks: islands shut off from the world because they had no landing places. An occasional clumsy rowboat that had put off from a marshy shore awaited the steamer in midchannel, and stood by while a passenger climbed over the rail; then, with long pulls of the oars, nosed in among the rushes again.

Harriet drummed on the bench with her strong musician's fingers and thought that some day she would make music that would carry this swish and fury of waters, and cry of birds, and insistent fluting of the whistle.

Mrs. Trindle brought out the box of food which she had provided, and Harriet's thoughts surged from music to eating.

'Mmmm!' she murmured contentedly, 'an ocean voyage gives you an appetite!'

She buttered buns; and Mr. Trindle opened a can of sardines, holding it out over the railing as he twisted the key that rolled back the top flap; and Mrs. Trindle slipped two silvery fish into each bun and laid a bun and two fig-bars and a banana on a paper napkin on each lap. From somewhere Mr. Trindle summoned a pop boy, and opened three root-beer and orange-crush bottles with enticing spurts of foam. They ate and drank with deep relish.

When she was done, Harriet wadded her napkin around her banana peel and tried to toss it out over the rail. Perversely it blew back and down. She heard a shout of laughter from the lower deck and peered over into the upturned face of a boy who grinned and waved the pink napkin as if it had been a rose.

She could not help laughing back, though he was one of those swaggering, assured boys whom she liked to snub. He had a dimple in one cheek, as if someone had screwed a fingertip around in it, and his teeth gleamed like new ivory. He twisted a corner of the napkin into a stem and stuck it behind his ear and thrummed an imaginary guitar. The banana trailed down out of the crumpled pinkness, so that Harriet and Mr. and Mrs. Trindle all laughed again, leaning over the rail.

But then, much too soon, the boat ride was over. The whistle uttered long pipings, and the three travelers straightened and looked ahead. The steamer was chugging up to the barnacle-crusted stilts of a dock; chugging up pompously while the water churned against its sides and surged away and back again.

This was Great-Grandmother's island.

Mr. and Mrs. Trindle and Harriet stood amid their luggage on the clattering dock and watched the flurry of landing. A few Negroes had lounged out of the COLORED deck with them, laughing and shouting to others who laughed and shouted from the shore. A few pieces of freight had been landed, with yells and laughter. Harriet

watched absorbedly as four Negroes, their bodies glistening wet and brown through ragged denim, made a living
chain down a cleated slope to the freight deck and dragged
huge cakes of ice up to the pier. One clasped another to
form the chain, the last one grappled the ice, and all together climbed the cleated slope, dragging the burden.

On the shore two little colored boys in ragged overalls
ran along the beach picking up shells. A white man in a
white suit glanced indifferently at the Trindles and got
into his car and puffed back through the sand.

Mr. Trindle hailed a Negro with a brimless felt hat
perched on the side of his head. The man grinned at him
in friendly fashion. 'Brother,' asked Mr. Trindle, 'are
there any taxicabs operating in this vicinity?'

The man took off his hat and scratched his head.
'Which?'

'Any automobile we can engage to convey us to Sister
Freeman's home? Are you acquainted with a lady by the
name of Freeman?'

'Sho'. Mis' Freeman,' the man said, replacing the hat
he had removed to scratch his head. 'Ain' no automobiles
fuh hire, but I reckon y'all can walk it. Mis' Freeman
ain' live such a far piece. Y'all just follow thisyere road
to the fork and go to the right twell y'all done pass a
cane patch. House nex' the cane patch is blue. That
Mis' Freeman's.'

'Whoosh!' said Mr. Trindle, after they had trudged
along for ten minutes without sighting the fork. It was
heavily hot, here on the island. Mr. Trindle plumped the
three suitcases down in the dust, and swung his thin
brown neck in a half-circle while he wiped it with a damp
handkerchief. His collar was a white rag that had long
given up the effort to stand.

Harriet, roused by the ejaculation, caught up her own
suitcase self-reproachfully. She had not even noticed that

Mr. Trindle was laboring along with the heavy luggage while she and Mrs. Trindle carried only their overnight cases. She was scarcely aware of the afternoon sultriness, and of the way the 'piece' had stretched on through minutes muffled in deep, white dust. As one held in an enchantment, she tramped on toward her only living kin.

The island was held in enchantment, too. All the charm, the sleepy antiquity, that she had seen scattered along the way from Washington to Bosquet were boiled down in this small island ringed round by palms and rushes and waves.

The whole place seemed asleep. One automobile passed them, and Mr. Trindle turned toward it a hopeful brown face, glistening with sweat, but it was a white people's car and passed without a sign. Horses jogged by, bestridden by ragged boys and men. A vehicle creaked up behind them, wheels squalling. Harriet's attention was fixed on a thicket of palmetto where a mocking-bird did a wild dance of song, and she was dreamily considering that the bird would form the motif for another composition, with its sweet full calls and its pixy variations, whimsical, peevish. She did not turn to see the complaining cart until a great horned head appeared at her elbow. She leaped aside into the weeds, the suitcase banging her knees and the prickers snagging her stockings. A piebald ox swayed by between sapling thills. The rude two-wheeled cart he pulled was heaped with long rods like purple fishpoles, and topped by assorted human beings.

The cart screeched to a stop. The driver, his back bowed, his forearms on his knees, asked, 'Cain' I tote yo' satchels, Mister?'

Mr. Trindle nodded gratefully and heaved the large ones up among the purple sticks, wheezing, 'Sister Freeman's, thank you.'

'Sho'! Mis' Freeman's,' the man said, and nodded. The

cart groaned onward again, and the little old granny in the back end nodded and grinned at them around her little black pipe, and lifted a gnarled black hand in farewell.

The cart had scarcely disappeared to the right, where the road forked, when a still more startling interruption occurred. With a crash of underbrush and a rustle of weeds a beast hurtled out of a thicket and careened onto the road, where it skidded to a stop, flinging up its heels almost in Harriet's face.

'Now-now-now-now, young one! Mind where you're going, please!' Mr. Trindle adjured the apparition.

The calf was ridden by an imp with bare arms and legs like brown wires. This imp stared back at them over her shoulder and her grin displayed a startling gap in her front teeth.

'Oooh — Lawzy!' she whooped, and clapping her hands to her mouth and her heels into the calf's sides, she was off in a scramble of hoofs and tasseled tail and rocking-horse motion fore and aft.

'Good gracious!' Harriet cried, thoroughly awake. 'If this isn't the weirdest place! Ox carts full of purple fishpoles, and imps riding calves — and whole fields of white roses.'

Mr. Trindle cackled. 'That field's not flowers, Harrie: it's cotton. And your fishing-rods were sugar cane.'

'I don't know whether I can endure another step,' Mrs. Trindle panted. 'These new shoes have made a blister on my heel — I didn't know we'd have to walk across whole islands — and I'm about to melt and run away besides. Can't we go and sit on that porch a minute?' Her round face was slick with sweat.

'Oh, but it's such a dreadful shack,' Harriet objected. 'I know it's picturesque, but — Don't you suppose that cornfield-looking place ahead is the cane patch the man told us about? With Great-Grandmother's house just beyond it?'

'Well — ' Mrs. Trindle's eyes fastened hopefully on the light silken shimmer of green, while she spread her toes and wriggled the heel of her shoe loose. A trickle of perspiration zigzagged down her nose.

Mr. Trindle contemplated the despised shack. '"The young folk roll on the little cabin floor,"' he sang wheezily. 'Reckon that is precisely the type of domicile to which the song writer had reference.'

As they approached the cane patch the imp on the steer dashed toward them again, swerved her bucking steed to one side, and rocked back.

'You don't reckon it's a reception committee, do you?' Mrs. Trindle took breath to wonder.

'Mrs. Trindle, I think you have hit the nail on the head with your customary accuracy,' said Mr. Trindle.

Harriet had eyes for nothing but the farther boundary of the cane patch. She was watching for the blue house, the only home in all the world that was really hers. Reaching the far corner of the green silk field, she jerked to a standstill and stared.

Like the shack they had just passed, except that this was bluewashed instead of whitewashed, Great-Grandmother's home sat back at the edge of the thicket and waited for them. And at the door, standing bent yet tall —

With a murmured 'Excuse me!' Harriet ran ahead of Mr. and Mrs. Trindle, in at the gate, up the path, across the rickety porch. Great-Grandmother was holding her off with big, trembling hands, and gazing at her with wet old eyes on a level with her own. Great-Grandmother was folding her close, against a white kerchief that smelled of soap and sun. Great-Grandmother was crooning huskily, 'My own li'l gran'!'

In a moment she was recovering her poise and bowing to the Trindles. 'Y'all come a far piece!' she said politely. 'I'm right glad fuh see you. Come in. Come in an' res' yo' hats.'

The imp appeared, surprisingly divested of her steer, seized their hats and bags, and deposited them on the bed, at whose foot already stood the suitcases that had gone on ahead. Soon Mrs. Trindle was swaying in the single old rocking-chair and chirping about the orange and brown velvet marigolds she could see through the open door, and Mr. Trindle was easing his trousers over his knees and sitting down on a stool and clearing his throat and asking the imp, 'And who might this young lady be?'

The imp, sheltering herself behind Great-Grandmother, squirmed as if she were going through setting-up exercises and inspected her hands as if they were brand new. Great-Grandmother dragged her forth with a large kindliness. 'Lily, ain' I tol' you-all to be mannersable to ladies and gentlemen? — E's de drift dat lives wid me, suh.'

'*Drift?*'

'Yessuh. No fader, no mudder, no home. Just a li'l drift.'

Harriet's eyes and brain were clearing and steadying. She was in the cleanest of cabin sitting-rooms. Its walls and ceiling, its doors and shutters, were tidily papered with fresh magazine and newspaper pages. The doors and windows were curtained with white cheesecloth, which blew out lazily because there was no glass. The uneven floor was gay with rag rugs, and a neatly quilt-covered bed filled a quarter of the floor space.

And Great-Grandmother? She sat on a stool before the fireplace, the drift between her knees staring goblinlike at the company. Granny, in a patched calico dress and a white kerchief and apron and headcloth. Granny, whose old face was like those of proud bronze statues Harriet had seen: high, carven nose flaring strongly at the nostrils; eyes deep-socketed; cheek planes flat; mouth long and cleanly cut, flexible for speech and laughter, firm for closure. Granny, fit child of Moses.

The rest of the day sped like a strange dream. Dreamlike, surely, that Harriet Freeman, of Minneapolis, should belong in this sleepy cabin with its fireplace of clay and sticks. Strange that her only kindred should be an old woman who looked like an Ethiopian princess and spoke a language bewildering to the ear.

Lily, the drift, showed Harriet the immediate surroundings. Grinning and darting ahead and capering back, she led the way down through the thicket where the mockingbirds sang, parting curtains of gray moss as she went. She darted out upon a sandy beach and the fiddler crabs scuttled into their holes with an elfin patter, lugging their grotesque 'fiddles.' She jabbed a small finger toward a gray shack standing on stilts above the water. 'Oystershuckin' fact'ry!' she announced, finding her voice again.

Far away a whistle shrilled. 'Da's where at ey cans s'rimps,' she said hoarsely.

Sea smells; lush swamp smells; perfume of unseen flowers. Harriet came up on her toes and spread her arms wide and sent her voice spiraling upward exultantly, as they turned back toward the cabin.

The deep dust of the back yard had been patterned like an engraved tablet by the feet of Granny's motley crew of hens. The hens pecked busily around the door, and a hound, Caesar, thumped his tail to greet them, and a cat, Snowball, stretched herself in the long rays of the sun. With her small stomach importantly thrust out, the drift picked up an armload of brush and deposited it beside the kitchen fireplace.

Granny was stooping above a kettle that swung over the fire. She smiled at Harriet.

'Hopes y'all hungry!' she said, uncovering an iron spider that steamed amid the embers. 'Granny done fry y'all a chicken, honey chile.'

'I never was so hungry in my life,' Harriet said with conviction. 'What's the other good smell, Granny?'

'Hoecake, honey? Sho' y'all knows hoecake? Or does you maybe mean de sweet 'taters?'

Granny served the supper on the crowded kitchen table. She took from her trunk a yellowed linen cloth and spread it with careful hands. The dishes she placed on the clean, darned fabric were cracked and miscellaneous. One plate was old blue, one was cheap pink, the rest were ten-cent-store white. But the flavors were such as famous chefs might lick their lips over.

After they had eaten, Harriet wiped the dishes, and they all sat on the porch a while, none of them saying much. Even Mr. Trindle's conversation petered out, and he politely covered one yawn after another until Granny, gently thudding in the rocker, rebuked herself.

'Y'all tired out. I ain' got no sense, neither no manners, tonight. Reckon I cain' study nothin' but my li'l gran' ' — she patted Harriet's shoulder — 'But y'all come a far piece an' you needs yo' rest.'

With ill-concealed eagerness they went in. Mrs. Trindle's eyes gleamed as she contemplated the bed. What can be more beautiful to the traveler than smooth, white pillows and a crisp, white sheet hem competently turned over the covers?

Granny folded back the pieced coverlet. It was far too warm for a quilt.

'Harrie, do look!' Mrs. Trindle exclaimed through a yawn. 'Wouldn't they be wild over that quilt in Minneapolis? And the bedstead, too. Hand-made. And — yes,

GRANNY

sir! cords instead of springs. — Mrs. Freeman, how long
have you had it?'

Granny chuckled deeply. 'Honey, don' go askin' me
how long. My fader fetch me here jest after Marse
Lincum turnt us loose. An' here I been ever since, an'
dat dere bed wid me. An' I pray de Lawd E lemme stay
here twell E call me home to Heaven.'

'If you were up North, they'd be pestering you to sell
that bed,' Mrs. Trindle said practically, caressing the well-
rubbed wood.

'Law, honey, don' nobody hanker after ol' truck like
dat when ey kin get shiny gol' ones,' Granny protested.

'But, Granny, haven't you read how crazy people are
for old furniture and things? In the cities up North?'
Harriet asked shyly.

Granny laughed a rich laugh that shook her tall body
and sent her earrings glinting in the lamplight. 'Y'all
funnin' yo' ol' granny?'

'Funning you? Why, no, Granny. Surely you've read
about it yourself.'

'Hab mussy!' Granny said amusedly. 'I cain' read,
honey chile.'

Harriet's heart plunged. It seemed — outlandish — to
have a grandmother who couldn't read. Harriet Freeman,
member of the Honor Society at Centennial High. Harriet
Freeman, whose father had been a university graduate
and whose mother had been valedictorian in normal school.

Without hope she murmured, 'You mean — your eyes
aren't strong enough, Granny?'

Granny shook her head comfortably. 'Ain' never read
an' write, honey chile.'

Harriet lay on her pallet on the floor a long time that
night, staring through the darkness that lay like a thick,
hot blanket over her, and thinking how strangely everything had turned out: Landers School and Granny's

'homestead' and Granny. No, not Granny herself. She was as stately and beautiful as an old woman could be. Even her folded coif was stately, not unlike an Egyptian headdress, when one got used to it.

But — Granny's illiteracy! Harriet could not subdue a sick shame at thought of it.

To live with it was unthinkable. She would be as good as she possibly could, during the few days before the Trindles must start homeward. Then she would go back with them and make better use of her opportunities than she had ever done. She would really work with all her might at her dear music, so that some day she could compose something that should hold the magic sounds of sea and wind and birds, and even of the frogs she could hear through the dark, drowsily; the magic sounds and the enchantment that held them all.

Once a week, regularly, she would write to Granny. She quivered at the thought that R. Corwin would have to read those letters to Granny. She hoped she need not meet R. Corwin.

The frogs piped and the chorus of the crickets rose and fell through the sultry darkness, and Harriet was asleep.

III

R. CORWIN

HARRIET woke reluctantly when Lily, all dressed, stepped carefully over her, carrying her own folded bedding to the rail of the back porch to air.

The atmosphere was still as steamy as a Turkish bath, but Harriet felt her hunger stirring when she sniffed the rich smells of coffee and baking breadstuff. Granny was bending over the hearth again, shifting a hot sheet of metal where the flat corncake was baking.

While the Trindles were bestirring themselves, Granny killed and dressed a chicken and set it frying in a three-legged iron spider in the fireplace. In another pot green pods bubbled, with a ham bone to flavor them.

'You mean y'all ain' know *okra?*' Granny answered her query in amazement. 'Honey chile, wha' kine of vittles does you-all eat up No'th?'

The church house, Granny told them at breakfast, was a far ways and the weather looked juberous — so heavily sultry. 'But Preacher Smith gwine fetch you,' she added with a pleased smile. 'So us better get ready tereckly.'

Five people preparing for church in two small rooms made a gentle bedlam: dressing behind doors, stumbling over each other in unconventional attire, continually needing something that had been left behind someone else's door.

Betweenwhiles Lily fed the hens and the young 'critter,' work ox, Nicodemus, and threw scraps to Caesar and set a saucer of milk for Snowball. And Granny stirred and tasted and seasoned savory dinner dishes and packed a huge basket and attended to the milk — 'Neighbor chile done milk fuh me.'

Lily had had her bath on Saturday, she informed Harriet. Today she needed only a washing and the rebraiding of her small pigtails. Harriet counted twenty of them, each rising straight from the center of its own little patch, each patch bordered by an even brown pathway. Granny unwrapped one braid at a time and combed it, while Lily writhed and rolled her eyes to make sure that Harriet appreciated her anguish; then Granny rebraided and rewrapped it. Clean long stockings were pulled on Lily's thin legs and held up with firm twists of cloth; a patched and skimpy dress, beautifully ironed, was dropped over the pigtails. She was finished.

Thereupon she flew around importantly, helping others. The pump was in the back yard, and she rode the squawking handle again and again, and lugged in pails of water. Dumbly she pointed out the two square inches of mirror on the kitchen shelf, and Granny's clean fragment of comb. Open-mouthed she watched Harriet use her own comb and toothbrush and powder puff and rouge.

'Preacher Smith,' tall and portly and golden brown, was tapping at the door during the last bustling hurry, and he bowed them out to the rusty automobile that chugged and shivered in the road. The two ministers and Lily crowded into the front seat, and Granny and Mrs. Trindle and Harriet wedged themselves into the back, smoothing themselves down as compactly as possible, so that the crowding and the moist heat together should not quite wreck the freshness of Sunday clothes. Even the moving car gave no illusion of coolness today.

'Approximately what would you opine to be the dimensions of this enchanting little isle?' Mr. Trindle inquired.

It became immediately apparent that 'Preacher Smith' also enjoyed conversing. He did not slacken till they drew up before the church, and by that time the guests found themselves as fully informed as if their noses had been buried in a guidebook.

The island, said the minister, was fifteen miles long and four wide, and had a population of some thousand Negroes and fifty white people. In early days the famous Sea Island cotton had been grown here, and made the plantation owners rich. Boll weevil and the fall in the price of cotton had ended its great value as a crop.

At the close of the Civil War the land had been sold to the freed slaves at a nominal price — about a dollar an acre — in small farm tracts. In many cases their descendants still held the same ground, growing garden truck, cane, a little cotton, a little rice. But many of them had fallen behind with their taxes, and much of the land had been sold from under them by Northerners who used it for winter homes and hunting preserves. Of late it had also been in demand for truck gardening.

'If our people could only hang onto their land,' Mr. Smith concluded. 'They could have a mighty nice life here, mighty nice. Fish and s'rimps and oysters for the catchin', and rabbits and partridges ——'

He sent his old car bucking and shivering through the white coral dust. Harriet was thankful that they were late. At the church house, set far from any other building in the misty, gray wood, she found swarms of new faces turned toward them. She was glad that they must press through the waiting groups and take their seats without pausing to talk. With smiling, gold-toothed bows right and left, 'Preacher Smith' led the visiting minister up to the platform and opened the service.

Jericho Church had no hymnals, no organ, no piano, but it had music that swept its oblong, whitewashed box like an ocean tide of splendid sound. Harriet had heard spirituals all her life, but never anything quite like the great ebb and flow of these. 'Great Day, the righteous marchin', God gwine build up Zion's wall!' — 'Oh, Lawd, come by here!' — 'Let your light shine over!'

Feet beat time, bodies swayed, the close, hot church throbbed with the rhythm like a pulsing heart.

The pastor introduced Mr. Trindle, who read the Scripture, looking smaller, darker, larger-eyed than ever in the dimness of the church. The pastor preached, and the whole congregation nodded and sighed and moaned and called, 'Amen!' and 'Hear him, Lawd!' The pastor called for prayers, and Harriet felt her great-grandmother stir at her side and gather herself together and stand.

Through half-open eyes Harriet could see the big dark hands clenched on the bench-back. Granny's husky voice broke on the murmurous congregation. 'Oh, dear King Jesus,' she prayed, 'we done come yere to praise Yo' Name!'

'Praise de Lawd!' someone echoed.

'When de way seem dark, Lawd Jesus, an' it look like us all alone in dis big worl', he'p us to remember dat You ain' never fuhgit us. Forgive us our foolishment, King Jesus!'

'Do, Lawd, do!' the voices chimed in, and the church pulsed again with the patting of feet.

Fans fluttered more and more rapidly as the service went on; and at its close people detached their shoulders cautiously, with a ripping sound, from the seat-backs, and went outdoors, where it was scarcely cooler.

Dinner was served under the great trees, on planks set up for tables. Busy, jolly women heated kettles and pails of food on a stove in the detached kitchen — though Harriet wondered how anything could possibly have got cool in this atmosphere. The congregation stood before the well-filled board and sniffed the savory steam that rose from a score of dishes, until Mr. Trindle had asked the blessing long and sonorously. Then hearty voices and high laughter were set free in a great burst of sound, and the busy, jolly women poured hot coffee and loquaciously urged food on the assembled people.

'Mo' collard greens, Rev'end? Mo' s'rimp?'

'Lawzy, Mis' Freeman, y'all ain' eat *nothin*'. Reckon you just too proud of yo' gran'.'

'Sis' Brown! Got some mo' Hoppin' John in that dish?'

The fat, jolly women waddled gaily to and fro with their savory dishes, their brown faces dimpling like pricked bread loaves. The thin jolly women skittered to and fro, quick as bantam hens, and shrieked with good-natured laughter. The men shouted and slapped their knees and guffawed. And everyone ate as fast as possible. To Harriet it seemed like a big, rollicking picnic; and she thought it was good to have it all tied to the little whitewashed church.

There were girls among the diners, but not many. They edged away from Harriet and averted their eyes when she looked at them. There were boys, in noisy clusters.

One boy Harriet particularly noticed. A grizzled hound with a tattered ear got up from the ground when this boy came out of church, and pressed an adoring nose into his hand. Lily had run to him, too, and he had swung her up on his broad shoulder as if he were used to teasing and petting her. He ate across the table from Harriet and some distance down, and she looked at him whenever she had a chance.

He was tall and slim, with a good, strong flash of white teeth in the warm brown of his face. His head was well shaped, and the tight rolls of curly hair that covered it made Harriet think of the curls of the old Greeks. His neck was a trifle too long, though it could stand extra length, it was so strong and round. He wasn't exactly handsome, but his eyes were: straight-looking, brown eyes with gleams of amber, almost hidden by thick lashes when he laughed. Harriet had observed that people with eyes like that didn't need much else to make folks enjoy looking at them. As to his clothes, his trousers had been worn shiny and his clean shirt was patched; but his orange necktie was knotted with firmness and a certain style.

Harriet cleared her throat two or three times before she succeeded in asking Lily: 'Who is the boy down the table? The one with the orange necktie?'

Lily had been eating with amazing speed and capacity. Now her well-picked drumstick shot out in the boy's direction. 'Who? Him?' she asked, her mouth full of chicken.

Harriet blushed. She looked down at her plate and pretended to be greatly interested in the collard greens there. 'Hush!' she whispered, and glanced furtively at the boy. He had heard Lily. He was grinning at her, a question in his glance.

'Dat-dah one?' Lily persisted.

'M-hm,' Harriet assented in a strangled voice. 'But, Lily, *don't point*. For goodness sake don't let him know we're looking at him.'

'Why, dat Richie,' Lily announced in a penetrating whisper, rolling her eyes cautiously toward the subject of discussion. 'E too nice, dat boy. E de bes' boy dey is.'

Harriet ate rice and shrimps as if there were nowhere in the world a tall, brown boy with laughing eyes and an orange necktie. She simmered with embarrassment.

RICHIE

She simmered with heat, too. The air was heavy and still, the trees motionless, the curtains of moss motionless.

'Isn't it — sort of breathless weather?' she asked Mr. Trindle, who stood at her other side.

The Reverend Mr. Smith leaned across the narrow table and answered, and his voice was anxious. 'It's portent-i-ous weather. My radio says this mo'nin' that the big sto'm's headed toward Florida, but I'm thinkin' we might get hurricane winds here.'

('Radio!' thought Harriet, 'how out of key with this sleepy island, this far Jericho Church!')

Mr. Smith was rapping the board with his knife-handle. 'I don' know but we-all better put out fo' home as soon as we are through eatin', brothers and sisters,' he announced in the hush that followed his gavel. 'Look a pow'ful lot like sto'm.'

The confusion of laughter and clattering dishes and talk gradually swelled again, but Harriet noticed that eating was quickened, and that people began to melt away, walking, or jogging through the woods in mule-drawn wagons or carts.

'Lily and I would just as soon walk,' Harriet suggested to Mr. Smith, 'and then there would be room for some other grown people. — I'd love to walk,' she added hastily, 'if Lily knows the way.' Mr. Smith looked dubious, but Harriet persisted; she wanted to see as much as possible of the island before she went back to Minneapolis.

'Sho' I knows de way,' Lily said indulgently.

'Thank you kindly,' Mr. Smith agreed. 'I'll likely meet you befo' you arrive and fetch you the rest of the distance.'

Because it was so hot, big girl and little one walked slowly. Lily strutted with pride and kicked up spurts of fine white dust with her clumsy little shoes. Harriet lifted her hat to let the air reach her damp forehead. A heavy silence blanketed the island; even the mocking-birds gave only an occasional fretful flute from the thickets.

'Y'all ever tas'e wil' grapes?' the child asked. 'I knows whah at dey's some big ol' vines.'

She darted from the road into a thicket where thick-bodied vines climbed high in the trees. 'Dasn't shin up in my Sunday clo'es,' Lily said wistfully, eyeing the clusters of shiny fruits overhead.

Harriet ran and leaped in air, swinging up a long arm. She clutched a cluster and handed it to Lily; got another for herself. The fruit was the more piquant because it had so little pulp and so much seed. Again and again Harriet leaped and brought down treasure.

A long pennant of moss brushed her cheeks as she stood eating, and she looked around her: everywhere the moss was swinging and the branches were waving.

'Reckon us better git goin'!' Lily said uneasily, and led the way through the copse.

Harriet went leaping along beside her. Heavy vines swung in her face. Long, thin vines caught at her ankles and twisted round her legs, pricking and tearing.

'I — didn't — know — these woods were — so deep!' she gasped.

Lily stopped stockstill. 'Dey — dey ain'!' she faltered. 'Reckon us done gwine de wrong way.'

Without discussion they wheeled in another direction. Still the woods stretched on. Harriet lifted her eyes apprehensively to the uneasy branches, for a sudden twilight fell, as if the sun had set or sea birds flown across the sky.

A new sound struck through the rush of wind and the creak of branches: a great roar of sound — boom — boom — boom! The woods thinned ahead of them and they dashed out upon a little ridge.

Lily burst into a wail. The ridge overlooked, not the

road nor someone's cane or cotton patch, but long lines of angry, steel-gray waves that came thundering in on the rush-grown beach.

'I don' know whah us at!' Lily sobbed.

The rising wind wrapped their skirts around their legs, turned Lily's over her head like an inverted umbrella, drove the salt spray into their faces. And then, as if the sky had broken, the rain poured down and sent them staggering back under the trees.

Lily cowered against Harriet, shaking with fright, and for a moment Harriet, too, gave way to panic. This was unlike anything she had ever known. Lost, it seemed, in a tropic storm!

She shook herself together. Lost on an island fifteen miles by four? Nonsense! They must have been running lengthwise of this narrow strip of woodland. If they struck a course at right angles to the beach, surely they would soon come out into the open.

An explosive report followed by a screech and swish sent them leaping. That sound could be nothing but the fall of a mighty tree limb, and a warning that the woods were no safe refuge. They pushed onward.

Wild screams of the wind lashing the trees, crack of branches, rush of rain, roar of driven bay waters! Harriet plowed on, Lily's cold, wet paw in hers. The grasp of the wind, suddenly seizing them and carrying them on across stubbly ground, told her that they had come out into a field, at last. She put her mouth to Lily's ear: 'Which way now?'

Lily, eyes screwed tight, shook her head and sobbed. The wind pushed them on until their lungs labored for breath. The rain drove through their clothes. Harriet braced her feet and tried to stand. She had never dreamed of such noise and fury. The whole world was one screech and bellow, one mad, buffeting, tearing clamor.

'Lie down!' she told Lily. 'Lie down till we can get our breath.'

A strong hand closed on her shoulder. She twisted around and looked up into the face of the boy Richie. The old hound cowered against him, head and tail tucked low.

'Oh, Richie!' Lily hiccoughed, burying her face against him. 'Oh — Richie!'

Tacking this way and that, Richie guided them across the stubble field, through a cane patch combed flat by wind and rain, in at a door that the wind almost snatched from its hinges.

'Praise de Lawd!' cried Granny. 'Mistah Trindle! Preacher Smith! Dey's here! De chillen here!'

For it was Granny's own cabin they had reached. Granny and Mrs. Trindle, gray-faced with fear, drew them into shelter, and Mr. Trindle and Mr. Smith turned back with obvious relief from the front door.

'Dey gwine fuh hunt y'all,' Granny explained, feeling Harriet and Lily with shaking hands. 'Go in behint de do' an' git you on some dry clo'es. Richie, reckon y'all do efn you wrap a coat roun' you? — Oh, praise de Lawd! I so purely scairt, honey chile!'

The seven people huddled round the fire as best they might, the girls and Richie shivering in spite of themselves. The storm was a monster, wrenching the trees, tearing the shakes from the roof, pulling at the doors, driving a spray of rain in at every crack. Above its wail and shout Harriet heard all at once the cackle of hens; and looking through the holes in the walls she dimly saw the henhouse turning somersaults across the yard; skittering along, bounding in the air, crashing against the fence.

The cabin was shadowy, with its windows shuttered. Granny lighted a lamp, muttering little prayers as she did so. The feeble flame flickered cheerlessly. The rag rugs rippled in the wind that blew through the broken floor, and lay in little drifts against the walls. Mr. Smith knelt by the bed and prayed aloud, and Mr. Trindle stood and added to his petition. Granny raised a spiritual and they all joined, though they could hardly hear their own voices. There was comfort in singing, 'Oh, Lord, come by here!' even to the accompanying screech of wind down the chimney, the battering of rain, the pelting of oranges on the roof; comfort, though the frail shack groaned and swayed around them.

Wind and rain lulled at last, and Granny opened a shutter and peered out. She fumbled it shut again, and when she turned, Harriet saw tears coursing down her face.

'Po' ol' fig tree!' Granny said huskily. 'Done went down dis time. Weathered lots of heavier sto'ms, but now it done fo'.'

Mr. Smith was buttoning his coat. 'Better go now, in this interval,' he said, and shook hands and departed.

The others grouped themselves round the door, which Richie held ajar, and listened till a series of muffled explosions told them the reverend car was still able to work.

Lily had been holding tight to Richie's sleeve, and when they turned back she demanded irrelevantly, 'Richie, how-come y'all fin' me 'n' Hayet?'

A deep flush reddened the smooth brown of Richie's face. He grinned, and the warm amber in his eyes glinted sidewise at Harriet through his furry black lashes.

'We-ell — reckon ol' Jess trail' you,' he improvised, twisting the old hound's ear gently. 'Couldn' make 'm quit, nohow. So I went along to see if she'd got track of a rabbit.'

Granny chuckled.

'I ain' like the look of the sky,' Richie said frankly, 'neither the feel of the air. And when Lily turned off through the woods, I reckoned Miss Harriet might get scared in the storm. It wasn' much outen my way.'

'Oh, do you live near?' Harriet asked. She wanted to say something casual: it was so silly to feel embarrassed before an ordinary island boy.

'Sho' nuff!' Lily answered promptly, nestling against him. 'E live nex' do'.'

'Why, honey chile, y'all knows Richie,' Granny said in her comfortable way. 'E done write letters to you-all.'

Harriet looked at him blankly and shook her head. 'You must be thinking of someone else,' she protested, her voice thin against the storm.

Richie pulled his close-cropped curls with his free hand and made a quaint, foot-scraping bow. 'No'm, Granny ain', Miss Harriet. Ain' you recognize me? I'm R. Corwin.'

IV

Young Granny

R. Corwin! It astonished Harriet to have her vague picture of a middle-aged woman fall suddenly to pieces and reshape itself into this boy with his slim length and broad shoulders and laughing eyes. She felt queer to think he knew so much about Granny and her, but she couldn't feel vexed with him.

And he looked definitely pleased with her. They stood staring at each other until Granny said: 'Richie, dis quiet spell cain' las'. Maybe y'all better ——'

'Sho' had!' he agreed, laughing at his own abstraction. 'Better go tell Mom we all safe.' He bowed himself out of the door and was gone.

'Oh ——' Harriet exclaimed.

'E come back tereckly,' Granny responded with a chuckle. 'E de chile dat milk our cow.'

She bent stiffly to straighten the heaped-up rugs, and then busied herself rebuilding the kitchen fire, using no small fuel that could make dangerous sparks. When she lifted the lid of a kettle that stood simmering in the ashes, Harriet unconsciously moistened her lips and swallowed.

'Hoppin' John,' Lily announced, widening her eyes in

anticipation and patting her small stomach. 'Bet Richie stay to supper dis night.'

It was an hour later that a fumbling knock heralded Richie's return. Lily whirled the wooden button and opened the door, clinging to it with both hands as the wind caught at it, and slamming it to and buttoning it as soon as Richie was inside. He bore a pail of foamy milk and one of water.

'Kind of early,' he apologized, 'but the sto'm ——'

'Dat cow all right?' Granny asked anxiously.

'Fine as silk,' Richard assured her. 'Only e don' let me get much milk. Scared, I reckon.'

'Ma li'l critter all right, too?' Lily asked, rummaging in his coat pockets while he was washing his hands, as if she were used to finding small gifts there.

Wiping his hands, Richie slanted his gay glance down at her, 'That Nebuchadnezzar ain' turned a hair,' he said, looking from her to the other room as if he wanted to go in but didn't know how.

Lily thrust out her lower lip at him. 'Nicodemus!'

'Nebuchadnezzar!' Richie teased.

'Nicodemus!' Lily whimpered.

'*Nicodemus* ain' eat no grass. — Oh, have it yo' own way. — Nicodemus.' He tousled her braids and went on in.

Mrs. Trindle was rocking, and Mr. Trindle was standing, hands clasped behind his back, teetering from heel to toe while he peered at the papers pasted on the wall. He was an inveterate reader, and the only print in the cabin was the wall-paper and the Bible on the three-legged stand.

From the kitchen where she was straining the milk, Granny called, 'Set down an' res' yo'se'f, Richie!'

He let himself down onto one of the stools and blinked rapidly at the scallops of newspaper that trimmed the mantel.

Harriet liked shy boys. With them she dropped the

scornfully indifferent manner she had for the more aggressive ones.

'I never did really thank you for saving us from the storm,' she said, raising her voice above the noisily increasing blasts.

Richard jerked his foot and tilted his chin as if he were making a bow sitting down. 'The pleasure was all mine!' he shouted.

Involuntarily they both laughed at his informal formality.

'Show him some of those kodak pictures, Lily,' Harriet suggested.

Lily, sitting on the floor with a sheaf of snapshots in her scanty lap, edged over to Richard's knee and thrust a picture at him.

'The Lincoln Memorial,' Harriet explained, leaning toward it. 'I took five rolls on the way, and had them finished while we were in Charleston. Lincoln Memorial came out pretty well, didn't it? It's — well, it's so beautiful it makes me feel awfully queer. I never felt that way about a building before, though the Empire State in New York — May I have the pictures a minute, Lily?' She shuffled through them and showed him the one she had taken from the tower.

'I seen Savannah oncet,' Richard said, looking respectfully from the picture to Harriet. 'Savannah's right pretty, but it ain' got nothin' like thisyere.'

The wind had risen high again, and Richard hitched his stool closer so that he could hear and be heard. Mrs. Trindle tied an apron over her chubby brown voile and joined Granny in the kitchen. Mr. Trindle made his way placidly across one wall, tipping up his head to read through the bifocals; when the wind rushed away for a moment they could hear his deep hum and Mrs. Trindle's cluck and Granny's husky murmur. Richie's voice, or

Harriet's, would blare out into the unexpected stillness.
Then the wind would be back again and the rain pounding,
and the two would raise their voices a notch higher, talking
as if to someone in the next house.

Lily stood first on one bare foot and then on the other,
behind the young people. Her mouth was open with
interest and wonder and her big eyes rolled toward
Harriet as she spoke, toward Richie as he answered, back
to Harriet, while she took them across the fifteen hundred
miles from Minneapolis, with the pictures for illustration.

'I ought to have a megaphone, and then I'd feel like a
sightseeing bus sure enough,' Harriet said, sitting back
and laughing weakly when she had reached Charleston
and her last snapshot.

'Y'all got any pictures from yo' home town?' roared
Richard.

'Oh, yes. I brought my memory book to show Granny.'
— Harriet prodded her suitcase from under the bed and
lifted a bulky scrapbook from it. 'This is Mr. and Mrs.
Trindle's house, where I live' — Richard stared hard at
the comfortable verandaed house — 'and here's our
school' — he sucked in his breath — 'and here's the
basketball team I play on. And Glee Club ——'

'*White* chillen?'

'We don't have separate schools. Separate places on
the street-cars and trains, either. There aren't so very
many colored people in Minneapolis. Goodness, I never
did see these — these Jim Crow compartments until I
came South. They make me feel like some kind of animal.'

Richie looked at her gravely. 'Minneapolis must be
like heaven,' he said.

Harriet laughed, shaking her head in vigorous dissent.
'Jiminy, no! We get snubbed plenty. — They are fair to
us in school, though. I played for the Glee Club, and all
the singers were white girls and boys. If you make good

you get the credit.' She tilted her stool sidewise to see what was on the page he was inspecting. 'Oh — those are our crowd: the kids I went round with. Iva and Helen' — she pointed to one after the other — 'are my best friends; and there's John and Dave and Jimmie.'

'Look mighty grand,' Richard said disconsolately. 'Dressed as nice as white folks.' He held the book closer, studying the boys' faces, their smart clothes. He glanced with polite interest at the girls, but returned to the page of boys.

'Which of theseyere —— ?' he asked constrainedly.

Harriet laughed. 'Which do I play around with? Well, mostly with this one: Jimmie. His dad's a doctor. Jimmie's going to be one, too, if he ever gets around to it.'

'Y'all spilin' yo' eyesight, chillen!' Granny shouted at them. 'Y'all better light de odder lamp.'

Richard, his face drooping, sprang to get the small lamp and light it with one of the twisted paper spills that waited on the mantel. He set the lamp on the three-legged stand beside the Bible and they drew their stools closer to its feeble yellow arc.

'You haven't told about your school,' Harriet remembered, thinking how strange memory book and pictures and favors and programs looked in this dimness of shuttered windows.

Richard's teeth flashed more happily. 'I go to Booker, over on St. Catherine's Island. Row myself over ev'y morning. Booker's great. Ain' no such a big place as yo' school, but it's sho' nuff great.'

'What kind? High school? Boys' school?'

'All kinds. Somethin' like Hampton. You-all knows Hampton. Booker teach us how to farm our land good and grow good critters and make good houses. Teach us how to mend our carts and make harness and fix shoes. Teach the girls how to cook and keep house nice.'

'But doesn't it have — well, lessons like algebra and history and — and English?' Harriet floundered, trying to be polite and at the same time to find out what she wanted to know.

Richard's face puckered in a rueful smile. 'Reckon y'all think we don't get no English, sho' nuff. It does seem like the islands and the coast got a diff'ent kind of talk, and it's hard to change it. Yes, m'm, we studies books along with crops and carpenterin'. It's a grand school.'

He unfolded from the stool as he spoke, and took from Granny's hands the bright pie tins of food she was carrying. Looking to see that Mr. and Mrs. Trindle had been served, he offered a tin to Harriet, 'pulling his foot' as he did so. The other tin he held out to Lily, with exaggerated deference. She giggled and shook her head. 'Gots to he'p Granny,' she said.

When all were provided, Mr. Trindle's resonant voice asked the blessing, and they ate.

Hoppin' John proved to be a concoction of rice and peas. Seasoned with slivers of red chili and hot from the kettle, it was no mean dish. The usual hoecake came with it, nutty and crisp; and hot cocoa.

Harriet sat at ease, relishing her food, feeling cozy and secure with the wind and storm trying to get at them and failing. She watched Richie thoughtfully in the dim light, her brows puckered. His eating manners were not repellent, even though he did break many rules of etiquette, holding the whole piece of cornbread on his palm to butter it, and dipping it carefully into the cocoa.

'Lily chile,' Granny rebuked the drift during the course of the meal, 'ain' I tol' y'all to don' leave yo' spoon in yo' cup?'

Richard hastily took his own tin spoon from his own tin cup and glanced sheepishly at Harriet. 'Yo' Granny is the most mannersable woman!' he murmured.

She leaned nearer him so that she need not speak so loudly, and said, 'I wonder why she should be!' She had noticed herself that Granny had no uncouth ways: some that were strange and old, of course, like taking snuff. But even the snuff Granny managed neatly.

'Maybe y'all can get her to tell about her great-grandpa,' Richard said, as if that would explain everything.

'Moses?'

He nodded, swallowing hoecake. 'Seems like Moses was quality. 'Sides which, Granny's folks was house servants. Mine was field hands. Made a differ'nce, that did. — Moses' white folks was dog-mean in they hearts, but they was mannersable, and they learnt their Negroes nice ways, and sense, too. Yo' Granny ain' even study signs like most island folks — good-luck things and bad-luck things. My land, she don't care if you put yo' hat on the bed, even!'

Harriet glanced abstractedly at the bed and her hat. 'And yet Granny can't read or write.' She spoke wonderingly, forgetting her shame. No one but Richie and Lily could hear, even with her voice pitched high, for the rain was roaring again and the wind furious after a brief lull.

'Folks say Black Moses could read and write some other talk like nothin' ever seen hereabouts. Like enough it ain' true.'

Harriet screwed thoughtful brows. Would there be any chance to get these stories from her great-grandmother before starting home? Not with Mr. Trindle talking on and on, gently, steadily, with a roll of fine, well-chosen words like a phonograph record. Mr. Trindle talked all the time he wasn't reading.

He had been talking between bites, though no one seemed to hear him. Now, when the noise outside suddenly withdrew as if it were worn out, his voice emerged placidly on the comparative stillness: '—— never experienced so violent a conflict of the elements.'

Granny bent an anxious gaze on him. 'I ain' exackly git de words,' she confessed.

'Mr. Trindle says he never saw such a storm,' Mrs. Trindle interpreted briskly. 'And I'm sure *I* didn't.'

Granny's eyes narrowed into a far look and she shook her head. 'Dis li'l wind an' rain ain' been nothin',' she said indulgently. 'Hit ain' been nothin'.' Her bowed shoulders quivered. 'De Gre't Sto'm, way back when my gran's was all bofe baby-chillen — dat was a sto'm, sho' nuff. One of 'm been dis chile's pa,' she recalled suddenly, with a fond look at Harriet. 'I could tell you-all big tales of dat sto'm, sho' nuff.'

Outside, the fury had remained a while away, leaving only a steady fall of rain on sodden ground. Inside, the fire crackled pleasantly. Plates and cups were empty.

'Oh, Granny,' Harriet begged, 'do tell us about it. We can wash up the dishes afterward.'

'Hit too old an' far off,' Granny dissented.

'Your personal reminiscences of the disaster would be of great interest to us all, Sister Freeman,' Mr. Trindle urged, tilting back his stool so that he could cross his knees.

Granny looked at him admiringly. 'Rev'end, you-all sho' got de gif' of tongues.'

'Granny, *please* tell us!' Harriet pleaded, hitching her stool over close to the old woman. Richard muttered, 'Excuse me!' and tiptoed to pile wood on the fire, for the storm had made the air clammy. Granny stroked Harriet's hair tenderly. Lily's head nudged jealously into her and she stroked it, also. Her eyes were on the flicker of flame.

'Hit de wuss sto'm ever I knowed,' she mused aloud. 'I mind it good. A young woman I was den — risin' thirty-fi' — ; an' pow'ful, else you wouldn' be here dis day, honey chile. — Us done pick de cotton, me and yo' gre-granddaddy, and ready fuh dig de sweet taters. Hit come like de sto'm today, on'y se'm times wuss ——'

The firelight sent the shadows leaping across the ceiling, shrinking down to the floor. It glittered on Mr. Trindle's gold spectacle rims and on Mrs. Trindle's brooch. It illumined Lily's wondering eyes and dropped mouth, and Harriet's intently knitted brow as she sat with elbows on knees and chin in hands, gazing into the fire while she listened, or turning to look with wonder and sympathy and admiration into the face of Granny, now impassioned, now anguished. It shone on Richard, whose eyes rested most of the time on Harriet; on her intense and lovely face; on her long, strong, sensitive fingers; even on her warm-colored, prettily made dress.

Granny told the story in vivid, simple words, as if she were thinking aloud, and the little group of listeners were so carried along by the narrative that they lost all sense of the cabin, the time, and were with Lucy Mary Freeman in 1893.

She had been living with her husband in a cabin on this very site when the great storm came. With them had lived their son and his wife — eighteen or nineteen years old — and their two children, Harriet's father and his baby sister.

The hurricane had come from the West Indies and smitten them with unleashed fury. The sea had risen twelve feet above the high-tide mark, covering much of Gentlemen's Island and the other islands. The sea swept up in a lashing fury of spray, and the skies opened and let down blinding torrents of water, and the wind hurled itself, shrieking, across the land.

— 'Us soon see hit ain' no common sto'm,' said Granny, shaking her head in fearful recollection. —

Her son went out to try to save the critter and the

cow. Minutes passed. The girl wife staggered out to look for her husband. Granny's man rushed after her. None of them came back.

Granny had looked down at the little baby, sleeping peacefully, 'in dis se'fsame bed, min' you!' and at Harriet's father, clinging to her knees and whimpering with fear, and she saw that their lives depended on her.

— 'I had it from de Lawd!' she said solemnly. —

She knew the cabin must go; but in the yard were trees; and in the trees, she felt, was her only hope. There was not time to get to the Big House — No, it must be the trees.

The chinaberry was out of the question: shallow-rooted, it would be jerked loose in an hour. But there was a live-oak, huge, old, clinging deep and tenaciously.

The cabin was groaning like a living thing, rocking as if in torment. Granny snatched up the baby, bundled her in a quilt, tore a stout homespun sheet with a mighty wrench of teeth and hands, and bound the strips around the cocoon of quilt and baby.

— 'E li'l brack head like a li'l brack flower in de midst!' Granny crooned, and her eyes were wet with tears after forty years. —

She opened the door, the baby girl in her arms and the two-year-old boy catching at her skirts. They were in the midst of a howling fury. She held the baby to her breast so that its breath should not be snatched away. Even Tommy's crying was wrenched from him and he was gasping and voiceless.

Granny ran for the oak tree, but even amid the harrying of the wind she lost the feel of Tommy's hands on her skirt. She went back and picked him up from the ground and carried him under one arm and the baby under the other. She fought her way to the oak and cowered against its trunk for breath.

How could she climb it? Climbing a tree took more than legs, and both arms were filled. Could she leave one child while she bound the other in the branches? She dared not. Pine shakes from the roof, stones from the chimney, hurtled through the air. Between her powerful teeth she gripped the strong homespun of the baby's bindings, swung Tommy like a sack under one arm, and climbed into the twisting, writhing, trembling tree.

Up among the broad branches, she tied the baby securely with the homespun strip, as she had planned. She tore her stout petticoat into more strips and trussed Tommy to another branch. She wedged herself into a place between them and waited. — She waited. Drenched and shivering, she waited.

Always she watched for any sign of her husband, of her son, of his young wife. But with no hope. For a while she could make out the dim shape of the cabin; then it was not there. The chinaberry tree was not there.

Shrieking clamor of wind. Pouring rain. Beating flood. Nightfall: grayness grown black. — Daybreak: blackness grown gray.

— 'But, Granny, what did you do all the time? What did you *do?*'

'Ain' do nothin' but pray de good Lawd Jesus. Ain' nothin' else fuh do.' —

Probably a day and a night she clung there. Then, doubtless, something struck her on the head, stunning her. At any rate, she found herself hurtling along in the wildness of black water and lost consciousness again. In the morning she was picked up among the wreckage on the shore near Bosquet, and carried into a building there.

— 'Honey chile, hit dat Wash'ton Hall at Landers School! Dat God's trufe!' —

When she was taken back, frantic, to Gentlemen's Island as soon as relief boats could go, they found the old oak one of the few trees standing on the island. Among its branches hung two-year-old Tommy, without sense or feeling, and the baby girl, dead.

— 'But Daddy never told me.' 'E ain' mo'n se'm year old when dem whi' folks took 'm up No'th,' Granny explained. —

No building on the island was left standing; not even the Big House; not more than a half-dozen trees. Half the people were dead. Disease took added toll because of the unburied bodies. That is, they were buried close to shore, and the tides soon uncovered them.

— 'My folks, dey says, "Die by water, Lie by water."' —

The few mournful, half-naked survivors worked painfully, burning the marsh sedge that had buried their farm tracts and their unharvested sweet potatoes, building shelters from the wreckage of cabins and houses, from the wreckage of a ship that was thrown ashore by the tempest. The Red Cross, with Clara Barton working in person, brought food and clothing. Granny and Tommy were given two pecks of grits and two pounds of pork each week.

With Tommy to live for, Granny had worked like a man. Neighbors had helped her raise a new cabin — this cabin.

'An' I root aroun' an' I root aroun', an' what y'all think I finds, all bruck up amongst de trash? Disyeah bed and deseyeah stools. Dat why I hope de good Lawd lemme keep'm twell I dies.'

Richard cleared his throat respectfully. 'Ever I hear tell that the first wild beanies came up on Gentlemen's after the sto'm.'

'Beanies?' Harriet asked, stirring like one waking from a long dream.

'Some calls 'em Po' John 'n' Polly. Them wild bean plants that stan's higher'n your head. — From seeds the waves fetched from far-off lands,' he added, dreamy eyes on the fire.

Young Granny

Mr. Trindle drew a long breath and pulled his watch from his pocket. 'Ten o'clock!' he proclaimed in his full round voice.

Harriet got up and staggered to the door, her feet sound asleep and heavy as lead. She pulled open the door a crack. After the tumult and confusion of the evening's story it was a surprise to find the wind almost dead and the rain falling heavily, quietly.

V

'SHO' NUFF?'

ALL that night the wind blew fitfully and the rain fell, but the next day dawned as peacefully as if storms had never been.

Granny and Harriet threw all the shutters wide to sun and air, and spread the bedding over the porch rails to catch the sunshine. Drenched ground and drenched wood steamed as the day drew on.

Green oranges sprinkled the scanty wet grass in the front yard, the mud in the back. The big-lobed leaves of the uprooted fig tree had not yet begun to droop. Granny hobbled around it, shaking her head, as she thought of the little green thumbs of fruit that would never thrust out from it, never ripen to richness, again.

The hens, which had perched disconsolately in their broken coop, came clucking and singing for food. Caesar thumped his lank tail in the sun, and Snowball rubbed against their ankles with a silken hum of flattery. Nebuchadnezzar-Nicodemus bunted Lily exuberantly. Butterflies like living flame danced on the orange and brown marigolds.

As soon as the old live-oak had dried out a little, Harriet clambered up among its branches. She clenched her teeth, holding the homespun strips that bound the soft bulk of the baby. She gripped the limp wriggle of little Tommy under her left arm until it ached. She dragged herself up with her right arm. She spread her toes inside her oxfords. — Here — here! this might be the right branch for binding the baby girl. This for the little boy. And here she could wedge herself ——

'Harrie, dear, do be careful of that good skirt!' Mrs. Trindle cautioned from below. Harriet's fierce frown relaxed and she laughed and adjusted the skirt and placed her feet more carefully, so as not to scar their smooth leather. She had been, not Harriet but Granny — Lucy Mary Freeman, barefoot, clothed in linsey.

She settled in the gnarled branches, among the polished little leaves and the long streamers of silvery moss that hung down like the silver trimmings on a Christmas tree. The hurricane could be the theme of a symphony. Its crash and moan and roar swept through her ——

Morning sped, and afternoon.

'Do you think you can adequately complete your visit with your great-grandmother by the day after tomorrow, Harriet?' Mr. Trindle asked.

Harriet soberly studied a rag rug. 'I feel as if it were sort of running away. When I think of Granny, with that baby and my father ——'

'My dear child, you must not cloud the issue with irrelevant facts,' Mr. Trindle advised. 'Some undertakings are unnecessarily onerous.' — Mrs. Trindle folded her small mouth tight, and her nod agreed with him — 'Even in the North, I grant you, we have our handicap. But there is no soul on this green earth who has not a handicap. Some have poverty. Some have the curse of great wealth. Some have ill-health. Some, my dear Harriet, have the greatest handicap of all, which is to have none — nothing to build bone and sinew of the spirit. Now we have the handicap of color in a white country. Some of us think about it so much that it hides all other handicaps from our minds, as a dime can hide the sun if held close enough to the eye. Color is not the only disadvantage; it is by no means the greatest one; but if you were to remain in the South, Harriet, you would double it, at least.'

Mrs. Trindle slid into his pause-for-breath. 'Granny is comfortable and contented, with Lily to love and to run errands for her, and this Richard ——'

'There is one matter' — Mr. Trindle rolled the words from his tongue slowly but without relish — 'that it may be necessary to investigate. I chanced upon it yesterday while following the course of a serial story around the walls. It has considerably troubled me.' He was pushing back behind the headboard of the bed as he spoke, and Mrs. Trindle was following. 'It may have been attended to long since,' he said doubtfully, laying a long forefinger on a newspaper pasted in the corner.

Harriet sidled along the bed so that she could see. The newspaper sheet held gray columns of fine print, and at the point of Mr. Trindle's finger the name, 'Freeman.'

Harriet read, her brows knitted: 'Freeman, Lucy Mary: Gentlemen's Island, twenty acres, improved.'

'What's it about, Papa?' Mrs. Trindle inquired.

The finger traveled to the top of the page and pointed out the caption, 'Real Estate Sold for Delinquent Taxes.'

'Y'all fin' sumpn eyesightin'?' Granny asked politely from the doorway.

Harriet gulped and blurted out her question: 'Granny, this says — Granny, did you know your place had been sold for taxes?'

She gazed at Granny desperately, but the old woman did not look surprised or frightened: only sad. She smoothed down her gingham apron and stared across the bed at the newspaper as if she could read it.

'So dat's whah e went to. Richie, fetch me de paper an' read 'm off to me, and I fold'm away on a shelf. Reckon I done pas'e 'm on by mistake sometime.'

'But, Granny ——'

'At what time was this occurrence, Mrs. Freeman, if I might be so bold as to inquire?'

'Long time ago,' Granny said vaguely.

'And have you heard no more about the matter? Has there been no attempt to — to remove you from your cabin?'

Granny's fingers shook as she straightened her head-cloth. 'No, suh, ain' nobody come near. Reckon de good Lawd gwine keep 'm off twell I's through wid dis earth.'

Harriet looked more closely at the paper. There was no date remaining. Rather blindly she stood staring while the others edged out into the room again. A small hand slid into hers.

'Hayet!' Lily whispered. 'Don' y'all crave to see de ocean? Spec' Richie want to take y'all, but I knows de way good as him.'

Harriet was glad to go, to get away where she could think, or maybe just feel. So she followed numbly as Lily capered on ahead. Burs rode her skirt hem, to claw viciously at her legs; thread-and-needle twined its tearing length around her ankles; cockspur worked in between oxfords and stockings; showers of water from the wet brush drenched stockings and draggled skirt. She gave them no heed.

And then Lily, grinning back at her, pressed through a tangle of vines, led up an unexpected bank of white sand and over a ridge, and presented the ocean.

'Ain' e *too* pretty?' cried the imp.

In long lines of jade the breakers swept in, topped by curling white foam as far as the eye could see. Endlessly they broke on the narrow strip of sand where lay no mark of man. On the landward side of the narrow strip the ridge was topped with a fringe of wild grain, slanted by yesterday's rain, its heads translucent in the low sun. There was no sound but the call of sea birds and the break of the waves.

Lily romped along the beach gathering shells into her skimpy skirt. Harriet stood looking as long as she could stand it, and then dropped on the sand and hid her face and cried.

It was beautiful here, but so different; so lonely. It was a world into which she did not fit. She could not stay here; she could not. She could not go to that school, with girls who spoke another language and had lived another life —

But neither could she take Granny up North. Her small annuity would not care for the two of them there. And what would become of Lily if they were to attempt it? Yet if Granny's home was in danger ——

Lily tugged at her arm, got down on her knees, and pulled away her shielding hand and stared solemnly.

'Y'all — hongry?' She clasped her thin hands reminiscently over her thin stomach, as if that were the first cause for tears.

Harriet dabbed at her tears and sniffed. 'No. Are you?' she asked, her voice thick with tears.

Lily shook her head. 'Never no mo'. But, Lawzy, ain' I use' to be befo' Granny took me, down to S'vannah.' She rocked back on her heels, her skirt drawn tight around her bare ankles, and her face assumed a look of grave experience.

'Savannah? Did Granny get you in Savannah?'

'Preacher Smif, e fotch me. Caze I ain' belong to nobody. E fin' me eatin' vittles somebody frow to de dogs.' She giggled eerily.

Harriet shivered.

'I don' min',' Lily assured her. 'I ain' hongry no mo'. But I use' to cry an' cry. An' Granny use' to cry an' cry, too. — E glad to God, sence you-all done come to'm.'

Harriet scrambled to her feet and washed her swollen face in salt water that stung. That was the heart of the trouble. She meant everything to Granny.

Lily had stayed where she was, squatting on the sand, watching Harriet with shifting elfishness and pity. Now her head pivoted like a bird's, and she jumped up and ran toward the sand ridge.

Harriet wheeled, face and hands dripping, as the child swung possessively on Richard's arm. He was carrying a banjo slung over his shoulder, and the old dog Jess shambled at his heels.

'Done milk Granny's cow,' he explained. 'She reckon Lily taken you down along this way. She say y'all might like to see the sunset — it mighty pretty — and then come home to supper.'

'You play?' asked Harriet, trying to divert his eyes from her tears. 'Do play something, please.'

Richard stood at ease and thrummed his banjo. Thrummed old tunes that fitted the blue-washed cabin over the hill; queer tunes that Harriet had never heard. With the twang of the banjo came the soft low croon of words in a voice as rich as Jersey cream, or liquid and exultant as a meadow lark's song.

She listened, fascinated, until he paused and stretched an arm seaward. The sun was dropping, copper-red, into a low bank of cloud. They watched it fire the immensity of water before it, spreading a burnished golden pavement to their feet.

'Richard,' Harriet asked suddenly, 'what do you know about Granny's place being sold for taxes?'

'Reckon I know all about it. Way back in 1928, must 'a' been, when I was a young chile. Rich white man from up No'th — Yankee — he come projecking round and buy up a heap of thoseyere small farms that's back on their taxes.'

'Isn't there some law about owners having the first right to redeem their own property, though?'

Richard shrugged. 'They call it "double tax." Ain' many got cash-money to pay double tax.'

'Then why's Granny still in possession?'

'Seems like the rich folks up No'th got pow'ful po' all of a sudden, and thisyere white man ain' got money to build the grand house and stables and all.'

'But any time he wanted to, he could just put her out?'

'Reckon so. Lots of other folks in the same fix. Only I got my plans.' — Richard's glance kindled — 'If he hold off a few mo' years, till I done learn enough at Booker, I'm gwine teach my people how to farm so good they can pay taxes and git back the land.'

He stood tall and straight, unconsciously plucking chords on his banjo, and the last rays of the sun lighted him to copper.

'No place on this whole earth better to live, seem like, if on'y my people learn the good ways. Y'all cain' hardly know how po' most of 'em live, Harriet. Ain' had no chance. And that's what I want to do. I want to he'p 'em get a Rosenwald School. You-all knows Rosenwald Schools?'

Harriet nodded. The wealthy Mr. Rosenwald had established a fund from which half the cost of an adequate school building could be drawn by any community which would raise the other half itself.

'Then I want to be a Gov'ment teacher right here on Gentlemen's, and lead my people out into a grand new life on their own land.'

He halted in his eloquence and grinned at her self-consciously.

Harriet stared at him. She'd never seen a finer-looking boy. He looked like a leader.

'But, Richie,' she protested, 'you oughtn't to stay on this little tiny island all your life! Why — why, with your voice and — and everything, you could make a name for yourself up North, where you'd have some chance.'

Richard shook himself as if his own bright dream were fading like the golden pavement across the water. But Lily broke the momentary silence. She hurled herself on Richard, glaring over her shoulder at Harriet.

'E ain' gwine up No'th. E ain'! Efn you-all got to go off an' leave me'n Granny, you anyways ain' got no call to take Richie, too.'

Richard let go a sigh. 'Y'all — gwine back, sho' nuff?' he asked wearily.

VI

First Day of School

Richard's face had been the face of a leader looking toward the deliverance of his people. Now the joy had dropped from it as the sun had dropped from the sky, leaving him somber as the sea.

He glowed again when Harriet spoke.

'I'm not going away,' she said slowly. 'I'm going to stay and go to Landers School.'

Harriet had not known that she had decided until her own words told her so. The rest of that evening it seemed to her a good decision. Granny was so happy — 'I glad to God, honey chile. I glad to God' — and Richard and Lily; and the night was so mysteriously beautiful.

After supper they all sat out on the front porch. The two young people sat at the end and talked softly, so as not to disturb the older ones — or be themselves disturbed. Harriet told of the wonders of Minneapolis and St. Paul; wonders she had never recognized before: the chain of lakes, the high, wooded banks of the Mississippi, Minnehaha Falls, the marble loveliness of the Capitol, the art galleries ——

Richard had never ridden on street-car or bus or train;

never even in an elevator. He had never visited museum or gallery. He sat clasping his knees and looking out through the dusk where mocking-birds continued to call now and then.

'It never seem real to me befo',' he said dreamily. 'Folks come a far piece — across the sea, even — and visit Booker and tell us suchlike tales; but ever befo' it seem like readin' in a book. When you tells it — a young chile like we-all — then it do seem real.'

He touched the banjo strings with a gentle finger, and the soft bite of the notes blended with the throaty voices of Granny and Mr. Trindle, the dove moan of Mrs. Trindle; with the contented munching of the cow, not yet put in her shed; with the calls of birds and the swelling and diminishing chorus of the crickets and the plaint of frogs — even with the glimmer of fireflies. Harriet could not untangle the elements that had bound her here: the drowsy mystery of island days and nights, the majesty and pride of Black Moses, and beautiful old Granny.

At the young people's end of the porch, talk ceased. The banjo went whispering on; Richard hummed, and Harriet joined in. For a little while the soft voices murmured together. Richard sighed deeply, happily.

'Why'n't you-all sing befo'?' he demanded. 'Girl, y'all sing good as me. Don't know but you sing better!'

Next morning, Harriet was less certain of her wisdom. Mr. Trindle talked to her soberly, rolling his eyes up through the upper section of his glasses because she was taller than he — a fact which he would not, however, acknowledge.

'In the North, little girl, we enjoy comparative freedom of motion and a sort of equality; while here — No, I am fearful — if you will pardon the colloquial term, my dear Harriet — I am fearful that you are biting off more than you can chew.'

'I'll chew it!' Harriet vowed. 'I ought to be able to

stand anything for a year. And in that time I ought to find out what can be done about Granny and her place.'

'And your music?' Mr. Trindle persisted, blinking rapid eyes up at her.

'There'll be something I can practise on ——'

But it was a heavy gray day, inside and out, and it grew heavier and grayer as they took their farewell of Granny and Lily and Richard; as they steamed across the steely waters to Bosquet; as they motored along the black highway to Landers; as they made arrangements in the office for Harriet's tardy registration.

Today the campus was humming with life and activity, yet to Harriet it could scarcely have been more desolate. When, early that afternoon, she turned from the entrance gate and hurried stiffly to Washington Hall, the air pressed down on her unendurably. It was not soft, today; it was sticky. Beyond the draperies of gray moss Harriet could see the heavy gray of the bay. Crows swept across the gray sky, cawing hoarsely, and buzzards wheeled endlessly above her. The wind moaned through the trees and the bay moaned on the same dull, suffering pitch. Harriet tightened her lips as she went in at the door and climbed the steep stair.

For Mr. and Mrs. Trindle's car had vanished down the leaf-dark tunnel of road. They were on their way to Minneapolis. And she, Harriet Freeman, was a student enrolled in Landers School and shut away on this morsel of an island off one of the most remote corners of her country.

She frowned ferociously and snapped open a suitcase. She had pushed aside the blue calico curtain of her corner closet and was inspecting its half-spools nailed up for hooks, when she heard a mouse-sound at the door. She wheeled. A small, thin girl in a sack-like dress of bright red and pink, stood in the entrance, bent under the weight of an ancient straw bag and a matting suitcase.

'I MOSSIE CLAPP, F'M GREEN CO'NERS'

The small girl said breathlessly, 'Dee say downstairs I duh come to disyeah room.' She leaned out into the hall, rapidly counted doors, and nodded. 'Disyeah room.'

'I suppose we're room-mates,' Harriet said without expression. 'I was just about to hang my things in this closet. Does the other suit you just as well?'

The girl stared at Harriet with a dropped lip, and rolled big eyes from one corner to the other. 'Dee all bofe nice,' she sighed.

'We'd better introduce ourselves,' Harriet said unsmilingly, slipping a dress on one of the wire hangers she had brought and hanging it in her triangular cubbyhole. 'I'm Harriet Freeman, from Minneapolis, Minnesota.'

Another of those doubtful, blinking pauses. — 'I Mossie Clapp, f'm Green Co'ners. — Ain' nevah lef' mah home befo'.'

There was a frightened catch in her voice. Harriet glanced at her and away again. She was thin and obviously undersized for whatever age she might be. She was the imp Lily with a few years added.

Methodically Harriet hung her dresses: a brown-and-white checked taffeta; a striped organdy; a white Swiss with blue dots; a brown-flowered tan voile; a print; a wool skirt; sweaters; a semi-formal frock of brown chiffon, swirling over orange. As she picked up the chiffon, she saw that Mossie was shielding her own garments from sight, thrusting her body between them and Harriet, while she scrutinized each of Harriet's dresses with astonished eyes. Mossie's clothes did not take up half the hooks in her small triangle: two dresses — Harriet shuddered at the purple-and-yellow, the poisonous green — and nightgowns and underwear of sturdy, plain muslin.

Harriet took last from her suitcase the framed photographs of her father and mother. She looked for a place to set them. There was not even a dresser in this cubicle.

But there were nails in the board walls, and she contrived a way to hang the pictures near her bed, where she could see them early and late. Below them she thumbtacked an enlarged snapshot of the Trindle house. She had to frown more ferociously than ever when she was fastening up the pictures, and at the first clamor of the gong, she turned and ran out of the room. A glance at her wrist watch had told her it was the dinner bell.

She had never felt more alone than when she strode swiftly, head high, the length of the campus. Mossie was scurrying behind her, but Harriet felt too desolate to speak to anyone. Miss Francis, the principal, met her and placed her at a table with four other girls and Mossie, introducing them all.

The dining-room was gray from the clouds. Half the girls at her table were new, and the other half laughed and talked among themselves. Harriet was not hungry, and the food did not tempt her: okra and tomatoes and boiled potatoes and small portions of pork, with applesauce for dessert. She played with her serving, and made herself look around the room as if she were happy and quite at ease.

Of course there were attractive girls within her range of vision. She picked out a serious little dumpling with wide-set eyes and pretty manners; a willowy girl with a beautiful, tragic face; a large-framed, kindly one who made her think of a young edition of Granny; an arrogant one, modishly dressed, who regarded the scene coldly, under drooped lids. But at her own table there was no one who attracted her; and when they had finished eating and filed out, Harriet marched back across the campus alone, her head a half inch higher than before.

When she stepped in at the door of Washington, that blended odor wrapped itself around her, adding to her sense of suffocation: the musty smell and the sweetish damp smell; smells of wet vines and wet flowers, and ancient, worm-eaten wood, and the salt sea.

She rushed into her room and started to slam the door so that she might throw herself upon that narrow little bed and cry. — But she must not close the door: this was Mossie Clapp's room as well as hers; Mossie Clapp, a being out of another existence. — Harriet would have liked to crawl under the bed, but her two suitcases were there, since there was no other place for them. She sat down on the edge of the bed instead, and clenched her hands tightly together.

'Well, where under the sun did you hail from?'

A light, clear voice sounded from the door, and Harriet looked up, astonished, and into the ironic eyes of a girl who might have come from Minneapolis. Jauntily she stood there, a thin hand on each side of the door and feet nonchalantly crossed, and grinned at Harriet in delighted surprise.

'Minneapolis,' Harriet said feebly. 'Where did you?'

The other girl lifted her eyebrows and tossed her head in a comical gesture of uncertainty. 'Why — just here and there,' she replied, dropping boyishly on the other bed. 'Born in Jamaica. School in New York and Charleston. Mother was teaching French in Charleston, but she got a sort of bug to come down here — that was from Miss Bates, the music teacher here. She goes to Charleston one day a week. So we're trying this for a year.'

Harriet studied her with quickened interest. 'You mean you're going to go to school right *here?*' she asked, unconsciously patting the bed beside her.

'Sister, you don't know the half of it. Mah room's raght nex' do',' she said, impishly imitating the regional accent. 'What's your name, neighbor? We might as well get set without wasting any time. I can see we're going to save each other's lives, practically.'

Harriet told her, still regarding her with relieved amazement.

'And I'm Johnnie La Rocque, in case you want to know. It started out to be Jeanne, because we're part French; but I'm all for Johnnie. Fits me a lot better.'

Johnnie wore a boyish shirt, a well-tailored jacket suit, sport oxfords. The outfit suited her clever, singular face and straight, black, short-cut hair, just as the nickname did.

And her cool breeziness had swept away the heaviest of the clouds in the little room. Harriet clasped her knee and smiled at Johnnie, and told her how she had been missing Helen and Iva and Jimmie and the rest. She told her about Gentlemen's Island and Granny, and how, forty-three years ago, a young Granny in drenched linsey had been carried half drowned into this very hall. She even told her about Black Moses.

Johnnie laughed delightedly. 'My gosh, it sounds like a story-book! It isn't going to be so hard to get going here, after all. There's a teacher that's keen, too: white, but she can't help that. I mean, she's awfully young, for a teacher, and ought to be fun. And there are some swell-looking girls. — Oh, hello there!' she broke off cheerfully as Mossie Clapp sidled into the room. 'Come along, Harriet, and have a look at my diggings. Then we can see whether Mother's in her room.'

Both girls smiled at Mossie as they departed, but the smile shut her out instead of taking her in. Already, thrust together by the strangeness of their situation, the two were practically a closed corporation.

Mrs. La Rocque had a small suite at the end of the hall. Johnnie signaled her with a tuneful triple knock and escorted Harriet in. In spite of the severe wooden walls and the common furniture and the bleak wind that rattled the old-fashioned windows, the room seemed flooded with

sunshine and gaiety. Harriet couldn't see why, except that
the thin yellow curtains made a sunny glow and a chubby
copper teakettle jigged and chuckled on an electric plate
on the stove. The three women who looked up at the
girls' entrance added to the sense of coziness, one of them
curled up on a divan among yellow and orange cushions,
and all of them sipping tea from yellow pottery cups.

'Mother,' said Johnnie, when she had greeted the other
teachers, 'just lookit what I've found!' She pinched
Harriet's sleeve between thumb and finger and led her
forward triumphantly. 'This is Harriet Freeman. She's
from Minneapolis, so she comes pretty near being a darn-
yankee.'

Mrs. La Rocque grinned piquantly. Her high-curled
pompom of hair and the style of her dress were French
in their suggestion, and she looked the urbane gentlewoman; yet her small, amber face with its enormous
dark eyes held a trace of Johnnie's *gaminerie*. 'I'm glad
you've come, Harriet,' she said. 'I told Johnnie she'd
find friends here. Miss Bates — Miss Anthony — may I
present Harriet Freeman?'

Harriet bowed. Miss Anthony, plump and sunny-colored and gay among the plump, sunny-colored gay cushions on the divan, showed two rollicking dimples and said
that Harriet had enrolled in her physics class.

'And Miss Bates teaches the music here and directs the
Glee Club and such matters,' Mrs. La Rocque observed.
'I don't know whether you're taking music or not, Harriet.'

Harriet murmured that she had not decided. She was
dubious about piano lessons at two dollars a month. Personally, this Miss Bates attracted her. There was an
obvious patch on Miss Bates's crisp gingham dress, as if
patches did not matter to her; but she carried herself
with distinction. She was so thin that her shoulder
blades showed plainly through her clothing, and the thin-

ness made her gentle, dark face even more sensitive-looking; yet with all the gentleness, her mouth was spirited and her eyes held fire.

'Won't you girls have some tea with us?' Mrs. La Rocque asked, pouring hot water from the chubby copper teakettle into the chubby pottery teapot.

Miss Bates had risen, glancing at her watch. 'A lesson,' she said, and sighed, with a significant, 'Ella Hooper!'

Harriet frowned determinedly. 'Thank you, Mrs. La Rocque,' she said, 'but I think I must go on. I wondered whether Miss Bates would let me walk over with her?'

She would ask to listen in on the lesson. How else was she going to find out what kind of teacher Miss Bates was — at two dollars a month? And it would be less embarrassing not to sign up for music at all than to sign and then cancel.

The lesson was as bad as Harriet could have dreamed. Ella Hooper folded herself on the piano bench in such a posture that Harriet wanted to sing her the song she had learned at camp:

> 'Are you a camel, or aren't you a camel?
> And say, do you have a hump?
> Do you sit at the table
> As straight as you're able,
> Or all in a lump,
> > lump,
> > > lump,
> > > > lump,
> > > > > lump?'

Yet Miss Bates did not correct the clumsy pose after a first patient suggestion. She did not correct the awkward position of Ella's hands. She let her go on, stumbling, faltering through the lesson without any form at all. Worse, she did not seem shocked or horrified or even bored. Her voice was gentle, patient; and if Ella approached a proper rendering of an exercise, the teacher clapped softly and said, 'Better, Ella; better!'

Harriet felt her face grow hot and her hands and feet large with embarrassment. When there came a pause, she rose hurriedly, mumbling a thank you, and that she would have to go and hoped Miss Bates would let her visit her again some day.

Miss Bates made as if to speak, and then nodded quietly, with a small smile folded into the sensitive mouth corners. 'Do visit me,' she said.

'Visit *her*, yes,' Harriet muttered fiercely to herself, as she was likely to be doing when she strode, head high and brows knitted. 'I do want to visit her, for I think she's lovely. But preserve me from listening to any more of her lessons. I can make some sort of excuse to Miss Francis about paying a dollar a month to use the piano in Jaynes Hall for practising; something about catching up because I'm behind. Goodness knows I am behind, away from a piano for weeks now.'

Miss Francis permitted Harriet the practice privilege, after the thoughtful scrutiny that always made Harriet stand straighter; and Harriet practised diligently, choosing times when there were few girls in Jaynes, or none at all.

The days went on with little change in the relations between Harriet and Johnnie and the rest of Landers.

'It's sure a lucky break that you and I have the same schedule,' Johnnie observed one day when they had got permits to walk beyond the school boundaries. 'When I have to cross that campus alone I feel as jumpy as if I were running the gauntlet. Or I feel like those dreams where you go to a party in the kind of knitted bedroom slippers your maiden aunt wears. You know: as if you were exposed to the public gaze and the public gaze was finding something awfully wrong with you.'

Harriet flicked her an incredulous glance. 'I thought it was just me that felt like that,' she said. 'No one would ever believe you gave one single hoot about anybody; not even the President of the United States.'

'That's hokum, though. A front you hide behind. You look, yourself, as if it would take the King of England to bow your proud head. That was what I noticed about you when first you came into classes: the way you stared down your nose at the world.'

Johnnie giggled impishly, but Harriet looked somewhat taken aback.

'*That's* a lovable manner!' she commented. 'Like Roseanne Gibbs.' Roseanne Gibbs was the modish and arrogant one she had noticed at her first Landers dinner.

Miss Senter was emerging from the office building as they passed it. 'Let's sort of loiter and see if she won't catch up with us,' Johnnie murmured. 'D'you know, there's another person that's lonesome, or I miss my guess. She's only here to fill a vacancy this semester. She's teaching Home Ec — the sewing part and dress design, and home decoration. Doesn't she look like a kid?'

The teacher did look as young as most of the high-school students: a slender, girlish type, with blonde curled hair.

She overtook them, and fell in step with them. 'Off for a walk?' she asked. 'So am I. Suppose we join forces?'

'That would be great!'

The three tramped down the black highway and into the woods, woods that plunged them at once into a deep strangeness. Single file they pressed ahead, weaving their way between great man-bodied vines and stepping high to avoid some of the burs and other prickly things that beset them. Mosquitoes rose in swarms, whining about their ears and stinging their ankles viciously. But there was a recompensing beauty in the green dimness, the trees arching so high as to form a green sky.

At the edge of a clearing Miss Senter stopped abruptly. The other girls bumped into her and peered over her shoulders. Under the high trees lay scattered mounds of earth, vine-grown, weed-grown: little six-foot, seven-foot mounds.

'A — clock?' Harriet questioned in bewilderment. 'A — a teapot?'

'Good gosh!' shrieked Johnnie. 'There's a swell piece of old luster, or I'll eat my hat. It's broken, of course, but ——'

'I wouldn't disturb them,' Miss Senter said quickly.

Both girls gaped at her.

'It's a graveyard,' she explained.

There was a silence, in which Harriet felt herself gripped by something alien. Johnnie gulped, but she struck an attitude and saluted. 'Our dark ancestors!' she chirped.

Silently they picked their way between the graves, looking at their homely and pathetic decorations, their borders of colored glass or bright stones, their vases and teapots and plates and cups. Both fantastic and gruesome was that small cemetery deep in the woods, far from a settlement. It laid a pondering silence on them all as they tramped back to school.

'Why do you suppose they do that — put clocks and things on?' murmured Harriet, half angry.

'I've heard that they think it's a safeguard to decorate the grave with favorite possessions of the one who has died,' Miss Senter said diffidently.

'How do you mean, safeguard?'

'Why, so that the spirit won't come back and trouble the living.'

'Our people have a sweet lot of superstitions down here.'

'*Our* people!' Harriet protested. None of the three seemed to think of anything more to say.

As they reached the campus they could hear gay talk and laughter, a booming voice and snatches of song. A group of girls were studying on a bench under the sassafras tree, and laughing until they leaned helplessly against each other. Silence fell as Miss Senter and Harriet and Johnnie came in sight. The talk and laughter were clipped off as with sudden scissors, and every girl bent studiously above her book.

'Good afternoon, Willie Lou! Good afternoon, Ella! Good afternoon, all the rest of you whose names I don't know!' Miss Senter greeted them smilingly, but not until after Harriet had heard her draw a determined breath and had seen her square her shoulders.

Her small pleasantry fell into silence like a stone into deep water. Willie Lou lifted her smouldering eyes and swept the three with a hostile glance. 'Good evenin', Miss Senter,' she said coldly.

'Good evenin', Miss Senter,' murmured the other students.

When she was well past the group, the teacher shrugged unhappy shoulders. 'That Willie Lou's *bright*. But how she does hate and despise me. Why, do you suppose?' she asked, her gray eyes searching the other girls'. 'Of course none of them like me much, except maybe that cute little round Phyllodoxia, and Hannah Tomotley, and Pearlie Randall and her sister. — But with Willie Lou Bennett it's just plain hate.'

'She hates you for being white,' Johnnie answered matter-of-factly. 'Just exactly the way most white folks despise us for being colored.'

'But it doesn't make sense,' Miss Senter protested indignantly. 'Why did I come down here except that I like them?' She jerked her small head defiantly and smacked one fist into the other palm. 'And now I suppose they'll hate you for taking a walk with me.'

Harriet shrugged. 'What does it matter? They don't like us anyway. We two against the world.'

'One little, two little Injuns,' Johnnie chanted. 'Say, Harriet, why couldn't you and I room together? Let's ask Miss Francis this minute. Your Mossie isn't so bad, but you ought to listen to my Deena May. Jiminy, you can hear her laugh clear across the campus.'

'You can ask, but that's all the good it will do,' Miss Senter warned them with conviction.

She was right. Miss Francis looked at them across her neatly ordered old desk, her blue eyes a little amused, a little sorry and detached, as if no one's opinion could unduly sway her judgment.

'It would be a grave mistake,' she said. 'School isn't endurable if you don't establish yourself on a friendly footing with the majority.' She moved a book into precise alignment with the edge of her desk. 'And besides, I had hoped some of you girls who have enjoyed such rich opportunities—There are a dozen girls in Landers to-day who could give as much, in different ways, as the faculty — if they would.'

She patted the book decisively and looked up. The smile warmed her eyes. 'No. I'm sorry,' she said, 'but you must remain as you are.'

VII

MOSTLY MOSSIE

THE girls made a polite exit from the principal's office, but they stormed mutinously along the walk to Washington Hall, and their rush up the stairs and along the squeaky corridor said more than words.

For once, Harriet slammed her door. It might be Mossie's room as much as hers, but even a dog wanted to be alone sometimes.

She was so sick of hostility; so sick of being surrounded by a hundred aliens. There was Phyllodoxia, the chubby one, of course, and Hannah, who looked like Granny, and the long-legged Randalls with their innocently wondering eyes. They might all be delightful if she knew them; but she didn't know them. And most of the girls had lived all their lives on the sea islands or on the coast, a background entirely different from hers. They neither liked nor understood her, and she neither liked nor understood them. Even Mossie stared at her with dropping jaw and scurried out of her way.

Harriet threw herself heavily on her bed. She would get a demerit at inspection for crumpling her spread, but she didn't care. She wadded her pillow and cried into it, letting loose all the tears that had been gathering since she had cried on the beach at Gentlemen's. She pounded the edge of her cot with her fists and kicked the foot of it with her shoes and then lay still for a long time, not thinking, only aching.

At last she sat up and began mechanically to smooth her hair. Of course Miss Francis meant well. In theory she was doubtless right. But couldn't she see that there was no common ground for Harriet and Mossie? for Johnnie and Deena May?

For the first time she noticed that the curtain of Mossie's closet bulged outward. She got up and lifted it. What she saw was funny, but it did not make her laugh.

Huddled in the cubbyhole with her dresses hanging around her, crouched Mossie. With swollen eyes she peered at Harriet between the skirt of a nightgown and that of her poisonous green Sunday dress. She sniffled forlornly and crept out. Trying not to look at each other, the girls sat on their beds, necessarily so close that their knees touched. Mossie sniffled again. Harriet blew her nose.

'I'm jest a-gwine die!' Mossie wailed suddenly. 'I wants to go home!'

'Well, why don't you?'

Mossie stared at her over a wad of handkerchief. 'I cain'. Mammy done pick cotton an' Pappy done pick cotton an' I done pick cotton; an' us all gone widout hoecake, even, fuh git de money. Cain' shame 'm all by gwine back.'

'Don't the other girls like you, either?' Harriet asked gruffly. 'They certainly don't have any use for me.'

'Dey scairt of you. You'n' yo' fine clo'es an' yo' gran' kin' — she nodded toward the photographs. 'An' me, I's scairt of *dem*.'

'But you certainly aren't afraid of me,' Harriet remonstrated.

'I — I cain' make out yo' talk noway,' Mossie said feebly. 'Y'all duh talk so funny.'

'Oh, well. . . . We'll catch on to each other's lingo if we try hard enough.'

Harriet was thinking that Mossie's feeble drawl and hanging lip were like Stepin Fetchit's in the films. She had always thought the character an atrocious caricature. Well, there were as many different kinds of colored people as of white. Harriet emptied the last drops of water from the granite-ware pitcher and laved her hot face.

'You string along with Johnnie and me,' she said resignedly, when she came out of her fluffy towel.

After all, Mossie was more like a draggled little cat than anything else, and you couldn't leave a draggled little cat helpless.

'Wha' — wha' y'all say?' Mossie queried.

If only she would pin up that lower lip!

'Walk with Johnnie and me — sometimes,' Harriet said slowly and distinctly. 'And — I tell you what! Go with us to the picnic Saturday!'

'Thank y'all kinely,' Mossie murmured in a frightened voice.

At the same instant Harriet felt herself briskly kicked in the bend of the knees so that she almost sat down. She glanced over her shoulder: Johnnie had come in and was making a face at her, beckoning her with an imperative chin.

'It's all very well to go humanitarian,' Johnnie scolded, when they were out of earshot of everyone else, leaning over the balcony railing. 'But there's such a thing as carrying it too far. If you have to take up a protégée at all, why don't you adopt Phyllodoxia, or the baby-faced Randalls?'

Harriet tried to think of a convincing answer.

Johnnie tapped her foot impatiently. 'Well? — And

the picnic. I was looking forward to that picnic. But if your foundling is tagging us every minute, in that gingham dress that looks for all the world as if a blind and deaf and dumb person had cut it out with a can-opener in a dark room at midnight' — she warmed to her subject, her face losing its irritation in the zest of creation. 'And the colors are like pink ice cream with cherries in it, or pink stick candy with red stripes.'

They went off in gales of laughter.

'But I say, Harriet,' Johnnie observed, 'wouldn't it be fun to see if she'd look human if we dressed her that way? Couldn't we ——?'

'My, but you're consistent!' Harriet observed. Johnnie pinched her with vigorous fingers.

The next night a hundred pairs of eyes anxiously considered the heavens. The dozen Seniors had gathered on the campus to sing, as was their Friday-night custom. It was one of the soft, mysterious hours when the birds called sleepily and the moon rose red out of the bay and fireflies meshed themselves in the streamers of gray moss that hung like enchanted veils before its ruddy lantern. Voices were full and sweet and mellow, and the world held no unloveliness. And when the whole school joined in the Negro National Anthem, singing from dormitory windows and balconies, Harriet felt her heart climb.

> 'Sing a song full of the faith
> That the dark past has taught us;
> Sing a song full of the faith
> That the present has brought us . . .'

Next morning a hundred girls pulled open sleepy eyes when the rising bell rang at half-past six, and dashed to their windows to see whether it was fair. It was.

Saturday was always busy. Girls who were earning their board by extra housework were wielding strenuous brooms and mops and dustcloths. Girls who earned by washing for the faculty must hurry across to Jaynes Hall with their bundles. All the girls had washing and ironing to do for themselves, anyway, unless they had managed to squeeze it in during the week. And it was not easy to do that in odd minutes at Landers, where there was no modern easy way to wash lingerie and hose in rooms or bathrooms.

Harriet and Johnnie and Mossie went flying with the rest, cleaning their rooms, making their beds according to the exact conventions of Landers students, doing their washing, rushing back to their rooms to dress.

Mossie's dark little face was more somber than usual, with a stocking top pulled down to the brows. She had been using pomade on her hair and combing it with a heated iron comb set like a poker in a coiled handle.

'Johnnie,' she asked timidly, 'how y'all keep yo' hair so straight an' shiny?'

'It grew that way.' Johnnie was almost regretful: Mossie had looked so hopeful.

Mossie's lip sagged mournfully.

'Why do you care?' Harriet asked. 'I don't — much. I'll admit it's a nuisance to go to all the bother of straightening it and then have it wind itself up as tight as the dickens the minute a damp breeze hits it. — Especially here, where all the breezes are damp.'

'Oh, well' — Johnnie treated the matter lightly, not being personally annoyed by it — 'did you ever see white girls with their hair all curled just so, and then after they'd been out in the rain and it looked like something the cat had dragged in? — Of course not with permanent waves. But did you ever see them getting their permanent waves? They have their hair all twisted up tight and clamped to the electric light, and there they have to *sit* — anyway in the old-fashioned kind they do — looking like Medusa, for hours on end, no matter how it pulls and burns. **And** then when the operator undoes it and combs it out, like enough they say, "Horrors! it's just like *wool!*"'

Mossie cringed. Wool was a word she and her friends did not allow in their vocabulary.

Johnnie laughed at her discomfort. 'Why on earth is it so much worse to have to *straighten* your hair than to have to *curl* it?' she demanded.

'Because it is,' Harriet said flatly.

'A fellow's own handicaps are always worse than the other fellow's,' Johnnie jeered.

Mossie, meanwhile, had taken her purple and yellow dress from its hanger. Suddenly she squeaked piteously and held the skirt up to view, a gaping tear in the back.

'That won't be much of a trick to mend,' Johnnie assured her crisply.

'Mend!' Mossie stared at her, face twisted. 'I **ain'** studyin' de mendin'. Lookit de shape!'

'Why, it's just an ordinary three-cornered tear,' Harriet briskly seconded Johnnie, her voice receding as she lifted her brown-flowered voile over her head and wriggled into it.

'But dis shape, hit bad luck!' Mossie wailed. 'Hit mean a inimy done lay a trap fo' me.'

'Oh, *Mossie!*'

Mossie looked at them as at benighted beings. 'Sho' nuff it do,' she said solemnly.

Here Harriet interrupted. 'Oh, good gracious!' she cried in studied consternation, like a girl speaking a part in a school play. 'I can't have grown so much as this! Kids, would you kindly look at this dress?'

Johnnie grinned behind Mossie's back, and Mossie clasped shocked hands. 'Oh, an' e too pretty!' she squealed. 'Cain' y'all leave down de hem, m'm?'

Harriet shook her head, tugging vainly to bring the

sides of the placket together. Then she blinked and frowned at Mossie. 'Why, I bet it would be just right for you!' she cried. 'I wouldn't feel half so bad if it didn't have to be wasted.'

While Johnnie stuck out her chin and her lower lip to button her collar, surveying the pair with judicial eyes, Mossie let the dress drop over her head. 'Why, e do fit!' she exclaimed.

'Isn't it amazing?' murmured the conspirators, who had feverishly stitched it by hand, hiding it under Johnnie's pillow when anyone approached the door.

'I say!' cried Johnnie, snapping thumb and finger. She whirled into her own room and returned with a cream-colored ribbon and a pair of brown ankle hose. 'Weren't these just made to go with that dress?' she crowed, and tied the ribbon about Mossie's round head with a bow sitting perkily atop.

Mossie stood on one foot at a time to change her stockings. Her eyes did not swerve from the mirror Harriet had set on the bed.

'I don' reckon it me a-tall,' she whispered.

At eleven the campusful was packed into trucks and cars and the last forgotten box of food had been remembered and run back after, and the caravan rolled out along the black highway toward the 'main.' When they had crossed the causeway from their island they were in territory new to Harriet.

They rolled past cabins set in autumn fields, all much alike and all like Granny's, with a lovely slope of roof from ridge to front eave of porch. People sat on the rickety porches, and banana trees ruffled ragged leaves in the breeze, or chinaberries spread dense shadows, or live-oaks towered gigantic above the squatting cabins.

They passed between dark cypress swamps and swept through a ruinous gateway into a magnificent avenue

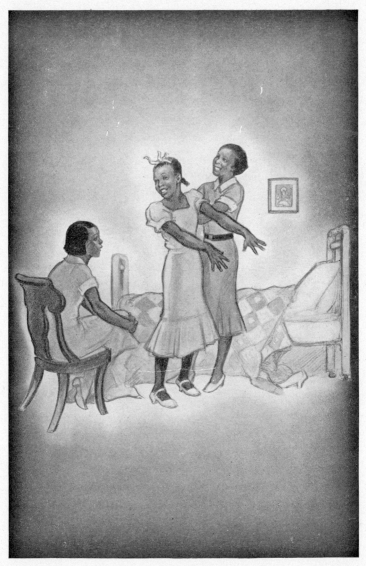

'I DON' RECKON IT ME A-TALL'

of oaks, their branches almost touching the ground and stretching along it fifty feet or more.

'Tolliver,' said Mossie.

'No!' Harriet spoke with a stifled scream. For Taliaferro — she sat erect and stared before her — Taliaferro was the plantation where Black Moses had lived and died.

She had not known that it was the goal of the day's excursion. Eagerly she stared across the broad stretches of tangled grass to the feathery clumps of bamboo through which the river glinted. Here, in an unbelievably far past, her own forebears had lived in slaves' quarters.

The picnic was served cafeteria style on the broad lawn, and when the girls had gathered up their sandwiches and salad and cups of cocoa, they formed groups for eating. Joan Senter — the girls were calling her Miss Joan, now, at her own suggestion — and Mrs. La Rocque, Harriet, Johnnie, and Mossie, made one circle. It was a congenial group, yet Harriet could scarcely keep her mind from the past to savor the present.

'*Qu'est-ce que c'est que ça?* — A penny for your thoughts, child!' Mrs. La Rocque challenged her.

Harriet unkinked her brows and looked embarrassed. 'Do excuse me. I was thinking about my great-great-great grandfather, Black Moses. He was a slave on this very plantation,' she said candidly. 'But I think he must have been a wonderful slave.'

Mossie emerged from her cocoon of silence. 'Tollivers y'all whi' folks?' she demanded. 'Dey us-all, likewise.' She sucked in her breath and stared at Harriet with the hanging lip Harriet so often itched to tap back into place. 'Y'all say *Black Moses?*'

Harriet nodded, wonderingly.

'M'mudder's granny tell 'bout Black Moses. Ever I git 'm mix wif Moses in de Good Book. A'mighty big, dey say, an' a'mighty strong, so e pull up trees wif e's han's when e mad. Y'all mean Black Moses, yo' grampa?'

Mrs. La Rocque laughed. 'Evidently he's become a colored Paul Bunyan, Harriet,' she observed.

She was studying the two girls. Harriet thought she understood that pondering scrutiny. Harriet's ancestors and Mossie's, slaves on the same plantations; and she and Mossie as widely different as any two girls in the world. After all, individuals were individuals.

And what an individual Black Moses must have been! What a personage! Harriet pictured him, a Joseph in the land of the Pharaohs: subject to them; captive; but treated with dignity, with respect, as became his rank in his own land, his personality anywhere.

They all dawdled around the grounds a while, Harriet repeopling it with great ladies and little, hoop-skirted, pantaletted girls and long-trousered boys; and dark faces above white kerchiefs; and dark arms plunged into the morass of the rice field: up — down, up — down, to the rhythm of barbaric chanting. She had to shake herself free from the phantoms of the past when Miss Francis called them to join in the games and races.

The three girls took part with equal reluctance. They probably would not have taken part at all if it had not been for Roseanne Gibbs. She primmed her little mouth and drew so far aloof as to make it clear that she had come to the picnic only because compelled, and *would not* demean herself by playing games. So Harriet and Johnnie stepped resignedly forward in response to the principal's summons, and Mossie, of course, trailed after them.

Mossie's hands shook so that she dropped all her peanuts in the peanut race; and she did not start running in the hundred-yard dash until the others were halfway to the goal. Johnnie sauntered amusedly through the events. But Harriet, though she had not wanted to contest with her hostile schoolmates, could not resist the joy of running when once she had started. She easily broke the day's record in the hundred-yard dash and in the standing jump.

'You actually impressed Willie Lou the Great!' Johnnie drawled. 'She has designs on you — she's captain of the basketball team, you know.'

Yes, Willie Lou was scowling darkly in Harriet's direction, from the center of the group that she had huddled around her for conference.

'I can't imagine that I'd want to play on a little team like this,' Harriet said stiffly.

VIII

WILLIE LOU

HARRIET, Johnnie, and Mossie filed into chapel one after the other. Except for her shoes, Mossie no longer looked as if she had been pulled out of the ragbag. She wore the brown-flowered tan voile everywhere and always, washing and ironing it with scrupulous care every two days.

'I hope to goodness she'll get her new dress done, in sewing class, before that voile is simply washed to pieces,' Harriet said to Johnnie. 'Otherwise I've got to outgrow something more, and she might catch on.'

'That dress has made a heap of difference,' Johnnie agreed. 'She's begun to clasp her arms across her chest now, when she marches, instead of trying to hide her hands somewhere. I think it's one step up from that scared scurry of hers.'

The three girls were still a study in angles. Johnnie, airily erect, sauntered with tailored skirt swinging. Harriet strode like a young goddess in bronze, head thrown back, gaze frowning. Mossie scurried forward and dropped back, round head tucked down, startled eyes rolling, shapeless shoes slapping flatly. She could not sit with the other two: they were in Senior section and she in

Eighth Grade. Separated from them, she sat hunched together as if fearing look or blow. Only when there was a general singing of spirituals was she released from her frightened self-consciousness.

Harriet, too, loved the spirituals, and because of them she liked the chapel hour. It was much like all chapel hours. Girls studied surreptitiously and passed notes and whispered with caution as students do in chapel everywhere. And the talks given by some of them were like those in Young People's meeting in Harriet's home church, when members rose and read from printed slips articles to which no one paid any attention. Here, in addition, the speakers were most of them unused to public appearance: they stood shaking and terrified and repeated their talks in high, breathless voices, having evidently learned them by heart.

Today it was different. Today the speaker was Willie Lou.

Willie Lou took her place on the platform awkwardly and began awkwardly, but her speech was no thing of rote, and it soon caught Harriet's grudging attention. 'The Uplift of Our Race,' Miss Francis had announced the subject; and Willie Lou of the smouldering eyes began like a slow fire that smokes and crackles at first and then leaps into a blaze.

'Some of yo' girls say yo' tired hearin' about race, race, race,' she accused them. 'You know when we gwine get rid of race? When we get rid of thisyere brown skin of ours!' — She thrust out her pale-palmed brown hands — 'What we got to study is how we gwine step up higher!'

She breathed hard, head forward, eyes burning. 'We got to step up higher by holdin' hands and climbin' all together. Hark to me! Every one of us that does something big; every one that writes a book or paints a picture or sings or acts or preaches — big! — we lift the whole

race. If we hang together! We don' have to try to be
white folks. We aren't white. And colored must be good
as white, or why did the Lord make 'em? But long as
nine-tenths of our folks live shiftless and know-nothin' in
dirty shacks — long as that keeps up the other tenth is
held down, too: nine hundred pounds is too big for one
hundred pounds to tote on its back. Not if it wants to get
anywhere.'

She stood for a moment, hands clenched on the reading
desk, chin belligerent. 'It's no use us sayin' the white
folks ought to educate us. White folks is a lot of 'em as
slack-twisted as colored. And down here most of 'em's dog-
poor. You know it. It's up to us to look after our own.'

Her voice rose. 'Quit lookin' to the white folks, I tell
you. They don' mind if they did drag us here in the first
place. They don' mind if they did take us away from our
people and our country. They think it's fine to spend a
couple dollars a year to teach a colored child and fifty to
teach a white ——'

Before Willie Lou had finished speaking, there were
murmurs and even hisses from various parts of the room.
The sound was like the wind after the sultry calm that
precedes the great storm. It was like flame breaking out
from beneath a blanket of smoke.

Harriet looked around her in astonishment. She had
not realized that these girls were tinder, ready for the
spark, or smouldering flames, ready for the breeze.

Johnnie nudged her, murmuring out of the corner of her
mouth: 'This gets bad, sometimes, so the teachers tell
Mother. Old grudges flare up and they lose control.'

Harriet's spine crept with uneasiness; but Willie Lou
had scarcely sat down when the tall, strongly built
Hannah got quietly to her feet.

'Hannah,' asked Miss Francis, 'have you something to
add to this spirited talk?'

'Yes, m'm. — I cain' talk like Willie Lou, but I just got to say right here that I agree with her, and I want to thank the white folks that give us a chanct to move up together like Willie Lou says. Startin' way back with Miss Landers who founded thisyere school, right down to Miss Francis and our teachers. *They* ain' never done us any harm. *They* don' owe us an education. I'm glad to God for 'em: they're givin' us all they got. If we use it like we ought to, I reckon we march up together, like Willie Lou say.'

Without a pause, her deep voice swelled out through the room in the spiritual that Harriet loved best:

'Great Day! The righteous marchin' ...'

A few at a time, uncertainly, other voices took their answering parts until at length the hundred were gathered in the tide of noble sound. Harriet did not sing: it would be awkward, she felt, to show musical ability where she did not mean to use it; but she listened with a full heart.

'Isn't that Hannah a grand person?' she asked under her breath as they rose. 'All along I've wanted to know her, but she sort of slips out of my way. — Listen! There's hardly any more of a murmur than usual. Hannah turned the trick.'

Hannah had, for the time; but Willie Lou was still simmering. She was still simmering when the Senior girls went swimming in the bay that afternoon.

The swimming instructor was Miss Joan. Harriet and Johnnie enjoyed being with her: she was almost like another girl; there was just enough distance between them to make her friendship a compliment. Harriet was eager for her first plunge in salt water, too.

The campus had its own little beach, so that the girls could put on their swimming suits in their rooms and run through the thicket and down a woodsy path to the water.

Miss Joan, being a teacher, had slipped into a robe which was a silken splash of color.

'It looks more ornamental than useful,' Johnnie objected, contemplating the orange chrysanthemum that bloomed on its back.

'That's what I'm thinking,' Miss Joan agreed. 'I'll hang it up on a hickory limb and not let it near the water.'

The tide was beginning to creep in and swish softly among the rushes. Harriet dashed through shallow water and swam the buoyant waves, Johnnie beside her, until they were well out beyond the group of neophytes.

For a long time they floated on their backs, looking up at the gentle blue of the Carolina sky, across at the columned white mansions of Bosquet.

'Aren't y'all frozen?' chattered Countess Waters from the boat, where she was sunning herself, gray with chill.

They swam over to her. She was a quiet little girl and had always held aloof from them. 'You ought to feel Minnesota water once,' scoffed Harriet, swinging the boat and splashing, while Countess's fingers gripped the gunwale. 'This is too warm if anything. But the only thing I really don't like is having to wear swimming shoes. They make me feel sissy.'

'You sure get your feet cut up with oysters if you don't,' Countess warned, watching admiringly if anxiously.

'I s'pose. Some day I'm going to try it, though. Gosh, isn't this pretty?'

Sweet gum and palmetto marched down to the beach, their green forming a crescent around the cove. Set in that frame the girls were nymphs, old ivory and gold and bronze and ebony.

'I always think we look a lot nicer than white people in bathing suits,' Harriet observed complacently.

'We sure make more noise,' Johnnie said.

The quiet place rang with shrieks, shouts, laughter. Few of the girls could swim — Harriet and Johnnie, Willie Lou and Phyllodoxia. The learners yelled with fear and delight while they balanced frog-like on Miss Joan's palm in the water and jerked inept arms and legs. They yelled with laughter when they stepped into holes. They hooted at each other. When they managed to flounder past their depth and in over their heads they came up blinded and choking and used the first breath from their aching lungs to shriek with merriment. It seemed impossible that so much noise could come from so few girls.

'I always think there's something wrong with one of our people who doesn't laugh easy and laugh a lot,' Johnnie observed, splashing Harriet enthusiastically.

'These South Carolinians are sort of different, though,' said Harriet, unexpectedly grasping Johnnie and holding her under.

'Gosh!' Johnnie spluttered, making fearful noises and blowing water out of mouth and nose.

'And I sometimes wonder whether girls like Willie Lou don't think they're crusaders or something,' Harriet went on, as if there had been no interruption, though she kept out of her companion's reach.

'Willie Lou can laugh hard enough, when there aren't any white people round. It's Ella ——'

Harriet nodded. 'I know. Bitter laughter, hers is. I don't think she's any too good for Willie Lou. — Look, Johnnie. Look at them now.'

Ella and Willie Lou stood where the water curled around their ankles, and watched Miss Joan. Harriet could see the lift and flare of Ella's nostrils, the scornful droop of her eyes. She said something to Willie Lou without turning her head. After a poised instant, Willie Lou gave a shout of laughter and leaped up the slope toward the gum tree where Miss Joan's gay coat was hanging.

'She's up to mischief,' Johnnie said with conviction.

Willie Lou was knotting the sleeves of the soft robe, the body, balling it up in her strong grasp. She took a ball-player's pose and wound up to pitch it toward the bay. But Harriet was moving swiftly, too. Before the bundle had left Willie Lou's hands, Harriet was swimming out to a point which would cross its course, and before it could reach the water her long arm shot up and caught it. With it strained above her head she swam to shore, one corner skimming the waves as she went.

She stamped up the slope and hunched the garment in the fork of a tree until she could shake her hands dry. While she was worrying loose the knots, Miss Joan ran up to her, surprise in her face.

'Why, what happened?' she asked, taking the robe and smoothing it ruefully.

Harriet met Willie Lou's glare evenly. 'I found it that way, Miss Joan. Somebody's idea of a joke.'

'Somebody had a funny idea,' Miss Joan snapped, her color flaming. Willie Lou transferred her glare to the teacher. 'Suppose you joke with my cotton one next time you feel a funny spell coming on,' Miss Joan warned, shaking the rainbow of silk and hanging it up again. 'Now who's next to try that first stroke?'

She ran back into the water, leaving Harriet and Willie Lou to confront each other. Roseanne Gibbs sauntered toward them, languidly curious, her turquoise swimming suit untouched by water. Hannah lingered near, and Countess and Johnnie.

'Teacher's pet!' Ella sneered at Harriet.

'I am not. But you think it's so smart to plague the white teachers. You knew very well it would ruin that robe to get it sopping wet.'

'Shucks! You-all are like babies that are sati'fied with a stick of candy when they've been turnt out of house an' home,' Willie Lou flung at her.

'And *you* remind *me*' — Harriet kindled with the fire of battle — 'of a dog that bites the person who pulls him out from under a car. Sure, somebody ran him down, and if he can't get at the one who hurt him, he'd just as soon take a nip at the one who saved him.'

'I don' think it was ve'y nice, Willie Lou,' Hannah added gently.

IX

BOARDING-SCHOOL BUSINESS

THE next Sunday evening service was in charge of the Seniors. They chose to hold it on the beach, since the weather was fine. Johnnie and Harriet and Phyllodoxia and Countess helped Miss Anthony gather wood for a fire, not to warm the languorous air, but to drive away a few of the millions of hungry mosquitoes. As soon as dusk had fallen, girls and faculty marched in a loose procession across the campus and down the slope. Some of them sat on logs that had been placed out of reach of the tide; most of them stood. Hannah lighted the fire, and it picked out the glint of eyes and teeth from the darkness.

'Hannah,' Miss Anthony asked, 'will you raise "Great Day"?'

Harriet loved the way Hannah 'raised' the spirituals. In chapel she always wanted to turn and watch her. The tall girl sat so serene and relaxed, her hands resting in her lap. When she was asked to lead, her gentle face glowed a little, but she looked aside, shyly, out of the window, and opened her mouth and let her great, sweet voice flow out, strong, quieting.

Tonight her voice was even lovelier than usual. Harriet felt herself carried by the harmony, and before she knew it she was singing herself. There was such beauty in the volume of sound. Even Willie Lou's voice, strident as it was, and Ella's, heavy and husky, added to the pricelessness of the whole.

Miss Anthony repeated, 'The heavens declare the glory of God, and the firmament showeth His handiwork...' Phyllodoxia shyly told a story that she had evidently memorized word for word. In her soft, breathless lisp she gave perfect finish to every sentence, every phrase.

A small breeze turned the smoke toward the log and stung the eyes of the girls there. Along with the lapping of the water and the crackle of the fire there was a gentle slapping of mosquitoes. The salt smell of the bay, the fishy tang, the sharp smell of smoke, the sweet of blossoms, all wove into story and song.

The National Anthem was the climax of the hour. As its stately words rolled out, Harriet forgot everything but the beauty of the night and the sea, and the yearning of her own people. Her round, sweet voice rang out without self-consciousness. When the anthem was ended, she was singing almost alone. Willie Lou's powerful voice and Ella's deep one were not to be heard, and Hannah was humming as if to listen at the same time.

'Good gracious, girl!' Johnnie murmured as they climbed back through the thicket. 'What a voice!'

'Chile!' shouted Deena May, 'that sho' was singin'. I mean *singin'!*'

Study hall was close and bright after the magic outdoors. All the girls in Washington and Douglass Halls were required to study in the largest classroom in the evening. The single small bulbs that dangled nakedly from cords in their cubicles were not bright enough for prolonged reading.

Harriet and Johnnie and Mossie sat in a row, and Harriet often looked up from her solid geometry to watch Miss Bates, the teacher in charge tonight. Harriet liked to study the resignation of that passionate mouth, the sadness of eyes that could light to such a dance of fun.

Now and then Miss Bates walked up and down the aisles to see that her charges were really studying. When Miss Anthony inspected, she folded her arms across her breast, and the dimple that slashed one cheek played in and out as she glanced from desk to desk. Miss Joan strode smartly in her low-heeled oxfords. Miss Bates was different from anyone else: she had a lovely walk; and her hands clasped each other loosely, lightly; and her head was high.

Tonight she stopped at Harriet's side. 'We must have you for the girls' chorus,' she said, nodding gently as she spoke. 'Aren't you ashamed, trying to hide a voice like that?'

Harriet flushed and bent her eyes on her book. Miss Bates didn't resent it, that Harriet had not enrolled with her for piano lessons. Had she heard Harriet practising at Jaynes Hall before breakfast?

The Jaynes Hall piano was not notably good, but Harriet was learning to love that morning hour. The campus was so still; trees and flowers were so watchful; and the sun came up so red out of the bay behind the industrial hall. Sometimes Mossie crept after her and sat huddled at the foot of the stair that led to the second floor. She was a strange audience, Mossie, with her feet toed in and her elbows on her knees and her fists punched into her cheeks while her big eyes wondered at Harriet's swift fingers.

Sometimes Harriet turned with a half-vexed laugh. 'Mossie, I don't see how you can *stand* listening to these scales and exercises.'

'Likes to watch yo' fingers,' Mossie mumbled. 'Likes to hear the soun's come so fas' and — and bright.'

'Listen to this, if you've got to be listening.'

Harriet improvised what was in her mind: still islands with lipping waves; the coming of storm; the scream of dying trees; the rain; peace. She looked round at Mossie. Mossie sat with lip fallen and eyes bewildered.

'It isn't any good,' said Harriet.

Now she wondered whether Miss Bates had heard her working on the Prelude in F, on the Moonlight Sonata, and had understood that Harriet couldn't waste her time with a two-dollar-a-month piano teacher who taught humped-over girls like Ella to play 'Lightly Row.'

Ella and Willie Lou were glancing at Harriet now and then. They did not usually come to study hall, but tonight they bent above their books with absorption, except when they covertly studied Harriet. Perhaps they disliked her still more, now that they had found she had a good singing voice.

In spite of them, this had been a pleasant evening, and the three companions loitered over to Washington Hall in a state of unusual contentment. Harriet lingered at Johnnie's door, the two laughing and talking. Mossie went on along the corridor, but she came hurrying back, round-eyed.

'Lawdy, Hayet!' she gibbered, 'y'all better come see what happen!' She twitched at Harriet's sleeve, scurried ahead of her, looked back at her, like a puppy trying to lead its master.

The two other girls were at the door in a moment. Confusion greeted them. The bedding had been jerked from Harriet's cot and tied by its corners into a huge, ungainly bundle which filled the space between the beds. The curtains had been tied in a series of knots. The pictures of Harriet's father and mother, of Helen and Iva and Jimmie, had been taken down and pinned on the wall again upside down. Harriet's suitcases sprawled open and empty on the dismantled cot.

95

'My — land!' gasped Harriet.

Johnnie stepped briskly over the bundle and undid the knots. Lingerie and nightclothes, costume jewelry, powder and cream, all manner of odds and ends that had been stored in the suitcases were heaped in a wild conglomeration.

'Mighty fine thorough job of stacking a room,' Johnnie commended dryly, as she began to lay the articles in place again.

'Done spill yo' powdah into yo' golden slippahs!' Mossie mourned, squatting on the other side of the heap. 'Done spill all yo' elegant perfume!'

'Stacking a room?' asked Harriet.

'Oh, I forgot you've never been to boarding-school before. Stacking a room is one of the intellectual pursuits of Betty Co-Ed. It's also a lovely way to get even in a light-hearted, girlish fashion. And when there's more in the room more can be accomplished. Such as emptying all the dresser drawers. — I wonder where Willie Lou got the idea?'

'Willie Lou?'

Bestriding the bundle, Johnnie shot Harriet a caustic glance. 'Don't be a poll parrot,' she advised. 'Surely you see Willie Lou's fine hand in all this. The criminal hasn't bothered Mossie. Also, Willie Lou was not down at the beach when we — when you — sang the Anthem.'

Mossie scuttled out into the hall, and Harriet leaped across her household goods to turn her pictures right side up. She snorted. 'I guess I can put up with tricks as well as the next one. — Only she hadn't any business touching Daddy and Mother.'

They had only begun to sort out the medley, a crowd of stocking caps and bathrobes offering suggestions, when a tap sounded at the open door, and Miss Francis's even voice: 'Well, well, young ladies!' Her nostrils were dilated.

and no wonder; the room reeked with lavender toilet water.

Harriet jumped up, anxiously untying the knots in her best chiffon hose and inspecting them to see if the rough handling had pulled their threads. 'Won't you come in, Miss Francis?' she stammered.

'Where?' Miss Francis asked — 'But I've brought you some help.' She motioned Willie Lou to come in. 'This isn't exactly my idea of Landers recreation, Willie Lou.'

Willie Lou glared at Harriet and mumbled something that carried an unmistakable sting of 'tattle-tale' at the end.

'Why, I never!' Harriet exclaimed indignantly, falling back on a childhood phrase.

Miss Francis had caught the muttered word, too. She turned back. 'No, Willie Lou. Harriet told me nothing.'

Under Miss Francis's arm peeped the round eye and dropped lip of Mossie, breathing hard.

'And I haven't the least complaint to make, Miss Francis,' Harriet said firmly, scowling at Mossie. 'Don't they always stack rooms at boarding-schools?'

Willie Lou lingered after Miss Francis had gone.

'There were two dresses you forgot to tie knots in, Willie Lou,' Harriet complained. 'And you're so good at knots.'

Johnnie snickered, a long, hissing giggle between her teeth. Somehow this time they were all laughing, except Willie Lou; and she wasn't there.

When the campus was still, that night, three girls in bathrobes crept out of the front door of Washington Hall. The buildings stood darkened, except for entrance lights and a bright window in the middle of Sarah B. — Miss Francis's window. Crickets chanted, and whippoorwills called mournfully.

The two girls were hurrying a third between them. 'I ain' done nothin',' she whimpered. 'I ain' mean nothin'.'

'Keep your little mouth tight shut for once!' Johnnie ordered.

Across the campus they hurried her, keeping in the shadows because the moon shone full and limpid. They rushed her through the thicket and down the slope and across the strip of sand, because the tide was out. The moonlight made an enchanting scene here, etching itself in the pools among the rushes.

The girls did not take time to look, but for a minute they stopped to listen. Did it come across the waters of the bay, that lovely, eerie sound? Was it sound, or was it a dream?

A phrase came clearly, a delicate march of notes — Bach. A Bach fugue. Harriet stood tranced until the music had been taken into the great orchestra of the night.

'Come on! We've got work to do,' she said.

Straight out across the wet sand they marched.

'Wha' y'all gwine do wid me?' begged Mossie.

'Do you want to gang up with us or don't you?' Harriet queried sternly.

'Sho' — sho' does.'

'Then it's high time you learned that our gang doesn't tattle. We settle our differences in more adult ways.'

They shucked off her robe and rolled up their pajamas; they made a chair of their hands and commanded her to sit on it; they walked out till they were knee-deep in the cool water.

'One for the money,' said Johnnie.

'Two for the show,' said Harriet.

'Three to make ready,' said Johnnie.

'And — four — to — *go!*' said Harriet.

Simultaneously they ducked their heads from under Mossie's encircling arms and unclasped their hands.

Splash went the water, sending silver rings widening —
widening ——

And back to Washington Hall presently dripped three
girls, arm in arm.

X

In the Library

'Anyway,' Johnnie commented, 'it makes Willie Lou seem just a spiteful, malicious girl. I thought you were a little off, calling her a crusader. The robe business, and then stacking the room; why, she's just childish.'

'Oh, well, we're all kind of childish,' Harriet said fairly. 'And as for the crusader business, isn't it sort of mixed up together? I shouldn't wonder if Willie Lou considers us traitors to a sacred cause.'

Willie Lou 'made Harriet mad.' She made her see red. Yet she could not help admiring Willie Lou's spirit and determination. Willie Lou, probably coming from a shack that held no printed page except those that papered its walls — Willie Lou, struggling up out of shanty schools and illiterate speech — Willie Lou saw visions and made her companions see them.

'But how can she help knowing that Miss Francis and Miss Joan and the others give up heaps for us all?' Johnnie fumed.

They were on their way to the old cottage which had been the home of Rachel Landers seventy-five years ago and which now housed the sewing-rooms. Here Joan

Senter was poking about in a barrel and hissing a thoughtful tune through her teeth.

'Oh. You two,' she observed when Harriet and Johnnie came in. 'Maybe you can lend me your alleged brains. I want a project, good, big, and different.'

'Expect it to pop out of the barrel, Miss Joan?' inquired Johnnie, swinging one leg from the corner of the table.

'Out of this barrel if at all,' Miss Joan assented. She dragged forth a wire lampshade frame, a stack of oilcloth samples, a mass of embroidery floss, hopelessly tangled, a swatch of tulle which crackled into a dozen breaks, like a handful of autumn leaves, when she shook it free of its folds.

'Where on earth does that junk come from?' Harriet asked, prodding with a gingerly finger. 'Look at this backless formal, would you?'

'It comes from up North. Landers simply hasn't money for Home Ec materials.'

Harriet snorted at the oilcloth samples. 'What under the shining sun could anybody do with those?'

'Oh, my. That shows how dumb you are' — the young teacher cherished them in her hands. 'These are easy. They'll make grand pot-holders to sell in the student store or the Carnival.'

'And the gunny sacks?'

'We *ask* for gunny sacks. Look, Harriet!' She pointed at a row of garments on hangers: a wine-colored dress, a small boy's suit, and another dress of hunter's green; all were of a material that suggested homespun.

Harriet twitched her brows at them. 'What's the connection, Miss Joan?'

Miss Joan jabbed a dramatic finger at them, at the gunny sacks. 'Product and source. Washed, ripped, dyed, cut, sewed, and there you are!'

'Gracious! That's what Mossie's brown and old-gold dress is? Miss Joan, you're a wonder.'

Miss Joan nodded abstractedly, picking up a comb that had flipped out of her curled topknot and thrusting it in again, while one arm went on probing in the depths of the barrel. 'Look at this,' she exclaimed, coming up with a stack of folded cretonne.

'Curtains? Somebody's whole sun parlor,' Johnnie guessed.

Miss Joan unfolded one and held it admiringly at arm's length. 'Not even faded!' she said gloatingly. 'Here's my Home Ec project in a nutshell!'

'How do you mean?' Harriet asked, tilting her head at the red and yellow flowers and the blue parakeets.

'The kitchen!' Miss Joan exploded the word at them, her small chin round with satisfaction. 'You know what the kitchen looks like.'

They did. Both had had to take their turn waiting on tables, and they had grown familiar with the huge, clean room. It was a giant room, with work-tables down the center and a giant stove and cupboards. Always in order, and always smelling pleasantly of fresh bread and meat and vegetables, it was gray and prisonlike, with its drab walls and furniture.

'Curtains would brighten it a lot,' Johnnie agreed.

'Mmmmm!' Miss Joan pounded the pile of cretonne. 'Dutch curtains, cute as a bug's ear. But that isn't all. Jersey-cream-colored walls. Furniture enameled Chinese red. The tin pails they get canned fruit in, and the lard cans and all such, painted cream and lettered for all sorts of supplies. — I think the school will allow us enough to buy paint and enamel,' she said jubilantly. 'And it exactly fits in with our section on interior decoration.'

During the succeeding class period, Harriet could see the kitchen project buzzing behind the young teacher's eyes. Sometimes it popped out of her mouth. — 'That buttonhole's puckered like a drawstring, Harriet. Didn't you ever learn buttonholes? See: like this.' — She took the doll's pajama coat that Harriet was working on. 'I think maybe it will be better to paint the containers first, so as to work the girls up to the walls by degrees.'

'Up is right,' Harriet agreed, frowning over her buttonhole. 'Those walls must be twelve feet high.'

Johnnie was making pajamas for herself, smart affairs with dizzy diagonal stripes. Willie Lou had been dissuaded from an especially violent plaid — Willie Lou was broad as well as tall — and beguiled to choose a print with shaded blue and orange stripes, up and down.

'Johnnie,' Miss Joan suggested, 'if you'd baste more you'd rip less.'

'I like an unstudied effect,' Johnnie objected.

Miss Joan smiled, and Willie Lou looked at them as if they were speaking a strange language.

'It would be pretty to line the curtains with flame color — there are so many gray days,' said Miss Joan; 'if we could afford it!'

Harriet had a free period after Home Economics, and she went into the library to do some collateral reading for her history class. That history class — Negro History, it was — made her think of the quotation about a liberal education — Mark Hopkins on one end of a log and the student on the other. Any log would be a grand school, Harriet thought, with Miss Francis on it. Harriet had always found history dull and lifeless. Now it was alive and absorbing. It even challenged her to do extra reading.

But the library did depress her. Back of its gray wood floors and pine tables always floated the tiles and waxed oak of other libraries she had known. Back of its meager shelves of books, most of them old books, glowed the well-filled stacks and huge card catalogues of Minneapolis. Here she felt the full contrast between past surroundings and present.

And today Willie Lou accented the contrast. Unspeaking, she had tramped along behind Harriet. Unspeaking, she sat down opposite her, opened a book, and rested her forehead studiously on her hands.

Ten minutes, fifteen, the two girls sat there. Harriet doubted whether Willie Lou had turned a single page. She herself read and turned pages to the end of a chapter, and then turned back to begin over again, her mind a blank. She looked across the table. Willie Lou dropped her hands to her chin and returned the look.

Willie Lou cleared her throat and asked angrily, 'Did y'all ever play basketball? The girls want I should ask yo' to come to practice. Y'all run good — an' yo' got plenty muscle.'

Harriet laughed nervously.

'Well,' she said, 'I don't know — When is practice?'

'You-all ever play?' Willie Lou repeated. 'We got a right good team. Don' need baby players.'

Harriet's face grew hot. This was one of the times when the other girl's insolence sent all her nerves hopping with anger. 'I played forward on a Centennial team. Centennial had only two thousand girls to draw from,' she said coldly.

'Why'n't you go back to yo' two thousand?' Willie Lou sneered. 'You-all sure don' fit in here so good. Why'n't you go back to yo' swell father and mother dressed up in their silks and di'monds? Why did they send you-all pokin' round to spy on us, anyways?'

Harriet's lonesomeness, her homesickness, seemed to flood over her in a great tide of pain at Willie Lou's taunting words. Her eyes were hot and she felt sick at her stomach.

'Don't you — don't you dare speak of my mother and father like that. It was a hateful trick to turn their pictures upside down. It was a low, mean thing to do!' she raged, leaning across the table to blaze into Willie Lou's face. 'They were the best father and mother that ever lived! They were the dearest ——'

Her head went down on her arms with a bump and she was crying; not silent, dignified weeping, but loud, hiccupping sobs, like a little child's.

She felt arms across her shoulders. She heard a deep, slow voice asking, '*Were?* Y'all ain' say "were"?'

She could do nothing but sob.

A gentle hand rested on her head. 'Y'all mean "were," honey?' the voice persisted.

Harriet bobbed her head a little.

'Last year — Mother——' she managed to stammer. 'Father — years ago. — Nobody in the world — but Granny — over on Gentlemen's Island ——'

'No kin but her Granny, over on Gentlemen's,' the deep voice relayed her words. 'Why, chillen, she's nothin' but a po' little drift. Fine clothes don' count — Why, honey ——'

The room had grown still. Harriet could hear nothing but her own sobs. She fumbled for her handkerchief and poked at her hidden face with it. At length she sat up, wishing that the floor would swallow her.

Girls were bent over books, tensely silent. Girls stood hunched before bookshelves. Close on one side of Harriet sat Hannah. Close on the other side sat Willie Lou.

'It — it might make y'all feel better to get out and practise on the team this evenin',' Willie Lou said gruffly.

XI

Paint Sandwiches

It was fun to play basketball again. Rules were different: Centennial used girls' rules, Landers boys'. Harriet soon grew accustomed to the change.

Johnnie and Mossie both tried out, because Harriet did. Johnnie was no player, and at first Mossie was worse. But gradually she developed something. She was small and elusive. She had a way of ducking and sliding and scurrying so that she never was where you thought she was going to be. Willie Lou said she might make a right good runnin' center if she didn't grow too much.

'Ain' gwine grow no mo',' Mossie confided to Harriet. 'Done tote too many heavy washin's fo' Mammy. I'm close on seventeen now.'

Harriet scrutinized the little creature in shocked surprise. In basketball bloomers and middy Mossie had more than ever the goblin look of Lily, the Drift.

Yet now, dressed alike, the girls seemed less alien to Harriet. Under the swaying ribbons of moss, shrieking like young savages and leaping and whirling and running in the game, they were all — just girls, whether they had come from Minneapolis or Jamaica, from New York, like

Phyllodoxia, from Charleston, like Roseanne, from Green Corners, like Mossie, from Dafuskey, like Willie Lou.

The other girls seemed to regard Harriet more as a human being, also. They had even elected her vice-president of the class in place of Lizzie Gill, called home by illness. That was almost immediately after the episode in the library. Hannah proposed her name and Countess seconded it, and Harriet felt that the vote was carried because she, Harriet, was 'nothing but a poor little drift.' — She would never have anything to do, since Willie Lou was president. Still, she did like being a class officer.

She was altogether happier. She began to feel as she had in Minneapolis, as if each separate twig on every tree she met had an especially joyous message for her; as if every smell and sight and sound were for her, personally; as if she would like to dance on tiptoe instead of walking; and as if she could eat twice as much as was on the table. In fact, she began to feel natural. She decided that it was outdoor exercise that had made the change: in fair weather basketball practice was always outdoors.

Basketball was not her only exercise: Miss Joan's kitchen project provided extra activity and promised more. As soon as the quick-drying enamel came, an evening was given to transforming cupboards and tables and stools, all the Junior and Senior girls convening the minute the supper dishes were done, and working in shifts. Miss Francis even let the last shifts work past the bedtime bell, while the ghosts of earlier shifts, in bathrobes and stocking nightcaps, watched their progress with giggles and murmured encouragement and criticism, skittering up the back stairs when their scouts gave warning of approaching teachers.

- An end of the gingerbready porch of the Home Ec cottage was fenced off with chairs, too, and carpeted with newspapers as a workshop. Here the girls painted con-

tainers and lettered them. In sewing classes they made
the cretonne curtains, lining them with flour sacks dyed
orange 'to make a sunshine on a cloudy day'; and hemmed
other sacks for dishtowels, cross-stitching them in gay
designs.

In other Home Economics class-hours Harriet was
working diligently on doll clothes, since Miss Joan agreed
that they offered good practice. Harriet had measured
the first garments and sent the size to Mrs. Trindle, and
in early November the desired doll came to fit them: a
cunning, long-legged little girl with bobbed yellow hair.
The girls flocked round Harriet when she unwrapped it,
exclaiming as they passed it from hand to hand. They all
liked dolls.

Not that they played with them; but, as other girls in
schools and colleges in other parts of the country have
had Kewpies on their dressers, or limber-legged French
dolls and grotesque cloth elephants and dogs among the
fluffy cushions on their beds, so the Landers girls had
dolls.

A Landers bed was made according to strict rule. The
spread was laid smoothly over the sheets, and the quilts
and blankets rolled or folded in neat patterns on top of the
spread. And sitting against these rolls or squares or
triangles were dolls.

Willie Lou was the only girl who did not admire
Harriet's doll without reservation.

'Oh, Lawdy!' she said, rotating it. 'Buckruh (white)
doll, just like the rest. Looks like we could have our doll-
babies colored. Looks like when we draw pictures of us fo'
the school paper we could anyways make us look tanned.
No suh! Ev'y one of those gals we draw is lily-white.
And ev'y one of them doll-babies is buckruh.'

She thrust the doll brusquely at Harriet. Harriet had
some sympathy with Willie Lou's viewpoint; she had

rather admired Willie Lou's round brown little doll, the only dark one she had seen at Landers. And she didn't resent the brusqueness: Willie Lou was cross because she was having 'the shakes.'

Harriet was anxious about the shakes. Willie Lou had had several attacks of malaria since she had come back to school in September, and each attack was a threat to the big game with Booker, scheduled for the last Saturday in November. So much depended on Willie Lou.

And not only in basketball was she important this fall. The Seniors were in charge of the Carnival, which was billed for the third Saturday, and Willie Lou was president of the Senior Class. Her malaria gave the whole school 'the shakes.'

On the second Saturday, she and Harriet were assigned, together with Roseanne Gibbs and Phyllodoxia, to paint one wall of the kitchen, Miss Joan having determinedly shuffled the usual cliques. A wall at a time was as much as the best-natured of cooks — Miss Mitty — could be expected to endure.

Roseanne and Phyllodoxia had been deputed for the part below the chair rail and Willie Lou and Harriet, both tall and agile, for the part above. They mixed the yellow paint out in the graveled space behind the kitchen, and divided it into four coffee cans. That is, three of them mixed and divided, while Roseanne looked down her nose and curled her lip at the process.

'I don't call this any Home Ec project,' she said haughtily.

'I call it a swell one,' Harriet retorted.

'Wisht I could paint up my own mother's house so bright and pretty,' Countess said wistfully from the doorway.

Roseanne led the way in, nostrils dilated. 'Where do I begin?' she asked languidly.

'Begin where you darn please!' Harriet snapped. But she cut off with a laugh the further remarks that crowded to her lips: Roseanne looked so funny in her borrowed suit of coveralls, her Lady Vere de Vere manner sticking up out of a rough-dried denim bib. 'You and Doxy can settle that,' Harriet added more amiably.

So Roseanne began in one corner and leaned forward at an angle of forty-five degrees and lifted a dripping brush from her coffee can.

'Golly, gal!' shouted Ella, stacking clean dishes in a cupboard. 'Gwine have that yeller paint all over the floor, and Miss Mitty skin you alive!'

Hannah, who also worked in the kitchen, twisted to see, while she wrung out a soapy dishcloth. Then she loped across the room with a newspaper she jerked from its storage place. 'Spread'm down good and thick, honey,' she advised, and then spread them herself. Roseanne watched from under the drooping lids of one who does a service in letting herself be served.

Meanwhile Phyllodoxia had scurried to place newspapers in her own corner, and now she began to draw the wet brush across the lead-gray wall in luscious, creamy strokes. Harriet and Willie Lou dragged a long table over against the wall, set two chairs on it, laid a plank across the chairs.

'Golly!' Ella observed. 'Y'all better make haste. Miss Senter won' like you go climbin' thataway.'

'It's perfectly all right if we keep balanced,' Harriet argued.

'Only way to reach thisyere high old wall,' Willie Lou grumbled, 'without we totes those heavy old ladders clean across the campus.'

She climbed on the plank first and balanced there, holding the can of paint in one hand and dipping the brush daringly.

'Whee!' squealed Countess Waters, cutting great loaves of homemade bread for the day's picnic and spreading them with peanut butter. 'Willie Lou, you-all mind what you're doing, or you eat paint sandwiches today.'

'I sho' got the shakes,' Willie Lou admitted. 'But you mix the paint up good with that grunnet butter and I won't mind.'

Harriet reached as high as she could and flowed a rich ribbon of color from her brush. She glanced appraisingly down at Roseanne's corner. Not so good. How could Roseanne make every brush stroke show, skimpy and stringy? Miss Joan had warned them to try to make one coat do; paint, she reminded them, cost money.

'Sort of flow it on, Roseanne,' Harriet advised.

Roseanne threw her a brief glance and went on without reply.

The four girls painted, and Hannah washed dishes and sang, and Countess made sandwiches and hummed, and Miss Mitty took from the oven pans of hot bread, which she set on a cupboard ledge almost under Harriet's nose. The savory steam rose to the top of the room and made Harriet swallow hungrily. Wouldn't a heel of that bread taste good, hot and a little soggy from being cut too soon, and soaked with butter?

'You've done your half of the high part, Willie Lou,' she said, staring at the loaves. 'Now let me do mine.'

'Just as lief,' said Willie Lou. 'Got the shakes so bad.'

Harriet had covered all but a square foot of her portion when Willie Lou, glancing over her shoulder, hissed, 'Jiggers, Hayet!'

Harriet looked at her inquiringly.

'Miss Senter. She gwine skin you, climbin' like that.'

Harriet slapped her brush convulsively down the decreasing gray rectangle. Again. Again.

'Mind the plank!' Willie Lou exclaimed, and her hand shot out toward it.

Harriet had no chance to mind anything. Just as she caught sight of Miss Joan's disapproving face, she felt the plank jarring from under her feet. Down to the table she came crashing, clutching can and brush as if they could save her. From the table to the floor she bumped, the paint making a geyser as she went.

'Harriet Freeman!' cried Miss Joan, darting in from the door.

'My fresh bread!' moaned Miss Mitty. 'Hope y'all ain' killed, honey!'

'Hayet, if you fix yo'se'f so you cain' play in the Booker game ——' howled Willie Lou.

Harriet dazedly felt of herself and shook her head. A thick stream trickled down her nose, feeling gruesome and gory. She wiped a hand across it. It was bright yellow instead of red.

'How on earth —— ?' Miss Joan demanded.

'Willie Lou pushed the plank,' Roseanne Gibbs remarked coolly.

Willie Lou's mouth fell open. 'My land, let me ketch you once, you little old ——' she stuttered.

Harriet looked quickly at Willie Lou, and the girl's eyes met hers squarely, holding them with a question that was at once defiant and anxious.

'Don't be silly, Roseanne,' Harriet said definitely. 'Willie Lou did no such thing. — I don't think I'm broken,' she added seriously. She looked at the loaf of bread beside her, on which, in some unexplained way, her hand had been planted. 'If I took off the top paint,' she said, 'it would still taste good, with butter.'

'Well,' said Miss Joan, 'you're going to have to take off some of the top paint from yourself — with turpentine and a bath. We're due to start on that picnic in an hour.'

'Anyway,' said Harriet, gingerly gathering herself together and getting up, 'our wall's painted.'

Countess, showing all her little white teeth in a smile, broke off the painty top crust of the bread and scraped the under crust, which had come in contact with the floor when Harriet's wideflung hand struck it. With a shy, 'Please, m'm, Miss Mitty?' and a glance under her lashes at the cook, she buttered the squashed loaf and held it out to Harriet.

'Won't some of you share it with me?' Harriet invited; 'Countess? Hannah? Ella?'

Everyone refused with thanks, and Harriet alternately munched and cleaned up her part of the painty mess. It was fortunate the linoleum had been well papered. Harriet wadded up the yellow-splashed paper and Hannah opened the range for her to crowd it in.

Presently she was walking across the campus with Miss Joan, Harriet consuming the rest of the loaf as she went. It *was* good, even though most of the crust had been lost.

'You'll not have any appetite for the picnic,' the teacher protested.

'Watch me!' Harriet replied thickly. 'I've got a whale of an appetite, Miss Joan. I never do get filled up.'

'That's always the way with girls in boarding-school,' said Miss Joan, smiling as reminiscently as if her girlhood had been past for twenty years.

The smile faded, however, and she studied Harriet with an uncomfortably cool keenness in her gray eyes. 'I really am disappointed,' she reproved. 'But perhaps I expected too much of you. I didn't suppose I needed to be on guard this morning to see that you didn't do anything foolish. That was my mistake. And if one of you had been injured by that silly stunt of a plank on two chairs on a table — well, I'd have been liable in all sorts of ways.'

Harriet threw the last quarter of her loaf into a clump

of bushes. It didn't taste so good. She walked beside Miss Joan, hot and miserable. Sometimes it took just that much to dash one's spirits to the ground. Miss Joan's disapproval shed a sudden, clear, cold light on the painting episode and made it look silly and childish.

'I'm sorry, Miss Joan,' she muttered. She wasn't good at expressions of repentance. 'But I do think I'm punished enough without your looking at me like that,' she added with a rush. 'You may think it's fun to come smashing down every which way. I feel like a dozen eggs and all of them scrambled. — I beg your pardon for speaking that way,' she added, remembering that this was, after all, a teacher.

Miss Joan laughed and peered at Harriet's battered elbow. 'You come right straight into my room and get that thing disinfected and dressed,' she said.

XII

THE CARNIVAL

BY THE middle of October the Carnival had been adver-
tised with posters in Booker and the high schools of
Bosquet and Yemassee and even Charleston and Savannah.
It was always one of the biggest social events of the Landers year.

Harriet was listed on the committee of arrangements,
but only because she was an officer in the class, she knew.
With Willie Lou in control, Harriet had nothing to do
with plans or preparations; she had only to plan her own
costume for the evening.

At first she had thought of representing Black Moses;
but there was no telling who might come — from Booker,
for instance; and in case anyone important was there,
Harriet didn't really want to be playing the part of a man.
So she decided to be Harriet Tubman, leader of her own
race, and she studied histories and novels of the period
for costume, and rooted through the odds and ends in
the attic of Sarah B. for materials with which to concoct
the quaint outfit.

To the attic of Sarah B. had been taken the most
fantastic offerings from the barrels sent to Mather: old

silk hats too dilapidated for selling in the Sales House, old party gowns, old canes, split umbrellas, odd gloves; besides contributions by generations of teachers and girls. After its decades of slow growth the collection was an amazing one. Harriet and Johnnie and Mossie reveled in their search, there under the eaves. Harriet and Johnnie soused their finds thoroughly in gasoline and aired them in the drying yard down behind Jaynes Hall, and Mossie imitated their fastidious care, though with the round eyes and dropped lip of bewilderment.

But Harriet was not to slip through the Carnival so easily. On Wednesday Miss Francis stopped her as she passed the faculty table after dinner.

'Harriet,' she said, in the soft, light voice which nevertheless held so much decisiveness — periods where periods should be — 'you are vice-president of the Senior Class.'

'Yes, Miss Francis.'

'Willie Lou is down with a really bad attack of malaria. You will have to take charge of the Carnival in her place.'

'Oh, Miss Francis!' Harriet protested, drawing down her brows. 'The girls only elected me vice-president because — well, they happened to be feeling sorry for me just then. I don't know but they felt sorrier for themselves when they'd calmed down.'

'Still, you are vice-president.'

'But it's only three days before the Carnival ——'

'Willie Lou had everything planned and moving. In the morning you can go to the infirmary and find out what she has done and what there is to do.'

But in the morning Harriet could find out nothing. 'Willie Lou's clean out of her head,' the nurse said, turning Harriet and Johnnie away from the door. 'We haven't had such a hard case in years.'

'I suppose we've got to ask that Ella where Willie Lou kept her notes,' Harriet said. 'Maybe I'll get a chance to do *some*thing that hasn't been done every year since the Civil War,' she added, brightening.

'Go easy, gal,' Johnnie advised lightly. 'You've been doing pretty well; don't upset the apple-cart.'

'Hm?' Harriet asked abstractedly.

'The cook doesn't like to have the caller come into the kitchen and tell her what seasonings to use.'

'Hm?' Harriet repeated. 'Oh, there's Ella. — Ella, where did Willie Lou keep her programs and arrangements and things? Notes, you know, about the Carnival?'

'She didn't keep notes,' said Ella. 'Reckon you-all got to fire ahead best you can. You're vice-president,' she conceded sourly.

'I guess I'd better give out a notice in chapel this morning,' Harriet planned, 'telling the committees to report after dinner. And everyone who's on the program.'

'Likewise the girls who've got charge of the booths and things,' Ella suggested unwillingly.

The announcement brought Roseanne, who was to sing, Phyllodoxia, who was to give a reading, and Countess, who was to have charge of the Chamber of Horrors. It brought also the managers of booths and other concessions.

'Why, this isn't going to be near enough of a program!' Harriet exclaimed, her brows fierce. 'Why, with people coming from as far as Charleston, we can't have a measly little program ——'

'We don't need such a great of a program,' Ella said resentfully, 'with the candy booth and the grunnet (peanut) booth and' — She ticked off a half-dozen attractions, bending back the long flexible fingers of one hand with a finger of the other — 'you-all give folks too much pieces and music and they don' get time to buy. Maybe it ain' thataway up No'th.'

Harriet gave scant attention to Ella's lowering face

and to the uneasy silence of the others. 'Wouldn't it be nice if we could have something striking and distinctive?' she asked eagerly. 'A waffle booth, maybe, with cane sirup and somebody dressed up with a white kerchief. Or a fried fish booth. Or maybe this benny candy.' Benny candy was a crisp rich with bene or sesame seeds instead of nuts. — Harriet was picturing how anyone who happened to come from Gentlemen's Island would admire her ability and originality if the evening sparkled with new and amusing features.

'But thisyere's Wednesday,' Countess reminded her timidly. 'There isn't time to change ev'ything, Harriet. And where'd we get waffle irons enough?'

'But how shall we fill in the whole evening?' Harriet persisted.

'There's the Grand March, so the visitors can see all the costumes,' Countess went on.

'And we can use a heap of time singin',' Hannah offered. 'And we always have singin' games fo' ev'ybody.'

'Singing games?'

'Like Git About Cindy, and String Them Beans. Ev'ybody knows 'em. We always play 'em.'

'That's it: you've played them forever!' Harriet exclaimed. 'This time let's have something brand new!'

Johnnie drummed her chair arm and hummed something under her breath and Ella and Deena May shuffled their feet noisily, but Harriet went on thinking.

'A scavenger hunt!' She exploded the words.

Johnnie chuckled ironically.

'Scag — ?' Countess murmured.

'We'd make out lists of things the people had to find, and of course in this case we'd have to hide them around Jaynes Hall.'

'What kind of things?' Ella demanded.

'Well, I remember one where we had to find a pair of

ear muffs and a mustache cup. — But we'd have to do it quite differently for the Carnival.'

'My father's got a mustache cup,' Hannah said in some perplexity. 'But he ain' got any mustache.'

'*Ear* muffs?' squealed Deena May. 'What you-all mean, ear muffs?'

'You think you-all can make our folks understand how you mean?' Countess asked, her soft little face troubled.

'Oh, that's easy!' Harriet waved away the difficulty with an enthusiastic hand. 'And think what fun it will be to have a change for once! Johnnie, you and Doxy and — and Roseanne can help with the lists.'

'Well,' said Johnnie, after a look at the blankly unresponsive faces about them, 'it's your funeral, Harriet.'

Harriet was too well pleased with her idea to notice. 'Who plays for the solo and the community singing and the Grand March?' she asked.

'Miss Bates does.'

'And who tends to decorating the hall?'

'Chairman does. — *You* do.'

'Well — maybe Miss Senter will take us out in her car early Saturday morning. I think loads of Spanish moss — And how about a big orange moon showing through a fringe of the moss? — What do you think, Ella?' Ella's throat-clearings and shufflings had at last pierced her absorption.

'Me? I don' have to think!' Ella rumbled. 'You-all can do the thinkin' for the lot of us.'

Harriet stared at her. 'One other thing,' she said icily. 'Wouldn't it be fun to sort of exhibit Miss Senter's kitchen project that night? Like a housewarming? What would you suggest, Countess?'

Countess looked up and down and smoothed her dress.

'You-all might put on a stunt,' Ella said, 'showin' how nice you can land in a loaf of light-bread.'

'We do have housewarmin's for new houses,' Countess said. 'Soon as the house is built, we ask all the folks and we sing and pray all night and have eats in the mornin'. — Maybe we could make the Grand March from Jaynes's to the kitchen —— '

'Then round the kitchen till they've all seen it,' Harriet agreed.

'What would you have for music?' asked Johnnie.

'When we got no fiddle, neither banjo, we just beat on the wall with a stick.'

'Ella,' Harriet asked determinedly, 'will you take full charge of the kitchen-warming? — Phyllodoxia, will you check up on the booths and see that they're going to be decorated and ready? It looks to me,' she finished complacently, 'as if things were going to go all right in spite of malaria.'

There were no more hitches than a school party has to have in order to be a school party. Harriet and Johnnie and Phyllodoxia and Roseanne labored till all hours on their scavenger hunt, typing two hundred lists and hiding innumerable objects throughout the hall after it had been decorated. Harriet was only vaguely discomfited by the grudging response of the Senior Class in general: she had too much to do to notice the atmosphere.

Saturday was rainy; all afternoon it drizzled and by dinnertime a heavy downpour had set in. Yet in the final hubbub of preparation, Harriet noticed that guests were steadily arriving, in cars, afoot, by team: families of the girls, boy friends, girl friends. Dashing into Jaynes Hall after a hasty inspection of the kitchen, Harriet found it buzzing with talk and laughter.

Most of the girls were excitedly greeting friends and relatives. Harriet's heart dropped as she looked round the clustering groups. How could she expect any friend or

even acquaintance? Granny couldn't make the trip, and
there was no one else unless ——

From a group of boys and girls a long, slim figure
detached itself and approached her hesitantly, hands
clasped before it, lips slowly parting over white teeth.

'Why — Richie Corwin!' she cried. They shook hands,
and Harriet found that her heart had sprung up a notch
and was beating a little fast, but happily, where it belonged.

'It sho' looks right pretty,' Richard said, standing
beside her.

It did. Harriet had stretched wires lengthwise of the
hall and hung them with streamers of silver moss, while a
few feet from the side wall an entire moss curtain had been
devised, with the moon glowing through it. Johnnie had
thought of having that moon rise realistically by means of
a pulley; but it had balked so badly when they rehearsed
it, and tangled up its electric wiring so completely, that
they had had to let time stand still. — 'Though I'll bet
Ella had something to do with the mixup!' Harriet
declared in private. — Across the end walls the booths
had been built and draped gaily with bunting and crepe
paper. The Landers girls, in costumes quaint or grotesque,
circulated among the guests, adding to the pictorial effect.

Harriet's cheeks burned with irritation as she located
Roseanne Gibbs. Catch Roseanne co-operating with a
costume when she had a gorgeous new formal of gold-
metal cloth! For a moment Harriet wished she had worn
her chiffon; but, after all, the Harriet Tubman dress was
becoming; and she had felt justified in using a little more
rouge and lipstick than every day. — Nobody was co-
operating very well, except the ironic Johnnie and Doxy
and Countess and Hannah. The others dragged on the
program like so many weights.

But — 'It sho' looks *awful* pretty,' Richard repeated,

and he was smiling shyly at her. 'I couldn' dress up,' he added regretfully, tucking his chin down to inspect his shiny, well-brushed suit.

'You look — grand!' Harriet assured him. She was thinking, 'every inch a man.' Richard was every inch a man, even if he was still only a boy.

She consulted her wrist watch. She'd lost track of time in the pressure of all the things she must do. That scavenger hunt — Looking at the older people who were gathering, she wondered feverishly whether it was going to be so easy to make them understand it. 'Why, we've got to start right now!' she exclaimed, turning toward Countess. 'Where can Miss Bates be?'

Miss Bates was not there. Miss Francis was not at the door, greeting guests. While their eyes searched for her, she came in with her quick, nervous step, and approached them. 'Harriet,' she said, 'Miss Bates is running a temperature of a hundred and one. With her health as it is, we can't let her take part tonight.'

'Lawzy!' Countess mourned. 'You reckon Roseanne Gibbs can play those pieces?'

'I can't wait to find out,' Harriet said abstractedly. She craned her neck to pick Deena May out of the crowd and beckoned her. Deena May came somewhat sulkily. — 'Deena May' — Harriet spoke in a rapid undertone — 'will you tell Ella that she and Hannah will have to help swing the singing games? And if I have to fake a lot of tunes I don't know, I don't want to worry over the scavenger hunt ——'

'You mean String Them Beans and such? — But who looks after the scag — the scagenver hunt?' Countess asked.

'It's out. There isn't going to be any,' Harriet said flatly. — Countess smiled and Deena May grinned.

Harriet lifted the whistle to her lips and cut short the

talk and laughter. 'Friends of Landers,' she said, her mouth suddenly dry, 'I'm speaking in place of Willie Lou Snyder, the president of the Senior Class. She is really in charge tonight, though illness keeps her away. She had planned the program, and we have made few changes in it.

'We are glad the rain did not keep you away, and we hope you'll enjoy the evening. In order to set the ball rolling, we will all join in the Grand March. Landers girls will pass twice round the hall so that the visitors may see the costumes and vote on the best one. Then they will lead the way across the campus to the kitchen — double-quick if it's still raining — and our guests will follow. We want you to see what the Home Economics Department has done to make the kitchen pleasanter for Miss Mitty and the girls.'

She turned, trembling from nervousness, and sat down at the piano. As soon as she spread her slim hands in a crashing chord, her nervousness vanished. Here she was quite at home.

Richard stood beside her, diffidently, watching the music with intent eyes and turning the page when the time came. She flashed a pleased glance at him: it was nice that he could read music; it was nice to have him there.

Over her shoulder she could now and then see the girls marching in couples, giggling and glancing at the audience. Johnnie was Toussaint, the famous Haitian general. She had made velvet kneebreeches out of an old skirt. Long white stockings and silver-paper shoe-buckles and lace ruffles at neck and wrists blotted out the modernness of the Norfolk jacket. She wore a cotton wig tied back with black ribbon, and a cocked hat with a feather. On her arm hung Mossie, in hoop skirt and poke bonnet.

Dresses of ten years ago, twenty, thirty, fifty, had been taken from the stores in the attic, and astonishing acces-

sories added to them. There were a George and a Martha
Washington with cotton wigs much like Toussaint's. Ella
wore a rakish silk hat and a Prince Albert coat with long,
sleek broadcloth skirts. The little Randalls were in sun-
bonnets and checked aprons.

Harriet played them out of the hall, the guests crowding
after them; played till the last one was out, and then
brought up the rear, with Richard. The marchers broke
rank and dashed across the intervening space to the
kitchen, which gleamed bright and welcoming in the rain.
Richard had only time to say, 'Harriet, yo' Granny got
good right to be proud of such a grand!' before they were
standing in the door with Miss Francis and Miss Joan,
surveying the scene.

'I do wish we could have painted the ceiling,' Miss Joan
sighed.

'I wish we could have done better lettering on those
cans,' added Harriet.

There was small criticism from the crowd, which had
formed in double line again and was marching round and
round and out into the hall and through the dining-room
and back again, to the vigorous tap-tap taptaptapping of
the Prince Alberted Ella. When they were not looking
at each other they were admiring the racks of dishtowels
spick and span and smartly marked; or the smoothly
gleaming Chinese red enamel on cupboards, stools, and
tables; or the ranks of containers, painted and lettered; or
the clean butter-yellow of the walls.

Harriet pointed out to Richard the small rectangle,
dimly discernible, which marked her disaster; and Ella
heard and paused in her poker-tapping long enough to
shout: 'Ought to seen 'm! Come down like Humpty
Dumpty!'

'You got the message about the games?' Harriet asked.
Ella nodded brusquely. 'Can you play 'm?'

'Not very well, but I'll do the best I can.'

'Reckon it'll do,' Ella muttered.

Harriet didn't point out the lard can, big as a barrel, which Hannah had so painstakingly lettered. With one swift movement, instead, Harriet shoved and turned it until almost all its vivid lettering was hidden. Why hadn't someone noticed in time that dear Hannah had spelled out in Chinese red: 'S – H – U – G – A – R'?

When the improvements had been thoroughly inspected, Hannah started a song in which everyone joined, and those who wanted refreshments were served lemonade by a clown and sugared doughnuts by a Dutch girl with a face like an ebony cherub's (Phyllodoxia), and clinked their nickels into a bright tin dishpan held by a languid lady in the long, tight skirt and high collar of 1912.

Back at Jaynes Hall again, the program went on, and the booths were opened for business. Boys bought pop and candy and grunnets for themselves and the girls, and carried paper bags to the middle-aged and old people who could not be coaxed to leave their seats. Boys bought bait at the fish pond and dangled hook and line over the curtained corner, drawing it up with roars of laughter over the baby dolls or strings of beads that they had caught. They ventured awkwardly into the tea-room and sat with knees pressed together and balanced a plate and a cup and a wafer. From below in Countess's Chamber of Horrors sounded squeals and shrill laughter and deep guffaws to indicate the success of phosphorescent ghosts with wet rubber gloves to shake hands with, and diets of worms and all the other nonsense that became so gruesome in deep darkness with cobwebs creeping across visitors' faces.

Harriet did not have time to be 'treated' much, and she thought perhaps Richard was glad: he had probably a lean purse. She drank a root beer with him, and he bought her a bag of grunnets and a bag of candy and insisted on baiting her hook at the fish pond. There was much giggling behind the curtain when she dangled the line, and, when she jerked it up, a ten-cent-store diamond glittered on the hook. She could feel the girls watching her to see what she would do; and Richard, his lips laughing but his eyes anxious.

Harriet laughed, too, and slipped the ring on her right hand.

Presently she blew the whistle once more and announced that the judges had awarded the costume prizes to Johnnie and Mossie: a handkerchief and a blue necklace. Then she called the crowd into a game of Steal Miss Liza.

Harriet got along fairly well with the accompaniment. Richie hummed the airs for her, and that helped; but the players did not need much accompaniment. Old and young they joined in the gay old dancing, singing games:

> 'Dat ol' man ain't got no wife,
> Li'l Liza Jane.
> Cain' git one to save he's life,
> Li'l Liza Jane.
> Now won' you steal Sis' Liza,
> Li'l Liza Jane?'

Cotton wigs were mussed now, and cocked on one side; ancient dresses had suffered from having their trains stepped on; but no one was ready to stop.

> 'Git about, Cindy, Cindy.
> My peach tree's all in bloom;
> My true love gwine to marry soon;
> Git about, Cindy, Cindy!'

The evening had sped by. The booths were empty and ragged. It was time for the final Grand March. The final Grand March was marched. . . .

'Gosh, how you sing *and* play,' said Toussaint, as the last of the visitors loitered out past Miss Francis. 'And you certainly showed good judgment, letting the scavenger hunt go — even if it did mean a lot of time wasted getting ready for it. But, Harriet, have you annexed you a man? What's that Jimmie of yours going to say?'

Harriet looked startled. 'Well — Jimmie's in Minneapolis, Richard's here. But, anyway, — well, don't be silly.'

She had very nearly said, 'Can you imagine me thinking seriously of a shabby island boy who can't even use proper English?'

She could not say it: she was surprised by the warm thrill of loyalty that would not let her belittle him.

He was only a poverty-stricken and ill-educated islander. Jimmie was the son of one of the most successful Negro physicians in Minneapolis, and booked straight through for the university and medical training himself. Jimmie was a letter man, and wore his school sweater with dash. He was fun, too. Yet these few weeks had made his face fade from her mind surprisingly. She had to get out his picture to remember how he looked.

XIII

'DOSE OF LANDERS!'

THE first of the year's big games was with the Booker girls, and was to be played at Booker during Farmers' Fair, the last Saturday in November. From the day Willie Lou was taken ill, the Booker game was the chief topic of conversation: the Booker game and, first, whether Willie Lou could possibly recover soon enough to captain it; the Booker game and, next, whether Landers could possibly win it under a substitute captain; the Booker game and, finally, who that substitute captain should be.

There were two logical candidates, Harriet and Ella. Harriet ended the discussion. 'Don't be silly,' she said flatly. 'Ella's been on this team four years and I've been on four weeks. She knows your tricks and your manners. There's only one answer.'

The last Saturday in November dawned bright and beautiful. The persistent languorous warmth had sharpened at last with autumn, though the hardier flowers still bloomed — Klondike cosmos, orange-yellow; marigolds; opopanax in fluffy yellow balls; sapphire-blue spider lilies. The broomstraw was feathery with seed; and enough trees had lost their leaves to make the forest floors lovely.

The Landers truck jolted with shouts and singing over

the causeway to St. Catherine Island. At Booker the girls announced themselves with a challenging yell:

'Going to give Booker yellow janders!
How we do it? Dose of Landers!'

Miss Joan reached up and patted Harriet's hand as the girl leaned against the slatted side of the truck.

'You look happy,' she said, rather wistfully, 'you one little, two little, three little Injuns!' — and she pointed at Johnnie and Mossie, crowded up against the slats with Harriet.

Harriet thought fleetingly that the teacher herself did not look so happy these days. The girls were not seeing so much of her. They had less leisure than earlier in the term; and, besides, Miss Joan hadn't been asking them to walk and ride with her as she had formerly done.

'This school is something else again,' Miss Joan said, and they all looked around them while they waited for the truck to empty out.

The buildings stood in the perpetual twilight of an old oak forest dripping with gray moss. Today people from this island and others trooped through the dimness. Boys and girls were gathered everywhere, and when the Landers truck had driven through the gate and burst into sound, the Booker students surged forward to meet them.

Harriet looked into the throng. Smiling that bashful, wary smile of his, but with more assurance because today he was a host, Richard appeared before her as if he had shot up out of the shadowy ground, in that shadowy place that wraiths might well love.

'Mighty pleased to see you-all,' he said, pulling his foot in his old-fashioned bow.

'Mighty glad to be here!' she answered. 'Girls, you met Richard the other night. Granny's neighbor.'

The three girls jumped down from the truck and they

walked together toward the administration building, where were most of the exhibits. Richard paced slowly, hands clasped before him, eyes smiling down at Harriet.

The hall was a wild medley of sound and color and odor. The people swarmed in streams and cross-currents, crying out and cackling with laughter. Small, dark children scurried at their mothers' skirts or stood with brown legs stoutly set and stared. Exhibits were of all imaginable sorts. There were intricate quilts — Star of Bethlehem, Statehouse Steps; dresses made by girl students; canned fruit and vegetables; jelly; fine cotton bolls, full heads of rice, enormously long okra pods. A forlorn bantam rooster, some child's pet, thrust a ruffled head through the bars of its box and crowed belligerently. A calf bawled for its mother.

Harriet stopped before a table of baskets, jerking the other three to a halt with her. 'What a strange kind!' she cried.

'Yes, m'm,' Richard said, 'exackly the kind they make in Africa. Palmetto and reeds.'

She touched a beautifully shaped wood basket for the hearth, and a big, simply curved waste basket. 'They're somehow awfully lovely. Can you make them, Richard?'

'Sho' nuff! And we boys built thisyere model house in the carpenter shop.' He directed her attention to a miniature cottage outside the window. 'It taken — took — first prize in the State Housin' Contest. You-all like to see it, Harriet? — And the other young ladies?'

'If you'll excuse us, we'd like to look at the quilts instead,' Johnnie replied with excessive politeness. Mossie began an indignant protest, but Johnnie, eyes shining with amusement, dragged her away.

Richard piloted Harriet through the medley and out to the tiny house, whose roof ridge was only a few inches higher than his head. Other people were peering through

'I WANT TO MAKE SOMETHIN' OF MYSELF. I WANT TO
GET AWAY WHERE THINGS ARE DIFF'ENT'

the windows, and so did they. Four rooms the cottage had, and simple furnishings.

'Us boys made the house and the chairs and tables and bed. Girls made the curtains and rugs and paint' the walls — but they didn' fall into no bread,' he teased. 'It took first prize,' he repeated.

He gazed through those windows with the pride of achievement. Such a humble little sitting-room; such a plain little bedroom; such a primitive little kitchen; and a cubbyhole with a high window and a tin washtub and a wash basin and pitcher.

'Da's whe' dey takes dey bafs!' squealed an excited small girl whose nose was flattened against the pane at the level of Harriet's elbow. 'A hull room jes' fuh take bafs! Mah-own sis tell me.'

'If all my people could have 'm nice comf'terble homes like that,' Richie yearned.

He showed her the barns, with the beginnings of a thoroughbred herd. He showed her the rice-thresher — an experiment that had not worked out so well as expected. 'Folks go on lickin' their rice out with a stick like they've always done.'

He showed her, with vast pride, the library.

'I've been readin' all I could,' he said. 'Of late I've been readin' a sight. Reckon you-all know why.'

'You're going to college after you're through here; that's why!'

'Well — first off I want to talk better, so I don' feel so funny talkin' to you-all. You see any diff'ence, Harriet?'

'Richie, I really do.'

'An' nex', like y'all say, I want to make somethin' of myself. I want to get away where things are diff'ent.'

They were back among the exhibits now, weaving this way and that, and so interested in their own conversation that they constantly bumped into other people.

'I should think you would want to get away!' Harriet responded vehemently. Her eyes frowned at the humanity that surged around her. White headkerchiefs, sometimes topped with disreputable hats, round, black heads, rags, rags, rags; a rank smell of tobacco, though pipes were hidden here; a gabble of talk almost unintelligible.

Joan Senter had been almost lifted from her feet and carried along by the human tide. She was washed up against Harriet, and her breathless laughter was sobered by Harriet's somber face.

'Don't take it so hard!' she said swiftly. She drew Harriet, and Richard with her, into a cove behind a rack of dresses. 'Harriet, remember it's like this with any part of *any* race that has no education and no higher contacts. Weren't you ever down in the slums of a big city? Wouldn't you a lot rather have the island people's life and chance? And what about our white mountaineers?'

Harriet smiled at her. Miss Joan understood how stifled she was feeling, how weighed down by the poverty and backwardness of a great mass of her people. She pressed the teacher's arm warmly, and the three stood a while almost silent.

But it was almost the hour for the game, with no more time for idle pain or pleasure. Reluctantly Harriet threaded her way through the exhibit hall to the corridor where she was to meet her team-mates. At the corridor door Richard said, 'I'll be shoutin' for you! And, Harriet, yo're comin' over to Gentlemen's to spend Christmas with yo' Granny?'

She nodded emphatically, tossing her hand in friendly promise, and slid into the crowd of girls. She hoped she'd have a chance to throw some of those showy baskets of hers. She always wanted to play a good game, but today the desire was sharpened. She wanted to help Landers overcome the handicap of Willie Lou's absence and win the trophy for keeps. And she wanted to show Richard!

The teams were jigging up and down and shouting as all teams do, so that it seemed impossible that order should ever be wound out of the tangled skein of noise. Parents and grandparents and brothers and sisters and uncles and aunts and cousins had filled every available seat and wedged themselves into all the standing space and were hailing each other gaily. The Landers girls pranced in a file below their basket, one after another tossing the ball up and in or up and out, according to their ability.

The shrill whistle cut through the clamor and brought the centers leaping with stretched finger tips for the ball. A small and solemn boy with a crooked foot pulled himself up on a stool before the scoreboard, chalk importantly ready. The game was on.

Harriet played well and fast. Tall and long-limbed and muscular, she seemed able to shoot straight up into the air, her arms stretching elastically toward the ceiling. In the first quarter she soared upward and intercepted a Booker ball as it flew toward its basket. She captured it, dribbled it across the floor till she could pass it to Hannah, who passed it to Ella, who made a basket.

The teams were well matched. Ella and Harriet were better forwards than Booker's, but Booker had the better defence. Her guards stuck like shadows, sidling, leaping, seldom betrayed into even an accidental foul.

There was the swift patter of soft shoes on the wooden floor, like the beginning of a rain, punctuated with shouts and shrieks from the players and applause from the audience. These onlookers could howl and stamp, even if they were hazy as to the details of the game. They could scream with laughter, too, when the ball pelted into their ranks, sending them bending and scattering out of the way. And then the whistle sounded the end of the half, and the small scorekeeper rolled his eyes solemnly toward a referee for confirmation and ground the chalk against the board in staggering white numerals: Booker, 13; Landers, 12. Then the gymnasium roared like the sea.

Harriet had early located Richard. She had flashed a glance his way after her first noticeably good play and had seen him yell and wave a long hand, his face lighted with laughter; had seen his Booker companions struggle to silence him, laughing also. — It was much more fun to win glory when someone was cheering especially for you! Now in the last half she wished with every beat of her pounding heart to make a score, a spectacular basket, for her own glory and for Landers.

Back and forth raced the ball, accompanied by the patter and rush of feet: up to one end, down to the other, too swiftly for accurate baskets. Mossie, doubling and running and making a long slide as if on ice, grabbed the ball beneath Booker's basket and dribbled it rapidly up the floor. Mossie almost never fouled in her dribbling: she seemed to dance with the bounce of the ball: step-bounce, step-bounce, quick and true.

Ella roared a 'Hy-ah!' that they had answered in a dozen practice games, and Mossie, feinting to pass the ball to the left, shot it, lightning quick, to the right and Ella. Harriet, just left of the center, poised unguarded, and the ball smacked into her hands. She swung around, gauged direction and distance for a long, tense moment, and then hurled the ball toward the basket. It hovered — it dropped — and the room rocked with cheers and groans. The solemn little boy, who had been staring at the game over his shoulder, turned back and erased the figures and slowly traced: for Booker, 13; for Landers, 14.

Again ball and team eddied to and fro. Playing was again too fast and excited for scoring, but Ella plunged against a Booker girl, and in the resulting penalty Booker made a free throw and tied the score.

Time was jumping past. Again Mossie had the ball, slid between opposing guards, step-bounce, step-bounce. Again she passed it to Harriet, well toward the center. Again Harriet, catching it, made swift calculation.

It was her chance for one more spectacular throw, and Landers' chance for victory. If she missed, the game would be a tie, or worse.

And almost under the basket, for an instant unguarded again, Ella waited tiptoe.

Swift and straight the ball flew toward Ella's hands. With the speed of light it rose from those hands, up, up above the basket, where it arched and fell gracefully into place. The whistle shrilled. The game was over.

The solemn boy, his very knickerbockers creeping dejectedly toward his toes, plaintively marked the final score: 16 to 14 for Landers.

High over the heads of the crowd Richard waved to Harriet. Ella said grudgingly, 'You sho' knows teamwork, Hat!' — The other Landers girls grabbed their forwards and hoisted them on their shoulders, where they rode, tilting, clutching, laughing, out to the truck. Joan Senter made a megaphone of her hands and shouted, 'Six little — hundred little Injuns!'

It was true: Harriet and Johnnie and Mossie no longer stood alone against Landers.

But next morning the depression which had beset Harriet in the exhibit hall engulfed her again. She was writing one of the three weekly letters permitted students: writing to Mrs. Trindle.

'Sometimes I feel as if I can't stand another day of this. Some things about it I'm getting to love, but others — ! Well, I suppose you've felt it yourself, like a big weight dragging you back — our people. "My people," Richard

Corwin would say. But it's too awful to feel that these thousands without hope *are* my people. And that, in a way, we can't any of us rise until they are all lifted up. It's like being crushed under a burden too heavy to bear.'

XIV

Miss Bates

DECEMBER'S three weeks of school had more than they could hold.

The classes were vying with each other in money-making projects. The cooking teacher let the Seniors make benny candy. Roseanne Gibbs brought out a box of the famous 'peach leather,' from Charleston. The rolls of it, like tiny orange-brown diplomas, had to be sold at a nickel apiece. The Juniors bought quantities of grunnets and roasted them and sold them, hot and good, for five cents a bag.

Peanut shells were everywhere, tumbling out of desks and littering grass and rolling from under beds. The art teacher had all her classes make posters:

KEEP LANDERS CLEAN!
Put the nuts into your mouths
and the shells into the wastebaskets!

Girls were chinking in the time with the making of Christmas gifts: needle and thread, pen and ink, paste, knitting needles, crochet hooks, were forever being thrust under pillows or into pockets or sat on when an intended recipient suddenly appeared. Harriet had finished an elaborate trousseau for her doll, and spent September on a present for Granny. She looked long at clever apron patterns and pretty nightgowns; but her sense of humor pictured Granny's dark dignity in them, and she laughed and cut long-sleeved, high-necked outing nightgowns, with conventional round collars. She sent boxes of peach leather and benny candy to her three best friends in Minneapolis; to the Trindles, besides more conventional gifts, sprays of holly and mistletoe and Spanish moss.

The Christmas tree, erected in the middle of Landers dining-hall at the final dinner before the holidays, was a gay affair. Everyone was well remembered. Harriet found on the tree a bunch of sugar cane from Mossie, a snapshot of Washington Hall, framed in seashells, from Hannah, a handkerchief from Willie Lou, a book from Johnnie, a carefully embroidered collar from Phyllodoxia. She had received several packages from Minneapolis — from the Trindles a beautifully knitted rust-colored dress which Mrs. Trindle must have had to hurry to finish.

Joan Senter stealthily slipped small parcels to Harriet and Johnnie. 'You know I got the dickens from the faculty,' she explained, with a puckered grin above her sober little double chin. 'That was for singling out favorite companions among the students. I suppose they're right. I'm not so grown-up and sensible as I thought I was. — But that's why I've seemed to be so busy lately.'

'Mother told me,' Johnnie said gravely. 'But she said not to repeat it. She said you were a dear, Miss Joan. She said the only thing wrong with you was youth, and she hoped you wouldn't be in any hurry to get over that.'

'Good gracious!' Harriet exploded. 'You don't have as much social life as we do, even.'

'Oh, well!' — the young teacher achieved a fairly

nonchalant manner — 'it won't be for long. They haven't any place for me in Landers after this semester, even if I wanted to stay. And my old school has offered me the crafts classes. It will be a lovely job, like a bed of roses, comparatively speaking.'

The climax of the campus celebration was the musical program that night. The girls, in white dresses or dresses as nearly white as they possessed, wound their way across the campus at first dark, each carrying a candle thrust through a cardboard disk, and sang. They sang the Christmas carols, and Harriet led. They sang the spirituals, and Hannah led. 'Ain' gwine study war no more...' — 'Oh, my lovin' sister, when the world's on fire...' How they loved to sing them! How Harriet thrilled to hear them, especially like this, looking back on the long misty line curving beneath the black trees, taper flames glimmering ——

In the big living-rooms at Sarah B., a fire burned in the fireplace and the candles were set everywhere, in decorative holders made by Miss Joan's classes from tin salvaged from the dump heap. Miss Francis read the Christmas story: 'And there were in the same country shepherds, keeping watch by night over their flocks...'

So quiet the rooms. So sweet and holy all the still-burning flames.

Harriet played. After her ability had been betrayed by the Carnival, it was a foregone conclusion that she should play. She played another carol, with the whole room crooning it. She played 'Humoresque,' 'Souvenir,' — proved popular by thousands of radios. And then she played Chopin's 'Prelude' in F, on which she had been working, together with Beethoven's 'Moonlight Sonata,' in those early morning practice hours all fall.

She did not know quite why she played it: perhaps it was a way of saying to Miss Bates, 'You see? I've gone pretty far to be expected to take lessons of a little music teacher who teaches beginners only.'

She played well. Even the girls, stirring uneasily, looked at her with wide eyes in the glimmer.

There was more singing, and Roseanne Gibbs rendered, not too badly, 'To a Wild Rose.' Miss Bates followed Roseanne at the piano. She also played popular classics: 'Herd Girl's Dream,' and 'Traümerei.' Then she paused for a long moment and played the 'Moonlight Sonata.'

Harriet listened in growing amazement. She had known that Miss Bates played correctly and with good touch, but until tonight she had heard her do nothing but accompaniments. The sonata, with its range of technique, its range of emotion, was done as she had never heard it. To a group of a hundred schoolgirls on a sea island of South Carolina ——

After most of the other girls had gone, Harriet waited, while the teachers went about putting out a hundred candles that were guttering down to inch-high mounds of white. When she approached Miss Bates, Miss Bates turned to her with a smile that was tender as well as amused.

'Your "Prelude" was beautifully done,' she said. 'I've heard you many mornings when I've gone down through the drying-yard to watch the sun rise out of the bay — The sun comes up as big and red and gorgeous when you see it from the drying-yard as anywhere else ——'

'Then it was really you I heard, one night in the fall, playing Bach. I thought the wind carried it from one of those mansions in Bosquet. Or that it was a fairy ——'

'I practise from ten to twelve, or thereabouts. And you from five to seven. And so we've kept apart, with the whole day between us.'

Harriet stood with compressed lips and downcast eyes. She had felt superior to this 'little music teacher.' And now, what could she say? She couldn't say, 'Oh, Miss Bates, you play so beautiful!' as the girls had done. She couldn't even echo Miss Francis: 'It was a privilege to listen.' Her feeling was too big for any expression she could give it.

She lifted troubled eyes. *'Why?'* she stammered. 'Why?'

'Why — *here?'*

Miss Bates sat down on one of the hard settles and motioned Harriet to sit beside her. Half consciously Harriet noticed again the grace of the sitting, in one long flowing movement; the grace of her beckoning hand.

'It's too long a story,' the teacher said. 'My father was a musician, too, and dreamed great things for me. And gave his life' — she laid a significant hand on her breast — 'to make them come true. Expensive teachers — schools ——'

'They did come true?'

'Yes, they did come true. For such a little while. And then — you know how susceptible our race has been to tuberculosis — then long months in a mountain sanitarium. And then this. — And I've loved it very much.'

'Teaching Ella Hooper to play "Lightly Row"?' Harriet demanded fiercely.

Miss Bates chuckled. 'Giving them all the music they can hold, in every way possible. That's going to make a difference to a hundred schoolhouses in the woods and fields; to a hundred hundred homes. — And here I am, living in all this beauty instead of going out quickly — like that candle — in another concert season or two. That's what the doctors said: a season or two of public life, gay and glamorous, and that would be all. Now I'm giving something. And having Beethoven, just the same. And going to Charleston every week, so that life doesn't become too — tight.'

'That's all, my dear. But mostly — I hate to sound priggish, but it's true — mostly happiness is *giving* something.'

Miss Bates had risen, with that sweet fluid motion, but Harriet sat dumbly looking up at her.

'Magdalen Bates!' she said, as one who speaks out of a dream. 'Mother used to speak of you. — And *I* can have lessons of — Magdalen Bates.'

'The pianos aren't so good,' said Magdalen Bates, 'but it might be worth two dollars a month.'

XV

'Go Tell It on de Mountains'

HALF of Christmas belonged to Landers. The other half began when Harriet again took boat for Gentlemen's Island, the day before Christmas. Huddled in her warmest coat she sat as before on the open deck, where now the wind blew keen.

It seemed perfectly natural for Richard to meet her at the dock and carry her suitcases for her. This time the air had a crispness that made the walk a delight. And immediately upon landing Harriet tasted Christmas. People were crowding round the one little store down near the shore — the store where R. Corwin had got the stale stationery — buying and shouting and laughing and shooting firecrackers. The cabins that sunned themselves along the road had their front doors and window shutters gleaming white, and no one was lounging on the porches.

'Because it's Christmas Eve,' Richard explained. 'Ever we whitewash with oystershell lime and clean up and trim up nice for Christmas.'

'I hope Granny has a big apron, so I can get right to work helping her!' Harriet cried.

'No need to spoil yo' nice hands,' he said, smiling his
big, kind smile. 'Lily and Granny and me, we've made it
pretty a'ready.'

They crunched through a short cut, where the keen
smell of fallen leaves rose around them. And there stood
the cabin. Granny's marigolds still bloomed bravely, and
late chrysanthemums were wine and snow. And never
were door and shutters more glisteningly white than
Granny's.

Harriet had only an instant to admire them before
Granny answered the creak of the gate and came hurrying
across the porch, her headkerchief and apron as dazzling
as the whitewash, her gold hoop earrings bobbing, her
face radiant. Lily, scrubbed and shining, too, ducked
under Granny's arm and dashed at them, grabbing the
suitcases and staggering into the house with them, grinning back over her shoulder.

Harriet went straight into Granny's outstretched arms.

'But come in, come in, Richie, 'n' res' yo' hat an' coat!'
Granny remembered to urge, wiping away the tears
with a starchy apron corner. 'Ain' got no manners, nohow.'

The cabin took them in with almost the same warmth
and welcome as Granny. Lily, when she had deposited
the suitcases and bustled away with Harriet's hat and coat
and gloves, went jigging around scrutinizing Harriet from
all angles and watching to see if she noticed with proper
appreciation the dressing up of the room.

All the walls and the ceiling and the insides of doors and
shutters had been papered with fresh newspapers, so that
no sharp breezes could come through anywhere except at
the cracks in the floor, where the freshly washed rag rugs
lifted a little. Door and window curtains were snow
white.

'Lily cut the trimmin's for the mantel,' Richard

murmured under his breath, nodding toward the cut-out newspaper.

Lily grinned whitely when Harriet exclaimed over those scallops, and rolled her eyes toward the 'big girl' from the tin can of chrysanthemums which she was regarding with sudden absorption.

'The flowers likewise,' Richard explained, and Harriet praised them to the child's satisfaction.

Beneath Lily's newspaper edging the fire snapped and sparkled and made the room alive. From the kitchen came mingled food odors of Christmas: grapy, fruity smells; smells of spice and molasses and fresh bread. Harriet's eyes filled with tears. She had not believed that Christmas could ever make her so happy again.

Proud to do the honors, Lily led her into the kitchen and showed her the bottles of colored juices and the glasses of jelly on the shelves; the strings of red peppers hanging from the walls.

'Traded me some hens fuh fresh hog-meat,' Granny said happily.

And — 'Don' e smell good?' demanded Lily, lifting the lid of a kettle and licking her lips with exaggerated delight.

It did smell good: rice, Harriet could see, bubbling deliciously with tidbits of meat and seasonings of scarlet pepper.

'But us gots chicken fuh Christmas,' Lily whispered loudly. 'And — Granny, kin I show 'm de fruit-cake?'

She hopped and skipped to the cupboard and lugged out a crock, hugging it in skinny arms. 'Smell 'm!' she commanded.

'Scuppernong wine on de crus',' said Granny, as if that explained the peculiarly delicate fragrance. 'Made tereckly after Thanksgiving.'

Harriet stood in the back door, flung open to the

December sunshine. The fallen fig tree had been cleared away and the henhouse rebuilt.

'And who ever chopped all that wood?' Harriet asked. 'E did!' Lily crowed, sighting impishly along her finger at Richard. 'E chop de wood and e white de do's and e fetch de scup'nongs and de hick'ry nuts and de wil' crabapples.'

'Care if I walk over to the meetin'-house with you-all tonight?' Richard asked hastily.

Harriet looked questioningly at Granny. 'Do we go to the meeting-house?' she asked.

Granny nodded as she stirred the savory rice. 'Sho' we does. It Chris'mas Eve. Please' to have y'all, Richie.'

Richard went home, and Lily watched with wide eyes and buttoned-up mouth as Harriet unpacked her suitcases. Harriet showed her the contents of some of the packages, with the result that Lily went dancing wildly around the cabin, making eyes at Granny and exploding with the laughter that she tried to hold in. Other packages Harriet sneaked carefully on the tiptop of the old wardrobe; yet not so carefully that Lily should not see them being hidden and go bouncing with a vehement joy that shook the cabin. Guessing but not knowing — that was a big part of a little girl's fun.

Supper was early. Granny filled and refilled the 'chillen's' plates and watched their zest with deep-eyed content. And as soon as the hens were shut up and the dishes washed and the fires carefully banked and clothes and hair tidied, the bong-bong-bong of a cowbell sounded from afar. Lily pranced, where she stood, like a jumping-jack whose string has been jerked.

'It de meetin'-house! It de meetin'-house!' she squealed, and dived for her red sweater on its nail behind the door. At the same moment Richard tapped and came in.

'Isn't there any way of locking up?' Harriet inquired,

when they were all ready to go. Her tissue-wrapped Christmas gifts were small enough, but she was uneasy at the thought of leaving them in an open house.

'Lockin' up?' — Granny chuckled richly — 'Don' got to lock no do's on Gentlemen's, honey!'

Mule teams, horse teams, ox-carts, and two or three rusty cars were massed around Jericho Church. It was packed with dark humanity. Its whitewashed walls were hidden by the people, and the dim kerosene lamps high along the side walls illumined the sharp glitter of teeth and eyes in the duskiness.

Harriet felt a million miles away from last Christmas Eve. Then a group of their young people had been carried around the Twin Cities in automobiles, to see the outdoor lighting and to sing carols in the crisp, snowy darkness. — 'The first Noël the angels did say!' How she had loved those archaic words, lifted down from the Middle Ages! How she had loved the revival of the old custom!

Yet there was something artificial about that revival. There was nothing artificial about this celebration. It was old custom coming down unbroken from the past.

The Christmas story was read from the Bible, while old voices and young murmured praise. Old hymns were sung, lined out by the leader because there were no hymnals, and many, to be sure, who could not read.

People prayed and gave testimony, with everyone else joining, as at that first church service Harriet had attended. Children sprawled over their mothers' laps and slept, or bobbed their heads against parental shoulders. Richard shyly directed Harriet's attention to a dark Madonna across the church from them, a delicious brown three-year-old sleeping in her arms, his dimpled knees bare. A boy of sixteen or so, beside them, grinned knowingly at Richard and let his eyes move on to Harriet. 'My-own folks,' Richard said. 'Mom wants you and

Granny should have dinner with us whilst yo' here.'
Harriet found her eyes irresistibly drawn to Mrs. Corwin
and Aaron and Baby Washington. The eyes played a
game across the crowded room all night.

Before the evening was far spent, Lily's head had
bobbed down on Granny's lap. Harriet felt her own eyes
drooping, her head nodding, even in all the rise and fall of
sound about her. Richard nudged her gently and she
came awake with a start, hoping she had not had her
mouth open. She looked at the boy beside her, in acute
embarrassment, and he smiled back gently, humorously.
The kindest person, Richard!

'It mos' midnight,' he whispered. 'I knowed — knew —
you'd want to listen for cock-crow.'

A hush held the congregation, and far off in the still
dark sounded the faint, high paean of a cock: another;
another.

Then indeed did the voice of petition change to the
voice of praise and joy. The frail building shook with
hallelujahs and the rhythmic patting of feet. Spiritual
after spiritual was led off and joined by the congregation.

Lily sat up with a jerk, muttering hoarsely: 'Granny, is
our cow kneelin' down fuh sho'? An' Nicky, too?'

'So they says, honey, so they says,' Granny answered
her softly.

Harriet looked a startled query at Richard.

'Ain' — haven' — you ever heard it?' he asked. 'All
the old folks say so: that the cows and the critters and all
the beasts, they kneel to pray at Christmas Eve, just like
humans. — Like enough it ain' so,' he added hastily, 'but
it's pretty.'

Lily dropped back to sleep. Granny's head swayed
forward till her chin rested on her white neckerchief, and
then jerked upright as she opened suspicious eyes. The

lamps smoked and grew dimmer. The air thickened. Harriet kept dozing, rocked by the vibration.

Again she wakened, finding Richard's smile upon her, hoping again that her mouth had not fallen open, feeling a rush of cool fresh air from the open doors. A thin light filtered into the church, paling the lamp flames. The voices of the people rose with fresh eagerness.

'Go tell it on de mountains, Dat Jesus Christ is a-born!'

'It's day-clean!' whispered Richard. 'The sun has come up, shoutin' the praise of the Lord.'

That cherry-red sun might have been shouting, but the tuneful clamor of the people would have drowned any sound but their own.

By the time Granny and her trio had left the throng and walked a little way, the keen air had washed away the night's stale sleepiness. Richard carried Lily pickaback, and Harriet walked arm-in-arm with Granny. Harriet thought there had never been anything so beautiful as this Christmas morning, edged with frost and animated by the early song of birds and the flash of rabbits across the road and the whirring of partridges from a thicket.

'Does us git our stockin's now?' Lily demanded, when Richard set her down on Granny's porch.

'You-all piles into bed an' has you a nap befo' breakfast,' Granny told her. '*Den* you kin see has Sandy Claw been here. Don' you look yit!'

Lily staggered sleepily through the room, face set rigidly ahead but big eyes rolling sidewise toward the mantel. 'Sandy Claw ain' came! E ain' came!' she whimpered uncontrollably.

'Jes' wait twell after breakfast and see!' Granny counseled, spanking her gently toward the bed.

'Cain' sleep nohow!' Lily protested, knuckling heavy eyes as Granny pulled the dress off over her twenty braids. 'Cain' —— ' The words were engulfed in a wide yawn and she rolled over into the big feather bed and was asleep.

Harriet and Granny filled the child's stocking, and while Harriet washed her face and combed her hair, she could hear Granny crackling starchily around the fire.

While Granny was cooking breakfast, Harriet filled still another stocking and hung it back in the shadows, where it would not be quickly observed. So when breakfast was ready and the shutters thrown wide to the good Christmas sun, and Lily wakened, three stockings hung in delightful distortion before that snapping fire. Little attention did the savory breakfast receive from little girl or big, though Granny urged and scolded.

A doll smiled from the top of Lily's Christmas stocking, as a doll should smile from the top of every little girl's. It was the yellow-haired doll which Harriet had dressed in sewing class. Its present costume was a pair of outing-cloth pajamas and bedroom slippers that Harriet had contrived from scraps of felt.

'E *too* pretty! Dis de clo'es de buckruh wear fo' Sunday bes', enty?' Lily asked rapturously, holding the doll at arm's length to admire her and snatching her to her breast to love her.

Harriet laughed. 'It's what "de buckruh" wear for sleepy-time. You just wait and see what else is in the stocking.'

Lily clawed out a polished apple and a poke of molasses candy, and probed among the nuts till she fished out a tissue-wrapped parcel soft to the touch. It disclosed small underclothes, nicely made to the last snap and buttonhole. Still farther down was a checked gingham dress, and below it a knitted coat and hat, socks, and slippers.

Under the stocking was a new dress for Lily herself, from Granny. And in the stocking's toe was a small box which revealed a silver ring set with a turquoise. It had been Harriet's ring, and she had remembered Mother's saying: 'A doll-baby in the top and a finger ring in the toe: that surely does make the right kind of Christmas stocking for a girl child.'

Ring on finger, Lily dressed and undressed her doll. Her hands trembled and her tongue protruded from the bud of her lips. She was dumb with joy.

'You-all ain' peek at yo' own stockin', Hayet,' Granny reminded her.

Apples. Nuts. A knitted scarf from Granny. A bottle of dreadful perfume from Lily, who woke up from her doll to beam when Harriet took it out. On the floor below the stocking, a bulky bundle: a quilt of beautiful old design, quilted with tiny stitches.

'For me?' cried Harriet.

Granny nodded, eyes moist with delight at the girl's surprise. 'E de Statehouse Steps pattern,' she said. 'Done began piecin' 'm when I got yo' letter las' summer.'

'And you haven't looked at *your* stocking, Granny!' Harriet reminded her in turn.

'Mussy me! I ain' hang no stockin' dis fifty year!' — Her eyes followed Harriet's finger, pointing to the black length in the shadows. — 'Why, honey chile, whenever did you-all —— ?'

Chuckling with embarrassment, Granny sat down in her rocker and held her aproned lap for the treasure. Lily had traded the eggs from her pet hens and bought a bottle of hair-straightener over which Granny giggled and clicked her teeth. Granny stroked her thick, fleecy nightgowns almost as delightedly as Lily stroked her doll, and examined the pink embroidery on the yoke of the blue one and the blue embroidery on the yoke of the pink one with indrawn breaths of admiration. And in the toe of Granny's stocking, too, was something small and precious in a jeweler's box: a small brooch that had been Mother's, with a chip diamond sparkling in its twist of gold. At sight of that, Granny threw a nightgown over her face and rocked to and fro, crying softly.

'What are you going to name your new doll, Lily?' asked Harriet, shy of tears.

Lily looked up solemnly: 'I name 'm Granny Hayet Queener Sheber.'

From the door Richard's laughter echoed theirs. He did not come empty-handed. He had one of the hand-woven wastebaskets for Harriet, a string of beads for Lily, and for Granny a sack of rice and a broom, hand-made from wild broom grass bound with split hickory.

Shyly Harriet handed him a parcel that had lain on the mantel, lovely in star-strewn blue wrapping paper and silver bows. Richard turned it over and over. 'E too pretty fuh spile!' he murmured, lapsing into Gullah talk. He sat with knees stiffly pressed together and awkwardly slipped off the ribbon and folded the paper, before looking at the book, 'American Cities.'

'Never did I own a book befo', cep'n' the Good Book and schoolbooks,' he said soberly.

Eyes shining with eagerness, Lily plumped Granny Hayet Queener Sheber down on the open pages of the book and followed her with all her wardrobe and waved the turquoise ring so close to Richard's eyes that he flinched involuntarily. Then she exhibited the perfume she had given Harriet and the hair-straightener that she had given Granny.

When all the presents had been inspected, Harriet looked longingly at the open window. 'Let's walk!' she proposed.

With Lily scampering around them, ahead of them, like a dog that runs three miles to its master's one, Harriet and Richard tramped around the island. Again squirrels and rabbits and quail darted through the underbrush, and fallen leaves crunched underfoot. Richard had a pocketful of peanuts and a length of white sugar cane apiece, and he showed Harriet a more satisfactory technique for chewing and sucking the oldtime Southern sweet.

'Got to get my book an' go home,' he said reluctantly, when they returned to the cabin. 'Promise' to take Mom an' li'l Washin'ton to Booker for the Mystery.'

He passed a loving hand over the book cover.

'You simply must see all those cities some day,' Harriet said eagerly.

'I'm gwine to,' he answered simply. 'Done made up my mind.'

XVI

'WE RE LUCKY!'

THE morning after Christmas Harriet was wakened by a flood of cool air and a red gleam full in her face. She snuggled down under the weight of quilts and stared sleepily. The sun was shining straight in at the window — an open window which had certainly been shuttered when she went to bed.

Granny was not beside her. She was kneeling before that window in her high-necked, long-sleeved nightgown — a patched nightgown, for she was saving the new ones. While Harriet blinked drowsily, the old woman bowed her grizzled head to the floor, once, twice, three times.

'La-la-la-la-la!' she intoned as if humming in her deep voice; and then, very simply, 'Blessed King Jesus, keep Yo' li'l chillen safe and good dis day, Amen!'

Harriet squeezed her eyes shut before Granny struggled stiffly to her feet and turned to dress. That morning obeisance was so strange!

The strangeness hovered in her mind through the hurry of washing and dressing. Richard was going to take her over to Saint Catherine's today, and when he came to milk they must make their plans.

We're Lucky!

While she was slipping her dress over her head she heard the boy's thumping at the back door, and when she ran out to the kitchen to say good morning the air was aromatic with warm milk.

It was a fine crisp day for an excursion. Richard's bateau was staked on the bay beach. They ran lightly across the strip of quaking sand and established themselves, and Harriet watched with eager interest as Richard set the oars in the oarlocks and pulled out with long strokes into the salt-smelling water.

'Set right still!' he warned her.

'Oh, I've been in rowboats before. We have lakes in Minnesota: pretty little ones all through Minneapolis and St. Paul and big ones with pine and white birch up through the north of the state.'

'Gwine see 'm!' he boasted, grinning at her. 'Gwine see 'm all!'

She puckered her brows. 'I — don't know whether I've ever seen anything lovelier than this, though!' She waved her arm in a comprehensive gesture.

'Shucks!' he deprecated. 'Y'all are just bein' mannersable.'

Saint Catherine's was lovely, too, in the afternoon sunshine. When Richard had tied his boat they tramped through the sweetness of it, he with his oars over his shoulder. The road that led to Booker was an even more shadowy tunnel than the Landers highway; and more ox-carts squalled past them, and more mule teams with no harness except rope reins and ropes to hold up the sapling thills.

Miss Locke's house stood in a sunny garden a stone's throw from the nearest of the school buildings. Walks made of great round stepping stones led between frosted chrysanthemums and marigolds with a few hardy blossoms, up to a deep-porched bungalow. Harriet set foot on a stone and paused. It was strangely grooved and marked.

'Millstones,' Richard answered her unspoken query.

'But I don't see ——'

'Old-style ones, somethin' like the kind in the Good Book, I reckon. Mom tells how there was a big flood back in 1911 and the island folks was in a bad fix. So the teachers at Booker say if they bring their old millstones to make Booker a walk they'll give 'em food and clo'es for 'em. You see there ain' no rocks on the whole of the island.'

Miss Locke, small, erect, blue-eyed and white-haired, met them cordially at the door. She had a welcoming hand for Richard and a questioning smile for Harriet. Richard made the introduction with simple dignity, and, seated in the quietly charming living-room, Harriet came quickly to the point.

'Miss Locke, what can be done about the island farms that are being sold for taxes? My great-grandmother's tract — it seems that it was sold years ago. Do you suppose I can get it back for her?'

Miss Locke's face shone. 'Are you one of the boys and girls who are going to work for their people here?' she asked. 'Richard is another. He's a real Booker lad, even if he has had only a few years with us. We're looking to such boys to play a big part on their own islands in a few more years. We need girls just as badly.'

Harriet shook her head. 'No, I haven't thought of staying more than this year. I mean to go back and enter the University of Minnesota. I'll be a music major, but I'm going to minor in Home Economics. — I do want to see what can be done about Granny's home, though.'

She glanced at Richard. He was twirling his cap, his face cloudy.

'Well,' Miss Locke conceded, 'there are other places to work. I suppose it's natural I see this one. There's a great deal to build on in these islands.' She smiled abstractedly past them out of the window. 'But your great-grandmother's home ——' She recalled herself.

'It's in that bunch of farms boughten up by Mr. Van Buren from up No'th,' Richard explained.

She nodded. 'Oh, yes, just before the Depression. I've looked into that. He lost practically everyting in 1929, and he hasn't paid the taxes on those farms since he bought them.'

'He hasn't?' Harriet's voïce was eager. 'Doesn't that mean that we could buy them back? Or would it cost too much?'

'A hundred dollars might cover your grandmother's tract. But after that there would be the problem again of making it productive enough to support her and whoever else is dependent on her, and pay the current taxes as she goes. Richard has it well planned. He can do it, too; and not only that, but help all the others on the island to do it.'

She smiled at them sparklingly and swept on.

'Richard harvested the prize crop of sweet potatoes on his school acre this fall. Seven times the average yield for South Carolina. You can see what such productiveness would mean to the farmers. That's why Richard wears a Booker sweater, like a letter man at home. — You work Mrs. Freeman's ground too, don't you, Richard?'

'My brother and me.'

'Well, you see they can make the farms pay if they work scientifically. Tell her how you apportion your crops, Richard.'

Richard went on twirling his cap, while he told Harriet, heavily, how they planted for provisions for the household and provisions for the animals and a 'money crop' that would give them the small amounts of cash necessary.

'But Richard's plan is much bigger than this. He's learning to do everything that's needed on a farm, from

re-tiring a cart and making harness to breeding good
stock; and as soon as he's through here and maybe had
an advanced year at Hampton, the Government will put
him in as instructor on his own island, to work through the
rural schools there. You can't measure his value!'

'But his music?' Harriet asked.

'His music will always be an asset beyond price.' Miss
Locke smiled again, expectantly, at Richard, but he was
still twirling his cap.

'These *are* your plans, Richard?' Alarm sharpened her
voice.

'Lessen I get me a good job up No'th — just for a
while — and make money enough to send back to my
people and help 'm thataway,' Richard answered.

Miss Locke's brows lifted in concern. 'I can't think you
would do that,' she said in a carefully controlled voice.
'You've too much vision, Richard. Money can't help your
people as you yourself can help them — help them to
help themselves.' She studied him anxiously, but he
would not meet her eye. 'I can't imagine where a boy or
girl could invest life better than right here. There's a
sounder basis here for most of our small landowners than
anywhere in the North, where life is so often tawdry and
sordid for them. Here you could be a sort of Moses ——'

Richard seized the name as an escape.

'Miss Locke, there's another thing Harriet wants to
find out,' he said quickly. 'Somethin' about her great-
great-great grandpa. Black Moses, he was called. On
Tolliver Plantation.'

Miss Locke still studied him, her eyes somber with
disappointment. Harriet helped him past the awkward
silence.

'They say strange things about him, Miss Locke.
Legends like the legends of Paul Bunyan of the Northwest,
about his size and strength. But the most interesting

things are about his being — well, the son of a priest somewhere in Northern Africa, and reading and writing in
another tongue. Yet Granny' — Harriet flushed —
'Granny can't read or write our own.'

Again Miss Locke had recalled herself courteously.
'Yes, I have heard of him. I've heard of him as a leader
not unworthy of his name. He was hampered by one of
the harder type of masters' — she broke off; began again
— 'but whatever his origin and whatever his condition
here, he was a nobleman. Any descendant of Black
Moses has reason to be proud.'

Harriet's high head was higher as she shook hands in
farewell; but Miss Locke was thinking less about her than
about Richard. Her blue eyes rested on him ponder-
ingly.

'Richard,' she said, 'your life is your own. But look
at some of the boys that have gone North. Don't they
seem — shoddy — compared to Sam Fripp, working on
Hilton's Head for his people?'

'Reckon it depends on what's inside 'm in the first
place,' Richard dissented. 'Looks like we-all ought to
see somethin' beyond our own islands, m'm.'

Unaccountably, Miss Locke's face had brightened. 'I
guess you're right in one thing, Richard,' she said more
serenely. 'It depends on what you really *are*, inside.'

As they walked back toward the bay and the boat,
Harriet's elation bubbled through a certain depression
that had settled upon her. 'It does seem marvelous what
you can do here! It's a — a profession. And something
that seems to be building for the future, too. Isn't it
stupid how we choose little things to do with our lives,
when we could just as well choose big ones? — Richard!'
she broke off to scold, 'why are you acting so funny about
it today?'

'Shucks!' He grinned down at her. 'Y'all get me eye-

sighted over seein' the world and then you scold me caze
I want to see it. Cain' do nothin' about it anyway,
Harriet. My lef' foot done itch for a week.'

'Your foot itches?'

'Sure sign,' he said, grinning. 'Gwine travel strange
ground.'

'Who's the swanky-looking boy?' Harriet interrupted
softly.

'Lawzy, if it ain' Jick Smith,' Richard answered without
pleasure.

Jick Smith was sauntering out to a dilapidated gateway,
smiling as he came. Richard tossed a hand in salute and
hastened his steps, but Jick did not take the hint. He
creaked open the gate and confronted them.

'Miss Freeman,' Richard said unwillingly, 'meet Jick
Smith. He just came from up No'th.'

Jick nodded. 'Seen you before, ain' I? Don't have to
ask are you from the No'th, Miss Freeman. Gwine back
in a hurry, too, I bet you. So'm I. Never could stan' the
sticks.'

'Oh, but I think these islands are lovely,' Harriet
replied coolly. She recognized Jick. He was the boy with
the round dimple in his cheek, the boy who had stuck her
pink paper napkin behind his ear on the boat.

She knew his type. He was present in every group of
society and in every color. There was something winning
about his impudence, something fascinating about his
cakewalking swing as he came to meet them, his feet
cutting little flourishes, with style and precision. But he
was spoiled and sure of himself. Harriet loved to take
that sort down a peg. So she looked at him 'down her
nose,' as Johnnie expressed it.

'We've got to hurry, Richie,' she said, 'or Granny'll be
worried. Good-bye, Mr. Smith.'

Richard kept glancing at her anxiously as they ap-

'WH' Y'ALL WANTS TO KNOW, HONEY CHILE?'

proached the bateau. 'Handsome, ain't he — isn't he?' ne asked.

'Who? That Jick person? Say, Richard, wasn't he one of the ones Miss Locke meant when she spoke of the fellows who had been living North?'

'Maybe so.'

'Well, I don't know Sam Fripp; but I kept putting this slick Jick up against — Black Moses,' Harriet said soberly. 'Richie, haven't you heard anything more about Black Moses?'

'Ask Granny,' he suggested, helping her into the boat. 'Ask her tonight. I fetched her some pa'tridges and she invited me to supper. I like to hear tales about Black Moses, my-own self.'

The sun was setting red when they reached the home beach and drove the boat in among the rushes. The air was so keen that Harriet snuggled her fur collar up around her ears and Richard slapped his hands together for warmth as they strode through the field and through the thicket to Granny's cabin. The opening door let out a rush of fragrant warmth. Supper was making, and by the time Richard had washed himself scrupulously and milked, the meal was ready to dish up.

The partridges were delicate morsels, and the pork chitterlings and rice supplemented them gratefully. Harriet ate until she was sure she could never eat again.

Yet after the dishes were washed and the fire was made up in the sitting-room fireplace, she was not sorry to see Granny putting grunnets to roast in the ashes.

'Granny,' she said, 'while the peanuts are roasting, won't you tell us about Black Moses?'

Granny looked at her questioningly, smoothing Lily's head with a big dark hand. 'Wh' y'all wants to know, honey chile?'

'Well — what language was it he read and wrote?

And why didn't he teach you reading and writing?
And ——'

'Ain' dat 'nough fuh start on, honey?' Granny asked,
shifting Lily to a more comfortable position on her lap.
'Why e ain' teach me? Caze e done dead befo' I done born.
Black Moses ain' so old when e dead,' Granny explained
somberly, and rocked creakingly back and forth before
she added: 'Mammy tell us stories, but I fuhgit 'm. But
I do know Ol' Mas'r beat e's darkies efn dey learn readin'
an' writin'.'

'Yet they keep telling us that most masters were kind,'
Harriet protested.

'Mebbe mos' of 'm was,' Granny agreed, stroking Lily's
head against her shoulder. 'Plenty was, I knows fo' a
fac'. De kind ones was kind and de bad ones was bad.
But dey ain' no human, honey chile, got de right to own
no odder human. Caze men and women is men and
women in de eyes of de good Lawd.'

'All men born free and equal,' Richard said oratori-
cally.

'But — Moses? Where do you think he came from,
Granny?'

Granny shook her head. 'I ain' know. Not where de
mos' of 'm come from. Mammy say e stolen f'm e's
father. I ain' know where.' She leaned to take a nut
from the hot ashes and test it. The fire lighted her strong
brown face; lighted Lily's wide bright eyes.

'Git up, honey!' Granny told Lily, and herself rose
stiffly from her rocking-chair and went to a corner of her
room where a third stool stood in the shadows. She
returned, walking painfully, carrying the stool and holding
its age-dark top to the firelight while she scrutinized it
with eyes and fingers. 'Ain' hardly a mark lef',' she said.
'Pappy carve 'm when e set in de dark. E say Moses teach
'm.'

With a quick intake of breath Harriet tilted forward and peered. Richard was crouching beside Granny, his eyes puzzled.

'There's A and B and C; but theseyere don' look like no letters ever I've seen,' he said slowly.

'Richie, they — they look like —' Harriet began eagerly, only to break off. 'Granny, why do you kneel facing east when you pray? And why do you bow three times as you do?'

'Lawzy, honey chile!' Granny's voice was flustered, and she began over again. 'Lawzy, I ain' know why. Cep'n my mammy and my pappy done so befo' me, an' it seem like a proper kind of prayin'.'

Harriet's brilliant gaze went to the stool, with its tracery of characters half effaced by time, and to Richard's face, still bent above it.

'It must be Arabic!' she cried. 'And Black Moses must have been really an educated Mohammedan. Like that Ben Ali you read about, who left a diary in a desert dialect of Arabia. Oh, Richie, think of being a free Arab to start with and ending up as a Negro slave!'

'I don' quite make out,' Richard said, puzzled.

'Richie, haven't you read that chant, Allah il Allah il Allah — There is no God but God? That's how you began your prayer, wasn't it, Gran?'

'La-la-la-la-la!' Granny hummed acquiescently. 'I ain' know what it mean befo', but dat de blessed trufe. On'y one Lawd and E's Son, King Jesus,' she said reverently. She pulled the kettle to a cooler part of the fireplace and stirred it again, the warm peanut fragrance expanding through the cabin.

'A Mohammedan!' Harriet repeated musingly.

'And a good man dat was willin' to lay down e's life fo' e's frien',' said Granny.

'Listen!'

Through the still night came the throb of measured beating.

'De drum!' Granny explained it.

'Askin' folks to a Christmas week frolic,' Richard added. 'Granny, Harriet might hanker to go.'

The three 'chillen' ran to the door and stood listening to the exotic pulse in the blackness.

'I've read how they use a drum like that in Africa, to call people. What do they do at the frolic?'

'Oh, they march, and they dance — mos'ly square dancin' — an' they eat. Crowd the cabin so you cain' hardly move. They'll be another one tomorrow night likewise, sposen you like to go.'

'Maybe. But not tonight. It's more fun here. Let's sing, shall we?'

She laughed exultantly, and Richard and Lily joined her.

'We're lucky one way,' said Richard; 'we're such a laughin' people.'

'We're lucky anyway!' Harriet declared. She flung her head high. 'We have so much life in us. We can do anything we try to. Anything.'

XVII

The Cabin in the Clearing

Richard's mother had invited Granny and Harriet and Lily to New Year's supper. Harriet dreaded the event. There was no longer any strangeness in having Richard for a friend, when Richard was a lone figure, good and gay and gifted. But how would it be when she saw him in his own home, a part of a family?

His own home was beyond another cane patch and another thicket, and the guests arrived in midafternoon, in the sweetness of winter sunshine. Single file they entered the path that slanted off from the road. Lily led the way, her stockings drawn taut and her dress crackling with starch under her faded red sweater. She carried Granny Hayet Queener Sheber in both hands, straight in front of her, but her old root-doll, Rebecca-Rachel, was tucked under her patched red arm. Rebecca-Rachel had fine roots for hair and a rag-wrapped weed stem for a body; Granny had made her and dressed her.

Granny wore her best black dress, very ancient, with a beaded collar, and her snowiest headcloth and apron. Harriet followed them, a slim dark princess, with the warm fur of her coat collar and the rust-red of her hat framing her face.

Tall dry weeds closed in around them as they went: a forest of weeds meeting over their heads. The tallest were the wild beanies, the beans still rattling in their dry pods. To Harriet those tropic fugitives were part of Granny's story. She recognized the wild fennel, too, and the wild broom straw that made most of the island brooms. And here and there an okra plant, escaped from a gar- den, lifted exquisite late blossoms.

At the end of the path a round head dodged into sight, with another far below its level: dodged into sight; dodged out of sight again. Lily paused with a swish of skirts and a richly indulgent giggle. 'Aa'on an' Wash'ton!' she announced importantly. 'All bofe scairt of Hayet.'

Almost immediately, Richard was striding forward to meet them. He twitched one of Lily's braids and 'pulled his foot' in a bow to Granny, while his eyes went past them both with a questioning smile for Harriet. It was an anxious smile, as if he, too, had been wondering how his home would impress her. He backed against the wall of weeds with his arms outspread to hold them back, and let his guests pass him, Lily strutting ahead, into the Corwin clearing.

Harriet stopped short and looked. Like Jericho meeting-house, the cabin was enclosed in shadowy woods. A vast live-oak spread its arms behind and looked down, down, down on the pine-shake roof, caressing it with streamers of moss. The wind murmured high overhead as Harriet had heard it in Northern pine woods.

Before it the dooryard was swept clean as a floor, and a holly tree, bright with berries, adorned it. Harriet drew a deep breath. Here lived both peace and beauty. She smiled at Richard, who had stood anxiously watching her, and his face cleared.

'Not much like where you-all live,' he said. 'There's Mom, Harriet.'

The face he turned to his mother held no doubt, no apology. She came across the porch to greet them, round and warm-brown and comely. 'Y'all sho' welcome!' she cried. 'Us proud to see you, dis New Year Day.'

Little Washington nearly tripped them in his efforts to keep hidden in his mother's skirts, but they were all finally inside the cabin. There Aaron was grinning and pulling his foot and his forelock, and a ragged old man, wizened and dry as a cricket, bowed deeply to Granny. This was Grampa; not Richard's grandfather; just a grampa-in-general, who had dropped in to sit by the fire a while and eat when eating-time came.

Harriet studied the small sitting-room, while Richard took her hat and coat and hung them in a corner. One of the windows held a shining pane of glass; otherwise this was much like Granny's sitting-room. The bed was big and puffy; the walls and ceiling were covered with fresh layers of newspaper; the mantel was trimmed with cut-out scallops. On the mantel, beside the faded picture of a man whom Harriet guessed to be Richie's father, was a snapshot of Harriet, neatly framed in sand dollars. On the center table with the Bible was the book of American Cities.

'Mis' Corwin — Mis' Corwin!' Lily was saying breathlessly, holding Granny Hayet Queener Sheber high so that her hostess might appreciate its splendors.

'My land to goodness!' Mrs. Corwin exclaimed. She looked the doll's clothes over with interest while Washington tried to climb up her to see better and Aaron tried to see without appearing to. 'Who ever done make y'all sech gran' doll-baby clo'es?'

Lily thrust her thumb backward at Harriet and then plugged her mouth with it.

'E too pretty fuh break,' Mrs. Corwin said anxiously. 'Lemme set 'm on de mantelpiece, honey. Wash'ton jest raven fuh git 'm.'

'I got Rebecca-Rachel fuh play wid,' Lily agreed, and she nestled the root-baby in her arms and watched delightedly as Mrs. Corwin enthroned the queen in her knitted coat beside Harriet's picture.

Mrs. Corwin excused herself with bobbing bows and went back to see to her dinner. Pot lids clattered and whiffs of savory smell came through the open door. Granny laid off her voluminous old coat and sat down across the fire from the old man, and Lily ran out with Washington.

'I'll show you the yard if you don' mind, Harriet,' Richard said, and held the door for her to precede him.

The habitual forest twilight was deepening into an enchanted dusk. Killdeers called plaintively and frogs chorused. Silently Richard pointed through a shadowy vista that led to a dark gleam of water. Among the rushes a white crane poised on one leg like an ivory carving.

'It's so lovely — so lovely!' sighed Harriet.

Lily dashed around the corner of the cabin. 'Hayet!' she begged, 'come see de house me 'n' Wash'ton build yes'day.'

The young people followed her. They passed the big iron wash-kettles standing on their dead embers. They passed the pile of rice waiting to be thrashed with two rough sticks hinged with a bit of rope; waiting to be polished in a mortar that was a hollowed section of tree-trunk. They passed the brick well of the cane mill, with its long pole where the 'critter' was hitched to revolve the millstones. They passed the clean, tight chickenhouse. They came to the staggering playhouse, like an African hut with cornstalk corner posts and straw-thatched roof, where Washington sat in cherubic dignity.

It was all Harriet could do to keep from picking up the master of the house and hugging him. He was the kind of child who sets fingers itching to touch him. At three years he had not lost his baby plumpness. His mouth was a moist, carnelian-colored pucker, his eyes big and solemn and velvety, his little body as straight-limbed and dimpled as a cupid's.

Lily asked him, 'De baby wake?' and peered past him at Rebecca-Rachel lying on a straw pallet in the corner. With eyes watching Harriet for the effect of her housekeeping, she seized a little broom of wild bamboo and twigs and swept her dooryard vigorously.

'I'm so glad to have made your acquaintance, Mrs. ——' Harriet turned to Lily with exaggerated courtesy — 'Let's see: I didn't catch the name.'

Lily snickered behind her hands. 'Name Mis' Co'win. Dis Mist' Co'win. E my husban'. Git up, Wash'ton, and make yo' manners.'

The gentleman plunged forward on his dimpled brown hands and scrambled thence to his feet. He rolled his eyes up at Lily and made an obedient bow, flopping down on all fours again in the process.

Lily rescued him and brushed broom straw from his tight, black curls. 'E awful li'l,' she said dubiously. 'Y'all think e ketch up wid me?'

The visit was interrupted by a stifled shriek from the cabin door. It was a shriek of pure terror, and both young people went leaping toward Mrs. Corwin, who stood shrinking back from the step with Aaron peering over her shoulder.

When they came up she was pointing with a shaking finger at the step. A small object lay there, indistinct in the dusk. Richard leaned over and picked it up.

'Now-now, Mom,' he coaxed. 'Ain' nothin' but some fool chile flung it here to skeer us.'

He dangled the small bag with attempted nonchalance, but his mother only chattered with panic, and Grampa, looking over her other shoulder, showed the whites of his eyes in like fear.

'Listen, Mom,' Richard went on, 'I take it and drown it and that's all they is to it. Ain' nothin' — never was nothin' — sho' won' *be* nothin' oncet the water's drownded it.'

He loped away toward the rushy gleam Harriet had seen a few minutes before. She walked slowly after him and stood waiting for his return, herself too puzzled for words. He returned, rubbing his hands together, and grinned sheepishly.

'Some smart chillen,' he scolded. 'Like to scare Mom clean outen her wits.'

'But what on earth —— ?'

'Conjure bag,' he said briefly.

'*Conjure bag?*'

He nodded. 'Somebody puts roots and a lock of yo' hair in a little small bag and puts it where yo' bound to step over it. To put a charm on you; make you die or have bad luck.'

'Richard, you don't believe any such thing!'

He shook his head. 'Booker chillen learn better,' he said without full conviction. 'But Mom still thinks the old way.'

When they went in, they found Mrs. Corwin moving jerkily around the kitchen, picking things up and setting them down, her brown face still ashen. Granny was saying, 'Sho', Mis' Corwin, dem signs an' conjures don' have no power over no true believer.' Richard patted his mother's plump shoulder and added soothingly: 'It done drownded, Mom. Nothin' to fear.'

'Could I help, Mrs. Corwin?' Harriet asked. 'I'd love to.'

Mrs. Corwin looked at Harriet's glowing knitted dress, at her well-groomed hands. 'Y'all too fine, honey,' she said, making a valiant effort at composure. 'Richie 'n' Aa'on, dey he'ps me most as good as gal-chillen.'

Nevertheless, Harriet and Richard both tied on clean aprons and helped set the table and dish up the food. Granny gossiped with Grampa before the fire and the children fell to playing again near them, still uneasy over the grown folks' fright. Richard talked with determined cheerfulness. He showed Harriet the stove he and Aaron had got their mother, and explained how he meant to seal the whole interior of the cabin with matched boards as soon as he could afford to, so Mom wouldn't have the bother of papering it every year. He intended to add window sash, with glass, one at a time, too.

'Dat chile got highfalutin ideas,' his mother said quaveringly, as she set a steaming dish on the table, but her glance at her tall son was an admiring one, mingling dependent wonder and pride.

'Would y'all please to come to supper?' she called to the old people, and they came with alacrity, Grampa stepping stiffly like rusted machinery, but with a mass of pleased wrinkles under his white thatch.

Dinner was good, with wild ducks that Richard had shot, and liver pudding, and fruit cake richly flavored. Grampa ate steadily but with an abstracted gaze.

'Mis' Freeman an' me wonders if it ain' dat no-count Mis' Jones done you like dat,' he mumbled with his mouth full.

'It was some no-count mischiev-i-ous chile!' Richard said quickly. 'Grampa, we ain' gwine think no more about it. They ain' no — any — magic anyway. Booker teach us that.'

Grampa cackled, eating again as fast as his toothless gums would allow. 'Might it was a chillen,' he conceded, 'caze yo' Mom ain' got no ill-wishers. But Booker don' knows ev'ything. Whi' folks mebbe ain' need signs, but de good Lawd gib 'em to colored. Colored folks ain' need book-learnin'.' He mumbled another delicately roasted morsel of duck, smackingly. 'Yo' Mom ain' need no receets fuh cook good. She ain' need no book-learnin' fuh raise three likely boy-chillen. Looka dat Wash'ton. Why e ain' puny an' crook-laig? Caze e mammy feed 'im pot liquor an' tie chicken bones round e neck so e don' suffer wid e teethin'.' He sucked the juicy flesh from a breast bone resoundingly.

The talk went on, talk about cooking and hunting and the white folks coming to the island for the winter season. White folks were so tender they couldn't come to their homes on the islands till after the hard frosts had set in.

Harriet sat looking at the delectable Washington, lost in thought. Pot liquor. That was the juices of boiled vegetables, rich in salts and vitamins. How recently the scientists had found out about those vitamins! How long the islanders had been making babies strong with them! But not all the islanders were wise, that was clear: too many of their babies had the bow legs, the winged shoulder blades, the large heads, of rickets; the span of life was still too short.

If you had sense, thought Harriet, you might get along pretty well without book-learning; but most folks didn't have that much sense.

Mrs. Corwin had sense; she was a fine person, even though she hadn't gone beyond the shanty schools. But her face was only now regaining its color, and Harriet felt very sure that it had required a heroic self-control for her to go on so quietly with the supper.

Granny and Aaron helped with the dishes. 'Y'all go 'long in an' make some music,' Mrs. Corwin bade Harriet and Richard.

So Richard made up the fire, with a polite word to Grampa, who was already nodding beside it, his sharp chin with its grizzle of sparse beard resting on his collarless shirt-front. Richard drew up a stool for Harriet, and took down his banjo and plucked it, and they sang. Lily and Washington were playing mysterious things on the floor with Rebecca-Rachel and some jackstones.

How music made homes of the humblest places! Harriet thought. She closed her eyes and tilted her head against the newspapered wall and sang, and didn't know where she was. She opened her eyes and watched Richard play, his feet wrapped round the front legs of his stool, his head on one side, his eyes dreamy and smiling. When both had stopped, breathless, she reached out her hand for the banjo.

'Y'all ever play one?' he asked, bringing the stool down on its front legs with a thump and handing her the instrument.

She shook her head, trying the banjo hesitantly. After a few moments, guided by her knowledge of music in general, she was plunking soft chords for one of the Landers songs. It was a song that teased her memory with its simple words and the haunting melody borrowed from an old spiritual. She sang, and Richie hummed a deep accompaniment, like bees in clover.

> 'Landers, Landers, Landers, Landers,
> I do love you for your name.
> Landers, Landers, Landers, Landers,
> I do love you for your fame.
> I would keep your banner,
> Ever keep your banner
> High!'

Richie's face was shining with happiness. He was looking toward the kitchen door, and Harriet turned and saw that Mrs. Corwin and Granny stood watching and listening, and Aaron peered over his mother's head.

'Y'all see?' Richie demanded. 'This girl ain' white folks. No. I know she can make the piano holler for dear life; but she can take my old banjo, likewise, and make it sweet-talk as good as I can. She ain' too grand,' he finished simply.

Hurriedly Harriet started another tune, her cheeks burning.

They sang on, and presently they heard outside a strident, monstrous cough. Grinning, Richard strode to the door. 'Booker boy,' he explained. 'Got an old automobile. When we got gasoline, we ride all round Gentlemen's. — Please excuse me.'

He was back in two minutes, clearing his throat uncertainly. 'I told Sam you-all don' want to ride in any old car without springs and doors,' he said.

Harriet sprang to her feet. 'Oh, don't I?' she mocked. 'If Granny doesn't mind — At home we call them jaloppies, and lots of kids have them.'

'I like it, too,' Richard admitted.

Harriet looked respectfully to Granny for consent, and Granny nodded. 'Reckon young uns has to be young uns. Put on yo' hat, honey chile, likewise yo' coat. — No, Lily, Wash'ton ain' gwine, neider Aa'on.'

'Ain' any mo' room,' Richie told her gently.

The jaloppie was waiting in the road, one yellow eye glaring through the blackness. Sam hopped out from under the steering-wheel and shook hands with Harriet, and Richie helped her in.

'Got to git some water,' Sam said, and ran with banging pail to the pump.

'Radiator does leak so bad,' Richie explained.

Sam poured the water into the radiator, Harriet sniffing the sharp smell as it promptly began to leak out upon the dusty road. Then he found a place to hang the pail, and dashed to the front of the machine and threw himself upon the crank till the engine began to cough purposefully. He wriggled under the wheel again and the jaloppie gave a big hump and a big bump, and lurched sidewise over a stone and leaped ahead.

It was the jaloppiest jaloppie Harriet had ever met. Its seat-cushions were gone, so they must ride on bare boards. Its doors were missing, so that Richie braced his long legs, with the skill of custom, across the opening.

Harriet jerked her hat down tighter and wished she had a way of tying it under her chin. She began to laugh. Bump! and they would all leap upward together as if from a springboard. Thump! and they would all come down as if they were trying to break through the boards. Bang! and the only thing that kept them from flying out of the car was the tightness of the front seat.

'I'm s-sure g-g-glad there isn't any t-top!' she stuttered through her laughter. 'Our h-h-heads would go r-right through! — Oh, my hat!'

But Richie had caught her hat just as she felt the cool draft of its departure. He caught it with a convulsive swing of the hand that had been holding to the place where there wasn't any door.

She pulled it down as tight as she could. 'If I c-could only t-tie it!'

After another amazing contortion, Richie produced a folded handkerchief. 'T-try that!' he shouted above the roar and rattle.

Harriet put it on cornerwise over her small hat and managed to knot it under her chin. As they came into a band of light streaming from an open cabin door, she saw Richard studying the improvised headcloth with a queer smile.

The car banged to a stop and Sam was out, with his pail, and dashing to the pump, while the jaloppie stood shaking itself like a wet dog.

'Sam must have to take a regular route,' said Harriet, 'to be sure of water.'

'Ain' got to go far fo' water, not on Gentlemen's,' Richie reminded her. 'Harriet, is this too rough for you-all? Sure you don' want to go back home?'

Harriet chuckled. 'It's such fun you couldn't hire me to go home.'

It was a wild ride. Sam drove hunched forward with a heavy foot on the accelerator, and the car roared through the deep dust of the road, to the tune of loud explosions. It hit an occasional little board bridge with a jolt that jarred the words out of the riders' mouths and the breath out of their lungs. The one headlight picked out the weeds by the wayside, the tangles of palmetto and oak, the pickets of a fence. Beyond the margins of the road was nothing but deep black, except where light glimmered through the cracks of an infrequent cabin. The jaloppie seemed boring through limitless dark a tunnel lined with light.

Sometimes Sam flung himself at the wheel and wrenched the car to the side of the road to avoid a 'critter' placidly ruminating in the middle of the way. Often the darkness gave back paired green lights, high or low, that were the eyes of beasts, big or little. But they met no other headlights: not a single car of any sort.

They did not try to talk much, for talking meant a stuttered shout. Once Sam, face straight ahead, did ask, 'G-girl name of C-c-countess at L-landers?' And Harriet shouted back, 'Y-yes! Y-you know h-her?' And Sam answered, 'M-met up with her oncet. — Wh-whyn't y-you bring her to G-gentlemen's sometime?' And Richie began to laugh. And Sam shouted, 'Aw, sh-sh-shut yo' mouth, Richie!' and laughed, too. He had a big, clean laugh like Richard's.

They laughed until Harriet could scarcely bear the ache

of it. And they sang funny tremolo songs. And then they
jolted up a ridge of sand and stopped short.

'Who says I cain' turn on the moon?' Sam asked, out of
a deep stillness.

There they sat, sole owners of those miles of beach, with
the breakers booming softly and a glow deepening at the
far horizon. Silently they watched as the glow sharpened
to a keen red sickle, to a broad blade, to a semicircle, to
a full round.

When it had really risen, so that its aching beauty and
magic were dimmed and it no longer seemed profanity to
speak or sing or laugh, Harriet softly sang 'Oh, Mammy
Moon,' the boys bumbling along below her. Then,
reluctantly, Sam backed down the sand ridge and ma-
neuvered his way around into the road again, and they
went bumping and snorting and galloping home.

It was not late when Richard and Harriet came, blown
and laughing, into the Corwin cabin, but Lily and Washington lay sprawled asleep, the plump feather bed rising
roundly about their small bodies. Old Grampa had gone,
and Mrs. Corwin, placid again, was showing Granny her
quilt pieces.

'Oh, Granny, we had the most fun. — And the moon!
Richie, I didn't suppose Sam would be like that.'

'Like what, Harriet? Sam's kind of human.'

Harriet dropped down beside Granny to look at the
quilt top spread out across her knees. It was a wonder of
intricate piecing.

'Has the pattern got a name?'

'Sho' nuff: Star of Bethlehem,' Mrs. Corwin said,
reaching over to smooth it fondly.

'Ain' — *haven'* we got plenty quilts, Mom? Why you
want to wear out yo' eyes piecin' mo'?' Richard teased,
standing with an elbow on the mantel, watching them,
while the old hound nosed his hanging hand.

177

'Y'all knows good and well what disyere quilt fo',' Mrs. Corwin scolded. 'I sells chances and makes a heap of money on it.'

'Tell 'em what fo' you want the money, Mom,' Richard persisted.

'We gwine git us a Rose'wald School on Gentlemen's!' Mrs. Corwin explained. 'I ain' got no book-larnin' my-own se'f, but —— '

Her eyes went past Harriet to the bed and she heaved herself hastily to her feet.

'Hab mussy!' she went on, all in the same breath; 'efn dey ain' a hat on dat bed!'

While Harriet watched, open-mouthed, Richard picked her hat from where she had dropped it beside Lily. With his eyes twinkling, he took a pin from beneath his coat lapel, and gravely stuck it into the hat. His mother loosed a sigh of relief and then looked sheepishly at Harriet.

'Cain' learn me no diff'ent now,' she said. 'I done growed up on signs, seems like. — But I reckon de book-larnin's good fo' de young uns. I sho' be glad to God if Wash'ton grow up good as Richie an' Aa'on. So it look like I got to put in some heavy licks, workin' fo' de white folks' schoolin'.'

XVIII

BIG MANOR SCHOOL

LETTERS awaited Harriet when she went back to school after the short Christmas holiday. Among them was one in Mrs. Trindle's finely formed writing. It said:

Dear Little Harrie:

Papa and I have been thinking of you so much the past month. Your letters have been pretty cheerful, all but the one in November after you had been over to Booker School. But we are afraid that that one just showed what was in your little heart all the time.

Yes, we do have a heavy burden in all the illiterates of our race; but we have a good chance, too, if we will stand up and face things.

However, Papa and I think you deserve the very best opportunities you can have, and not to be crushed by too much of a burden, either, especially while you are so young.

So we have been looking into the matter of your going to that Charleston school this next semester. I know what you're likely to say: that there is not enough money. If there weren't, we'd be glad to help out; but with your little annuity and the education insurance, you can make out, by being very careful. A payment should be reaching you within the week.

Then you can visit your great-grandmother, the dear old soul, in the summer, and return to us and your university course next fall.

When Harriet had read and re-read the letter, she tapped at Johnnie's door and showed it to her. Johnnie skimmed swiftly through it, and then sat gazing through the bright black slits of her eyes into a sassafras tree outside.

'It seems the sensible thing to do, doesn't it?' Harriet asked.

'Yes. Oh, yes, it does seem — sensible.'

'You don't know how let down and soothed I feel' — Harriet spoke with a vehement rush — 'and as if that old load had been dumped off my back.'

'You and Miss Joan both going —' Johnnie meditated aloud. 'Let's go tell Miss Joan, shan't we?'

Together they clattered down the stairs and over to the next hall, where Miss Joan and another of the younger teachers had two small bedrooms and a sitting-room.

'Sit down and make yourselves at home,' Miss Joan called from her bedroom. 'I've just come home from borrowing me a bathtub!'

'Won't you be tickled to death to get back to the kind of living you've been used to?' Johnnie asked.

'Mmmm! Tickled pink!' the young teacher gloated. 'Cold bath every morning, hot bath every noon, shower in betweentimes. Soft beds. And — hey! would you look at this!' She emerged in slip and robe, tragically holding out a silk dress spotted with mould. 'Just hanging in the closet! I found a pair of shoes ruined today.'

'My very best handbag has mould in all the creases. But what I hate more is having those silverfish sort of slither away every time you open a book. And I never had seen a cockroach before,' Harriet said meditatively. 'I caught one that measured four inches — including the feelers,' she added hastily.

'*She's* going away from here, too,' said Johnnie, kicking at Harriet.

'I'll read the letter to you while you finish,' Harriet offered. 'Shall I, Miss Joan?'

'It's the only thing to do. Isn't it?' she said, folding the letter when she had read it, and sticking it back in its envelope.

'What about your lessons with Magdalen Bates?' Miss Joan asked.

'She goes to Charleston once a week anyway,' Harriet reminded them. 'So that's as long as it is short. — Of course I'm going to miss the Negro History course with Miss Francis. I'll miss practically all the teachers. But ——'

'What about Granny's farm?' Johnnie inquired negligently.

Harriet felt suddenly empty. She hadn't yet stopped to think that Charleston would leave her no margin for saving that hundred or so dollars.

'I don't know why we should expect that that Northerner would push the matter now,' she said uncomfortably. 'Why would he, when he's let it slide eight years?' But I hope to goodness nobody will try to nab it for a truck garden! she was thinking miserably.

'Have you told Miss Francis?' Miss Joan asked, coming out and stooping to peer into a small mirror while she combed her damply curling corn-colored hair. 'It will make a vacancy for some other girl.'

'I'll — tell her.' Harriet went slowly over to the office.

Miss Francis took a long time to read the letter, while Harriet stood waiting in the shabby office, thinking that it would be only a half-year or so before she would be free to enter beautiful up-to-date buildings again: adequate buildings.

She read this year's Senior poster:

'Do you want something $\begin{cases} \text{made?} \\ \text{cleaned?} \\ \text{repaired?} \end{cases}$ Ask us!

Do you want Charm? Visit the Senior Beauty Salon!'

Miss Francis folded the letter and tapped the desk with it, musingly. 'Won't you take a little time to think it over?' she asked. 'Of course I see Mrs. Trindle's point; but I don't believe you're wasting your time here, even scholastically. Nor pining away with melancholy.'

Harriet shook a vehement head. 'No, but I do get awfully depressed by the poverty and hopelessness.'

'You and Johnnie bring viewpoints that are fresh and wholesome, now that you've adapted yourselves to the situation. Please wait a few days before you decide. And — Harriet!' she sent her clear low voice after the departing girl, 'wouldn't you and Miss Joan like to go with me on the semiannual visit to the rural schools this week? Since neither of you will be here much longer you might like the opportunity.'

Harriet regarded her suspiciously.

'The party always includes one or more students,' Miss Francis went on with a flicker of amusement. 'I think little Clapp wouldn't be bad: she comes from somewhere off in that direction. We'll go in on the main, to Grand State, and Jerusalem; and maybe to Mossie's — Big Manor, I think it is, though we've never been there.' She pivoted her chair to look at the school schedule on the wall. 'Friday. Meet here at eight-thirty.'

The first schoolhouse where they stopped that Friday morning was Grand State, and it was a cabin on stilts with a rickety pair of steps at its front door. As she approached those rickety steps, Miss Francis laid a finger to her lips and stood listening. The girls listened, too. Voices came unmuffled through the thin walls.

'Firs' three grades stan' up!' the teacher ordered. The consequent bumping and shuffling gradually subsided.

'Say yo' ABC's,' the teacher directed.

The voices responded in swelling chorus, some round with certainty, some ragged with doubt.

'Count to one hunderd!'

Again the voices obeyed, shouting at first and gradually waning to a murmur.

'Be seated!' said the teacher.

'Don't look so shocked,' Miss Francis murmured. 'What can you expect, with school only four months a year?'

She knocked at the door and introduced herself, and led the way inside, somewhat to the confusion of the teacher, since hers was the only chair and all the benches were filled.

The day was rainy and chill, and the wooden shutters had had to be closed, so that the schoolhouse was dim. Harriet peered around her, dodging a drip of rain through a hole in the roof. Fifty pairs of eyes turned as if by machinery from Miss Francis to Joan, to Harriet, to Mossie. Fifty pairs of feet scuffed or padded on the floor when fifty children rose and said, 'Good mo'nin', m'm!'

The smallest boy and girl could not have been more than five years old, and they were padded fat with clothes, like Chinese children. The little boy's stocking came rumpling down over his shoe, and the little girl straightened it with motherly pattings, and tied it with the twist of rag that was the garter, while he stared, uninterested in clothing, at the strangers. The biggest boys, in the back of the twilit room, looked sixteen or more. The whole fifty, five years old to sixteen, sat down, crowding the backless benches.

Covertly Harriet appraised the broken floor; the round red stove which made a hot ring of air around itself and then gave up the struggle; the patch of wall painted grayish black and serving as a blackboard. On it the teacher had lettered:

Time is To Costly Too Waste.

The teacher's homemade desk held a few ragged books and a cowbell. Hats and sweaters covered an end wall. A bucket of water and a dipper occupied one end of a rickety bench, and a huddle of paper lunch bags the other.

Miss Francis was telling about Landers. Joan told them a story, to which they listened open-mouthed. In conclusion Miss Francis beckoned the teacher to the door, and Harriet helped her lift a tied and labeled carton from the back seat. They drove on.

'What sort of things do you bring them?' Miss Joan asked.

'Oh — pencils, tablets, old readers from up North. And clothing, of course. One thing I wish we could get a lot of is United States maps. I wonder if one of the filling station companies wouldn't donate them. Just notice how few you see on the walls of these schools.'

'But — pencils and paper!' Pencils and paper had seemed to Harriet the irreducible minimum of equipment, taken for granted.

'Some of 'em chillen sho' be t'anksful fo' de clo'es,' Mossie observed. 'It awful col' dis time of year, gwine barefoot to school.' She wriggled her feet reminiscently.

The next schools they encountered were much like the first. Noon came, and the Landers party found a pump where they could wash their hands, and drew up beside the road to eat their lunch before they set out for the fourth school on their list.

'Now,' said Miss Francis, as they came out of that fourth school, 'we'll have to hurry if we hope to make Big Manor. We've never taken it in, because there aren't any real roads.'

'Big Manor my school,' said Mossie. 'I knows jest where e at. — On'y I don' know where's we!'

Following Mossie's wavering finger, Miss Francis drove off into the woods and stopped at the nearest cabin to call from the car. At her hail a woman peered through the window and ducked a bow and listened to her query. Her answer was fluent, but Miss Francis looked bewildered.

'Mossie, can you understand what she says?'

'Sho', m'm. E say we duh go long disyere road to de fo'k, an' den to de right twell we cross de track, an' den crost de field an' over de crick on de boa'd bridge an' crost anodder field an' through de crick; an' den we gots to walk a sma't piece twell we gits to de quarters an' den past de quarters twell we dere!'

The ride that followed was a strange one. The car sidled and creaked through stubble and ventured timidly on the two planks that formed the bridge — one for each pair of wheels. The four occupants heaved a fourfold sigh when it crossed with a final bang. It lurched through another field, straddling a faintly marked cart road. It dipped into another creek and splashed through it and reared up out of it. It settled down with a sigh and a shiver, and Miss Francis got out.

She hoisted out another carton, and the four took turns carrying it, two at a time, through a dry cottonfield.

'How much farther do you think, Mossie?' Miss Francis asked, easing her side of the burden down and wriggling her tired shoulders.

'Jest a li'l piece now, m'm,' Mossie answered, straining eagerly ahead.

It was really only a little piece to the quarters, a village of whitewashed cabins facing each other across a hard-trodden road. The quartette skirted its borders, seeing only an old man and an old woman, and a young man 'licking out rice.' All three bowed and grinned and called greetings and stood watching them as they went.

And then it was only another little piece to the school-house on the hill.

From the stovepipe a wisp of smoke trailed languidly. Mossie ran up the steps and pushed at the door.

'E gone home!' she wailed. 'Ain' nobody here!'

The others followed her in, the floor quaking so ominously under them that Harriet went flying, hop, skip, and jump, to avoid the most perilously teetering of the boards.

'Disyere where I mos'ly set,' Mossie told them, sliding along the handhewn bench to the window. 'So I could git out when ey fit. An' likewise so I could look outdo's.'

Harriet felt her throat tightening as she surveyed Big Manor. It was really the worst of the five. Planks nailed across the back corners of the room formed two of the seats. The window shutters creaked dismally. She could not see a single bright or lovely thing.

'But there is a map!' Miss Joan exclaimed, as if her thoughts had been following the same furrows. 'It's the second one I've found today.'

It was a packing company's map of the United States, and its dimensions were perhaps twelve by sixteen inches.

Harriet's gaze was pulled past it to a pair of eyes like brown and white agates in the back window. A small boy was hoisting himself up to the sill. He was a clean enough little boy, but his cumbersome trousers were held up by twisted strings tied to safety pins on his shoulders, and his feet were bare to the cold. His eyes were trained on

Miss Joan, in the most intent and astonished stare that Harriet could remember. When the young teacher smiled at him he dropped out of sight as if he had been shot.

Harriet turned around. A dozen youngsters were sitting quietly on the benches, and others were stealing in at the door on cautious tiptoe.

Miss Francis regarded their expectant faces, their hands spread primly on their knees.

'Where did you fall from?' she asked. 'Would you like to hear a story?'

'*Yes*, m'm!' they chorused after an instant's pause. '*Please*, m'm.'

'Harriet,' Miss Francis suggested, 'are you ready with a story?'

Harriet stood up and gathered her courage. At first her voice came thin and husky. 'I'm going to tell you about some Indian children,' she began. 'These Indian children are called Hopis and they live in Arizona.'

'Mmmmmm!' said the children in chorus.

Harriet stopped, rather taken aback. 'How many of you know where Arizona is?' she asked, trying to get her bearings.

Hands remained fixed on knees and eyes on Harriet. Two big boys in the back seat nudged each other.

'Will one of you point out your own state for me, on the map?'

A big boy raised his hand and shuffled up to the little map. Once there, however, he was lost. He looked at the north, at the east, at the west, at the south. He trailed a forlorn finger across the prairie states in the middle. He rolled eyes of dumb appeal at Harriet.

Coloring hotly, she pointed to South Carolina, and to Arizona, straight across from it. Then she began her story:

'Once upon a time, long ago, the Indians in Arizona were fighting with the Mexicans just south of them ——'

'Mmmmmm!'

'— and one of the Indians found a little Mexican baby boy that had been left behind on the trail when his parents were running away ——'

'Mmmmmm!'

Now it was Harriet who cast a look of appeal, and at Miss Francis. Miss Francis looked as astonished as Harriet was feeling. There was nothing to do but labor on, though she found herself hurrying when it was time for that periodic response. All the children, even down to the smallest, gave her the most painful attention. The boy who could not locate his own state watched her and listened with alert interest. The teacher, informed of their coming, stood by the door and listened almost as eagerly as the pupils.

When Harriet had finished, dizzy and out of breath, Miss Francis said: 'One of your own old neighbors is with us today: Mossie Clapp. She has been in Landers only a few months, but she is doing well. Mossie, don't you want to tell them something you've learned at your new school?'

Mossie, too, had known that this request was coming, yet her face went gray with fright as she stood clutching the desk.

'I — maybe tell 'm what ey should eat for breakfast, an' how fuh set de table.'

Miss Francis nodded, and Mossie addressed herself to her principal, as if there were no one else in the room. She told Miss Francis that she should have cocoa and hominy grits and milk, and that she should use oilcloth on the table, or else a tablecloth — 'flou' sacks makes good tablecloths' — and put the plates and cups and spoons on just so, and sit down together — 'stead of grab yo' food like dogs an' run wid it,' she reproved Miss Francis.

She concluded with eloquence, undisturbed by the

regular chorus of 'mmmmm's.' Shifting her eyes for one instant to a small boy, she demanded, 'Wha' y'all had fuh breakfas', Frankie?'

Frankie rose, thrusting out his small stomach self-importantly. 'Coffee 'n' hawgmeat,' he announced.

'You-all tell yo' mammy give you cocoa an' grits an' milk an' make you strong chile!' Mossie adjured Miss Francis, and sat down, quivering with fear and triumph.

Her talk had been a copy of one of the school nurse's. The pupils had watched her with wonder — Mossie Clapp, very spruce in her second sewing-class dress, a red and white checked gingham with red revers and red buttons on its double-breasted blouse. Her looks, from the red ribbon drawn through her rolled hair to her black oxfords and red-striped anklets, spoke much louder than words. They even drew attention somewhat from Miss Francis and Miss Joan, who had apparently made such a sensation. When Miss Francis had dismissed the postscript school, it clustered around Mossie. The smallest girl went around behind her, as if to make sure that the glory was not all in front, like a paper doll.

Harriet sat very still as they rode toward home. 'You know,' she exploded at last, 'I wouldn't have believed there were such schools in the United States.'

'This particular school has one unusual feature,' Miss Francis said mildly. 'Some of the children have never seen white people before.'

Miss Joan gasped and sputtered. 'But Miss Francis —! Will you say that again? You don't mean —? Why, how many miles is it from the highway?'

'I know; but I do mean it. It's true, isn't it, Mossie?'

'Yes, m'm. Dey plenty dem chillen ain' saw no whi' folks twell dis wery day.'

'But — how could that *be*?' Harriet demanded.

'Mostly the lack of roads, I suppose. No roads to

bring the white people in and nothing to take the colored people out. — I know it's almost unbelievable. But the whole school situation is pretty hard to believe. The last statistics I've seen showed that our state spent an average of $7.84 per colored child per year for education. Some counties spend less than that.'

Harriet gulped. 'What is the average for the whole country?'

'I don't know exactly. Somewhere under a hundred dollars.'

'How can they expect us to rise when we've no more chance than that?'

'And the mountain white schools aren't a bit better than Big Manor, either,' Miss Joan commented.

'Whi' folks' schools? Sho' nuff?' Mossie's face was pure amazement.

'It's the whole South that's suffered, these seventy-five years,' Miss Francis observed. 'Not just one class: Negroes, rich whites, poor whites.'

'I often wonder what became of — of our white people,' Harriet said slowly. 'The Taliaferros.'

Mossie listening hard, as she still must to follow this unfamiliar tongue, gasped and rolled her eyes at Harriet. 'Tollivers? Ey live in house ain' far f'm Tolliver Plantation,' she said. 'Efn y'all take de nex' turnin' ——'

Harriet clasped her hands hard. 'Would it be too far out of our way, Miss Francis?'

Miss Francis glanced at her watch. 'It might not be a bad idea,' she said.

Between swamps where the frogs sang eerily, past little gray church houses staggering on stilts, past the crossroads store — 'Datdere's Tolliver's!' announced Mossie, who had sat well forward in the back seat, directing.

Miss Francis slowed the car. 'Would you like to get out and see Mrs. Taliaferro, Harriet?'

Harriet frowned earnestly. 'Yes, Miss Francis, I think I really would.'

A very small Negro girl answered the jangle of the old-fashioned bell and ushered them into the chilly, high-ceilinged parlor. Silently she scurried to call her mistress, and presently Mrs. Taliaferro came in, a little girl clinging to her skirts and whimpering to be carried.

Miss Francis introduced herself with the calm that was a part of her poise. She never needed vivacity for emphasis. Her quiet was emphasis in itself. 'And these two Landers students,' she said, 'wished to greet you because their ancestors served yours on Taliaferro Plantation.'

Harriet had risen at once, as she had been taught to do when an older person entered the room; and Mossie had slid off the edge of her chair and was busily making herself small.

Mrs. Taliaferro sat down and waved a hand toward the sagging mahogany sofa. 'I'm glad to make your acquaintance, Miss ——,' she said to Miss Francis. 'Y'all are Maum Clapp's little grand, aren't you?' she asked Mossie with mild interest. 'But the other one — she isn't a Clapp? — Hush, Betty!' The fair-haired little thing was whimpering and shivering.

'No, Mrs. Taliaferro. I'm Harriet Freeman, and I've been living in Minneapolis.'

'Freeman? — Freeman? — Betty, run and tell Lishy to make a fire if you're that cold.'

'Black Moses Freeman ——' Harriet said tentatively.

Mrs. Taliaferro raised her eyebrows and nodded. 'I've heard them speak of Black Moses. He was a smart darky, Grandmother Taliaferro always said.'

Harriet steeled herself to ask a question. 'Did you ever hear where he came from? What he was? They say he was educated in his own language.'

Mrs. Taliaferro said politely: 'But you know there were

so many such stories. This one was a chief or a king, and that one was a great warrior. But they all look pretty much alike now, don't they? — Black Moses was smart, though; I've heard that.'

The child pattered in behind small brown Lishy, who trailed splinters and chips after her as she came, her big eyes solemn above her double armload. Betty ran to Mossie's beckoning hands. Mossie was not shy with white babies. She had had much to do with them before she moved to the vicinity of Big Manor School.

'Such a lovely child!' Miss Francis commented, rising to go.

The mother rested a slender hand on the foam of blond curls. 'If she didn't have so much malaria,' she said anxiously.

'Wouldn't it be better for her up North?' Harriet inquired with her intense frown. 'I never heard of malaria in Minnesota.'

'Mistah Taliaferro's business interests,' the young mother replied vaguely. 'Must you-all go? Do come back again some day.'

Lishy opened the door for them, ragged shoes slapping scarred floor, and they crossed the porch, avoiding the missing board.

In the car again, no one spoke until they were bowling along the road toward the causeway. Then Harriet said, '*Worse!*'

Mossie gawped. Miss Joan looked inquiring. Miss Francis smiled at the narrowing road.

'They have a worse time of it than we do, those Southern white people who were used to being rich,' Harriet explained. 'That little girl — she looks poorly nourished, and she's chockful of malaria. And even the mother is sort of trapped.'

'What a wise young thing you're getting to be,' Miss

Francis observed in her light, level voice. 'Did you ever hear the characterization of Charleston: "Too poor to paint and too proud to whitewash"?'

'You mean,' Miss Joan interpreted, 'that they're bound by their past glories?'

'Won't do what they can because they can't do what they want to!' said Harriet. 'Oh, Miss Francis, everything about the North makes it easier to break loose and go ahead there!'

'Yes,' said Miss Joan, 'and today has made my decision for me. I'm going to teach in the mountain school.'

Again the three listeners reacted in three ways. Harriet folded her lips resentfully tight. Mossie's face was a complete blank: everything these outlanders did was mysterious. Only Miss Francis looked both comprehending and content.

'Well,' Harriet declared at length, 'I'm going to begin packing, myself. That's what *I'm* going to do.'

XIX

The Majesty of Moses

Saturday was too busy a day for packing or even for planning. Sunday morning found the girls walking into town to church in a long queue of galoshes and raincoats and rain caps. Sunday afternoon was calling time.

During dinner the rain stopped. Patches of robin's egg blue showed through the gray clouds. When the sun glinted out, a thousand diamonds quivered on tall grasses and long mosses. Birds went wild with song. Girls broke into gay little runs as they crossed the campus to their dormitories.

For Sunday afternoon was calling time.

From two to six the girls were permitted callers: 'home folks,' 'boy friends.' With a teacher acting as hostess, they gathered in the big living-rooms of Sarah B. Soon little girls, too small to have callers, would come scurrying to knock at dormitory doors and say, 'Deena May, young man askin' for you-all' — 'Roseanne, yo' folks is here,' — 'Le Misher, you've got a caller.' Sad the hearts of those to whom no messenger came; loud and defiant their laughter together, or else frank their tears.

All along Harriet's corridor girls were primping. They

dashed into and out of each other's rooms with brief preliminary taps.

'Deena May, you-all gwine wear those blue beads? Mind if I borrow 'em?'

'Le Misher, cain' you tie my hair bow like yours?'

'Got any high-brown powder, chile? Somebody spilt mine.'

'Which you reckon looks best: this dress or this?'

Harriet pulled off her checked taffeta and pulled on a brown wool skirt and a furry orange sweater. She was changing her silk stockings for smart thin wool when Mossie came racing down the corridor.

'Hayet!' she gasped, 'Pearlie Randall say tell y'all you gots a caller. Big tall one. Reckon it dat Richie?'

Harriet puckered her brows. 'You don't suppose anything's the matter with Granny?' She thumped into her brown and tan oxfords, knotted the ties with swift fingers, and ran down the stairs and over to Sarah B.

Already the big rooms milled with young people. There were big country boys, ill at ease among all these dressed up and chattering girls, and their girls as ill at ease as they; two young sailors from a naval base not far away, their round dark heads rising cockily from precisely creased blue collars. There was Richard, sitting somewhat self-conscious in a straight chair, watching the door.

Harriet thought it was nice to see him spring up at sight of her; nice to see him 'pull his foot' in his old-fashioned bow, when she introduced him to Miss Francis. He was much nicer than any of the other boys gathered in clusters throughout the room.

The two young people wove their way toward a pair of chairs in a far corner. Progress was slow. Willie Lou accosted them with a shout: 'Hattie, meet my friend Georgie Clarke!' Round little Phyllodoxia, all aglow, lisped: 'Oh, Harriet, my brother from Atlanta Univerthity! Thith ith Paul, Harriet.' Roseanne did not stop them; she stood aloof with her handsome mother — the woman Harriet had met at Landers entrance the first day — and drooped scornfully amused eyes at the others.

When at length they reached their safe haven, Richard was breathing convulsively, as if he had been swimming a stormy sea.

'It was so nice of you to come!' Harriet said. 'This is probably my last Sunday at Landers. Next week I was coming over to see Granny. And then — Charleston!'

Richard seemed scarcely to hear her. 'Harriet,' he broke in, 'we been having tur'ble lot of this flu sickness break out on Gentlemen's.'

'*Granny?*'

He nodded. 'She's bad sick. Mom's been doing what she could, but — well, you saw how it was: Mom don' know the new ways.'

'*I* know them. — How soon can we get a boat?'

'Efn we make haste ——' Richard was on his feet and Harriet weaving through the throng again, this time blind and deaf to salutations.

She told Miss Francis of Richard's errand, and received permission to go to Granny at once. While Richard roved round the campus, she threw together the clothes she thought she should need; found the treasurer and from her obtained money for the boat trip and for supplies she would get at the Bosquet drugstore. She silently gave thanks that the instalment of her annuity had come the day before — a money order, cashed and deposited with the treasurer. Checks were of little use here, as no banks had survived the depression. She was rather glad she was not tempted by checks: it was so easy to write too many of them, and she must use as little money as possible. The trip to Charleston, tuition, books — these would strain her resources.

By this time Miss Joan had learned of the emergency and backed out her car to take the young people to town and to the boat. All the way Harriet was ticking off lists of supplies on her fingers.

'A hot-water bottle — Granny wouldn't have a hot-water bottle, would she, Richie?'

Richard looked blank.

'A rubber bag to put hot water in to keep on their lungs or wherever there's an ache,' she explained.

'We use a hot brick. Or a bag of hot salt.'

'And just as well, too,' the teacher commented.

'We-ell. Mentholatum to rub on her chest.'

'Ain' lard 'n' turkentine good enough?'

'We-ell. Plenty of oranges and lemons to make fruit juices for her to drink ——'

'Granny's got plenty oranges from her own tree.'

Even in her anxiety Harriet laughed. 'And of course she has mustard, for mustard poultices.'

'You might take some canned things for yourself, and canned soups to feed Granny when she can eat them,' Miss Joan suggested. 'And some changes of sheets. — It's Sunday, but maybe I can coax a storekeeper to break into his store for us.'

By their combined efforts they had the revised list of necessities all together in time for Harriet and Richard to run, panting, upon the boat just before it tooted and frothed away from the dock. They stood and waved at Miss Joan until she turned back to her car, and then they settled down in Harriet's favorite bow seat.

'Now!' said Harriet. 'Richie, how long has Granny been in bed?'

'Ain' been in bed till day befo' yesterday,' he told her. 'Been a-coughin' round for a week — ever since y'all went back to Landers, I reckon. But now she's a sight worse. Fair burnin' up with fever.'

Harriet smote her knee. 'I should have got a thermometer!'

'Cabin's nice and tight,' Richard objected. 'Got
plenty of wood to keep it warm.'

'Thermometer for Granny's fever,' she explained.

'So now Granny an' Lily are both two in bed,' he went
on after a puzzled pause.

'Have they had the doctor?'

'Ain' no doctor on Gentlemen's.'

'Well!' Harriet ejaculated; 'thank goodness I've had
courses in the care of the sick. And thank goodness I had
influenza last winter, so I know the best ways of taking
care of it. Probably I can get her well in time so I won't
have to be much late for Charleston. I'm sure Miss
Francis will let me make up this week's exams.'

Richard crossed and uncrossed his knees and laced his
long fingers over them. He looked through his lashes at
Harriet, the brightly expectant look of one who springs a
delightful surprise. 'Like enough I'll be seein' y'all in
Charleston.'

'What do you mean, Richie?'

He grinned. 'We just got it fixed up. Jick did.'

'Jick?' she asked, her mouth wry as if the name tasted
unpleasant.

'Jick's smart, Harriet. He even got the truck painted up
fine and marked "Cotton-Blossom Kids."'

'*Cotton-Blossom Kids?*'

'Yes, m'm. "Cotton-Blossom Kids. Jazz Orchestra
and Quartet." That's me and Jick and two other chillen.
One boy, he tap dances like a hen on a hot griddle and all
the time lookin' like he's clean out of his head with joy.
Me an' Jick, we play the banjo and the other boy's got a
sax; and we all sing good. — We're gwine shoot straight
for Charleston while the white folks are there from up
No'th; and when we've got all the loose money in Charles-

ton, we're gwine on up along the coast. Maybe, like y'all say, we make a big hit in Harlem.'

He stopped, eager for applause, but Harriet's mouth was tight and her brows were twisted. 'Oh, Richie!' she flared, 'do you think you'll like anything so — so —— ?'

He stared at her, crestfallen, and she shook her head and flung out her hands.

'What about the work you're planning here, Richard? What about helping your people redeem their little farms?'

'Reckon it's too late to help them thataway,' he said soberly. 'Another fellow's been around lookin' 'em over, studyin' to buy 'em up to raise garden stuff. — And if it ain' too late, I got mo' chance to help by earnin' money — seems like. Besides seein' the world the way y'all said, Harriet.'

'But the work — the *work!* Don't you remember what Miss Locke told us that day —— ?' Her voice dwindled. After all, how could she object? She who had roused his ambition for travel in the first place? She wriggled around on the bow seat, with her back to him and her foot tucked under her and going to sleep. 'I've got to try to think what I'll do first for Granny,' she said ungraciously. Her eyes stung with tears, and she kept her head turned away: her nose got lavender-colored when she cried.

Heat a sack of salt — in a covered spider in the ashes? Give Granny a sponge bath to make her more comfortable — she should have got bathing alcohol!

(What a contrast, Richie standing by the sea like a statue of young Moses, planning the deliverance of his people, and Richie in candy-striped trousers and a tilted hat, playing jazz for dimes!)

Squeeze oranges and give Granny the juice ——

(Richard might get the taste for that dusty excitement; might keep on with that sort of life! And she had loved to hear him say, 'my people.')

Clean the cabin and air it ——

(How cheap a calling seemed if it had no real service in it. She shook her shoulders and covertly wiped her eyes and nose.)

Almost before the boat had docked, Richie was helping her down the gangplank, and they were clattering over the loose boards of the pier and loping through the dust. Harriet had never yet felt it necessary to 'walk like a lady' when haste was needed. She carried her parcels and Richard her suitcase, and the greater weight handicapped him just enough to keep his pace equal to hers.

He grinned at her as he stretched out a long arm and opened Granny's gate; an anxious grin, like a whipped puppy's overtures of friendship. 'We — run — good together!' he panted.

Harriet didn't smile back. She gave him a swift, frowning glance and clattered across the porch and into the cabin.

Granny sat straight up in bed, burning eyes on the incomer. 'Chile of Moses!' she said in a cracked, husky voice. 'I pray de good Lawd an' E sen' me de chile of Moses!'

'Hayet, e do talk so funny!' wailed Lily, rolling over against the girl and hiding her hot little face in Harriet's cool coat. 'I skeered.'

But Granny had lain down, long dark hands crossed on tumbled counterpane. 'Chile of Moses — An' 'im flogged to deaf fo' e's people. Flogged twell e done dead ——'

Harriet flashed a startled look at Richard.

'Yes. I done hear that, likewise. Granny wouldn' have told you if she had her wits. — Flogged to death caze he taught them to read and write. — Don' take shame, Harriet. Don' take shame, honey.'

Harriet's head went up. 'Shame? I'm proud as th' dickens.'

'RICHARD, SHE REALLY IS BETTER'

She had no time to stop and meditate on a martyr forebear. 'Richie, would you build up the fire and get fresh water? And then stay out a little while?'

Harriet had learned the technique of bathing the sick and putting fresh linen on the sickbed, but she had had a doll for the patient. She was hot and breathless and aching of back by the time she had two live patients cool and fresh between clean sheets.

Granny went on talking, talking, gazing with uncanny eyes at the rafters. Occasionally she sang.

Richard knocked diffidently.

'Come in,' Harriet invited from the stool where she had dropped. 'Excuse the mess.' She nodded toward the sheets and pillow cases she had piled in a corner. 'As soon as I catch my breath I must sweep the dust out from under the bed. Queer. It's clean everywhere else but there.'

Richard twisted his cap. 'My people think it's a bad luck thing to sweep under sick folks' bed. Kill 'em sho'. — Or to wash their face, either.'

'Was the piece of rag tied around their front hair one of the old ways, too?' she asked. 'Lily's was pulled so tight her eyebrows were screwed up into the middle of her forehead.'

'Yes, m'm. It's s'posed to hol' up the palate and cure the sore throat and the cough.' He grinned uncertainly, and they laughed together, more at ease again after the stiffness that had lain upon them.

But the laughter roused Granny, who had lain quite still, her lips moving as she picked at the knot of a comfort. She sat up again. 'Ain' not'in' — fuh laugh about!' she protested. 'Ain' not'in' — not'in' — not'in' ——'

Gently Harriet urged her back on the pillow. 'There, Granny. Lie still and Harriet'll make you some orange juice. And in a little while you'll be all well again — all well again.'

Granny gazed at her soberly, rationally. 'No. Ain' gwine git well no mo'. De good Lawd gwine fetch me home. — White man come projeckin' roun' after dis li'l ol' farm. Gwine buy it up fo' de taxes. Say I got to git out dis spring.'

The hoarse voice creaked to silence, while the two young people stared at each other and Lily stared from them to Granny, nodding affrightedly and whispering, 'Hayet, yes, m'm, white man did say thataway.'

Again the old woman opened her parched mouth, speaking painfully. 'Ain' never gwine leave dis place cep'n to go to Heaben.'

Harriet and Richard tiptoed out to the kitchen and Harriet began to squeeze the oranges Richard had brought in and heaped on the table. 'You think that's really so?' she asked in a dry voice.

'Reckon so, Harriet.'

Tight-lipped, she carried a jelly glass of juice to Granny and one to Lily, who smacked eager lips over it. Then she filled a kettle with water and dropped in a spoonful of healing benzoin and set it in the fire so that it should send its steam into the room.

Meanwhile Richard went home and changed to work clothes. When he came back to milk the cow he brought a covered bucket with hoecake and rice and a crisply fried fish for Harriet. By the light of the log fire she ate hungrily, and Richard sat back on his heels and watched her.

'Have you eaten anything?' she remembered to ask.

'No, not yet. Reckon I got to be gettin' along. But, Harriet, if you need Mom, either me, you just toot Granny's old horn, will you?'

Richard did not even get out of the yard. Harriet had buttoned the back door and gone in to Granny's bedside, feeling small and young and fearful, when a hoarse shout from Granny herself brought him running back. Lily launched herself upon him, terrified, as soon as he stepped into the room.

For Granny was sitting up again, brandishing her arms and gasping on the top of her shallow breathing: 'Gwine home! Gwine home! Look away yander, chillen; buckruh done come a'ready to run po' Granny off. E cain' come. E cain' come!'

Wildly she clung to Harriet, staring over the girl's shoulder at the darkest corner. Her old face writhed with fear and sorrow.

And then Harriet spoke, steadily. 'He isn't coming, Granny. He isn't coming, ever. Harriet's going to keep your little farm safe for you.'

The old woman listened, and her frightened eyes turned to the girl's face, searchingly. Frowningly serious, that face; calm and sure Harriet's voice.

'First thing tomorrow Richie's going to Bosquet and get Harriet's money for her,' the girl went on, soothingly. 'And pay the taxes. And then the place will be yours for good and all. You'll go for us, won't you, Richie?'

Richard nodded. 'Sho' will,' he said dazedly. 'Do anything for you-all, Harriet. — Either Granny.'

Granny's eyes still searched her grandchild's face. 'You-all got de cash-money?' she quavered.

Harriet swallowed hard and nodded. 'Sho'!' she said emphatically: and did not even notice how she had said it.

Quite suddenly and simply, Granny curled down in her bed and slept.

Richard stood tall and somber with his arm on the mantel and looked down at Harriet, rocking in Granny's old chair, a quilt-wrapped bundle that was Lily filling her arms. Lily had crept over and climbed up into Harriet's lap, pleadingly silent as a puppy.

'Y'all mean it, sho' nuff?' Richard asked. 'About the money and buyin' back the place?'

'Do you think I'd have said it if I hadn't meant it?'
Harriet rocked harder and then stopped because a board
creaked too loudly. 'I'll write a note to Miss Francis.
She'll understand.'

'But — does it leave you enough fuh go to Charleston?'
She shook her head.

'But ——'

'I don't *want* to go to Charleston. I — I want to finish
at Landers. Afterward I'll go somewhere not too far
away — maybe Spelman, in Atlanta — where I can learn
lots more about Home Ec — nursing, cooking, diet,
babies. And then' — her voice thickened with earnestness — 'I'm coming back to Gentlemen's and help my
people *live.*'

'Harriet, *your music?*'

'Oh, I'd keep up my music, every way I could.' She
laughed out suddenly. 'Wouldn't a Steinway look funny
here? We'd all have to move out.'

'It ain' no joke, honey. *Common* folks could teach my
people ——'

Harriet didn't protest that she was common folks.
Maybe the common folks weren't common, either: but
she knew *she* wasn't. She felt bigness, sureness, strength,
within her.

'What I really want is to compose, Richie. Music, you
know. You reckon I'd do more if I was in big cities,
whirled around and gay? No. I'll do bigger things on
Gentlemen's. I know it.'

Granny turned and muttered, and Richard was beside
her in one stride, a firm hand on her head to quiet
her.

'Harriet,' he asked, 'ain' it a good sign when they begin
to sweat?'

Harriet rose and thrust Lily into his arms. Eagerly
she bent above the bed, laying her palms against Granny's

neck, listening to her breathing. 'Richard, she really is better. — I'll fix another salt bag ——'

Richard laid Lily on the bed and went after more wood. When he had finished making up the night's fire, he straightened, dusting his hands, and looked at Harriet, a long, wondering look. 'You mean it, sho' nuff. — Comin' back to Gentlemen's.'

'It took me so long to see it.' Harriet spoke in a vehement soft rush, while she adjusted the salt bag and poulticed Granny with brown paper buttered with lard and turpentine as Richard had advised. 'But it's the most wonderful chance to do something — big! I might have to teach a while, to earn a living. But I'm young. There's time. And I'd get my people working for a Rosenwald school, like your mother, and' — She let out a long breath and looked at him shiningly. A cricket chirped loud and near and again they heard the reiterant chorus of frogs, the sigh of the wind, high in the trees, as if it had mysteries and wisdoms beyond mortal knowing. 'Such a place to make music, Richie! Such a place! And likely I could go away often enough so I'd love to come back — so I'd always know how beautiful it is.'

'Chillen, cain' y'all sing sump'n' fo' Granny?' The deep old voice came suddenly, quietly. 'Seem lak I kin sleep good efn y'all sings.'

They sat on the old handhewn stools on each side of the fire and Richard began, his voice big and sweet:

> 'Great Day,
> The righteous marchin'——'

Harriet sang, too, gazing deep in the fire. From one song to another they passed, before Richard, tiptoeing to the bedside, lifted a long finger. 'Bofe two asleep! Reckon I gots to go, Harriet.'

'Richard! You haven't had a bite of supper!'

He shrugged careless shoulders, as if his mind were on matters far from food. But he did not go.

'My people are so stubborn,' he warned her. 'It ain' gwine be no easy work, Harriet.'

'Don't I know it?' She struck her hands together. 'What do I want of easy work? I'm strong enough for hard. If Black Moses could die for my people, I guess I can work for them.'

'I thought you'd be shamed,' Richard muttered. 'Y'all thought he was king-proud — Black Moses — and him flogged like a horse.'

Still her eyes shone in the firelight. 'It took just that to make me see. — Only I can't teach them to farm their tracts so they won't lose them,' she conceded, her triumphant voice flagging, 'or grow good cattle or build good houses.'

A pocket of resin bubbled and spat on the fire. A shutter banged. A cricket chirped and the wind was still. The cat rubbed its arched back silkily against Richard's big shoe. Granny was breathing in deep, quiet rhythm.

'That will have to be somebody else,' Harriet said wistfully.

'*Me*,' said Richard.

He flung his arms wide, and his face, with its dark planes sharp-cut by the firelight, held the leader look she had seen before. Then it relaxed, and his teeth flashed white.

'Girl,' he said, 'it's gwine be fun, likewise!'

THE END